Democracy and Dictatorship in Europe

SHERI BERMAN

Democracy and Dictatorship in Europe

From the Ancien Régime to the Present Day

OXFORD
UNIVERSITY PRESS

OXFORD
UNIVERSITY PRESS

Oxford University Press is a department of the University of Oxford. It furthers
the University's objective of excellence in research, scholarship, and education
by publishing worldwide. Oxford is a registered trade mark of Oxford University
Press in the UK and certain other countries.

Published in the United States of America by Oxford University Press
198 Madison Avenue, New York, NY 10016, United States of America.

Library of Congress Cataloging-in-Publication Data
Names: Berman, Sheri, 1965– author.
Title: Democracy and dictatorship in Europe : from the Ancien régime to the
present day / Sheri Berman.
Description: New York, NY : Oxford University Press, [2018]
Identifiers: LCCN 2018027023 (print) | LCCN 2018044301 (ebook) |
ISBN 9780199373208 (updf) | ISBN 9780199373215 (epub) |
ISBN 9780199373192 (hardcover)
Subjects: LCSH: Europe—Politics and government. |
Democracy—Europe—History. | Dictatorship—Europe—History.
Classification: LCC JN8 (ebook) | LCC JN8.B47 2018 (print) | DDC 320.94—dc23
LC record available at https://lccn.loc.gov/2018027023

9 8 7 6 5 4 3 2 1

Printed by Sheridan Books, Inc., United States of America

To those who have struggled to get rid of the ancien régime.

CONTENTS

ACKNOWLEDGMENTS

This book has been long—too long—in the making. Indeed at many points I was not sure it would get done. The only advantage of having taken so long is that I have read and learned more about European political history and political development than I ever thought possible. During the many years I worked on this book I tried out parts of the argument on many audiences. To those who came to my talks, panels, and seminars, I offer immense thanks— your questions and criticisms pushed me to think harder about what I wanted to say and how to say it better. During the time this book was percolating I have also published versions its arguments in various venues. I would like to thank the *Journal of Democracy* and *Dissent* in particular for publishing several of these essays and their editors for proving feedback on them. My greatest intellectual debt, however, goes to the many Barnard and Columbia students who have taken my "Democracy and Dictatorship in Europe" class over the last decade. This book grew out of this class; after teaching it for several years I realized there was no single book that covered what the course was trying to achieve and that maybe I could be the one to write that book. And each year I taught the course I re-worked the lectures to better communicate important arguments and themes to my students and these lectures provide the intellectual infrastructure for the book that follows. Without this process of constant revision and re-thinking I would never have been able to put the many pieces of the puzzle that is European political development together, so again thank you to the students who pushed me to keep revising and improving. I would also like to thank the many teaching assistants who helped me teach this class and the research assistants who helped me put together the figures in the book that follows. And finally, I am grateful to Oxford University Press and David McBride for publishing this book and being patient while I struggled to finish it off.

Although they did not directly help with the book, I would like to thank Isaac and Lucy for pushing me and making me determined to show that if you work hard and do not give up you can accomplish what you set out to do. I would also like to thank my wonderful fuzzies for comforting me when I wanted to throw another book I realized I needed to read against the wall or chuck another chapter revision in the trash bin. And finally thanks to the friends who helped me get through my own process of overcoming the ancien régime. Just as this book shows that liberal democracy cannot be consolidated without undergoing this long and painful process, so too did this book's completion require it.

Democracy and Dictatorship in Europe

CHAPTER 1 | Questions about Political
          | Development

You have to know the past to understand the present.

—Carl Sagan[1]

IN NOVEMBER 1989 the place to be was Berlin. History was being made.
Dictatorships were collapsing and, as George H.W. Bush put it, "America
[had] won the Cold War."[2] The bloody twentieth century with its horrible
violence and titanic ideological battles was coming to a close. Liberal democracy was triumphant, and the West was about to lead the way towards progress and prosperity. Many felt in 1989 as Wordsworth did about the French
Revolution exactly two hundred years before: "Bliss was it in that dawn to be
alive, / But to be young was just heaven."[3]

Europe, of course, was particularly euphoric. The downfall of communism
in Eastern Europe combined with the collapse of dictatorships in Southern
Europe during the previous decade left the continent more united than ever
before. For the first time in its modern history European countries shared
the same political (democratic) and economic (capitalist) system; Germany
and Russia—the great powers that had caused so much instability in the
past—were no longer threats; and the European Union was on the verge of
incorporating much of Eastern Europe and creating a single currency. At the
end of the twentieth century, the view that a united Europe was on its way
to becoming "the next global superpower," and the model for a new type of
peaceful, prosperous, post-national polity, was widespread.[4]

How fickle is History. Today the optimism of 1989 is long gone, replaced by fears that Europe and the West have entered a period of decline. Liberal democracy has faltered in Eastern Europe and is threatened by populism in Western Europe and the United States. Scholars and commentators no longer talk about the triumph of liberal democracy, the "end of history," and "post-national" politics, but worry instead about "illiberal democracy," "global authoritarianism," virulent nationalism, and democratic "deconsolidation."[5] As Viktor Orbán, Hungary's current prime minister, whose political career began in 1989 as an opponent of dictatorship but who has since morphed into an opponent of democracy, recently proclaimed: "The era of liberal democracy is over."[6]

How did we get from there to here? How can we understand the fate of today's new democracies and the problems facing its older ones? What makes liberal democracy work well in some places and some times, but not others?

These are questions of the utmost theoretical and practical importance. The rapid spread of democracy at the end of the twentieth and beginning of the twenty-first century combined with its current problems has placed questions concerning the origins, evolution, and fate of democracy at the forefront of contemporary debate. This book will add a fresh perspective to this debate. From historians we have gotten superb studies of particular countries' politics at particular points in time. From political scientists we have gotten theories about what it takes to make democracy work.[7] And more recently, scholars and commentators have provided analyses of democracy's current crisis.[8] This book draws on and aims to complement the work of historians, political scientists, and contemporary analysts of democracy. It is grounded in the view, as Carl Sagan put it, that one "has to know the past to understand the present." It will integrate questions being asked about democracy today with a re-consideration of European political development in order to gain a better understanding of how and why democracies and dictatorships developed in the past. And by reconsidering how democracies and dictatorships developed in the past it will add a historical perspective that will enable us to better understand what is going on in the world today.

Europe is the perfect place to ground such an examination: it is the place where modern democracy was born and is currently the home of a large crop of well- and not-so-well-functioning democracies. In addition, Europe has also been the home of dictatorships of all kinds—monarchical, military, populist, hybrid, competitive, fascist, and National Socialist. These democracies and dictatorships emerged, moreover, at various times and in various economic and social contexts. Indeed over the course of the modern era, European countries have differed in almost every way political scientists identify as causally significant for democratic development: timing, nature, and rapidity of economic development; levels of economic inequality; strength of national states; degree of ethnic and religious diversity; and more. That so many types of political regimes and such immense economic and social diversity have existed in Europe provides an opportunity to study how democracies and dictatorships develop and decay over time and in various contexts.

In addition to placing the European experience in broader context and bringing a historical perspective to the consideration of contemporary cases, a re-examination of political development in Europe can help us understand the problems its own democracies face today. After a half century of unprecedented political, social, and economic success, Europe is once again experiencing profound political malaise and even political disorder. Most commentary on Europe's present problems has focused on contemporary causes like globalization, technological change, the financial crisis, technocracy, immigration, and refugee flows. This book will show, however, that short-term analyses misunderstand or at least oversimplify what is going on. In particular, the historical perspective adopted in this book will help us see how Europe's current problems have their roots in the decay of the foundations upon which liberal democracy was (re)built after the tragedies of the interwar period and the Second World War.

Before moving on, it is necessary to briefly define some key concepts used throughout the book: democracy, democratization, and consolidation. The first seems straightforward, but in fact students of democracy have almost as many definitions of it as there are regimes in existence.[9] The latter two, meanwhile, although conceptually and practically related, represent different stages or parts of the political development process; too often contemporary commentary conflates or fails to clearly differentiate them, leading to confusing analyses, assertions, and policy recommendations. Some conceptual brush-clearing, in short, is necessary before the analysis begins.

Key Concepts

The term "democracy" derives originally from the Greek word for popular rule, *demokratia* (*demos* = "common people," and *kratos* = "rule" or "power").[10] Although defining democracy as "rule by the people" seems uncomplicated, it is actually too ambiguous to be used to analyze or compare political systems. For example, who are "the people"? Does rule by "the people" mean *all* "the people" or just some subgroup of them? And how about "rule"? Do "the people," however defined, have to rule directly in order for a system to be considered democratic or should indirect, mediated, or technocratic rule also be considered democratic? Must "the people" agree on all political decisions or at least share a conception of the "common good" in order for a political system to be considered democratic or can there be conflicts among "the people" on what "rule" should entail in a democratic system?

Because of questions like these, social scientists have tried to come up with definitions of democracy better suited to empirically analyzing and comparing political regimes. Perhaps the one most oft used by scholars and policy makers today is a "minimal" or "electoral" definition which characterizes political regimes based on their procedures, particularly those used to pick rulers. In this view, the central procedure of democracy—and the feature that distinguishes it most clearly from other types of political regimes—is the selection of leaders through competitive elections by the people they govern. The most important modern statement of this definition of democracy was given by Joseph Schumpeter in his classic *Capitalism, Socialism and Democracy*. According to Schumpeter, "the democratic method is that institutional arrangement for arriving at political decisions in which individuals acquire the power to decide by means of a competitive struggle for the people's vote."[11] For Schumpeter, in other words, the need for leaders to compete for support or win elections rather than coming to power via coercion or heredity is the most important distinction between democracy and dictatorship. It is important to note that while its focus on elections is fairly simple and straightforward, this definition of democracy also implicitly includes a number of civil and political rights, such as some degree of freedom of speech, assembly, and organization since without them, elections could not be considered truly competitive, or "free and fair."

This "minimal" or "electoral" definition of democracy has many advantages. First, it is intuitive; most people recognize free and fair elections as the central feature of democracy. Second, it provides concrete, empirical benchmarks that can be used to differentiate democracy from dictatorship: if a country denies the right to participate in free and fair elections to its citizenry, then it is not democratic. Third, in addition to enabling us to judge the nature of any particular political system at any particular point in time, this definition also helps us analyze whether it is moving in a democratic or non-democratic direction: as elections become "freer and fairer" and/or increasing numbers of citizens are able to participate in them, countries can be characterized as becoming more democratic, or democratizing.

The "minimal" or "electoral" definition of democracy thus allows for relatively clear-cut and straightforward comparisons of political regimes. Some scholars, however, think the benefits of this definition's parsimony are outweighed by costs in terms of accuracy. In particular, critics assert that proponents of this definition are guilty of the "fallacy of electoralism"—of assuming that relatively free and fair elections indicate a well-functioning democracy. Surely anyone who reads a newspaper today can come up with examples of relatively free and fair elections gone awry. For example, many currently worry about the growing popularity of populist parties and politicians in the West whose commitments to liberalism and perhaps even democracy are uncertain. Similar concerns were voiced during the Arab Spring when many worried that elections would bring to power Islamists whose commitments to democracy were weak or instrumental. Indeed, such concerns were invoked in Egypt to help justify the overthrow of the Muslim Brotherhood's Mohamed Morsi and when the Algerian government voided the results of a democratic election that was about to be won by the radical Islamic Salvation Front (FIS) in 1992. Commenting on the United States' support of the Algerian government in this latter case, then Assistant Secretary of State Edward Djerejian explained that the United States favored democratization but did not support groups that believed in "one person, one vote, one time."[12] Such concerns, of course, are nothing new. Infamously, both Hitler and Mussolini pursued an "electoral path" to dictatorship; this book will discuss many other cases from European history where elections brought to power politicians and parties with at best tenuous commitments to democracy.

In addition to worrying about elections leading to governments that subsequently undermine democracy, critics also worry about democratically elected governments using their power in "non-democratic" or illiberal ways. Once again anyone who pays attention to current events could come up with numerous contemporary examples of such behavior. For example, Orbán in Hungary, the Law and Justice party in Poland (led by Jarosław Kaczyński), and Recep Tayyip Erdoğan in Turkey all came to power via relatively free and fair elections and then used their power to reward supporters and punish detractors, and more generally undermine democratic procedures and institutions. And also in the still fairly recent European past, democratically elected leaders in the former Yugoslavia sanctioned or incited violence against minorities in their own countries. As Richard Holbrooke famously asked before the 1996 elections in Bosnia, "Suppose elections are free and fair and those elected are racists, Fascists, separatists? That is the dilemma."[13]

Because it is not hard to find cases of democratic elections gone awry, and because many believe that while necessary, free and fair elections are not sufficient to make a political system fully democratic, many scholars argue for going beyond a minimal or electoral definition of democracy and favor a "liberal" one instead. As the term "liberal" indicates, proponents of this view argue that democracy is not merely a political system that chooses its leaders in a particular way; it is also a political system where government and citizens act in particular ways, namely in accordance with the tenets of liberalism. As the American Declaration of Independence declared: "We hold these truths to be self-evident, that all men are created equal, that they are endowed by their Creator with certain unalienable Rights, that among these are Life, Liberty and the pursuit of Happiness." In this view, in order to be considered truly or fully democratic, a government must be willing and able to guarantee the rule of law; and must protect minorities and individual liberties; and leaders and citizens must respect the democratic "rules of the game," and treat all members of society as political equals. The "liberal" definition of democracy is thus deeper than the electoral or minimal one. It incorporates into our understanding of democracy a set of values or goals that cannot be secured by political procedures alone. Democracies differ from dictatorships, in other words, not only in the way in which they choose their leaders, but also in the way they treat their citizens and their citizens treat each other.

The liberal definition of democracy has real advantages. First, it avoids the "fallacy of electoralism": it does not assume that particular procedures, most importantly relatively free and fair elections, are all it takes to make democracy. Second, it explicitly incorporates a wide variety of liberal rights that many view as inherently part of any truly democratic system. Third, it allows us to engage in more fine-grained and multifaceted, if somewhat fuzzier and more complicated,[14] comparisons of political regimes than does the minimal or electoral definition of democracy. Indeed, the more stringent requirements of liberal democracy clearly eliminate countries like Hungary, Poland, and Turkey and many others from the democratic category.[15] Precisely to capture the fact that many democracies are not liberal, another political label— illiberal democracy—is often invoked. Like electoral democracies, illiberal democracies have relatively free and fair elections but few if any of the other trappings of liberal democracies: they do not fully or indiscriminately apply the rule of law, protect minorities, or ensure individual liberties.

European history offers the perfect context within which to examine the nature, dynamics, and implications of different types of democracy. The following chapters investigate how common these different types of democracy have been; the factors determining whether a country develops an electoral, illiberal, or liberal democracy; and whether and how the development of illiberal democracy affects the development of liberal democracy down the road.[16] Some scholars, for example, assert that countries that democratize before the conditions to sustain liberal democracy are in place are likely to become "stuck" in illiberalism. As one influential treatment of the topic puts it, "Premature, out-of-sequence attempts to democratize may make subsequent efforts to democratize more difficult and more violent than they would otherwise be."[17] Is this true? Has electoral or illiberal democracy precluded progress towards liberal democracy in the past? Are electoral or illiberal and liberal democracy "competing" regime types or rather different stages of political development?

Alongside investigating the nature, dynamics, and implications of different types of democracy, two other key foci of *Democracy and Dictatorship in Europe* are democratization and consolidation.

Democratization refers to the transition from dictatorship to democracy. It is a process, not a stable condition. Democratization implies nothing about the durability or health of democracy. Democratization may occur and the new democracy may be weak or short-lived. Once again, European history provides a great context for investigating how and why democratization occurs and how often it leads to stable democracy. The following chapters examine many cases of democratization in Europe from the seventeenth century on in order to shed light on how and why dictatorial regimes are replaced by democratic ones and to determine how common it has been for democratization to lead to consolidation rather than instability or democratic failure.

Consolidation is what potentially happens after democratization: it is when the collapse of a dictatorship leads to the formation of a successful democracy. But how should democratic success be measured? Some scholars and observers focus on durability. In this view, democracy should be considered consolidated if it lasts for some significant period of time. But what should that period be? Five years? Ten years? A generation? Because any particular time period might seem arbitrary, some prefer a measure of durability that defines a democratic regime as consolidated when it has successfully carried out a certain number of elections.[18]

If one rejects, however, an electoral or minimal definition of democracy, then a purely quantitative definition of consolidation focused on durability or elections will be insufficient. Many scholars and observers accordingly favor a qualitative definition of consolidation that focuses on the attitudinal and behavioral shifts that comport with liberal democracy. In this view, a consolidated democracy requires that all groups are allowed to participate in political life and voice their demands, as long as they do so within the "rules of the game"; the basic rights of minorities and individuals are respected by the government as well as other citizens; and support for democracy is principled rather than conditional—that is, leaders and citizens view it as the only legitimate political system, not merely suitable because it produces particular policies or electoral outcomes, but rather because it comports with a society's deeply held values and preferences.[19] The following chapters will investigate how and under what conditions democratic consolidation has occurred in the past. As we will see, consolidated liberal democracy is a rare and recent phenomenon, with a much more difficult and turbulent backstory than most contemporary observers recognize. This brings us to some of the book's major themes and arguments.

Key Themes and Arguments

Based on the belief that we need to know the past to understand the present, *Democracy and Dictatorship in Europe* takes questions people are asking about democratic development and decay today and places them into historical perspective. One obvious advantage of a historical perspective is that without it we cannot know whether the problems facing democracy today are distinctive to the contemporary period or fairly common characteristics of political development. Indeed one argument this book will make is that much commentary on the state of democracy today is implicitly based on mistaken assumptions about how political development unfolded in the past. Another advantage of a historical perspective is that it enables us to recognize and understand the long-term causes and consequences of critical political events. This book will argue that political development is best understood as a marathon and not a sprint: it can take a long time for certain transformations to work themselves out and for the implications of distinct decisions or dynamics to become clear. Any attempt to understand the fate of a particular democratic experiment must take into account not only conditions surrounding the transition, but also the deep historical legacies from previous regimes that each attempt must wrestle with. Understanding how this process unfolded in Europe in the past can help us understand it in other parts of the world and during other periods.

This book's analysis begins in the seventeenth century, during the period of the ancien régime, when modern states began to emerge in Europe. As we will see, the nature of Europe's old regimes, and in particular whether and how they engaged in state-building, dramatically affected subsequent political development. Few political scientists delve this deeply into history, and this has produced a distorted picture of Europe's modern political development. The old regime was more than a type of dictatorship; it was a social and economic system as well. Eliminating it would therefore require more than a change in political institutions; revolutionary transformations in society and economy would also be necessary. Beginning with the French Revolution, many political transitions took place across Europe but, as we will see, almost all these democratic experiments failed because more representative political systems were grafted onto societies and economies in which the institutions, relationships, and norms of the old regime remained. Moreover, while dissatisfaction with the old regime in general and dictatorship in particular became increasingly widespread during the nineteenth and early twentieth centuries, a consensus on what should replace it did not emerge until the second half of the twentieth century, at least in some parts of Europe. Indeed, *Democracy and Dictatorship in Europe* will show that the best way to understand modern European political history is as a struggle to eliminate the vestiges of the old regime and build a consensus about the type of regime that should replace it. This process began in 1789 in France (even earlier in Britain) and then spread across the continent, reaching its climax during the interwar period and only being settled after 1945 in Western Europe, during the latter part of twentieth century in Southern Europe, and the process continues in Eastern Europe in today. We will see, in short, that getting rid of an old regime is a necessary but not sufficient condition for constructing a liberal democratic one. European history offers us many examples of times when an old order has died or is decaying but a new one has not yet arisen. Such periods are interregnums, and precisely because they are dominated by conflicts over what a new order should look like, they tend to be disordered and even violent. We may, in fact, be living through one today, so understanding how they have played out in the past is crucial.

In addition, beginning the analysis in the seventeenth century will make clear that in politics as in economics there is no "free lunch," that is, the idea that a gradual, liberal, non-violent path to democracy exists is based on a misreading or misinterpretation of history. Although such a path is certainly attractive in theory, there are in fact very few cases of stable liberal democracies that developed in this manner. Indeed, we will see that the political backstory of most democracies is one of struggle, conflict, and backsliding. More optimistically, we will also see that problems and even failures do not preclude later democratic success. Indeed, in Europe problems and failures turned out to be integral parts of the long-term processes through which non-democratic institutions, elites, and cultures were delegitimized and eventually eliminated, and their democratic successors forged. Many contemporary analysts do not seem to realize this because of a lack of historical perspective: they often ignore or misread the frequently messy and unattractive manner in which the current crop of liberal democracies actually developed and their analyses of democracy today are accordingly faulty.

This book will also focus on the connections between state- and nation-building and the development of democracy. There is much discussion today of the importance of strong states and national unity for well-functioning liberal democracy. Again, Europe provides a great context within which to study this, since the development of and relationship among states, nations, and democracy varied greatly in its past. In Western Europe fairly strong states and nations emerged before capitalism began reshaping societies or the challenge of democratization appeared on the political agenda. In other parts of Europe, the sequence differed. In Spain state- and nation-building began in the early modern period, but stalled and so the challenges of economic development and democratization had to be faced with a weak state and weak national identity. In Italy a national state emerged only in the late nineteenth century and then had to quickly confront the challenges of nation-building, economic development, and democratization. And in Eastern Europe independent countries only emerged after World War I, and, as in other newly decolonized regions, the challenges of state-, nation-, and democracy-building had to be confronted simultaneously. As we will see, how countries dealt with the legacies of their old regimes and how easy it was to build a consensus around a new one was profoundly influenced by the sequencing of state-, nation-, and democracy-building.

A final theme of *Democracy and Dictatorship in Europe* is the distinctiveness and import of the new order constructed by the United States and Western Europe after 1945. Although many forget it now, this postwar order was the foundation upon which consolidated liberal democracy was finally built in Western Europe. It was only after the chaos and devastation of the interwar years and the Second World War that a consensus emerged on the desirability of liberal democracy as well as on what it would take to make it work. This consensus undergirded the construction of international, regional, and domestic structures and relationships that finally generated peace, prosperity, and political stability in Western Europe. Understanding the postwar order, in short, is necessary to understand why democracy consolidated in Europe after 1945 but not before. And this order's decline over the past decades helps explain the problems liberal democracy is facing in Europe today.

In short, *Democracy and Dictatorship in Europe* will take the reader through a tour of the European past not in order to re-tread well-worn historical territory, but rather to provide an integrated and coherent story of European political development, making clear how episodes from the French Revolution to the collapse of the Weimar Republic to the building of the postwar order in Western Europe to the construction and destruction of communism in

Eastern Europe relate to each other and the larger story of the development of liberal democracy.

Book Outline

Democracy and Dictatorship in Europe will examine the development of democracies and dictatorships in Europe from the ancien régime up through the present day. It does not cover every European country in depth but instead focuses on countries that enable variations on certain critical factors that influence political development—including the nature and sequencing of state-, nation-, and democracy-building; the timing, type, and rapidity of economic development; and the degree of ethnic, religious, and linguistic diversity—to be considered. France, Italy, Germany, Britain, Spain, and East-Central Europe are covered extensively; other European countries are considered briefly, and Russia only enters the analysis when its own political development directly affected that of other European countries, for example, after the First and Second World Wars.

Chapter two focuses on the early modern period. It examines the type of political regime that dominated Europe during this time—monarchical and particularly absolutist dictatorships—as well as the era's most important feature—the emergence of modern states. The focus is on understanding the main features of the French ancien régime, with comparisons to developments in other parts of Europe. The chapter analyzes the type of state-building that occurred in France and other parts of Europe and highlights some of the ways this process influenced subsequent political development.

Chapter three examines early modern Britain and in particular the civil wars, regime changes, and Glorious Revolution of the seventeenth century. It analyzes how Britain's conflictual seventeenth century reflected previous state- and nation-building efforts and how seventeenth-century conflicts laid the foundation for the unusually peaceful and gradual political trajectory Britain would follow from the eighteenth century on.

Chapter four examines the French Revolution, taking up the story where chapter two left off. It analyzes why the French monarchy became vulnerable to collapse by the end of the eighteenth century and why, when it did collapse, a revolution, rather than a less tumultuous transition occurred. It also examines why the first modern democratic experiment produced by the revolution[20] led to state terror and a populist military dictatorship rather than consolidated liberal democracy. And it begins considering how the revolution would influence subsequent French and European political development.

Chapter five examines 1848, the next major turning point in Europe's political development. During this year a democratic wave swept across much of Europe, quickly toppling monarchical dictatorships. Yet barely two years later, this democratic wave had receded and Europe was back under dictatorial rule. The chapter explains why this democratic wave succeeded and then failed so spectacularly, focusing on the role played by class and communal conflicts in determining political outcomes.

The next three chapters examine European political development during the late nineteenth and early twentieth centuries, focusing on the development and growing conflict between nationalism and democracy. Chapter six examines the French Third Republic. It analyzes the transition to and the nature of the Third Republic. This Third Republic turned into France's longest-lived regime since the revolution and achieved important successes but was also marred by critical weaknesses. The chapter investigates the Third Republic's weaknesses through the prism of the Dreyfus Affair, the most important crisis the Republic confronted before the First World War.

Chapters seven and eight examine the unifications of Italy and Germany, respectively. These chapters analyze the states produced by these unification processes and how they influenced subsequent German and Italian political development, particularly via their impact on nation-building and by shaping the way the struggle for democratization would play out during the late nineteenth and early twentieth centuries.

The next five chapters focus on European political development during the interwar period. Another democratic wave swept Europe after the First World War, toppling dictatorships across the continent. However, by the end of the interwar period many of these new democracies had collapsed, some into a new and virulent type of dictatorship—fascist or National Socialist. Chapter nine examines the struggle for democracy in interwar France. It considers the main challenges confronting the Third Republic after the First World War and investigates why French democracy was able to survive until 1940, but in a weakened and troubled state.

Chapter ten examines British political development during the nineteenth and early twentieth centuries. It analyzes why Britain remained fairly stable during the nineteenth century when the rest of Europe was characterized by turmoil and upheaval as well as why it proved relatively immune to the extremism and democratic decay plaguing much of the rest of Europe during the interwar years.

Chapter eleven returns to Italy, asking why Italian democracy collapsed so quickly after the First World War. It investigates the causes of the political instability and violence Italy experienced after 1918 and the reasons why Mussolini and the fascists were able to take advantage of democracy's problems. The chapter also examines the nature and consequences of the fascist dictatorship in Italy.

Chapter twelve examines the interwar Weimar Republic. It investigates the causes of the Republic's collapse and the reasons why Hitler and the Nazis were the eventual beneficiaries of it. The chapter also analyzes the nature and consequences of the Nazi dictatorship.

Chapter thirteen examines Spanish political development. It begins with a consideration of state- and nation-building during the early modern period and analyzes how these influenced Spain's subsequent political development. The chapter focuses on the instability and violence plaguing Spain during the nineteenth and early twentieth centuries and asks why traditional conservative forces were able to retain immense power in Spain, while their influence was waning in much of the rest of Europe. The chapter also analyzes why Spain's interwar democratic experiment failed and why this failure led to civil war and a relatively traditional conservative dictatorship rather than fascism.

The next four chapters of *Democracy and Dictatorship in Europe* examine the second half of the twentieth century. Chapter fourteen examines postwar Western Europe, examining why liberal democracy was able to consolidate after 1945, having failed so often in the past. It focuses on how the Second World War and the changes that occurred after it at the international, regional, and domestic levels enabled Western Europe to put the instability, conflict, and violence of the previous 150 years behind it.

Chapter fifteen examines the transition to communism in East-Central Europe after 1945. Like Western Europe, East-Central Europe's postwar political development diverged greatly from the prewar period. But while this divergence landed Western Europe finally in the liberal democratic camp, East-Central Europe ended up ruled by communist dictatorships. The chapter investigates the domestic and international reasons for this political outcome and the main features and consequences of communist dictatorships in East-Central Europe.

Chapter sixteen investigates the background, timing, type, and consequences of Spain's transition to democracy in the 1970s. It examines the Francoist dictatorship that ruled Spain after the civil war and how it transformed Spain's economy and society, the nature of the transition to democracy, and the reasons why democratic consolidation occurred relatively quickly and easily in Spain during the late twentieth century.

Chapter seventeen examines the transition to democracy in East-Central Europe. It asks why attempts at political liberalization failed in East-Central Europe in the 1950s, '60s, and '70s, but democratization succeeded in 1989. It also investigates why, when democratization occurred, it was peaceful and negotiated in some East-Central European countries but accompanied by mass protests and elite intransigence in others. And finally, it considers how legacies of communism continue to influence the region's political development today.

Chapter eighteen, the conclusion, summarizes the book's findings and discusses the implications of the European experience for contemporary debates about democratization and consolidation. In particular, it lays out several crucial lessons European history provides about the development of democracy and dictatorship and reiterates the contributions a historical perspective on political development can provide to those struggling to understand the challenges facing democracy in Europe and many other parts of the world today.

| The Ancien Régime

Ancien régime society was [Ancien régime society was] divided into closed, self-regarding groups whose members have so few links between themselves that everyone thinks solely of his own interests, no trace of any feeling for the public weal is anywhere to be found.

—Anne Robert Jacques Turgot, minister to Louis XVI[1]

UNDERSTANDING MODERN EUROPEAN political development requires understanding the ancien régime: it was the system against which revolutionaries in France rebelled in 1789, and its characteristics shaped the nature of the French Revolution and the course of subsequent French political development. As Tocqueville pointed out over a century and a half ago, "without a clear idea of the old regime . . . it is impossible to comprehend" either the French Revolution "or the history of the . . . years following its fall."[2]

What, then, was the ancien régime? Although today the term refers to any regime that no longer exists, originally "ancien régime" referred to the order that existed in France before the French Revolution. Indeed, the term itself dates from this great upheaval: it seems to have first been used in a 1788 pamphlet celebrating the new regime that was about to be born with the meeting of the Estates-General.[3] The nature of the ancien régime is difficult for us to understand today. It was, most obviously, a political dictatorship—an absolutist monarchy, where subjects owed loyalty to a hereditary king whose rule was justified by the "divine right of Kings"—the belief that the king was God's representative on earth and his subjects were duty-bound to obey him.[4]

But the ancien régime was not only a type of political dictatorship justified by a particular ideology; it was a social, economic, and cultural system as well. This presented revolutionaries in France and other parts of Europe with a daunting task: getting rid of the institutions of political dictatorship, including the king himself, was only the first and, as it turned out, the easiest of the many steps that would be necessary to fully eradicate the ancien régime. Indeed, as we will see, destroying the ancien régime proved to be a longer and more difficult process than any revolutionary at the time could have predicted.

Understanding why this was so requires understanding the ancien régime. And in order to do this we must examine the context within which it developed—the early modern period in general and the seventeenth century in particular.[5] The key challenge French and other European rulers faced during this time was asserting authority over territory, subjects, and competitors. However, even when French and some other European rulers succeeded in meeting this challenge and building the foundations of modern states,[6] traditional, pre-modern social and economic relationships remained in place. The early modern period was thus an interregnum or transitional era: an old order was dying and features of a new order, most notably modern states, were beginning to emerge. An etymological reflection of the era's transitional nature is reflected in the term "state" itself, which is derived from the word "estate," which was, as described below, the dominant form of social organization before modern states emerged. (Such a situation, with traditional social and economic relationships co-existing with features of modern states, characterizes many parts of the developing world today.) As conditions changed over time in France and other parts of Europe, conflicts or tensions between aspects of the old order and the emerging new one grew, creating instability and, in some cases, violence and revolution. A full appreciation of the backstory of French and European political development must therefore begin with an analysis of the ancien régime and the conditions characterizing France and Europe during the early modern period.

The Ancien Régime's Background

Up through the early modern period Europe was divided into a large number of small political units. In 1500 Europe contained hundreds of entities claiming some authority over people or territory; for every one of these that survived, like France or Spain, there were several that did not, like Burgundy or Lucca.[7] During this time the borders between political entities were porous and poorly defined, and kings' control over border areas tenuous.[8] While border areas were particularly unstable, a king's[9] hold over the rest of his territories was often not much stronger; indeed, most of the "countries" of the day were really loose collections of provinces, regions, and people, with their own legal systems, cultures, languages, and traditions.[10] In short, where kings existed they were more titular than actual rulers, at least by contemporary standards: they had little power outside of a "capital" city; most people had little contact with or even knowledge of the king and his court; and the king's authority was constantly challenged. Most crucially, to maintain power kings needed the loyalty and support of the nobility.[11]

Indeed, the dominant authority in most people's lives during this time was local or religious. Direct responsibility for the provision of defense and welfare up through the early modern period lay mostly with the nobility rather than kings. In general, kings could not engage in warfare on their own; instead, they needed the support of nobles who provided the resources and men necessary for battle. Far from any king having a "monopoly over the use of violence," to use Max Weber's classic definition of "state-ness," control over violence in pre-modern Europe "was dispersed, overlapping and democratized."[12] Nobles had their own private arsenals, armed forces, and fortresses and used them to defend their land and the people who lived on it. In addition, the Catholic Church and ecclesiastical figures exerted immense social, cultural, and political influence and carried out many of the functions we would today associate with "states," including education, care for the poor, and running hospitals. In short, up until the early modern period, authority in Europe was segmented and fragmented and most Europeans' identities accordingly remained local or religious rather than national.[13] The geographical, ethnic, or linguistic unity that we associate with modern nation-states did not exist in Europe at this time.

The lack of a single central ruler with a monopoly over the means of violence or overarching authority made the seventeenth century disordered and violent. In addition to endemic banditry and piracy,[14] domestic and international conflict abounded. The Thirty Years' War (1618–1648) was among the most important of the latter. Although its origins lay in religious conflict between Catholics and Protestants, it developed into a more generalized conflagration that destroyed entire parts of Europe. For example, in the area of Central Europe that would later become Germany, war and the famine and disease that followed it reduced the population by perhaps one-third.[15] The period was also marked by domestic revolts, rebellions, and uprisings[16] that were largely a response to attempts to centralize authority. As monarchs attempted to consolidate power, local, regional, and religious elites as well as ordinary people engaged in various forms of resistance. The *Fronde* in France (see below), the English Civil War (see chapter 3), and revolts against the Spanish crown in Portugal and Catalonia (see chapter 13) were all consequences of this dynamic. Indeed, so frequent and severe were center-provincial-local confrontations, and so acute and disorienting was the larger debate about the nature and locus of authority, that many historians view them as the cause of a "general crisis" Europe experienced during the seventeenth century. As one influential treatment of the period put it, "Behind the internal conflicts in the European countries in the middle of the seventeenth century, we find the same factor: the growth of state power."[17] Indeed, the violence and instability caused by attempts to centralize authority were so substantial that many wondered if Europe would survive; as a contemporary observer wrote, "If one ever had to believe in the Last Judgment . . . I believe it is happening right now."[18]

War and domestic conflict led to a longing for an end to instability and violence. This is reflected in the work of major theorists of the era like Jean Bodin and Thomas Hobbes who argued that only strong, unitary sovereigns who had "high, absolute and perpetual power over . . . citizens and subjects" could "prevent society from lapsing into the 'state of nature,' a constant war of everyman against every man that made life solitary, poor, nasty, brutish, and short."[19] And indeed during the seventeenth century some monarchs did begin centralizing power, undermining that of the nobles and religious authorities, building their own militaries and developing the institutions that would enable them to finance and administer these endeavors. Such monarchs began, in other words, developing the foundations of what would become modern states. The way in which states were built and the relationships among the monarch, nobility, and church embedded in them would critically influence subsequent political development.

Even where successful, state-building was extremely difficult, marred by constant conflicts and setbacks, and, as we will see, requiring endless tradeoffs and bargaining. This is because even when faced with a desperate need for revenue to fight wars,[20] most European monarchs were unable to completely defeat those opposed to the centralization of authority. They therefore had to make a variety of compromises to get the job done. Although these compromises varied from case to case with critical implications for subsequent political development, one common feature was that rulers left many of their opponents' social and economic privileges in place while undermining or at least weakening their political power.

Privilege was a central feature of this time. Today this word has a pejorative connotation, but in pre-modern Europe it simply described rights people enjoyed by virtue of belonging to a particular social group or estate. Privilege was sanctified by law; one contemporary definition described it as "distinctions, whether useful or honorific, which are enjoyed by certain members of society and denied to others."[21] These distinctions extended into almost all spheres of life, governing everything from access to economic resources in general and property in particular, to the payment or non-payment of taxes, to the type of justice system and punishment one was subjected to. In contrast to the contemporary world, in other words, where rights are generally viewed either as national, deriving from membership in a particular state, or universal, inhering in all human beings, in pre-modern Europe rights were inherited or, as we will see, bought, and depended on membership in a particular group or estate. The privileged groups during this era were the nobility and the clergy, and their privileges originally derived from functions they served—providing justice, defense, and other social services. The world of privilege was thus marked by inherent inequalities and divisions: access to political, social, and economic resources and rights was largely determined by group membership. People identified accordingly with their status group or religious or local community rather than a particular country.

Beginning in the early modern period, however, kings in France and elsewhere began to change this system—or rather, parts of it. Eager to centralize power, early modern monarchs in France and elsewhere made a tradeoff—they exchanged support for or at least acquiescence in some centralization of political power for a re-confirmation, and in some cases even augmentation, of the social and economic privileges of the nobility and church. Although such tradeoffs enabled monarchs in France and elsewhere to centralize power, it also embedded crucial weaknesses or even contradictions in emerging states. As France and the rest of Europe changed over the course of the early modern period, privilege became harder to maintain and justify. In addition, and most pointedly in France, the inextricable intertwining of the king's power and the system of privilege made the ancien régime extremely difficult to reform since changes in one sphere had inexorable consequences on the others.

To better understand these dynamics, this chapter will examine France in depth and some other cases in comparison. France is often held up as the first modern, centralized state, and it is certainly the one contemporaries viewed with the greatest awe. It is also, of course, the country that gave us the French Revolution, and understanding the Revolution's backstory is critical. Furthermore, although much about France was distinctive, as was the case in all European countries, the basic challenges that arose from its state-building experience would critically affect its political development throughout the modern era.

The French Case

When Hugh Capet, the first king of the Capetian dynasty that would eventually create what we now think of as France, came to power in 987 he ruled over an assortment of lands, towns, and fortresses that were collectively much smaller than the territory we now recognize as France.[22] In addition, of the territory within France's borders, much of it was out of the king's direct control; "large parts of what subsequently would become the territorial state of the French monarchy were in practice independent and often belligerent states, imperial cities, and principalities, dependent on the counts of Flanders, the dukes of Burgundy, the kinds of England and of Aragon, to name but a few of the long series."[23] Hugh Capet's kingdom also lacked well-defined frontiers, a common language, or a unified legal system.[24] Given the obstacles to the centralization of power in France—strong traditions of local sovereignty, powerful nobles, and institutional, linguistic, and legal diversity within its provinces—it is not surprising that kings only gradually and fitfully expanded their territorial reach over the following centuries. And many of the areas incorporated into France kept their old customs, currencies, and languages, and kings also confirmed and often enhanced their traditional privileges, most notably their ability to control how they were governed and taxed.[25] The Church also retained control over education and poor relief, and French nobles remained powerful and obstreperous.[26] In short, up through the sixteenth century France did not resemble a modern state, much less a modern nation-state at all. Instead it was "a collection of 'nations,' pays, seignories, fiefs and parishes," each of which kept its own customs, privileges, and even languages.[27] Given this history of independence, attempts by kings to centralize power often provoked bloody reactions by elites and peoples.[28] Indeed, during the sixteenth and early seventeenth centuries conflicts over centralization became so frequent and serious that the "French monarchy seemed to be disintegrating in civil and religious war."[29]

Yet this gradually changed.[30] During the reigns of Louis XIII (1619–1643) and especially Louis XIV (1643/54–1715) the monarchy made great strides in subduing the opponents of centralization and expanding its military forces, lawmaking authority, and bureaucratic apparatus.[31] When Cardinal Richelieu looked back on his service to Louis XIII he wrote that when he became chief minister in 1624 "the Huguenots shared the state with [Your Majesty] . . . the *grands* (essentially the nobility) behaved as if they were not your subjects, and the governors of the provinces as if they were sovereign powers."[32] However, by the end of Louis XIV's reign these forces were greatly weakened and the French monarchy and state were the envy of Europe. How did this transformation occur?

Perhaps the most obvious characteristics of this period were violence and conflict. As Charles Tilly noted, "During the seventeenth century France passed through a significant revolutionary situation almost one year in two."[33] Peasant revolts, uprisings by the Protestant minority, and obstinate resistance by provincial authorities and local nobles marked the period.[34] However, the most consequential conflicts for French state-building were the series of civil wars known as the *Fronde* (1648–53).

The *Fronde* was a result of the monarchy's centralizing aspirations. In the years preceding its outbreak, the French monarchy had to deal with domestic unrest as well as the Thirty Years' War, straining its finances. The king thus needed to raise revenue, which would require expanding his control over individuals, areas, and corporate bodies previously largely free from central interference. The response was predictable: violent rebellions led by those committed to protecting privileges from the expansion of royal authority. The first of these, referred to as the first *Fronde* or the *Fronde Parlementaire*, was led by the Paris *Parlement*, which refused to pay proposed taxes and, in order to avoid future incursions, called for explicit limits on the king's powers. This revolt was eventually put down when the king's army returned home after signing the Peace of Westphalia, but the turmoil did not end. In 1650 a second *Fronde des noble* broke out. As the name indicates, this was a more directly noble-led affair, spurred by the nobility's determination to protect its power and privileges from the monarchy. These *frondeurs* were gradually beaten back, and by 1653 the *Fronde* was over. The cost, however, was very high: provinces were devastated and trade and economic life disrupted.[35] Nonetheless, the *Fronde* opened a new political era.[36] It did not eliminate opposition to centralization nor clear a direct path to more extensive taxation or the construction of other institutions associated with modern states, but it did change the dynamic between the king and nobility. Many nobles, after losing a military confrontation with the king, recognized the advantages of compromise. And the king, although victorious in the *Fronde*, recognized that defeating the nobles through coercion alone was very costly. The *Fronde* ultimately therefore "led both king and nobles to realize that cooperation could be mutually advantageous. After decades of revolts and conflict, this realization came nearly as an epiphany to both sides."[37]

Instead, therefore, of relying purely on coercion, Louis XIII and Louis XIV and their ministers began enticing key opponents into a new relationship with the crown using venality, bribery, patronage, and the distribution of privileges.[38] Such tools were not new in France, but the Louises made more extensive and innovative use of them than had their predecessors.

For example, even after his military victory in the *Fronde*, Louis recognized that he could not pay off the debts and expenditures associated with war through taxation alone. In the past, attempts to expand taxation had caused rebellions,[39] and so the king understood the need to move slowly and indirectly. Louis XIII, Louis XIV, and their successors therefore turned to a less politically problematic way of raising funds—the sale of offices. Venality has obvious advantages to leaders desperate for money. First, it is quick and easy, requiring limited personnel to administer and little in the way of institution-building. Second, it does not require directly confronting the nobility or other taxation-resistant actors. Accordingly, the sale of offices went into overdrive after the *Fronde* to the point where, by the eighteenth century, everything from the right to be an auctioneer, a bailiff, or an oyster seller to the ability to collect taxes and or be a judge was auctioned off.[40]

Many offices were lucrative, bringing an annual income as well as revenue produced by the office itself and some conferred privileges on the holder, including ennoblement, and eventually the ability to pass the office to descendants. The holders of such offices accordingly developed a strong stake in maintaining this system. And because offices were for sale to those who could afford them, they were often purchased by what we might now consider to be the well-off middle class. In addition, therefore, to providing quick and easy access to funds, venality enabled the king to create a new nobility as a counterweight to the old[41] by turning rich and ambitious local merchants, businessmen, and so on into his own clients.[42] The sale of offices thereby became a "key prop of royal absolutism."[43]

Alongside the sale of offices, the king also doled out or confirmed a variety of other privileges to increase loyalty to the crown and expand his authority.[44] One of the most important of these was exemption from certain taxes. The nobles, for example, did not have to pay the hated *taille* (a land tax) as well as other direct taxes such as the *capitation* and *vingtieme*.[45] The Church, meanwhile, was allowed to keep the revenue generated from its land (between 6 percent and 10 percent of the country's total), making modest "gifts" to the king in lieu of many taxes. The Church also collected the *tithe*, which theoretically entitled it to a tenth of every person's livelihood. Such measures helped the king buy off his opponents, but the price was high, not merely in lost revenue[46] but by creating deep divisions and inequalities in society.[47]

Other tradeoffs were required to expand the king's administrative capacity throughout his realm. Precisely because they had traditionally lacked the authority or institutional infrastructure to run the territories ostensibly under their control, French kings had relied on brokers to govern. The problem was that these brokers, often the great nobles, were not fully loyal or subservient to them. As one observer noted, "Of all the dangers that menace France there is none greater . . . than the tyrannical enterprises of the governors . . . who by means of their governments of provinces and towns have made themselves lords, practically sovereign lords of their regions."[48] Richelieu in particular recognized that successful centralization meant replacing this system, and so he created his own network of brokers, purposefully bypassing the *grands* and instead searching out men with connections and ties at the local and provincial level (people we might today call "joiners" or "connectors") who were not members of the old nobility. Lacking the independent power of the *grands*, these men became Richelieu's *creatures* alone.[49] Richelieu then funneled resources to his brokers, who then bought the support of other key figures at the local level. In addition to expanding the reach of central authority, these brokers acted as Richelieu's eyes and ears, facilitating information flows, acting as mediators between different interests, and lobbying for the king's policies.[50] Richelieu's successors, Mazarin and Colbert, continued along these lines, bypassing and undermining the *grands'* networks, and creating a new web of relationships that reached into provincial France. French kings thus initially relied on traditional means (funneling resources) and networks (local notables)[51] to expand control and were only gradually able to construct something that resembled a modern administration with the *intendants*, a sort of royal bureaucracy that operated parallel to the system of venal offices dominated by the wealthy.[52]

Alongside venality, patronage, and clientelism, the king also used the palace of Versailles to co-opt and control the nobles. After the *Fronde*, Louis XIV made presence at Versailles a key prerequisite for the currying of favor and commercial advantage. Once at Versailles, the king created an elaborate court and set of rituals that emphasized the king's differentiation from the nobles. The king devoted immense time and energy to cultivating social distinctions that played to the aristocracy's belief in a natural and clearly differentiated social hierarchy—but one with the king firmly at the top.[53] By assembling the nobility at Versailles Louis XIV was better able to "control them. Those who came were richly rewarded" but also "domesticated and made dependent."[54] In addition, from the king's perspective, bringing the nobles to Versailles had the advantage of physically removing them from their local power bases.[55] With more time spent at Versailles, noble households, entourages, gendarmes, and so on shrank.[56] Versailles, in other words, helped direct nobles' wealth and energy away from the administration of their land and people and toward trying to impress the king and other aristocrats. Conspicuous consumption, rather than politics, became the French aristocracy's focus.[57]

These tradeoffs were in many ways very successful. During Louis XIV's reign in particular the monarch's power vis-à-vis the adversaries of centralization increased. Although Louis XIV confirmed the Church's enormous financial resources he also declared his right to make ecclesiastical laws; to approve all declarations by the pope before they took force in France; to regulate bishops' travel outside of France; and to protect royal officials from excommunication as a result of their official duties. Similarly while the king confirmed the nobility's social and economic privileges, their political power was undermined. As nobles lost authority at the local level, they were increasingly viewed as parasites by the wider population. Tocqueville's remains the classic analysis of this transformation:

> [W]hen nobles had real power as well as privileges, when they governed and administered, their rights could be at once greater and less open to attack. In fact, [in a previous age] the nobility was regarded . . . much as the government is regarded today; its exactions were tolerated in view of the protection and security it provided. [By the eighteenth century, however they had ceased] to act as leaders of the people [but had] not only retained but greatly increased their fiscal immunities and the advantages accruing to them individually.[58]

Having co-opted or weakened his opposition, Louis XIV made great strides in centralization and state-building: he expanded France's territory by nearly 10 percent and added one and a half million new subjects to his realm;[59] he gave his territories something resembling a single system of civil law for the first time and eliminated some local, provincial, and municipal institutions;[60] he made his population more religiously homogenous by revoking the Edict of Nantes[61] and forcing two or three hundred thousand Huguenots who had previously resisted centralization to flee the country.[62] It is worth remembering that during this time it was widely accepted that religious diversity made a country unviable—as the old proverb had it: "one faith, one law, one king."[63] And Louis XIV expanded the monarchy's administrative and military power by making increasing use of *intendants* and expanding and professionalizing the army.[64] In short, during the seventeenth century French kings were able to centralize authority and lay the foundations of a modern state. By so doing, they transformed France from a kingdom that had seemed on the verge of disintegration, dismemberment, and anarchy at the beginning of the seventeenth century to one that possessed a monarchy and state that were the envy of Europe by the century's end.[65] Although the monarchy's political power increased greatly, a nobility and Church with immense social and economic privileges, were embedded within the ancien régime creating critical, perhaps even fatal, flaws. These flaws would come back to haunt French kings and the French people during the late eighteenth century and beyond.

Other Cases

Although there is much distinctive about the French case, the basic challenge confronting French kings during the early modern period—centralizing authority—was confronted by all European rulers. Not all rulers succeeded, however, in outmaneuvering or undermining the opponents of centralization. Indeed, the majority did not, which is why most of the political entities existing in Europe in 1500 were gone by 1900.

One particularly consequential, if unusual, example of state-building failure was Poland.[66] Indeed, during the early modern period Poland went in the opposite direction from many of its neighbors, with its nobility consolidating its dominance over the king. The nobility preserved and even strengthened its traditional social, economic, *and* political power at the local and national levels. It retained authority over its own lands and peoples as well as its own independent military capabilities; it also controlled a national political assembly, the *Sejm*, which elected the king, thereby ensuring that his independence and power were limited. Poland thus became known as "The Paradise of the Nobility"—because here the nobility reigned supreme.[67] Although many at the time favorably contrasted the Polish nobility's "Golden Liberty" to the absolutism developing in France and other parts of Europe, its ability to block the centralization of authority was calamitous. Lacking a strong central authority, Poland failed to develop the national-level administrative, fiscal, or military resources or the consistent, forceful foreign policy that would allow it to successfully confront its neighbors. As any modern victim of European imperialism could predict, it was thus gobbled up by them.

Poland and France were on opposite ends of the state-building spectrum during the early modern period, but there were many variations in-between. In Spain, for example, the centralization of authority went in reverse: at the beginning of the early modern period the country had some well-developed proto-state institutions, especially a strong military and a fairly strong monarchy, but by the period's end, both were in decline (see chapter 13).[68] The Spanish nobility and Church held on to political as well as social and economic power, and the Spanish crown was unable to develop administrative institutions under its own control or complete authority over Spain's provinces.[69] During the seventeenth century, centrifugal tendencies increased, and the crown faced revolts in Portugal, Catalonia, and elsewhere. Indeed, by the end of the century "the focus of loyalties for . . . Spaniards was becoming increasingly diffused" with identities becoming narrower and more localized.[70] As one of Charles III's (1759–1788) ministers put it, Spain remained "a body composed of other smaller bodies, separated and in opposition to one another, which oppress and despise each other and are in a continuous state of war."[71]

The Spanish state that emerged from the early modern period was thus weak—Spanish kings were not as powerless as their Polish counterparts, but neither were they able to undermine or co-opt the opponents of centralization as had their French counterparts. Without a strong central authority or national institutions Spain embarked on a long period of international decline and domestic disorder. "By the mid-seventeenth century, banditry was widespread . . . and there were enormous crime waves in both the countryside and the cities. In the 'dark corners of the land' . . . gang warfare and clan faction were the rule. Even in the capital Madrid, it was impossible to go out at night except in large numbers and armed to the teeth." Many began to fear that "royal jurisdiction" was on the verge of "extinction."[72] Spain thus entered the modern era with an un-integrated territory, a recalcitrant and fractious nobility, and an unreformed and reactionary Church—all of which critically affected its political development up through the twentieth century (see chapter 13).

Another interesting case is Prussia. Up through the early modern period Prussia was composed of discontinuous territories lacking natural boundaries or strong economic or cultural ties. Indeed, so disjointed were these territories that they were not yet generally even known as "Prussia."[73] The titular rulers of Prussia, moreover, had historically been weak and faced extremely powerful nobles. Little seemed to suggest, in short, that Prussia was an auspicious candidate for state-building.[74] Yet during the late seventeenth and early eighteenth centuries a series of remarkable Hohenzollern rulers—the Great Elector, Frederick William (1640–1688), Frederick I (1688–1713), and Frederick William I (1713–1740)—managed to achieve what the Prussian historian Otto Hintze referred to as "the perfection of absolutism," creating a strong state ruling over consolidated territories.[75] Prussian absolutism differed, however, in important ways from its French counterpart.[76] Rather than the monarch undermining the nobility as in France, or the nobility undermining the monarchy as in Poland, in Prussia a symbiosis emerged between the crown and the Junker aristocracy.

The Hohenzollerns eliminated the nobles' assemblies and created a national-level bureaucracy and army. Indeed, so formidable did both become that Prussia eventually became known as a "bureaucratic-absolutist" state; a famous quip had it that "Prussia was not a country with an army, but an army with a country."[77] But rather than severing the central state from the nobility, Prussian kings integrated them into it, allowing them to dominate high-status posts especially in the bureaucracy and army, and turning them into a "class of hereditary state servants."[78] This facilitated state-building by offering the nobility "something of value, the prospect of a salary that would assure a higher standard of living than many noble households could otherwise afford, an intimate association with the majesty and authority of the throne, and the status attaching to an honourable calling with aristocratic historical connotations."[79] It is important to note, however, that while the Hohenzollerns strengthened their own power at the national level, they left the nobility's local political power, including their authority over their lands and the people on them, largely intact.[80] And since the Junkers controlled a higher percentage of land during this time than almost any other nobility in Europe,[81] this meant that much of rural Prussia remained dominated by them up through the nineteenth century. As the great German historian Gerhard Ritter put it, "The Prussian sovereigns compensated their landed nobility for the loss of their political rights . . . by supporting their position as patrimonial lords."[82] And so despite losing power to central rulers, the Junkers remained "miniature kings" on their own lands and traditional social and economic hierarchies remained relatively untouched.[83] Prussia thus entered the modern age in paradoxical way—with a strong monarchy *and* a strong nobility, and with a comparatively modern state as well as deeply entrenched pre-modern social and economic relationships. As we will see, this played a crucial role in shaping Prussian and later German political development up through the mid-twentieth century (see chapter 8).

Lest we assume that the only successful states during the early modern period were absolutist, the British case presents another political trajectory. In comparison to France or Prussia, the obstacles to territorial centralization were relatively low in England since it had a fairly small territory that was easily navigable and somewhat removed from the main power struggles of the continent.[84] And indeed the country we now think of as England was unified much earlier than France or Prussia.[85] Nonetheless during the early modern period the British Isles were violent and chaotic, with kings constantly driven from the throne, rulers often meeting violent ends, and endemic riots and rebellions. One sociologist calculated that "between 1450 and 1640 there were more internal disturbances in

England than in any other European country."[86] This instability peaked with the War of the Roses (approximately 1455–1485), a decades-long series of conflicts between powerful magnates for control of the Crown. When the war finally ended with the victory of a somewhat obscure Henry Tudor, Earl of Richmond, a crucial task facing the new king was to assert himself vis-à-vis his "over mighty subjects" and (re)centralize authority. As one analyst of the period put it, "A poor and weak crown was confronted by wealthy and arrogant magnates: there lay the crux of the problem."[87] Henry VII (1485–1509) and his successors did increase the power of the Crown and began what some scholars refer to as a "Tudor revolution" in government.[88]

Henry VIII (1509–1547) continued along the path laid out by his predecessor, and took a major step forward by "nationalizing" the English church, thereby removing a potential opponent to his authority and using land expropriated from the Church to fund expenditures and buy the loyalty of elites. Meanwhile, Cromwell, Henry VIII's key minister (1532–1540), reorganized the government, making it less an extension of the king and his household and creating new institutions to handle various administrative functions. The process picked up under Elizabeth (1558–1603), who further strengthened loyalty to the Crown.[89] Under the Tudors, in short, government became less personalistic and more bureaucratic; whereas Henry VII had himself managed most governing functions from his private chambers, Elizabeth left much day-to-day governing to advisers and administrators. Reflecting this, whereas the word "state" had "possessed no meaning in English beyond the 'state or condition' of the prince or the kingdom, by the second half of Elizabeth's reign it was used to signify the 'state' in the modern sense."[90]

In short, in the years after the War of the Roses the Crown reasserted its authority in England. However, when seventeenth-century English monarchs tried to centralize their authority further by moving towards the type of absolutist dictatorships that their counterparts in France and elsewhere were developing, they failed. Indeed, by the end of the seventeenth century, the absolutist option had been firmly rejected in England. That Britain avoided the absolutist wave that swept over other parts of Europe during the early modern period profoundly influenced its subsequent political development, as we will see in the next chapter.

CHAPTER 3 | English Exceptionalism I

In the seventeenth century men killed, tortured, and executed each other
for political beliefs; they sacked towns and brutalized the countryside.
They were subjected to conspiracy, plot, and invasion. [By the eighteenth
century] this had all vanished.

—J.H. Plumb[1]

THE PREVIOUS CHAPTER analyzed the ancien régime and the rise of an
absolutist dictatorship in France during the early modern era. English
kings tried to imitate their French counterparts but ultimately failed, pushing
English political development in a very different direction from France's
and indeed the rest of Europe's. The price, however, was very high: during
the seventeenth century the British Isles suffered through civil war, religious conflict, military dictatorship, regicide, and a Glorious Revolution.
These political upheavals transformed the political infrastructure and power
relationships of England's old regime.[2]

This early transformation turned out to be crucial. As Europe embarked
on a period of rapid and disorienting change in the eighteenth and nineteenth centuries—with capitalism transforming societies and new social
groups demanding political power and representation—Britain already
had crucial political battles behind it and a national political institution in
place—Parliament—capable of integrating new groups into the system and
responding to new demands and challenges. As we will see, this helped make
Britain's political development exceptional during the modern era: gradual
and evolutionary as opposed to conflictual and violent.[3]

This chapter will examine the seventeenth-century political upheavals that contributed to British exceptionalism. At the heart of these upheavals lay three interrelated issues. The first concerned power: would England move in an absolutist direction with power increasingly centralized in the Crown, or would a more "balanced" political regime develop where power was shared among different political actors? The second issue concerned money: where would the financial resources necessary to meet state-building and war-making challenges come from? And the third issue concerned religion: how would religious differences within England and the territories of the British Isles be dealt with?

The Background

Before the seventeenth century a parliament existed in England, but it was not a permanent institution of government like the parliaments that exist today; it met irregularly, summoned by the king for advice or to deal with particular problems, like preparation for war.[4] English kings, like their counterparts elsewhere, were wary of Parliament since it could potentially restrict their power; in particular, Parliament had a nasty habit, from the king's perspective, of asking for concessions in return for money. English kings therefore tried to raise money on their own, either by exploiting their personal resources or via other means that did not require parliamentary approval. If, however, expenditures increased, the monarchy's existing resources and tools might no longer suffice. This happened often during the seventeenth century.

England's first Stuart king, James I (1603–1625), found himself in financial difficulty soon after coming to power due to the extravagance of his court and foreign policy misadventures. These financial difficulties led to a tug-of-war with Parliament. In 1610, for example, James was presented with a scheme known as the "Great Contract," which proposed granting the king an annual payment in return for the forfeiture of some of his traditional rights. However, once negotiations over the precise terms of the deal got under way, reaching an agreement on either the amount of money to be granted or the specific rights to be surrendered proved impossible. The deal therefore collapsed, and James dismissed Parliament. Since this did not end James's financial problems or Parliament's insistence on concessions in return for helping solve them, a pattern of summoned and dismissed parliaments continued throughout James's reign.

Such struggles intensified during the reign of James's son and successor, Charles I (1625–1649). One cause of this was Charles himself. An inflexible believer in the divine right of kings, Charles was not interested in compromise or bargaining. The king's personal preferences might not have mattered so much had the need for compromise and bargaining not increased—but it did, due partially to escalating financial pressures. One source of these was the Thirty Years' War. Parliament had grown frustrated with the cost and handling of English involvement in the war and rejected Charles's request for additional funding. This and other matters led Charles to dismiss Parliament in 1626. Now forced to raise money on his own, Charles turned to a number of unpopular measures, including forced loans; when some of his subjects refused to go along with them, Charles had them imprisoned and declared martial law to deal with the discontent and rioting breaking out in various parts of the country. Charles also increasingly made use of the Star Chamber, a royal court of justice, to punish opponents outside of the existing legal system.[5] Such measures, and the shift towards absolutism they represented, led to increasing dissatisfaction, and Charles was forced to call Parliament back into session in 1628. Almost immediately Parliament began debating resolutions to restrict the powers Charles recently employed and eventually proposed a "Petition of Right," calling for freedom from forced loans and taxes, guarantees of due process, and restrictions on the use of martial law. Unwilling to accept these demands, Charles dismissed Parliament in 1629 and began a long period of personal rule, sometimes referred to as the "eleven years' tyranny" since he refused to call Parliament for eleven years.[6] With Parliament no longer available to raise revenue, Charles again resorted to "innovative" measures to raise money, including the particularly unpopular "ship money."

Ship money traditionally referred to funds that the Crown collected from coastal towns to fund naval expenditures necessary to defend them in times of war. In 1634 Charles attempted to expand the use of ship money to inland towns and for the "possibility" of war, rather than because an actual conflict was at hand. (Underlying the king's need for increased funds lay changes in the nature of warfare and military technology which had rendered England's military, particularly its navy, out of date.[7]) Despite real military and financial needs, Charles's request for ship money was widely reviled[8] as an attempt to impose new taxes without parliamentary approval, and refusal to pay was widespread. The failure of ship money and other royal schemes to provide the funds to meet England's military and other obligations made it increasingly difficult for Charles to rule without Parliament; what made it impossible was that existing financial problems collided with other state-building challenges.

As noted in the previous chapter, it was generally accepted during this time that religious diversity made a country unviable—as the old proverb had it: "one faith, one law, one king."[9] Religion was "a public duty,"[10] and deviations from the state religion were seen as potentially subversive in England as in other parts of Europe. In the years after Henry VIII nationalized the English church and placed it under control of the state, all Englishmen were legally obligated to become members of the Church of England and attend services; Protestantism became central to England's identity, and Catholicism was prohibited.[11] However, during the early seventeenth century many, most importantly the Puritans, came to believe Protestantism was under threat.

As the name implies, Puritanism aimed to "purify" religious, personal, and social life of corrupting influences. In particular, Puritans believed that the Reformation in England had not gone far enough and that the Church of England remained tainted by traditions and practices that smacked of Catholicism. But in a world where religion was not merely a personal preference but a social force and where the King was the head of the state Church, criticism of religious traditions and practices had implicit and sometimes explicit political implications. By the early seventeenth century Puritanism had gained many adherents, particularly among the gentry and merchant and professional classes.[12] In addition to religious beliefs, Puritans developed strong internal networks and associations. Indeed, by the 1630s Puritanism had become a sort of "sub-culture, which began in the cradle of the family hearth, embraced and enclosed men, women and children within its godly vision and conditioned the way they saw the political world."[13] This combination—of shared beliefs, broad social appeal, and robust internal linkages—gave Puritans the resources for organized collective action.[14] And as Charles's reign progressed, growing numbers of Puritans and others came to believe that collective action was necessary.

From early on, Puritans and other Protestants suspected Charles of having Catholic sympathies. In 1625 he married a French Catholic princess and allowed her and her entourage to openly practice their faith, thereby raising fears that restrictions on Catholicism would be loosened. (In fact, Charles had signed a secret marriage treaty with Louis XIII of France promising concessions.) In addition to his marriage, Charles also embraced Arminianism, a movement that aimed to restore some pre-Reformation traditions and rituals to the English Church and strengthen clerical authority—which would, by extension, increase the power of the Church's head, the King, over religious life. Whatever Charles's personal religious inclinations, his support for Arminianism had a clear *political* rationale: he preferred religious practices that stressed obedience and deference to authority and a Church with strong internal hierarchies at whose apex would be the king. However, by involving the Crown directly in ecclesiastical matters and by calling for reforms that clearly aimed to enhance royal power, Charles increased and fused religious and political dissatisfaction. Puritans, for example, had previously concentrated most of their attention on religious reform. But the actions of Charles and his ally Archbishop Laud convinced them that their religious goals were threatened by the Crown's absolutist aspirations and therefore that political as well as religious changes would be necessary. Charles and Laud, meanwhile, convinced themselves that all those opposed to Arminianism were Puritans and unreasonable radicals and responded accordingly. These beliefs created a self-fulfilling prophecy: within the space of a decade Charles's and Laud's actions "succeeded in creating a new, large and radical Puritan party out of the hard core of the old one plus a mass of new alienated Anglicans."[15]

By the end of the 1630s Charles's financial, religious, and other policies had generated widespread dissatisfaction; bad economic conditions then made the situation even more volatile. Harvests during the 1630s were poor and came after a period of economic prosperity, thus frustrating the expectations of many.[16] What sent the whole situation spiraling out of control, however, was the fusing of Charles's absolutist aspirations with the "unfinished business" of state-building in the British Isles.

As noted in chapter 2, political centralization and territorial unity were achieved earlier in England than in many other European countries[17] and after the War of the Roses (approximately 1455–1485) Henry VII and his successors had re-asserted the Crown's authority vis-à-vis the nobility and the Church. However, the story in other parts of the British Isles was different. Scotland, for example, although united with England under a single Crown (the ruling Stuart dynasty was in fact Scottish) was essentially a sovereign state, retaining its own administration, institutions, laws, and culture. Warfare between the two countries was common, and "both sides engaged in persistent terrorism, marauding at will and reinforcing cultural stereotypes and racial animosities. Four of James's six immediate Scottish predecessors had died as a result of these struggles: two in battle, one on the scaffold, and one heartbroken after a devastating defeat. Indeed, there was so little respect between sovereigns that the decapitated skull of a Scottish king was used as a flowerpot in the English royal conservatory."[18] Hostility between the two peoples could thus be intense. As one early traveler noted that "nothing pleases the Scots more than abuse of the English . . . when the English taught their children archery they encouraged them to take good aim—so at least a Scot believed—by saying 'There's a Scot! Shoot him!' "[19] Despite all this, Charles decided to barrel ahead and increase his control over Scotland.

Again, it is important to note that although Charles's moves in Scotland and his larger absolutist aspirations were viewed as an unwelcome attempt to change the status quo by most Scots as well as others throughout the British Isles, they were in line with the broader trends of the day. As noted in chapter 2, during the seventeenth century monarchs in many parts of Europe were trying to centralize their power and move towards absolutist rule. In addition, given the centrality of religion at the time and the related conviction that religious diversity rendered a state unviable, it is also not surprising that Charles viewed religious homogeneity as necessary.[20] Moreover, Scotland's religious practices were particularly "problematic" from Charles's perspective not only because they differed from England's, but also because they were difficult to reconcile with absolutism. The Scottish reformation had gone further than its English counterpart, eliminating more of the rituals and practices associated with Catholicism, and had been "achieved against the State," not by it.[21] The Scottish Church, in other words, was not subservient to the Crown as the Anglican Church had become after Henry VIII's break with Rome.

Thus alongside attempts to impose his preferred religious doctrines and practices in England, Charles also demanded that the Scots bring their Church more in line with the English one and thus under greater royal control. The spark here seemed to be Charles's imposition of a new, royally authorized Prayer Book in 1638. The reaction to this was swift: when an attempt was made to read from this Prayer Book in St. Giles Cathedral in Edinburgh, shouting, wailing, and the throwing of foot stools resulted. From there, things got worse. Protests snowballed into a nation-wide revolt, and in 1638 members of the nobility, gentry, and clergy signed a Covenant committing to defend the Scottish church from Charles's impositions. The Covenant movement led to the outbreak of the Bishops' Wars in 1639 (so-called because Charles wanted to replace the Scots' Presbyterian system, which lacked bishops, with the English High Anglican one, in which bishops figured prominently). Lacking a strong military or the financial means to create one, Charles's initial attempts to squash the Scottish revolt failed, and he found himself in the unenviable position of facing military catastrophe and bankruptcy.[22] With his back up against the wall, Charles called Parliament to ask for funds.

Any hopes Charles may have had that Parliament would hand him the money to crush the rebellious Scots evaporated immediately. When Parliament met in April 1640 even moderates insisted that Charles address long-standing grievances related to the abuse of royal power before consideration would be given to his financial requests. Unwilling to accept Parliament's conditions, Charles dismissed it in May, only three weeks after it came into session, thus leading it to become known as the "Short Parliament." Meanwhile, the situation was deteriorating with discontent growing among soldiers and the broader population and the Scottish Covenanter army making its way to England. Unable to figure out any other way to finance a campaign against the Scots, Charles called Parliament back into session. This Parliament turned out differently than its predecessor.

The Parliament that came into session in November 1640 sat for twenty years, until 1660, and thus came to be known as the "Long Parliament"; its members included men like John Pym and Oliver Cromwell, who would play important roles in subsequent English political development. Although this Parliament was determined to press forward, initially its demands were not revolutionary—there were no calls to do away with the monarchy or enact far-reaching social or economic reforms. Instead, Parliament's goal was to check the Crown's absolutist tendencies and put in place what we would today consider a constitutional monarchy with authority shared between the executive and legislature. Indeed, reflecting its residual respect for the monarchy, the Long Parliament did not initially place full blame for the proceding years' events on Charles himself, faulting instead his "wicked" advisers. Indeed, two key ones, Archbishop Laud and Earl of Strafford, were quickly impeached and subsequently killed. Parliament did, however, quickly pass several acts with profound political implications. The Habeas Corpus Act (1640) abolished the Star Chamber and gave the imprisoned the right to demand a writ of habeas corpus; the Triennial Acts (1641) required that parliament be called at least once every three years;[2] and ship money was forbidden without parliamentary consent. Cumulatively, these acts would dramatically strengthen Parliament, giving it critical agenda setting, financial, and other powers.

The trigger for these changes and the calling of the Long Parliament more generally was Charles's absolutist and state-building aspirations, particularly his attempt to extend his authority over Scotland. Scotland was not, of course, the only territory in Charles's realm that he lacked full control over, and revolts in another of these, Ireland, pushed political upheaval further out of control. Indeed, because the English civil war cannot be untangled from the conflicts in Ireland and Scotland it is sometimes referred to as "The War of the Three Kingdoms."

Irish revolts began in 1641 and had a number of triggers, including the particularly harsh rule of Sir Thomas Wentworth (the most recent English

Lord-Lieutenant of Ireland), poor economic conditions, and probably most importantly, Irish (Catholic) fear of the growing power of the anti-Catholic Long Parliament and Scottish Covenanters. However, as was the case with Scotland, the deeper cause was the nature of Ireland's relationship with England.[24]

After the Tudor re-conquest of Ireland in the early sixteenth century, the English king became the king of Ireland, but English control over Ireland was contentious and incomplete. In order to increase the Crown's authority, a number of measures later used in other British colonies were employed, including martial law and plantations. Catholics in Ireland were discriminated against and their land taken away and given to Protestant colonists loyal to the metropole. Irish Catholics appealed to English kings for religious toleration and other rights, and the Irish upper classes argued for a restoration of their property and the same privileges enjoyed by other upper-class subjects of the English Crown. In the summer of 1641 Charles I's troubles seemed, momentarily, to offer the Irish a golden opportunity. Facing rebellious Scots and a Parliament unwilling to grant him funds to deal with them without concessions, Charles offered the Irish religious toleration, property, and other rights in return for raising an army that he could use against the Scots. However, Charles's attempt to raise a Catholic army confirmed suspicions of his Catholic intentions and untrustworthiness.

Over the course of 1641 tensions between Crown and Parliament increased. In November the latter passed the "Grand Remonstrance" cataloging Charles's perceived "misdeeds," calling for religious reforms along Puritan lines, the expulsion of bishops from Parliament, and a Parliamentary veto over Crown appointments. The Remonstrance had several critical effects. First, some parliamentarians who had previously been critical of Charles viewed it as a step too far and moved into what was becoming a "royalist" camp. Second, Charles's delay in responding to the Remonstrance led Parliament to take the unusual step of distributing it widely in an attempt to whip up popular support. And third, Charles ultimately rejected the Remonstrance and soon after made a move that sent the country careening towards civil war.

Fed up with Parliament, Charles attempted what was essentially a coup in January 1642, marching his soldiers into Parliament and arresting five of his key opponents, including John Pym, who had first proposed the Grand Remonstrance. Parliament had, however, been warned in advance, and the five fled before soldiers arrived. With the coup's failure and the further loss of popularity accompanying it, Charles decided to leave London and set up a new court in York; he also sent his family out of the country with the royal jewels to drum up foreign support. The king's coup attempt and flight hardened Parliament's stance. In March it passed the militia ordinance, declaring Parliament in control of the country's armed forces, and in June it sent Charles the "Nineteen Propositions" demanding that he relinquish control over defense and foreign policy, enforce restrictions on Roman Catholicism, make royal ministers and new peers dependent on parliamentary support, and allow parliamentary supervision of the education and marriages of royal children. Charles rejected the "Propositions," and by the end of the summer the king and the Parliament were at war.[25]

Parliament's forces were led by Oliver Cromwell. Cromwell was a devout Puritan who believed that God had chosen him for the tasks at hand. He developed the New Model Army, a disciplined, professional fighting force that was remarkably successful. By 1645 more than 10 percent of the adult males in England were in arms; the number is even higher if the British Isles are included.[26] However, as the New Model Army got closer to defeating the royalist forces, divisions about what should replace Charles and his regime grew. By the summer of 1647 the King was a prisoner of the New Model Army, the old regime was disintegrating, splits within the opposition in general and the army in particular were growing, and debates about England's political future were reaching a fever pitch.

Among the most important were the Putney Debates set up by the New Model Army at the end of October 1647. With the king gone and the old regime in tatters, the New Model Army had become a power separate from the Parliament it had been raised to serve. During the debates a group known as the Levellers called for universal suffrage, parliamentary supremacy, and the protection of a variety of "native rights," including freedom of conscience and equality before the law; they called, in other words, for what would have been Europe's first real democracy. As Colonel Rainsborough, the Leveller spokesman, put it: "I think that the poorest he that is in England hath a life to live, as the greatest he; and therefore truly, Sir, I think it is clear, that every man that is to live under a government ought first by his own consent to put himself under that government; and I do think that the poorest man in England is not bound in a strict sense to that government that he hath not had a voice to put himself under."[27] Most in the army viewed such changes as a recipe for "anarchy," but could not agree on an alternative to them. And then, in November, Charles escaped from his prison, plunging the country back into civil war.

With Charles's flight and the renewal of hostilities, calls increased within the army for him to be brought to trial for treachery and misdeeds. Parliament would not agree to this, instead hoping that continued negotiations with Charles could achieve peace and reform without political revolution. The army, however, was no longer willing to tolerate Charles or accept Parliament's primacy in political matters, viewing it now as a "decayed body" and the army as the real representative of the people.[28] The army thus presented Parliament with a Remonstrance, demanding Charles be brought to trial and that Parliament disband. Political developments in England thereby took a dramatic turn: what had originally begun as a conflict between Crown and Parliament over absolutist versus constitutional government had morphed into a battle between Parliament and the army over whether England should completely destroy the old regime.

The army, however, had the guns, and with political chaos engulfing England this gave it the upper hand. On the morning of December 6, 1648, troops marched into Parliament, commencing what may have been the first military coup in early modern European history. The troops were led by Colonel Pride who, armed with a list of MPs "hostile" to the army, proceeded to "purge" Parliament, leaving only a pliant rump behind. This episode accordingly became known as "Pride's purge" and the resultant parliament as the "Rump Parliament." In January 1649 Parliament put Charles on trial; within ten days he was beheaded. The impact of these events was momentous. As Thomas Carlyle put it, "I reckon it perhaps the most daring action any Body of Men to be met with in History ever, with clear consciousness, deliberately set themselves to do."[29] The Rump officially declared the monarchy and House of Lords abolished and England a republic, now to be known as the Commonwealth. With this latest political transition power now resided the hands of an unelected armed force. As Simon Schama colorfully notes, England had become "a vacuum filled by an uproar";[30] or as a popular ballad of the time put it, the "world [had] turned upside down."[31] It was against this backdrop that Hobbes wrote *Leviathan,* and once one understands the period, his concerns, if not necessarily his solutions to them, are easy to understand.

England was not the only part of the British Isles in an "uproar." The situation in Ireland was particularly grim. During the 1640s the revolt in Ireland had grown, fed by hopes of securing religious toleration and other concessions from Charles and fear of the anti-Catholic New Model Army.[32] When Charles was executed in 1649, the Irish proclaimed his son, Charles II, king in Ireland. One of the first acts undertaken by the new Commonwealth, therefore, was sending Cromwell to Ireland. The campaign by Cromwell and his successors was devastating: the Irish were slaughtered in a gruesome, bloody struggle that was as much a communal as a political conflict. Although estimates vary, hundreds of thousands of Irish ultimately lost their lives.[33] And if that was not enough, the 1652 "Act for the Settlement of Ireland" imposed at the conflict's end subjugated Ireland further, expropriating so much Irish land that by 1656, four-fifths of it was owned by Protestants.[34] The native, Catholic Irish were basically reduced to a subservient labor force for Protestant landowners.

Conflict also raged in Scotland. Although the Covenanters had opposed Charles I's religious and political moves, the Scots were unhappy about the ending of the Scottish Stuart dynasty and viewed the Commonwealth and New Model Army as major threats to their independence. The Scots therefore decided to back Charles II's claims to the throne in return for promises to respect Scotland's religious and political traditions. Cromwell came back from Ireland to deal with this threat, re-conquering Scotland by 1651 and expelling thousands of Scots to colonies. Although the Scots were not punished as punitively as the Irish, they had clearly been conquered and their long fight to maintain their independence was coming to an end.[35] The cost of the wars in the three kingdoms was very high: recent estimates suggest that England may have lost 3.7 percent of its population (more than in WWI and WWII), Scotland as much as 6 percent, and Ireland perhaps over 40 percent.[36]

Cromwell's victories in Ireland and Scotland may have fed his sense of destiny as well as the faith of many in him. In any case, he became convinced that even the Rump Parliament was corrupt and inefficient, and in April 1653 he and his allies did away with it entirely via another coup. With this, the Commonwealth was replaced by the "Protectorate" and Cromwell became "Lord Protector,"[37] thereby ironically achieving two of Charles's key goals—eliminating Parliament and creating a powerful, modern army—by returning the country back to a dictatorship, although of the military rather than the monarchical-absolutist variety.

Cromwell's Protectorate was an anathema to both Parliamentarians and Royalists and clearly obviated the entire rationale of the civil war, which had been to protect Parliament from royal overreach. While alive, Cromwell was able to suppress opposition, but when he died in 1658 things started to fall apart. The Protectorate was handed over to Cromwell's son Richard, but he lacked his father's power and charisma and was therefore unable to maintain the unity or support of the army; without it, the Protectorate was doomed. By 1659 Richard was gone, and in 1660 Charles II, son of the executed Charles I, was back on the throne. English political development now seemed to have come full circle, transitioning from one monarchical regime to another, with a republic and a military dictatorship in between. To an observer in 1660 it therefore might well have seemed as if two decades of violence, warfare, and political chaos had achieved very little.[38]

But that was not entirely true. Despite the restoration of the monarchy, there was no going back to the status quo ante. During the previous decades a king had been brought to trial and beheaded in the "name of the people," the House of Lords had been abolished, the established Church reformed, the lands of the king and Church confiscated, and rule "by the people" declared; new ideas about liberty, equality, and the nature of governance spread[39]; and England's relationship with Ireland and Scotland transformed (the "three kingdoms" were united under a single government for the first time during the Commonwealth era). And within England the political balance of power in 1660 differed from that in 1640. The Crown reclaimed by Charles II was "a different crown from the one that had tumbled into the basket in 1649. By withstanding attacks from monarch and army, Parliament had made good its claim to be the representative of the people, even if the concept of representation and the definition of the people remained elusive. If it had previously been an event, Parliament was now an institution."[40] The basic goal of the Triennial Act—ensuring regular parliaments—remained in force as did the abolition of key elements of personal rule, like the Star Chamber, and many of the Crown's feudal rights and revenues. Perhaps most importantly, parliamentary control over taxation was strengthened and the king's right to levy prerogative taxes like ship money eliminated. The restoration settlement was thus something of a mish-mash. Parliament was stronger, but the monarchy had been re-established and the balance of power between the two remained unclear. In addition, the political role of religion and the Church remained contentious; and although England's control over Ireland and Scotland had increased, these relationships were unsettled. In other words, many of the tensions that had tormented England during the previous decades—over regime type, religion, and state-building—remained embedded in the restoration order.

Not surprisingly, therefore, the first restoration king, Charles II (1660–1685), quickly found himself involved in some of the same conflicts that had bedeviled his father. Religion, for example, returned quickly as a source of controversy. Many in Parliament were suspicious of Charles II's pro-Catholic foreign policy, support of Catholic France, involvement in the Third Anglo-Dutch war, and issuance of the Royal Declaration of Indulgence, which would have granted significant religious liberty to both Roman Catholics and Protestant dissenters. Parliament was, however, able to force Charles II to back down, refusing to provide funding for involvement in the Anglo-Dutch war and compelling him to withdraw the Declaration of Indulgence and agree to the Test Act, which required officeholders to swear allegiance to the Church of England and denounce Catholicism.

Parliamentary and societal fears were sharpened not only by Charles II's purported personal religious preferences, but also by his family situation. Charles and his wife, Queen Catherine, had been unable to produce an heir, leaving Charles's Catholic brother James, the Duke of York, next in line for the throne. Given the widespread and vehement anti-Catholicism of the time, a movement to exclude James from the throne emerged. It is from this movement that the terms "Whig" and "Tory" derive, with the former advocating exclusion and the latter opposing it. To some degree, this also represented a socioeconomic divide, with the middle class and merchant groups over-represented among Whigs and the Tories having a more aristocratic air. Although ostensibly about religion, the exclusion conflict was at its heart political: would royal prerogative or Parliament determine the occupant of the throne? During the late 1670s and early 1680s Charles and Parliament tussled over an Exclusion Bill that would have barred James from the throne. So heated was this conflict that a group of Protestant conspirators launched the "Rye House Plot" to murder Charles II and James. The plot failed, but less than two years later Charles was dead anyway, and lacking an heir, his brother James assumed the throne as James II.

Despite this background, when James came to power his position seemed secure. His first parliament was dominated by Tories, and although his Catholicism was an issue, he had no sons and all his daughters were Protestant, so the belief was that the throne would return to Protestant hands. In addition, James initially promised to respect English law and the existing Protestant Church. When a challenge to James's rule broke out soon after his accession in the form of a rebellion by Charles II's eldest but illegitimate son, the Duke of Monmouth, it was rapidly put down. The army remained loyal to the Crown and no major areas or social groups rose up against the king. At least in James's early period of rule, therefore, it seems "that the vast majority of English men and women were willing to accept a Catholic king as long as he was willing to rule within the parameters established by the English constitution in Church and State."[41]

The problem was that James had no intention of so doing. Like his father and brother, James had Catholic and absolutist tendencies and aspired to the type of absolutist rule his cousin, Louis XIV, was perfecting in France (see chapters 2 and 4). James attempted to augment his power in myriad ways. He increased revenues by modernizing the Treasury and also benefited from a "trade boom" that increased customs returns, limiting the need to ask Parliament for funds.[42] In addition, recent research indicates that during James's reign "English taxes began their 'steep and almost continuous ascent,' "[43] thereby also increasing money available to him. One crucial outlet for these financial resources was the military. James recognized that a great power and a strong state required a powerful army and navy, and he modernized and increased spending on both. James gave key military positions to Catholics, which violated the Test Act, and was clearly an attempt to increase the military's loyalty to him.[44] James used the army for domestic political purposes as well, dispersing it across the country, providing both a visible manifestation of state power and a potent tool for social control.[45] James also extended his hold over other parts of the state apparatus like the courts, applying "litmus tests" to new judicial appointees and removing judges who did not agree with him, and over local government, purging "town corporations, commissions of the peace and country lieutenants."[46] James also increased spending on domestic intelligence gathering and made use of government spies and the post office to keep an eye on the opposition.[47] One contemporaneous ditty captured the reality of this early modern surveillance state: "In former time / Free conversation was no crime / But now the place / has chang'd its face."[48]

As was the case with his father, it is difficult to detangle James's absolutist aspirations from his religious ones. In late 1685 James adjourned Parliament when it resisted his attempts to exempt Catholics from the Test Act. In spring 1687 he then issued a Declaration of Indulgence, which would have greatly expanded religious freedom for Catholics and Protestant Dissenters. Although this seems progressive today, it was viewed as radical and threatening in seventeenth-century England. Alongside the Declaration, James used royal prerogative to place Catholic supporters in key social and political positions. For example, he caused a major kerfuffle by trying to force a Catholic president on Magdalen College, Oxford, a traditional Anglican bastion. These provocative moves aimed to advance the cause of Catholicism and to boost James's political power by planting Catholics in influential positions and trying to build a coalition between Catholics and Protestant dissenters. James also tried to "pack" the Parliament that was due to come back into session in 1688 with his supporters. And to top it all off, in the fall of 1687 rumors began to spread that James's wife, Mary, was pregnant, raising the specter of a Catholic heir to the throne.

Thus by 1688 tension was already high when James re-issued his Declaration of Indulgence and ordered all clergy to read it in their churches. When the Archbishop of Canterbury and six other bishops refused, James had them arrested them for "seditious libel" (essentially rebellion against the Crown) and sent to the Tower of London, causing an uproar. After a trial the bishops were acquitted, but the damage had been done. "The Trial of the Seven Bishops, the greatest historical drama that ever took place before an authorized English law court, aroused popular feeling to its height."[49] By this point, the worst fears of the exclusionists seemed to have been confirmed. James's desire to change the religious and political status quo and construct the type of Catholic, absolutist regime that his cousin was perfecting across the channel was obvious to all.[50] As historian Steven Pincus perceptively put it, James

> carefully, methodically and above all bureaucratically promoted a series of centralizing policies that were both modern and proven to be successful. James followed a blueprint that had been perfected by Louis XIV in France. James was not merely seeking equal standing for his coreligionists. His total reshaping of English government at every level was much more ambitious than that. . . . [He] built up a modern army, and a modern navy, made all branches of government subservient to royal authority, and extended the power of the government deep into the localities. . . . He went a long way towards transforming the English state into a centralized, efficient, and bureaucratic machine.[51]

By 1688 James had alienated even most of his erstwhile Tory supporters, but they could at least console themselves with the thought that his rule would eventually end and the throne would revert to James's Protestant daughters—and then presumably to the political status quo ante. However, these hopes were dashed in the summer of 1688 when James's wife gave birth to a baby boy. With this birth the country now faced the possibility of a Catholic and potentially absolutist dynasty on the throne in perpetuity, something intolerable to even the monarchy's hitherto most ardent supporters.[52]

Having lost elite and mass support, James was a dead man walking. A coalition of influential figures sent a letter to William of Orange, Stadholder of the Dutch Republic and the husband of James's eldest daughter, Mary, basically inviting him to invade England and rescue the country from James. In November William landed in England, famously proclaiming "the liberties of England and the Protestant religion I will maintain." The fighting force William arrived with was relatively small; he could not have succeeded without popular support. And this he clearly had. Almost as soon as William landed, Protestant officers in the army began defecting and popular uprisings and anti-Catholic rioting spread across the country. Faced with an invasion and evaporating support, James attempted to flee; he was recaptured but then allowed by William to escape to France. "It is undoubtedly true that William's invasion was what finally toppled James' monarchy. But it would be misleading to conclude that the Glorious Revolution was therefore brought about from above and outside, or that it was, first and foremost, a foreign invasion. William's invasion was itself predicated upon the fact that James' regime had already begun to collapse from within. . . . The Glorious Revolution was thus equally brought about from within and from below."[53] Indeed, a key reason why the country did not descend into civil war as it had in the early 1640s was that by 1688 Tories and Whigs agreed the king had to go.

James's flight provided a convenient fiction for the transition: it was proclaimed that by fleeing the country, he had abdicated, leaving the throne vacant.[54] In January the House of Commons passed the following resolution:

> That King James the Second, having endeavoured to subvert the Constitution of this Kingdom, by breaking the Original Contract between King and People; and, by the Advice of Jesuits, and other wicked Persons, having violated the fundamental Laws; and having withdrawn himself out of the Kingdom; has abdicated the Government; and that the Throne is thereby vacant.[55]

In February, Parliament offered the throne to William and Mary.[56] And with this, British political development began a new era. Although this was not fully clear at the time, the Glorious Revolution solved many of the conflicts that had bedeviled England, Britain, and much of the rest of Europe during the early modern period.

Politically, the Glorious Revolution eliminated the absolutist option and transformed the political infrastructure of the old regime. Throughout the seventeenth century English kings tried to move towards the type of absolutism developing in France and other parts of Europe. But with the transition from James to William and Mary, British absolutism was dealt a fatal blow and Parliament, constitutionalism, and the rule of law were strengthened. Even the coronation oath taken by William and Mary reflected these changed expectations and power relationships, binding "them, in a pointedly contractual phrase, to govern 'according to the statues in Parliament agreed on'— the first time a reference to Parliament and . . . law had figured in this ancient ceremony."[57] More significant was the new monarchs' acceptance of the Bill of Rights in 1689 which committed the Crown to governing in accordance with the rule of law.[58] As historian W.A. Speck put it, with the acceptance of the Bill of Rights, the Crown was now clearly "beneath and not above" the law. In addition the Bill of Rights confirmed Parliament's status not as "an event" but "an institution" and enumerated and enhanced its powers,[59] perhaps most importantly its control over taxation and the military. The Bill of Rights also enumerated liberal rights held by citizens, thereby changing England from a nation where "liberties were based on tradition to one where they were based in part on positive law."[60] And the Bill of Rights made the transition from James to William a constitutional settlement rather than a coup,[61] presenting government as a sort of contract, where rights and responsibilities were based on law and not the whim of the monarch.

In short, the Bill of Rights and the larger political transition it was part of represented a fundamental break with divine right views of monarchy and old regime norms of governance. This was, to be sure, no transition to democracy. What Britain became after the Glorious Revolution was an aristocratic oligarchy, but one with a constitution institutionalizing some liberal rights and a strong, *national* parliament that provided representation to the elite and could check the Crown. Thus by the end of the seventeenth century England had behind it political conflicts that most other European countries embarked on during the nineteenth and even twentieth centuries—a time, as we will see, when these political conflicts became inextricably tied up with economic and social ones.

In addition to putting crucial political conflicts behind it and entering the modern era with a constitutional political order and a powerful Parliament, the Glorious Revolution also opened up a new era in state-building. Most efforts at state-building during the early modern period failed; those that succeeded often did so under absolutist auspices (see chapter 2)—precisely why, of course, James and his predecessors were so enamored of this political option. But with the Glorious Revolution, Britain's state-building continued on a constitutional and parliamentary path.[62] By the early eighteenth century the British state was extracting more resources, had more effective administrative institutions, and controlled a more powerful military than other European states.[63] (In Michael Mann's terms, it was both infrastructurally and despotically powerful.[64]) In addition, problems related to territorial control or integration entered a new phase after the Glorious Revolution. In 1707 the Act of Union ended Scottish political independence and created the United Kingdom of Great Britain.[65] Ireland, meanwhile, was further reduced to colonial status, ruled over by the military and a Protestant elite, thereby foreshadowing the treatment Britain and the rest of Europe would mete out to other colonies in centuries to come.

The economic consequences of this post–Glorious Revolution state-building were profound. The constitutional and parliamentary system checked the power of the king without allowing the aristocracy to run rampant (as it did, for example, in Poland and to a lesser degree Spain; see chapters 2 and 13), provided a forum where emerging social and economic groups could find a voice, and institutionalized the rule of law and the protection of private property. For these and other reasons this system is often viewed by social scientists as a—or even the—main reason behind England's rise to hegemony during the coming centuries.[66] After 1688 England's constitutional and parliamentary political order oversaw a "financial revolution," creating the Bank of England and a new system of public credit that raised money more cheaply and efficiently than other European countries. And the stability and legitimacy generated by the new constitutional and parliamentary order enabled the British state to dramatically increase taxation to the point where by the early eighteenth century "Britain's population was generating a level of revenue per capita exceeded only by the Dutch Republic."[67] (See Figure 3.1.) These increased revenues, in turn, enabled the development of a vast military apparatus and ambitious foreign policy.[68]

In addition to solving critical political and state-building challenges, the Glorious Revolution also helped end the religious conflict that had

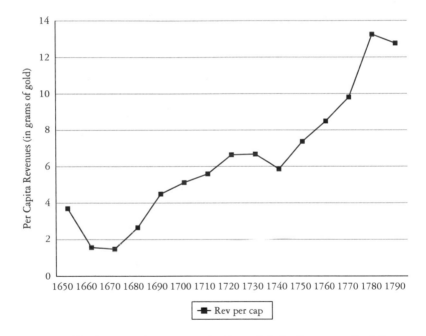

FIGURE 3.1 Yearly per capita revenues in Great Britain (in grams of gold), 1650–1789.

Source: Mark Dinecco, "Fiscal Centralization, Limited Government, and Public Revenues in Europe, 1650–1913," *Journal of Economic History* 69, 1 (2009): 48–103. Dinecco, *Political Transformation and Public Finances, Europe 1650–1913* (New York: Cambridge University Press, 2011); K. Kivanç Karaman and Şevket Pamuk, *The Journal of Economic History* 70, 3 (September 2010).

plagued England during the seventeenth century and that would continue to plague other parts of Europe in the centuries to come. In 1689 Parliament passed the Toleration Act granting freedom of worship to most Protestant dissenters—but not Catholics. This was a major change from the beginning of the seventeenth century when, as noted above, all English men and women had to be members of the state church and dissent was punishable by law. In 1701 Parliament passed the Act of Settlement banning Roman Catholics, or anyone who married a Roman Catholic,[69] from the throne, eliminating from British political life a long-standing cause of instability. The Act of Settlement also re-confirmed that the occupant of the throne was governed by law, not heredity or divine right. Catholics thus still faced immense discrimination in England, and religious conflict continued in other parts of the British Isles, most obviously in Ireland where the Catholic majority was denied basic rights like the ability to vote or sit in Parliament, own or purchase land, get a university degree, or gain entrance into key professions. Despite these injustices, it is important to note that for the time and in comparison to the rest of Europe, England did at least have the principle of toleration enshrined in law—a condition that "stood in stark contrast" not only to England's past but also "to the enforced religious uniformity of France and most of the German states" and was even different from "the Calvinist domination of Protestantism in the Netherlands or the monopoly of the established Lutheran churches . . . in Scandinavia."[70] Indeed these post–Glorious Revolution changes would provide a foundation upon which future expansions of religious toleration could be built (see chapter 10).[71]

Conclusions

The year 1688 was a critical turning point in British political history. Whether this turning point should be considered a true "revolution" on a par with what occurred in France in 1789 has long been debated by historians.[72] One obvious thing to note is that while the conflicts of the seventeenth century transformed the political institutions of England's old regime, they left its social structure essentially intact. In particular, the English "landed upper class was not in any way displaced" by the upheavals of the seventeenth century—as its French counterparts were after 1789. Indeed, as we will see, without a strong monarch to counterbalance it, this landed upper class became the most powerful in all of Europe with critical implications for Britain's subsequent political development.[73]

However by the end of the seventeenth century Britain was dramatically different politically than it had been at the beginning of the seventeenth century, and it was also dramatically different politically from most of the rest of Europe. And its new political order worked: whereas during the seventeenth century England had been wracked by violence and instability, from the eighteenth century on it was an island of political stability and became commercially and militarily the dominant power in Europe. But the price paid for this had been very high. During the seventeenth century, "men killed, tortured, and executed each other for their political beliefs; they sacked towns and brutalized the countryside. They were subjected to conspiracy, plot and invasion." By 1688 it almost seemed as if "violence in politics was an Englishman's birthright . . . conspiracy and rebellion, treason and plot were part of the history and experience of at least three generations of Englishmen."[74] But by the eighteenth century, Britain had put this legacy behind it, having fought crucial political battles and transformed the political infrastructure of its old regime. Its political development during the modern era therefore turned out to be more peaceful and gradual than in most of the rest of Europe. This early political transformation had other equally important consequences, the most obvious being that it enabled Britain to go out and subjugate a larger area of the globe than any other European country. Another critical, and perhaps ironic, consequence of this early political transformation is that it enabled the social and economic vestiges of its old order to remain in place longer than in most of the rest of Europe (see chapter 10). The contrast with the French case, which jump-started the modern era in Europe, and is in many ways Britain's polar opposite, is instructive. It is to this case that the next chapter turns.

| The French Revolution

Since 1789 European and indeed world politics has been a struggle for
and against the principles of the French Revolution.

—E.J. Hobsbawm[1]

B RITAIN WENT THROUGH a series of upheavals during the seventeenth
century that transformed it politically and placed it on a different political development path from most of the rest of Europe. But however dramatic and consequential Britain's seventeenth-century upheavals were, they
were nothing compared to what occurred in France at the end of the eighteenth century. The French Revolution not only transformed France more
profoundly than the Glorious Revolution or civil wars did Britain, it also
exerted a direct and lasting impact on the course of European and world history in a way the British upheavals did not. Indeed, to paraphrase the great
historian Eric Hobsbawm, since 1789 European and indeed world politics
can be understood as a struggle for and against the principles of the French
Revolution.[2]

Why was the French Revolution so pivotal in French, European, and
world history? France's position in Europe during this time is surely part
of the answer. Unlike England during the seventeenth century, France at
the end of the eighteenth century was continental Europe's most powerful
and admired state; its absolutist monarchy was viewed by other European
monarchs with awe. Its culture and language dominated Europe, and elites
across the continent were intensely Francophone. Moreover, the revolution
spilled beyond France's borders, as Napoleon marched across Europe and its
ideas spread around the globe. For these and other reasons, events in France

influenced eighteenth-century Europe in a way events in seventeenth-century Britain did not. But most important was the nature of the French Revolution itself: it was not merely a transition from one type of political regime to another, but rather the greatest, most radical threat the ancien régime had yet experienced, challenging not merely its political structures, but its social and economic ones as well.

This chapter will examine the French Revolution and how it changed the course of French and European history. Although the revolution had many causes, at its heart lay the nature of the ancien régime. By the 1780s the weaknesses embedded within the ancien régime, along with economic, demographic, and ideological developments, helped create a crisis. However, once change began, so interconnected were the political, social, and economic structures of the ancien régime that any attempt at reform in one sphere inexorably impacted the others. And once the system began to unravel, deep divisions in ancien régime society, the radical goals of the revolutionaries, and the dangerous domestic and international situations created by the monarchy's collapse sent the situation spiraling out of control.

The Background

As noted in chapter 2, the ancien régime in France achieved many successes, particularly in the realm of state-building. During the seventeenth century absolutist monarchs ended a period of chaos, confusion, and instability and turned France into the dominant power in Europe. They did so by asserting dominance over their territory, subjects, and competitors, particularly the nobility and the church, and by centralizing authority. However, the price paid for these accomplishments was high. In essence French monarchs bought acquiescence in the centralization of authority by confirming, and in some cases augmenting, the privileges of particular provinces and groups. Although this did enable kings to stabilize France after a period of intense disorder (see chapter 2), as conditions changed during the eighteenth century the tradeoffs and compromises built into the French state began destabilizing the ancien régime instead.

One critical change occurred in the realm of ideas. French kings based their claim to rule on divine authority ("the divine right of kings," see chapter 2), and political power was inherited. The social order accompanying this form of rule was, as noted, based on privilege: everything from access to economic resources to the payment or non-payment of taxes, to the type of justice one was subjected to, was determined by membership in a particular group or residence in a particular province. In this world, the privileged and non-privileged were not just politically, but also socially and economically distinct. As Abbé Sieyès, who would play a critical role in the French Revolution (see below), once wrote, "The privileged individual considers himself, along with his colleagues, as constituting a distinct order, a nation of the select within the nation. . . . The privileged actually come to see themselves as another species of man." Similarly, Tocqueville said of the aristocracy that "[t]hey scarcely even think of themselves as belonging to the same humanity"[3] as the rest of us. In addition, in the ancien régime people were subjects rather than citizens, duty bound to obey their ruler as God's representative on earth. Challenges to this political and social order began as early as the Reformation, which began breaking down ideas about divine sanction and inequality before God. Such challenges grew more widespread and forceful from the eighteenth century on, expanding from the religious to the intellectual and political spheres.[4] The Enlightenment, of course, took aim at many aspects of the old regime, including the legitimacy of absolutism and inherited social hierarchies.[5] Perhaps most importantly, "natural rights" advocates, social contract theorists, and others began asserting that the right to rule depended not on birth but on fulfilling certain obligations or ensuring certain outcomes. John Locke, for example, famously declared "life, liberty and [property]" to be fundamental rights, meaning they could not, therefore, be subject to the whims of monarchs."[6] Rousseau, meanwhile, although a very different thinker, similarly shook up traditional beliefs about governance by laying out a "revolutionary notion of equal citizenship and the concept of public opinion that would be a court of appeal against the unjust actions of the state. Society, through the social contract, granted the state its autonomy in return for the state's recognition of the innate natural rights of the individual."[7] In addition to questioning the nature or foundations of the right to rule, Enlightenment thinkers also advanced a vision of a community made up of autonomous and equal individuals that offered a stark alternative to the hierarchical and privileged social order at the core of the ancien régime. Alongside these new ideas, the basis of privilege had also changed: in the past social hierarchies had been justified by services that the privileged groups rendered to king and country, but by the eighteenth century the nobility in particular no longer performed these functions, so there was "very little justification by way of social utility to support [their] lofty and parasitic position."[8] Enlightenment thinking was undoubtedly most prevalent among members of the educated elite, but as Robert Darnton and other scholars have shown, radical and subversive ideas spread fairly rapidly and widely in late eighteenth-century France, even without the benefit of Twitter and Facebook.

Alongside ideational changes, economic development during the late eighteenth century also proved destabilizing as it re-shaped France's social structure. Traditionally, society was divided into three estates—the church, the nobility, and the rest—but by the end of the eighteenth century this tripartite structure no longer corresponded to the distribution of interest, property, or productive capacity. The third estate, for example, had grown dramatically in size and economic importance and included a growing middle class or bourgeoisie that saw itself as the most industrious and dynamic sector of society. By some estimates, for example, there were "more than twice as many bourgeois under Louis XVI as in the last years of Louis XIV"[9] and this group resented the privileges enjoyed by the first and second estates—or at least disliked being kept from them.[10] The first and second estates, meanwhile, had become more differentiated and internally divided. The nobility, for example, included, members of the "nobility of the robe" and "nobility of the sword" (the former being more recently ennobled state servants and the latter's nobility emanating from feudal military service), and the economic resources, interests, and viewpoints of different parts of the nobility became less homogenous over time. Within the Church, meanwhile, differences between wealthy bishops and relatively poor local clergy increased. Economic development, in short, made the ancien régime's tripartite organization of social, economic, and political power anachronistic and generated tensions within and between various groups.

In addition, although the eighteenth century was generally prosperous, the benefits of growth were unequally distributed. Urban wage earners, for example, did less well than others since prices rose more than wages. Small peasants also did relatively poorly. Furthermore, economic growth was uneven and the economy stagnated about a decade before the revolution. The effects of this slowdown were aggravated by a major economic crisis in 1787, triggered, as these things often were in pre-capitalist times, by bad harvests. By the late 1780s, in short, economic suffering was extensive and concentrated in the lower orders; economic development had exacerbated social tensions and resentments; and the Enlightenment had corroded the legitimacy of the ancien régime and the system of privilege that supported it. But dissatisfaction alone does not a revolution make. As one of history's great revolutionaries once noted, "The mere existence of privations is not enough to cause an insurrection; if it was, the masses would always be in revolt."[11] Instead, the real problem was that by the 1780s the ancien régime faced both growing domestic and international challenges *and* was unable to respond successfully to them.[12]

The clearest and most consequential example of this was in the realm of finances.[13] The French ancien régime was built upon a system of financing that seems peculiar to us today (see chapter 2). As the great historian Albert Cobban characterized it, Louis XIV bequeathed to France a fairly modern state paired with a semi-medieval system of financing.[14] As we know, this financial system was a result or manifestation of the tradeoff that lay at the heart of the ancien régime: in order to keep the support or at least acquiescence of the adversaries of absolutism, the crown preserved and even augmented many privileges. (As one scholar sardonically put it, absolutism can therefore be viewed as "no more than a gigantic system of bribery of those whom the crown found it worthwhile to bribe."[15]) And one of the most tangible benefits of privilege was exemption from many taxes. But since taxes are generally the modern state's primary source of revenue, French kings were financially constrained by the privileges they depended on to rule. The tension or even contradiction between a fairly modern state and a semi-medieval financing system became increasingly clear over the course of the eighteenth century. Ironically, this was partially a consequence of the ancien régime's success: as France's absolutist monarchs grew more powerful, so did their international aspirations. In particular, in order to maintain its great power position France became involved in wars throughout the eighteenth century. Making matters worse—from the French perspective, that is—the ancien régime found itself facing new international rivals, particularly Great Britain, which, partially as a result of developments discussed in the previous chapter, had a more flexible and efficient political and financial system than France. The French confronted the British in the Seven Years' War (1756–1763), which ended with France losing most of its overseas holdings and navy and accumulating debt that by the end of the 1760s was devouring more than 60 percent of state expenditures to service.[16] France then got involved in the American War of Independence, taking the side of the rebellious colonists against the British. (If there was ever a good example of the blind force of international ambition, France's absolutist regime taking the side of the liberty-loving, democratically minded colonists was it.) Although the colonists' victory against the British bought some revenge for France's loss in 1763, the price paid was very high. French participation in the American War of Independence made the ideals of the American Revolution widely known and fashionable in France, further undermining the legitimacy of the ancien régime. One aristocratic observer remarked, "I was singularly struck . . . to see such a unanimous outbreak of lively and general interest in the revolt of a people against a king. . . . I was far from being the only one whose heart then throbbed at the newborn liberty reawakening to shake off the yoke of arbitrary power."[17]

In addition, participation in the American Revolution worsened the ancien régime's finances. The limited taxation capacity of the ancien régime meant that participation in the war was financed primarily by borrowing. The ironies here are delicious, with the ancien régime's inability to raise taxes reflecting "inversely, the well-known American principle of 'no taxation, without representation,'" since the privileged groups took "the position that if they were not represented in government they were under no obligation to pay taxes to it."[18] On top of an already very high debt burden, additional expenditures for this war helped push the state near bankruptcy.[19] It is important to stress, however, that this was *not* due to the absolute amount of expenditures, but rather to the inability of the ancien régime's financial system to pay for them. A comparison with Britain is illustrative. Although France was richer and more populous, the British state taxed more extensively *and* borrowed more cheaply. By the end of the 1780s the British tax burden was higher in absolute terms than the French and took up nearly twice as high a share of per capita incomes (see Figure 4.1).[20]

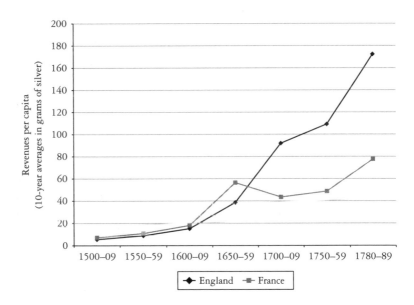

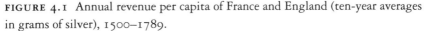

FIGURE 4.1 Annual revenue per capita of France and England (ten-year averages in grams of silver), 1500–1789.
Source: Mark Dinecco, "Fiscal Centralization, Limited Government, and Public Revenues in Europe, 1650–1913," *Journal of Economic History* 69, 1 (2009): 48–103. Dinecco, *Political Transformation and Public Finances, Europe 1650–1913* (New York: Cambridge University Press, 2011); K. Kivanç Karaman and Şevket Pamuk, *The Journal of Economic History* 70, 3 (September 2010).

Moreover both levels *and* rates of increase in taxes were higher in Britain than France: in fact, despite growing need, the share of taxes collected per capita seems to have fallen in France over the course of the eighteenth century.[21] The French state's relatively limited taxation capacity influenced the cost of its borrowing as well: since it was unable to raise taxes as easily or efficiently as the British to repay loans, markets extracted "a risk premium for holding even the most secure debt obligations of the French monarchy."[22] These differential financial capabilities help explain why Britain was able to pay off the cost of war, recover quickly from defeat in the American War of Independence, and even go on to improve its international position afterwards, while France ended up crippled by its "victory." It also explains why taxation created more resentment in France than England: in the former, privileged groups and provinces avoided paying taxes, whereas in the latter everyone, including the aristocracy, paid taxes.[23]

Although the financial fallout from participation in the American War of Independence pushed the ancien régime to its breaking point, these structural problems had been clear to perspicacious reformers for some time. The problem was that by the 1780s it was no longer possible to solve these problems without a "renegotiation" of the tradeoff that lay at the heart of the ancien régime: the system of privilege.

Towards the end of Louis XV's reign (1715–1774), for example, his principle adviser, Maupeou, tried to reform the system of privilege and the *parlements* that protected privileged groups and provinces.[24] These reforms were, however, vociferously resisted and cost Louis XV much of his popularity. Indeed, largely as a result of these efforts, Louis XV became so disliked that when he died in May 1774 he had to be buried quickly for fear that prolonged ceremony or mourning might provoke a popular outcry.

Given this, one of the first moves made by Louis XV's successor, Louis XVI, was dismissing Maupeou and restoring the *parlements*. This increased Louis XVI's popularity, but the problems facing the ancien régime were too great to be avoided, no matter how much the new king preferred to do so. Louis XVI's subsequent appointment of Ann Robert Jacques Turgot as his controller-general (essentially, minister of finance) indicated that he recognized the need for a new approach. Turgot was an economic theorist and a former civil servant and therefore seemed to have the intellectual and practical experience necessary to tackle the ancien régime's financial challenges. In particular, Turgot understood the danger posed by French involvement in the American War of Independence and warned the king that without reforms "the first gunshot will drive the state to bankruptcy."[25] Despite such warnings, the king entered the war, and to deal with the financial fallout, Turgot proposed restructuring the taxation system by ending some monopolies, guilds, and other restrictions on economic activity; cutting government handouts; and creating a national body to advise the king on taxation. In response, aristocratic society united "from top to bottom"[26] and the king, under pressure from the queen and other anti-reform aristocrats at court, backed down. By the end of 1776 Turgot and his reforms were gone.

Turgot's successor was Jacques Necker, an immensely rich and popular Swiss Protestant banker.[27] Necker understood the need for reform and began modernizing the financial bureaucracy. But Necker was unwilling to directly confront the system of privilege and so financed French participation in the American War of Independence with loans carrying increasingly high interest rates. Necker also made a fateful move in 1781, publishing his report to the king (*Compte rendu au roi*) and thereby bringing public opinion into the debate about state finances for the first time. The report presented a probably misleading picture of the ancien régime's financial health, making it appear as though state revenues met expenditures.[28] As a result, when the inevitable financial reckoning came, it shocked a now-activated public opinion. However, despite the relatively moderate nature of Necker's reforms, he too displeased the queen and other reactionaries and was thus ultimately dismissed by the king.

Necker's eventual successor was Charles Calonne. Calonne understood the desperate situation, but attempted to put off reforms as long as possible because he understood their social and political costs. By 1786, however, the game was up: Calonne informed Louis XVI that the state was insolvent and reform could not wait. As he put it, "The only effective remedy, the only course left to take, the only means of managing finally to put the finances truly in order, must consist in revivifying the entire State by recasting all that is vicious in its constitution."[29] Calonne suggested calling an Assembly of Notables, stocked with handpicked members of the privileged orders, to provide the crown with the support and financial aid it needed.

Much to Calonne and the king's chagrin, however, when the Assembly convened in 1787 it refused to play along. Calonne told the Assembly that "the special provisions, exemptions and immunities . . . made the task of Government impossible,"[30] but the notables insisted that changing part of the tradeoff at the heart of the ancien régime without the other was a nonstarter: financial and political reform had to go hand in hand. In particular, the nobles were unwilling to give up privileges without a devolution of political power back to them.[31] What began, in other words, as a financial problem quickly morphed into a political one,[32] and the options available to the ancien régime, as we will see is so often the case with dictatorships, for

dealing with its problems had narrowed to either widening political participation or resorting to greater repression.[33]

Faced with the notables' demands, and under pressure from the queen and
other advisers, Louis XVI's resolve broke and he dismissed Calonne. By now,
however, the dire financial situation was out in the open and the country was
in the midst of its worst economic crisis of the century, with unemployment
above 50 percent, rising prices, and a disastrous harvest causing widespread
suffering—all of which made it harder, of course, for subjects who had to pay
taxes to do so. As Ernest Labrousse, an eminent scholar of the crisis, wrote,
"It was not so much that [taxes] increased, but that he who had to bear
it weakened."[34] Against this backdrop, the privileged orders made another
critical move, insisting that only an Estates-General, a national assembly
representing the three estates of the realm that had not met since 1614,
could deal with the challenges at hand. Finally recognizing there was no way
out,[35] the king relented and announced he would call an Estates-General for
1789. The notables assumed that the Estates-General would enable them to
force through political changes they had long desired. Instead, of course, the
airing of their demands unleashed a chain reaction of pent-up dissatisfaction
that made limiting changes to the political realm impossible; what began as
an attempt at political transition led instead to the greatest revolution the
world had ever known.

The Course of the Revolution

Louis XVI's consent to the summoning of an Estates-General in August
1788 confirmed that the ancien régime could not meet the challenges it
faced.[36] The question now became: what would come next? In order to answer this question we need to understand some crucial legacies or features
of the ancien régime. The ancien régime, like most dictatorships, did not
allow the development of any authoritative national political institutions
capable of challenging the dictator's (monarch's) authority. Citizens, therefore, lacked experience in public affairs or popular organizing and "hardly
understood what 'the people' meant."[37] In addition, and again, like many
dictatorships, the ancien régime fostered a society where citizens were
"divided into closed, self-regarding groups"[38] where little "trace of any
feeling for the public weal is anywhere to be found."[39] The result was that
pre-revolutionary French society was divided and dissatisfied but lacked
institutions or traditions of political activity, compromise, or accommodation capable of dealing with these divisions and discontent. As a result,

once the king stepped into the background with the calling of the Estates-General, the country descended into a political vacuum and—without national political institutions, traditions, or norms to guide or respond to it—the discontent and divisions that had been brewing under the surface exploded. Initially, the goal was reforming the ancien régime. That there was, by this point, a widespread recognition of the need for reform is confirmed by the lists of grievances (*Cahiers de Doléances*) members of the three estates had been invited to submit to the king in the period leading up to the Estates-General. These *Cahiers* revealed a fairly broad consensus on the need to end absolutist rule. Most also insisted on the principle of "no taxation without representation": going forward, only taxes approved by the Estates-General would be considered legitimate.[40] However, despite this broad *negative* consensus on the need to end absolutist rule, as time went on, reaching any *positive* consensus on what type of regime should replace the existing one became increasingly difficult. Indeed, as we will see, once the ancien régime began to crumble, a vicious cycle developed, as long-repressed social, political, and economic divisions and grievances led to mass mobilization which, combined with a lack of legitimate national-level institutions capable of responding to them, led to growing disorder and eventually violence.[41]

The vicious cycle is illustrated by the fate of the Estates-General. The Estates-General had been called to deal with two significant but limited tasks: remedying the fiscal situation and reforming absolutism. However, the nature of the ancien régime made it difficult, if not impossible, to limit reform to the financial and political realms. When the Estates-General last met in 1614 it was organized around the traditional semi-feudal, tripartite division of society, but by the end of the eighteenth century this organization was obsolete. As a result, almost as soon as the Estates-General was called, conflicts broke out about what form it should take and what procedures it should follow.

Particularly problematic was representation. Traditionally, each of the three orders had equal weight in the Estates-General, ensuring that the privileged orders could always outvote the third estate. Given the social, economic, and ideological changes that had occurred since 1614, the third estate was unwilling to accept structural subservience: "equality" for emerging Third Estate leaders "was the overriding moral and legal" goal.[42] (This was a good reflection, as one revolutionary leader put it, of how a "revolution in ideas" preceded the "revolution in fact."[43]) In the period after its calling, innumerable pamphlets appeared demanding a new voting system in the Estates-General that would "correctly" reflect the nature of contemporary society. The most famous of these was Abbé Emmanual Joseph Sieyès's *What Is the Third Estate?*, which famously declared:

What is the third estate? Everything.
What has it been heretofore in the political order? Nothing.
What does it demand? To become something therein.

Sieyès demanded that the privileged orders grant the third estate political power commensurate with its social and economic import—if they did not, they should be abolished.

Debates about representation soon superseded fiscal reform as the main source of controversy. As noted above, many of the privileged had expressed a willingness to give up at least some privileges in return for political reform in the 1787 Assembly of Notables—the assumption, of course, being that political reform would work to their benefit.[44] The demands of the third estate for increased political representation threatened this assumption. In May, the nobility and clergy rejected the third estate's voting plan (the nobility voting 188 to 46 against and the clergy 133 to 114), as did the crown. In response, the third estate walked out[45] and reconstituted itself as the Commons (*Communes*), declaring that as the elected representatives of 95 percent of the nation they had both the right and the duty to take control of its affairs. In June the third estate went further, pronouncing itself the *National* Assembly—the title itself rejecting the particularism and privilege that lay at the heart of the ancien régime—and asserting its right to reform France. With this what had begun as a revolt by the privileged against absolutism had become something different. Power and initiative had passed from the privileged to the third estate, and the agenda had expanded from financial and political reform to a broader questioning of the ancien régime.

Furious, the king closed the hall where the National Assembly met. When the deputies arrived on June 20 and found the doors locked and guarded by soldiers, they moved to a nearby tennis court where they took an oath (the "Tennis court oath") to continue meeting until France had a new constitution. In response, Louis XVI made another of the vacillating moves that over time aggravated even those sympathetic to him, asserting his authority and then backing down under pressure. In this case the king announced that he would accept reforms but not the separation of the orders; accordingly, he demanded that the Assembly disburse and re-assemble as Estates. The third estate rejected this and its supporters rioted. Faced with the third estate's refusal and growing social disorder, the king conceded and on June 27 declared that remaining members of the first two estates should join the third in the National Assembly. But rather than stopping the revolution, continued mass mobilization combined with critical miscalculations on the part of the crown sent events spiraling further out of control.

This is exemplified by the storming of the Bastille. On July 11, 1789, Louis XVI, under pressure from conservative advisers, decided again to dismiss his popular finance minister Jacques Necker, who had been called back in 1788. Parisians interpreted Necker's firing and the growing concentration of royal troops in key areas as the beginning of a conservative counter-reaction and rioting broke out. On July 14 crowds descended on the Bastille, which stood in the center of Paris as a potent symbol of royal authority (although by this point it was almost devoid of prisoners). By the end of the day the Bastille had fallen and the head of its Governor, de Launey, was on a pike. This caused the king to back down again: he promised to disburse his troops, recall Necker, and return to Paris from Versailles.[46]

After the fall of the Bastille, mass mobilization continued, not only in Paris but also in the countryside, helping to push the revolution further from its initial fiscal and political goals into social and economic transformation. The peasantry was by far the nation's largest social group, and its mobilization shifted the revolution's momentum and trajectory. Particularly important were the peasant rebellions that broke out in the summer of 1789 known as the "Great Fear." These rebellions had their roots in the peasantry's anger at the nobility's and Church's domination of land ownership, right to tithes, and various other feudal obligations, but these long-standing resentments were aggravated by the intense suffering caused by the agrarian crisis that hit France in the late 1780s. The combination of long-standing resentments, short-term suffering, and disintegrating national political authority created the perfect conditions for an explosion.

In order to appease the peasants, the National Assembly moved beyond fiscal and political issues to social and economic ones. The Assembly's "August Decrees" abolished the privileges of the first and second estates as well as those enjoyed by many French provinces; feudal obligations, tithes, the sale of offices, and corporate-based judicial and taxation regimes were now gone. As François Furet put it, "A juridical and social order, forged over centuries, composed of a hierarchy of separate orders, corps and communities, defined by privileges somehow evaporated, leaving in its place a social world conceived in a new way as a collection of free and equal individuals subject to the universal authority of the law."[47] The "August Decrees" were followed by other changes. The first was the adoption of the Declaration of the Rights of Man and Citizen on August 26. Reflecting the influence of Enlightenment ideals, the Declaration's first article proclaimed: "Men are born equal and remain free and equal in rights. Social distinctions may be founded only upon the general good." Whereas in the ancien régime "rights" were the result of birth or membership in a particular group, rights were now declared to be something to which all citizens were entitled.[48] The Declaration then enumerated as "natural, unalienable and sacred" a range of classic liberal rights including equality before the law, the sanctity of property, and freedom of speech and the press. In addition to renouncing the privileges and status hierarchies at the heart of the ancien régime, the Declaration also repudiated its notions of sovereignty, asserting that "sovereignty resides in the nation. No body nor individual may exercise any authority which does not proceed directly from the nation." With this, Louis XVI ceased being a divine right monarch and became instead "King of the French" (*roi des Français*), whose authority emanated *from* the people and whose rule was to occur in accordance with law.

In November the National Assembly further undermined the foundations of the ancien régime by declaring the property of the Church (and later of the Crown and noble émigrés) "national property" (*Biens nationaux*). Church land was sold in small lots, which appealed to peasants. The great French historian Jules Michelet argued that the nationalization of Church lands helped "put the seal . . . on the wedding of the peasant and the revolution."[49] In addition, Church property was used to back a financial instrument called *Assignats*, which were used to pay down the national debt. A political benefit of these moves was that anyone who purchased *Assignats* or nationalized lands more generally developed a "material stake in the revolution."[50]

As a result of these changes, by the end of 1789 France had been radically transformed from even a year earlier: sovereignty had been transferred from the crown to the nation, and the three Estates had been abolished along with the larger system of privilege they represented. Reflecting this, people were already referring to the "old regime" as that which existed before the constitution of the National Assembly.[51] With much of the institutional infrastructure of the "old regime" gone, focus turned to constructing a "new regime" to take its place. And while there had been broad consensus, at least within the third estate, on desirability of getting rid of the old regime, there was not much agreement on what should replace it. In particular, by the end of 1789, conflicts within the third estate and the "reform coalition" more generally over whether to stick with the original, somewhat limited aims of the National Assembly—eliminating absolutism and the social and economic privileges that went along with it—or to push France's transformation even further came to the fore. Over the coming months these conflicts deepened as a result of social disorder, the threat of foreign intervention, and several decisions taken by the National Assembly.

One was its passing of the Civil Constitution of the Clergy in July 1790. Given the close connection between the Church and the ancien régime, any attempt to transform the latter inevitably involved changes to the former.[52] The process of reforming Church-State relations had already gone quite far since the clergy's privileges had been eliminated and the Church's property had been nationalized. However, the Civil Constitution went a fateful step further, turning bishops and priests into officials paid by the state, rather than ecclesiastical appointees, and demanding that they swear an oath of loyalty to the new regime. Despite widespread resentment of the Church's wealth, privileges, and support for the ancien régime, many found this unacceptable. The lower-level clergy, for example, who had generally been sympathetic to the third estate and reforming the ancien régime, split, with approximately half refusing to take the new oath and some continuing their parish duties even though this was now technically illegal. This measure also divided the third estate, with the generally religious peasantry particularly resenting this move.

Another critical event was the king's attempt in June 1791 to flee with his family to Austria (the queen's birthplace) to foment counter-revolution. Like so many of the king's moves, this was poorly implemented and counterproductive. The royal family was recognized on their journey, arrested in Varennes, and returned to Paris under guard where they were confined to the Tuileries palace. The "flight to Varennes" (as it became known) embittered both the crown's detractors and supporters. For the former, it confirmed the king's untrustworthiness and unwillingness to reconcile with the revolution; calls for a transition to a republic and even for putting the king on trial for treason grew louder. The latter, meanwhile, along with foreign monarchs, were infuriated by the treatment meted out to the royal family and the growth of republicanism and radicalism. In July Emperor Leopold II of the Holy Roman Empire and Frederick William II of Prussia issued the Declaration of Pillnitz, which stated that Louis XVI's fate was of concern to all European monarchs and threatened intervention if he was further harmed.

Against a backdrop of heightened domestic and international tension the National Assembly presented its draft constitution in 1791. It was fairly moderate,[53] calling for a constitutional monarchy, with a king subservient to the rule of law and balanced by a powerful legislative branch. Indeed, under this constitution the legislative branch would dominate since it had the right to initiate and enact legislation, ultimate say over declarations of war and treaty making, and control over taxation and public expenditures. The king, on the other hand, was granted a "suspensive veto," which would enable him to delay but not fully block legislation. In addition, the 1791 constitution called for a reorganization of the French state, eliminating the privileges of many provinces and creating a new system of departments (*Départements*) under the national state. Also notable was the constitution's enshrining of liberal values by making the Declaration of the Rights of Man its preamble.

The 1791 constitution would, in short, have created a constitutional France. The problem was that by this point the constituency for moderation had shrunk dramatically. Reactionaries, émigrés, and foreign monarchs believed that things had gone too far and that the time for counter-revolution was at hand. Others, meanwhile, believed that things had not gone far enough, and wanted to move the revolution in a republican or democratic direction.[54] To deal with the former, in November 1791 the National Assembly declared that all French citizens who had fled abroad would be considered potential counter-revolutionaries; any who did not return and thereby prove their loyalty to the new regime would be guilty of a capital offense. Later that month the Assembly declared that priests who refused to take an oath of loyalty would be considered politically suspect and therefore at risk of losing their pensions as well as subject to official surveillance and perhaps even exile. After some vacillation, Louis XVI vetoed both decrees, further convincing many that he was in cahoots with émigrés and foreign powers.

Particularly important during this time was the republican *Girondist* faction (sometimes called the *Brissotins* after Jacques Pierre Brissot, a leading member of the movement and head of the legislative Assembly), which favored a pre-emptive attack on France's enemies. In March 1792 the king gave in to Brissot and others and filled his cabinet with "a team of outright warmongers"; a month later he declared war on Austria to a "delirious" Assembly.[55] Soon after, the Duke of Brunswick, commander of the Prussian and Austrian forces, issued the Brunswick Manifesto, threatening the French with revenge if the king or royal family were harmed. Given the fear of foreign invasion and the already high level of suspicion against the king, the manifesto was interpreted as further proof of the king's secret collaboration with foreign forces. (And indeed the manifesto had been sent to him in advance for approval.) On August 10 a mob stormed the Tuileries Palace, killed the Swiss Guards, and arrested Louis XVI and the rest of the royal family. A wave of revolutionary and counter-revolutionary violence now threatened to overwhelm France. In addition to advancing foreign armies, royalist revolts broke out in a number of French provinces, and in Paris a complete lack of authority combined with growing fear of counter-revolution led to more mob violence (the "September massacres") against those viewed as "enemies of the revolution."

More changes followed. By the end of September a republic was declared; a few months after that a decision was made to put Louis XVI on trial. This turned out to be a show rather than a real trial. Maximillien Robespierre, for example, who would play an increasingly important role in the revolution, made clear his view that a trial was unnecessary since "Louis has already been judged. He has been condemned, or else the Republic is not blameless."[56] And so in January 1793 Louis XVI was condemned and executed, physically eliminating the most important remaining connection to the ancien régime.

Although perhaps apocryphal, the quote often attributed to Louis XIV, "L'État, c'est moi," was true in one important sense—the king had been at the center of an interconnected web of political, social, and economic institutions and relationships; with him gone, what was left of these collapsed.[57] With the country in chaos—the 1791 constitution was moot since it was based on constitutional monarchy and the monarchy was now gone—and foreign armies threatening France, the situation spiraled further out of control.

In order to protect France from its internal and external enemies, a "Committee on Public Safety" was set up by the National Convention in the spring of 1793.[58] In the summer of 1793 the committee put forward another constitution. Whereas the 1791 constitution had called for a constitutional monarchy, the 1793 constitution (sometimes referred to as the Constitution of the Year I or the Montagnard Constitution[59]) laid out the framework for a transition to democracy. Like its 1791 predecessor, the 1793 constitution was based on the Declaration of the Rights of Man but went beyond it, calling for universal manhood suffrage, an end to slavery, a right to subsistence, public education, and rebellion against unjust governments. This would have given France a more democratic order than existed in the United States at the time. In keeping with its democratic spirit, the constitution was presented to the public in a referendum and approved by an overwhelming majority.

France's first democratic experiment was extremely short-lived. Threatened by enemies within and without, the convention delayed the constitution's implementation and turned dictatorial powers over to the Committee on Public Safety. Within the committee power passed to the radical Jacobin faction and from there to Robespierre, who moved mercilessly against all perceived enemies. The moderate Girondists were pushed out of power; many were eventually put on trial and some executed. Similar ruthlessness was displayed towards other "enemies of the revolution": thousands were sent to the guillotine and revolts in various parts of the country were brutally suppressed; the most significant of these, the royalist uprising in the Vendee, was crushed in a bloody campaign that claimed the lives of hundreds of thousands.[60] And these numbers, as terrible as they are, do not fully capture the horrors of this time: hundreds of thousands were accused of political crimes and subject to mock trials, and friends and neighbors spied on and denounced each other. Terror became an instrument of state policy. Robespierre argued, "Terror is only justice: prompt, severe and inflexible; it is then an emanation of virtue; it is less a distinct principle than a natural consequence of the general principle of democracy, applied to the most pressing wants of the country."[61] Alongside attempting to eliminate all perceived enemies and vestiges of the ancien régime, the committee also tried to create a "new nation" and a "new man" to replace them, undertaking a unprecedented campaign of social engineering that included imposing a new calendar, concretely symbolizing the dawning of a new epoch in human history; instituting a new system of weights and measures that would eventually become the metric system; replacing traditional holidays with ones celebrating revolutionary values like virtue and labor; trying to eradicate patois and homogenize and systematize the French language; and attempting to eliminate remaining vestiges of Catholicism and make a "cult of reason" or "Cult of the Supreme Being" the new state religion instead.

Against its external enemies, the committee was ruthless. The most important innovation during this time was the *levée en masse*, essentially, the mobilization of the entire nation or mass conscription, which translated the democratic politics of the revolution into the military realm. Whereas under the ancien régime, most people were excluded from political, social, and economic power and wars fought by professional armies with minimal attention to public attitudes and needs, now France belonged to the nation and defense was accordingly the responsibility of all. And so in order to deal with a desperate situation—the country was at war with Austria, Prussia, Spain, Britain, and other European powers—the National Convention declared in August 1793 that

> From this moment until such time as its enemies shall have been driven from the soil of the Republic, all Frenchmen are in permanent requisition for the services of the armies. The young men shall fight; the married men shall forge arms and transport provisions; the women shall make tents and clothes and shall serve in the hospitals; the children shall turn old lint into linen; the old men shall betake themselves to the public squares in order to arouse the courage of the warriors and preach hatred of kings and the unity of the Republic.

The effect was momentous. The number of men in the army increased dramatically, reaching a peak of perhaps 1,500,000, and other citizens were put to work in support roles and war industries. Remarkably, the combination of larger armies infused with revolutionary patriotism helped turn the tide against foreign invaders.

Because of the contrast between the democratic and egalitarian aspirations that ushered in the First French Republic and the horrors perpetrated during it, scholars have long debated why a transition from democracy to the Reign of Terror occurred. Some view it as an inevitable consequence of the unrestrained rise of mass politics and the idealistic, and perhaps unrealistic, desire to put in place a political order based on abstract notions of the "common good" or "collective purpose."[62] Others view it as a response to the outbreak of war and the threat of foreign invasion[63]: in such a situation a dictatorship willing to employ all means necessary to defend France was required. Others argue that in assessing the "Reign of Terror" "one has to keep in mind the repressive aspects of the social order to which it was a response".[64] in this view, the roots of the ancien régime were so deep and its defenders so intractable that extreme means were necessary to eradicate them. There is surely something to all these views: revolutionaries were indeed seized by a belief that a new order had dawned and that any and all means might be necessary to protect it from those eager to restore the old one. In addition, the threat of war and invasion created desperate challenges and widespread fear—a combination that often leads to extreme measures. And finally, there is no doubt that the ancien régime's social, economic, and political roots were so deep and its legacies so vast that any new regime would face immense challenges eradicating or overcoming them. Perhaps, therefore, the best way to understand the transition from democracy to dictatorship in France during this time is by combining insights from all these perspectives: faced with an existential threat from invading armies and the almost complete breakdown of domestic order that followed the collapse of the political, social, and economic institutions of the ancien régime, many of the country's leaders and citizens concluded that a ruthless dictatorship was the only way of saving the revolution from its external and internal enemies. R.R. Palmer, for example, in his classic study of the Reign of Terror described the situation thus:

> Paris was in turmoil. Street orators and demagogues, secret agents both of the government and of its enemies, radicals and counter-revolutionaries of every description roamed the streets. Deserters from the army, disguised priests and strange foreigners jostled with half-crazed patriots and self-appointed saviors of the nation. On the frontiers the armies of England, Holland, Spain, Prussia and Austria were thrusting themselves into France. The ports were practically closed by the British navy. Beyond the battle lines lay a Europe

unanimously hostile, stirred up by French émigrés, by conservatives of all nationalities almost hysterical with fear, by the pope and the Catholic hierarchy, and by Catherine the Great of Russia, an old woman near death who urged on the Allies while declining to join them.

Anarchy within, invasion from without. A country cracking from outside pressure, disintegrating from internal strain. Revolution at its height. War. Inflation. Hunger. Fear. Hate. Sabotage. Fantastic hopes. Boundless idealism. And the horrible knowledge, for the men in power, that if they failed they would die as criminals, murderers of their king. And the dread that all gains of the Revolution would be lost. And the faith that if they won they would bring Liberty, Equality and Fraternity into the world.[65]

But by the middle of 1794 fear of the fanatical Robespierre and a widespread desire for an end to ever-escalating violence helped turn the tide again. In July the convention ordered the arrest and then quick execution of Robespierre, ushering in another regime change. During the following period, known as the Thermidorian reaction,[66] French armies held off their adversaries and the Reign of Terror ended. The new regime could not, however, stabilize the country and violence continued, but was now directed against Jacobins and others on the "left" rather than counter-revolutionaries on the right. The Thermidorian regime also drew up another constitution, which eliminated many of the progressive and democratic reforms of the 1793 constitution. The 1795 constitution, sometimes referred to as the Constitution of the Year III, called for a republic with limited suffrage and indirect elections, a bicameral legislature with an upper house to "check" the lower, and a five man directory as its executive.

This satisfied neither the right nor the left, and these divisions, sharpened by years of violence, made stability and compromise difficult. In October 1795 a royalist attack on the convention was put down with the help of a young upstart general named Napoleon Bonaparte who then bolted to fame and increasingly important military posts. The convention handed off power to the directory, which was increasingly reliant upon military force and the prestige and lucre it gained from military victories abroad to stay in power. (After many years of war and domestic upheaval, France's economy was in almost complete shambles and the state's budget had become dependent on revenue extorted from foreign territories.) In short, despite ostensibly coming to power to correct the excesses of Bourbon absolutism and the Reign of Terror, the directory's own unpopularity combined with continued domestic instability led it to abandon legal and constitutional methods and rely on force.[67] In September 1797 this was taken a step further when, after an election that returned gains for the right, three members of the directory mounted a coup and annulled the elections. This triumvirate then assumed emergency powers and began purging purported royalists from governmental and judicial posts as well as undertaking other punitive measures against alleged enemies. The triumvirate could not, however, gain significant popular support or deal with the country's myriad problems and deteriorating military situation, and so pressure for change continued. This time, however, the spark for yet another of the revolution's transitions was provided by a man who played a key role in its first one.

The Abbé Sieyès remained a crucial figure throughout the revolution, with his latest position being a director. Despite his leadership in it, Sieyès was convinced the directory could not deal with France's problems and began plotting its end. Sieyès fixated on Napoleon as the man to implement his coup, due to the popularity the latter had gained as a result of his military adventures. What Sieyès did not recognize was that Napoleon was not interested in playing second fiddle. On November 9, 1799 (18 Brumaire VII on the revolutionary calendar), deputies were told that a Jacobin plot was underway and that they needed to leave the center of Paris. By the next day, however, they realized this was a coup rather than a Jacobin rebellion. Now facing resistance, Napoleon marched into the chambers and chased out the opposition; from this point forward he, rather than Sieyès, was in charge.[68]

Playing on France's exhaustion and widespread desire for order, another constitution was drawn up—the constitution of the Year VIII/December 13, 1799—establishing a new regime called the Consulate. This latest transition was critical: just as France had provided Europe with its first modern democratic experiment and perhaps its first totalitarian one as well, it now pioneered yet another new and totally modern type of political regime—the populist dictatorship—that would finally bring some stability to France for the first time in over a decade. The 1799 constitution mixed democratic and dictatorial elements in novel ways. It paid lip service to universal suffrage and popular sovereignty, but centered power in the executive branch, particularly in the hands of the First Consul (Napoleon). Voting was popular, but indirect, with voters electing "notables" who then served in various governing bodies. The new constitution was submitted to a plebiscite and approved by the extraordinary vote of 3,000,000 in favor and 1,500 against. Plebiscites became Napoleon's favored way of invoking popular legitimacy—allowing him to claim support for his initiatives without having to deal with institutions that might constrain him or regular interventions in his governing. In 1802 and 1804 he again used plebiscites to expand his authority, becoming "First Consul for Life" and then emperor.[69] Napoleon's coronation was full of symbolism (and immortalized in the famous painting by Jacques-Louis David, *The Coronation of Napoleon* [*Le Sacre de Napoléon*]). Most famously, he crowned both himself and the queen, making clear his independence from the Church (normally the pope would place the crown on the king's head) and that his power derived from the "unanimous will of the French people and Army."[70] In addition, his oath went as follows:

> I swear to maintain the integrity of the territory of the Republic, to respect and enforce the Concordat and freedom of religion, equality of rights, political and civil liberty, the irrevocability of the sale of national lands; not to raise any tax except in virtue of the law . . . and to govern in the sole interest, happiness and glory of the French people.[71]

Although the idea of a republican emperor seems like an oxymoron, Napoleon's empire was more popular and more successful than any of the post-revolutionary regimes preceding it. To be sure, Napoleon's military genius had much to do with this: his accomplishments in this sphere were of truly historic proportions, bringing France power and glory it would never again achieve. Napoleon's military accomplishments fed his reputation, enhanced his charisma, and provided him with a level of domestic support that previous regimes did not have. But although Napoleon's military accomplishments were extraordinary, his domestic accomplishments were remarkable as well.

These accomplishments cannot be understood separate from the man; in many ways, Napoleon embodied the spirit of the revolution. He viewed himself as a supporter of the Enlightenment, opposed to the obscurantism and traditionalism of the ancien régime and was determined to shape his country's destiny.[72] In addition, he was committed to many of the revolution's goals and was a product of it: Napoleon's military position was a consequence of the emigration of much of the noble officer corps during the early stages of the revolution and the subsequent emergence of leaders based on talent rather than birth. Napoleon had, in short, the will and desire to continue transforming France as well as the qualities that enabled him to gain the support necessary to do so. Napoleon can thus be seen as the last of the enlightened dictators of the early modern period as well as the first thoroughly modern one, since he both sought and achieved a remarkable degree of popular legitimacy. Reflecting this, Tocqueville characterized his regime as "the despotism of a single person resting on a democratic basis."[73] This combination of authority *and* popular support[74] eluded all previous post-1789 regimes and explains why Napoleon was able to achieve what the others had not: during his rule the coups, rebellions, food shortages, inflation, and overall lack of order that had plagued France for a decade ended, and the long and arduous process of consolidating the revolution's achievements began. Never one for modesty, when once asked what his impact had been on the revolution Napoleon responded, "I finished it."[75]

It is perhaps not surprising that Napoleon's most notable domestic accomplishments were in the realm of state-building, since it was precisely flaws or contradictions in the ancien régime state that set off the chain reaction that led to his rise to power. In essence, Napoleon continued the process of state centralization and modernization that began under the ancien régime.[76] During the Napoleonic period the venality, clientelism, and privilege that pervaded the ancien régime state were eliminated and the foundations of a professional bureaucracy and administration put in place. These reforms enabled Napoleon to achieve goals that the ancien régime could not. For example, societal-wide tax collection began, which, along with the development of the Bank of France, gave France a degree of financial stability the ancien régime did not have. In addition, under Napoleon the state could enforce its will over France's entire territory. Key here was the Napoleonic code. Reflecting his outsized ambition and energy, Napoleon provided France, and subsequently many parts of Europe, with its first uniform legal code that enshrined equality before the law for all men (but not women and children); eliminated the welter of corporate and provincial privileges that had previously divided France; proclaimed freedom of religion; institutionalized property rights; and mandated equal property inheritance for all sons. The Napoleonic code permanently eliminated, in short, the legal underpinnings of the privileges that lay at the heart of the ancien régime. Napoleon once wrote, "My motto has always been: a career open to all talents"[77]—something his own life, of course, exemplified. Napoleon opposed privilege, distinctions based on birth, and other socioeconomic features of the ancien régime, and during his regime wealth or service rather than birth began determining social status and power. A concrete way in which Napoleon tried to cultivate this shift was through the Legion of Honor, the first modern order of merit and a replacement for the chivalrous orders that had existed under the ancien régime: the new "aristocracy" would be based on wealth and state service rather than birth or privilege.

Another key accomplishment of the Napoleonic period was in the realm of Church-State relations. Although the ancien régime had limited the independence and political power of the Church, the two remained inextricably intertwined, and the latter's social power and economic resources were largely left in place. The revolutionaries concluded that in order to eliminate the ancien régime, it was necessary to eliminate Catholicism. With the Concordat signed with Pope Pius VII in July 1801 Napoleon confirmed the revolution's undermining of Church power, but backtracked on its extreme secularism.[78] The Concordat institutionalized the state's dominance over the Church, but allowed religion to be practiced freely. In addition, Catholicism became the "religion of the great majority of the French," but not the official state religion. Moreover, religious freedom was written into the Napoleonic code, and Protestants and Jews were promised the right to practice their religion. Also important was the Concordat's official acknowledgment of many other revolutionary changes, including the clergy's position as state employees, their need to swear an oath of allegiance to the state, and the irrevocable nationalization of church lands.

In addition to his accomplishments in France, Napoleon spread many of the ideas and institutions of the revolution across Europe. Indeed, the French revolutionary armies saw themselves not as "conquerors, but as liberators, at the service of a universal ideal of liberty, equality, and fraternity. Their mission was to free subject peoples from tyranny, aristocracy, and fanaticism."[79] In the lands of his empire Napoleon abolished feudalism, privilege, and serfdom; put in place new tax structures and fiscal systems; imposed state control over religion; instituted the Napoleonic Code and proclaimed equality before the law; standardized weights and measures; modernized state bureaucracies; and more. In short, not only did Napoleon reorganize the map of Europe—coming closer to integrating Europe into a single empire than at any time since Rome—he also reorganized the countries he conquered. By the "close of the Napoleonic era in 1815 there was hardly a country west of Russia and Turkey and north of the Pyrenees . . . that had not been profoundly affected" by the expansion or imitation of the French Revolution.[80]

Even after Napoleon's military overreach caused his regime to collapse and monarchies to be restored in France and elsewhere in 1814/15, there was no going back to the status quo ante. Many of the administrative, fiscal, and juridical reforms instituted under Napoleon's empire were maintained by restoration monarchs—who had learned from Napoleon how powerful a modern state could be.[81] In addition, the experience of war and occupation transformed much of Europe in ways no restoration could roll back. Mass conscription created armies motivated not merely by paychecks but by patriotism that had marched across the continent, changing forever the way wars were fought and experienced. In addition, occupation by foreign armies and rule by foreign leaders who proclaimed universal rights and freedom of the people but denied the conquered self-government and violently suppressed opposition helped spur nationalism across Europe. This was particularly true in Germany and Italy, the territories of which were not just conquered but also reorganized and consolidated. We will see the consequences of these developments in chapters 5, 7, and 8. That the post-Napoleonic restoration of Europe re-organized the continent's borders without much concern for the wishes of the people involved inflamed nationalism further. And finally, the overthrow, however temporary, of the ancien régime in many places broke traditional habits of loyalty and showed that such a thing could be done. The long-term effects were momentous:

> It was now known that revolution in a single country could be a European phenomenon, that its doctrines could spread across frontiers, and what was worse, its crusading armies could blow away the political system of a continent. It was now known that social revolution was possible, that nations existed as something independent of states, peoples as something independent of their rulers, and even that the poor existed as something independent of the ruling classes.[82]

In short, the French Revolution and its Napoleonic aftermath began what would turn out to be a long and arduous struggle to eliminate the ancien régime and replace it with a new one.

Conclusions

Understanding the outbreak and development of the French Revolution requires two things: understanding why the ancien régime was unable to deal with the challenges it faced and thus collapsed, and understanding why this collapse led not just to a political transition but to social and economic revolution as well.

The chapter began with Tocqueville's insight that "without a clear idea of the old regime . . . it is impossible to comprehend" either the French Revolution "or the history of the . . . years following its fall."[83] As we saw in chapter 2, the early modern period was an interregnum, a sort of half-way house between the pre-modern and modern eras. During this period French monarchs began constructing a modern state, but left many pre-modern social and economic relationships and institutions intact. By the mid- to late eighteenth century this schizophrenic mix of modern and pre-modern elements, combined with changing social, demographic, economic, and ideational conditions, made it difficult for the ancien régime to respond successfully to the challenges confronting it. The clearest and most consequential example of this was in the financial realm.

By the 1780s the ancien régime state's flaws had caused growing financial problems, which combined with an economic downturn to create a crisis. Solving this crisis would require renegotiating the system of privilege that lay at the heart of the ancien régime, thereby bringing the crown into conflict with groups upon whose support it depended. French kings therefore tried to avoid this for as long as possible, but by the late 1780s this was no longer possible.

The nature of the ancien régime combined with changing social, demographic, economic, and ideational conditions thus explains why it could not deal with the challenges it faced and thus collapsed. The chaotic revolution that followed this collapse was also shaped by the ancien régime's nature. Dependent on a complex and deeply entrenched system of privileges, French monarchs found it ideologically and politically difficult to reform. When finally forced to reform, the interconnectedness of political, social, and economic spheres in the ancien régime made limiting change to any one of them difficult, especially once mass mobilization was added to the mix. And since the ancien régime did not allow any authoritative national political institutions to develop, French citizens had little experience organizing politically, compromising, or working across social boundaries.[84] When a national assembly, the Estates-General, finally did meet in 1789, France was already in the midst of crisis and it quickly collapsed into internal bickering over basic questions regarding form and procedure, rendering it unable to deal with the rising discontent in French society.

In addition to a lack of national-level institutions, another legacy of the French ancien régime was an extremely divided country. Not only was French society split into "closed, self-regarding groups" which had little "trace of any feeling for the" common good,[85] French provinces had very different administrative, legal, and cultural traditions. In 1789, in other words, various groups shared little beyond discontent with the reigning order. Long-standing societal and territorial divisions, moreover, had been aggravated by demographic, economic, and ideological trends as well as a deep economic crisis in the 1780s. And, later on, fears of émigré-inspired counter-revolution and foreign invasion were layered on to this toxic mix. As a result, once the ancien régime collapsed, France descended into a political vacuum and—without national political institutions, traditions, or norms to guide or respond to it—discontent and divisions that had long been brewing under the surface exploded. Indeed, as the contrast with 1848 makes clear (see chapter 5), a key feature of the French Revolution was the extent and duration of this "explosion": the entire "third estate"—the vast majority of the population—became involved, including, most critically, the peasantry, whose continued mobilization propelled the revolution past political reform and into more radical social and economic transformations.[86]

The contrasts between the English ancien régime discussed in the previous chapter and its French counterpart are telling. In the former, aspiring absolutist monarchs were unable to eliminate the national Parliament, enabling it to act as a "coordinating mechanism" or focal point for political opposition, activity, and organization during and after England's tumultuous seventeenth century. In addition, the existence of a national parliament gave opponents of absolutism an "alternative" governance system to rally around, that is, a "balanced" or constitutional monarchy. Furthermore, in addition to absolutism never taking hold in England, neither privilege nor particularism were entrenched in the ancien régime English state as deeply as they were in the French; also critical is that England did not have a mass reservoir of discontented peasants to propel violence and disorder forward. These factors help explain why the Glorious Revolution was less violent and chaotic than the French Revolution and remained largely limited to the political realm, rather than spiraling into the massive social and economic revolution that occurred in France between 1789 and 1815.

Alongside understanding the outbreak and development of the French Revolution we also need to understand its consequences. Whether the revolution was the most "glorious" event in European history or "a total disaster" is a debate that has been carried on by historians since the revolution began.[87] Clearly, there is something to both perspectives. The revolution performed the "salutary" task of freeing the modern world, as one historian put it, "from its medieval fetters,"[88] but the violence it took to accomplish this left France scarred and divided, hindering its ability to consolidate many of the revolution's gains or achieve political stabilization more generally.

Beginning with the "positive" side of the ledger, the revolution eliminated absolutism and much of the rest of the political and legal infrastructure of the ancien régime. Although the Bourbons were restored after Napoleon's fall, their rule (see chapter 5) was very different from that of their predecessors: constitutions, separate legislative and executive branches, and an electoral system were all now parts of the political system, and the "nation—composed of citizens stripped of corporate distinctions and officially equal before the law—replaced hereditary, divinely sanctioned monarchy" as the source of sovereignty.[89] In addition, popular participation was a genie that could not be put back in the bottle. Even though France's first democratic experiment came to a quick, ignominious end, from this point forward neither rulers nor conservatives could ignore popular opinion. Also immense was the revolution's effects on the French state and nation. As a result of the revolution, a "modern" state emerged in France. Although the ancien régime appeared strong and powerful to contemporaries, it could not fully or directly control its people, territory, or the Church. After 1815 social and territorial privileges were gone; nationwide systems of law, taxation, and customs were in place; the bureaucracy, administration, and military were professionalized; the corporate and intermediary structures that had stood between people and the government were eliminated; and the Church was made subservient to secular authority. The post-revolution state, moreover, was now the tool of the people or the nation rather than the monarch, enabling its power to be applied more effectively and ruthlessly than ever before.[90]

> Before 1789, France was a crazy-quilt of overlapping and incompatible units, some fiscal, some judicial, some administrative, some economic, and some religious. After 1789, those segments were melted down into a single substance: the French nation. With its patriotic festivals, its tricolor flag, its hymns, its martyrs, its army, and its wars, the Revolution accomplished what had been impossible for Louis XIV and his successors: it united the disparate elements of the kingdom into a nation and conquered the rest of Europe. In so doing, the Revolution unleashed a new force, nationalism, which would mobilize millions and topple governments for the next two hundred years.[91]

There is a great historical irony here: although a key goal of absolutism was centralizing power, as the English and even more the French case shows, it was only with absolutism's demise that truly modern nation-states emerged.[92]

In addition to eliminating absolutism and much of the rest of political and legal infrastructure of the ancien régime, the revolution transformed France's society and economy.[93] Post-revolutionary society was no longer composed of corporate groups but of individual citizens, equal before the law. The big loser in this transition was the nobility. As we saw in chapter 2, it had lost most of its political power with the rise of absolutism. The revolution now robbed it of its social and economic privileges as well: its monopoly of high offices in the state, church, and military; feudal dues and services; much of its land; and its special fiscal and legal rights.[94] If the nobility was the revolution's main loser, the revolution's main beneficiary was probably the middle class or bourgeoisie. Careers became open to talent, or at least wealth, rather than being reserved for those from a particular group or background, and critical legal and institutional barriers to the emergence of capitalism were removed: guilds, monopolies, and communal lands were eliminated; the rule of law strengthened; and the right to property institutionalized.[95]

Besides the middle class or bourgeoisie, the revolution's other main beneficiary was probably the peasantry, which also got much of what it wanted, namely an end to feudal rights and ecclesiastical tithes, and most importantly, control of their land.

Alongside these positive or "progressive" consequences, the revolution had negative ones as well. The chaos and violence of the revolution crushed the French economy and made dealing with fiscal and economic problems carried over from the ancien régime difficult. Historians estimate that French GNP in 1799 was only about 60 percent of what it had been in 1789.[96] Over the longer term, the revolution's economic impact was mixed. As noted above, the revolution swept away many legal and institutional barriers to the emergence of capitalism, but many of its other consequences were less beneficial. For example, selling off noble and Church lands may have reinforced a preference among the wealthy to invest in land rather in business, commerce, or industry. Probably more important was the revolution's establishment of a class of small and middle peasant proprietors fervently tied to their land, which slowed urbanization, the expansion of the domestic market, and economic modernization overall.[97]

Like its economic record, the revolution's political and social impact was mixed. Most obviously, the modern world's first democratic experiment failed, leading to chaos, terror, and an eventual transition back to dictatorship, first of the military populist and then eventually of the monarchical variety. The revolution also left behind a society scarred by social divisions and violence. Pre-revolutionary French society was also deeply divided, but by the end of the Napoleonic era the country had suffered through over twenty-five years of warfare, economic decline, coups, and civil conflict, layering new social fault lines and fears on top of the old. Two groups in particular emerged from the revolutionary years dissatisfied with the status quo. Royalists, nobles, and other conservatives resented the changes wrought by the revolution and were determined to reverse many of them. The working class, democrats, and radicals, meanwhile, were frustrated that some of the revolution's changes had been reversed and were determined to push France in a more democratic and egalitarian direction.

Although the revolution, in short, destroyed the foundations of the old order, the process of building up a new one had just begun. However, the deep social divisions and resentments left over by the revolution, as well as a tradition of social revolt if not upheaval, made achieving a consensus on what this new order should be extremely difficult. In retrospect it is clear that the French Revolution was not the end, but rather the beginning of the end of an era.

CHAPTER 5 | 1848

1848 was the turning point at which modern history failed to turn.
—G.M. Trevelyan[1]

T HE FRENCH REVOLUTION was the beginning of the end of the ancien
régime in Europe. By the time Napoleon exited the scene in 1815 the
political and legal infrastructure of the ancien régime was gone in France,
and the experience of war and occupation had shaken the foundations of
the ancien régime in many other parts of Europe as well. Although a monarch returned to France after 1815 and the Congress of Vienna attempted
to roll back the clock in the rest of Europe, there was no going back to
the status quo ante. The example of 1789, and the even more incendiary
one of 1793, along with the rise of nationalism had dramatically changed
Europeans' views and expectations about politics, authority, and sovereignty
while Napoleon's march across Europe had led to a reorganization of political, social, and economic institutions and relationships within his empire
and restructured the map of Europe. During the years after 1815, therefore,
the old regime came under increasing pressure from the forces unleashed by
the French Revolution.

The next major stage in the struggle against the old regime came in 1848.
Sparked again by events in France, a democratic wave spread across the continent. The year 1848 became known as the "springtime of the peoples"—a
time when Europeans demanded self-determination and self-government,
and the continent once again seemed to be on the verge of a glorious new
era. However, despite the initial optimism, the democratic wave receded

quickly; within eighteen months it was replaced by a dictatorial undertow. It was, as Trevelyan put it, "the turning point at which modern history failed to turn."

This chapter examines the 1848 wave and why it succeeded and failed so dramatically. Although the wave had many causes, along with the shakiness of old regime foundations after the French Revolution, two general, cross-national trends were crucial. The first was a process of economic development that was beginning to transform European societies during the first half of the eighteenth century. The second was the growth of nationalism. These trends combined to increase the number, diversity, and power of the groups dissatisfied with the old order. Growing discontent was then sharpened by a severe economic crisis that hit Europe in the period 1846–1847. Thus by time the French once again took to the streets in February 1848, political dissatisfaction had been rising for years and much of the continent was a tinderbox ready to explode.

The year 1848 did not, however, put an end to the old order or put in a place a new democratic one. As we will see, this was largely because the oppositional coalitions turned out to be more divided than they first appeared. Although by 1848 a broad range of social groups shared deep-seated grievances against existing regimes, they did not share much else. And so despite widespread dissatisfaction and mobilization, almost as soon as the old order retreated, the glue that held the opposition together began to dissolve and various groups began fighting among themselves. Perhaps ironically these conflicts were largely the consequence of the same forces that had propelled the democratic wave forward—demands for political reform and nationalism. As 1848 progressed, liberal and middle-class frustration with the old order's denial of political rights, social status, and economic freedom became overwhelmed by a fear of democratization and the radicalism they believed would follow it.[2] And in parts of Europe where issues of national unity or state formation also appeared on the agenda, oppositional coalitions proved particularly fissiparous and fragile as the retreat of the old order allowed the often conflicting claims of various ethnic, religious, and linguistic groups to explode. The result of these divisions was that, within about a year of the initial democratic wave in 1848, all the oppositional movements had fallen apart. And this turned out to be the opening the forces of the old order had been looking for. Taking advantage of divisions among their erstwhile opponents, conservatives were able to co-opt some of their former adversaries and re-install new forms of dictatorship. Nevertheless, the Europe that emerged from the wreckage of 1848 was not the same Europe that existed before.

The Background

During the first half of the nineteenth century European economies and societies changed dramatically.[3] The continent's population, for example, grew rapidly: in 1800 there were about 187 million Europeans; by 1840 there were perhaps 266 million. Indeed, in some parts of Europe, like Great Britain and Prussia, population probably doubled during this time. This population increase may have helped stimulate unprecedented economic growth. Although nineteenth-century European economic growth rates were modest by contemporary standards, what made them revolutionary was that they began consistently outpacing population growth, allowing for sustained economic progress for the first time in modern history. Along with increased economic growth came striking changes in technology, transport, and communications. Road networks expanded dramatically; the Austrian Empire, for example, built 30,000 miles of road between 1830 and 1847. Canals, steamships, and railroads began transforming the way people and products traveled: the total shipping tonnage of the Western world more than doubled between 1800 and the early 1840s; the number of letters sent annually in France increased from 64 million to 94 million between 1830 and 1840; and travel times between major European cities and between cities and parts of the hinterland began to precipitously decline: for example, between 1830 and 1840 it became possible to get from Berlin to Magdeburg in fifteen hours, rather than the two and a half days it took at the beginning of the century.

European societies were also transformed. During the first half of the nineteenth century, and especially after 1830, urbanization increased. In 1800 about 15 percent of Europeans lived in cities; by 1850 the rate was approximately 20 percent and rising, particularly in the more economically advanced regions of Europe like Britain, France, and various German states.[4] Urbanization was fueled by the migration of people from the countryside to the city looking for work; it was during this period, in other words, that an urban working class began to appear in Europe (see Figures 5.1–5.5.).[5] This migration was not matched by a rise in government services, planning, or regulation, and the result, as anyone who has read Charles Dickens's *Hard Times* knows, is that the condition of the poor and workers were grim: lower-class districts were squalid and unhealthy; disease outbreaks common; life expectancy low; workplaces dictatorial and dangerous; and, to make matters even worse, real wages were declining.[6] Such conditions helped set the stage for organized working-class and socialist movements.

Workers were not, however, the only group suffering. Indeed, as is the case today, countries mired in the early stages of economic development

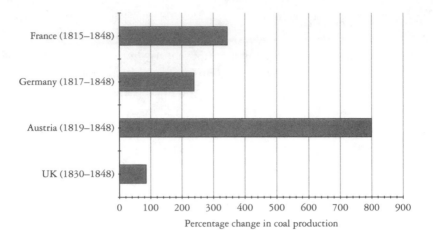

FIGURE 5.1 Change in coal output in select countries, 1825–1848.
Source: B.R. Mitchell, *European Historical Statistics 1750–1970* (London: Macmillan, 1978).

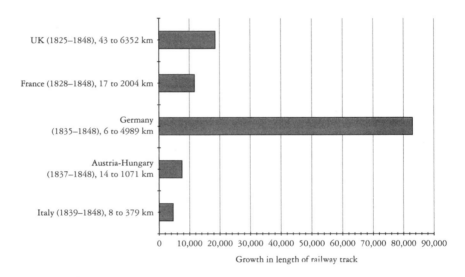

FIGURE 5.2 Change in length of active railway track in select countries, 1825–1848.
Source: B.R. Mitchell, *European Historical Statistics 1750–1970* (London: Macmillan, 1978).

tend to experience capitalism's least attractive features. Industrialization and the spread of markets disrupted and in some cases destroyed the livelihoods of artisans, small craftsmen, and shopkeepers; those who survived the economic upheaval often experienced status and income declines.[7] This combination of grievances against the emerging socio-economic order and a long-standing tradition of organization produced growing mobilization and

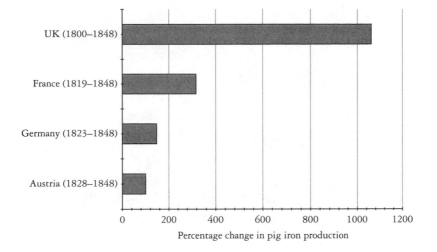

FIGURE 5.3 Growth of pig iron production in select countries.
Source: B.R. Mitchell, *European Historical Statistics 1750–1970* (London: Macmillan, 1978).

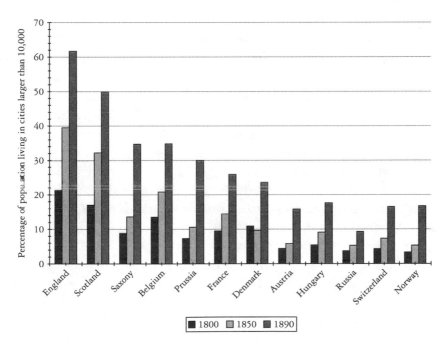

FIGURE 5.4 Rates of urbanization in select countries, 1800–1890.
Source: B.R. Mitchell, *European Historical Statistics 1750–1970* (London: Macmillan, 1978).

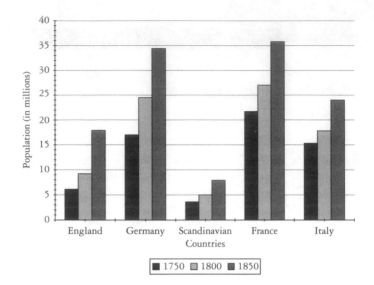

FIGURE 5.5 Growth of population in select countries, 1750–1850.
Source: B.R. Mitchell, *European Historical Statistics 1750–1970* (London: Macmillan, 1978).

even uprisings in the years preceding 1848.[8] Peasants meanwhile, still by far the largest group in European societies, also found themselves under immense strain: commercial farming encouraged the enclosure and privatization of the common lands and forests they depended on; new farming techniques and technology were more easily utilized by large rather than small farmers; and, especially in Eastern Europe many of the nobility's feudal privileges remained. The result was that in the years before 1848 expressions of peasant discontent (for example, land occupations and uprisings) proliferated.[9] In short, while overall economic growth increased during this period, so did poverty and inequality, and living standards probably declined for a majority of the population.[10] Not unlike today, therefore, during the decades preceding 1848 some groups benefited greatly from growth while others felt disadvantaged by the emerging economic order. In addition, the groups suffering most lacked basic political and, in many parts of Europe, even civil rights. The combination of increased suffering, dissatisfaction, and mobilization with unresponsive and unrepresentative political institutions was potentially explosive.[11]

If, however, dissatisfaction had remained limited to the lower classes, it probably would not have represented a major threat to the existing order. The problem was that by 1848 the middle class was increasingly dissatisfied as well. Although this group was still relatively small, especially in Europe's less developed areas, economic development was increasing its size, wealth, and diversity. This group's discontent, however, stemmed less from economic concerns than political and social ones. At its top levels, large businessmen and financiers were amassing fortunes that rivaled those of landed elites, but growing numbers of professionals, merchants, businessmen, and white-collar workers were also becoming more prosperous, educated, and informed. However, despite the growing size and wealth of the middle class, in most parts of Europe this group lacked the right to vote and was excluded from prestigious governmental and social positions, for example in the army and bureaucracy. (Revealingly, the exceptions to this rule—Britain and Belgium, where the middle classes had been enfranchised and government had been more responsive to their demands—were not engulfed by the 1848 wave.[12] See chapter 10.) Thus by the 1840s the disjuncture between the unrepresentative and unresponsive dictatorial regimes that reigned in most of Europe on the one hand and changing economic and social realities on the other had created, as Eric Hobsbawm put it,

> a world out of balance. The forces of economic, technological and social change released in the past half century were unprecedented, and, even to the most superficial observer, irresistible. Their institutional consequences, on the other hand, were as yet modest. . . . It was inevitable that landed aristocracies and absolute monarchies must retreat in all countries in which a strong bourgeoisie was developing. . . . [It was] inevitable that the injection of political consciousness and permanent political activity among the masses, which was the great legacy of the French Revolution, must sooner or later mean that these masses were allowed to play a formal part in politics.[13]

Alongside the increasing size and dissatisfaction of the middle and working classes, frustration with the existing order was also fueled by another trend of the era—the growth of nationalism. As discussed in chapter 4, the spread of nationalism was one of the many transformative consequences of the French Revolution. The Declaration of the Rights of Man and Citizen had proclaimed, "the principle of sovereignty resides essentially in the Nation," forever changing discourse and thinking about political legitimacy. The revolution and the success of the *levée en masse* provided concrete evidence of the power potentially embedded in communities inspired by national sentiment. As the great military theorist Clausewitz noted, "in 1793 a force appeared that beggared all imagination. Suddenly war . . . became the business of the people—a people of thirty millions, all of whom considered themselves to be citizens. . . . The people became a participant in war; instead of governments and armies as heretofore, the full weight of the nation was thrown into the balance."[14]

Napoleon then reorganized the map of Europe, consolidating parts of the Italian Peninsula and the central European German states into larger units and breaking down many long-established political relationships, dynasties, and institutions. And of course the experience of occupation by foreign (French) armies and rule by foreign leaders who proclaimed freedom of the people and national sovereignty but then denied conquered peoples self-government and used violence to suppress opposition, helped stimulate nationalist sentiment as well. And when the Napoleonic era ended, most of the territorial settlements arranged by the Congress of Vienna were as artificial and had as little to do with the wishes of the people involved as had those of Napoleon's empire (or for that matter any other empire), thus setting the stage for future nationalist mobilization. As Joseph de Maistre, himself a conservative, said, "Never before have nations been treated with such contempt, or kicked about in so infuriating a fashion."[15]

In the years after 1815, economic and social change further fueled nationalism. Migration began breaking down traditional local identities and creating a space for new "national" ones.[16] The expansion of education fed the growth of an intelligentsia interested in and capable of championing nationalist projects[17] and a general rise in literacy and the spread of new forms of communication extended and systematized vernacular languages and made it possible for people to "imagine" themselves as part of national linguistic and cultural communities.[18] Although the growth of nationalism was a continent-wide trend, its effects were particularly disruptive the farther east one traveled. By the mid-nineteenth century, state-building projects and the political centralization and linguistic, religious, and ethnic homogenization that accompany them had progressed further in western than in central or eastern Europe. By 1848 the English and the French had already achieved national unity; the peoples living in the Austrian Empire or the areas that would later become Germany and Italy had not. Hence the rise of nationalism meant that by mid-century rulers in these latter regions confronted not only challenges to their political and social institutions but also the form and existence of their realms, as demands for the formation of new states or a dramatic reorganization of existing ones proliferated.[19]

Thus by the 1840s widespread dissatisfaction with the reigning order existed in much of Europe. Two sparks helped detonate an explosion. The first was a major economic crisis. Beginning in 1845 a series of bad harvests hit Europe; particularly devastating was the failure of the potato crop, on which the lower orders in many parts of Europe depended. These crop failures were accompanied by an economic recession and a financial panic. Together these produced food shortages and even famine in some places, rising prices,

growing unemployment, and overall worsening living conditions, particularly for the poor.[20] Indeed, the years 1846–1847 were "probably the worst of
the entire century in terms of want and human suffering."[21] Into this situation appeared the second "spark": the French. Propelled by many of the forces
discussed above as well as the particular dynamics generated by the country's
own distinctive history, France rose up in revolt in early 1848. More colorfully expressing what political scientists would later call the "demonstration
effect," Klemens von Metternich, chancellor of the Austrian Empire, noted
that "when France has a cold, all Europe sneezes."[22]

The French Volcano

After Napoleon's defeat, Louis XVIII, the brother of the executed Louis
XVI (see chapter 4), was restored to the throne in France.[23] However, Louis
XVIII's monarchy was very different from his brother's. Most obviously, the
politically sanctioned and legally entrenched social and economic privileges
that lay at the foundation of the ancien régime were gone. In their place,
Louis XVIII ruled under a constitution that confirmed key achievements
of the revolution, including equality before the law; the Napoleonic Code;
freedom of expression, the press, and religion; and the revolutionary land
settlement. Politically, the restoration monarchy also differed from its pre-
revolutionary predecessor: in addition to being a constitutional rather than
an absolute monarch, Louis XVIII now had to rule along with a bicameral
legislature, consisting of a Chamber of Peers appointed by the king and a
Chamber of Deputies elected by a very restricted franchise.[24] The restoration
monarchy thus represented a sort of political half-way house between traditional monarchy and more representative government, and this left many—
royalists, republicans, liberals, and democrats,—dissatisfied. However, the
balance of power in society had changed radically since the pre-revolutionary
era. The number and power of royalists had diminished, while the number
and strength of republicans, liberals, democrats, and others opposed to monarchy grew over the first half of the nineteenth century. The result was that
although many groups disliked the restored monarchy, those favoring a
more representative political order became increasingly difficult to contain
over time.

    After Louis XVIII died and was replaced by his younger brother Charles
X in 1824 things took a turn for the worse. Charles X was more intransigent and reactionary than his brother. After elections in 1830 returned
a liberal Chamber of Deputies, Charles dissolved the chamber and called

for new elections. When elections again returned a chamber opposed to his policies, Charles X and his ultra-royalist premier Prince Jules de Polignac issued the July Ordinances dissolving the chamber, disenfranchising about three-quarters of those currently eligible to vote, censoring the press, and chipping away at other post-revolutionary gains. It was, however, no longer the eighteenth century; the constituency for royalist reaction was simply too small to support such a move. And so the July Ordinances almost immediately produced another political transition in France, the "July Revolution": barricades went up in Paris, troops were unwilling to fight for an unpopular regime, and Charles left for England.[25]

After Charles's departure, liberals offered the throne to Louis Philippe from the younger, Orleanist branch of the Bourbon family as "king of the French"—indicating that his authority came from the people. Louis Philippe ruled under a constitution imposed on him by the chamber that was more liberal than its predecessor; it abolished, for example, hereditary peers in the upper house and doubled the number of citizens eligible to vote for the second chamber, essentially expanding the franchise to include much of the upper middle class.[26] Despite this, the suffrage remained very restricted: less than 3 percent of adult males were eligible to vote, compared, for example, to about 18 percent in England after the 1832 reform act (see chapter 10). The "July Monarchy" was, in other words, constitutional and more liberal than its predecessor but still far from democratic. Louis Philippe famously characterized his goal as remaining "in the just middle" (juste milieu), equally distant from the excesses of popular and royal power. The problem once again was that the liberal and constitutional aspects of the regime alienated royalists, particularly supporters of the elder branch of the Bourbon family, while restricted political participation angered the vast majority of citizens excluded from political life. It is perhaps not surprising, therefore, that political stability was elusive. As Ernest Renan would later write: "So light was the illness which brought an end to the July [monarchy], that one must ascribe to it an extremely poor state of health."[27] The July Monarchy had to deal with attempts on the king's life and consistent expressions of discontent from the disenfranchised. Louis Philippe occasionally tried containing the opposition with repression; the so-called September laws (1835), for example, curbed freedom of assembly and the press. Such moves did not eliminate the underlying causes of opposition but rather limited the forms through which it could be expressed. Indeed, pressure continued to grow until a series of "exogenous" shocks combined with continued government intransigence caused the situation to explode.

Beginning around 1846 bad harvests, a financial crisis, and an economic depression hit France, causing increasing suffering, especially among the lower classes. The government, meanwhile, continued to resist calls for reform, rejecting, for example, attempts to expand the suffrage in the spring of 1847. Perspicacious observers recognized that this mixture of growing dissatisfaction and an unwillingness to respond to it was creating a volatile situation. In January 1848 Alexis de Tocqueville, for example, warned his colleagues in the Chamber of Deputies that they were "sleeping on a volcano. . . . Do you not feel . . . that the earth is quaking once again in Europe?"[28]

With political assemblies outlawed, the opposition decided to hold a series of "banquets" to air grievances. Initially the tone of these "banquets" was moderate, but they became increasingly radicalized as the king refused to respond to them. The situation came to a head in February 1848 when the government banned the banquets, some soldiers fired on a crowd of protestors, and barricades once again went up in Paris.

The stage was thus set for another political transition. Yet despite the barricades and widespread popular mobilization,[29] initially the transition was neither particularly chaotic nor violent because the regime backed down. The foundations of the July Monarchy were fairly weak—it did not rest upon the complex web of social and economic privilege that its ancien régime predecessor had, and so its fate was not directly tied up with the fate of myriad social and economic institutions. But perhaps most important, the July Monarchy lacked the support, disposition, or capacity to resist by force.[30] As noted above, many conservatives and royalists disliked the July Monarchy almost as much as liberals, republicans, and democrats. Louis Philippe also lacked the ideological convictions of his absolutist predecessors. In addition, several units of the National Guard made clear their unwillingness to fight for the regime.[31] And so rather than defend the existing order, Louis Philippe initially attempted to placate growing protests by dismissing his Prime Minister Guizot; when this did not do the trick, he simply abdicated and left France. At this point, the Chamber of Deputies appointed a provisional government, and in February transition to the Second Republic with universal suffrage occurred.

This provisional government, however, was an uneasy coalition of moderate liberals, radicals, and socialists, who shared an antipathy to the July Monarchy but not much else.[32] Indeed although there was a general acceptance of the need for a transition to a republic rather than another constitutional monarchy, many liberals would have preferred a republic with an expanded but not universal franchise, that is, one limited to those who could meet income and/or education requirements. Many workers, socialists, and others, meanwhile, insisted not only on full democratization, but a "social" republic as well—one committed to significant social and economic reform, particularly the "right to work." Such demands, combined with growing working-class organization and fears of further upheaval, led the provisional government to create a commission to investigate the conditions of the working class and set up "National Workshops" to provide work to the unemployed. These workshops, however, were unable to deal with extremely high unemployment and widespread economic suffering, and protests continued. These developments, combined with memories of the French Revolution, led many liberals and members of the middle class to fear that France was sliding into chaos and bloodshed. In addition, peasants became quickly disillusioned with workers' demands as they feared anything that might threaten private property and, given their own economic problems, resented taxes being spent on make-work and other programs that provided no direct benefit to them. And so unlike in 1789, in 1848 mass protesting and mobilization did not ignite the countryside; instead, the action remained largely limited to Paris. Indeed, within the space of a few months fears that democratization and the demands of workers and radicals threatened the social order and the interests of other groups in society dramatically changed political dynamics in the country. As one scholar put it, "The euphoria of February gave way to the anxiety of the spring."[33]

The Wave Spreads

Although pressure had been building, and scattered revolts had occurred in Switzerland and parts of the Italian Peninsula before February 1848, it was the overthrow of the July Monarchy that ignited a wave of uprisings against the old order. And, as was the case in France, the rapid mobilization of their populations, concerns about the reliability of their troops, and fear of meeting the same fate as Louis Philippe, or even worse, Louis XVI, led most European monarchs to conclude that they lacked the support or capacity to resist demands for change with force. Indeed, the extent and rapidity of the political transitions that took place after February was remarkable. The wave "spread more rapidly and widely than any [before or since], running like a brushfire across frontiers, countries and even oceans. . . . All governments in the revolutionary zone were swept away or reduced to impotence. All collapsed or retreated virtually without resistance."[34] Even some of the continent's seemingly sturdiest monarchical dictatorships, like those in the Austrian Empire and Prussia, were overwhelmed by the wave that spread across Europe in 1848.

But transitions are not the same thing as consolidation. As we already saw in 1789, getting rid of an old regime is one thing, building a new one is something else. And in 1848 the discrepancy between the surprising ease with which the old regime collapsed and the unexpected difficulty of consolidating a new one was particularly stark. The most obvious problem in 1848 was that almost as soon as the old order retreated, the coalitions opposed to them began to fall apart. As we already saw in France one division concerned the extent of political reform and whether it should be accompanied by significant socioeconomic reform. In many other parts of Europe, political and socioeconomic divisions were compounded by national or ethnic ones. This dynamic was clear in the Austrian Empire and the German Confederation.

Indeed the Austrian Empire[35] was probably the epicenter of national contention in 1848. Although there were attempts, particularly under the "enlightened" eighteenth-century Habsburg monarchs Maria Theresa and Joseph II, at political centralization and state-building, they were only partially successful. This meant that on the eve of 1848 the empire was ruled by an autocratic monarch, but feudalism remained and along with it immensely powerful nobles. In addition, neither the empire's territories nor peoples had been homogenized; instead the empire remained a collection of ethnic and linguistic groups lacking a strong sense of national unity. These features provoked growing discontent in the years leading up to 1848, but the French example sent things spiraling out of control.[36]

On March 3 Louis (Lajos) Kossuth, a liberal Hungarian statesman, gave an electrifying speech to the Hungarian Diet (essentially, parliament) demanding an end to absolutism and feudalism as well as autonomy for Hungary.[37] Soon after this speech Kossuth and other liberals put forward a reform program, sometimes referred as the March or April Laws,[38] that would free Hungary from internal domination by its powerful nobility and foreign domination by Austria, end feudal privileges, transition to a constitutional and parliamentary regime, and give Hungary control over its own budget, finances, and foreign policy—thereby leaving the emperor as the only tie between it and Austria. The Hungarian nobility initially felt it had no choice but to accept this program, viewing it as the best way of avoiding peasant unrest in the countryside and further uprisings in the cities. Indeed Kossuth warned the nobility "to act . . . or it will fall victim to those whom it should free, and that day of massacre will spell death to the Constitution and to the Hungarian nation."[39] Reinforcing this point, on March 15, radicals, led by Alexander Petöfi (Petőfi Sándor), a poet, democrat, Hungarian nationalist, and determined foe of the Hungarian nobility, marched through Buda-Pest[40] demanding a series of reforms (the "Twelve Points"), and chanting Petöfi's National Ode, which proclaimed:

> We swear by the God of Hungarians
> We swear, we shall be slaves no more.[41]

Kossuth's speech, which was immediately translated into German, helped inspire crowds in Vienna to rise up: workers, members of the middle classes, and even some liberal nobles joined together to demand reforms and the dismissal of Chancellor Metternich, the most hated symbol of the old regime. The emperor at the time, Ferdinand I, was feebleminded and had epilepsy and was incapable of formulating an effective response to the brewing crisis. His key advisers, however—in addition to Metternich, his uncle, Archduke Louis—opposed giving in to mass pressure. The archduke initially reacted to protests by calling in the cavalry, which led to several deaths and more rioting. The Citizens Guard (*Bürgerwehr*) was then summoned, but as was the case with the Parisian National Guard, some troops refused to defend the regime, even joining the Viennese protestors. Complicating matters, by this point the rest of the empire was in turmoil. Uprisings in the empire's Italian provinces began early in 1848 and troops had been sent in to defend the empire; by March Piedmont had declared war on Austria in the name of Italian independence and troops became bogged down there. In Prague, meanwhile, Czechs and Germans came together to demand constitutional government, civil liberties, and other reforms. And many of the empire's other Slavic peoples (in addition to Czechs, the empire included Poles, Slovaks, Slovenes, Croats, Serbs, and others) also began demanding political reform and greater autonomy.

Faced with multiple and cascading demands and with its troops disbursed and disorganized, the court felt it had no choice but to give in. By the end of April the emperor had approved the March laws, thereby legalizing Hungarian autonomy; Metternich was gone; and a constitution, civil liberties, and an end to feudal obligations and privileges promised. These changes largely corresponded to the demands of liberals and peasants. Workers and radicals, however, wanted full democratization, as well as further socioeconomic reforms, and so continued protesting throughout the spring, culminating in a massive uprising in Vienna on May 15. Unable to control the situation in the capital, the court abandoned Vienna for the more hospitable environment of Innsbruck and left the city in the hands of an Austrian "Committee on Public Safety." The flight of the emperor and the radicalization in Vienna frightened many liberals, moderates, and others who had previously supported reform but who now found themselves marginalized observers of a process they felt was slipping out of control.

Alongside divisions over the nature and extent of political and socioeconomic reform, once the old regime began to retreat, conflicts among the empire's ethnic groups grew as well. Indeed, some of the court's initial concessions ended up aggravating rather than calming tensions. For example, the acceptance of significant autonomy for Hungary exacerbated ethnic conflict since the newly autonomous Hungarian state was itself composed of various ethnic, linguistic, and religious groups. Indeed, Hungary may have had the "most diverse confessional and ethnic composition of any state in . . . Europe" at the time, with Magyars, who were themselves divided among Catholics, Calvinists, Lutherans, and Unitarians, making up only about 45 percent of the population, the rest being Romanian, Croat, Serb, or other.[42] Moreover, despite their own long struggle for autonomy, the Magyars had no intention of allowing full recognition or self-rule to their own minorities. Many Magyars, particularly from the upper classes, simply did not believe that Slavs, Romanians, and other "backward races" deserved the same rights and consideration as they did,[43] and the new Hungarian state committed itself to a process of Magyarization to ensure the domination of Magyars and the Hungarian language.[44] In contrast, the constitution the Habsburg emperor offered his people in April promised "all peoples of the Monarchy [would be] guaranteed the inviolability of their nationality and language."[45] As the Czech leader František Palacký put it, how could any Slav assent to being part of a state "which declares that a man first be a Magyar before he can be a human being?"[46] Hungary's own minorities were thus unhappy with the prospect of exchanging domination by one set of overlords (Austrian) for another and perhaps even worse one (Hungarian).[47]

In addition to conflicts with Magyars, the Slavs also quickly found themselves in conflicts with each other as well as with the empire's German-speakers.[48] Czechs and Germans, for example, who had united in Prague during the early spring to demand liberalization soon found themselves at odds over the future of Bohemia, whose large minority German population made it a candidate for inclusion in a new German state (see below), something the area's Germans generally favored since it would make them members of a national majority but the Czechs vehemently opposed since it would turn them into a minority. And so when Palacký was invited to participate in the preliminary meeting of an all-German pre-parliament as a delegate from Bohemia to discuss the formation of a unified German state, he refused, noting that despite speaking German, he was not German at all but rather "a Czech of Slavonic blood."[49] (One scholar called Palacký's reply the "moment when the ethnic worm turned in central Europe."[50]) Soon after the Czechs refused to participate in a German parliament, the Germans decided they no longer wanted to participate in the Prague National Committee, which had been set up to plan elections and other political reforms in Bohemia.

In addition to conflicts between Slavs and other groups within the empire, the Slavs themselves were divided. In order to strengthen their position vis-à-vis Germans and Magyars, Slavs called a Pan-Slavic congress in Prague in June. When it met, however, it divided into three main groups—the Czecho-Slovaks (the largest group), the Poles and Ukrainians, and the South Slavs—each of which had its own views about how the existing order should change. Palacký, for example, particularly fearful of the threat from German nationalism, concluded that rather than working for the formation of new states, the Czechs and other Slavs should instead support the maintenance of the multi-ethnic empire, albeit in a liberalized form. His belief that central Europe's diverse and intermingled populations, and its Slavic communities in particular, had much to lose from attempts to form new nation-states led Palacký to famously quip that if the multiethnic "Austrian state had not existed . . . it would have [been] in the interests of Europe and indeed humanity to . . . create it as soon as possible."[51] Such views were not, however, shared by all Slavs. The Poles, for example, did not trust the Czechs or the Habsburgs and, having once had their own state, preferred independence to being part of even a liberalized, multiethnic empire. And even among those willing to consider a liberalized and perhaps even federal empire, disagreements arose over the precise structure this reformed empire would take: should its constituent units, for example, be divided along historic or ethnic lines? Such differences made it difficult for the Pan-Slavic Congress to issue more than a fairly broad declaration in favor of liberty and equality for all nations and individuals.[52] By the summer of 1848, therefore, the empire's various communal and socioeconomic groups had already begun bickering over the type of order they wanted to replace the old one, providing counter-revolutionaries with opportunities to pick off some of their former adversaries.

As was the case in the Austrian Empire, a combination of political and national demands shaped the outbreak and evolution of the 1848 wave in the German Confederation. At this point, there was no "Germany," but rather dozens of states, city-states, and duchies containing German-speaking populations in Central Europe. Napoleon's march across Europe reshaped the region, bringing an end to the Holy Roman Empire, incorporating many of the empire's German-speaking territories into a new entity, the Confederation of the Rhine, and subjecting these territories to a crash course in modernization which included eliminating many institutions of the old regime, reshaping legal systems and bureaucracies, and separating church and state.[53] After Napoleon's fall, the Congress of Vienna reorganized the region again, bringing a loose grouping of almost forty German-speaking states into the German Confederation. The weakness of this confederation combined with rising German national consciousness led to growing support for a unified German state in the years before 1848.[54] And since most of the lands of the confederation were ruled over by monarchical dictatorships, demands for unification became tied to demands for political change. Thus, during the *Vormärz* period (that is, the years leading up the March 1848 transitions), challenges to the old order grew and then uprisings in France, Vienna, and elsewhere caused an explosion of popular mobilization. The most important events occurred in Prussia, which, alongside Austria, was the most powerful state in the confederation.

As noted in chapter 2, during the late seventeenth and early eighteenth centuries a series of remarkable rulers had created in Prussia the "perfection of absolutism" based on a strong state, nobility, and army.[55] Indeed, in the decades before 1848 the nobility had strengthened its position,[56] and the army had become so formidable that one government minister quipped that "Prussia was not a country with an army, but an army with a country."[57] In 1848 Prussia was ruled by an absolutist monarch, Friedrich Wilhelm IV, who, like his counterparts in much of the rest of Europe, was initially surprised and overwhelmed by the rapidity and extent of popular mobilization. Within days of the overthrow of Louis Philippe immense demonstrations broke out in Prussia, the most consequential of which occurred in Berlin on March 18: barricades appeared in the streets, crowds surrounded the Royal Palace, and fighting threatened to get out of hand. Despite his absolutist convictions, widespread popular mobilization in his own lands combined with the transitions that had already occurred in other parts of the confederation and Europe led Friedrich Wilhelm to decide that discretion was the better part of valor, and so he acceded to demands for a constitution, other liberal reforms, and German unification.[58] These developments, in turn, led to the calling of an all-German National Assembly, elected by broad, if not quite universal, suffrage,[59] which met in Frankfurt's St. Paul's Cathedral in May 1848 and was tasked with coming up with a constitution for a unified Germany. Despite widespread enthusiasm for unification, the Parliament soon began bickering over the form and extent of this new state.

Most members of the Frankfurt Parliament came from the educated middle classes[60] and favored a new German state governed by a liberal, constitutional monarchy that would provide the political, social, and economic opportunities denied to them by the old regime. Their ideal, as the historian Theodore Hamerow put it, was "the *juste milieu* between absolutism and mob rule, between the anachronisms of autocracy and the horrors of revolution."[61] There was, however, a minority within the Parliament as well as vociferous and mobilized groups within German society demanding complete democratization as well as extensive socioeconomic reforms.[62] In addition to debates about a new political and socioeconomic order, questions about the territories and populations to be included in a German state proved vexing. Far from being natural, the borders of any new German state were disputed, not least because the area had long been manipulated and reshaped by outside actors. The German Confederation that came into being at the end of the Napoleonic era left many Germans outside its borders and included populations within them who did not consider themselves German. As we saw, this had already caused tensions when many who considered themselves Czech, Slovene, Polish, Italian, etc., rather than German were asked to participate in a pre-Parliament for a German state that they had no interest being part of. The most obvious problem facing those tasked with German state-formation was the Austrian Empire.

One way to conceive of Germany was as the home of all Germans. This *grossdeutsch* or "greater German" solution meant incorporating Austria as well as Bohemia and other parts of the Habsburg Empire with significant German-speaking populations into the new state. This approach would end the Austrian Empire, at least as currently constituted, and require incorporating into a new German state many people who did not consider themselves German, since the empire's German-speaking territories contained mixed populations. In addition, this *grossdeutsch* solution would create an Austrian-dominated and strongly Catholic Germany, since the Austrian Empire was overwhelmingly Catholic. An alternative approach to German state-formation would exclude Austria and the lands of its empire, avoiding many potential conflicts and entanglements, but at the price of leaving many German-speakers outside the new country's borders. This *kleindeutsch* or "lesser German" solution would create a Germany dominated by Prussia, rather than Austria, and be overwhelmingly Protestant rather than Catholic. Debates between the *gross-* and *kleindeutsch* camps thus touched upon a variety of divisions: between Catholics and Protestants, between north and south Germans, or Prussian and Austrian partisans, and between those with an expansive, romantic view of nationalism and those with a more pragmatic approach to state-formation. As one observer put it, the *grossdeutsch* solution appealed to emotion, the *kleindeutsch* to reason.[63]

Although the Austrian Empire represented the most obvious problem facing those tasked with determining the nature and borders of a new German state, it was far from the only one.[64] Another problem was the Duchy of Posen, an area originally part of the defunct Kingdom of Poland but which had been awarded to Prussia at the Congress of Vienna, although not included in the German Confederation. Posen had been promised some autonomy under this arrangement, but over time this was largely abandoned in favor of a Germanization process that repressed the use of Polish, promoted the use of German in schools, excluded Poles from positions of authority, and colonized the land with Germans. The result was that by 1848 Posen included a large German minority. Marx, for example, criticized these moves as an early example of German imperialism.[65] Whether or not to include Posen in a new German state thus brought liberal and national principles into conflict. Another problem was Schleswig and Holstein, two provinces in Denmark with significant German-speaking populations and a complicated legal and constitutional status. When a new Danish king, Frederick VII, announced his opposition to Schleswig joining Germany in 1848, Germans in the province revolted and called upon their fellow Germans in Frankfurt for help. Almost immediately upon convening, therefore, the Frankfurt Parliament found itself confronting many complicated, if not contradictory, challenges that brought it into conflicts with Denmark, the rulers of Austria and Prussia, and many of its own people.

The Wave Recedes

The 1848 wave began in France, and events there shaped and foreshadowed developments across the continent during the post-transition period. Almost as soon as the old order collapsed in France the oppositional coalition began to dissolve as liberals, members of the middle class, and peasants became increasingly concerned about the "radicalism" of workers and others on the left. These fears were reflected in the outcome of parliamentary elections held in April 1848: moderate Republicans and conservatives/monarchists were the big winners while relatively few radicals or socialists won seats. The Assembly that emerged from these elections moved the republic to the right, electing an Executive Commission that excluded radical and socialist representatives; appointing a conservative, General Cavaignac, minister of war; and perhaps most provocatively, winding down the National Workshops. The latter move had immense symbolic and practical significance since the workshops had been a central demand of the left and, although costly and not particularly effective at eliminating either unemployment or poverty, had at least provided some relief to approximately 100,000 citizens. This, combined with the general rightward trend of the republic, led to an immense uprising: during June 23–26 tens of thousands took to the streets of Paris. The "June Days" were pivotal: born in the midst of an uprising, the republic's fate would now be determined by one against it. This uprising turned out to be more bitter and bloody than its predecessor in February since the republic turned out to be sturdier and more determined than the July Monarchy, able to rely on the National Guard and troop reinforcements and support from the provinces and rural areas. The rebels, meanwhile, although committed, lacked leadership, organization, or much backing outside of Paris and so were fairly easily crushed, although at a high cost: at least 1,500 killed, while another 3,000 insurgents were captured and 12,000 later arrested. The June Days sealed the break in the initial oppositional coalition: workers and others on the left, embittered by the violence and repression unleashed against them, became convinced that the middle class and liberals could not be trusted, while many liberals and members of the middle class and peasantry became more convinced that workers and others on the left were radicals bent on social revolution.[66]

In the aftermath of the June Days the assembly put forward a new constitution for the republic that called for a strong president, elected every four years by universal manhood suffrage. When elections were held in December 1848 the true beneficiary of the June Days became clear: Louis-Napoleon Bonaparte, a man whose name and program promised the French a return to the order and stability many now clearly craved.[67] Beyond the family name, Louis-Napoleon shared with his famous uncle a dislike of democracy but an instinct for populism. And so almost as soon as he came to office, Louis-Napoleon began undermining the foundations of the republic: using opposition to his rule as an excuse to chip away at civil and political liberties and harass and repress the left.[68] But these partial changes were not enough. As his four-year term was due to expire, Louis-Napoleon pressured the assembly to revise the constitution to allow him another. When it refused, he attacked it head-on: in December 1851 he had forces loyal to him occupy Paris, arrest his opponents, and declare a state of martial law. After brutally suppressing uprisings against his *autogolpe*, Louis-Napoleon offered the public an opportunity to ratify his rule via referendum. When an overwhelming majority voted in his favor,[69] Louis-Napoleon was emboldened to go a step further. About a year later he asked the public once again via referendum to approve him as emperor for life. And so in December 1852 Louis-Napoleon became Napoleon

III,[70] "Emperor of the French," thereby transitioning France, as had his uncle, to populist authoritarianism. Observing these developments Marx famously remarked that "all great world-historic facts and personages appear, so to speak, twice . . . the first time as tragedy, the second time as farce."[71]

The crushing of the June Days and the renewed appeal of the "forces of order" in France encouraged counter-revolutionaries elsewhere in Europe.[72] In the Austrian Empire liberals and members of the middle classes and peasantry had grown increasingly wary of workers and other "radicals" and more willing, accordingly, to consider a deal with conservatives. In addition, infighting among the empire's various ethnic, linguistic, and communal groups provided myriad opportunities for the Habsburgs to return to their tried-and-true policies of "divide and rule."

The counter-revolution's first major victory occurred in Prague. Some weeks before the ending of the Pan-Slavic Congress in June 1848, Prince Windischgrätz, a steadfast supporter of the old regime and the use of force to defend it, was sent back to Prague by the court with a new plan to combat urban insurrections. When the Pan-Slavic Congress came to a close, workers, students, and others held a huge demonstration during which protestors marched on army headquarters in the city. Eager to try out his new tactics, Windischgrätz used this demonstration as an excuse to begin a counter-offensive against the protestors; the ensuing "battle of Prague" lasted several days and ended with Windischgrätz's victory. This outcome depended not only on Windischgrätz's new tactics, but also on the weakness of the opposition. When the battle broke out, the city was divided: Germans and Czechs were estranged, and some moderates and liberals, frightened by growing radicalization, were willing to compromise with the old regime.[73] In addition, the urban rebels did not receive much support from the countryside or other parts of Bohemia, enabling Windischgrätz to focus his troops on crushing the rebellion in the city itself. Once Prague was "pacified," the population collapsed into further infighting, with some blaming German and Magyar agents for instigating the uprising and German-speakers celebrating the end of the "anti-German" Czech nationalist movement.[74]

Since the old regime's initial concessions had been conditioned by the unreliability and unavailability of troops, Windischgrätz's victory provided a major shot in the arm. In addition, the situation on the Italian peninsula had shifted. Conflicts within and among states on the Italian peninsula combined with the decision of some key actors, including the pope and King Ferdinand of the Kingdom of the Two Sicilies, to withdraw from the fight against the Habsburgs, helping Austrian troops under General Radetsky win back lost ground. By the end of the summer Piedmontese and other Italian forces had been routed at Custozza, leading Piedmont to sue for an armistice (see chapter 7). With the army having turned the tide on the Italian peninsula and emboldened by Windischgrätz's victory, attention turned to the empire's biggest problem: Hungary. During the previous months counter-revolutionaries had encouraged the grievances of Romanians and a variety of Slavic groups against Hungary; during the fall these moves began to pay off. In September the emperor reinstated Count Josip Jelačić as Ban (essentially, chief government official or governor) of Croatia. A strong supporter of Croatian autonomy, Jelačić was a known foe of Hungary, since he, like many other Slavs, saw Hungarians, rather than Austrians, as the main threat to this goal. As one observer noted, "animosity toward Hungary was . . . [perhaps] the only unquestioned fact of Croatian politics"[75] since the Hungarians had repeatedly rejected Croatian demands during the pre-1848 period and the rhetoric and policies following the granting of Hungarian autonomy in 1848 promised more of the same. Soon after his appointment, Jelačić led his troops into battle against Hungary. And when the man the court sent to Hungary to take over its armed forces, Field Marshal Franz Philipp von Lamberg, was lynched by an angry mob, the court had an excuse to declare war against Hungary as well. Just as Hungarian demands for autonomy helped set off a chain reaction in the spring of 1848, so did Hungary's fight against the counter-revolution play a critical role in determining the fate of the Austrian Empire.

Events in Hungary immediately impacted Vienna. When Viennese troops were ordered to reinforce Jelačić's Croatian forces, an uprising broke out in the capital. But now, unlike in the spring, the Habsburgs had reliable forces at their command: by the end of October troops under Jelačić and Windischgrätz marched into Vienna and, after several days of fierce fighting, crushed the insurrection. With Viennese radicals defeated, a conservative ministry under Count Felix zu Schwarzenberg was installed to reassert imperial authority. In order to do so, Schwarzenberg insisted that Ferdinand I had to go; in December 1848 Ferdinand's nephew, Franz Joseph, ascended to the throne.

As for the Hungarians, although they fought bravely and fiercely, their struggle was ultimately doomed by a combination of internal divisions and external enemies. At the outbreak of war, Kossuth turned to a *levee en masse*, quickly forming a popular national army that initially achieved remarkable success. The liberal Kossuth was not, however, beloved by the Hungarian nobility, and some pro-Austrian officers deserted to the enemy.[76] More important, however, was that the Hungarians had to fight a war on many fronts: against the Austrians, internal adversaries, including their Croatian and Romanian minorities,[77] and ultimately an overwhelming external foe.

Throughout the period 1848–1849 Czar Nicholas I had looked uneasily upon developments in Central Europe, concerned that uprisings might spread to his own territories and/or reconfigure the balance of power in Europe to Russia's disadvantage. He had therefore encouraged the Habsburgs to deal forcefully with their subject nationalities. When the Habsburg's war effort against the Hungarians faltered, and the former "requested" Russian assistance, the czar was happy to oblige; during the summer of 1849 Russian troops poured into Hungary.[78] Kossuth desperately appealed to European liberals, who had long viewed Russia as the bulwark of reaction, and other European states for support, but his pleas were ignored. By the fall of 1849, Hungary's bid for independence was doomed and a dictatorship was back in control of the empire.

Developments in the Austrian Empire critically affected events in the neighboring German states. Here divisions between liberalism, nationalism, and democracy emerged in a particularly stark and tragic way. Regarding the extent or borders of a new German state, the Frankfurt Parliament's initial instincts were to allow its nationalist urges to overwhelm its liberal ones, voting to incorporate most of Posen into Germany, to "invite" the German provinces of the Austrian Empire to join the new German state, and to support the Germans against the Danes in Schleswig-Holstein. The latter two decisions thrust the Parliament into international difficulties. Soon after the Frankfurt Parliament voted in favor of a "greater Germany" in October 1848, it was confronted with the Austrian Empire's newly appointed Chief Minister Schwarzenberg's declaration that he intended to keep the empire intact, thereby barring Austria or any other territories from joining the new German state and essentially vetoing the Frankfurt Parliament's "greater German" solution. The decision to incorporate Schleswig Holstein also created difficulties for the Parliament, as it raised the ire of both Britain and Russia. Both worried about German nationalism upending the European order, and the former also worried about German access to North Sea seaports, while the latter worried about potential German designs on its Baltic provinces. And so at the end of August 1848 Prussia, under British and Russian pressure, signed the Malmö armistice dropping its support for the German nationalists in Schleswig and Holstein and withdrawing its troops from Denmark. Prussia did this, however, without consulting the Frankfurt Parliament, thereby making a mockery of its authority and popular sovereignty more generally. Prussia's decision enraged the Parliament and the left more generally, since the latter viewed it as a sign of the former's timidity vis-à-vis Prussia and the forces of counter-revolution. Reflecting what would become a fairly typical left-wing view of the Parliament, Friedrich Engels colorfully characterized it as an "Assembly of Old Women [that] was, from the first day of its existence, more frightened of the least popular movement than of all the reactionary plots of the German governments put together."[79] After initially condemning Prussia's decision, the Parliament gave in and accepted the armistice, setting off a series of protests and uprisings throughout the confederation that came to be known as the "September Crisis." In Frankfurt, for example, democrats, workers, and others marched upon St. Paul's Cathedral demanding that representatives on the left resign from the Parliament to protest its concessions to Prussia and failure to live up to the ideals of popular sovereignty. This uprising, as well as others, was eventually defeated, but in the aftermath of the September Crisis, divisions within the opposition hardened. Democrats and others on the left condemned Parliament and moderates as traitors, while many moderates vilified the democratic movement as "radical" and began calling for prohibiting many of its activities. The dynamics and outcome of the September Crisis were ominous: "All at once, the educated and proper-tied Liberal middle classes realized they had taken on the role of the sorcerer's apprentice, who is incapable of dismissing the forces he has conjured up. Unity and freedom had been on the agenda, not revolt, bloodshed and danger to property; faced with radical uprisings . . . they were inclined hastily to consolidate what had been achieved and to combine with the old powers to ensure security and order."[80]

The polarization that followed the September Crisis was further deepened by spillover from events in the Austrian Empire in November. As noted above, when Viennese troops were ordered to reinforce Jelačić's Croatian forces in their fight against Hungary, an uprising broke out in the capital. During this uprising Robert Blum, a left-wing representative of the Frankfurt Parliament who had been sent to Vienna, was arrested, court-martialed, and executed by the imperial authorities. Blum's arrest, trial, and execution challenged the authority of the Frankfurt Parliament since Blum should have had diplomatic immunity and again highlighted the Parliament's weakness vis-à-vis the forces of reaction. And the fact that Slavic troops played a crucial role in crushing the Viennese uprising added nationalist and ethnic resentments to the mix. Thus by the time the Parliament issued the "Basic Rights of the German People" proclaiming equality before the law; freedom of speech, press, assembly, and religion; and the end of feudal privileges and obligations in December 1848 it had already lost the support, or at least the enthusiasm, of democrats and others on the left. This disillusionment, in turn, helped seal the fate of the constitution the Parliament proposed for a new Germany in March 1849.

The Frankfurt Parliament's constitution called for the creation of a unified, federal Germany that would include only those lands of the German confederation that did not belong to the Austrian Empire; that is, it now embraced the "little German" solution since the "greater German" had been rejected by the Austrians. It also called for a Germany that would be ruled by the King of Prussia—as "Emperor of the Germans"—along with two houses of Parliament, one representing the individual states and the other elected by manhood suffrage. This constitution appealed to neither the left, which among other things objected to a hereditary emperor as the head of a new Germany, nor the right, which among other things objected to limits being placed on the emperor's powers. The stage was thereby set for a battle between the forces of revolution and counter-revolution.

After being offered the crown of a new Germany in March, Friedrich Wilhelm IV stalled in responding to the Frankfurt Parliament, allowing frustrations within the Parliament and divisions between the Parliament and the left to harden. At the end of April he decided the time had come to make his move, turning down the crown, rejecting the constitution, and denying the authority of the Parliament more generally, notoriously proclaiming that it "had no right at all to offer me anything whatsoever . . . in order to give [the Parliament would] have to be in possession of something that can be given, and this is not the case."[81] In response to Friedrich Wilhelm's declaration, uprisings broke out across Germany. The situation in April 1849 differed greatly, however, from that of March 1848: the Parliament was weakened by defeats and disillusionment and unable to act as a rallying point for opposition; the initial opposition was now divided between moderates and liberals on one side and democrats and radicals on the other; and Friedrich Wilhelm was emboldened by the success of the counter revolution in other parts of Europe and the renewed reliability of his troops. And so by the end of the summer Prussian troops crushed the various uprisings, the Frankfurt Parliament dissolved, and conservative regimes were back in power in Prussia and other German states. By the end of 1850 another major step backward was taken with the restoration of the German Confederation. The dream of a liberal, unified Germany had come to an end.

Conclusions

After 1789, 1848 was the next major stage in the struggle between democracy and dictatorship in Europe. The democratic wave that swept across

Europe in 1848 toppled even some of the continent's seemingly sturdiest dictatorships. Yet despite the speed and relative ease of these transitions, democratic consolidation proved elusive. Indeed, perhaps the most striking feature of the 1848 wave was how much easier it was to get rid of the old order than it was to build a new one. As we saw, this was largely due to divisions within the oppositional coalitions and how they were eventually exploited by the old regime. Liberals, moderates, and members of the middle class generally wanted a liberal and representative, but not fully democratic, order to replace the old one. Peasants were generally less interested in political reform than in protecting their livelihood and property (France) or securing it via the abolition of feudal privileges and landholdings (much of the rest of Europe). Unlike in 1789, but influenced by the memory of what had happened during the French Revolution, European monarchs rapidly gave in to moderate demands in 1848, thereby largely demobilizing the peasantry and the middle classes. In 1848, therefore, revolution did not spread to the countryside nor did a breakdown of social order along the lines of what happened in France after 1789 occur. Instead, almost as soon as the old order gave in, moderates, liberals, much of the middle class, and the peasantry grew increasingly frightened that full democratization and the demands of workers, radicals, and others on the left for further socioeconomic reforms threatened their interests. The clearest and perhaps most tragic manifestation of this class-based conflict occurred in France during the June Days, which many analysts have therefore viewed as the "first battle" in the European "civil war . . . fought between the two classes (workers and the bourgeoisie) that split modern society."[82] Alongside political and socioeconomic conflicts, nationalist disputes also weakened the opposition in those parts of Europe where nation-states did not yet exist. The Austrian Empire, for example, "was the very heart of nationalist contention in 1848–9, yet rather than a crescendo of nationalist demands tearing the realm to pieces, the different national movements fought each other, and cancelled each other out."[83] In Germany, meanwhile, the Frankfurt Parliament was critically weakened by divisions between liberals and democrats, as well as by disagreement over which peoples and territories to incorporate into the new Germany. These political, socioeconomic, and national conflicts ripped apart the opposition and drove parts of it back into the arms of conservatives, creating an essential precondition for the reverse wave that swept across the continent during the last half of 1848 and 1849.

Indeed by the early 1850s there seemed little left of the wave that had swept across the continent in 1848. The year 1848's combination of great promise, wide scope, almost immediate initial success, and then rapid backsliding led many to view it as a complete failure. And surely, if we take as our standard of measurement the consolidation of democracy, then 1848 certainly failed. If, however, we take a longer-term view this assessment should change.

Although 1848 did not produce consolidated democracies, the Europe that emerged from the ashes of 1848 differed greatly from that which existed before. Perhaps most importantly, 1848 weakened the old order and forced its most perspicacious defenders to recognize that times were changing. In 1849, for example, the Prussian minister Otto von Manteuffel declared that "the old times are gone and cannot return. To return to the decaying conditions of the past is like scooping water with a sieve."[84] The most obvious blow to the old order was the abolition of serfdom and other feudal privileges that occurred in 1848; these were not reinstated during the reverse wave. As with the French Revolution, the abolition of feudal privileges after 1848 had dramatic political, social, and economic consequences: it was the beginning of the end of the politics of tradition and a society of orders and eliminated remaining hindrances to capitalism in many parts of Europe.[85] In addition, in 1848, for the first time in many parts of Europe, elements of modern democracy appeared—popular mobilization, freedom of the press, assembly, and association, an open public sphere, parliaments, elections, and more. Although many of these changes were rolled back during the reverse wave, many of the political organizations, civil society associations, and publications that appeared in 1848, perhaps most importantly those associated with workers' and socialist movements, re-emerged and played critical roles in European politics during the coming decades. As Charles Tilly and other scholars have argued, 1848 "modernized" protest and other forms of collective action in Europe.[86] Partially reflecting these changes, post-1848 political dictatorships also differed significantly from their pre-1848 predecessors.

In the Austrian Empire, for example, the diminution of the nobility's power facilitated a program of political centralization and state modernization, and the upper reaches of the government and economy gradually became the preserve of the upper middle class rather than just the nobility. In addition, Emperor Franz Joseph and his chief ministers began a cautious reform program during the 1850s and in 1860 even agreed to the formation of a constitution and parliament.[87] In Prussia, meanwhile, after doing away with the Frankfurt Parliament, Friedrich Wilhelm put forward his own constitution that, while much less liberal than its predecessor, did make the country a constitutional state.[88] And in France, monarchy disappeared forever after 1848, and although not democratic, Louis-Napoleon's empire was constitutional and rested at least in part on popular consent; during this period almost universal manhood suffrage became a feature of French political life.

In addition many post-1848 conservatives recognized that the era of feudal privileges was at its end, that constitutional rather than absolutist monarchy was the form of government best-suited to protecting their interests, and that they needed to expand their support base if they were to retain power.[89]

In addition, as we will see in coming chapters, the second half of the nineteenth century and the early part of the twentieth century were defined by many of the same struggles that appeared in 1848.[90] Most obviously, the contest between the forces defending the old order and those advocating a new one continued. As the great contemporary historian Leopold von Ranke put it, the struggle between monarchical dictatorship and popular sovereignty that began in 1789 became "the fundamental tendency" or defining feature of the second half of the nineteenth century.[91] Layered on top of this was another struggle that emerged in full force in 1848: that between classes. The fateful split between workers and socialism on one side and the middle-class and liberalism on the other that appeared during 1848 deepened over the coming decades. For Marxists and others on the left, 1848 came to be seen as the time when the middle class "discovered that it preferred order to the chance of implementing its full program when faced with the threat to property. Confronting 'red' revolution, moderate liberals and conservatives drew together. . . . [And so after 1848] the bourgeoisie ceased to be a revolutionary force."[92] In response to the actions of the middle class and liberals during 1848, workers and socialists came to view them, and not just monarchical dictatorship and conservatives, as their enemies. As we will see, the political consequences of this split were profound, driving a wedge between erstwhile opponents of the old order, isolating and radicalizing the growing working class, and hindering the formation of cross-class coalitions in favor of liberal democracy in many parts of Europe.[93]

Alongside political and socioeconomic conflicts, another force that emerged in 1789 and then again in 1848—nationalism—also defined European politics during the second half of the nineteenth century. In the Austrian Empire, Germany, Italy, and other places where nation-states did not yet exist, the struggle for the formation of new states or the reorganization of existing ones resumed after 1848. (These struggles are examined in chapters 7, 8, and 15.) But even in places where national state-building projects had progressed comparatively far, nationalism became an extremely disruptive force during the second half of the nineteenth and first half of the twentieth centuries. However, as we will see, late nineteenth- and early twentieth-century nationalism differed in important ways from its late eighteenth- and early nineteenth-century predecessor. Most importantly whereas nationalism, liberalism, and democracy had been united in opposition to the old order before 1848, after 1848 they diverged. We have already seen how 1848 helped split democrats and liberals; after 1848 nationalists became estranged from their erstwhile allies as well. Indeed, during the late nineteenth and early twentieth centuries nationalism morphed from a foe of the old order into an enemy of democracy and liberalism. The changing dynamic between nationalism, liberalism, and democracy in the continent's most politically advanced country—France—is the subject of the next chapter.

CHAPTER 6

The French Third Republic

The Republic endured because it was the form of government that divided us the least.

—Adolphe Theirs[1]

A LTHOUGH BY THE early 1850s the democratic wave of 1848 had receded, it had introduced democracy, however briefly, to parts of Europe that had never experienced it before (see chapter 5). For the first time, many Europeans acted collectively to demand political change, participated in elections, and witnessed the convening of parliaments. This was not enough to consolidate democracy, but mass politics and pressures for political change were not eliminated by the reverse wave. The other force threatening the old order in 1848—nationalism—also did not disappear with the reverse wave. Indeed, during the last half of the nineteenth century the pressures and conflicts that had caused the 1848 wave re-emerged, albeit in new forms and combinations, eventually creating an explosive mix that would send Europe careening towards the wars and revolutions of the early twentieth century.

This chapter will examine these dynamics in France. As the birthplace of modern democracy and nationalism, France differed in important ways from the rest of Europe. The French Revolution had destroyed the foundations of the ancien régime, thereby accomplishing what in many other countries happened only after 1848. The destruction and violence of the French Revolution also, however, left behind deep social divisions that hindered the formation of a stable new order to replace the old one.

During the first half of the nineteenth century France went through several political transitions: from the First Republic to the First Empire (1804–1814/5); from the First Empire to the Bourbon Restoration (1814/5–1830); from the Bourbon Restoration to the July Monarchy (1830–1848); from the July Monarchy to the Second Republic (1848–1852); and from the Second Republic to the Second Empire (1852–1870). During the second half of the nineteenth century, France experienced another transition, to the Third Republic. Reflecting the frequency of political upheaval in France, a long-standing joke had it that the National Library kept its copies of the constitution in the "periodicals" section.[2] The Third Republic was France's third try at democracy and was more successful than the previous two, not least because of the legacies left behind by these earlier attempts. Not only had the political and legal infrastructure of the ancien régime been eliminated and a central state constructed, the Third Republic did not have to build democracy from scratch: many of the institutions and practices necessary for democracy already existed in France when another transition occurred in 1870. However, also in accordance with what by this time had become a French tradition, the transition to the Third Republic was tumultuous, leaving a large number of dead bodies and a reservoir of social resentment in its wake. Furthermore, despite turning out to be France's longest-lived democratic experiment and the only major democracy in Europe at the time,[3] the Third Republic should not be considered fully consolidated since, despite lasting for many decades and achieving myriad accomplishments, a significant number of French citizens never accepted the legitimacy of the Republic or the democratic rules of the game.

A backlash against liberal democracy was not limited to France. Indeed, anti-liberal and anti-democratic forces that had their roots in movements that first appeared during 1848 appeared in all European countries by the end of the nineteenth century. Largely because France had made great strides in the struggle against the ancien régime and towards democracy and state-building early on, these forces were less powerful than in many other European countries. Nonetheless, forces opposed to the Third Republic, particularly of the populist, anti-Semitic, nationalist variety, did emerge with critical consequences for French political development during the late nineteenth and early twentieth centuries. Before examining these developments through the prism of their most spectacular nineteenth-century manifestation—the Dreyfus Affair—it is necessary to examine the emergence of the Third Republic itself.

"The Government That Divides Us the Least"

As discussed in chapter 5, after the collapse of the Second Republic, France transitioned to the Second Empire. Although this regime has often been parodied most famously by Marx, who derided Louis Napoleon's attempt to recapture his famous uncle's glory as history repeating itself this time as farce,[4] or presented as a mere interlude between the Second and Third Republics, in fact during the Second Empire (1852–1870) France experienced important changes that contributed to the relative success of democracy during the late nineteenth and early twentieth centuries.[5] Although neither liberal nor democratic, because of France's previous history the Second Empire was also not a traditional dictatorship; today we might call it a populist or "competitive authoritarian" regime. A perverse version of popular sovereignty was embedded in the Second Empire: the constitution made the emperor "responsible to the French people," and Louis-Napoleon claimed the people were "the only sovereign I recognize."[6] In addition, during the Second Empire, French citizens gained further experience in voting and other aspects of competitive politics.[7] For example, although the powers of the national legislature were limited and basic civil liberties like freedom of the press and association restricted,[8] elections with universal manhood suffrage were held, civil society organizations existed, and a republican "counter-elite practiced in the arts of democratic politicking" developed during the Second Empire.[9]

Alongside the development of crucial political institutions and practices, France's economy and society also changed significantly during this period. Louis-Napoleon was eager to promote economic development, and between 1852 and 1870 France experienced significant economic growth, its banking system was modernized, manufacturing and industry expanded, and rural migration and urbanization increased.[10] France's class structure shifted accordingly, most notably via the continued growth of the middle and urban working classes. And public works programs transformed and tied the country together: road, rail, and port networks expanded, and Baron Georges Haussman re-designed Paris, giving Europe perhaps its first truly modern city of magnificent buildings, stunning monuments, and grand boulevards.[11]

After France recovered from the disorder of the early 1850s, Louis-Napoleon began facing pressure within Parliament and from society for political liberalization. During the 1860s he moved the Second Empire into a phase of "liberalizing authoritarianism," loosening restrictions on public assembly and the press, recognizing workers' rights to strike and organize, expanding public education, and increasing the powers of Parliament.[12] These reforms were popular—in 1870 a plebiscite asking the French whether they "approve[d] the liberal reforms carried out since 1860" returned over 83 percent voting "yes" with a turnout of over 80 percent[13]—but Louis-Napoleon had become less so. Legislative elections held in 1869 returned strong gains for the liberal opposition, especially in Paris. Concerns about his popularity may have led Louis-Napoleon to make some risky moves.

Like his more talented uncle, Louis-Napoleon committed his empire to international glory and the "liberation of peoples" and involved France in a variety of foreign policy escapades. But by the 1860s the balance of power in Europe was changing, most crucially as a result of the rise of Prussia and its push to unify and dominate German-speaking Europe (see chapter 8). This created tension between France and Prussia, and the Prussian chancellor, Otto von Bismarck, was able to manipulate Louis-Napoleon to bring these tensions to a head. Taking advantage of Louis-Napoleon's too-easily injured honor and desire to whip up support for his empire, Bismarck maneuvered a Franco-Prussian dispute over the candidate for the vacant Spanish throne into a war, which led to France's rapid and stunning defeat. Since dictatorships must depend on their performance (or repression) to stay in power (as opposed to democracies, which can derive legitimacy from reflecting the "voice of the people"), this international humiliation proved fatal for Louis-Napoleon. Within two days of the battle of Sedan on September 2, 1870, that ended with the surrender and capture of Louis-Napoleon, a Paris mob forced the legislature to proclaim the end of the empire, and another tempestuous political transition began in France.

After the fall of the empire, a provisional government took charge as Paris came under siege by the Germans. When the government finally surrendered in January 1871 and elections were held, they revealed an extremely divided country—Paris voted Republican and socialist, while the rest of the country voted conservative and monarchist. When the new National Assembly took office, with Adolphe Theirs as the head of a new government, conflicts began almost immediately between it and workers and radicals in Paris. By March, these had grown so intense that the Parisian rebels decided to elect their own government, which came to be known as the Paris Commune, plunging France into civil war. Karl Marx memorialized this episode in one of his most famous writings, "The Civil War in France," in which he characterized the Commune as the first example in history of a "truly working-class government" or "dictatorship of the Proletariat." The reality was somewhat different. Having come to power quickly and unexpectedly and during a period of chaos, the leaders of the Commune lacked a unifying ideology, coordinated plan of action, or organizational infrastructure. Nonetheless, the Commune's perceived extremism combined with a long-standing fear in the French provinces of Parisian radicalism left it vulnerable. And indeed, when government forces began their final offensive against Paris on May 21, 1871, the Commune fell rapidly but not before a bloody week of street fighting, mass executions, and terror. Although the exact toll is unclear, certainly tens of thousands of French citizens lost their lives during this week and the brutal government reprisals that followed the Commune's fall.[14]

The Commune and its aftermath layered on to an already divided society further bitterness and suspicion. Although it was not the harbinger of socialist paradise envisioned by some, the Commune was supported by a significant sector of the emerging working class, which viewed its fate as further proof that the bourgeoisie would never tolerate working-class or socialist government. For conservatives, meanwhile, the Commune represented a violent threat to property and order whose recurrence needed to be avoided at all cost. The Third Republic thus began with a stunning military defeat, foreign occupation, the signing of a punitive treaty which included a heavy war indemnity, the loss of two of France's provinces, Alsace and Lorraine, and civil war. In short, the Third Republic was ushered in by a war "that shattered national myths of grandeur and cohesion" and "set off a dynamic of defeatist hysteria" and a collapse into the "worst civil violence in Europe since the 1790s."[15] Given this, it is perhaps not surprising that the post-transition Republic got off to a rocky start.

The first National Assembly had a conservative monarchist rather than a republican majority, but because of divisions within the former camp, republicans won out. [16] As the Republic's first leader, Adolphe Theirs, put it, the Republic initially endured not because it was enthusiastically embraced by the vast majority of French citizens but rather because it was the form of government "that divide[d] us the least."[17] However, despite its inauspicious beginnings, Theirs placed the Republic on a moderate course and support for it gradually solidified. Evidence of this came during the so-called *le seize-Mai* crisis, a sort of monarchist coup attempt, when the Royalist President MacMahon dismissed the prime minister and attempted to appoint a new royalist prime minister and government. The parliament passed a vote of no confidence in the new government on May 16, 1877, to which MacMahon responded by calling new elections. Much to his chagrin these elections returned a strong Republican majority. During the subsequent years the Republic expanded its reach and activity or, to use social scientific terms, its infrastructural power,[18] one reflection of which was a continued growth in the per capita revenue extracted by the state (see Figure 6.1).

In addition, during this period "peasants became Frenchman," in Eugen Weber's evocative phrase: nation-building took a major step forward as French

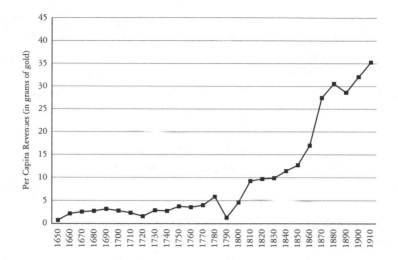

FIGURE 6.1 Yearly per capita revenues in France (in grams of gold), 1650–1910. Source: Mark Dinecco, "Fiscal Centralization, Limited Government, and Public Revenues in Europe, 1650–1913," *Journal of Economic History* 69, 1 (2009): 48–103; Dinecco, *Political Transformation and Public Finances, Europe 1650–1913* (New York: Cambridge University Press, 2011); K. Kivanç Karaman and Şevket Pamuk, *Journal of Economic History* 70, 3 (September 2010).

society was further homogenized and millions of isolated, uneducated rural French citizens were integrated into the national polity. The Third Republic expanded France's rail, road, and canal networks, enabling citizens to communicate and engage with each other to an unprecedented degree,[19] and free, mandatory, secular primary education was established via the Jules Ferry laws (1881 and 1882), creating a citizenry tied together by common language,[20] values, and traditions and cultivating a cadre of teachers devoted to creating republican citizens.[21] By the end of the 1880s the Third Republic had also reintroduced universal military conscription, which provided citizens from across the country further education in a common language and socialized them into national, patriotic values.[22] However, despite its growing strength and accomplishments, during the late nineteenth century the Republic faced significant challenges as well.

Some stemmed from the general turmoil of the era. The last decades of the nineteenth century were a period of rapid and disorienting change for France as well as the rest of Europe. During the mid- to late 1870s Europe and North America experienced a prolonged depression that ended the steady economic growth of the previous decades. So severe and prolonged was the downturn that it came to be known as the "Great Depression," a characterization it kept until the 1930s when an even more severe downturn took over the title. This depression hit France hard and was layered on to the economic shocks generated by the Franco-Prussian war. The 1870s depression was followed by a period of economic globalization that re-ignited growth, but also generated destabilizing social trends including a decline in the relative import of agriculture and small, family-owned businesses in the economy,[23] an unprecedented increase in migration both internally from rural to urban areas and externally from the "old" world to the "new," and a growing sense on the part of workers, artisans, farmers, and others that the ruthless pressures of the capitalist system were leaving them further and further behind. As we will see in subsequent chapters, these developments led to a backlash across Europe, and the rise of movements on both the left and right that rejected key features of the emerging modern order.

On the left, the consequences of unfettered capitalism fed the rise of workers' movements; by the late nineteenth century Marxism had become the dominant doctrine within most working-class, socialist parties. Marx, of course, rejected capitalism and was also skeptical about democracy since he did not believe the bourgeoisie would ever permit democracy to truly function and allow workers to take power; these views were solidified by 1848 and the Paris Commune. In France, the first truly Marxist party, the *Parti Ouvrier Français* (POF), was formed in 1879 under the tutelage of two of France's best-known Marxists, Jules Guesde and Paul Lafargue.[24] Guesde and Lafargue championed a particularly crude version of Marxism that stressed the inexorable decline of capitalism and the inevitability of class conflict, and belittled the Third Republic and democracy more generally since they were convinced that the bourgeoisie would never allow workers to truly threaten their interests. As Lafargue once put it with his characteristic bluntness, "The bourgeois republican order is the most corrupt and dishonest regime which could possibly exist."[25] To believe that it could be used to fundamentally improve the lives of workers was an illusion. Or, in Guesde's word, it was a waste of time to pursue democratic change since "in multiplying reforms, one only multiplies shams."[26]

Alongside the growth of a Marxist left that rejected capitalism and denigrated democracy, the other and far more dangerous beneficiary of the discontent and dislocation that swept across Europe during the *fin-de-siècle* was nationalism. In France as well as the rest of Europe (see chapters 7 and 8), the constituency for and appeal of traditional conservative movements that aimed to revive the ancien régime diminished during the late nineteenth century; instead, the right became dominated by nationalist movements. Unlike their 1848 predecessors, who fought the ancien régime in the name of liberty, equality, and democracy, *fin-de-siècle* nationalist movements viewed liberalism and democracy as well as capitalism as the main threats to national unity and identity.[27] In France this new type of movement first appeared during the Boulangist crisis.

General Georges Boulanger was a French general and later politician who thrived on and encouraged the generalized discontent of the era as well as the discontent with the Republic arising from scandals, bank failures, corruption, and an inability to take revenge against Germany and reclaim France's "rightful" place at the head of Europe. Reflecting this last obsession, Boulanger was sometimes referred to as General Revenge. Boulanger's solution to France's problems was an aggressive anti-liberal, anti-Republican, populist, and pseudo-socialist nationalism. This odd mixture attracted the support of a broad range of dissatisfied French citizens: prominent conservatives supported the movement as well as many who viewed themselves as socialists. Indeed, within Parliament Boulangists championed policies traditionally associated with the left, supporting extensive social reforms and cooperating with socialists in Parliament; indeed, notes one observer, "the only issue which . . . distinguish[ed] the Boulangist from the socialists was nationalism."[28] In addition, Boulangists saw themselves as champions not of a narrow elite, but of France's "disinherited" and "little people."[29] Indeed, so popular did Boulanger become that after winning a significant victory in the 1889 elections, coup rumors spread; when the time came to act, however, Boulanger hesitated, and shortly thereafter the government charged him with treason and conspiracy. To the dismay of his supporters, Boulanger fled rather than fought, and his support thereafter quickly diminished. Boulanger then died an ignominious death, committing suicide in 1891 at the grave of his mistress in Brussels.

Although the Boulangist episode was relatively brief, its significance should not be underestimated. It marked the birth of a new type of right-wing movement in France: nationalist, anti-liberal, and anti-democratic, but also appropriating many of the themes, appeals, and policies traditionally associated with the left and able to attract a mass constituency. Boulangism thus represented a trend away from elite-based, traditional conservative movements on the right, aiming instead to unite a broad coalition behind a strongman who would "clean house" and eliminate the "weak" Republic.[30] Boulanger's success made clear that a significant number of citizens were at least willing to consider alternatives to the democratic status quo.[31]

The Dreyfus Affair picked up where Boulangism left off. As one observer remarked, "Boulangism drew up nationalism's birth certificate, the Dreyfus Affair its baptismal record."[32] The basic facts of the Dreyfus case are these: in 1894 a French spy in the German embassy discovered a handwritten note in a wastebasket listing French military secrets, which became known as the *bordereau*, received by a German military attaché in Paris. The handwriting on the note was linked to an artillery officer named Alfred Dreyfus. Dreyfus was arrested for spying, court-martialed, convicted, and sentenced to degradation and deported for life to Devil's Island off the coast of French Guiana. But rather than ending there, the Dreyfus case turned into the greatest scandal of nineteenth-century France, mobilizing and aggravating existing divisions within French society and creating almost civil war–like conditions. The reason is that although the Dreyfus Affair was ostensibly about Dreyfus's guilt or innocence, at its heart lie a more fundamental controversy about France's political future. The controversy penetrated almost all areas of French political and even private life—courtrooms, Parliament, the arts, the street, salons, and dining rooms became sites of heated conflict—and once again divided the country into pro- and anti-democratic camps. The Affair also made clear that despite the Republic's many successes, significant opposition to it remained and was, moreover, no longer limited to monarchists and traditional conservative institutions like the church and military but was spreading to populist, anti-Semitic, nationalist movements.

The Dreyfus Affair

Alfred Dreyfus's background is crucial to understanding the controversy. Dreyfus came from a wealthy Alsatian Jewish family, which made him a double outsider. Although anti-Semitism had long been a part of European culture, by the late nineteenth century it had begun changing from a religious to a racial or national sentiment. Jews were no longer portrayed "only" as a threat to Christian beliefs and teachings, but also increasingly as "foreigners" exerting a disproportionate and debilitating influence over national life. In France, Jews were scapegoated for almost every problem facing the Third Republic, from scandals, to economic crises, to its decline vis-à-vis Germany; many members of the middle and upper classes also resented the rapid rise and success of Jews in France.[33] Making matters worse, Dreyfus came from Alsace, a region lost by France after the Franco-Prussian war, making it a symbol of French decline and its inhabitants—particularly its Jews—of suspect loyalty to some.[34] After Alsace's annexation by Germany, the Dreyfus family moved to Paris, where Alfred attended military school. After finishing, Alfred joined the French Army, eventually ascending to the army's general staff office in 1894, the only Jew to achieve that status. Thus, when a cleaning woman in the pay of French counterespionage found the *bordereau*, a document that contained information that seemed to link it to someone inside the general staff office, widespread anti-Semitism along with the "paranoia" pervading the military establishment at the time[35] led many to assume Dreyfus's guilt.

Counterintelligence officers were called in to compare the note's handwriting to Dreyfus's and that of others in the general staff office. Despite an inept investigation and the inability of counterintelligence officers to come to a definitive conclusion about the note's author, Dreyfus was charged and carted off to prison. Dreyfus had little motive to commit such a crime—he was wealthy, married with children, had no known vices, and had worked his way up through elite military schools—but as a Jew he was seen by the military as "not really French" and "a traitor by nature."[36]

Although the arrest was initially secret, word leaked out and the right-wing press exploded in paroxysms of anti-Semitism. The Church, which played a crucial role in fanning anti-Dreyfus, anti-Semitic, and anti-democratic sentiment, published descriptions of Dreyfus as "the enemy Jew" and an agent of "international Jewry" whose goal was the ruin of the French people. Its largest paper, *La Croix*, called for the expulsion of Jews from France.[37] And Edmund Drumont's *La Libre Parole*, perhaps the principal mouthpiece for Parisian anti-Semitism, declared Dreyfus's absolute guilt and its certainty that he was part of a vast plot to betray the French people and deliver them into the hands of Germany.[38] In addition, even before Dreyfus's trial began, the war minister, General Mercier, declared in interviews with French papers that he was certain of Dreyfus's culpability.

Despite the drumbeat of condemnation and the non-public trial, the lack of actual evidence against Dreyfus led the military to fear an acquittal. To avoid this, a file was concocted containing "absolute" proof of Dreyfus's guilt and presented to the court on General Mercier's orders in secret. Presented with this "evidence," which neither Dreyfus nor his counsel were allowed to examine, the court found Dreyfus guilty on December 22, 1894, and sentenced him to the maximum penalty allowed by law. Before being sent off to serve his sentence on Devil's Island, Dreyfus was humiliated by being stripped of his military insignia, badges, and sword in a courtyard filled with soldiers while a large anti-Semitic crowd called for blood outside. The nationalist Maurice Barrés described the scene:

> Judas! Traitor! It was a veritable storm. . . . The poor wretch releases in all hearts floods of intense dislike. His face that marks him as a foreigner, his impassive stiffness, create an aura that even the coolest spectator finds revolting . . . he was not born to live in any society.

Only the branch of a tree grown infamous in an infamous wood offers itself to him—so that he could hang himself from it.[39]

At this point the case might have ended but for two factors: the unwillingness of Dreyfus, his family, and a small band of supporters to accept this miscarriage of justice, and a fortuitous change in counterintelligence personnel.

After Alfred Dreyfus's conviction, his brother Mathieu continued to proclaim Alfred's innocence. Mathieu did not find much of an audience until 1895, when Colonel Georges Picquart became the new head of counterintelligence. Soon after taking over, Picquart was given another document discovered by the same French spy in the German embassy who had found the original *bordereau*. This document, which came to be known as the *petit bleu*, was addressed to a Major Walsin Esterhazy, a dissolute and dishonest gambler and swindler who was however Catholic and aristocratic, and had high-level military connections. Eventually coming to suspect that Esterhazy might be the author of the original *bordereau*, Picquart collected samples of his handwriting. Realizing that Esterhazy's handwriting matched that of the *bordereau*, Picquart began an inquiry which led him to conclude that Esterhazy had indeed been working for Germany. However, when Picquart reported the results of his investigation to his superiors, they made clear that they had no interest in exonerating Dreyfus. General Charles-Arthur Gonse, deputy head of the general staff, asked Picquart, "What do you care if that Jew rots on Devil's Island?"[40] Picquart was told to keep quiet; soon after he was removed from his position and then shipped off to Tunisia. In addition to getting rid of Picquart, the military gave Major Hubert-Joseph Henry the task of strengthening the case against Dreyfus. Unable to do so legitimately, Henry manufactured further evidence, in particular a letter naming Dreyfus as the German spy, which came to be known as "*le faux Henry*."

By this point, the case was becoming increasingly difficult to control. In order to protect himself, Picquart gave the results of his investigation to a lawyer friend named Louis Lebois, but asked him not to publicly reveal his findings, probably because he did not want to be seen as betraying the army to which he had devoted his life. Lebois then met with the vice president of the Senate, Auguste Scheuer-Kestner, who was also an Alsatian, who then began his own investigation; Scheuer-Kestner also eventually concluded that Dreyfus was innocent and Esterhazy the real culprit. However, like Picquart, Scheurer-Kestner's initial attempts to convince others of Dreyfus's innocence met with little success; indeed he became the subject of vitriolic attacks in the anti-Semitic press. In November 1896 Dreyfus's small but growing band of defenders received two boosts with the publication of Barnard Lazare's brochure "A Judicial Error: The Truth about the Dreyfus Affair," which picked apart the case against Dreyfus and the French daily newspaper *Le Matin*'s publication of a leaked copy of the original *bordereau* which enabled several people who knew Esterhazy to recognize his handwriting. One of these, a banker named Castro, contacted Mathieu Dreyfus. Mathieu then went to Scheurer-Kestner and asked him to confirm that he too believed Esterhazy to be the author of the *bordereau*—an identity Scheurer-Kestner had not originally wanted to reveal because of promises of secrecy made to Lebois. Armed with growing evidence, Mathieu made an open complaint about Esterhazy.

With the charges now public the military felt compelled to open an investigation, which amazingly concluded that Picquart rather than Esterhazy was the true culprit. By this point, interest in the case had grown. When *Le Figaro* published a series of letters by one of Esterhazy's former mistresses in which Esterhazy proclaimed his hatred of France and faith in Germany at the end of 1897, the general staff became convinced that only a full trial of Esterhazy could bring the uproar to an end. The trial occurred in January 1898 behind closed doors and resulted in the rapid acquittal of Esterhazy. After this, Émile Zola, perhaps the most influential French novelist of the day, published his famous "I accuse . . . !" (*J'accuse . . .!*): an open letter in the newspaper *L'Aurore* to the president of the Republic, Félix Faure, which accused key figures in the military of lies, cover-ups, and anti-Semitism and those in the government who supported the military or simply allowed its miscarriage of justice to stand of betraying the Republic. "Truth and justice," Zola wrote to Faure, "have been slapped in the face."

> France's cheek has been sullied . . . and History will record that it was during your Presidency that such a crime against society has been committed. . . . The Republican government should take a broom to that nest of Jesuits [in the military] and make a clean sweep! . . . what a den of sneaking intrigue, rumour-mongering and back-biting that sacred chapel has become—yet that is where the fate of our country is decided. People take fright at the appalling light that has just been shed on it all by the Dreyfus Affair, that tale of human sacrifice! Yes, an unfortunate, a "dirty Jew" has been sacrificed. . . . [These officers] have crushed the nation under their boots, stuffing its calls for truth and justice down its throat on the fallacious and sacrilegious pretext that they are acting for the good of the country! . . . [They have also] led public opinion astray, manipulat[ing] it for a death-dealing purpose and pervert[ing] it to the point of delirium. It is a crime to poison

the minds of the humble, ordinary people, to whip reactionary and intolerant passions into a frenzy while sheltering behind the odious bastion of anti-Semitism. France, the great and liberal cradle of the rights of man, will die of anti-Semitism if it is not cured of it. . . . The Affair is only just the beginning, because only now have the positions become crystal clear: on the one hand, the guilty parties, who do not want the truth to be revealed; on the other, the defenders of justice, who will give their lives to see that justice is done. I have said it elsewhere and I repeat it here: if the truth is buried underground, it swells and grows and becomes so explosive that the day it bursts, it blows everything wide open with it. Time will tell: we shall see whether we have not prepared, for some later date, the most resounding disaster.[41]

Within twenty-four hours, hundreds of thousands of copies of the newspaper had been sold. *J'Accuse* rallied intellectuals, socialists, youths, and others into a *Dreyfusard* movement, and demands for a retrial of Dreyfus grew. However, rather than gaining Dreyfus a retrial, Zola was charged with libel. Zola's trial was mobbed, anti-Semitic riots broke out across France, Catholic and Church groups protested "this Jewish campaign besmirching France," " 'France for the French' became a ubiquitous slogan," Jewish stores and synagogues were attacked, and Jews were assaulted in the streets with the police often standing by. According to reports "the crowds were not only crying slogans related to the Dreyfus Affair, but also 'Death to the Jews.' "[42]

Zola's trial and then conviction for libel further inflamed and divided the country into lines familiar since the revolution—between the supporters and opponents of liberalism, democracy, and the Republic, now in the guise of *Dreyfusards* and anti-*Dreyfusards*. The anti-*Dreyfusard* camp included, of course, traditional conservative forces like the military and the Church but much of the sound and fury surrounding the affair—the constant anti-Semitic and anti-Republic protests—came from new populist, right-wing movements.[43] Drumont, for example, the founder of the anti-Semitic *La Libre Parole* and the author of a number of extremely popular anti-Semitic tracts, including the runaway hit *La France Juive* (Jewish France)—which sold 100,000 copies in 1886 alone and was premised on the idea that "France was falling under the control of Jews [who were] responsible for every French ill"[44]—founded the Anti-Semitic League of France (*Ligue antisémitique de France*) during the Dreyfus Affair to disseminate anti-Semitic literature and mobilize demonstrations against the Republic. The Patriots' League (*Ligue de la Patrie Française*), meanwhile, originally formed to promote nationalism and revenge against Germany, morphed during the Dreyfus Affair into an anti-Semitic, anti-*Dreyfusard* movement that staged disruptive and sometimes violent protests against Zola and the Republic. And *Action Français*, which would go on to play an important role during the early twentieth century, also had its origins in the Dreyfus Affair, calling for a "purification" of France's "foreign elements," attacking democracy and joining "the popular radicalism of nationalism with the reactionary elitism of the royalists."[45]

In the summer of 1898 a new cabinet came to power with Godefroy Cavaignac as minister of war. Cavaignac wanted to end the controversy and so dug up the old file of evidence originally compiled against Dreyfus and presented it to the Chamber of Deputies as proof of Dreyfus's guilt, not knowing that it was fake. In August Captain Louis Cuignet from Cavaignac's staff was going through evidence and realized that a key document—"*le faux Henry*"—was a forgery. When confronted by Cavaignac, Henry immediately confessed and was sent to a military prison but before he could incriminate any higher-ups, he was found dead, an apparent suicide, his throat slashed by a razor. Henry's death elicited an outpouring of anti-Semitic vitriol from the nationalist right. Common among nationalists was Charles Maurras's view of Henry as a "hero of the state" and his vilification of the Republic for its "Jewishness." (Maurras would go on to become the chief ideologue of *Action Français*.) Henry's death occasioned an "orgy of anti-Semitic insults and calls for the massacre of French Jews."[46] Typical was the following declaration from the *Jeunesse Antisémitique* (Young Antisemites):

> To the Nation!
> Citizens!
> For a year the hirelings of foreign enemy powers, all enemies of our race, have been unleashed against our army, which alone stands above our unhappy country, looted and dishonored by Jews for the last century. . . . The youth of France will march in tight ranks around the flag . . . [and] will chase the foreign hordes from the soil of France.[47]

A fund was taken up for Henry's widow, and Drumont's *La Libre Parole* launched a campaign to erect a monument to him.

After the confession and death of Henry, Cavaignac resigned[48] and Dreyfus's family once again petitioned for a retrial. During the last months of 1898 and first months of 1899 conditions reached a fever pitch, as the *Dreyfusards* made political headway and the country was rocked by anti-Semitic and anti-Republic demonstrations. In February 1899 Faure died suddenly in office and was replaced by Èmile Loubet, who was sympathetic to the *Dreyfusard* cause. Loubet was bitterly attacked by the nationalist right, and members of the Patriots' League attempted a coup soon after he came to office. However, in the summer of 1899 Loubet and the *Dreyfusards* were strengthened by the formation of a "government of Republican defense" under Prime Minister René Waldeck-Rousseau, which included representatives from across the political spectrum, including Alexander Millerand, the first socialist to serve in a "bourgeois" government.

During the summer of 1899 a new trial for Dreyfus was ordered, but because the situation in Paris had become so volatile, it was moved to Rennes in Brittany. However, by this point much of the rest of the country, including Rennes, had become a tinderbox: a week or so into the trial one of Dreyfus's lawyers was shot by a fanatic, and police and the military had a hard time containing anti-*Dreyfusard* demonstrations. When the military court once again found Dreyfus guilty of treason despite the fake evidence, the confessions of Henry and Esterhàzy, and all the rest, albeit this time "with extenuating circumstances," neither *Dreyfusards* nor anti-*Dreyfusards* were satisfied: fears grew that France was sinking into civil war–like conditions. Worried about the explosive domestic situation as well as the damage being done to France's reputation abroad, the government decided to pardon Dreyfus to placate the *Dreyfusards* while also passing an amnesty law, protecting all those involved in the Affair from prosecution, to placate the military. Dreyfus's pardon did not, however, exonerate him, and he and his supporters continued to fight for a declaration of innocence—something he only received in 1906.[49]

The Affair and the Third Republic

Why does the Dreyfus Affair merit so much attention? First, because it revealed important weaknesses and vulnerabilities in the Third Republic. Even in France, the country with the longest democratic tradition in Europe, a significant number of citizens were so dissatisfied with the Republic that they were willing to support anti-liberal, anti-democratic, anti-Semitic, and often violent opposition to it. Second, and relatedly, the Affair profoundly impacted the main political actors in France. On the left, the Dreyfus Affair forced socialists to confront head-on their ambivalence about liberal democracy: Should socialists defend the Republic because liberal democracy was critical to the achievement of socialism, or stay on the sidelines because the fate of the bourgeois state did not really concern them and had little to do with socialism's ultimate victory? On one side stood Guesde and Lafargue, who simply could not defend the bourgeois Republic and accept the open modification of their understanding of socialism that defense would entail. They insisted "the proletarians have nothing to do with this battle which is not theirs."[50] On the other side stood those for whom the institutions and ideals of the Republic were a critical component of their socialist vision. The undisputed leader of this camp was Jean Jaurès, who argued,

> the democratic Republic is not, as our self-styled doctrinaires of Marxism so often say, a purely bourgeois form . . . it heralds Socialism, it prepares for it, contains it implicitly to some extent, because only Republicanism can lead to Socialism by legal evolution without break of continuity.[51]

Jaurès's defense of the Republic during the Dreyfus Affair thrust him into the political spotlight. Indeed, from then until his assassination in 1914, he became one of the most important and beloved figures in the French and international socialist movements. The anti-Republican fervor stirred up by the Affair helped Jaurès convince a majority of French socialists that their overriding goal had to be protecting democracy from anti-*Dreyfusard* forces. This is part of the backstory to the formation of the "government of Republican defense" in 1899 under Prime Minister René Waldeck-Rousseau mentioned above. In return for socialist support, Waldeck-Rousseau asked the socialist Alexandre Millerand to join his cabinet. This request triggered a crisis within the socialist movement since having socialists not merely support but actually join a non-socialist government indicated an acceptance of cross-class cooperation and the bourgeois state that challenged the reigning Marxist orthodoxy head-on. In response, Guesde, Lafargue, and other socialists called for the convocation of France's first all-socialist congress since 1882. Not surprisingly, at the congress Jaurès emerged as the strongest defender of Millerand and of socialist support for democracy. The congress's outcome was ambiguous. Two resolutions were adopted, the first declaring the participation of socialists in a bourgeois government incompatible with the principle of class struggle, and the second saying that under "exceptional circumstances" such a tactic might be permitted. The controversy continued to simmer even after Millerand's departure from the government, and spilled over into International Socialist meetings. The Affair and its aftermath marked a crucial stage in the grappling of French as well as European socialists with democracy.[52]

In addition to forcing socialists to confront head-on their views of democracy, the Affair convinced all Republicans that defending the Republic required more concerted and coordinated effort. The Dreyfus Affair thus "rekindled the Republic spirit" and helped spur the formation or expansion of a number of pro-Republican organizations, including the Masons, *Libre-Pensée* (Free Thought) groups, and the League of the Rights of Man

(*Ligue des droits de l'homme et du citoyen*), that provided meeting grounds for Republicans from different parts of the political and class spectrum.[53] Perhaps even more important was the formation of the Radical party in 1901. This party was pro-republic, national in scope, and positioned itself in opposition to conservatives and monarchists as well as socialists by adopting a socially conservative, pro-property, and individualistic stance that enabled it to attract middle-class, lower-middle-class, and peasant support. The Radical party became the largest party for much of the remainder of the Third Republic, serving in almost all its governments and providing significant stability.[54] Also notable was that the Radicals were willing to work with other pro-Republican groups to defend democracy. Particularly consequential was Radical participation in a 1902 left-wing bloc (*Bloc des gauches*) that included socialists and enacted critical legislation, most notably the 1905 law separating Church and State that formed the foundation of France's twentieth-century commitment to *laïcité*.

The separation of the social and political goals of the French Revolution that the Radical party represented and the growing acceptance of democracy by the middle classes and peasantry that this separation facilitated was a striking difference between the First, Second, and Third Republics. As one influential observer put it, during the Third Republic, "The Republic and the left stopped identifying with each other . . . and consequently the right and hostility to the Republic were no longer confused. There was now, and would be for a long while, a republican right or, if you prefer, republicans on the right."[55] The strengthening and broadening of the Republic's support base was accompanied by a weakening of its traditional enemies. Monarchism, for example, "if not dead, had been routed and relegated to the camp of lost causes." The Church and the army were significantly weakened, and "the system of national education was completed, expanding the Republic's ability to shape the norms and values of its citizens."[56] In the years after the Dreyfus Affair, in other words, the Third Republic made significant progress.

Nonetheless, threats remained. In addition to strengthening the resolve and accomplishments of pro-Republican forces, the Affair influenced the anti-Republican right. Although some of the organizations that had flourished during the Affair declined after it was resolved, others did not, and the ideas and strategies they employed during the Affair remained part of French political life during the early twentieth century. In addition, the Affair marked a transition on the right: the traditional forces opposed to the Republic—monarchists, Bonapartists, the Church, and the military—were no longer the "cutting edge" of the anti-democratic movement. Instead, these forces continued to decline or became subsumed into more modern and dynamic nationalist movements. These nationalist movements took from the Affair the lesson that overthrowing the Republic would require more proselytizing, organizing, and political activity. And so as opposed to previous anti-democratic movements, late nineteenth- and early twentieth-century nationalist movements became mass-based, populist, and cross-class. Particularly useful in this regard was anti-Semitism, which allowed nationalist movements to appeal to traditional religious prejudices, resentment of post-emancipation Jewish success, and the large numbers of citizens discomforted by what they viewed as France's decline. These movements and appeals would eventually form part of the foundation upon which the fascist and National Socialist movements of the interwar period would be built.

The Dreyfus Affair's status as the most spectacular manifestation of the growing power and popularity of anti-Semitism in Europe during the *fin-de-siècle* is another reason it warrants attention. Indeed, the Dreyfus Affair opened up a new chapter in the history of Jews in Europe. Although, as noted above, religious anti-Semitism had long existed, it took on a new, more virulent, and more dangerous form during the late nineteenth century as part of a more general backlash against democracy, liberalism, capitalism, and other aspects of modernity. That this new form of anti-Semitism appeared even in France, Europe's most democratic nation, where Jews had been emancipated early on and had accordingly achieved a comparatively high degree of assimilation, highlights how pervasive and portentous this trend was.[57] Dreyfus and his family represented precisely the type of assimilated, secular, patriotic Jews that many hoped were paving the way for full Jewish integration into European culture and society. But the Dreyfus Affair and the paroxysm of anti-Semitism it unleashed forced many to reconsider the future of European Jewry. Among those influenced by the Dreyfus Affair was Theodor Herzl, the Paris correspondent for the Vienna newspaper, the *Neue Freie Press*. Herzl was Jewish, but he came from a family that took pride in its secular, assimilated nature. By the end of the nineteenth century Herzl was dismayed by rising anti-Semitism in his native Vienna, but his experiences in France during the Dreyfus Affair shocked him: if acceptance and assimilation were impossible in France—the home of the French Revolution and the Enlightenment—how could there be hope for it elsewhere? The Affair thus helped convince Herzl that Jews had no choice but to establish a state of their own. After the Dreyfus Affair Herzl went on to become a father of modern Zionism: penning some of the movement's foundational texts, organizing and becoming president of the World Zionist Organization, and tirelessly pursuing international support for a Jewish state.[58]

A final reason the Dreyfus Affair merits attention is that it reflected pathologies and problems facing not only France but, as subsequent chapters make clear, much of the rest of Europe as well. The *Dreyfusard* and anti-*Dreyfusard* camps sprang from and represented divisions in French society that reached "back to the French Revolution and forward to the Holocaust."[59] *Dreyfusards* were the defenders and anti-*Dreyfusards* the opponents of democracy and liberalism, that is, the ideals of the French Revolution in general and the Third Republic in particular. As we have seen, to some degree the former triumphed with the Third Republic, which turned out to be the longest-lived and most successful French regime since the revolution and the only democracy in a major European country at the time. Nonetheless, the Third Republic faced significant threats from traditional defenders of the ancien régime, like monarchists, the Church, and the military as well as from the growing populist, anti-Semitic nationalist organizations that drew energy from the anti-*Dreyfusard* struggle. These organizations reflected a portentous shift in the nature of nationalism and the right that occurred across Europe: the former morphed from a progressive force arrayed against the ancien régime into an opponent of liberalism and democracy, and the latter became increasingly dominated by populist, anti-Semitic nationalist movements. This transformation of nationalism and the right profoundly influenced European political development, perhaps nowhere more so than in Italy and Germany, the cases to which this book now turns.

CHAPTER 7 | Italian Unification

We have made Italy, now we must make Italians.

—Massimo d'Azeglio[1]

T EMPORALLY HALFWAY BETWEEN 1789 and 1917, 1848 was also politically a midpoint—a time when the "old had not yet been overcome, and
the new was still being born."[2] As discussed in chapter 5, 1848 did not completely eliminate the old order or give rise to a new one, but the reverse wave
that swept the continent between 1849 and the early 1850s did not return
Europe to the status quo ante either. Most obviously, neither the national nor
democratic pressures that propelled the 1848 wave forward disappeared with
the reverse wave; during the last half of the nineteenth century these pressures
re-emerged in new forms and combinations. In the previous chapter we saw
how these pressures shaped political development in France, giving rise to
the Third Republic—the country's longest-lived regime since the revolution
and the only major democracy in Europe at the time—as well as the Third
Republic's most potent challenger, an anti-liberal, anti-democratic nationalist movement. This chapter will examine how these pressures shaped political development in another part of Europe—that which would become Italy.

It is common to bemoan the weak states and national identities that
characterize many contemporary developing states. Often forgotten is that
at some point all states were "new," even those currently viewed as "natural" or "inevitable," and building national identities and strong states
has always been a lengthy and difficult process. Chapter 2 discussed how
beginning in early modern Europe most attempts at state-building failed,
helping to explain why the 500 or so political entities that existed at

this time were reduced to a couple of dozen over the following centuries. Subsequent chapters examined the successful but arduous processes of state- and nation-building in Britain and France. These countries developed fairly strong states and national identities comparatively early. In contrast, many countries that exist in Europe today only arose in the nineteenth or twentieth centuries, forcing them to confront the challenges of state- and nation-building, capitalism, and mass politics in a relatively short period of time. This is true of Italy, for example. Its emergence, moreover, was neither natural nor inevitable; few people before the nineteenth century viewed it as a nation or an obvious candidate for statehood. Reflecting this, Italian unification was driven at least as much by the manipulation of elites and foreign policy opportunities as it was by popular demand or any inexorable historical, economic, or social logic. Modern Italy, accordingly, came into existence unwanted by many of its "people" and lacked a strong national identity or political institutions capable of dealing with the new country's myriad problems. As we will see, the unfinished business of nation- and state-building combined with the challenges of economic development and mass politics played havoc with Italian political life well into the twentieth century and indeed up through the present day.

The Background

In Italy, as in much of Europe, the French Revolution set modern nationalism in motion. Alongside Germany (see chapter 8), no other part of Europe was as affected by the revolution and particularly its Napoleonic aftermath as the Italian peninsula. Before Napoleon, Italy was divided into many political entities with different rulers, political, social and legal systems, economies, and traditions. In the south was the Kingdom of Naples and Sicily, ruled over by Spanish Bourbons, geographically, politically, and economically distinct from the rest of the peninsula. In the middle of the peninsula were the Papal States, ruled over by the pope as a theocratic autocracy. The north was occupied by political entities of various sizes and strengths. Some of these were under foreign, that is Austrian, control, others were ruled by independent dynasties; the most important of the latter was Piedmont-Sardinia. In the years before the French Revolution autocratic rulers on the peninsula, as in the rest of Europe, struggled with the nobility and Church over centralization efforts.[3] State-building was most successful in the north, particularly in Piedmont, and least successful in the south, a divergence that would play a crucial role in the formation and nature of the future Italian state.

During the period of French rule (1796–1815), state-building and modernization accelerated: the peninsula was consolidated into three parts; feudal and ecclesiastic privileges abolished; uniform legal and bureaucratic institutions established; a peninsula-wide conscription system set up; civil liberties, legal equality, and religious freedom declared; internal restrictions on trade eliminated and a single currency, commercial code, and system of weights and measures put in place; and the Church weakened through the confiscation of its lands and the taking over of many its functions by secular government.[4] Initially, the French Revolution and the Napoleonic invasions inspired many to rise up against the old order, but over time foreign rule spurred resistance. The Napoleonic Empire eventually collapsed, but territorial changes and social, economic, and political reforms undertaken during this time undermined the legitimacy and traditional structures of the old order and spurred the growth of nationalism.[5]

After Napoleon's fall, the Congress of Vienna attempted to turn back the clock in Italy as in the rest of Europe. Metternich, the Austrian chancellor and key architect of the restoration system, was eager to restore Austria's power on the Italian peninsula and had little interest or belief in the national aspirations that emerged during the Napoleonic period. Indeed, he famously denigrated Italian national aspirations by referring to Italy as a mere "geographical expression."[6] After 1815 the Italian peninsula returned to its fragmented condition: the pope was back in power, the Bourbons returned to rule what was now known as the Kingdom of the Two Sicilies, and Austria gained control of the peninsula's richest regions, Lombardy and Venetia, which because of their strategic position in the north gave Austria effective control over the entire peninsula. Nonetheless, it was impossible to put the genies that emerged during the Napoleonic period back in the bottle. Administrative, legal, and fiscal changes and the abolition of traditional rights and privileges had laid the foundation for more efficient and powerful states, and most rulers therefore kept in place at least some Napoleonic reforms.[7] For the people of the peninsula, the restoration of monarchical dictatorships and in many cases foreign rule was a hard pill to swallow. Uprisings quickly resumed, many of which could only be put down with Austrian help.

During 1848, uprisings exploded across the peninsula, but with a greater force and broader geographical spread than previously.[8] Reflecting the peninsula's fragmented nature, these uprisings, although often sharing some similar goals, had disparate leaderships and visions of what the new order should look like. During the early months of 1848 these uprisings forced the departure of or concessions by rulers across the peninsula. However, once the old order retreated, problems quickly appeared (see also chapter 5).

The opposition included charismatic revolutionaries like Giuseppe Mazzini and Giuseppe Garibaldi who favored mobilizing the masses and replacing the peninsula's various dictatorial regimes with a unified republican or democratic one. Mazzini was probably the greatest nationalist of the day, admired throughout Europe, and the inspiration for copycat revolutionaries across the globe. Part of his appeal was based on his advocacy of what we would today consider terrorist methods to achieve his ends. He believed, for example, that "insurrection by means of guerrilla bands is the true method of warfare for all nations desirous of emancipating themselves from a foreign yoke. It is invincible, indestructible." He also believed that until Italians were willing to die for their faith, their national goals would not be taken seriously. "Ideas," as he once famously put it, "ripen quickly when . . . nourished by the blood of martyrs."[9] In 1831 Mazzini founded the "Young Italy" movement to bring "the people" together to liberate Italy, but it was in 1848 that he achieved his greatest triumph, helping lead a short-lived radical Roman Republic—modern Italy's first democratic experiment. Garibaldi, like Mazzini, was a colorful figure, perhaps literally, since his followers came to be known for their red shirts, and raised his own army to defend some of 1848's revolutionary gains. Garibaldi's exploits in Italy and other parts of the world made him famous: he went on to be showered with honors in England, was offered a Union command in the Civil War by Abraham Lincoln, and got elected to the French national assembly.[10]

Alongside charismatic revolutionaries like Mazzini and Garibaldi, another key figure in the Italian story was King Charles Albert of Piedmont. Piedmont was the most powerful state on the peninsula and one of the few with a "native Italian" ruler. After Napoleon's fall, reaction had perhaps gone further in Piedmont than in the rest of the peninsula, with then king Victor Emmanuel I doing away with the reforms introduced during the period of French rule and re-establishing absolutism and the power of the aristocracy and church. Recognizing the way the wind was blowing, however, Charles Albert, who became king in 1831, quickly agreed to a new constitution in 1848 that established a constitutional rather than an absolutist monarchy and guaranteed equality before the law as well as other basic liberal rights. Charles Albert shared with Mazzini and Garibaldi a desire to rid the peninsula of foreign rule but differed from them in favoring a Piedmont-dominated new order rather than a democratic and/or republican one. When the 1848 wave broke out, Charles Albert took advantage of the chaos spreading across the Austrian Empire (see chapter 5) to send troops to Lombardy and Venetia to push out the Austrians. However, despite ruling over the peninsula's most powerful state, without the chaos in the empire Charles Albert was no match for the Austrians. Once the Habsburgs regained control over their armed forces Charles Albert was quickly forced to give up the areas he had conquered. He retained, however, control over Piedmont-Sardinia and did not roll back the constitutional system instituted in 1848. The reverse wave that swept over the rest of the peninsula ended reform experiments elsewhere: the French restored theocratic, papal rule to the Papal States; the Bourbons returned to the Two Sicilies; and other peninsular rulers reversed the concessions they made only months earlier.

Despite its failure, the 1848 wave turned out to be a critical stage in the *Risorgimento*—the rising or resurgence of Italy. Although the old order was neither eliminated nor a new one created, the uprisings had more popular support than previous ones and placed the question of Italian unification squarely on the European political agenda. In addition, the wave and its aftermath reshaped Italian nationalism. During 1848 many of the uprisings had democratic/republican as well as radical social and economic agendas, and in the years after the reverse wave, other "Mazzinian" uprisings occurred. That all ultimately failed led many nationalists to conclude that a single, united national movement rather than various uncoordinated ones was necessary and that this movement would have to be led by Piedmont, since it was the only state on the peninsula with the interest in leading and military and political power to a lead a drive for unification.[11]

Piedmont's evolution after 1848 strengthened its attractiveness to nationalists. Although conservative by today's standards, after the reverse wave Piedmont was "easily the most liberal and progressive state on the peninsula"[12] and a magnet for intellectuals and other exiles from more repressive regions.[13] In addition, although Piedmont's first years of constitutional government were rocky, with seven premiers during the years 1848–1849, particularly under Prime Ministers Massimo d'Azeglio and Camillo Benso (generally known as Cavour), Parliament's and the government's power vis-à-vis the king grew, and economic reforms, investment in communication and transport, and the end of the Church's control over education and ability to censor certain publications and place limits on religious minorities "modernized" the country further. Piedmont remained, however, a monarchy, and Cavour, in power almost continually from 1852 to 1861, although liberal, was no democrat; placing the unification movement under Piedmont's auspices thus meant jettisoning the radical socioeconomic and political goals and mass-based strategies that played a prominent role in 1848 and in Mazzini's revolts afterwards. But by the 1850s many republican and democratic nationalists were willing to accept this trade-off. Perhaps the most notable was Daniele Manin, who led the revolutionary Republic of San Marco between 1848 and 1849 and became a founder of the Italian National Society (*Società Nazionale Italiana*), the main organization advocating unification during this period. As Manin put it:

> Convinced that above all Italy must be made, that this is the first and most important question, we say to the House of Savoy [Piedmont's ruling dynasty]: Make Italy and we are with you—If not, not.[14]

And so in the years after 1848 the push for unification resumed, but rather than being linked, the national and democratic struggles now separated with the former taking priority over the latter. The shift away from radical and democratic goals was reflected in Manin's Italian National Society, led by an educated elite hesitant to mobilize or even engage the masses who would be the new country's citizens. As Raymond Grew wrote in his study of the National Society, "the concept of the Risorgimento was being changed from a revolution that would remake society to merely political change brought about by the force of arms."[15] Liberal fear of democracy and the "radical" demands of the masses carried over into the post-Risorgimento period and critically shaped Italian political development.

Alongside highlighting the weaknesses of a divided unification movement and the tension between national and democratic goals, 1848 and its aftermath made clear that Austria stood in the way of Italian unification and that ending its rule on the peninsula required the assistance or at least acquiescence of other European powers, particularly England and France.[16]

With Piedmont in the lead, the key figure in the unification process became Cavour. Cavour's interest in Italian unification stemmed as much from a desire to rid the peninsula of Austrian rule and augment Piedmont's power as it did from a romantic commitment to Italian nationalism. Cavour viewed Italian unification[17] as a political problem requiring careful international maneuvering and was forthrightly opposed to mass-based "Mazzinian" tactics or "radical" socioeconomic or political goals (that is, democracy). Recognizing Austria as the immediate obstacle in Piedmont and Italy's path, Cavour concluded that Napoleon III was the way around it.

Fortunately, Napoleon III had some sympathy for the Italian cause[18] as well as an interest in weakening Austria and the restoration order that ended his uncle's rule. By the summer of 1858 Cavour had enticed Napoleon III into signing a secret pact (the "Pact of Plombières") that promised French aid should Piedmont be attacked by Austria; in return, France would get Savoy and Nice from Piedmont, and Piedmont would get Lombardy, Venetia, and some other territories from a presumably defeated Austria. After some effort, Piedmont provoked a war with Austria in 1859 and France attacked Austria, forcing it out of Lombardy with surprising ease. Soon after, several states on the peninsula formed the United Provinces of Central Italy and asked to join Piedmont, largely out of fear of growing disorder. By this point Napoleon III was having second thoughts, concerned about the emergence of a too-powerful Piedmont/Italy as well as intervention by other German states in the conflict. Napoleon III's original intention had been to kick the Austrians out and create a strengthened Piedmont-led northern Italian kingdom as a French satellite, along with two or three other states on the peninsula. However, since Napoleon III was unwilling to use force to stop the unification of Italy, by 1860 Piedmont controlled the entire peninsula except for Venetia (still held by Austria), the Papal States, and the Kingdom of the Two Sicilies.

The Two Sicilies were the next to go. In early 1860 uprisings broke out in Sicily, bringing Garibaldi back onto the scene. These uprisings were the latest manifestation of a general breakdown of order that followed Bourbon state-building efforts. After Napoleon's defeat, the Bourbons attempted to build on French reforms to strengthen their authority and diminish the nobility's.[19] These efforts, however, were partial—the remnants of feudalism were eliminated and a class of non-noble landowners created but other corporate structures and the bureaucracy were not reformed—which created a Bourbon regime that was an "uncomfortable half-way house . . . neither a feudal nor yet a national monarchy."[20] This made it repressive and inefficient, leading William Gladstone, for example, to famously condemn it as "the negation of God erected into a system of government."[21] Or as historian Lucy Riall notes, this partial "political modernization" destroyed

the structures of the old regime along with its old bases of support. Traditional social relations, with their attendant rights, obligations, and privileges were undercut by the abolition of feudalism and administrative centralization. The reforms introduced by the Bourbon government weakened the old nobility and alienated the Church. They also undermined what loyalty had existed to the Crown. Crucially, however, few stable social and political relationships developed to replace those of the old regime.[22]

The Bourbons' state-building efforts thus weakened rather than strengthened central authority, creating divisions between new and old landowning elites and between landowning elites and peasants over land. (The end of feudalism and the creation of modern property rights meant peasants lost the common lands, water supplies, grazing areas for livestock, and wood for fuel they had previously depended on.) Peasant uprisings and land occupations also became endemic, and landowners began resorting to private militias to deal with them.[23]

Thus by the time Garibaldi landed in Sicily in May 1860 with his "thousand" red-shirted volunteers, central authority had already evaporated and unrest was widespread. Garibaldi famously proclaimed upon landing, "Either we make Italy here or we die!" but most of those who joined him probably had no idea what "Italy" meant. The historian Denis Mack Smith suggests, for example, that many Sicilians thought "Italy" was the name of the king's wife (*L'Italia* vs. *La Talia*[24]) and joined Garibaldi not out of a desire to fight for "Italy," but rather to further their own particular interests: landowners wanted a regime that protected their property, peasants wanted a regime that provided them with property, and almost everyone wanted to get rid of rule from Naples. Garibaldi promised something to everyone, vowing to restore order, give land to all who fought, and end Bourbon rule. With little local support, the Bourbons quickly fell, and Garibaldi took over Sicily; by the fall Naples was his as well. As it turned out, getting rid of the Bourbons was relatively easy. What turned out to be difficult was establishing a new order capable of solving the crisis that had led to the collapse of the Bourbon regime in the first place.[25]

Worried by Garibaldi's success, Piedmontese troops headed south to protect their control over the unification movement. Along the way they defeated the pope's forces, eliminating the "barrier between northern and southern Italy."[26] In October 1860 Piedmontese troops met up with Garibaldi's forces, helping beat back the remains of the Neapolitan army.[27] On October 26 Garibaldi and Victor Emmanuel II, the current king of Piedmont-Sardinia, met on a bridge in Teano and the former, accepting the inevitability of a Piedmont-led Italy, handed over the areas he controlled and leadership of the unification movement to the latter.[28] In March 1861 the Kingdom of Italy was proclaimed.

At this point only two pieces of the Italian puzzle—Venetia and Rome—remained out of Piedmont's hands. Both came to Italy as the result of the formation of another European state—Germany (see chapter 8). When the Austro-Prussian war broke out in 1866, Italy took Prussia's side in return for Venetia, and when the Franco-Prussian war broke out in 1870 Napoleon III was forced to call his troops back from Rome, allowing Italian forces to take over the city. By 1870 Italian unification was complete.

Although there had been uprisings, particularly in the south, and initial enthusiasm across the peninsula, unification was primarily an elite-, particularly a Piedmontese-elite-, driven process that took advantage of the weakening of France and Austria and benefited from a series of wars in which

Piedmont/Italy played a subordinate role.[29] That Italy's destiny depended heavily on the interests and actions of more powerful European states rather than its own efforts and ended up excluding the masses left many disillusioned. Mazzini, for example, bemoaned that Italy had not "made herself" or been placed in the hands of its people. Devastated, he referred to Italy as

> a living lie . . . [having] been put together just as though it were a piece of lifeless mosaic, and the battles which made this mosaic were fought by foreign rulers. . . . Italians are now without a new constitution that could express their will. We can therefore have no real national existence or international policy of our own. In domestic politics . . . we are governed by a few rich men. . . . Ordinary people are disillusioned. They had watched . . . as Italy . . . began to rise again; but now they turn away their eyes and say to themselves; "this is just the ghost of Italy."[30]

Similarly, Pasquale Villari, a great Italian historian, politician, and later student of the "Southern Question," warned his fellow parliamentarians that

> We brought about a revolution, which was largely the work of an intelligent, educated, and disinterested bourgeoisie. . . . The people were in such conditions as not to be able to participate in the revolution, and were in a sense therefore dragged along by us. But precisely because we stood alone in this effort, because we alone were intent on completing the creation of a free Italy . . . we found ourselves . . . isolated in a closed circle and we almost came to think that our little world was the whole world, forgetting that outside our narrow circle there is a vastly numerous class, to which Italy has never given a thought, and which it must finally take into consideration.[31]

The new country faced significant challenges. The peninsula lacked the linguistic, cultural, political, economic, or social unity that facilitates nation-building. The one thing Italy seemed to have going for it was geography, but this was not as favorable as it seems today since the eastern and western seaboards of the peninsula were divided by mountains, few of the peninsula's rivers were navigable, and some areas, particularly in the south, lacked roads or access to the rest of the peninsula.[32] Few spoke Italian—in the early 1860s probably only about 2.5 percent of the population[33]—and those who did mostly came from the small, educated elite. The vast majority of the peninsula's inhabitants were illiterate, making it hard for them to "imagine" themselves as part of a larger national community.[34] Relatedly, the peninsula's peoples lacked a shared culture or identity, defined as "a common way of thinking, a common principle, a common goal."[35] The peninsula's regions had dramatically different political histories and institutions: there were city-states, areas ruled over by a religious authority (the pope), and independent kingdoms and duchies; some areas had also long been under foreign rule. In addition, the peninsula lacked a dominant city or area to act as the natural cultural, economic, or political core of a new nation. And economically the peninsula was diverse and divided. Unlike the future Germany, for example (see chapter 8), where economic integration preceded political unification, there was little trade, or for that matter communication or transport, among the various parts of Italy. The regions varied enormously economically, with parts of northern Italy having economic and social conditions that resembled the more advanced regions of northwestern Europe, while the south remained among the poorest, backward, and most isolated regions on the continent. Italy, as d'Azeglio put it, may have finally been "made" by the 1860s but it still remained to "make Italians."[36] Unfortunately, "making Italians" or nation-building as well as state-building proved very difficult indeed.

Piedmont extended its constitution to the rest of the peninsula, giving Italy a fairly liberal but undemocratic political system that excluded most of the new country's citizens from political life. Piedmont's 1848 constitution created a political order of the *juste milieu*, in between the "extremes" of reactionary conservatism and democracy. The king retained sole right to declare war, make treaties, and nominate members of the upper house of Parliament, and ministers were responsible to him rather than the elected (albeit by a very narrow suffrage) lower house (the Chamber of Deputies). The king shared legislative power with the two-chambered Parliament and ruled in accordance with a constitution that created an independent judiciary and guaranteed equality before the law, habeas corpus, property rights, and other liberal rights.[37] In addition to extending its own constitution and political system to the rest of Italy, Piedmont also extended its administrative and juridical institutions, largely populated primarily by Piedmontese personnel, creating a centralized rather than federal system. The Italian state was, in short, "Piedmontized" from "its summit to its periphery."[38]

There were good reasons for this: Piedmont led the unification movement, and many of the peninsula's other political entities lacked modern infrastructure or institutions.[39] Nonetheless "Piedmontization" had significant downsides for state- and nation-building. Most obviously, Piedmont was considered foreign by many Italians; in addition to the administrative, political, and legal differences already mentioned, Piedmont's people, including its monarchs and elites, spoke in French or local dialects,[40] and many had little interest in or experience with other parts of the peninsula, having more extensive cultural and social ties with Western Europe than with its more backward southern neighbors. Cavour's native language, for example, was French, and he never visited southern Italy. In addition many, particularly in the south and especially in Sicily, had been led to believe that unification would bring significant autonomy.[41] Sicilians had long fought to get rid of their foreign rulers and so bitterly resented the loss of their particular institutions and traditions. The "Piedmontization" of the new Italian state, in short, left many Italians feeling they had once again been colonized or taken over by foreigners. The Milanese federalist, Giuseppe Ferrari, for example, referred to Piedmontization as the "last of the barbarian invasions."[42] In addition, few seem to have recognized the potential pitfalls in extending Piedmont's political, administrative, and juridical institutions to areas with very different customs, histories, and problems.[43] This proved particularly problematic in the south, where, as we will see, Piedmont's institutions were especially difficult to graft on to the region's lawlessness, factionalism, and underdevelopment.

Another challenge to state- and nation-building was the stance of the other great authority on the peninsula—the Church. Italian unification ended the pope's temporal rule; he was left only with control over Vatican City. Pius IX immediately proclaimed his opposition to Italy; like some Arab states today vis-à-vis Israel he even refused to mention it by name, calling it the "Subalpine usurper," threatened any Catholic who participated in its political life with excommunication (indeed he excommunicated Victor Emmanuel and his ministers), and appealed to foreign powers (France and Austria) to topple it on his behalf. Given the religiosity of many Italians, the Vatican's refusal to recognize Italy robbed it of legitimacy and led some citizens to withdraw from political life. In addition, since popes and much of the Church hierarchy were often Italian, part of the peninsula's educated elite had an international or religious allegiance that may have hindered the development of a secular Italian identity.[44] The pope's reaction to the formation of Italy did not stop with a rejection of the country itself; in his 1864 *Syllabus of Errors* he proclaimed the doctrine of "papal infallibility" and anathematized liberalism, democracy, rationalism, and toleration, forces he saw as contributing to the loss of his temporal power. The Church's "rejectionist" stance set up a conflict between religious and secular authorities and identities that plagued Italy for many years to come.

Italy thus began its existence with a deeply divided citizenry as well as deep divisions between its citizens and their state.[45] As one observer only semi-jokingly characterized the situation: "the Catholics hated the liberal democratic unified secular kingdom, men from all other regions hated the domination of the Piedmontese, Milan hated Rome, the Tuscans hated everybody else, the south hated the north, the republicans hated the monarchists, [and] the middle classes feared the revolution."[46]

One obvious manifestation of the lack of national unity and state weakness was the violence plaguing the country. Almost as soon as unification occurred, the new state faced rebellions and full-scale civil war in the south. "Piedmontization" was the ostensible cause for the latter in particular, but the civil war's roots lie in the breakdown of order that began before unification. With the Bourbons and Garibaldi gone, it fell to the new Italian state to stabilize the south. Doing so would require dealing with the underlying social and economic problems—recalcitrant landlords, land-hungry peasants, the privatization of violence, factionalism, and familialism, the pervasiveness of criminal activity—that were at the root of disorder. However, the primarily Piedmontese liberal elite running the new Italian state knew little about the south and, being unable or unwilling to come up with alternatives, resorted to force to deal with the region's problems. As one observer put it,

> The ruling class of the North showed a total lack of understanding of the culture and institutions of the South. . . . The good, rationalizing Piedmontese administration was going to solve everything. Once the tumour of Bourbon corruption has been excised, everything would return to [a] gentle and happy state. . . . When the Piedmontese realized that the Southerners were rebelling against them and rejecting them, they changed their tune and reverted to the idea of a paradise inhabited by devils.[47]

The army did eventually restore some semblance of order, but without addressing the underlying problems, violence and unrest could not be permanently eradicated. The Mafia and banditry grew, feeding off the resentment many Southerners felt at "being enslaved by Italy as they had formerly been enslaved by" the Bourbons.[48] During the coming years martial law and other illiberal forms of rule became the default responses of the Italian state to these problems, deepening the resentment and alienation of the south and fostering a sense among many northerners, as is often the case with "colonizers," that the south was racially different, "barbaric," "primitive," "irrational," and in need of colonization rather than an integral part of the national community.[49] The first viceroy or governor in Naples, Luigi Farini, for example, referred to the area as a "hell-pit" and claimed that "out of the seven million people" he ruled over, "he had found fewer than a hundred genuine believers in national unity. The country here is not Italy but

Africa, and the Bedouin are the flower of civic virtue when compared to these people."[50] Nino Bixio, an officer in Garibaldi's army and then a parliamentary deputy sent to work on a commission of inquiry into brigandage, wrote to his wife that the south "is a country which ought to be destroyed or at least depopulated and its inhabitants sent to Africa to get themselves civilized."[51] D'Azeglio, meanwhile, characterized the incorporation of Naples into Italy as akin to "sharing a bed with someone who has smallpox" and lamented, "in Naples we drove out a King in order to establish a government based on universal consent. But we need sixty battalions to hold southern Italy down, and even they seem inadequate. What with brigands and non-brigands, it is notorious that nobody wants us there."[52]

Alongside violence and disorder, another troubling manifestation of the lack of national unity and state weakness was widespread corruption. Unable or unwilling to deal with the hurly-burly of mass politics or many of the deeply troubling problems facing their new country, Italy's liberal elites relied on a system that came to be known as *trasformismo* to stay in power. (It was called this because it involved "transforming" potential opponents into supporters by parceling out power and patronage.[53]) Italian politics was thus driven by elites cooperating in return for material gain; election results, the "will of the people," or some vision of how to deal with the country's problems were not the paramount determinant of policy. Once in place *trasformismo* further weakened and sapped the legitimacy of liberalism and the Italian state by limiting governments' willingness and ability to respond to the country's problems.

Trasformismo, for example, negatively affected one of Italy's most obvious problems—the "southern question." Southern elites elicited promises that the status quo in their area would be preserved in return for supporting unification[54] and after the formation of Italy such promises continued as prime ministers found southern elites willing to make deals in return for assurances that their local power and prerogatives would not be undermined.[55] Such tradeoffs meant, however, that the south's unequal and unproductive landowning patterns, widespread crime, and overall socioeconomic backwardness[56] would not be attacked head-on, contributing to the perpetuation of the north-south divide and the alienation of the southern masses from the national community.[57] Indeed, at least initially, the formation of Italy worsened conditions for the south. After unification Piedmont's free trade, tax, and tariff policies, designed to benefit its own fairly developed and industrialized economy, were extended to the south, straining the region's uncompetitive, agricultural economy and the socioeconomic relationships embedded in them.[58] In addition, whereas during the Bourbon era the crown could check the predation of local elites, after unification local elites used the vote, which they but not the poor had, and corruption to control local government, policy making, and law enforcement. By the mid-1870s observers were already warning of the dangerous consequences of these developments. For example, a report on post-unification Sicily by two early students of the "southern question," Leopoldo Franchetti and Sidney Sonnino, noted,

> what exists here is a system of real slavery, and not just economic slavery but personal bondage. . . . The new dispensation after 1860 has confirmed or increased this dependence. Local affairs have now been completely given over by law into the hands of the possessing classes. Village councils, as well as town and provincial councils, are elected by the few taxpayers from among their own number. Education, local charities and other executive functions are carried out by the same people; and though the mayor will be chosen by the government, he will be one of the elected councilors. These men are then given complete control over everything.[59]

In addition to limiting politicians' willingness and ability to deal with the "southern question" and other problems, *trasformismo* and corruption more generally warped the development of political institutions. For example, politicians had little incentive to create political parties since governments were formed and policies passed via the exchange of favors rather than via the mobilization of mass support. Similarly, *trasformismo* limited the appeal of consistent or coherent party platforms since they hindered politicians' ability to support whatever governments or policies offered the greatest material payoff. The pernicious connection between corruption and the under-development of the Italian party system was recognized by Vilfredo Pareto, the great Italian social scientist "who described with remarkable precision the vicious circle ensnaring Italian . . . government: the absence of a stable party structure made patronage necessary to forge a majority, but [in turn] kept society weak and disorganized and thus impeded the formation of parties."[60] In addition to hampering the growth of liberal political parties, *trasformismo* also undermined the functioning and legitimacy of parliament. Since the formation of parliamentary coalitions and policies depended on backroom deals as much if not more than on election results, parliament came to be seen as corrupt, unrepresentative, and ineffectual. Thus even as the suffrage widened over the late nineteenth and early twentieth centuries culminating in a transition to essentially universal manhood suffrage before the Great War, many Italians had little reason to believe that participating in elections would make a difference. Lacking strong, mass liberal or centrist parties, an effectual or responsive Parliament or meaningful elections led many Italians to conclude that extra-parliamentary and anti-system movements were the best way to get their voices heard.

By the 1890s Italy had reached a critical juncture. Although progress had been made since unification, the country remained plagued by intense regional differences, poverty and underdevelopment, continual uprisings, and criminality. Its economy, moreover, was in the midst of a major recession and state bankruptcy was a possibility. Its population, meanwhile, had become more politically aware and mobilized since unification—education had grown and illiteracy declined, the use of Italian had spread, transport and communication infrastructure had improved, and electoral reform had expanded the suffrage to about 7 percent of the population[61]—but *trasformismo* and undemocratic political institutions excluded the masses from real political influence. The exclusion and alienation of the masses from political life was not of course new, but by the *fin-de-siècle* it was generating increasing instability as mass mobilization grew.

During the 1890s governments responded to eruptions of discontent with martial law and the suspension of civil liberties; some prime ministers even considered doing away with the parliamentary order entirely. As one contemporaneous observer noted,

> Successive governments . . . systematically and abusively interfered in the administration of justice, . . . "turned magistrates into soldiers," and [gave] a corrupt and depraved police force wide and arbitrary powers. Behind the façade of liberalism the realities of the unified state were authoritarian and arbitrary with the result that "In Italy there is nothing more uncertain than the boundaries that separate what is legal from what is illegal."[62]

Not surprisingly attempts to deal with discontent and disorder with repression and illiberalism backfired. By the *fin-de-siècle* an influential school of Italian thinkers, including Gaetano Mosca, Vilfredo Pareto, Pasquale Turiello, Vittorio Emanuele Orlando, Ruggero Bonghi, and Robert(o) Michels were penning powerful critiques of liberalism, parliamentarism, and the Italian state. Even more troubling and consequential was a backlash at the mass level with popular extremist movements resolutely opposed to the reigning order gaining increasing support throughout Italian society.

The first of these was the Italian Socialist party (the PSI, *Partito Socialista Italiano*, founded in 1892) and workers' movement. Socialist parties and workers' movements emerged in all European countries during the late nineteenth century, but the Italian versions were more intransigent and revolutionary than most. Syndicalism and anarchism, which rejected political activity and favored direct and if necessary violent action to overthrow the reigning order, were popular among Italian workers. And while the PSI eventually rejected syndicalism and anarchism, it remained opposed to cooperating or compromising with liberal elites or the Italian political system more generally and proclaimed its adherence to a version of Marxism that insisted on the inevitable and desirable collapse of the reigning order.[63]

Alongside a growing socialist party and workers' movement, an even more dangerous threat developed on the right, in the form of a radical, populist nationalism. Many historians trace the intellectual roots of this movement to a small journal called *Il Regno* (the Kingdom) founded in 1903 by Enrico Corradini. Corradini attacked the reigning order for its failure both to "make Italians" and to assert the country vis-à-vis stronger European powers.[64] Corradini insisted that meeting these challenges required mobilizing all Italians and including them in a great national project. Impressed by socialism's ability to inspire and organize workers, Corradini borrowed many of its themes, most notably the idea of class struggle, substituting conflict between rich and poor nations for conflict between capitalists and workers. He portrayed Italy as a "proletarian nation" engaged in a desperate struggle for unity and development at home and power and respect abroad.[65] Succeeding in this struggle, he argued, would require "mass organization, mass mobilization, and mass heroism"[66] and attacking the reigning domestic and international orders.[67] In the years after its founding, *Il Regno* attracted a wide range of contributors and helped spawn other nationalist journals and groups.

The last and best chance to deal with growing extremism and the social discontent underpinning it came during the "Giolittian era." Giovanni Giolitti was the dominant figure in Italian political life during the late nineteenth and early twentieth centuries, prime minister five times between 1892 and 1921, and in office, with only short interruptions, from 1903 to 1914. Unlike many of his predecessors, Giolitti recognized that repression and a failure to confront the country's problems had radicalized workers and the PSI. In 1901, for example, he proclaimed that Italy was

> at the beginning of a new period in history. . . . the lower classes can [not] be prevented from acquiring their share of economic and political influence. The friends of existing institutions have one duty above all: it is persuading these lower classes . . . that they have more to hope from existing institutions than from any [socialist] dreams of the future.[68]

And so in the decade and a half before 1914 Giolitti committed himself to reversing these trends. He was a determined advocate of economic development and modernization; although it is difficult to tell how much his specific policies mattered, during this time Italy had among the highest growth rates in Europe.[69] Giolitti also strengthened liberal rights, began some social policy initiatives, set up committees to suggest other legislation to help the downtrodden, and ended government strike-breaking.[70] Giolitti hoped these efforts would entice at least some workers and sectors of the socialist movement to cooperate with him.[71]

Giolitti's efforts furthered a debate within the PSI and workers' movement between those willing to consider some cooperation with him and the ruling order more generally and those opposed to any accommodation at all. The latter argued that Giolitti was trying to "transform" workers and the PSI via deal-making and bribes, a charge that Giolitti was vulnerable to, since despite a genuine interest in reform he was a master of *trasformiso*, regularly interfered in elections, made deals with reactionary southern elites, and relied on backroom deals and personal bargains rather than an institutionalized political party to stay in power. Indeed, so tied was Giolitti to traditional, corrupt practices that Gaetano Salvemini, one of his most powerful critics, famously tarred him with the nickname "Minister of the Underworld."[72] That radicals could point to these practices helped them overwhelm moderates within the PSI. In the years leading up to the First World War the PSI thus refused to cooperate or compromise with Giolitti or renounce its commitment to violence and a revolutionary overthrow of the reigning order.

Unable to entice the PSI to cooperate, Giolitti tried to blunt the growth of radical nationalism. But extremists of right and left were joined in their hatred for Giolitti, whom they viewed as personifying the corrupt, exclusionary, and ineffectual reigning liberal order. (Think of the common disgust left- and right-wing populists proclaim for the "establishment" today.) Indeed, nationalists claimed to speak for those people neglected and disgusted by Giolitti and the Italian political system more generally.[73] Nationalists claimed Giolitti represented "the old Italy" that had failed the *Risorgimento*. They also attacked his outreach to workers and socialists, which is perhaps ironic since this outreach led many businessmen and members of the middle class to see the "advantages" of the type of forceful authoritarian order favored by the nationalists over the existing liberal, parliamentary one.[74] In addition, nationalists fed off the "cultural malaise" and rejection of liberalism that grew during the *fin-de-siècle*. As Carlo Rosselli later recalled, "The whole of Italian life in those years . . . although they were years of great economic development, appears troubled by a serious moral crisis, by a morbid anxiety, by an increasing spirit of revolt against the existing order of things."[75] Disgusted with the direction taken by Italy during the Giolittian era, nationalists formed the Italian Nationalist Association (*Associazione Nazionalista Italiana*) in 1910. In his keynote address to the association's opening congress Corradini stressed that Italians needed to overcome their differences and "recognize that their interests lay not in competition against each other but in a struggle against others." To help Italy achieve the national unity and renewal it desperately needed, nationalists had to reach out to and gain the support of all Italians—the movement needed to advocate, as Corradini portentously put it, a truly "national socialism."[76] And indeed, the new Italian Nationalist Association grew to attract supporters from across society and the political spectrum.[77]

It is against this backdrop—the growing strength of socialism and nationalism and his failure to entice either into cooperating with him—that Giolitti made the fateful decision to go to war with the Ottoman Empire in 1911 (known in Italy as the Libyan war since Italy gained Libya as a colony as a result). Giolitti hoped the war would solve his political problems, appeasing the nationalists and forcing moderate socialists to openly support him and break with their revolutionary colleagues during wartime. Giolitti's calculations went tragically wrong. For socialists the war seemed to prove once and for all that Giolitti and the reigning liberal order were nefarious and imperialistic. The war thus helped bring revolutionaries firmly back into control of the PSI and ensured that Italy would enter the run-up to the First World War with its largest political party—by this point the PSI was receiving about 20 percent of the vote—firmly opposed to participation in or compromise with the reigning order.[78] In addition to further radicalizing the socialists, the war also radicalized the nationalists and in the run-up to the First World War, the Italian National Association began to evolve from a movement into a political party.

Alongside the war, Giolitti made another fateful decision during this time: with conscripted soldiers dying in Libya and desperate to spur national unity, Giolitti introduced a law in 1912 to bring universal manhood suffrage to Italy.[79] Having failed, however, to build a center-liberal party of his own or entice socialists or nationalists to cooperate with him, democratization ended up complicating rather than facilitating governance for Giolitti. Indeed, partially because socialists and nationalists were already committed to and capable of mobilizing and organizing the masses, they ended up being democratization's biggest beneficiaries (see chapter 11). Italy thus found itself in a very precarious position as Europe began its mad descent into the First World War.

Conclusions

During the nineteenth century the old order came under attack on the Italian peninsula. During the Napoleonic era the political, social, legal, and economic institutions of much of the peninsula were redesigned; some of these changes were reversed after Napoleon's fall, but the forces of nationalism and mass politics unleashed during this time grew during the coming decades. These forces helped generate numerous uprisings after 1816, and in 1848 they almost brought the old order tumbling down. After the failure of the 1848 wave, attempts were again made to repress the national and democratic movements, but both reappeared, albeit no longer as allies. The decision to prioritize national goals over democratic and social ones may have contributed to the success of the Piedmont-led national project in the 1860s, but the cost to the Italian state- and nation-building projects turned out to be very high. The formation of a unified Italy destroyed the existing political order on the peninsula, but constructing a new one turned out to be very difficult. Creating a unified, cohesive, developed, and assertive country required the type of wide-ranging economic and social transformation that the new Italian state was unwilling and unable to achieve.

As we saw earlier in European history, in Italy too the construction and nature of the Italian state profoundly influenced subsequent political development. Indeed, much scholarship on the *Risorgimento* criticizes Italian state-building, particularly the failure to transform the social and economic structures of the old order along with its political ones. From its birth, Italy was denounced in Mazzini's memorable phrase as "a living lie"—weak, illegitimate, and unable to solve the country's problems. Indeed many scholars, Gramsci being perhaps the most famous, view the *Risorgimento*'s and the Italian state's flaws as so fundamental as to be the root cause of fascism.[80] At the very least, it is very hard to understand fascism's obsession with creating a strong state and national identity without an understanding of the *Risorgimento* and the nature of the Italian state (see chapter 11).

While the flaws of the *Risorgimento* and the new Italian state were real, when assessing Italy's formation and political development it is important to remember the inherent difficulties involved in state- and nation-building. It is very hard to build states and nations, and Italy had to construct these under extremely difficult conditions: the territories incorporated into the new state had vastly different geographies, economies, cultures, political histories, and legal systems, and some had fallen into violence and disorder. State- and nation-building in Italy also faced a difficult religious challenge.

Although Church-state conflicts affected state- and nation-building in all European countries, by explicitly forcing Italians to choose between religious and national loyalty, the Church hampered state- and nation-building in a particularly profound way in Italy.[81] More generally if we compare state- and nation-building in Italy to what occurred in Central and Eastern Europe or other areas where these processes occurred in the twentieth century, Italy's post-unification development does not look so bad—in much of Central Europe, for example (see chapter 13), state- and nation-building were accompanied by violence, conflict, and myriad political setbacks and remain incomplete until the present day.

Most scholars and observers, however, implicitly or explicitly compare Italy to northwestern Europe (for example, France or England) where by the late nineteenth century states and national identities were fairly strong. These countries, however, had begun their state- and nation-building projects a century or more before Italy even existed, and so comparing the latter to the former is misleading. Moreover, Italy, unlike its counterparts in northwestern Europe, arose *after* the emergence of capitalism and mass politics. This complicated state- and nation-building, since by the late nineteenth century mobilized and organized mass citizenries made demands that leaders and governments during previous eras would not have confronted or would have had more time to deal with. During the late nineteenth century Italians themselves probably suffered from unrealistic expectations. As one contemporary put it, when assessing their new country too many Italians "contrasted present conditions with memories of past greatness or with dreams of impossible primacies."[82] As with many emerging countries, Italians thought that once unification occurred their country would achieve "great things immediately"[83]—economic growth, land reform, political stability, national solidarity, respect on the international stage—but such things take decades or generations to achieve. Nonetheless, when by the late nineteenth century the Italian state proved unable to deliver these things, Italians turned their backs on it in droves, pledging allegiance to socialist and nationalist movements that promised to destroy it. When there is a mismatch between citizens' demands and expectations and the willingness or ability of political institutions to respond to them, the outcome is disorder and instability.[84] (In Italy another outcome was emigration—exit rather than voice—which was massive by the *fin-de-siècle*.)

The growth of socialist and nationalist movements was not unique to Italy; however, whereas in France (see chapter 6) the growth of left- and right-wing extremism provoked a counter-movement among liberals, democrats, and social democrats, in Italy the state and its defenders were weaker, allowing socialists and nationalists to become a more dangerous threat to the existing order. Italy was not alone in this, of course; similar dynamics occurred, for example, in the other European country formed during this time—Germany. It is to this case that we now turn.

CHAPTER 8 | German Unification

> It was not through speeches and majority decisions that the great
> questions of the day will be decided—that was the great mistake of
> 1848 and 1849—but by iron and blood.
>
> —Otto von Bismarck[1]

As ACROSS THE rest of the continent, the forces underpinning the 1848
wave continued to shape political development during the second half
of the nineteenth century in German-speaking Europe. In 1848 nationalism
and liberalism came together in the Frankfurt Parliament and attempted to
form a unified German state. This attempt failed but did not extinguish the
desire for German unification. However, when the unification drive resumed
in the second half of the nineteenth century it took a very different form than
it had in 1848. After 1848 the alliance between liberalism and nationalism
collapsed, and the task of creating a unified Germany fell to conservative
Prussia and its chancellor, Otto von Bismarck.

Bismarck was true to his word, relying on war rather than parliaments
or democratic processes to bring about German unification. As discussed
in previous chapters, state-building profoundly impacts subsequent political development. Having led the drive for German unification, Bismarck
made sure that the new German state protected Prussia's interests. Prussia
entered the modern age in paradoxical way—with a strong monarchy *and*
a strong nobility (see chapter 2). During the seventeenth and early eighteenth centuries Hohenzollern monarchs centralized power at the national
level, but rather than undermining and enfeebling the nobility as in France,
the Hohenzollerns co-opted them, allowing them to dominate high-status

posts in the army and bureaucracy. They also allowed the nobility to hold on to authority over local administrative, juridical, educational, and religious institutions. Although Prussia changed in important ways by the late nineteenth century, the legacies of its state-building process continued to shape its interests and thereby the nature of German unification and the state formed by it, and thus subsequent German political development

Herein lies a great tragedy of German history: it took Prussia and Bismarck to finally complete German unification, but the state this process created hampered the formation of a cohesive national community and legitimate political institutions, thereby contributing to the country's horrific demise. By the early twentieth century Germany was among the most economically advanced countries in Europe and its population was increasingly politically aware and mobilized. The German state, meanwhile, enabled a conservative elite to retain enormous power and stymie demands for political change. The result was deepening social divisions, rising political frustration and discontent, proliferating radical nationalist movements, and deadlocked government. These dynamics characterized much of the rest of Europe, but they took a particularly virulent and dangerous form in Germany.

The Prussian Background

Although neither democracy nor national unification was achieved in 1848, German-speaking Europe was profoundly changed by the "springtime of the peoples." Before 1848 a key issue bedeviling German nationalism was whether a German state should include Austria—the *gross* vs. *kleindeutsch* versions of Germany (see chapter 5). After 1848 this issue was solved as Austria re-dedicated itself to maintaining its empire, taking the *Grossdeutsch* solution off the table and leaving Prussia, the strongest state in non-Austrian German Europe, as the logical leader of any renewed drive for German unification. Prussia, meanwhile, was also critically affected by 1848. The remaining vestiges of feudalism in Prussia were eliminated after 1848. Although the land-owning aristocracy, the *Junkers*, retained important powers, particularly at the local level including over government, police, school, courts, and churches, it was no longer a legally recognized "caste," and peasants, although still vulnerable to and dependent upon the nobility, were legally emancipated. In addition, after 1848 Prussia became a constitutional state. The constitution issued by Friedrich Wilhelm in 1850 provided for an immensely powerful monarchy but one that shared legislative power with a two-house parliament, with the lower house elected by tax payers with votes weighted by the amount of tax paid and the upper house appointed by the king and consisting primarily of conservative *Junkers*. Executive power belonged to the king; government ministers were responsible to him, and he was commander-in-chief of the army. The constitution enshrined some liberal rights, including equality before the law, the inviolability of property, freedom of religion, and the openness of public offices to all "competent to hold them."[2] After 1848, in short, many features of Prussia's old order remained, most notably the power of the monarchy, aristocracy, military, and bureaucracy, but some had been eliminated and what existed was no longer an absolutist dictatorship.[3]

These changes brought Prussia more in line with other German states and further away from Austria, which, at least initially, moved back towards absolutism after 1850. In addition, after 1848 the *Zollverein*, a customs union that removed obstacles to trade and fostered economic exchange and coordination among its members, expanded to include almost all German states except Austria (since its economic activity was focused on its empire). Against this backdrop, Prussian history reached a critical juncture in 1862 with the appointment of Otto von Bismarck as its minister-president (essentially, chancellor). Like Napoleon, Bismarck is one of those "great men" who change the course of political development. Henry Kissinger, for example, characterized Bismarck as a "white revolutionary": "few statesmen," he argued, "have altered the history of their societies as profoundly as Otto von Bismarck."[4] When Bismarck came to power in 1862 Prussia was the leading state in non-Austrian German Europe, but he was determined to enhance its power further. In this, he was remarkably successful, creating a Prussian-led Germany that reshaped the map as well the political trajectory of Europe. The long-term cost of Bismarck's success, however, was extremely high. Despite his vaunted realism in international affairs, domestically Bismarck was anything but, putting in place a political order and engaging in political practices that obstructed rather accommodated emerging reality, thereby helping set in motion social and political tensions that would eventually rip apart the country he did so much to create.

German Unification

After coming to power Bismarck maneuvered Prussia into a series of wars designed to reshape its position in Europe.[5] The first, in 1864, reprised a conflict from 1848 (see chapter 5) with Denmark over Schleswig-Holstein and ended with Denmark's defeat and loss of the duchies. The second war emerged out of the first, pitting Prussia against Austria in 1866 ostensibly over control of these duchies but really over which state would enjoy primacy in Central Europe. The Austro-Prussian war ended quickly with Prussia's victory, bringing Schleswig and Holstein into the German fold, replacing the German Confederation, which had included Austria, with a Prussian-dominated North German confederation that excluded it, and establishing Prussian dominance in Central Europe.[6] Next, in 1870, Bismarck manipulated a dispute over the heir to the Spanish throne to provoke the French Second Empire to declare war on Prussia. Bismarck calculated that this declaration, combined with growing German nationalism, would lead south German states to join the North German Confederation against France. This Franco-Prussian war also ended quickly with a decisive Prussian victory that re-shaped the map of Europe as well as its power hierarchy. France's defeat led to the collapse of the Second Empire and ushered in a period of chaos that ended with a transition to democracy and the Third Republic (see chapter 6). As the French Empire fell, a new German one arose: in January 1871 Wilhelm, the King of Prussia, was proclaimed German emperor in the Hall of Mirrors at Versailles. The new German Empire included the states of the North German Confederation, the southern German states that had allied with it in the Franco-Prussian war, and the territories of Alsace and Lorraine, which the treaty ending the Franco-Prussian war forced the French to turn over to Germany. A new country and a new great power now existed in the middle of Europe.

In comparison to its Italian counterpart (see chapter 7) Germany began with some important advantages. Germany was created by Germans, or Prussians, rather than being the result of the actions and interests of foreign powers, and this, along with the decisive military victories accompanying it, enhanced German patriotism and the willingness of the smaller German states to join a larger union.[7] These military victories also gave the new German state an international stature that most other new states, including Italy, could not match. The various states that joined together to form Germany were already economically (via the *Zollverein*) and partly politically (via the German and then the North German Confederations) integrated at the time of unification. They were also comparatively economically devel-oped and politically modern, much more so than their Italian counterparts, with constitutions, parliaments, and fairly well-developed administrative systems in place before unification occurred.[8] In addition, in 1870 Germany's population was about 80 to 90 percent literate (compared to 20 to 30 percent in Italy[9]) as well as largely linguistically homogenous. However important these advantages, Germany faced challenges as well.

Most obviously, despite Bismarck's limited war aims—beyond the formation of a unified Germany he was uninterested in conquering the countries he defeated or overthrowing their governments—the unification of Germany reshaped power relationships in Europe and ensured the new German state was surrounded by states wary, if not openly hostile, towards it. In addition, nation and state did not coincide in Germany: there were German speakers living in Austria, Switzerland, and elsewhere, and minorities (for example, Poles, Danes, Jews) living in Germany. The country's population, moreover, was divided between Catholics and Protestants. However, at least as consequential as these social and political characteristics was the nature of the new German state. Some argue it was "an autocratic semi-absolutist sham constitutionalism" that sustained a "traditional absolutist regime hidden behind a more liberal façade."[10] Others contend that Bismarck "made Germany a constitutional country. Not only was the franchise the widest in Europe, with the only effective secret ballot. The parliament [also] possessed every essential function. It was the seat of power."[11] Although both assessments capture aspects of Germany's political order, they oversimplify its nature and implications. Perhaps Carl Schmitt captured its essence best in describing it as a "dilatory compromise between monarchism and parliamentarism";[12] today we might characterize it as an "electoral authoritarian" or "hybrid" regime[13] since it featured some representative elements like elections and other avenues for mass participation, and some dictatorial ones, like an executive branch insulated from popular pressure and a deeply entrenched and politically powerful conservative elite. Concretely, Bismarck constructed the new German state so as to satisfy various constituencies while protecting the power of Prussia and its conservative elites. One constituency Bismarck had to satisfy was the twenty-five states of varying sizes and regime-types that constituted the new German Empire. Prussia was the largest and most powerful of these by far, containing about two-thirds of Germany's territory and population, making it much larger and much more powerful than Piedmont, for example (see chapter 7); other German states and their rulers were thus wary of being completely swallowed by it. Partially to assuage such concerns but also to protect Prussia's autonomy, Bismarck made Germany a federal state, essentially extending and expanding the constitution and many of the other arrangements of the North German Confederation to the new German Empire. That this could be done was facilitated by the comparatively modern nature of the various German states—unlike in Italy, there was no need to extend the laws, institutions, or administration of the new country's most powerful state, Prussia, to other areas of the country already capable of governing themselves.[14] Federalism allowed the German states to retain significant autonomy as well as their own parliaments, constitutions, and other political arrangements, which varied from very conservative in Prussia to more liberal in the south and southwest.[15] In addition, many matters affecting the everyday lives of German citizens—including education, police, and health—were left to state and local governments. Also critical was that the right to levy taxes was left to the states (*Bundestaaten*). The national government had to rely on tariffs, fees from postal and telegraph services, and whatever indirect taxes could be agreed upon by the legislature. Over time, this severely constrained the national government and became an important source of political and social conflict.

At the national level the government was composed of an executive branch, including the emperor or *kaiser*, his chancellor, and their staffs; a federal council, the *Bundesrat*, sometimes referred to as the upper house; and a national parliament, the *Reichstag*. The emperor controlled foreign policy and the army, although in reality the latter often acted independently of him. Indeed, throughout the empire's existence the army played a powerful role in German political life and remained dominated at the highest levels by the land-owning elite.[16] The emperor's power was enhanced by also being king of Prussia. In the domestic sphere executive authority was more circumscribed, since bills required the assent of both the *Bundesrat* and the *Reichstag* to become law. In case of legislative deadlock, the emperor could dissolve the *Reichstag* in the hope of gaining a more compliant majority later on. But he could not dissolve it permanently and was required to set a date for new elections upon its dissolution. The emperor's influence over the German political system was not direct, moreover, but rather exerted through a chancellor. The chancellor was ultimately dependent on the emperor, who could appoint and dismiss him, yet he was rarely a mere puppet. During Bismarck's twenty-eight-year tenure, for example, he was without question the key figure shaping the country's course both at home and abroad.

Of the two legislative bodies created by the constitution, one was distinctly conservative and the other more representative. The *Bundesrat* was composed of delegations from the twenty-five states, elected on the basis of local suffrage systems that ranged from relatively representative in the southern and southwestern states to highly undemocratic in Prussia.[17] Prussian males over the age of twenty-five were divided into three classes depending on the amount of property taxes paid; each class got the same number of votes even though the number of voters in each class varied greatly: during the late nineteenth and early twentieth centuries about 5 percent of the voters were in the first class and 80–85 percent in the third. Voting in Prussia, unlike at the national level (see below) also occurred without the secret ballot, and electoral districts were gerrymandered to favor rural areas, which were conservative.[18] Since Prussia controlled seventeen of the *Budesrat*'s fifty-eight votes and only fourteen were needed for a veto, and conservatives were heavily favored by the Prussian voting system, conservative Prussian *Junkers* could essentially block proposed national legislation they did not like.[19] Along with the Prussian king's status as German emperor, the Prussian prime minister's status as German chancellor, and the nobility's power at the local level and within the army and bureaucracy, these features of the German state ensured that Prussia acted as a "conservative anchor" of the empire "just as Bismarck had intended."[20]

In addition to placating the various German states and protecting Prussia and its conservative elites, the empire's political institutions also made some concessions to the empire's other key constituency—its citizens. This was clearest in the design of the *Reichstag*, which was elected by universal manhood suffrage and had important powers that initially were largely unexploited. Its assent was required for all legislation, including budgets, even those for the military, and it could amend, delay, or defeat bills. The *Reichstag* could not select or dismiss the chancellor, but it could force him to explain and justify his policies, criticize him, and refuse to cooperate with him. Even Bismarck, a master at manipulating the *Reichstag* and its parties, could not rule without it. During the Iron Chancellor's tenure in office, "almost all the significant pieces of legislation that were enacted . . . [were] modified by varying constellations of votes in Parliament, sometimes to such an extent that the original intentions of Bismarck and his colleagues were no longer recognizable."[21]

Indeed, much to Bismarck's chagrin, it was clear almost from the outset that the system he designed would not work as planned. Bismarck counted on having a free hand politically, thanks to support from a stable conservative coalition built around the *Junkers* and some sectors of the upper and middle classes; he also assumed that universal suffrage would strengthen rather than undermine the reigning order since he expected the masses to vote conservatively if given a chance. "In a country with monarchist traditions and a loyal mentality," Bismarck believed, "universal suffrage, by removing the influence of the liberal bourgeoisie, will result in monarchical elections, just as anarchism is the outcome of elections in countries where the masses harbour revolutionary sentiments."[22] Over time, however, these assumptions proved incorrect. The growing working class increasingly threw its support to the social democrats (SPD), while economic development began to drive a wedge between the *Junkers* and much of the upper and middle classes and between conservatives and liberals. Bismarck therefore had to resort to various ploys to hold together a pro-government alliance that would enable him to govern.

Post-Unification Politics

One ploy used by Bismarck was his (in)famous policy of "iron and rye"—an attempt to lock in a coalition between certain agrarian and industrial interests. Faced with the "stupendous achievement" of Prussia's successful unification of Germany, the German liberal movement "broke in pieces."[23] Some liberals made their peace with Prussia's non-liberal Germany and became "National Liberals." Others remained loyal to liberal ideals and became "Progressive Liberals." When an economic downturn hit Germany after the European economic crash of 1873 Bismarck exploited these divisions to engineer a logroll between National Liberals and the heavy industrial interests they represented and *Junkers* based on providing protective tariffs for products produced by each, iron and rye, respectively.[24]

A second ploy utilized by Bismarck was "negative integration"—uniting disparate groups based on fear or dislike of others. Bismarck was not content merely to keep those opposed to his vision of Germany out of power; he also demonized them as "enemies of the Empire," questioning their loyalty to Germany and actively mobilizing other groups against them. This is an insidious tactic and while certainly not unique to Bismarck—indeed we are very familiar with it today—it became a "trademark" of his rule and was used in a situation—a young state with a fragile sense of national unity—where its consequences were particularly pernicious. As historian Hans-Ulrich Wehler put it, as a result of "negative integration," "German domestic politics, along with broad sections of public opinion, became accustomed to the notion that a deep division existed among the citizens of the state."[25]

Bismarck's first target was Catholics, who during the late nineteenth century made up about one-third of Germany's population; the rest, with the exception of the small Jewish population, was Protestant. Bismarck recognized that many Catholics would have preferred an Austrian and thus Catholic-majority Germany to a Protestant-majority Prussian one, and believed Catholics would never be fully loyal to the new Germany. That two of Germany's minorities—Poles and Alsatians—were Catholic made matters worse. Bismarck manipulated the anti-Catholic prejudices of many Protestants as well as the anti-religious sentiment of liberals to launch a *Kulturkampf* (culture war) against Catholics during the 1870s, eliminating the Church's role in education, expelling Jesuits from the country and abolishing other "suspect" religious orders, placing the training and appointment of clergy under state supervision, introducing compulsory civil marriage, and confiscating Church property. In addition, many Catholic bishops, priests, and other ecclesiastical figures were exiled or put in prison. Although during this time tension between the Catholic Church and secular governments was widespread in Europe (see, for example, chapters 6 and 7), the *Kulturkampf* was distinguished by being a systematic, state-led "attack not merely on the church but on the entire Catholic way of life."[26] The other main group targeted by Bismarck was the Social Democrats (SPD), which by 1877 was already receiving half a million votes and placing growing numbers of deputies in the *Reichstag*. Bismarck manipulated a couple of attempts on the emperor's life in 1878 to whip up anti-socialist hysteria and get conservatives and National Liberals to pass laws denying freedom of assembly, association, and the press to the SPD. These laws did not, however, ban the SPD from participating in elections.

Despite some short-term success, ultimately these political ploys failed: neither protective tariffs nor the demonization of Catholics, Socialists, and others created a stable Protestant liberal-conservative coalition that could enable Bismarck or his successors to govern the empire freely. The main problem was that such a coalition required holding back economic, political, and social trends that were too powerful for even the Iron Chancellor. By the end of the nineteenth century, agriculture's share of the German economy was in steady decline and the industrial, commercial, and service sectors were growing steadily (see Figures 8.1 and 8.2).

Not surprisingly, industrial interests and the middle class grew frustrated at having to sacrifice to protect the *Junkers'* economic and political prerogatives, straining the conservative-National liberal coalition. In addition, Germany was becoming increasingly urban and the size of its working and middle class was growing (see Figure 8.3).

Partially for these reasons, the anti-socialist laws and the *Kulturkampf* ended up strengthening rather than weakening the very forces that Bismarck viewed as the greatest threats. The SPD in particular emerged from the anti-socialist laws stronger than before. Government repression meant that workers had more reason than ever to view the SPD as its main defender, and the party's share of the vote almost tripled. In addition, the party developed a network of affiliated associations—libraries, educational groups, burial societies, social clubs—that allowed workers to live within a socialist subculture from "cradle to grave."[27] Thus rather than eliminating the socialist "threat," the anti-socialist laws alienated what was becoming Germany's most politically popular party, and by extension

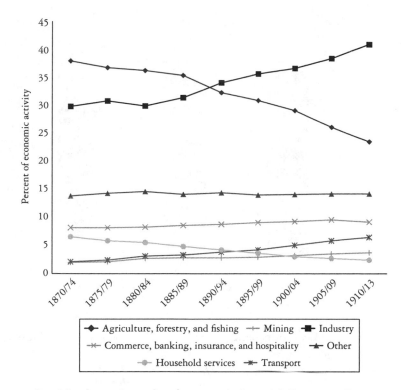

FIGURE 8.1 Net domestic product by sector in Imperial Germany, 1870–1913.
Source: Hoffman, Walther G. (ed.), with Grumbach, Franz, and Hesse, Helmut. *Das Wachstum Der Deutschen Wirtschaft Seit Der Mitte Des 19. Jahrhunderts* (Berlin: Springer-Verlag, 1965).

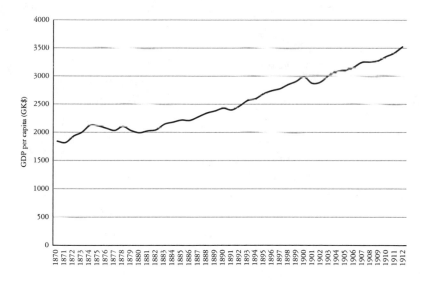

FIGURE 8.2 German GDP per capita, 1870–1912.
Source: The Maddison-Project, http://www.ggdc.net/maddison/maddison-project/home.htm, 2013 version.

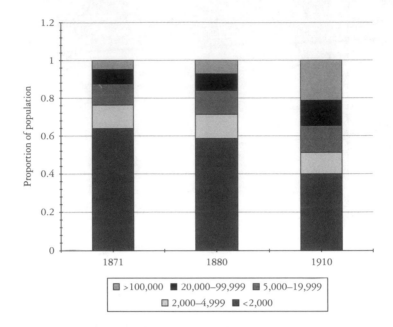

FIGURE 8.3 Population distribution by size of locality: German Reich, Prussian Provinces, and Federal States, 1871–1910.
Source: *Statistisches Jahrbuch für das Deutsche Reich 1915* [*Statistical Almanac for the German Reich 1915*], pp. 4–5 (for the year 1910); 1880, pp. 6–7 (for the year 1875), and Richard Tilly, "Popular Disorders in Nineteenth Century Germany: Preliminary Survey," *Journal of Social History* (Fall 1970), 1–40.

many of its supporters, from the existing state as well as other groups in society. In addition, Bismarck's actions and the anti-socialist laws in particular provided ammunition to radicals within the SPD at a time when the party, like other socialist parties in Europe, was divided between revolutionaries and those favoring democracy and reforms.[28] Repression also failed to eliminate the Catholic "threat," but it did help cement a religious divide in Germany. As Catholics recognized their vulnerability, their solidarity increased and a separate Catholic subculture that included newspapers, libraries, cooperatives, and other civil society organizations expanded as did Catholic political participation and support for a Catholic political party, the *Zentrum* or Center.[29] Ultimately the growing strength of the Catholic movement and Bismarck's inability to form governments based on "traditional" conservative support led him to shift course, ultimately reconciling with a new pope and enticing the Center party to support him. Bismarck's negative integration thus failed to create a stable, conservative coalition, strengthened the Catholics and Socialists, and set back the cause of national unity by increasing distrust among different groups in society and reinforcing the idea that Germany was threatened by internal (*Staatsfiende*) as well as external enemies.

By the end of the 1880s it was getting increasingly difficult even for Bismarck to maneuver within the German political system. In the 1890 elections the SPD got almost 20 percent of the vote, Catholics almost 19 percent, and parties representing various minorities (Poles, Alsatians, Danes) several percent more. In other words, despite economic growth and a strong international position, over 40 percent of the population, more if one includes the 18 percent received by the left or progressive liberals, supported parties significantly dissatisfied with the reigning order. One way to deal with this opposition would be via repression or a coup (*Staatsstreich*, in German)— Bismarck could use his powers and the support of the army to revise the constitution and strengthen the chancellorship while eviscerating the *Reichstag* and getting rid of other institutional outlets for mass participation. Despite toying with the idea, Bismarck ultimately rejected it[30] and by 1890 he was gone, forced to resign at the insistence of a new emperor, Wilhelm II, who disagreed with him on important matters and preferred a less domineering chancellor. In the years after Bismarck's resignation tensions grew, partially because without a master manipulator like Bismarck at the helm but rather the pompous and impetuous Wilhelm II and his weak chancellors, the conflicts and contradictions built into the German state became harder to handle.[31] The fundamental problem was that changing socioeconomic and political conditions were making the conservative "safeguards" built into the state increasingly difficult to defend and work around.

One indicator was increasing participation in *Reichstag* elections, which were held under universal suffrage.[32] The extent to which Germans voted is remarkable (see Figure 8.4). As one scholar notes, "It was an extraordinary feat, but Wilhelmine Germany was on its way to making non-voting unusual. In 1871, 52 percent of those eligible voted. In both 1907 and 1912, the last two imperial elections, the figure was about 85 percent." Furthermore,

> massive turnouts substantially reduced, if not eliminated the different rates of voting due to class, status, occupation, urbanization and region or residence. Moreover, the higher turnout rates were matched by corresponding rises in the more intensive forms of participation that required a greater expenditure of time, money and energy. There was a substantial increase in the membership of political and parapolitical organizations, in the distribution of printed campaign materials, in campaign activities of all kinds, including rallies

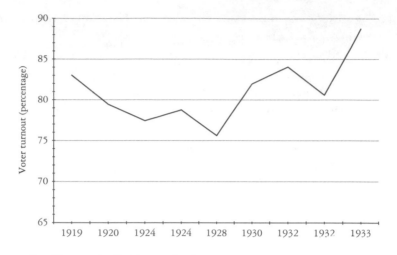

FIGURE 8.4 Turnout in Reichstag elections, 1919–1933.
Source: Dieter Nohlen and Philip Stover, *Elections in Europe: A Data Handbook* (Baden-Baden, Germany: Nomos, 2010).

and personal solicitations, in the numbers of party workers active on election-day, and in the amounts of individual contributions to parties and candidates.[33]

Largely as a result of growing political awareness and participation, the German party system changed dramatically during the late nineteenth and early twentieth centuries, as the more modern Catholic and social democratic parties gained ground at the expense of their liberal and conservative rivals. As the SPD was permitted to compete more freely, its impressive organization combined with the growth in its natural constituency produced by Germany's economic development improved its fortunes: with only one exception its vote share increased in every German election between 1890 and 1912 (see Figure 8.5).

Taking a page from the SPD, meanwhile, during the 1890s the Center party modernized, making "institutional and organizational density . . . a hallmark of the *Zentrum* as much as of the SPD."[34] In addition, the Center's leadership changed, as some of the clergy and old notables were gradually pushed aside in order to make room for more professional leadership.[35]

While the SPD and Center party were thriving, Germany's liberal and conservative parties were floundering.[36] The liberal parties gradually lost their hold over their natural constituency, the Protestant middle classes, while the conservatives also saw their national vote totals plummet—at least partially because economic development was sending rural labor fleeing to the cities for better-paying jobs and eroding the relative import of the *Junkers* in the German economy.[37] (See Figure 8.5.) But another crucial source of

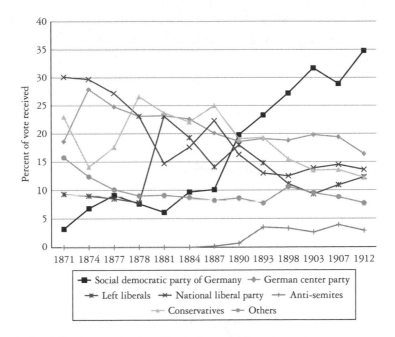

FIGURE 8.5 Election results by party in Imperial Germany, 1871–1912.
Source: Gerd Hohorst et al., *Sozialgeschichtliches Arbeitsbuch*, Vol. 2—1870–1914. Second revised edition
(Munich: Beck, 1978), pp. 173–76.

liberal and conservative decline was these parties' unwillingness or inability
to adjust to the age of modern mass politics. Up to the 1890s most parties,
with the notable exception of the SPD and to a lesser extent the *Zentrum*,
were informal collections of notables (*Honoratioren*) with little formal organization, especially at the grass roots level; their institutional structures were
not up to the task of competing in the hurly-burly of German politics.[38]
Unwilling to modernize, some conservatives attempted to stave off electoral
decline via voting fraud. As Daniel Ziblatt has shown, "Even in the presence
of uniform rules of universal male suffrage . . . landed elites were [able] to
capture key local institutions of the state, providing them with the coercive
and material resources to disrupt fair and free elections in order to defend the
countryside from oppositional mobilization efforts."[39]

The decline of the conservatives and especially the National Liberals left
many of their potential constituents, particularly in rural areas and among
sections of the middle class, searching for other ways of expressing their
social and political aspirations. This helped spur the growth of nationalist
associations that appealed to a wide variety of disaffected groups during
the *fin-de-siècle*. The growth of nationalist associations was not, of course, a

distinctly German phenomenon (see chapters 6 and 7), but they were very popular in Germany, drawing on a politically active and aware citizenry, and benefiting from widespread disillusionment with traditional conservative and liberal parties.[40] Many German nationalist associations peddled a particularly virulent nationalism—biological/racial, social Darwinist, anti-Semitic, deeply suspicious of many aspects of modernity, and obsessed with the idea that the country was weak, divided, and threatened by enemies within and without.[41]

On one end of the spectrum were apolitical organizations such as the *Wandervogel*, which organized youth hiking trips throughout the countryside, and aimed to counter "the sense of frustration, alienation, and loneliness which mass industrial society induced" and satisfy the nationalist longing for community so typical of the era.[42] On the other end of the spectrum were nationalist associations focused on German expansionism and the situation of the German *Volk*. Two of the most important of these were the Pan-German League (*Alldeutscher Verband*) and the Agrarian League (*Bund der Landwirte*). The former opposed the mixing of the German "race" with "inferior" ones like Slavs and Jews, and advocated imperialism and eventually the ethnic cleansing of territories to make way for German colonists.[43] The latter, although ostensibly a Junker-led pressure group for agricultural interests, became a mass organization that defended small businesses and other parts of the mainly Protestant middle class threatened by industrialization and modernization; it also blamed Jews for Germany's problems.[44] Alongside nationalism, another prominent feature of these groups was their eagerness to appeal to a wide variety of social groups; reflecting this, they often referred to themselves as "people's organizations" (*Volksvereine*). Such appeals, of course, characterized nationalist associations across Europe; what made such appeals particularly powerful in Germany was the explicit contrast nationalist associations made between themselves and mainstream political parties and organizations which they accused of dividing the *Volk* and alienating many Germans from the national community. The constitution of the Pan German League, for example, stated, "The League strives to quicken the Germanic-national . . . sentiment of all Germans in particular to awaken and foster the sense of racial and cultural kinship of all sections of the German people."[45] These nationalist associations, as Geoff Eley and other scholars have argued, are best viewed as "symptoms and agencies of change. They were formed as distinctive organizations within a space which the difficulties and obsolescence of an older mode of dominant-class politics had opened up."[46] They targeted their appeal directly to the "people" or the "masses" and their leaders were those who showed talent and effort. They were also very good at using modern methods of political organizing and propaganda to expand their appeal and support base.

By the early twentieth century, in short, the "electoral-authoritarian" or "hybrid" balancing act Bismarck bequeathed to Germany was increasingly unbalanced. The "outsider" parties—the SPD and the Center—had impressive internal organizations, ties to myriad civil society organizations, sophisticated electoral machines, and loyal members. The former, in particular, was on its way to becoming Germany's most popular party, while being openly opposed to the reigning order and alienated from the country's other political parties. The traditional government parties, by contrast—the Conservatives and National Liberals—were in decline, forcing chancellors to rely on the Center or ad-hoc coalitions to pass legislation. Germany's citizens had become more active, better informed, and increasingly mobilized, many through civil society associations that fed off dissatisfaction with the reigning order and promulgated an often aggressive and anti-Semitic nationalism. The government's policies, meanwhile, particularly military expenditures and the associated budgetary strains, deepened social and political divisions. These developments sparked occasional rumors of a *Staatsstreich* during the *fin-de-siècle*.[47] None materialized, however, and the system stumbled on, but problems became increasingly difficult to resolve.

For example, the erratic and irresponsible behavior of the emperor, Wilhelm II, furthered debates about the role of a monarchy. These came to a head in 1908 with the *Daily Telegraph* affair. Wilhelm's off-the-cuff remarks on foreign policy to the British newspaper caused a full-fledged domestic crisis, strong condemnation from almost all parties, including the Conservatives, and an insistence from Chancellor Bernhard von Bülow that the emperor refrain from such pronouncements in the future. In his memoirs Bülow wrote, "The Emperor's political observations and statements, published by the *Daily Telegraph*, were but the drop that brought the kettle of public exasperation to overflowing, filled to the rim as it was after all the careless remarks and gaffes His Majesty made time and time and again."[48] Wilhelm released a statement saying that in the future he would "ensure the stability of imperial policy by respecting his constitutional obligations." However, despite the emperor's backpedaling and the widespread condemnation of him, no move to place foreign policy under the control of a foreign minister answerable to the *Reichstag* occurred since this would require or least imply parliamentarization, which the Conservatives would not accept. And without Conservative co-operation "the great national movement against the Emperor vanished like a puff of smoke."[49]

The next year a budget crisis exposed further weaknesses. With the growth of the national government and military spending, the empire became increasingly short of funds since, as noted above, the German constitution initially gave the national government only limited means of raising revenue. In order to finance a modern and internationally ambitious state Bülow proposed a substantial tax increase in 1909, including the introduction of an inheritance tax. Conservatives, however, opposed direct taxation since they feared it would increase pressures for more popular say in policy-making; inverting the American adage, the German Conservatives' could be: "no taxation therefore no representation." Bülow's proposal would also take a power currently held by the states (read: Prussia) and hand it over to national government where a democratically elected *Reichstag* might gain control over it. Defying the government's wishes and those of their liberal allies the Conservatives thus refused to support the bill, joining instead with the Center to put forward legislation based on indirect taxes on mass-consumption items and business-related expenses—which of course only emphasized the divergence of interests between Conservatives and middle- and working-class groups. "The finance reform of 1909 thus came to symbolize the refusal of Germany's aristocracy to recognize and accept the consequences of economic decline."[50] His tax plan rejected, Bülow resigned and was replaced by Theobald von Bethmann-Hollweg. Reflecting upon unfolding events, the Bavarian ambassador Lerchenfeld wrote: "I am witnessing my fourth chancellor crisis. . . . We have come one step closer to a parliamentary regime in Germany."[51]

A step, to be sure, but only one. It was still the emperor and his advisers, and not the *Reichstag*, who chose the chancellor. Nonetheless, the tax crisis seemed to augur a potential political realignment. The National Liberals found themselves estranged from their erstwhile Conservative allies and aware that the interests of agrarian and industrial groups were growing increasingly difficult to reconcile. They also recognized that they had at least some overlapping interests with the Progressive People's party (essentially the old left liberals) and even the SPD.[52]

Desperately seeking to avoid pushing liberals and social democrats closer together, Bethmann-Hollweg sought conservative acceptance of some direct taxation while simultaneously trying to placate the left with some social legislation and political reform. But the Conservatives refused to budge and also rejected the chancellor's half-hearted attempt to reform the Prussian voting system in a more democratic manner. This led groups on the left, including the SPD, to stage the largest demonstrations for political reform yet seen in Germany.

Bethmann recognized . . . that the franchise reform debate had widened "the chasm between Conservatives and National Liberals" and driven the latter further to the left. More pointedly he observed that the Conservatives, "with their personal, social, religious, and political hubris and intolerance . . . have succeeded in focusing everyone's disgust and dissatisfaction on the three-class suffrage, which is generally seen as an expression of Junker predominance."[53]

It was against this background of political stalemate and frustration that voters went to the polls in 1912. The elections were a disaster for the government and the Conservatives, as the main winners were the parties of the left, particularly the SPD. In fact, the SPD emerged from the 1912 election as the most popular national party by far, with twice as many votes as its closest competitor (see Figure 8.5).

Breaking down the numbers, the future implication of voting trends was even more important: the SPD's dominance of urban areas continued to grow—it won over 50 percent of the votes in areas with a population of one hundred thousand or more, to the Conservatives' 2.2 percent—and it made some inroads into the Catholic electorate. Furthermore, the SPD ran a pragmatic campaign, focusing on issues with wide appeal, such as the inequities of the government's taxation policies, the need for democratization of the government and army, and social reforms. This pragmatism carried over into electoral agreements with the Progressives to ensure that their candidates would not run against each other in the second round.[54] By contrast, the National Liberals and Conservatives could only look upon the electoral outcome with dismay as their vote shares stagnated or declined.

Yet dissatisfaction alone does not cause change. Although the election suggested a clear rejection of the government parties and policies and the emergence of an overwhelming, if potential, anti-government majority, critical divisions with their roots in German unification and Bismarck's policies after it, hindered the formation of a progressive coalition capable of championing a common reform agenda. The SPD refused to recognize that as the largest party by far and the one with greatest stake in democratization it would have to moderate its rhetoric and make important tactical concessions in order to lead the charge for parliamentarization and full democratization.[55] The Progressives, despite their electoral agreements with the SPD, remained suspicious of the socialists, and vice versa. The Center party, despite an internal realignment that brought working-class leader Matthias Erzberger onto the party's executive committee, could not bring itself to explicitly join with "anti-religious" parties of the left. The National Liberals were pulled in two directions by their commitment to increased military spending on the one hand and their recognition that the Conservatives would not back the fiscal measures necessary to support it on the other. And the Conservatives grew more intransigent in defeat. When legislation was introduced after the national election in May 1912 in Prussia to reform its three-class voting system—which enabled Conservatives to remain the largest political force in Prussia despite their decline at the national level—the vote was 188 against and 158 for, with all 188 votes coming from conservative parties.[56]

Thus, despite the political mobilization and dissatisfaction that the elections and civil society activity revealed, the German political order remained stalemated. With continued conservative intransigence and without a unified progressive coalition, parliamentarization and democratization were impossible; but lacking a reliable conservative majority, the chancellor could not govern. The 1912 election and its aftermath thus left Bethmann-Hollweg in a very difficult position. As Volker Berghahn put it: "After 1912 it was not only the finances of the Reich and the Federal Government that were coming apart at the seams, but the political system in general."[57]

The government's situation worsened during 1913. After a dispute broke out between soldiers and civilians in the small Alsatian town of Zabern, the colonel of the local regiment gave orders to confine some of the demonstrators to the barracks for the night. Since the colonel had no juris-diction over civilians, he had clearly overstepped his authority and the public was enraged. A storm broke out in Germany, eventually forcing the army to sanction its officers and reconsider its practices. On December 4, 1913, the overwhelming majority of Reichstag delegates passed a vote of no confidence in the government.[58] The chancellor was still formally accountable to the emperor and so had no legal obligation to resign but his position had become even more tenuous. As Vladimir Lenin, an astute observer of political crises, once noted, "there are 'incidents' in public life that somehow illuminate the inner nature of a certain order of things by the flash that emerges from a com-paratively trivial event with unusual force and clarity."[59] Zabern was just such an "incident," illuminating tensions that had long been pulling the German political order apart: between its parliamentary and monarchical features, be-tween an increasingly assertive citizenry and Reichstag and an army largely free of civilian oversight, and most fundamentally between those remnants of the old order implacably opposed to change and those favoring a more lib-eral, even democratic, Germany.

Debate on military and financial matters after Zabern exacerbated these tensions further. As noted above, it was clear that the government's budgets and military spending could not be financed solely by indirect taxation and other means at its disposal. It is important to stress that the problem was not that Germany lacked the resources to finance these expenditures, it was that the national government lacked the ability to extract them. We encountered the same problem in ancien régime France (see chapter 4). Like the French ancien régime, in other words, what Germany faced was a political rather than economic challenge stemming from tensions built into its state to protect Prussia and conservative interests. (It is worth noting that by this time some federal states and communes had modernized their fiscal systems by introducing income taxes, but the national government "remained almost entirely dependent [for 90 per cent of its revenue] on the old taxes on consumption and imports."[60]) Despite growing pressure from chancellors and other parties, the Conservatives refused to budge even though this impinged upon military and foreign policy and increasingly divided them from the national government and almost all political parties and groups in society. After desperately trying to get the Conservatives to agree to some sort of compromise and failing, Bethmann gave in and passed a finance bill in June 1913 with support from liberals, Catholics, and social democrats.

He realized, however, that if allowed to solidify further, such an alliance would threaten the structure of the entire political system, and so he never repeated the move and was afterward unable to pass major legislation. Indeed this move was seen "on the Right as a victory for the 'power-hungry Reichstag democracy,' and a 'move towards a democratically governed unitary state.'"[61] Bethmann-Hollweg would later write of this period: "While the storm clouds gathered ever more heavily on the world horizon, an almost inexplicable pressure weighed on the political life of Germany. . . . The word 'Reichsverdrossenheit' [dissatisfaction or fatigue with the Reich] rose up out of the darkness."[62]

By 1914, therefore, Germany had reached a critical juncture. A state designed to protect Prussia and its conservative elites had become extremely difficult to reconcile with the changing nature of German society, an increasingly political aware and mobilized population, and the country's great power aspirations. The government was becoming paralyzed; tensions between agrarian and industrial interests and between conservatives, liberals, and almost everyone else were deepening; popular frustration and extra-parliamentary activity was on the rise, and the SPD—the party most opposed to the existing system—was going from triumph to triumph. National leaders faced the same basic options they had a generation earlier, but it was becoming increasingly difficult to put off choosing between them. The government could opt for repression, unilaterally revising the constitution with the support of the military[63] or it could pull away from the Conservatives and permit political reforms that would lead to full parliamentarization and democratization. Unwilling to engage in the massive domestic repression that would have been necessary to eliminate growing pressure for change but also unwilling to reform, national leaders dithered and the German political order stumbled on until the madness of the First World War intervened and brought the empire tumbling down.

Conclusions

After the failure of the liberal-led unification movement in 1848 the task of creating a unified Germany fell to conservative Prussia and its chancellor Otto von Bismarck. That unification occurred under conservative Prussian rather than liberal auspices critically affected Germany's subsequent political development. As a result of its own state-building, Prussia entered the nineteenth century with a strong monarchy *and* a strong nobility, and the German state it founded in 1871 was designed to protect the interests of both.[64] After unification, tensions between this state and evolving socioeconomic and political conditions emerged, worsening after Bismarck's departure.[65] By the early twentieth century Germany had among the most advanced economies and educated and politically aware populations in Europe, but many of its political institutions were unable or unwilling to respond to their needs and demands. The result was increasing political frustration and dissatisfaction and the rise of forces opposed to the reigning order. The two most important of these were the SPD and nationalist movements. By the early twentieth century, the former had become Germany's most popular political party as well as its most modern, with a sophisticated political machine, expansive network of affiliated associations, and a large membership and voting base. The lack of parliamentarism and full democracy meant, however, that the SPD was unable to assume governing responsibility commensurate with its growing electoral support. And while the SPD was less intransigent than some other European socialist parties like the Italian PSI, it was divided between revolutionaries who wanted to destroy the reigning order, and revisionists and reformists who wanted to gradually improve it and were willing to cooperate with other groups to do so. These divisions made it unable to lead a progressive coalition capable of spearheading the movement for full democratization during the imperial era. German nationalist associations, meanwhile, also grew increasingly popular, organized, and politically influential. These associations peddled an aggressive and virulently anti-Semitic nationalism[66] as the solution to the Germany's problems and offered disaffected citizens the sense of community and political efficacy that mainstream political institutions were unable or unwilling to provide. These associations were already shaping crucial policy debates over agricultural protection and imperialism and, as the conservatives and National liberals lost hold over the electorate, were becoming the dominant force on the German right.

In the years leading up to the First World War tensions mounted, coming to a head in conflicts over finances and taxation. This is not surprising, of course, since such conflicts often make transparent the socioeconomic and political fault lines in society. The clearest and most consequential example of this occurred in France during the late eighteenth century when the monarchy's need for revenue and an expanded taxation base helped set in motion a struggle between it and the nobility that pushed the country down the slippery slope to revolution (see chapter 4). While landed elites in imperial Germany did not enjoy the power or privileges of their eighteenth-century French counterparts, they had also embedded themselves in the old regime in a way that hindered its ability to adapt to changing circumstances. Indeed, by the early twentieth century conservative intransigence made it difficult for chancellors to govern in general and finance their budgets and military expenditures in particular.[67]

By 1914, in short, Germany had reached a critical juncture, something contemporaries were aware of.[68] Some argue that this led conservatives to rush headlong into the madness of the First World War as a way to overcome increasingly intractable social and political divisions and forestall democratization.[69] Others go even further, arguing that the tensions or disjuncture between economic and political development during the imperial era pushed Germany onto a special path or *Sonderweg* to National Socialism.[70] These are difficult debates to resolve,[71] but a comparative perspective does shed light on some crucial issues.

For example, from a comparative perspective imperial Germany appears quantitatively rather than qualitatively different from other West European countries during the late nineteenth and early twentieth centuries—more like an extreme case than a unique one. Many features stressed by *Sonderweg* scholars as leading inevitably to the tragedies of the interwar period—intense conflict between defenders of the old order and advocates of a new one, a traditional conservative elite as well as much of the middle class adamantly opposed to democratization, rising nationalism, weakening liberalism, mounting extremism—were present not just in imperial Germany but in most European countries by the late nineteenth and early twentieth centuries (see, for example, chapters 6 and 7).[72] What seems notable about imperial Germany, in other words, is not the *presence* of these features but rather the *form* they took—and in order to understand this it is necessary to understand political development before the imperial era. The nature of Prussian state-building during the early modern period, the failure of liberal-led unification in 1848, the relationship among the various German states before 1871, the historical lack of correspondence between German-speaking peoples and existing states and how this influenced German nationalism, the position of Germany in the middle of Europe—these factors and others shaped the unification process, the nature of the state formed by it, and subsequent German political development.[73]

As tensions within imperial Germany grew during the early twentieth century the state's legitimacy and national cohesion diminished. Nonetheless the political order stumbled on until 1914. Having hindered democratization before the First World War, the imperial political order ensured that Germany would make its first transition to democracy only upon its collapse at the end of the war. Transitions to democracy—particularly *first* transitions to democracy—are always difficult, but it is hard to imagine a transition occurring under less auspicious conditions than those facing Germany in 1918. These conditions are discussed in chapter 12, but it worth emphasizing that many of them were legacies of the imperial order itself.

The German people and the *Reichstag* knew little about the machinations surrounding the outbreak of the war or the progress of it since foreign policy and war-making were controlled by the kaiser, the chancellor, and the army. Indeed, by 1917 the army had sidelined the kaiser and chancellor, and Germany became essentially a military dictatorship. This explains why the country's defeat came as such a surprise and why the "stab in the back legend" seemed plausible to many: the military dictatorship simply hid the truth about the war from the German population until it collapsed in 1918. And, having sidelined other political actors and institutions, when the military dictatorship collapsed and the kaiser was forced to abdicate in 1918, a political vacuum and chaos engulfed the country. The enormous challenge of leading a transition to democracy in these circumstances fell to the SPD, a party the imperial order left woefully unprepared for this task. Alienated from the state, distrustful of other parties, itself distrusted by many Germans, and having never previously participated in national government, the SPD had to build a democratic Germany out of the rubble the imperial order left behind.

CHAPTER 9 | The Struggle for Democracy
in Interwar France

The lamps are going out all over Europe. We shall not see them lit again
in our lifetime.
—Sir Edward Grey, British Foreign Secretary on the eve of Britain's
entry into the First World War in August 1914.[1]

GREY'S UTTERANCE TURNED out to be an understatement. Europe
survived the First World War, but many of the structures, institutions,
and traditions that had defined it up through the time did not. In particular,
the war delivered a blow to the ancien régime from which it would never
recover.

The first major attack against the ancien régime came in 1789 (see
chapter 4) and throughout the nineteenth century it came under increasing
pressure, but the First World War brought its political superstructure
crashing down. But while monarchical dictatorships and empires disappeared
from Europe's political landscape after 1918,[2] the ancien régime's economic,
social, and cultural legacies lingered on.[3] Moreover while few mourned the
passing of monarchical dictatorships and empires, agreeing on what should
replace them proved impossible across much of Europe. The interwar period
was thus an interregnum—a period when an old order is dead or dying but a
new one has not yet arisen to take its place. And like most interregnums, the
interwar period was disordered and violent, consumed by a struggle among
liberals, democrats, communists, fascists, National Socialists, anarchists, and
others over what the nature of Europe's new order should be. This struggle

ushered in what Eric Hobsbawm called the "age of catastrophe":[4] a period when conflicts over Europe's political path pushed it into a war of almost unimaginable brutality that ended the period of European dominance that began with the rise of nation-states during early modern period (see chapter 2). In order to understand these conflicts and the different political trajectories of European countries during the interwar period, it is necessary to begin with the event it began with: the First World War.

The First World War

The First World War was truly a "world" war: what began as a confrontation between essentially France, the United Kingdom, and Russia on one side and Germany and Austria-Hungary on the other, spread to include all European countries except Spain, the Netherlands, Switzerland, and Scandinavia; it eventually also dragged in the Ottoman Empire, Japan, the United States, and various members of the British commonwealth (Canada, India, Australia); its impact was felt in Latin America and Asia as well. The First World War was immensely brutal and destructive: approximately 10 million died and perhaps three times as many were injured. Because of these staggering numbers, the war came to be known as the "Great War" in Britain and France—more terrible and traumatic in some ways than even the Second World War would be. All told France lost more than 10 percent of its men of military age (1.4 million dead) and if prisoners of war, the wounded, and the permanently disabled and disfigured are included, not more than one in three French soldiers escaped the war unharmed. Britain lost half a million men under the age of thirty, with perhaps surprisingly heavy losses among the upper classes. Germany, even though it lost more men than the French, lost a smaller percentage of its military-age men—13 percent—but this still translates into 2 million dead and almost 7.5 million casualties. The war also destroyed Europe's economic system. The prewar era had been one of increasing trade and globalization but all of this was lost: trade and other indicators of openness did not return to their prewar levels during the interwar years. The huge domestic costs of the war also generated high debts and then hyperinflation and massive unemployment after the war. And if this was not enough, an influenza pandemic spread across Europe and the globe at the end of the war, killing perhaps millions more Europeans and more than 50 million people worldwide. By end of the war, in short, Europe was shattered, exhausted, and demoralized. The term "lost generation" became associated with the war and its aftermath, reflecting the unprecedented death and destruction as well as the sense of those living at the time that the prewar world was gone forever. Thomas Mann, for example, whose own life and work echoed many Europeans' desperate attempt to come to grips with what was happening around them, wrote: "For us in old Europe, everything has died that was good and unique to us. Our admirable rationality has become madness, our gold to paper, our machines can only shoot and explode, our art is suicide; we are going under, friends."[5] John Maynard Keynes, meanwhile, who devoted himself to trying to build a new Europe out of the wreckage of the old one, characterized postwar Europeans as being "at the dead season of our fortunes. Our power of feeling or caring beyond the immediate questions of our own material well-being is temporarily eclipsed. . . . We have been moved beyond endurance, and need rest. Never in the lifetime of men now living has the universal element in the soul of man burnt so dimly."[6]

Concretely, the war and its aftermath propelled forward the two great forces that had been shaping political development in Europe since 1789—democracy and nationalism. The latter, of course, provided the immediate cause of the war in the form of a Serbian nationalist's assassination of the heir to the throne of the Austro-Hungarian Empire. Despite the devastation ultimately caused by this act and the war produced by it, nationalism became even more powerful and destructive after the war than before. Ironically, this was partially because the war accomplished one of the long-desired goals of Serb and other prewar nationalists: the destruction of Europe's great continental empires. However, rather than quenching nationalist passions, the end of empires enflamed them since when the map of Europe was redrawn after 1918 it proved impossible to make state and national boundaries coincide (see also chapter 15). To some extent, this was the fault of the Allies, who, despite an ostensible commitment particularly by Woodrow Wilson to self-determination, let self-interest trump the interests of the people involved when drawing up the boundaries of the new Europe. For example, a desire to punish and weaken the Central Powers meant Germany was forced to give up 25,000 square miles of territory containing over 7 million people. Austria was made into a rump state that encompassed little more than Vienna and its hinterlands, excluded many of the Austro-Hungarian Empire's German speakers, and was not allowed to join Germany, despite its clear desire to do so. Hungary, the other main successor state of the Austro-Hungarian Empire, was also downsized, losing two-thirds of its territory and three-fifths of its population. The Ottoman Empire, which had joined the Central Powers, was carved up by the Allies, with pieces awarded to Greece, Italy, France, and Britain. (The same process, of course, occurred in the Middle East at around the same time, when the Sykes-Pikot Agreement divided former Ottoman territories between France and Britain. Much scorn has, correctly, been placed on that agreement in the century since, but disregard for the wishes of the people living in conquered or defeated territories was, as previous chapters and chapter 15 on East-Central Europe make clear, the norm at the time.[7])

But even if the Allies had been committed to self-determination, aligning state and national boundaries would have been difficult if not impossible given how mixed-up populations in much of eastern, central, and southeastern Europe actually were. And so, as would be the case later in the century when Europe's overseas empires collapsed, the breakup of Europe's continental empires after 1918 led to the formation of countries that did not correspond to the preferences of many inside them.

Even before the war ended, the decline of the Ottoman Empire provided a frightening preview of what could happen when an attempt was made to align state and national boundaries in places were populations were mixed-up and geographically dispersed. Beginning in 1915, millions of Armenians, as well as Greeks, Assyrians, and others perceived as non-Turkish, were systematically eliminated via genocide and ethnic cleansing from the emerging Turkish state.[8] After the war, the "misalignment" of state and national boundaries in the countries that emerged out of the Austro-Hungarian Empire set the stage for conflicts that would eventually escalate to genocide and ethnic cleansing during and after the Second World War (see chapter 15).

It was not only in the new countries of Europe where nationalism generated immense political instability. Since the French Revolution and particularly 1848 nationalism had been growing in Europe's older states as well, and by the end of the nineteenth century nationalist movements had become among democracy's most vociferous opponents as well as the dominant force on the right. The First World War and its aftermath accelerated these trends. In the countries that lost the war, most notably Germany, the humiliation of defeat and the punishments meted out by the Treaty of Versailles inflamed nationalism; but even in countries on the winning side, nationalism grew as a result of the war and its aftermath. The brutality of war created a generation inured to violence and conflict and a cohort of veterans—many injured and disfigured—came back to societies often unsympathetic to and unable to care for them and quickly became disillusioned with the postwar world, unfavorably comparing its perceived immorality, indiscipline, and lack of direction with the camaraderie and sense of sacrifice characterizing their wartime experiences. Both Mussolini and Hitler fell into this category, and veterans like them disproportionately supported nationalist movements during the interwar period. More generally, the destruction and dislocation caused by the war and its aftermath left a generation of Europeans searching for new ways of understanding the world and convincing plans for changing it. In many European countries, nationalist movements stepped into this void and became the most potent adversary of the other great force unleashed at the end of the war—democracy.

Between 1917 and 1920 a wave of democratization swept across Europe, bringing an end to monarchies in Russia, Germany, and Austro-Hungary and sweeping away the last hindrances to democracy in other parts of Europe as well (see Table 9.1).

However, while this wave marked the end of monarchical dictatorships in Europe, it did not mark the beginning of a period of democratic con- solidation. Although the political infrastructure of the ancien régime was destroyed, many of its social and economic legacies remained,[9] and many Europeans were deeply suspicious of liberalism and capitalism. In addi- tion, many countries caught up in the post–World War I democratic wave were trying democracy for the first time and some had just been formed at the war's end, which meant they faced the challenges of democratic con- solidation and state- and nation-building simultaneously. (This is the story of East-Central Europe and is told in chapter 15.) Making matters worse, the interwar period presented democracies with almost unimaginable eco- nomic, social, and political problems. Understanding why some democracies overcame these challenges while others did not, and why some democratic failures gave rise to an entirely new form of revolutionary dictatorship—of the fascist or National Socialist variety—is the task of the next five chapters. A good place to begin is with Europe's most important, longest-standing de- mocracy—the French Third Republic.

Postwar France

France had, of course, eliminated the political and legal infrastructure of its ancien régime during the French Revolution, but had struggled ever since to come to a consensus on the type of regime that should replace it. This caused political disorder during the century following the revolu- tion but with the Third Republic France finally achieved some stability. Going into the First World War, the Third Republic was among the few full democracies in Europe and had existed since 1875—making it France's

TABLE 9.1 The Survival of Democracy in Interwar Europe.[1]

Survivors	New country?[2]	Democratized before war?
Belgium	No	Yes
Czechoslovakia	Yes	No
Denmark	No	Yes
Finland	No[3]	Yes[4]
France	No	Yes
Ireland	Yes[5]	No
Netherlands	No	Yes
Norway	No	Yes
Sweden	No	No
Switzerland	No	Yes
United Kingdom	No	No[6]

Casualties	New country?	Democratized before war?
Austria	Yes	No
Bulgaria	Yes	No
Estonia	Yes	No
Germany	Yes	No
Greece	No	No
Hungary	Yes	No
Italy	Yes	Yes[7]
Latvia	Yes	No
Lithuania	Yes	No
Poland	Yes	No
Portugal	No	Yes
Romania	Yes	No
Spain	No	No
Yugoslavia	Yes	No

1. *Essentially universal manhood suffrage and leaders/governments chosen by elections (rather than appointed by king or other non-democratic entity).*
2. *Coming into existence or gaining independence from second half of the nineteenth century on.*
3. *Had existed as an autonomous political entity, but had previously been controlled by Russia.*
4. *Universal suffrage instituted in 1906, but as it was controlled by Russia and its government was not fully autonomous.*
5. *Ireland existed before the interwar period, but only gained independence after the war.*
6. *More or less universal manhood suffrage in 1918, but a majority of men were able to vote before the war (see chapter 10).*
7. *Universal manhood suffrage in 1912.*

longest-lived regime since the revolution. This longevity, combined with legacies from France's earlier democratic experiments, meant that by 1918 France already had much of the infrastructure of democracy—political parties, civil society, a free press, functioning judiciary, and so on—in place. France also had a relatively strong state and sense of national identity—the French Revolution had accelerated state- and nation-building (see chapter 4) and during the prewar Third Republic the French state's strengths increased further (particularly with regard to what Michael Mann has called "infrastructural" power), and it expanded education, transport and communication networks, and military service, thereby strengthening national cohesion. (Or, in Eugen Weber's famous phrase, finally turning "peasants into Frenchmen."[10]) The prewar Republic did have to contend with left- and right-wing extremist groups that questioned its legitimacy and the desirability of democracy overall, but particularly after the Dreyfus Affair, extremist groups were countered by committed and organized pro-democratic forces that spanned the center-left to center-right (see chapter 6). In what could be seen as a logical culmination of this, when France declared war on Germany, parties across the political spectrum agreed to a Sacred Union (*Union sacrée*), forming a national-unity government that even included the old Marxist Jules Guesde.

This national-unity government fell apart before the war ended, and during the interwar period the struggle over democracy resumed. That this struggle continued 130 years or so after France's first transition to democracy reflects the inherent difficulty of building stable liberal democracy, especially in immensely challenging contexts like the interwar period.

Economically, France transitioned from a being rich nation and world banker "into a debt-ridden country with" an enfeebled economy.[11] Much of the First World War was fought in France, leaving considerable parts of the country's agricultural and industrial areas in ruins; the war may have set back French economic growth by a decade.[12] France was also heavily invested in Russia, and when the Soviet regime refused to honor the czar's debts, significant overseas investments vanished.[13] Exacerbating economic problems was the manner in which France financed the war and postwar reconstruction. Because it was politically easier than raising taxes, and because governments assumed much of the war's cost would be passed on to Germany after it, France financed its war effort primarily with debt and by printing money. Facing its own interwar difficulties (see chapter 12), Germany could not fully repay reparations, and so France was burdened with debt and inflation. Within a year of the armistice, the value of the franc fell by over 50 percent and the downward trend continued, transforming the franc from one of the world's "most solid" currencies to one of its most "unstable."[14] Increasing tax revenue would have been the logical way to deal with budgetary and financial problems, but this was politically and economically difficult. An income tax was instituted in 1916, but it was filled with loopholes and rates were very low; attempts to raise rates during the interwar period were stymied by tough economic times, which made raising rates particularly painful, and a general unwillingness on the part of various political parties to take responsibility for unpopular actions. The result was a vicious cycle as governments borrowed and printed money to deal with budgetary and financial problems that were largely caused by borrowing and printing money in the first place.[15]

The war and its aftermath also exacerbated the country's demographic problems, already serious before 1914.[16] As noted above, France suffered proportionately more deaths (1.4 million) and casualties (3 million) than other Western belligerents. Over 1 million of the latter were permanently disabled, and these men, called *mutilés*, became a common sight during the interwar period. Wartime deaths and disabilities, concentrated so heavily among young men, had a devastating effect on marriage and birth rates. France's population growth fell below Europe's other great powers, Germany, Italy, and Britain; by the end of the interwar period, France had proportionately Europe's fewest young and most old people. This demographic profile was "not a recipe for enterprise, for enthusiasm or self-assurance."[17] Only immigration stood between France and negative population growth; during the 1920s two million immigrants arrived, an increase of 77 percent over the course of the decade.[18]

Politically, the Third Republic continued to be plagued by anti-democratic movements on the right and left. Some nationalist groups, like *Action française*, were carry-overs from the prewar period, but after the war a "wave" of new nationalist groups appeared on the scene, the most important of which were the *Légion* (led by Antoine Rédier), the *Jeunesses Patriotes* (JP, led by Pierre Taittinger, into which the *Légion* merged in 1925), and the *Faisceau* (led by George Valois). These groups were mostly organized as *Ligues* (leagues), or civil society associations, rather than political parties and engaged in protests, marches, and brawls rather than organized electoral activity.

Although generally placed on the right, these groups had little in common with traditional conservative parties or movements and thus continued the prewar trend of a radical reshaping of the right.[19] Almost all these groups vociferously attacked democracy as well as the left and Jews, but favored replacing the Republic not with a monarchical dictatorship and a social and economic system based on privilege and status hierarchies, but rather with a corporatist political order that would foster national unity and be "truly" responsive to "the people."[20] Moreover these groups attracted a mass-base and a cross-class constituency; indeed they stressed their desire to represent "all France" as opposed to traditional parties that only represented particular groups—like workers. The *Légion*, for example, claimed it stood "above the interests of a single group," and sought "to gather all those . . . who put the salvation of France above all else."[21] The JP's 1926 program, meanwhile, declared that the movement wanted not "class struggle but class collaboration,"[22] and its program criticized the "egoism of the rich" and supported social reforms, including health and unemployment insurance, retirement plans, and improved housing. Its leader, Taittinger, declared that the JP differed from the traditional left in that it was "inspired by . . . [a] social nationalism . . . which recognized a solidarity uniting the interest of all Frenchmen, not by a Marxist internationalism which pitted one class against another."[23] Similarly, the *Faisceau* and Valois took great pains to convince the French that they were "not lackeys of capitalism" but rather "friends of the worker." Reflecting this, the group's paper denounced the "'yoke of money' that 'plutocracy' had imposed on the nation and proclaimed its devotion to 'social justice.'" Valois proclaimed that "big business was as decadent as parliamentary democracy."[24] None of these groups called for the complete destruction of capitalism; what they wanted instead was to temper it and create an economy that took societal needs into account.[25] As Valois once remarked, fascism properly understood "was 'neither of the right nor of the left,'" but instead simply "a friend of the people."[26]

Alongside a new "wave" of right-wing extremist groups, the Third Republic also confronted a new anti-democratic force on the left during the 1920s: communism. France's socialist movement had long had an ambivalent relationship to democracy, but especially after the Dreyfus Affair a pro-Republic faction, with Jean Jaurès as its head, defended the Republic (see chapter 6).[27] The formation of the Soviet Union re-ignited deep divisions within the socialist movement about democracy as well as other theoretical and practical issues. Despite desperate attempts to hold the movement together, particularly by Léon Blum, in 1920 the socialist party (SFIO) split, with radicals forming the French Communist party (PCF, *Parti communiste français*) and committing themselves to the overthrow of the Republic, if necessary by violent and insurrectionary means. Initially, the PCF seemed like it might become the dominant force on the left with its membership outnumbering the SFIO's and its daily newspaper, *L'Humanité*, outselling its socialist counterpart, *Populaire*. But by the mid-1920s the SFIO had regained its dominant position on the left, partially due to the PCF's constant infighting, unwillingness to brook dissent, and hardline Soviet stance. In the 1924 and 1928 legislative elections, for example, the SFIO and PCF got 20 percent and 10 percent, and 18 percent and 11 percent, respectively. The SFIO remained divided between those favoring cooperation with "bourgeois" groups and further integration into the Third Republic and those suspicious of both. Under pressure from its left wing, during the 1919 election the SFIO shunned alliances with center-left parties, facilitating the formation of a right-wing (*Bloc National*) government. In response, the party shifted course for the 1924 election, cooperating with the Radicals. The result was a resounding victory for the left-wing *Cartel des Gauches*, but when the Radical (considered a moderate center-left party) leader Edouard Herriot offered the Socialists some cabinet positions, writing to Blum that "the Socialists and Radicals have together campaigned against the coalition of high finance and slander. The evident will of the country is that this collaboration continue in the councils of government,"[28] the Socialists turned him down. The result was a succession of short-lived cabinets, unable to address the country's financial and economic problems. The left was punished in the 1928 elections, which returned a solid majority for the center and right. The conservative Raymond Poincarè returned to power—this time with the support of a Radical party that had given up on its erstwhile Socialist partner.

By the end of the 1920s the SFIO had reached an impasse. Unwilling to accept the revolutionary fantasies of the communists or fully commit to democratic practices and institutions, the party found itself sitting on the sidelines. That the SFIO could maintain these positions was due to the relative stability of the Third Republic up through the 1920s. Despite the presence of right- and left-wing extremists, centrist, pro-democratic parties held on to their voters and control of government up through this period. (The Third Republic's prewar pattern of weak and short-lived governments continued after 1918—there were approximately forty cabinets during the interwar period, some lasting for no more than a few weeks[29]—but almost all were made up of the same parties and recycled much of their personnel.) Socialists could, in other words, refuse to take responsibility for the Republic up through the 1920s because other parties did. As we will see, this was a key difference between France and many other European countries where democratic centrist parties began to collapse during the 1920s.

Beginning in the 1930s things began to change, forcing socialists and other political actors to rethink their priorities and strategies.[30] One reason, of course, was the Great Depression. Although the Depression hit France later and less severely than it did many countries, it also lasted longer and recovery was slower. Between 1930 and 1932 France's industrial production fell by about 30 percent (compared with about 47 percent in the United States and 42 percent in Germany) and its GDP declined by about 15 percent (compared with about 29 percent in the United States and 21 percent in Germany). Unemployment never reached the catastrophic levels it did in Germany or the United States, largely because France had comparatively few working-age men and a comparatively large number of small shopkeepers and farmers who simply cut back when the Depression hit and therefore never officially became unemployed. However, by 1936 when almost all European countries had begun bouncing back from the Depression, France's industrial production and GDP were still stuck below their 1929 levels and unemployment was reaching its peak.[31]

The suffering caused by the Depression combined with an increasingly threatening international environment—in 1933 Hitler became chancellor of Germany and announced his intention to leave the League of Nations—shifted the calculations of the SFIO and other Republican parties; in 1932 they once again joined in a *Cartel des Gauches*. The *Cartel* won the 1932 elections, but the SFIO was still unwilling to join a "bourgeois" government. Partially due to the SFIO's inconsistent support, between 1932 and 1934 five premiers came and went. Political instability made it more difficult to come up with forceful responses to France's growing economic and financial problems, providing fodder for denunciations of the Republic as weak and ineffective. If the Depression was not enough, in 1934 the Republic was hit with the Stavisky affair.

Alexander Stavisky was a serial con-man with friends in high places. He finally committed one con too many when he floated millions of francs of worthless bonds. When they came due, he fled and was found dead in January 1934. The police claimed Stavisky took his own life but his high level connections and an attempt by the sitting premier, the Radical Camille Chautemps, to hush the whole thing up made it look as if he had been killed to conceal the involvement of Republican elites in his shenanigans. The affair was a godsend for the nationalist movement. Joining anti-Semitism and anti-immigrant prejudice (Stavisky and his family were Jewish immigrants) with charges of government corruption, nationalist groups seized on the affair to re-energize their campaign against the Republic. The uproar eventually drove Chautemps and several ministers connected to Stavisky from office. When Chautemps's replacement, Éduard Daladier, fired the Paris Préfecture of Police, who had right-wing sympathies and was suspected of encouraging anti-government demonstrations, nationalist groups sponsored a massive riot, which some called a coup attempt,[32] on February 6, 1934, that left fifteen dead and forced Daladier to resign—a sitting premier felled not by elections but by extra-parliamentary activity—reflecting and furthering the power of nationalist groups.

Feeding off growing discontent and drawing inspiration from the rise of fascism in Italy and National Socialism in Germany, a second "wave" of nationalist groups appeared during the early 1930s.[33] Among the most important of these were *Solidarité Française* (SF) and the *Croix de Feu* (CF, which later morphed into the *Parti Social Français*, or PSF—see below). These second-wave groups shared several critical characteristics. Like their earlier "first-wave" counterparts, they were vehemently opposed to liberal democracy and profoundly anti-Semitic, but differed from traditional conservative movements in that most advocated some sort of fascist or National Socialist alternative to the reigning order rather than monarchy or a return to the past. All claimed to be working in the interests of the nation rather than any particular group or class and tried to attract a broad constituency. Most advocated state intervention in the economy and promised to protect bourgeois and peasant interests. Although their economic plans were often vague, they generally promised to control or manage capitalism and ensure the "health" of society.[34] However fuzzy and unrealistic, their vows to forcefully respond to the Depression and the dislocation and instability caused by capitalism, re-unite society, and protect France from its internal and external "enemies" proved attractive.

The growing popularity of nationalist groups combined with a rapidly deteriorating international environment (during 1934 Hitler consolidated his power in Germany, problems were growing across the border in Spain (chapter 13), and Austria collapsed into civil war and transitioned to dictatorship) led to another course shift by the SFIO, Republican parties, and the PCF.

Up through 1934 the PCF had steadfastly opposed the Republic and the parties supporting it. The PCF, like other European communist parties, took particular glee in attacking socialists, referring to them as "social fascists" and "social democratic vomit."[35] This reflected Soviet policy, which was directed towards undermining democracy and competitor parties on the left. However, especially after the Stavisky riots, the PCF's position began to change. Soon after February 6, which much of the left viewed as a coup attempt, the socialists and C.G.T. (the socialist trade union) called for massive counter-demonstrations as a warning to the Republic's enemies and the PCF urged its followers to join in. Behind the scenes, the Soviets had begun re-evaluating their stance towards democracy and socialist parties. Frightened by the situation in Europe and particularly the Nazi rise to power in Germany, which had been facilitated by communist intransigence and attacks on the

SPD (see chapter 12), Stalin instructed European communists to join with other parties on the left to defend democracy from the right. The PCF thus began pushing for cooperation with the SFIO. Meanwhile the Radicals also favored the formation of a broad pro-democratic coalition. The result was the Popular Front, a coalition including the PCF, SFIO, the Radical party (Republican, Radical, and Radical-Socialist party, *Parti républicain, radical et radical-socialiste*), and miscellaneous left groups. The Popular Front fought the 1936 elections on a relatively moderate program that promised to defend the Republic and institute significant reforms—but not threaten capitalism. The 1936 elections were a great victory for the Popular Front, which received 57 percent of the vote. The PCF's new-found restraint proved attractive: it experienced the largest gains of any Popular Front party, going from about 8 percent of the vote and 10 seats in 1932 to 15 percent of the vote and 72 seats in 1936. The SFIO, however, was the Popular Front's largest party and had the most seats in the Parliament; it was now willing to accept the consequences of this, forming a government with "bourgeois" parties (the communists remained outside the government), and its own leader, Léon Blum, became prime minister.

Despite the relative moderation of its program and constant conciliatory utterances by Blum, the right viewed the Popular Front as the coming of the apocalypse. Blum's becoming prime minister was viewed as particularly horrifying since in addition to being a socialist he was also Jewish and something of an intellectual, thereby pushing almost all of the right's buttons. Indeed, so toxic had the environment become that Blum was almost beaten to death by right-wing fanatics during the election campaign. After recovering, Blum was subject to almost constant abuse. Charles Maurras of the *Action Française*, for example, called him "a man to shoot in the back" while Robert Brasillach, an influential fascist-sympathizing author and journalist wrote: "The morning when Blum is led out to be shot will be a day of rejoicing in French families, and we will drink champagne."[36] The slogan "Better Hitler than Blum" became popular on the right. As the scholar of France Stanley Hoffman put it, during this period, rather than a stable democracy "the French political 'community' looked . . . like two armed camps preparing for a fight."[37]

Almost as soon as the Popular Front came to power, workers, frustrated by the Depression, the rise of the right, the sense that previous governments had ignored their needs, and fear that the Popular Front would be "too moderate," unleashed a wave of strikes and factory occupations, which generated counter-demonstrations and frightened the business community. Blum hoped reforms would calm the situation. Among these, the Matignon Accords were particularly notable, granting workers the right to strike and collective bargaining, a forty-hour work-week, and paid vacations; Blum also reformed the tax code, the structure of the Bank of France, and the French civil service. But perhaps because these reforms were not presented as part of a strategy for reshaping the French economy or as part of a distinctively socialist vision of the future, they did not satisfy workers. Blum's constant assurances, meanwhile, that he was committed to acting as the "loyal manager" of capitalism[38] did not placate the business community or the right. In the end, therefore, Blum's attempt to find a compromise between the demands of the left and right and workers and business ended up satisfying few and alienating many. The government's policies did little to address France's underlying problems, and the country's economy continued to deteriorate.

Hoping to tamp down on disorder, Blum moved to dissolve the *Ligues* but this had the perverse effect of encouraging the emergence of nationalist parties instead. The two most important of these were the PSF (*Parti Social Français*, French Social party), founded by François de La Rocque after the dissolution of the Croix-de-Feu league, and the PPF (*Parti Populaire Français*, French Popular party), founded by Jacques Doriot and other former members of the PCF. Like other "second-wave" nationalist movements, the PSF and PPF differed greatly from traditional conservative parties. They claimed to be working in the interests of the nation as a whole and tried to attract a broad constituency. The PPF, at least during the early stages of its development, did attract a relatively large number of workers as well as other defectors from the left,[39] and the PSF, which grew to be the largest of the interwar nationalist movements,[40] attracted support from almost all socioeconomic groups. As one observer notes, the PSF became the "first modern, cross-class, mass-mobilized French rightist party. . . . Its initial membership was strongly middle class, but as the movement grew, farmers made up 25 percent of the total, and an increasing number of workers were mobilized."[41] Reflecting this, de La Rocque proudly proclaimed that his was the only movement that could not be considered either "right or left." "Instead it had achieved a fusion of all classes. . . . One sees generals, great artists, great scholars, [and] high dignitaries of the Legion of Honor proud to obey workers and clerks who wear the Military Medal or the Croix de Guerre."[42] The PSF advocated a mix of nationalism and socialism, promising to defend the nation against the excesses of capitalism and the predatory behavior of (Jewish) financiers but also promising to protect the property of true "citizens." Both the PSF and PPF were quite popular. As historian Robert Soucy pointed out, "when Hitler came to power in Germany in 1933, the total membership of the NSDAP was about 850,000 . . . that is, about 1.5 percent of a national population of about sixty million. In 1937 the CF[/PSF] alone had nearly a million members in a population of forty million. France was not as allergic to fascism as some scholars have claimed."[43]

These parties fed off fear and resentment of the Popular Front, and so its demise took some of the wind out of their sails. Already reeling from challenges from the extreme left and right, when new international threats in the form of the Spanish civil war (see chapter 13) and an increasingly aggressive Nazi regime were added to the mix, the Popular Front was overwhelmed. Blum requested special powers to deal with the country's deteriorating situation, but he was turned down, and in response resigned. In June 1937, after just over a year in office, Blum's government came to an end. Weary and disgusted, Blum told the American ambassador, "I have had enough! Everything that I have attempted to do has been blocked."[44]

During the subsequent years, the Popular Front alliance fell apart, anti-Republican attacks by extremists, particularly on the nationalist right, continued, and divisions in the country deepened. Despite its problems, however, the Third Republic did not fall apart as did many other interwar democracies, but growing disorder and the rapidity of its collapse to Germany in 1940 raises questions about its underlying strength. Gordon Wright, one of the preeminent American historians of modern France, was probably correct in arguing, "the Third Republic [most likely] would have endured—by force of inertia, if nothing else—if spared the impact of depression and war. Yet the real test of any regime is how well it can face up to crisis. A nation that collapses as quickly as France did in 1940, a nation where consensus disintegrates when confronted with the economic and social stresses of a depression decade, is clearly suffering from some deeper sources of weakness."[45]

Conclusions

During interwar years Europeans engaged in a titanic struggle over what the nature of their new world would be. The ancien régime had been under attack since 1789, but it was not until the end of the First World War that its political infrastructure—monarchical dictatorships and empires—came crashing down. The end of the First World War also propelled forward the two great forces that had been driving European political development since 1789—democracy and nationalism. In the decades after the French Revolution these forces worked together to weaken the foundations of ancien régimes, but after 1848 (see chapter 5) they diverged. By the end of the nineteenth century, nationalist movements had become opponents of democracy and liberalism and were becoming the dominant force on the right. The year 1848 was also, of course, a critical juncture in the emergence of the European workers' movement. Initially, workers had been part of the coalition opposing the ancien régime, but when the middle classes and liberals realized that democratization might mean giving power to workers, they balked, helping usher in the post-1848 reverse wave. After 1848 the alliance between workers and the middle class fell apart in much of Europe, and the former turned to organizing their own unions and socialist parties. During the late nineteenth century, workers' movements in many European countries became ambivalent towards democracy, at least partially because after 1848 they were convinced that middle classes and liberals would never allow them to fully participate in or benefit from it.

During the interwar period, the conflict among these great forces—democracy, nationalism, and socialism—came to a head. When monarchical dictatorships collapsed at the end of the First World War democracy initially triumphed. But the First World War also radicalized the nationalist and workers' movements, giving rise to fascism and national socialism on the right and communism on the left—both of which offered Europeans political, social, and economic alternatives to monarchical dictatorships and democracy.[46]

Democracy proved particularly fragile and publics particularly susceptible to anti-democratic alternatives in Europe's new states, where state-, nation-, and democracy-building were compressed into a relatively short period of time (see Table 9.1). But even in many older states, democracy ran into trouble, and left- and right-wing extremism attracted mass support. This was true in France, the home of Europe's first modern democracy. Democracy did not collapse in France, but if support for democracy must be principled rather than conditional—that is, the vast majority of the population must accept democracy's legitimacy in both good times and bad—in order for it to be considered consolidated, then it would be hard to characterize democracy as fully consolidated in France during the interwar period.

There were, however, some countries in Europe where democracy did weather the interwar period fairly well. It is to one of those places—Britain—that we now turn.

| English Exceptionalism II

Reform so that you may preserve!

—T.B. Macaulay[1]

T HE KEY PUZZLE of interwar Europe is why some democracies survived while others did not. The last chapter analyzed France, one of the survivors. The Third Republic began the interwar period in a seemingly strong position: it had existed for several decades, could build upon democratic experience dating back to the late eighteenth century, and was supported by a comparatively strong state and sense of national identity. Yet despite these advantages, democracy faced serious challenges in interwar France. Understanding why this was so required examining the pre- and post-war periods. During the interwar years the Third Republic confronted significant demographic, social, and economic problems, and its inability to fully solve them contributed to disillusionment with it. But the Third Republic's difficulties were not merely a product of the interwar years. They were also manifestations of long-standing divisions in French society. Although the French had eliminated the political and legal infrastructure of their ancien régime in the late eighteenth century, they had thus far been unable to reach a consensus on whether democracy or some other type of political regime should replace it.

In contrast to France and much of the rest of Europe, Britain was politically stable during the interwar years. Indeed, among large European countries only in Britain can liberal democracy be considered fully consolidated during this period: it was not threatened by significant right- or left-wing extremism, did not have to contend with extra-parliamentary violence, and major political actors respected the democratic "rules of the game." Understanding why this was so requires examining the pre- and interwar periods. Britain faced fewer and less serious demographic, economic, and social problems during the interwar years than did many other European countries. However, equally if not more important is that British democracy was better prepared than most of its European counterparts to deal with the problems it confronted during the interwar period. The reason for this, in turn, is to be found in the country's political development during the previous century.

As we know, the nineteenth century was a period of political turmoil. Economic development, changes in social structure, growing political participation, and increasing demands for political liberalization and even democratization met fierce resistance from the defenders of the old regime, which contributed to rising social conflict, extremism, disorder, and violent political transitions in many parts of Europe. Britain also experienced economic and social change, growing political participation, and increasing demands for political liberalization and even democratization during the nineteenth century, but rather than destabilizing or destroying the reigning order, these trends were accommodated by and within it. To a large degree, this was a consequence of the comparatively puzzling behavior of its landowning elites. Unlike their counterparts in much of the rest of Europe, these elites gradually, if grudgingly, accepted reforms that slowly transformed the reigning order and eliminated their dominance of it. The comparatively moderate response of British landed elites to the challenges of modern politics had several critical and counter-intuitive consequences. First, it enabled these elites to hold on to political, economic, and social power longer than most of their European counterparts. Second, it ensured that by the time a full transition to democracy occurred in 1918,[2] Britain was less politically and socially divided and its political institutions stronger and more legitimate than those in almost any other European country.

Political Development during the Tumultuous Nineteenth Century

Since 1688, Britain had a constitutional and fairly liberal political order (see chapter 3) but not a democratic one. Up through the early nineteenth century Britain was essentially an aristocratic oligopoly dominated by an Anglican landowning elite.[3] Indeed, with the elimination of the "absolutist option" in Britain in 1688, and thus the countervailing power of a dominant monarch, British landowning elites became the most politically powerful in Europe. They were, for example, more powerful than either their Russian or German counterparts, the two groups to which they are most often compared. The Russian nobility was subordinate to the czar, and the German nobility also had to contend with a powerful monarchy during the modern period (see chapters 2 and 8). The British landowning elite also dominated all high-status positions in the British civil service, military, judiciary and church, almost all cabinet positions, the House of Lords, and the House of Commons (see Figures 10.1–10.3).[4]

And while the British landed elite did not reign over serfs as did its Russian and at some points German counterparts, its power at the local level was profound: it controlled political, administrative, and juridical functions in the countryside.[5] It was also immensely wealthy: indeed it was richer and controlled more of its country's economic resources (land) than any other elite in Europe; its estates, as anyone who has read the novels of the period knows, were the size of "little kingdoms"[6] and were ruled accordingly. Up through the nineteenth century, in short, the British landowning elite enjoyed a combination of political, economic, and social power unrivalled in any other part of Europe (see Figures 10.4–10.6).[7]

The landowning elite's power was protected by property and religious restrictions on the right to vote and by gerrymandering. By the early

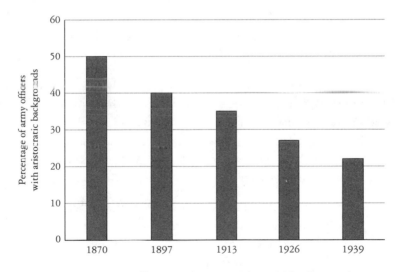

FIGURE 10.1 British army officers with aristocratic social backgrounds, nineteenth and twentieth centuries.

Source: David Cannadine, *The Decline and Fall of the British Aristocracy* (New York: Vintage Books, 1990).

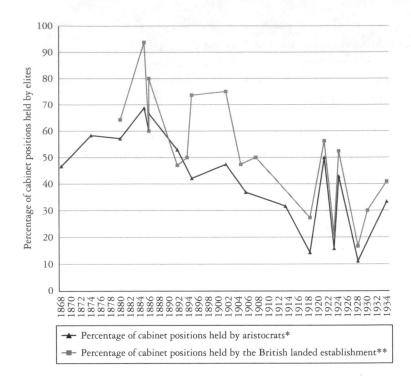

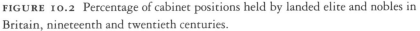

FIGURE 10.2 Percentage of cabinet positions held by landed elite and nobles in Britain, nineteenth and twentieth centuries.

Notes: * Guttsman; aristocrats defined as those descended from a holder of hereditary title in the grandparent generation. ** Cannadine; British landed establishment defined as the landowning class more broadly.

Source: W.L. Guttsman, *The British Political Elite* (New York: Basic Books, 1963); David Cannadine, *The Decline and Fall of the British Aristocracy* (New York: Vintage Books, 1990).

nineteenth century only about 5 percent of the population was enfranchised, and rural areas were heavily over-represented in Parliament. Indeed, by the early nineteenth century some rural districts had few voters left in them while many highly populated urban areas, including Manchester, Birmingham, Leeds, and Sheffield, did not have a single MP. As Lord John Russell, an influential Whig politician and twice prime minister, noted,

> a stranger who was told that this country is unparalleled in wealth and industry, that it is a country that prides itself on its freedom and that once in every seven years elects representatives from its population to act as the guardians and preservers of that freedom, would be anxious and curious to see how . . . the people chose their representatives. . . . Such a person would be very much astonished if he were taken to a ruined mound and told that that mound sent two representatives to Parliament; if he were

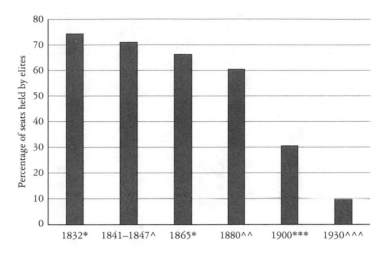

FIGURE 10.3 Members of the House of Commons with elite landowning backgrounds in Britain, 1832–1930.

Notes: * 489 of 658 seats; ^ 467 of 658 seats; ** 436 of 658 seats; ^^ 394 of 652 seats; *** 204 of 670 seats; ^^^ 61 of 615 seats.

Source: David Cannadine, *The Decline and Fall of the British Aristocracy* (New York: Vintage Books, 1990); Mary Ransome, "Some Recent Studies of the Composition of the House of Commons," *University of Birmingham Historical Journal*, 1, 2, 1958.

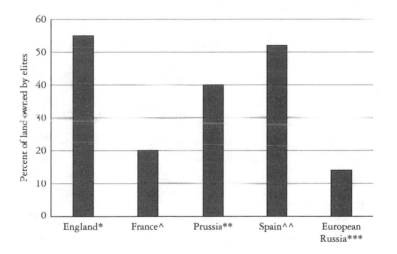

FIGURE 10.4 Percentage of land owned by landed elite in European countries of the nineteenth century.

Notes: * 1874; 1,000 acres minimum for landed elite; ^ early 19th century; landed elite more or less equivalent to French nobility; ** 1858; 375 acres minimum for landed elite; ^^ 1860; 250 acres minimum for landed elite; *** 1877; 270 acres minimum for landed elite.

Source: David Spring, ed. *European Landed Elites in the Nineteenth Century* (Baltimore, MD: Johns Hopkins University Press, 1977).

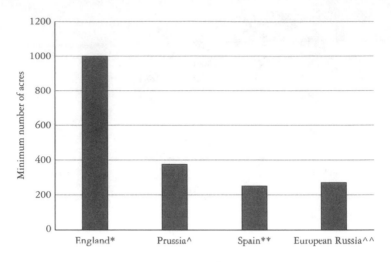

FIGURE 10.5 Land ownership requirements for consideration as landed elite in respective European countries.

Notes: * 1874; ^ 1858; ** 1860; ^^ 1877.

Source: David Spring, ed. *European Landed Elites in the Nineteenth Century* (Baltimore, MD: Johns Hopkins University Press, 1977).

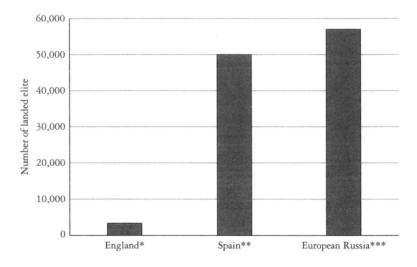
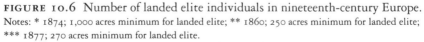

FIGURE 10.6 Number of landed elite individuals in nineteenth-century Europe.

Notes: * 1874; 1,000 acres minimum for landed elite; ** 1860; 250 acres minimum for landed elite; *** 1877; 270 acres minimum for landed elite.

Source: David Spring, ed. *European Landed Elites in the Nineteenth Century* (Baltimore, MD: Johns Hopkins University Press, 1977).

taken to a stone wall and told that three niches in it sent two representatives to parliament; if he were taken to a park where no houses were to be
seen, and told that that park sent two representatives to parliament. But
if he were told all this, and were astonished at hearing it, he would still be
more astonished if he were to see large and opulent towns and were told
that these towns sent no representatives to parliament.[8]

Accompanying gerrymandering was pervasive corruption. Rural, depopulated
areas were often referred to as "rotten boroughs" since they were controlled by
landowning elites who used them to send their own hand-picked representatives
to Parliament. In other constituencies, large landowners simply used their wealth
and influence to control electoral outcomes.[9] Such areas were sometimes referred
to as "pocket boroughs" since they were "in the pocket" of local elites. Elites
often spent thousands of pounds in bribes and other inducements to ensure their
preferred electoral outcome and the lack of a secret ballot facilitated intimidation
and vote-buying.[10] For example, in the years just before the First Reform Act
about 177 individuals influenced the return of about 355 MPs, just over two-
thirds of the representatives from England and Wales (see Figure 10.7).[11]

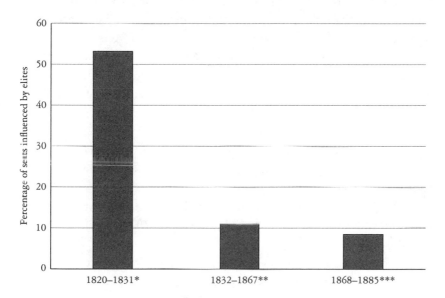

FIGURE 10.7 Seats in the House of Commons influenced by landed elites.
Notes: * 350 of 658 seats; 213 influenced by peers with seats in the House of Lords, 137 by others;
** 72 of 658 seats; 59 influenced by peers with seats in the House of Lords, 13 by others;
*** 55 of 652 seats; 40 influenced by peers with seats in the House of Lords, 15 by others.
Source: F.M.L. Thompson, *English Landed Society in the 19th Century* (London: Routledge and Kegan
Paul, 1963).

By the mid-nineteenth century unrepresentative political orders were coming under pressure across Europe (see chapter 5), and Britain was no exception to this trend.[12] Although Britain had experienced massive economic and social change since 1688—its population had increased fourfold, it had experienced an "Industrial Revolution," it was more urbanized (Manchester, Birmingham, Leeds, and Sheffield were small towns in 1688 but great cities by the early nineteenth century), and closely knit together by railways, roads, and newspapers—politically it had changed relatively little. What turned out to be exceptional about Britain during the late nineteenth century was not that its reigning order and ruling elites faced challenges, but rather how those challenges were met. During the nineteenth century the landowning elite that ruled Britain accepted gradually, if grudgingly, a sequence of reforms that eliminated the religious and political barriers inherited from the late seventeenth century, allowing new groups to be incorporated into the reigning order and eventually undermining their own power.

The first restrictions to go concerned religious minorities. Despite the long-standing bond between Anglicanism and the British state, religious prejudice, particularly against Protestant Dissenters, had declined over the previous decades, making the Corporation and Test Acts' (see chapter 3) limiting of public office to members of the Church of England appear unjust and anachronistic.[13] Thus despite the opposition particularly of many Tories, in 1828 the Sacramental Test Act giving non-Anglican Protestants the right to hold public office passed Parliament. In addition to being "a great victory over the 'principle of persecution and exclusion,'"[14] the Sacramental Test Act focused attention on those still excluded on religious grounds, most obviously Catholics—an outcome its opponents had feared. As a reporter for a Tory newspaper hysterically lamented: "where is the constitutional boundary to be fixed? At this side of Judaism? Or Mohammedanism? Or Deism? Or Unitarianism? Or Atheism? Or Devil Worship?"[15]

Catholic Emancipation was a harder sell than incorporating Protestant Dissenters since anti-Catholic prejudice had deeper roots in English society and any policy change towards Catholics would have implications for England's relationship with Ireland. However, declining religious prejudice[16] combined with fear of increasing unrest in Ireland and the growing organization of Catholics, particularly under the great Irish political leader Daniel O'Connell and his mass-membership Catholic Association, helped convince many elites that emancipation was the best way to ward off disorder. O'Connell brought the situation to a head in 1828 when he ran for and won election to a seat in Parliament that he could not hold. Recognizing that barring O'Connell might very well cause rebellion in Ireland, key Tories including the prime minister, the Duke of Wellington, and the home secretary, Sir Robert Peele, helped convince a reluctant House of Lords and King George IV to accept the Emancipation Act of 1829 giving Catholics the right to become MPs and hold other public offices.

Although the practical impact of the Sacramental Test and the Catholic Emancipation Acts on the landowning elite's domination of the reigning order was limited,[17] these reforms ended the long-standing link between Anglicanism and the British state. In addition, Catholic Emancipation split the Tories—many of whom believed that emancipation represented, as the newspaper *John Bull* put it, "the complete subversion of the principle upon which our Constitution has been founded"[18]—thereby dividing the anti-reform forces and helping to bring the Whigs—the more pro-reform group[19] although still firmly based in the landowning elite—into office (see below).[20] And, finally, the Sacramental Test and Catholic Emancipation Acts, combined with the 1830 political transitions in France and Belgium, boosted pro-reform organizing and agitation (see chapter 5).[21] Thousands of British citizens, including members of the middle and working classes, joined pro-reform associations, hundreds of thousands turned out for pro-reform meetings, and franchise expansion became a major issue in electoral campaigns.[22] Such developments helped convince some elites once again that reform was necessary. T.B. Macaulay, British historian and Whig politician, for example, criticized anti-reformists in Parliament for their "stubborn denial to risk everything until, in a self-induced crisis" you will be forced humiliatingly to give in. Do you want to "wait for that last, most violent paroxysm of popular rage . . . ?" "You know," he continued, "what happened to Charles X in France" (see chapter 5). In order to avoid this fate, Macauley urged his colleagues to "Reform so that you may preserve!"[23]

In 1830 the Tory Duke of Wellington's opposition to reform contributed to his downfall and replacement as prime minister by the Whig Earl Grey. The Whigs were generally more pro-reform then the Tories, but the debate was more about means than ends: both Whigs and Tories wanted to preserve the existing system and the landowning elite's dominance of it, but differed on how best to do so, with the Whigs viewing reform as the best way to ensure political stability. Grey, for example, declared that "The principle of my reform is, to prevent the necessity for revolution . . . there is no one more dedicated against annual parliaments, universal suffrage, and the [secret] ballot, than I am." The point of reform, he stressed, "is to preserve and not overthrow."[24] Similarly, Henry Cockburn (Scottish literary figure, judge, Whig, and drafter of the first Scottish reform bill), for example, argued,

> the Elective Franchise [must be] extended to those classes who possess property and knowledge. Much more is demanded by many, but it is hoped that it is not too late to make a change . . . the limit of which shall be possession of property and intelligence . . . any plan must be objectionable which, by keeping the Franchise very . . . exclusive, fails to give satisfaction to the middle and respectable ranks of society, and drives them to a union founded on dissatisfaction, with the lower orders. It is of the utmost importance to associate the middle with the higher orders of society in the love and support of the institutions and government of the country.[25]

In March 1831 Grey's government put forward a bill including districting and franchise reform; when it went down in the House of Commons Grey resigned and took his case to the voters. The 1831 elections were a huge victory for the Whigs: the party won 370 seats to the Tories' 235. The Whigs quickly put forward another reform bill, which, since they now dominated the House of Commons, passed by a large majority. The House of Lords rejected the bill, leading to protests, rioting, attacks on landed elites and their property, and an explosion of pro-reform activity and organizing.[26] At the end of 1831 the Whigs put forward another slightly modified reform bill, which passed the House of Commons by an even greater majority than its predecessor. The Lords tried to bury this bill with amendments and delays, leading the Whigs to propose swamping them with new pro-reform peers in order to end to the upper house's obstructionism. King William IV rejected this proposal (the monarch had the prerogative of creating peers); in response, Grey again resigned. The king then asked the Duke of Wellington to form a government, but since he did not have a majority in the Commons, the king was forced to call back Grey.[27] Recognizing that Grey and the Whigs' triumphant return would leave the king little choice but to pack the Lords, and fearing political and social upheaval if electoral results and the will of the House of Commons were again thwarted, the Lords backed down and in June 1832 the Reform Bill became law. It is important to note that the landowning elite dominated the Whig government that passed the Reform Bill (see Figure 10.8). Grey is reputed to have boasted, for example, that the members of his government "owned jointly more [of the country's land] than any previous administration."[28]

The Great Reform Act had symbolic and practical significance. It was the "first thoroughgoing attempt to redraw the political map and define which

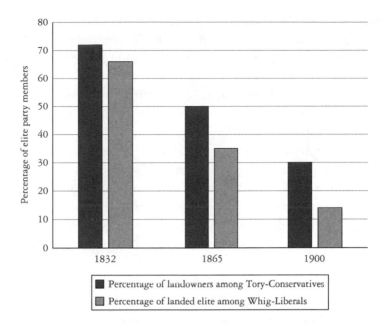

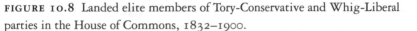

FIGURE 10.8 Landed elite members of Tory-Conservative and Whig-Liberal parties in the House of Commons, 1832–1900.
Source: Mary Ransome, "Some Recent Studies of the Composition of the House of Commons," *University of Birmingham Historical Journal*, 1, 2, 1958.

categories of person should, and which should not, have the right to vote" since the Glorious Revolution.[29] The act also made clear that it was possible to expand the franchise while maintaining the basic structure of the existing order, increasing the electorate by almost 50 percent to include a significant sector of the middle class and reorganizing electoral districts.[30] Britain now had probably the widest suffrage in Europe. The battle over the Great Reform Act also presaged future battles between the elected Commons and the unelected Lords: it was the first time the latter had been forced against its will to agree to legislation it disagreed with as a result of threats by the former.

While the political liberalization achieved by the Great Reform Act of 1832 is noteworthy, from a comparative perspective it is the *way* this reform occurred rather than its extent that is unusual. In France, for example, it took the upheaval of 1830 and the transition to the "July Monarchy" (see chapter 5) to achieve less than was achieved by the 1832 reform bill in Britain (the latter enfranchising a significantly greater share of the population than the former).[31] Also unusual was the relative foresight or at least pragmatism of at least some sectors of the British elite. As one observer put it, "from the standpoint of the ruling classes the Reform Bill was 'one of the transactions of which history does not present many examples, when the right thing was done in exactly the right way at exactly the right time.'"[32] Recognizing the way the wind was blowing, not just many Whigs but even some Tories threw their support behind what they explicitly viewed as a "conservative reform," that is, one that would help conserve the existing order via reforms that would forestall more radical challenges to it.[33] And after the reform was passed, the Tories made their peace with it, beginning their transformation into the Conservative party. While in retrospect the Great Reform Act may appear as the first step on Britain's long path to democracy, it is important to remember that its supporters viewed it in the opposite way: as a way of preventing democratization and preserving the reigning order by bringing into it those who could be trusted to support it and defer to the elites dominating it.

In the years after 1832, the calculations of its supporters were partially vindicated—the groups enfranchised by the Great Reform Act defended the reigning order and thereby helped ensure relative political stability at a time when much of the rest of Europe was in upheaval. In addition, the 1832 Act did not end the landowning elites' domination of the cabinet, civil service, army, or the Lords or Commons (see Figures 10.1–10.3 above). But the 1832 reform act could not check the rise of the middle class nor eliminate pressure for further reform. Perhaps the most important reflection of the former was the repeal of the Corn Laws and of the latter the Chartists.

The Corn Laws protected domestic agricultural producers via tariffs, duties, and restrictions on imported grain. The Laws were generally supported by landowning elites but opposed by industrial, commercial, and urban interests, which favored cheaper food. In 1838 the Anti–Corn Law League began mobilizing public opinion against protectionism.[34] Although the Conservatives (as the Tory party came to be known) had generally supported the Corn Laws and the landowning elite that benefited from them, rising anti–Corn Law agitation and the horrific fallout from the failure of the Irish potato crop in the mid-1840s, when over one million people died of starvation and another million were forced to emigrate, led a Conservative prime minister, Sir Robert Peel, to shift course. With the support of Whigs, free-traders, and about one-third of the Conservative MPs, the Corn Laws were repealed in May 1846.

The repeal of the Corn Laws had critical consequences. First, it split the Conservatives between those who considered the Corn Laws to be an "essential bulwark of the order of society" and those who recognized that the Irish famine and the Anti–Corn Law League had made the cost of retaining the laws very high—that is, between those implacably opposed to reform and those who believed that only through reform could more radical change be prevented.[35] With the repeal of the Corn Laws, many in the latter group eventually migrated to the Liberal party (see below), weakening the Conservatives and leaving them more narrowly based in the landowning elite. Second, the repeal of the Corn Laws made clear the rising power of industrial, commercial, and urban interests. Third and relatedly, the repeal of the Corn Laws once again displayed the ability of at least some members of the existing elite to adjust to changing reality. As one observer put it, "Common sense had once again saved the British upper classes . . . In 1848 while revolutions were raging on the Continent, Peel remarked that by abolition of the corn laws he had spared Britain a major upheaval. He had also saved the aristocratic elements from the gathering social revolution."[36] Indeed, the repeal of the Corn Laws combined with earlier political reforms helps explain why Britain was not swept up in the 1848 wave. In other parts of Europe middle and working classes came together in opposition to unrepresentative and unresponsive old orders, but by 1848 at least part of the British middle class already had what other middle classes wanted (see chapter 5).[37]

The British working class, however, remained disenfranchised and did demand further reforms after 1832.[38] The main vehicle for working-class agitation during this time was Chartism, which got its name from the 1838 "People Charter" calling for universal manhood suffrage, the secret ballot, the abolition of property requirements to serve as MPs, payment for MPs, equal electoral districts, and annual parliamentary elections.[39] The Chartists arranged mass meetings, supported pro-Chartist candidates in elections, and presented petitions with millions of signatures to Parliament. The last of these petitions was presented in 1848 as much of the rest of Europe was in turmoil. (While the French and others stormed the barricades, the English presented petitions.) Ultimately the Chartists were unsuccessful, but during the second half of the nineteenth century the reform drive continued. Interestingly, however, while liberals and conservatives in many other parts of Europe retrenched after 1848 (see chapter 5), in Britain Liberals, Parliamentary Radicals,[40] and even some Conservatives eventually accepted further reform.

This position was spurred by the growth of pro-reform mass membership organizations during the 1850s and 1860s like the Reform League and the National Reform Union[41] and an acknowledgment of persistent inequities within the reigning order. For example, by the 1860s Britain no longer had the most democratic franchise in Europe,[42] corruption remained pervasive, and inequitable districting still skewed outcomes in favor of the countryside and the landowning elite.[43] After 1848 all parties put forward various reform schemes, but as before the main goal of almost all was to preserve rather than overthrow the reigning order.[44] Thus the main difference between Liberal and Conservative proposals reflected their varying assessments of the degree to which proposals would affect political stability and their own party's political fortunes.[45] In 1866, for example, the sitting Liberal government proposed enfranchising "responsible" and "respectable" members of the working class, arguing that this would not threaten the reigning order or the elites who ran it.[46] William Gladstone, for example, who would play a large role in the unfolding drama, urged his colleagues in Parliament to recognize

> since 1832 every kind of beneficial change has been in operation in favour of the working classes. There never was a period in which religious influences were more active. . . [In addition,] the civilizing and training powers of education have" significantly improved the character of the mass of the people. [And] "as regards the press, an emancipation and extension has taken place" [that has provided all classes access to] "accounts of public affairs, enabling them to feel a new interest in the transaction of those affairs." [In short], "there is not a call which has been made upon the self-improving powers of the working community which has not been fully answered. . . . Parliament has been striving to make the working classes progressively fitter and fitter for the franchise; and can anything be more unwise, not to say more senseless, then to persevere from year to year in this plan, and then blindly to refuse to recognize its legitimate upshot—namely the increased fitness of the working classes for the exercise of political power?"[47]

If, moreover, "the best of the working men,"[48] were not incorporated into the system, they might become alienated from it and radicalized. Gladstone therefore argued that reform was the best way to avoid the social discord and upheaval that plagued much of the rest of Europe:

> It has been given to us of this generation to witness . . . the most blessed of all social processes; I mean the process which unites together not the interests only but the feelings of all the several classes of the community, and throw back into the shadows of oblivion those discords by which they were kept apart from one another. I know of nothing which can contribute . . . to the welfare of the commonwealth [more] than that hearts should be bound together by a reasonable extension, at fitting times, and among selected portions of the people,

of every benefit and every privilege that can justly be conferred on them.[49]

Despite the efforts of Gladstone and others when the time came to vote, the Liberals split with their more conservative wing (the Adullamites) joining with Conservatives to defeat the bill. As a result, the Liberal government resigned and was replaced by a Conservative one in June 1866. The bill's defeat and the transition from a Liberal to a Conservative government spurred public protest.[50] In June, for example, a pro-reform meeting in Trafalgar Square organized by the Reform League attracted hundreds of thousands of participants. In July another gigantic meeting in Hyde Park resulted in rioting when police tried to prevent participants from entering it, leading it to become known as the "Hyde Park Railings Affair" because some railings were pulled down when participants forced their way into the park.[51] (Not a storming of the barricades, but about as close as the English got.) The Conservatives found themselves at a critical juncture. The party was in power but lacked a majority in the House of Commons. More generally, the party had not recovered from its split years ago over the Corn Laws. (The last election won by the Conservatives was in 1847.) Now, however, its main foe was divided and defeated, and its powerful leader, Palmerston, dead.[52] Particularly committed to taking advantage of the opportunities this situation offered was Benjamin Disraeli, the chancellor of the exchequer. Disraeli was a committed Conservative but also a pragmatist: he understood that reform was inevitable and the party that achieved it would be well rewarded.[53] "Our party," he once told the Earl of Derby (past and future Conservative prime minister) "is now a corpse" and "only a bold and decided course" would put us on our legs.[54] And so, eager to strike a blow against the Liberals, in 1867 the Conservatives introduced a reform bill that was more far-reaching than the Liberal one they helped defeat the year before.[55] The Conservative bill would roughly double the electorate, enfranchising all "householding" adult males in urban areas (that is, those who owned or rented a house or occupied lodgings worth ten pounds) and reducing the threshold for voting in rural areas; it would also redistribute more than fifty Parliamentary seats.[56] Disraeli argued the bill would "popularize" the constitution "without democratizing" it:[57] it would enfranchise more voters, but as long as the Conservatives remained true to their historic task of "representing the national feeling"[58] (see below) they had nothing to fear. Thanks in no small measure to Disraeli's efforts, in 1867 the Conservative bill passed. When Derby resigned in 1868 for health reasons, Disraeli became prime minister.

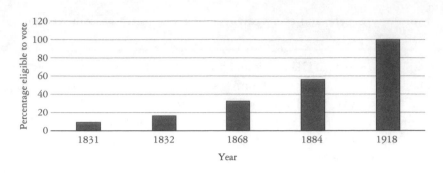

FIGURE 10.9 Percentage of adult male population (21+) eligible to vote in Great Britain and Ireland, 1831–1918.
Source: House of Commons, "The History of the Parliamentary Franchise," https://researchbriefings. parliament.uk/ResearchBriefing/Summary/RP13-14.

The Second Reform Act had critical consequences. First, and most obviously, it expanded the electorate, enfranchising some members of the urban working class and overall approximately doubling the number of adult males eligible to vote (see Figure 10.9).[59]

But the Second Reform Act marked a qualitative and not just quantitative shift in the franchise since it overturned "the principle embodied in the First Reform Act that property was the sole indicator of the fitness to vote."[60] The expansion of the electorate also spurred political party modernization. As discussed in previous chapters, in much of Europe liberal and conservative parties had difficulty adjusting to modern, mass politics. In Britain, however, the Liberals and Conservatives created more centralized and disciplined party organizations to help them pass legislation and govern more effectively, and they expanded their local-level networks and ties to a variety of civil-society associations in order to mobilize voters and fight increasingly contested elections.[61]

The Second Reform Act also ushered in a renewed period of reform, particularly under Liberal governments, that transformed the aristocratic oligarchy that had ruled Britain since 1688.[62] But although Britain's landowning elite was more powerful than almost any other, its decline did not elicit the intransigent and reactionary behavior so common among its counterparts (see chapters 7, 8, and 9). That the Liberal party led the attack on Britain's aristocratic oligarchy during the late nineteenth century must be understood against the backdrop of the larger transformation it underwent during the late nineteenth and early twentieth centuries.

As we saw in previous chapters, by the late nineteenth century widespread discontent with the inequities and dislocation caused by capitalism placed liberalism under strain across Europe. As one of the great observers of the liberalism of the era, the British intellectual L.T. Hobhouse, noted, if "the nineteenth century might be called the age of Liberalism . . . its close saw the fortunes of that great ideology brought to its lowest ebb. . . . It had the air of a creed that [was] becoming fossilized as an extinct form."[63] In an attempt to stem liberalism's decline, "social" or "new" liberals began calling for a re-evaluation of the movement's traditional ideology and programs. These liberals advocated abandoning liberalism's traditional skepticism towards government intervention in the economy and accepting a role for the state in protecting citizens and society from the vicissitudes of the market; they essentially wanted to maintain the basic structure of the liberal, capitalist order but to ameliorate its worst excesses. Such "social" or "new" liberals appeared in all European countries (and in the United States, where they were called Progressives), but only in Britain did this version of liberalism take over a governing party.[64]

Although outflanked by the Conservatives in 1867, the Liberal party won the first election after its passage in 1868. Led now by Gladstone, between 1868 and 1874 the Liberals passed the Elementary Education Act of 1870, providing essentially universal elementary education; the Trade Union Act of 1871, legalizing membership in trade unions; abolished religious tests for Oxford and Cambridge; modernized the civil service and army by, for example, increasing the role of examinations rather than patronage in the former and abolishing the purchase of officers' commissions in the latter; and reorganized the court system. Gladstone's first ministry also passed several critical voting and electoral reforms. The Ballot Act[65] of 1872 finally gave Britain the secret ballot, thereby striking a major blow against electoral corruption and intimidation and greatly diminishing the ability of the landowning elite to control electoral outcomes. During Gladstone's second ministry from 1880 to 1885 the "Corrupt and Illegal Practices Act" of 1883 further limited the elite's local power by regulating how much and on what candidates could spend money. And finally in 1884 the Parliamentary Reform Act expanded the franchise again, tilting political power "more markedly and more irrevocably than ever away from notables to numbers."[66] Two in three men in England and Wales, about three out of five in Scotland, and about one out of two in Ireland could now vote (the act also equalized franchise provisions across rural and urban areas).[67]

After Gladstone's departure from the political scene, the Liberals moved firmly into the "social" or "new" Liberal camp and struck two critical, perhaps even fatal, blows against what remained of aristocratic oligarchy: the 1909 People's Budget and the 1911 Parliament Act. The key figures in the Liberal party during this time were David Asquith, who became prime minister in 1908, and David Lloyd George, who served as his chancellor of the exchequer. In 1908 Lloyd George proclaimed:

> British Liberalism is not going to repeat the errors of Continental Liberalism. . . . [It] will not abandon [its] traditional ambition to establish freedom and equality; but side by side with this effort it promotes measures for ameliorating the conditions of life for the multitude. . . . The new Liberalism . . . must devote [itself also] to removing the immediate causes of discontent. It is true that men cannot live by bread alone. It is equally true that a man cannot live without bread. . . . [When] poverty is due to circumstances over which the man has no control, then the State should step in to the very utmost limit of its resources, and save the man from the physical and mental torture involved in extreme penury. . . . No country can lay any real claim to civilization that allows . . . its sick, infirm, unemployed, widows and orphans . . . to starve. . . . I do not think the better-off classes, whose comfort is assured, realise the sufferings of the unemployed workmen. What is poverty? Have you felt it yourselves? If not, you ought to thank God for having been spared its sufferings and its temptations. Have you ever seen others enduring it? Then pray God to forgive you, if you have not done your best to alleviate it.[68]

The most important manifestation of this "new" liberal turn came with Lloyd George's 1909 "People's Budget," which proposed financing extensive welfare measures by increased direct taxation of the wealthy, land, and luxury items and the perhaps even more frightening creation of new government bureaucracy to catalog and value landed property.[69] Lloyd George said his budget aimed to wage

> warfare against poverty and squalidness. I cannot help hoping and believing that before this generation has passed away, we shall have advanced a great step towards that good time, when poverty, and the wretchedness and human degradation which always follows in its camp, will be as remote to the people of this country as the wolves which once infested its forests.[70]

Lloyd George took aim at Britain's landowning elite and went on a publicity offensive to rally opposition against them and for his budget. At a speech at Limehouse in July, for example, he referred to the landowning elite as "gentlemen who do not earn [their] wealth. . . . [Their] chief sole function . . . [and] chief pride, is the stately consumption of wealth by produced by others."[71] In October in Newcastle, meanwhile, he quipped that "a fully equipped Duke costs as much to keep up as two Dreadnoughts, and Dukes are just as great a terror, and they last longer." Concerned that the land-owning elites' representatives in the Lords would block his budget, Lloyd George went on to ask, "whether five hundred men, ordinary men, chosen accidentally from among the unemployed, should override the judgment of millions of people who are engaged in the industry which makes the wealth of the country."[72] But override they did, rejecting Lloyd George's budget in November, overturning an over two-hundred-year tradition of the Lords not blocking "money bills" and triggering a showdown between the Upper House and the Liberals. After winning the election triggered by the budget's defeat, the Liberals introduced a "Parliament Bill" that would officially elim-inate the Lords' veto over "money bills" and leave it with only the power to delay legislation for a limited period. To ensure the act's passage, the Liberals secured a promise from the king to create new peers should the Lords reject it. Left with little choice, the Lords passed the Parliament Act in 1911, formally establishing the dominance of the Commons over the Lords, eliminating one of the last and most important political-institutional bulwarks of elite power and marking a definitive break with the aristocratic oligarchic order that had ruled Britain since 1688. If the 1909 People's Budget took direct aim at the landed elite's economic resources and power, the 1911 Parliament Act took direct aim at its political power.[73] As David Cannadine, perhaps the foremost chronicler of the decline of the British landowning elite, has written, "sym-bolically and substantively" with the Parliament Act "the political power of traditional landed society had been broken for good."[74]

However, despite an impressive reform record and their role in dismantling Britain's aristocratic oligarchy, it was not the Liberals but rather the Conservatives who benefited most from the new political reality created by the Second Reform Act. This was partially because the Liberals ended up divided and weakened by the most vexing problem Britain faced during this time—Ireland (see below)—but also because the Conservatives successfully adjusted both their appeal and organizational infrastructure to the decline of aristocratic oligarchy order and the rise of mass politics.[75]

An important figure in the Conservative reorientation after 1867 was Disraeli. Disraeli viewed the Conservatives as Britain's truly "national" party, one that stood "for the interests of the nation as a whole."[76] In his famous 1872 Crystal Palace speech, for example, he said this meant Conservatives must be dedicated to "maintaining our institutions, upholding the empire, and elevating the condition of the people."[77] In addition to its obvious elec-toral benefits, this vision of the Conservatives as a "national" party stemmed from Disraeli's genuine albeit paternalistic belief in the elite's obligation to the less fortunate. Already in 1845, for example, in his well-known novel *Sybil; or the Two Nations* Disraeli brought attention to the horrific conditions facing much of the English working classes and foreshadowed the idea of "one nation conservatism," that is, a Conservatism that overcame societal divisions and re-created a strong sense of community.[78] Disraeli's efforts to create a Conservative party that could compete in the post-1867 era paid off in 1874 when it swept rural areas, made critical gains in urban areas, including among the working class, and formed its first majority government since the 1840s.[79]

In addition to refashioning its appeal, after 1867 the Conservative party also increased its membership, professionalized its campaigns and voter outreach efforts, and strengthened its ties with a variety of affiliated associations, most notably the Primrose League, named after Disraeli's favorite flower, to attract and mobilize voters. By 1886 the Primrose League had two hundred thousand members and by 1890 almost a million; it was a broad-based association "embracing all classes and creeds except atheists and enemies of the British Empire."[80] During the late nineteenth century the Conservatives became something highly unusual: a party that appealed to the working class, middle class, business, and landed elites, making it not merely a "patriotic party" but also a truly national one.[81]

On the eve of the First World War Britain was politically distinctive in critical ways. First, it had a Liberal party that championed suffrage expansion and social reform, and provided a home for Britain's first Labour MPs in the 1870s.[82] The Liberal party in Britain avoided the estrangement from the working class that plagued and diminished the electoral fortunes of so many of its European counterparts by the early twentieth century. A second, and perhaps even more remarkable feature of Britain during this time was its Conservative party, which responded to the decline of the old aristocratic oligarchic order and the rise of the new mass one by modernizing its organizational infrastructure and appeal rather than retrenching into reactionary or extremist political activity.[83] So successful was the Conservative party's modernization that it won more elections in the decades after 1867 than before. It also managed to make the ostensible oxymorons "Tory democracy" and "working class Tory" realities in Britain. The distinctiveness of British liberalism and conservatism helps explain a third unusual feature of prewar Britain: its relatively moderate working class. In contrast to much of the rest of the Europe, neither Marxism, syndicalism, anarchism, nor any other revolutionary ideology gained much traction in Britain. By the early twentieth century much of the working class seemed to believe that it was not necessary to overthrow the country's reigning order, violently eliminate its elites, or definitively separate themselves from other political parties and social groups in order get their demands heard and responded to. And finally, and related to the above, before 1914 Britain's reigning aristocratic oligarchic order had been transformed and the political power of its landowning elite undermined without generating the intransigent, reactionary, and destabilizing political behavior that characterized this process in much of the rest of Europe. There was, however, an exception to this—an issue where many landed elites were willing to stray outside the democratic rules of the game, thereby threatening to create the type of institutional and social upheaval that was so prevalent in much of the rest of Europe during this time. That issue was Ireland.

Although part of the United Kingdom, Ireland was treated like much like a colony with its majority Catholic population subordinated to an "alien," ruling elite that controlled the vast majority of the country's resources (land). By the end of the nineteenth century resentment of British rule had generated growing disorder and violence in Ireland. Unfortunately for Britain and Ireland this issue rose to the top of the political agenda at the same time as the landed elite's political dominance came under sustained attack. Beginning around the 1880s but especially after the 1909 People's Budget and the 1911 Parliament Act, the landed elite felt beleaguered, and attempts to change Ireland's status therefore came to be seen not merely as an assault on the Union and by extension the empire, but also as an attempt to overthrow what remained of the political order that had underpinned British exceptionalism and greatness since 1688.

Once again, the main driver of change was the Liberal party. Gladstone was committed to dealing with, or as he put it "pacifying,"[84] Ireland. During his time in office he tried carrots—disestablishing the Anglican church in Ireland (a church to which few Irish belonged but which was nonetheless their official state church and to which they had to pay tithes) and instituting a long-overdue process of land reform to protect Irish tenant farmers from abuse by their landlords and increase the number of Irish peasant proprietors—as well as sticks—repression—to quell Irish discontent; when neither worked, he concluded that Home Rule was the only solution. In 1866 he therefore introduced a bill that would grant Ireland control over all its affairs, with the exception of defense, foreign policy, and foreign trade.[85]

Home Rule, by threatening the sanctity of the union and by extension raising questions about the empire more generally, elicited an almost unprecedented response. Debate over Gladstone's 1866 bill generated "scenes of excitement for which no parallel could be found since the days of the great Reform"[86] act; it was voted down in the Commons when not only

Conservatives but also ninety-three of Gladstone's fellow Liberals voted against it. So uncompromising was opposition that anti–Home Rule Liberals left their party, forming a new "Liberal Unionist" party that allied with Conservatives in subsequent elections.[87] Home Rule thus became for the Liberals what the Corn Laws had been for the Conservatives a generation or so earlier: an issue that split and weakened the party.[88]

Gladstone managed to come back to power once more, this time as the head of a minority government dependent on the support of Irish Nationalists, and again put forward a Home Rule bill that was defeated in the Lords by the largest majority hitherto recorded there. However, after the passage of the Parliament Act in 1911 the Lords could no longer act as a conservative bulwark, and so when a Liberal government introduced another Home Rule bill in 1912 the stage was set for the gravest challenge to Britain's political stability in modern times.

In response to the threat of Home Rule, Unionists in Ulster[89] began forming militias, and hundreds of thousands of Ulster Unionists pledged to resist Home Rule by force if necessary. Irish Nationalists were also organizing and arming. What made the situation a threat to the Union as well as Britain's overall political stability was the behavior of British elites and Conservatives, who finally seemed willing to embrace the type of intransigent, reactionary defense of the old order and extremist political behavior that characterized so many of their European counterparts. Portraying the Ulster Unionists as defenders not merely of the union and the empire but of the entire tradi-tional political order, many members of the elite and the Conservative party pledged to support them in their fight against Home Rule, even if they resisted with force decisions made by a legitimately elected government. The Conservative leader Andrew Bonar Law, a descendant of Ulster Scots and a staunch Unionist, was particularly provocative. At a huge rally in Belfast in 1912, for example, he and Edward Henry Carson, an Ulster-Unionist leader, declared they would "never under any circumstances . . . submit to Home Rule. . . . We will be ready, when the time comes, to protect our demand with our own right arm and with the manhood of our race."[90] In a July 1912 speech Bonar Law continued pressing this theme, declaring, "I said so to [the Liberals] and I say so now, with the full sense of the responsibility which attaches to my position, that if the attempt be made under present conditions, I can imagine no length of resistance to which Ulster will go, in which I shall not be ready to support them, and in which they will not be supported by the overwhelming majority of the British people."[91]

The situation degenerated until it came to a head in 1914 when the Lords' ability to delay legislation ran out, an unprecedented incident of military

insubordination occurred when some British Army officers threatened to resign rather than fight against the Ulster Unionists, and a "British Covenant"
originally signed by prominent members of the elite but eventually including millions of signatures was presented at Hyde Park and published in
every leading British paper stating that its supporters "feel justified in taking
or supporting any action that may be effective to prevent [Home Rule] being
put into operation, and more particularly to prevent the armed forces of the
Crown being used to deprive the people of Ulster of their rights as citizens of the United Kingdom."[92] Desperate to de-escalate a situation spinning
out of control, the Liberal prime minister, Asquith, proposed a variety of
compromises—for example, to exclude several counties in Ulster from Home
Rule for an unspecified period of time—but was unable to gain agreement on
any. With the United Kingdom facing potentially civil war–like conditions,
the First World War intervened.[93] On the same day the king assented to the
Government of Ireland Act, Asquith suspended it to enable the government
to focus on the war.

The First World War and Its Aftermath

The war allowed Britain to temporarily push aside the most destabilizing
and divisive issue it faced—Ireland—and for most of the war the country was
ruled by a coalition including Liberals and Conservatives. This unity guided
Britain through the final stages of its transition to democracy. Although
many Conservatives were uncomfortable with full democratization,[94] the social leveling and joint suffering that occurred during the war[95] and in particular a recognition that it would be hard not to enfranchise remaining
members of the working class after so many had fought and died for Britain
in the trenches, blunted opposition to universal manhood suffrage. The 1918
Representation of the People Act, sometimes referred to as the fourth reform
act, therefore passed with broad, cross-party support,[96] enfranchising all men
over the age of twenty-one, as well as most women over thirty, thus tripling
the size of the electorate, from about 7.7 million voters in 1912 to 21.4 million in 1918 (see Figure 10.9).

Given how relatively unproblematic the passing of the Representation of
the People Act had been, it is perhaps ironic that it helped bring Britain's
most problematic political issue—Ireland—roaring back to the top of the political agenda.[97] When the first elections under the new suffrage were held in
1918 the Irish Republican party, Sinn Féin, won the Irish vote in a landslide
and declared Ireland's independence from Britain. The British government

responded by pronouncing this move and Sinn Féin illegal and sending in a volunteer fighting force composed largely of British Army veterans[98] to crush the Irish Republican Army. After over two years of fighting, with atrocities committed on both sides,[99] Prime Minister Lloyd George concluded that the only solution was independence and partition. And so in 1922 the Irish Free State was declared, with six counties of Ulster remaining part of the United Kingdom.[100]

Although the reactionary, even extremist, behavior exhibited by the landed elite and Conservatives in conjunction with Irish Home Rule should not be underplayed, what stands out in a comparative perspective is how exceptional this episode was and how few challenges British democracy otherwise faced during the interwar years. With the exception of Ireland, Britain was never threatened by significant right- or left-wing extremism, did not experience significant extra-parliamentary violence, and major political actors respected the democratic rules of the game. To be sure, the war created somewhat fewer problems for Britain than it did many other European countries: it was on the winning side, the war was not fought on its territory, and it experienced fewer deaths percentage-wise than most other combatants.[101] Nonetheless Britain did face challenges besides Ireland. The war turned Britain from a creditor into a debtor nation and its economic performance was poor, even in comparison to the unimpressive record of most other European countries during this time.[102] In addition alongside the loss of Ireland, World War I and its aftermath helped trigger the decline of the British Empire and the country's loss of great-power status. But perhaps most potentially destabilizing was the precipitous demise of the landed elite. This process began before the war with the elimination of the political-institutional bulwarks of the aristocratic oligarchic order, but the war and its aftermath dramatically accelerated prewar trends.

During the war the landed elite sacrificed more of its sons than any other social group: not since the War of the Roses "had the English aristocracy suffered losses such as those which they endured during the Great War."[103] And during the postwar years the landed elite's political, social, and economic power declined further. After 1918 its dominance of the state and bureaucracy came to an end. Before the war, prime ministers were almost always members of the landed elite, but during the interwar years they ceased to be. Before the war almost all cabinets had a clear majority of members drawn from the landed elite, but between 1919 and 1937 only two out of seven did.[104] Up through the late nineteenth and early twentieth centuries the vast majority of MPs in the House of Commons were members of the landed elite or their close relatives, but by the 1930s less than one-tenth of even Conservative MPs were.[105] The landed elite's domination of high-status posts in the army, civil service, and Church was also over.[106] Accompanying the landed elite's political decline was an economic one. This too had its roots in the late nineteenth century—particularly in the economic depression of the 1870s and the cheap agricultural products from the "new" world that began flooding into Europe during this time—but accelerated after the First World War as Britain's general economic difficulties, the continued weakening of the agricultural sector, and vastly increased taxation forced landed elites to sell off their land at an unprecedented rate: one-quarter of the land of England, about one-third of the land in Wales and Scotland, and even more in Ireland was sold during this time, representing a "territorial transfer rivaled only by two other landed revolutions in Britain . . . the Norman Conquest and the Dissolution of the Monasteries."[107] During the interwar period, in short, the landowning elite was in terminal political as well as economic decline.[108]

In many parts of Europe like Germany, Italy, and Spain (see chapters 11, 12, and 13) such a decline spurred a furious backlash by the landed elite against liberal democracy, the working class, and other forces viewed as "responsible" for the collapse of the traditional order and the social and economic hierarchies accompanying it. Although disillusionment with democracy and resentment of the working class certainly existed among the British elite, with the exception of Home Rule this never resulted in the headlong embrace of reactionary, extremist, anti-democratic movements that characterized so many of Britain's European counterparts during the interwar years. The most significant such movement in Britain, Oswald Mosley's British Union of Fascists, was never more than a marginal political force, having perhaps twenty thousand members at its height and achieving derisory electoral results. Instead, during the interwar period Britain remained dominated by two comparatively moderate political parties,[109] both of which played by the democratic rules of the game and helped integrate into the existing political order groups that in other parts of Europe ended up alienated from it.

Perhaps surprisingly, the largest beneficiary of Britain's transition to universal suffrage were the Conservatives: between 1918 and 1935 they gained the largest share of the vote in six out of seven general elections. The Conservatives' remarkable electoral success reflected the party's continued evolution: during the interwar years it further shed its image as the representative of the landowning elite and became a center-right party anchored in business and the middle class. The party continued to stress "one nation" conservatism, embracing nationalism and communitarianism, which enabled it to attract a wide range of voters, including a not insignificant amount from the working class.[110] Alongside the dominance of the Conservative party, the other major electoral development that occurred during the interwar years was the replacement of the Liberals by Labour as Britain's "second" party.

The Liberal party's problems began in the prewar period, but the war divided and weakened the party further, splitting it between supporters of Asquith and Lloyd George, with the former staying outside the coalition government that the latter led. The Labour party, on the other hand, was greatly strengthened by the war and its aftermath. Between 1914 and 1919 Britain experienced immense social leveling, as the country drew together as a result of the war and the sacrifices it required.[111] Between 1914 and 1918 the government also dramatically increased its control over the economy, transforming a "planned economy" from a great fear into a reality. And the demands of a war-time economy and the labor shortages associated with it dramatically increased the power of labor and the trade unions. And of course, after 1918, the working class was fully enfranchised. Somewhat similar developments increased the electoral fortunes of other European left parties after 1918, but the postwar boost experienced by the British Labour party was not dissipated by the devastating splits and revolutionary fantasies that plagued so many other left parties during the interwar years. This was probably because during the prewar period Labour had been comparatively unencumbered by radicalism in general and skepticism of "bourgeois" democracy in particular, and so it was less susceptible to the siren song of communism. Thus when Labour formed its first government in 1924 it could focus on placating the "center" and convincing the electorate that it was committed to "governing in the interests of the nation as a whole"[112] without having to worry about protecting its flank from an extreme left competitor as did socialist parties in France, Italy, Germany, and elsewhere.

On the eve of the Great Depression Britain was thus in a very different position than most other European countries. Most notably, it was dominated by two comparatively moderate parties: the Conservatives on the right which had successfully cultivated a large and comparatively broad electoral base by stressing its commitment to Britain's constitution and Empire, leaving little room for the rise of a populist right-wing alternative, and on the left by Labour which had successfully avoided the radicalism and divisions that alienated much of the working class from democracy and weakened and in some cases destroyed the left in so many other European countries during the interwar years. Although the Great Depression did not hit Britain as hard as it did other countries in Europe, what is most distinctive about the country during this time is the political response to it. Rather than generating centripetal political tendencies and destroying the center, as it did in most other European countries, the Great Depression had a centrifugal effect and brought mainstream parties together. The first political "beneficiary" of the Depression was Labour, which formed its second government after the 1929 election. But when Labour proved unable to stem rising unemployment, growing deficits, and the collapse of the pound,[113] it was succeeded by a "National Government" formed by prime minister Ramsey MacDonald that included Labour, Conservative, and Liberal members. Two months after its formation this National Government won a huge vote of confidence in national elections (although the Conservatives rather than Labour were the big winners) and such National or coalition governments proceeded to guide Britain not only through the Great Depression but also through the even darker hours of the Second World War.[114]

Conclusions

Why was Britain not rocked by the political instability that characterized so much of Europe during the interwar period? World War I and its aftermath created fewer problems for Britain than for some other countries, but equally if not more important was Britain's ability to successfully confront them— something that can only be understood by examining the country's prewar political development. Across much of Europe the immensely difficult interwar period deepened and exacerbated already existing social, economic, and political divisions. Many European countries were also forced to construct new political institutions, and in the central and eastern parts of the continent, new nations and states (see chapter 15) when they made transitions to democracy after the First World War. Although Britain also made a transition to democracy in 1918 with the achievement of universal suffrage, it retained essentially the same political institutions it had since 1688, institutions that had already adapted to the social, economic, and political challenges of the nineteenth and early twentieth centuries and consequently were stronger and more legitimate than those characterizing most other European countries. This unusual political development trajectory, in turn, was largely the result of the comparatively puzzling behavior of Britain's landowning elites.

At the beginning of the nineteenth century Britain's landowning elite was the most powerful in Europe, enjoying a degree of political, social, and economic power unmatched by its counterparts in other European countries.

> About 7,000 families owned about 80% of the land in the British Isles. . . . The top . . . families had estates and treasures virtually

without comparison anywhere in the world. . . . Their social status was intact and alone. They dominated the church, the judiciary, the army, the law, the civil service, the House of Commons, and of course, the House of Lords. By any measure, the [British] aristocracy were an [incomparable] elite in terms of status, power, and wealth.[115]

Yet by the end of the interwar period this was all almost gone. As Tocqueville once put it, as a general rule "an aristocracy seldom yields without a protracted struggle, in the course of which implacable animosities are kindled between different classes of society,"[116] and certainly in most of the rest of Europe, landowning elites responded to their political, economic, and social decline with intransigent and reactionary defenses of the reigning order that created deep social divisions and political and institutional upheaval.[117] In Britain, however, a different pattern emerged. When faced with growing demands for political, economic, and social change during the nineteenth and early twentieth centuries the British elite behaved relatively moderately, gradually, if grudgingly, accepting reform. It is important to stress that this acceptance was strategic: many elites believed that by allowing limited or controlled change, they could forestall radicalism, promote political stability, and preserve the essence of the country's aristocratic oligarchic order. The British elite seem thus to have taken to heart the counsel given to one of their Sicilian counterparts in Giuseppe di Lampedusa's great novel of aristocratic decline, *The Leopard*: "For things to remain the same, everything must change." The main exception to this pattern was Home Rule, where members of the landed elite did exhibit intransigent, reactionary behavior. However important this episode was, from a comparative perspective what stands out is its exceptional nature: the response to Home Rule was not part of a broader extremist reaction to political, economic, and social change dating back to the late nineteenth century nor did it accelerate into a full-blown embrace of anti-democratic, pseudo-fascist radicalism during the interwar period.[118]

Ultimately, of course, just like its counterparts in the rest of Europe, the British landed elite was unable to preserve either the old order or its dominance of it. Britain's aristocratic oligarchic order was eventually transformed into a democratic one, although if we take 1688 as the starting point, it took an extremely long time—at least 230 years—for this transformation to be completed. However, in critical ways the British elite's strategy was a remarkable and certainly a comparative success. As noted, its gradual if grudging acceptance of reform helped forestall radicalism and promote political stability during the nineteenth and early twentieth centuries, a time when most of the rest of Europe was plagued by the former and lacking in the latter. In addition, the relative moderation of the British elite helped it hold on to its dominant position longer than most of its European counterparts. Up through the late nineteenth century the British elite enjoyed a combination and concentration of political power, economic resources, and social status unrivaled in the rest of Europe. It was really only with the First World War that this came to an end, and even after losing its political power, the landed elite did not entirely lose either its wealth or social status—and of course for another generation at least, it also had the empire to fall back on. Its relative moderation, in short, allowed the British landowning elite to go into a sort of "voluntary retirement"[119] during the twentieth century, whereas in much of the rest of Europe it took violence and conflict—often of an extreme and revolutionary nature as in France, Germany, or Russia—to bring the old order and the landed elites who were its main advocates and beneficiaries to an end.[120]

CHAPTER II

The Collapse of Democracy and
the Rise of Fascism in Italy

[Italy's crisis] consists precisely in the fact that the old order is dying
and the new cannot be born; in this interregnum, a great variety of
morbid symptoms appear.

—Antonio Gramsci[1]

DEMOCRACY SURVIVED IN both France and Britain during the interwar years but collapsed in many other European countries. In some
places democratic collapse led to the rise of an entirely new type of dictatorship. Unlike traditional dictatorships that aimed to restore or protect
the institutions and elites of the old order, fascist and National Socialist
dictatorships aimed to get rid of them. Also unlike traditional dictatorships,
fascism and national socialism were revolutionary as well as reactionary: they
championed traditional views of gender, family, and other aspects of personal
and communal life, but also aimed to mobilize and transform their citizens
and societies in hitherto unimaginable ways. And also unlike traditional
dictatorships, fascism and National Socialism were truly modern political
phenomena: they were masters and products of mass politics; garnered broad,
cross-class support; provided ideological justifications for their actions; and
claimed to be the legitimate representatives of "the people."

This chapter examines why democracy collapsed and was replaced by fascism in interwar Italy. In Italy, as in France and Britain, understanding interwar political outcomes requires examining both the pre– and post–World
War I periods. Italy entered the First World War with a deeply divided

society and a relatively weak and illegitimate state (see chapter 7). The war and its aftermath intensified existing social divisions and problems and created new ones. By the early 1920s the Italian state had lost control over parts of its territory, and its citizens had lost faith in mainstream political institutions. Fascism, meanwhile, had transformed itself from a marginal movement of disgruntled nationalists, syndicalists, and ex-veterans into a mass movement promising to provide what Italy's post-unification liberal and democratic orders had not: a strong state capable of uniting Italians and asserting the country internationally. Although the Fascist regime was not able to fully achieve its goals, it did change the nature of and relationship among Italy's state, society, and economy more than any previous regime. In order to understand how and why it was able to do this, we need to pick up the story of Italian political development where chapter 7 left off: on the eve of the First World War.

The First World War and Its Aftermath

By the early twentieth century Italy was in a precarious political position. Many had hoped or assumed that unification would solve Italy's problems: economic growth and land reform would occur, social and regional divisions would disappear, national cohesion and identification would increase, and the country would be propelled into great-power status. Although there was progress, improvements were slow and uneven, and disillusionment and dissatisfaction grew during the late nineteenth and early twentieth centuries. The nature of the post-unification political order made things worse: initially highly unrepresentative, even as the suffrage expanded during the late nineteenth and early twentieth centuries, deep-seated corruption and political elites' penchant for deal-making and collusion meant average citizens had relatively little impact on political outcomes. As a result, Italians began throwing their support to socialist and nationalist movements committed to destroying the reigning order. Onto these challenges, the First World War layered new ones.

Most immediately, the war produced a new cleavage between abstentionists and interventionists. Italy initially stayed out of the war, but disagreement over whether it should participate in a conflict that rapidly dragged in much of the rest of Europe grew, with a sizable minority of Italians, including nationalists, some dissident socialists, including Benito Mussolini, and parts of the liberal elite agitating for intervention. Italy did eventually join the war on the Allied side, but the way it did so set the stage for problems down the road: Italian leaders negotiated the country's entry without consulting the public or Parliament and ultimately agreed to bring Italy into the war against Austria and Germany in return for territorial gains agreed upon in the secret 1915 Treaty of London. As a result, unlike in most other European countries Italy did not enter the war buoyed by mass enthusiasm or the support of its main parties.

And the war proved a fiasco. Italy's army fared poorly against the Central Powers, suffering over six hundred thousand deaths and a million casualties; hundreds of thousands of its soldiers were permanently disabled. In addition to the war's immense material and human costs, its end created new problems. Italy's poor military performance led the British and French to regret the territorial promises they made in the Treaty of London and Woodrow Wilson was infuriated by these secret agreements in any case. And so, despite protests and even a walk-out, Italy's leaders were forced to give up most of the territories they had been promised; when they returned home, they were met with outrage and disappointment. Nationalists in particular viewed Italy's treatment as humiliating and further proof that the reigning order and its elites had to go.

The end of the war also brought immense economic challenges. Italy financed the war largely via borrowing and monetary expansion, and so by its end the country was highly indebted, its currency was weakening, and it was prone to high inflation.[2] By 1919 price increases were causing widespread rioting. GDP fell dramatically, by about 14.5 percent in 1919, 7.6 percent in 1920, and 1.8 percent in 1921,[3] and by the end of the war Italy's north-south divide had worsened, since most war industries and the boom that followed them were located in the already industrialized north. And when the war ended and these industries collapsed, unemployment shot up. This along with an explosion in union membership—in 1918 about 250,000 Italians were union members, by 1919 the figure was 1.2 million—spurred a wave of strikes. The situation in the countryside was also dire. Between 1915 and 1918 millions of peasants and agricultural laborers were forced to serve in the army, and to keep them happy the government promised them land reform and other benefits. When these promises went largely unfulfilled, peasants began seizing land.[4]

Dealing with such challenges would have required a strong, united government, which Italy did not have. As in most other European countries, the Socialists (PSI) emerged from the war as Italy's strongest party but it had long been skeptical of democracy and uninterested in cooperating with "bourgeois" parties (see chapter 7); the war and the Russian Revolution radicalized the party further. The postwar PSI included factions ranging from an extreme left led by Amadeo Bordiga that supported the Bolsheviks, insisted that revolution was "right and around the corner," and rejected democracy and all compromises with "bourgeois" institutions,[5] to a right-wing, led by Filippo Turati and committed to democratic socialism, but it was dominated by its "Maximalist" faction.[6] Maximalists supported the Russian Revolution and were committed to "revolution," but differed from the extreme left in believing that this might occur without violence and insurrectionism. Maximalist dominance was reflected in the resolutions passed by the PSI's first postwar congress in 1919, which proclaimed the party's support for the "dictatorship of the proletariat," condemned the national parliament as a "bourgeois" institution, and declared that "the proletariat would resort to the use of force to defend itself against bourgeois violence, or conquer power" while also permitting socialists to participate in elections—although not national governments—which it justified by claiming that victory at the polls would only "hasten the destruction of parliament and 'the organs of bourgeois domination.'"[7]

Italy's second-largest postwar party was the *Partito Popolare Italiano* (PPI), or Catholic party. As discussed in chapter 7, after Italian unification the pope barred Catholics from political participation. By the end of the First World War, however, it was clear that Italy was not going away and socialism was a growing threat. As a result, the pope decided to accept the formation of a Catholic party to defend the Church's interests.[8] From the perspective of democracy, however, the new party had critical drawbacks. It was extremely heterogenous, supported by Catholics from various classes and regions who shared little beyond their religious identity and loyalty to the Church. This, along with the Church's long-standing distrust of democracy and secular political parties, hindered the PPI's ability to form stable political alliances or coherent policy positions and attenuated its commitment to democracy. Its loyalty to democracy, using concepts discussed in chapter 1, was not principled but conditional—dependent on the adoption of policies that satisfied its particular constituency.[9]

Italy's first postwar election in 1919 made clear how much the nature of the PSI and PPI complicated the functioning of democracy. These elections confirmed the PSI as Italy's largest party with 32.3 percent of the vote and the PPI as its second, with 20.5 percent. Together these parties had a majority in Parliament, but the Catholics disliked the Socialists, and the Socialists had already made clear that they wanted nothing to do with "bourgeois" parties and were uninterested in governing in any case. As a result, the government formed after the 1919 elections was led by Francesco Saverio Nitti, whose new Liberal-Democratic-Radical party had come in third, receiving

15.9 percent of the vote. The absence of the country's largest party from government, and indeed its hostility to democracy overall, was particularly problematic. As Mussolini, who had by this time left the party to build his own revolutionary movement (see below), perceptively noted:

> The marvelous victory at the polls has simply shown up the ineffi-
> ciency and weakness of the socialists. They are impotent alike as
> reformers and revolutionaries. They take . . . action . . . [n]either [in]
> the parliament [n]or the streets. The sight of a party wearing itself
> out on the morrow of a great victory in a vain search for something to
> apply its strength to, and willing to attempt neither reform nor revo-
> lution, amuses us. This is our vengeance and it has come sooner than
> we hoped![10]

The consequences of the new government's weakness, the PSI's absence from it, and its antagonism to democracy more generally were quickly tested by a massive wave of unrest that hit Italy between 1919 and 1920 and came to be known as the *Biennio Rosso*, or Red Biennium. Worker discontent was already on the rise when a factory council movement sprang up in Turin, a stronghold of an extreme left-wing socialist faction headed by Antonio Gramsci.[11] These councils were organizations of workers, seen by Gramsci's group as proto-Soviets preparing for the not-too-distant day when the prole- tariat would control the economy. The council movement spread throughout 1920, generating massive strikes, factory occupations, and lockouts. By the end of the year almost 1.3 million workers had participated in these movements "and many had begun to insist that they, and not the owners and managers, were in charge of their industries."[12] As one commentator noted, to many "this seemed to be nothing short of the revolution itself."[13]

The Italian left was divided over how to respond. The PSI claimed that the situation was revolutionary, but union leaders argued that pushing be- yond economic issues to initiate a political transition would be disastrous. At one point, the union leader Ludovico D'Aragona offered the socialists leadership of the movement, telling them, "You think that this is the time to begin a revolutionary action, well, then, you assume the responsibility. We who do not feel able to assume this responsibility of pushing the prole- tariat to suicide, we tell you that we retire and submit our resignations."[14] Ultimately workers voted to limit the movement's aims, and although os- tensibly thwarted, the PSI leadership was also somewhat relieved: Having long proclaimed their advocacy of revolution but never preparing for it, its leaders had no idea how to actually bring about the end of the reigning "bourgeois" order.[15] Still, after having been continuously told that revolution was imminent, many workers felt robbed of their victory and betrayed by their leaders. The PSI's rhetorical commitment to revolution combined with its inability or unwillingness to actually make one fed resentment against the Maximalist leadership and deepened divisions within the party.

If workers were upset, employers and many parts of the middle class were horrified. The council movement's threats to property and management prerogatives, combined with an impressive showing by the Socialists during local elections in 1920 (see below), confirmed their worst fears. Making matters worse from their perspective, during the crisis the national government had chosen not to intervene at least partially because its current leader, Giolitti, calculated that the council movement would burn itself out and the use of troops would only play "into the hands of the revolutionaries."[16] He was right, of course, but his refusal to take action led many to believe that liberals and the existing democratic order more generally could not or would not defend their interests.

As discontent with the government grew and the situation in the country became increasingly chaotic, the Socialists remained wrapped up in their own internecine battles. Although enthusiasm within the PSI for joining the Communist International had been high, when Moscow informed the party that in order to join, it would have to expel all its "reformists" (that is, Turati and his supporters), end its relationship with the labor unions, and change its name to "Communist," some balked. At the PSI's 1921 congress, leftists favored accepting these conditions, but the Maximalists, while claiming to be committed to Moscow's objectives, were reluctant to launch a purge. When the congress voted to support the Maximalists' position and reject the deal, Bordiga, Gramsci, and their allies walked out and formed the Italian Communist Party (PCI).[17] Italy's left now included a party committed to insurrectionary activity and even more opposed to liberal democracy than the PSI. With the formation of the PCI, Turati and other reformists tried to convince the PSI to join a coalition with other democratic parties to counter the growing turmoil in the country, but the party's Maximalist leaders refused.

While growing social conflict and political disorder increased disarray on the left, it had the opposite effect on the right. Indeed, Italy's turmoil invigorated a marginal fascist movement. Benito Mussolini and like-minded colleagues formed the fascist movement in March 1919. (The Italian term *fasci* comes from bundles of sticks wrapped around an ax carried by magisterial attendants in Ancient Rome and was therefore meant to invoke the unity, power, and glory currently eluding Italy.) Mussolini began his political career as a socialist, but never fit easily in the party. During the prewar period he advocated a syndicalist-influenced socialism that rejected the economic determinism and political passivity of orthodox Marxism and instead favored direct action as the means to achieve revolutionary ends.[18] Mussolini called for a "revolutionary revision of socialism" and moving beyond socialists' traditional focus on the working class in order to become the representative of "the people" or "the nation."[19] Mussolini's shift away from mainstream socialism was accelerated by the First World War. The inability of the Socialist International to prevent the outbreak of hostilities and the decision by almost all of its constituent parties to support their own country's war effort confirmed for Mussolini the strength of nationalism and the bankruptcy of internationalism. He was soon speaking of the "necessity of shaking oneself free of 'dogma'" and declaring that "We Socialists . . . have never examined the problems of nations. The International never occupied itself with them," and as a result was overtaken by events. "We must find . . . a conciliation between the nation, which is a historic reality, and class, which is a living reality."[20] At the end of 1914, he called for a reconsideration of Socialist support for neutrality and was finally expelled from the PSI.

As the war progressed, Mussolini drifted further away from mainstream socialism, and by its end he had openly abandoned the notion of class struggle, which he now referred to as "a vain formula, without effect and consequence,"[21] and replaced it with nationalist rhetoric and an emphasis on national solidarity. Drawing on the idea of Italy as a "proletarian nation" (see chapter 7), he argued that Italians must be united in order for Italy to reach its potential. This required expanding economic production and defending the country against enemies and competitors—endeavors that would, in turn, create a national cohesion that transcended class conflicts.[22] Mussolini thus abandoned an emphasis on the proletariat, instead increasingly talking about "productive classes" rather than "oppressed" and "oppressors."[23] When Mussolini finalized his break with socialism and helped form the Fasci di Combattimento in 1919, his new movement combined nationalist and socialist themes, rejected liberalism and democracy, and said it aimed to represent "the people."[24]

Initially the Fasci met with little success. In 1919 it faced a socialist movement at the height of its popularity, while on the right Gabriele D'Annunzio was capturing the imaginations of veterans and Italian nationalists.[25] D'Annunzio had established himself before the war as a flamboyant literary figure, but when the war broke out he increasingly turned his attention from literature to politics, becoming a prominent nationalist and agitating for Italy's entry into the war, which he saw as an opportunity to "reinvigorate" and "cleanse" a feeble and decadent society.[26] Then he proudly entered military service, reveling in the excitement of the new flying machines, from which he threw his own propaganda pamphlets. Like many others, however, he was angered that Italy was not given the spoils secretly promised by the Allies. In order to right this perceived wrong and in defiance of the Italian government, in 1919 D'Annunzio led a few thousand veterans and disgruntled nationalists to seize the city of Fiume, a formerly Habsburg Adriatic port city with a large Italian-speaking population that the nationalists felt rightly belonged to Italy. (It had instead been awarded to the Kingdom of Serbs, Croats, and Slovenes established after the war.) D'Annunzio's Fiume adventure collapsed by the end of 1920, although not without highlighting the weakness of the Italian government, which had not been able or willing to capture Fiume itself or, at least initially, stop D'Annunzio and his supporters from doing so.

During its first two years of existence (1919–1920) the Fasci's support was limited to a few thousand workers from urban industrial areas, dissatisfied veterans, and a ragtag bunch of former revolutionary syndicalists.[27] The collapse of D'Annunzio's Fiume adventure and the chaos that began consuming Italy during 1920 handed the Fasci a golden opportunity. The deepening of the country's postwar problems, culminating in the Red Biennium, further divided the left and made much of the business community and middle classes fearful of the Socialists. The liberal government's seeming unwillingness to take a forceful stand against factory occupations, and the Socialists, meanwhile, convinced many Italians that neither the liberals nor the democratic regime more generally could or would protect their interests. And with D'Annunzio's star in decline, there was a space open on the right. As one observer notes:

> it seems fair to say in the early 1920s the majority of Italians of all classes lost confidence in the [democratic] regime. The masses of urban and rural workers were hostile to it, and their militant leaders had been openly defying it on numerous occasions. The Nittian and especially Giolittian formulae of neutrality followed by compromise . . . failed to win over the workers while alienating the employers. . . . [T]he landowners, much of big business, and lower middle class people were . . . envious of the workers whose economic status had risen in comparison with theirs, and who feared that any new "concessions" would further threaten their already precarious position in Italian society. Part of [the problem stemmed from these groups'] feeling of bewilderment and helplessness in the face of rapid changes that they did not understand and that seemed to be passing them by.[28]

Since liberal parties were most directly associated with the reigning political order—being in power at the national level up through 1921 and providing Italy's first postwar prime ministers (Orlando, Nitti, and Giolitti)—they paid the heaviest price for growing discontent. During the postwar years, the liberal movement grew increasingly divided.[29] In addition, although they had ruled the country since unification, during the interwar period liberals could not govern alone, initially relying on the support of the PPI. Alongside their tenuous hold on power at the national level, liberals also lost support at the local level. By the November 1920 municipal elections the PSI and PPI controlled about 50 percent of town councils and regions.[30] The growing power of the former in particular combined with the fears created by the Red Biennium and the sense that liberal governments would not or could not protect them, led businessmen and especially large landowners to look for new ways to defend their interests. Into this breach stepped Mussolini and the Fasci, asserting themselves as the force that could restore order and stability and champion the people who felt they lacked one.

Focusing more now on agricultural and rural areas, which felt ignored by the government and threatened by the socialists, and under the banner of a "war against Bolshevism," fascists took control of towns and villages and offered jobs and other resources to potential supporters. Fascists used what we would today consider terrorist means to achieve their ends: armed bands regularly beat and killed their opponents and/or destroyed their homes and property. These Fascist campaigns were remarkably successful. While over one million strikers stalked the Italian countryside in 1920, the number dropped to eighty thousand a year later. This triumph, combined with movement's general vigor—which stood in stark contrast to the government's passivity—brought it support from both landowners and nervous agricultural workers resentful of the socialists' power and particularly their control over employment in many rural areas.[31]

The Fascist moved quickly to lock in rural support. In 1921, for example, the fascists published an agrarian program that played on the deep unpopularity of the PSI's calls for nationalization of the land and began to chart a new course—one that exploited widespread fears of capitalism, while promising to protect private property. Mussolini declared:

> in opposition to the social-communists we want the land to belong not
> to the state but to the cultivator. Whereas social-communism tends to
> disinherit all, and to transform every cultivator into an employee of
> the State, we wish to give the ownership of the land and economic

freedom to the greatest number of peasants. In place of the sovereignty of a central political caste, we support the sovereignty of the peasant.[32]

The program also promised the "creation of a new 'rural democracy' based on peasant landownership," and criticized absentee or "parasitic" landlords.[33]

If rising disorder and government inaction provided an opportunity for Fascism, another was provided by the miscalculation of political elites. As noted above, lacking enough support to govern alone, by 1920 Italian liberals needed allies to govern. When time came for general elections to be held in May 1921, Giolitti made a fateful decision to include the Fascists in his electoral coalition. Given Giolitti's and Italy's history, this decision made some sense. Giolitti had long been the master of *trasformismo* (see chapter 7): throughout his decades in power he had coopted political opponents via compromises and deals, and he believed he could do the same with Fascists. He told a colleague, for example, that he would make Fascists respectable and acclimatize them to the rules of the game just as he had other groups.[34] Giolitti also believed he could use the Fascists to neutralize or counterbalance the Socialists, who, despite his previous efforts, had remained immune to his charms[35] (see chapter 7). This time, however, Giolitti's machinations did not pay off. The election resulted in diminished support for liberals and an increasingly fragmented party system. Together parties of the liberal-center got fewer than 30 percent of the parliamentary seats, 9 percent fewer than in 1919. In addition, whereas before the election liberals were divided into three different groups, after there were five factions, hindering coordination and coalition building. Among the other main parties the Populari gained eight seats and the PSI lost thirty-three. Alongside the growing proliferation of parties and factions, the Parliament was made more unworkable by the growth of explicitly anti-democratic parties: thirty-five fascists, fifteen communists, ten nationalists, and twenty-seven semi-loyal agrarians were also elected.[36] Alongside giving the fascists an electoral boost, Giolitti's inclusion of them in his "national bloc" also gave them an air of "respectability."[37]

By the time the Fascists held their next congress in Rome in November 1921, the movement had been transformed. Two years earlier, it was a small urban group with 870 members; now it was a mass movement with over 300,000 members. Fascism's shifting profile was reflected in the new program adopted at the congress, which aimed to appeal to a wide range of voters: it toned down some of the socialist radicalism of the 1919 program while still playing to widespread fears of the market and capitalism; it also forcefully emphasized the need to create a strong state that could foster national solidarity. The program declared that "disorderly clashes between divergent class and socioeconomic interests [had to] be disciplined," and recognized "national society" as the most fundamental "form of social organization." It offered various ways of reducing class conflict, emphasizing corporatist solutions such as the granting of legal recognition to organizations "representing workers and employers so that they may, in turn, be made legally responsible," and promoting "national solidarity and . . . the development of production." The program also called for various social welfare measures and promised that the movement would act for the good of the nation rather than any particular group.[38]

With regard to capitalism and private property, the program presented a mixed message in order to appeal to those eager to protect their property as well as those who felt the current economic order was stacked against them. The program declared that "The National Fascist party advocates a regime that would strive to increase our national wealth by unleashing individual enterprises and energies—the most powerful and industrious factor in economic production—and by abolishing, once and for all, the rusty, costly, and unproductive machinery of state, society, and municipality-based control." It promised to return some state-owned or controlled enterprises to the private sector and to support small landowners. It also, however, made clear Fascism's intent to "restore the ethical principle that governments ought to administer the commonwealth as a function of the nation's supreme interest," and stressed that private property carried responsibilities as well as privileges. "At once a right and a duty, private property is the form of management that society has traditionally granted individuals so that they may increase the overall patrimony."[39]

Fascism had morphed from a marginal group of discontents into a mass movement with an appeal, program, and support base that differed from its competitors. Not easily placed on either the left or the right, its rhetoric and policy offered something to practically all groups dissatisfied with the existing liberal-led democratic order. The Fascists presented themselves as opponents of "Bolshevism" and the best guardians of private property,[40] while stressing the "social duties" of property, emphasizing the collective good, and criticizing absentee landlords and "exploitative" capitalists. They also promised to finally provide Italy with a state that could unite Italians and promote the country internationally. The ability to link a fundamental critique of the reigning liberal democratic order and capitalism's "excesses" with a commitment to private property and a promise to achieve an "active" revolution that would finally create a strong, united Italy (see chapter 7) helped fascism become the country's first true "people's party"—one that "came close to representing the overall social structure of Italy."[41] Emboldened by its growing support and the government's toleration of its terrorism, during 1921, fascists continued their street-level violence and takeover of towns and villages.

While the Fascists were growing stronger and bolder, other parties sank further into disarray. As already mentioned, the liberal parties had been losing the hearts and minds of Italians for some time. By July 1921 even Giolitti, the great survivor, had lost his majority in Parliament and resigned. The PSI, meanwhile, had neither the will nor ability to mount a strong defense of the system, and the other main force in Italian political life, the PPI, was plagued by divisions and disagreements.[42] There was, in short, no clear foundation upon which to build stable democratic majority governments. After Giolitti, Ivan Bonomi became prime minister. Bonomi had been a member of the PSI before the war, but had joined the interventionist camp and become a leader of a group of Socialists expelled from the PSI. It was hoped his background might enable him to mediate between left and right. Neither side, however, was truly interested in cooperating, and Bonomi's cabinet quickly collapsed in February 1922. Bonomi was replaced by Luigi Facta, who came from the Liberal Union party. By this point, Fascists controlled entire areas of Italy. Early in 1922, for example, Italo Balbo, a Fascist leader, wrote about the situation in Ferrara, which he had occupied with his forces: "We are masters of the situation. We have not only broken the resistance of our enemies, but we also control the organs of the state. The prefect has to submit to the orders given by me in the name of the Fascists."[43] The main challenge facing Facta, therefore, was re-establishing the government's authority over its own territory, but without the support of the PPI and/or PSI, this could not be done via parliamentary majorities—so Facta began considering constitutional revisions to enhance the government's power. Political, business, military, and Church elites, meanwhile, had concluded that the only way to restore order and beat back "Bolshevism" was by reaching an understanding with Mussolini and the Fascists.[44]

The final stage in his drama began in October 1922 when the sitting government fell into crisis and Rome buzzed with talk that the Fascists were mobilizing for a seizure of power. Prime Minister Facta resigned after the king refused his request for a declaration of a state of siege so that he could move forcefully against the Fascists. Few scholars believe that the Fascists were strong enough to seize power on their own had the army been called out.[45] As Umberto Banchelli, a Fascists squad leader in Florence, wrote in 1922: "It must be admitted that the reason fascism developed so quickly and was given so free a hand was that in the breasts of officials and officers beat Italian hearts, which welcomed us gladly as we marched to the rescue."[46]

Perhaps recognizing that a coup attempt would likely fail, Mussolini was initially prepared to accept participation in a coalition government, but as the weakness of other forces and the willingness of many elites to tolerate him became clear, he declared that he would accept nothing less than the prime ministership. At this point the king, who had been more or less sidelined from politics, played an important role. Over-estimating perhaps the strength of the Fascists (there was talk that one hundred thousand Fascists were ready to march on Rome when in reality there were only a few tens of thousands and these were divided into different poorly armed and resourced groups) and perhaps fearful that if he resisted and failed, the Fascists would replace him with his more militaristic and dashing cousin, the Duke of Aosta, and with myriad voices urging him to bring the fascists into the government, the king decided not to call out the army and instead invited Mussolini to Rome. On the night of October 29–30 Mussolini took the train to Rome, arriving on the morning of the thirtieth and making his way to the palace. Rather than a coup, for Mussolini the March on Rome was a nice train ride; he came to power via the connivance of elites, rather than by winning an election or firing a shot.[47]

The Fascist Regime

After coming to power Mussolini faced three main challenges: dismantling the remnants of liberal democracy, gaining full control over his movement, and creating the strong state and national unity he promised Italians. He was very successful at the first, fairly successful at the second, and less successful at the third.

Once he became prime minister Mussolini began eliminating his opposition using the decree powers he had been granted by Parliament after coming to power and taking advantage of the weak, indeed, almost non-existent resistance initially put up by most other parties.[48] Mussolini gradually purged non-Fascist ministers from his government, passed an electoral law that all but guaranteed Fascists control of Parliament (the Acerbo Law),[49] and chipped away at parties and organizations not already under fascist control.[50] A critical stage in fascism's consolidation of power began on May 30, 1924, when a socialist deputy named Giacomo Matteotti gave a speech bitterly denouncing the recently held 1924 elections, claiming (correctly) that there had been widespread fraud and violence. Some days afterward, Matteotti disappeared, and was later found with a knife stuck in his chest. Five Fascists were eventually arrested for the attack. The murder elicited a storm of protest; the main opposition parties walked out of Parliament, and the press accused the fascists of barbarism. The affair prompted Fascist extremists to threaten a new wave of violence unless Mussolini took forceful action against the opposition. But rather than folding in the face of pressures from within his own movement and without, Mussolini went on the offensive. In January 1925, he proclaimed that he alone "assume[d] the political, moral, and historical responsibility for all that has happened. . . . If fascism has been a criminal association, if all the acts of violence have been the result of a certain historical, political, and moral climate, the responsibility for this is mine."[51] Mussolini then used the uproar created by the Matteotti crisis to tighten his hold over the fascist movement and then Italy itself.

Given Italy's extreme regionalism it is perhaps not surprising that Fascism evolved not as a centralized political movement but rather as a collection of local and regional units that shared the broad goal of creating a strong state and a powerful, unified Italy but were otherwise somewhat disparate. Although Mussolini was Fascism's leader, up through the mid-1920s his control over the party was not absolute.[52] The Matteotti crisis made this clear: while the penchant of many *squadristri* (members of the fascist squads) for independent action and violence had been useful in destabilizing democracy, the tendency of local and regional leaders to "go it alone" threatened Mussolini's hold on power. After Matteotti's murder Mussolini moved to centralize his control by reigning in the fascist squads, purging intransigents, appointing a new party secretary, and establishing a more top-down, hierarchical command structure within the National Fascist party (PNF, *Partito Nazionale Fascista*).[53]

With his control over the party more firmly established, Mussolini then turned to subordinating the party to the state. During the second half of the 1920s Mussolini stressed the "'solemn subordination of the party to the State' and insisted that it was essential not to confuse the 'Partito Nazionale Fascista, which is the primordial political force of the regime, with the regime itself.'"[54] With this began what is sometimes referred to as Fascism's totalitarian phase or "second wave,"[55] during which Mussolini began using the state to construct the "New Italy"[56] Fascism had long promised.

As noted above, much of Fascism's appeal and particularly its ability to attract supporters from a wide range of backgrounds came from its promise to provide what the *Risorgimento* had not: a strong state that would unite or finally "make Italians" and begin the national "regeneration" so many felt the country needed.[57] Indeed, strengthening the state was an obsession for the Fascists: "Everything within the state, nothing outside the State, nothing against the State" became Mussolini's well-known maxim.[58] During the second half of the 1920s and early 1930s Mussolini increased his control over the national state by "fascistizing" key institutions like the police, eliminating any remaining opposition, and exerting greater influence over the appointment of local and provincial officials.[59] Mussolini also strengthened the state by removing a long-standing thorn in its side—the Church. The 1929 Lateran Pacts finally settled many of the conflicts that had kept the Italian state and the Church estranged, legalizing the Vatican's status as an independent city-state, making Roman Catholicism the "official" religion of Italy, and financially compensating the Vatican for territories it lost as a result of the *Risorgimento* (see chapter 7). The Lateran Pacts were "wildly popular in Italy and made Mussolini the man who had brought peace between the state of Italy and the Church and who reconciled the political and spiritual identity of the majority of Italians."[60]

In addition to strengthening the national state and reaching a modus vivendi with the Church, the Fascist regime also developed a wide variety of para-statal organizations and programs to increase the state's penetration of Italian society. Perhaps the most well-known of these was the mass leisure organization, the *Opera Nazionale Dopolavoro* or OND, which was designed to bring Fascism "toward the people," "adhere the masses to the state," and create a new Fascist identity by involving workers in a wide variety of activities, including recreational circles, student and youth groups, sports, and excursions.[61] The desire to generate a single national, Fascist-inspired identity also motivated the regime's involvement in cultural production, including architectural projects, art exhibitions, and film and radio productions. Through these and other endeavors the Fascist regime effected not merely a political but a social

> mobilization of the population on a scale never seen before. People participated massively in fascist sponsored activities. . . . By March 1940 the PNF had more than 3.5 million enrolled and around 20 million Italians—little short of half the population—were involved in its various capillary organizations. . . . The fascist youth organization, [for example], had a membership of over 8 million in October 1940—more than the Hitler Youth at the same time. . . . The message conveyed through the varied activities was that the paternal party was interested in you and was on your side—a total political novelty for large parts of the population, effectively excluded from any form of political socialization before the advent of the regime.[62]

The Fascist regime made mass politics a reality in a way previous liberal and democratic regimes had not.[63]

In addition to reshaping the relationship between state and society, Fascism also dramatically expanded the state's role in the economy. The Fascist regime insisted that the state had the right—indeed the duty—to intervene in economic life. As one Fascist put it: "there cannot be any single economic interests which are above the general economic interests of the State, no individual, economic initiatives which do not fall under the supervision and regulation of the State, no relationships of the various classes of the nation which are not the concern of the state."[64] This did not mean that Fascists rejected capitalism or private property. Instead fascists claimed they wanted to ensure economic growth while ensuring that the nation's "needs" and "goals" were not threatened by unregulated markets or "selfish" capitalists.

During Fascism's early years in power, the regime did not make major changes in the economy. But after Mussolini's consolidation of power in the mid-1920s, the outlines of a new type of corporatist social and economic order emerged.[65] The first step toward this new order was taken with the Palazzo Vidoni pact signed by the Confindustria (or CGII, the Italian business association) and the Confederation of Fascist Unions in October 1925. The CGII and the Fascist Unions agreed that all labor negotiations would occur between them and that strikes and lockouts were banned since, "as expressions of class interests, they failed to take into account national needs."[66] If for some reason the labor market partners were not able to reach an agreement, the matter would be referred to labor courts for compulsory arbitration. If business was initially hesitant about the pact, fearing it would lead to further state encroachment on its prerogatives, employers soon realized that their loss of autonomy was balanced by other advantages, most notably the elimination of independent labor organizations.

Another piece of the corporatist edifice was laid the following year with the passage of the Rocco Law, which divided the country's economy into seven branches (industry, agriculture, banking, commerce, internal transport, merchant marine, and intellectual community) and set up "syndical confederations" for employees and employers in all but the last. And in 1927, the government put forward the Charter of Labor, which laid out the rationale for the corporatist system and the principles governing relations between capital and labor. It proclaimed the right of the corporations "as representatives of the unified interests of production" to oversee the establishment of production rules, the adjudication of labor disputes, the control of labor exchanges, and the regulation of occupational safety standards. The Charter described the corporatist system as one that promoted capitalism and private initiative while at the same time establishing the state's primary role in ensuring that the economy worked for society as a whole.[67] Corporatism, the charter proclaimed, considers that private enterprise in the sphere of production is the most effective and useful instrument in the interests of the nation:

> In view of the fact that private organization of production is a function of national concern, the organizer of the enterprise is responsible to the State for the direction given to production. Collaboration between the forces of production gives rise to reciprocal rights and duties. The worker . . . is an active collaborator in the economic enterprise, the management of which rests with the employer who is responsible for it. . . .
>
> In the [corporate system] individual initiative is always the fundamental impulse. [E]conomic activity, however . . . had important social reactions [and therefore] must be developed within given juridical limits. . . . [I]t is obvious that the individual must be considered responsible to Society and therefore to the State. . . . [W]hen private initiative is lacking or . . . the interests of the State are involved . . . intervention . . . which may take the form of control, assistance or direct management . . . will [therefore] be necessary.[68]

Alongside corporatism other initiatives increased the state's role in the economy. Beginning in the late 1920s, the government established a number of parastatal institutions, such as the Italian Credit Institute (*Instituto Mobiliare Italiano*) and the Italian Financial Society (*Societa Finanziaria Italiana*), that funneled funds to businesses and banks suffering from the economic downturn. In 1933, in response to the Great Depression, the government created the Institute for Industrial Reconstruction (*Instituto per la Riconstruzione Industriale,* IRI) to rescue the banking system. The IRI took over the stockholdings of banks and relieved them of their debts to the Bank of Italy, thereby saving much of the private sector from collapse but making it dependent on the state for capital. By 1939, the IRI "controlled 77 percent of pig iron production, 45 percent of steel, 80 percent of naval construction, and 90 percent of shipping."[69] And banking reform laws passed in the mid-1930s—which among other things nationalized the Bank of Italy—furthered state control over credit allocation.

In the agricultural sphere, meanwhile, the government protected the property of landowners but also extended its control over them by setting production targets and stockpiling important commodities. The Fascists also put in place health insurance, old-age and disability pensions, paid national holidays, the forty-hour workweek, family/maternity benefits, and other social policies designed to tie workers to the state and partially compensate them for their loss of autonomy and stagnating wages.[70] The state also sponsored public works, including highway construction and the draining of the Pontine marshes. These programs immensely increased the number of public employees and doubled state expenditures between 1922 and 1930–1933,[71] and by the outbreak of the Second World War the Italian state may have had "a control over the economy that was unequalled outside the Soviet Union."[72]

In short, the Fascist regime dramatically reshaped the nature of and relationship among the state, economy, and society in Italy. These changes seem for the most part to have been popular up through the late 1930s when Mussolini threw in his lot with Hitler, got involved in the Second World War, and turned the regime towards a more overtly "racialist" understanding of fascism.[73] Internationally, meanwhile, the changes wrought by Fascism also briefly gave Italy the international stature it had long desired. In addition to its pathetic but bloody forays in empire-building in North Africa, Fascism's domestic policies initially drew attention from across the globe. As one leading contemporary critic of Fascism, Gaetano Salvemini, noted, during the regime's early years Italy became a "Mecca for political scientists, economists, and sociologists looking for the basis of a new order in a world trapped between capitalist depression and communist autocracy."[74] The United States ambassador to Italy, for example, wrote in 1928,

> No man will exhibit dimensions of permanent greatness equal to Mussolini. . . . He has not only been able to secure and hold an almost universal following; he has built a new state upon a new concept of a state. He has not only been able to change the lives of human beings but he has changed their minds, their hearts, their spirits. He has not merely ruled a house; he has built a house.[75]

Conclusions

Understanding why democracy failed and was replaced by fascism in interwar Italy requires understanding the weaknesses of the former and the strengths of the latter. Italy entered the interwar period with serious problems, most notably a weak state and sense of national unity. These are, of course, problems facing many new countries, and they were exacerbated by the challenges Italy confronted as a result of the First World War and its aftermath. The war further divided Italians and many found the country's treatment by the Allies at its end humiliating, and they blamed democracy and its ruling elites for it. After the war Italy was also plagued by massive economic problems and social unrest. By the early 1920s the country seemed on the verge of chaos. The inability or unwillingness of liberal-led democratic governments to respond forcefully to these and other problems led businessmen, landowners, members of the middle class, and others to lose faith in liberals and democracy more generally. The country's two largest parties meanwhile—the socialist PSI and the Catholic PPI—were unable or unwilling to reach outside their "natural" constituencies or take over from the liberals the task of leading Italy's young democracy.

The failures of existing political elites and institutions were necessary but not sufficient for Fascism's rise. Also critical was the nature and appeal of Fascism itself. Initially fairly marginal, the Fascist movement seized the opportunities created by the failures of existing elites and institutions to reorient itself to capture growing dissatisfaction. By the early 1920s Fascism promised to restore order and protect private property while at the same time controlling capitalism's worst excesses, and to provide Italy with the strong state, sense of national unity, and international stature that previous liberal and democratic regimes had not. Fascism thus had a very different profile than traditional conservative movements: it mixed national and socialist themes and was profoundly illiberal but not entirely "anti-democratic"— by 1921 it was a mass movement with hundreds of thousands of members that claimed to represent "the people." However, even given fascism's unusual profile, without the support or connivance of existing elites its rise to power might not have happened. By the early 1920s many business, agricultural, Church, military, and even liberal elites had become convinced that the Fascists were the key to restoring order and eliminating the socialist/communist threat; some of these elites helped convince the king to offer Mussolini the prime ministership. This turned out to be a tragic mistake. Assuming they could use Mussolini to achieve their own goals, Mussolini instead used and destroyed them on the way to dragging Italy into the most shameful period in its history.

Just as it is necessary to understand the failures of the previous liberal and democratic regimes in order to understand fascism's rise, so too is an understanding of these failures necessary to fully understand what fascism did when it came to power. Fascism promised to provide precisely what previous regimes had not: a strong state capable of uniting Italians and asserting the country internationally. Although Fascism did not achieve these goals, it changed the nature of and relationship among Italy's state, society, and economy more than any previous regime: it also mobilized more Italians than ever before, and the Fascist state reached down deeper into society and exerted a greater control over the economy than had been possible before. Many of these changes outlived fascism's demise and shaped the development of Italy's second try at democracy after 1945.

| The Collapse of the Weimar
Republic and the Rise
of National Socialism in Germany

In this first year of Nazi rule the German people is assembled in unanimous, unswerving loyalty to the state, the race (*Volk*), and the German nation to which we all belong. Every difference is wiped away. The barriers of class hatred and the arrogance of social status that for over fifty years divided the nation from itself have been torn down. . . . Finally, the idea of the national community rises above the ruins of the bankrupt liberal-capitalist state.

—Hermann Göring[1]

UNDERSTANDING THE FATE of the Weimar Republic is perhaps the most important and difficult task facing a student of European political development. During the early twentieth century, Germany was among Europe's most economically advanced countries with a politically active and highly educated population, ruled over by an increasingly sclerotic and divisive semi-authoritarian regime. Germany finally made a transition to democracy at the end of the First World War, but democracy collapsed after a decade and a half, plunging the country into one of the most monstrous dictatorships the world has ever known. Why did democracy fail in Germany? And why did this failure give rise to a new type of dictatorship—National Socialism—that ushered in the most tragic and destructive period in modern European history?

To answer these questions we must return to where chapter 8 left off, with the old regime on the eve of the First World War. The legacies of the old regime dramatically shaped Germany's political development after 1918. By 1914 a majority of Germans favored some political reform, but various institutional safeguards enabled conservatives to resist changes that threatened their power and prerogatives; the ensuing political stalemate increased tensions within German society and diminished the legitimacy of reigning political institutions. The outbreak of the war temporarily paved over political and social divisions, but as the conflict dragged on, and the myth of a defensive war became increasingly untenable, dissension grew. By 1917 this dissension combined with growing disagreements between military and civilian authorities led the High Command to take the military's traditionally privileged position in Germany a step further, sidelining the kaiser and other political actors and instituting essentially a military dictatorship.[2]

When the war ended, the challenge of leading Germany out of the chaos of defeat and through its first transition to democracy fell to the SPD, a party the old regime and wartime dictatorship left ill-prepared for this task. Alienated from the state, distrustful of other parties, itself distrusted by many Germans, and having never previously participated in national government, the SPD had to build a democratic Germany out of the rubble the High Command and the old regime left behind. Transitions to democracy—particularly first transitions—are always difficult, but it is hard to imagine a transition occurring under worse conditions than those facing the SPD and Germany in 1918. Not only did the Weimar Republic inherit myriad political and social problems from its prewar predecessor (see chapter 8 and below), Germany was in a disastrous situation at the end of the war. The Allied blockade, which lasted until 1919, stopped foodstuffs and other basic materials from reaching the country, causing hundreds of thousands of deaths from disease and malnutrition. The weakened population was then particularly vulnerable to the influenza pandemic that exploded at the end of the war: hundreds of thousands more Germans died as a result in the years 1918–1919. In addition, even before the war officially ended, Germany experienced a wave of domestic violence that reached civil war–like conditions in parts of the country. And of course, the young Weimar Republic was quickly saddled with a punitive peace, which exacerbated the country's already desperate economic situation and generated outrage and humiliation among significant sectors of the population.

Despite this, the Republic managed to get through the immediate postwar period, but things did not improve much afterwards. During the 1920s the Weimar Republic was buffeted by further economic, social, and political crises. The Republic survived these as well, but when the Great Depression hit, many Germans no longer believed that democracy or the political parties associated with it could solve their or their country's problems. This disillusionment created a golden opportunity for a movement capable of taking advantage of widespread anger and frustration. That the Nazis were able to do this was a consequence of the party's evolution in the years leading up to the Great Depression. By the early 1930s the NSDAP had transformed itself from a marginal right-wing, anti-Semitic nationalist group into a powerful political movement that had infiltrated Weimar's civil society and attracted broader support than any other political force in the country. As was true of its fascist counterpart in Italy, the NSDAP promised to provide what democracy had not: a strong state capable of uniting "the people," eliminating their "enemies," and recovering the country's "rightful" international position after the humiliation of the First World War. Once in power, the Nazis turned out to be much more radical, ruthless, and effective than their Italian counterparts, transforming Germany's state and society as well as Europe to an astonishing and appalling degree.

The Transition to Democracy in Germany

Although initially greeted with much enthusiasm as a way to re-unite the country and assert itself vis-à-vis its competitors, the First World War was disastrous for Germany. Almost two million German soldiers died, and another four million were wounded. By the winter of 1917–1918 deteriorating conditions on the home front combined with anger over Germany's treatment of Russia in the Treaty of Brest Litovsk ratcheted up domestic tensions: strikes exploded in many parts of the country, and disturbances within the army and navy grew. During the spring of 1918 the High Command ordered a final massive offensive, but by August it was clear that all was lost. When the admiralty nonetheless called for a last-ditch battle against the British Royal Navy in October, German sailors mutinied and popular unrest engulfed the country. With the domestic and international situation in dire straits, the kaiser resigned on November 9. Phillip Scheidemann, an SPD leader, appeared on the balcony of the Reichstag and proclaimed, "Long Live the Republic!" and the office of the chancellor was handed over to another SPD leader, Friedrich Ebert. With this, democratization occurred in Germany.

Democratization eliminated the political institutions of the old regime but left behind deeply pernicious legacies, including politically and socially powerful anti-democratic elites embedded in the military, civil service, and judicial apparatuses, and deep societal divisions. Unlike its counterparts in Italy, the German Social Democrats accepted responsibility for leading Germany's new democracy, but the party moved haltingly into this position having no previous experience governing the country or plans for how to achieve consolidated liberal democracy. Indeed debate continued within the SPD over basic issues like the desirability of "bourgeois" democracy and co-operation with bourgeois parties up through 1918.[3] As Max Cohen-Reuss, a prominent Social Democrat, later remarked: "It was unfortunate that we found ourselves in a situation that we were not prepared for. . . . We had not fought for it ourselves. [I]t had, so to speak, fallen in our laps."[4] A similar criticism came from Friedrich Stampfer, a member of the SPD executive: "We should have emphasized to the masses that with the realization of democracy half of the program of Social Democracy had been achieved, and that the task facing the party now was to extend the position that we had won. We should have impressed upon our party comrades that democracy was not just a pre-liminary stage on the way to socialism, but rather a valuable achievement on its own."[5] The SPD's hesitancy and lack of preparation might have mattered less had the challenges it faced not been so great, but in 1918 it had to lead the country through political, social, and economic chaos.

In 1918 the SPD had to deal with a population devastated by the war and the blockade, troops streaming back from the front, and various groups staging uprisings in parts of Germany. Workers' and soldiers' councils (*Räterepubliken*) claimed authority in some cities,[6] and Germany's second largest state, Bavaria, was taken over by a left-wing group led by Kurt Eisner and declared an independent, Soviet-socialist republic. On November 10 General Groener, who had succeeded Erich Ludendorff as quartermaster-ge-neral of the army and was thus the lead military figure during the immediate postwar period,[7] called Ebert to propose a logroll between the military and the new government to deal with the turmoil. Groener told the new chan-cellor that the officer corps was particularly concerned to fight Bolshevism and was at the government's disposal for this task. In return for Ebert's preserving the authority of the general staff and officer corps, Groener offered vague promises of loyalty to the new regime.[8] Ebert, also fearing Bolshevism and chaos, agreed to the deal. But the pact was lopsided; the military leader-ship retained almost complete control over the armed forces, while Groener's loyalty proved fleeting, a disparity with fateful consequences for the Weimar Republic.

Meanwhile the Social Democrats and the Council of People's Deputies (the name given to the government that took over in November 1918) ap-pointed a national assembly to make decisions about the future development of the political system. This assembly[9] met in Berlin in December to decide on a date for national elections. Nearly two-thirds of the delegates were members of the SPD and fewer than one-fifth came from the USPD (*Unabhängige Sozialdemokratische Partei Deutschlands* or Independent Social Democratic party of Germany, which had broken away from the SPD in 1917 largely as a result of the latter's unwillingness to more openly oppose the German war effort). Despite its domination by the SPD (often referred to during this time as the MSPD, or Majority SPD, to differentiate it from the USPD) the assembly demanded rapid and extensive change. For example, it called for some socialization, the "disarming of the counterrevolution," an end to the wearing of badges of rank and uniforms off-duty, a voice for the soldiers in the election of their officers, and the formation of a "People's Militia." These demands, known as the "Hamburg points,"[10] reflected a relatively broad consensus on the need for social and economic reforms to accompany the political changes that had already occurred.

Faced with cascading demands and with little planning to guide it, the SPD government hesitated; its failure to act led to heavy criticism particularly from the left during December. Wilhelm Dittmann of the USPD warned his SPD colleagues that "the workers and soldiers councils would not stand by idly if the government and [party leadership] nullified the most important resolutions of the entire congress."[11] Similarly, Hugo Haase, a key figure in the prewar SPD and then the USPD, argued that all it would take to decimate the Spartacists (an extreme left-wing group that would morph into Germany's communist party) was to push through the social and economic measures being demanded by the masses.[12] On December 28 the USPD withdrew from the Council of People's Deputies because of the MSPD's unwillingness to reform the army, and the government's use of anti-democratic troops to quell disturbances in Berlin. The withdrawal of the USPD led to the dismissal of civil servants who were USPD members; when the USPD chief of police in Berlin refused to resign in January 1919 and the pace of reforms continued to plod, another bloody confrontation occurred.

This "January" or Spartacist uprising—a movement led by the far left, including the newly formed Communist party (KPD, *Kommunistische Partei Deutschlands*)—resulted in a large workers' demonstration in Berlin and the storming of the offices of the SPD newspaper. A counter-demonstration called by the MSPD succeeded in largely neutralizing the movement, and the USPD offered to call the whole thing off. While Dittmann tried to find a formula satisfactory to both sides, Ebert decided "to teach the radicals a lesson they would never forget."[13] In order to put down what was actually a somewhat pathetic affair, Ebert's colleague Gustav Noske relied chiefly on troops made up of reactionary ex-soldiers—the *Freikorps*. These troops went on a rampage, violently suppressing the workers and murdering the two best-known radical leaders, Karl Liebknecht and Rosa Luxemburg; total casualties exceeded one thousand.[14] This episode further tarnished the MSPD's standing and strengthened the conservative and independent inclinations of the military.

Protests against the government continued, but the elections of January 19, 1919, were a victory for the forces of democracy. The SPD emerged as the largest party by far, receiving 38 percent of the vote. The USPD received 7.6 percent of the vote; the left liberals (DDP) 18.5 percent; the Catholic Center (*Zentrum*) 19.7 percent; and the right liberals (DVP) 4.4 percent. The only other party to receive significant electoral backing at this election was the hard-right DNVP, which got about 10 percent of the vote (see Figure 12.1). The USPD refused to enter a coalition with the MSPD, so the MSPD joined with the DDP and Center party; together they had over 76 percent of the vote.[15] The National Assembly chose Friedrich Ebert as Germany's first president; Ebert then called on Philipp Scheidemann to form a government. In this government the MSPD held almost all the important portfolios, including defense, economics, food, and welfare. But the new government, and

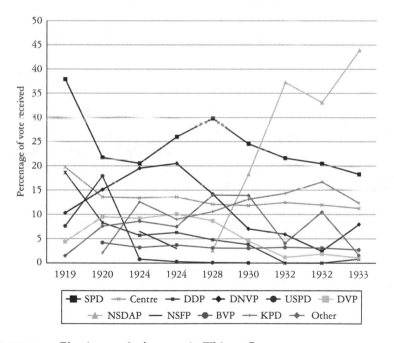

FIGURE 12.1 Election results by party in Weimar Germany, 1919–1933.
Source: Dieter Nohlen and Philip Stover, *Elections in Europe: A Data Handbook* (Baden-Baden, Germany: Nomos, 2010).

the SPD in particular, had little chance to savor its victory. From the left came strikes and Council Republics, as well as a vociferous campaign against democracy by the KPD.[16] The new government felt it had no choice but to deal with some left-wing disturbances with the help of *Freikorps*, infuriating the left.[17] More worrisome, however, was the growing radicalism of and attacks by the nationalist right, especially after the signing of the Versailles treaty in June 1919. This treaty forced Germany to "accept . . . responsibility . . . for causing all the loss and damage" of the war, give up its colonies and as well as parts of its own territory to France, Belgium, and Poland; drastically limit the size of its army and navy; turn over a large amount of military material as well as coal and other resources to the Allies; and pay twenty billion goldmarks in reparations. These provisions fed a pernicious "stab in the back" legend, which held the new republic, and the SPD in particular, responsible for the "humiliation" of Versailles and the military defeat that caused it. That so many Germans believed this legend was partially a legacy of the power of and eventual dictatorship by the army during the war. By keeping the country's true military situation from the public for as long as possible, the army leadership made Germany's defeat in 1918 appear sudden and unexpected. And, by urging the kaiser to turn over power to the Reichstag and its parties only once defeat was inevitable, the military leadership ensured that the unenviable task of having to negotiate with the Allies would fall to the new Republic, and the SPD in particular, rather than representatives of the old regime.[18]

On March 13, 1920, a group of right-wingers under the leadership of Wolfgang Kapp and General Ludendorff attempted a putsch. Among the leaders of the military only a single figure, General Reinhardt, was prepared to forcibly fight the insurrection, and so despite their attempts to appease the army, Ebert and Noske were now left without troops to defend the government. Some members of the bureaucracy also refused to support the republican forces, while members of the old conservative elite received news of the putsch with glee. The continued power of many reactionary structures left over from the old regime consistently haunted the Republic.

The MSPD responded indecisively to the putsch. This led the trade unions under their leader Carl Legien to step up to defend democracy. Deciding that a show of mass force was necessary, the unions called a general strike. This was hugely successful, rallying workers as well as members of the middle class; the putsch quickly collapsed. Despite clear demands from the strikers for reforms, including the resignation of Noske and two other ministers with ties to the military, harsh punishment for right-wing participants in the coup, a purge of the army and civil service, and the socialization of certain "ripe" industries, little action was taken: Of the 705 people officially listed as having taken part in the coup, only one, Kapp, got a prison sentence; nothing much was done to deal with either the military or the bureaucracy and no socialization occurred.[19]

The collapse of the Kapp putsch did not end the disorder. Indeed, on the heels of the putsch another uprising occurred in the Ruhr, this time instigated by the extreme left. This was also crushed by troops from the army and *Freikorps*.[20] By the time the next elections rolled around in June 1920 support for the moderate parties most associated with the Republic—the SPD and DDP—had eroded dramatically while support for parties further to the left (the USPD and to some degree the KPD) and right (DNVP and DVP) had increased. Indeed, the parties most closely associated with the new republic lost their majority less than two years after having been swept into office and only a year and a half after they had enjoyed the support of 76 percent of the electorate.[21]

The 1920s

Turmoil persisted during the early 1920s. Violent far-right attacks on the Republic, including high-profile assassinations of Matthias Erzberger, a left-wing leader of the Catholic party, and Walter Rathenau, Germany's foreign minister and a leading German-Jewish industrialist, continued. Many of the far-right groups that plagued the Weimar Republic had their roots in the prewar nationalist movements that had peddled an aggressive and virulently anti-Semitic nationalism as the solution to Germany's problems (see chapter 8). Of these far-right groups, one deserves particular mention because in 1919 a young Austrian named Adolf Hitler attended its meetings and by the end of the year had become its propaganda chief. In early 1920, the party changed its name to the National Socialist German Workers' Party (NSDAP) and published a program that mixed nationalist, socialist, and anti-Semitic themes. In addition to calling for "the union of all Germans in a greater Germany," a redefinition of the German nation that would include only those of "German blood," and promising to combat "the Jewish-materialist spirit," the program included planks to help the party fight Marxism and the SPD, in part by appropriating some of its main themes, particularly its critique of capitalism.[22] This combination of nationalism, anti-Marxist socialism, and anti-Semitism was fairly common in late-nineteenth- and early-twentieth-century Europe (see chapters 6, 7, and 8).[23] In 1923 the NSDAP attempted to overthrow the Republic with the Beer Hall putsch. This putsch was a flop that ended with Hitler in jail and the party banned, but reflecting the sympathies of the court, the sentences given the putschists were very mild. Hitler, for example, served only nine months, during which time he reconsidered his strategy for capturing power and wrote down his thoughts about his struggle in what would become *Mein Kampf*.

Alongside the Beer Hall putsch, the Weimar Republic was rocked by other crises in 1923. Communists in Saxony and Thuringia used their positions in provincial parliaments to plan a general uprising, and in Hamburg the KPD unleashed an unsuccessful insurrection. Most traumatic of all, however, was the invasion of the Ruhr. When Germany was declared in default of its reparations payments, France and Belgium invaded the Ruhr, sending nationalists into a frenzy and aggravating the Republic's already difficult economic situation.

In order to compensate citizens who refused to cooperate with the invading authorities, the German government printed money, thereby contributing to the outbreak of the Great Inflation.[24] Probably everyone has seen pictures of Germans pushing paper money around in wheelbarrows or using it as fuel; by the end of 1923 the currency was essentially worthless. The Great Inflation was followed by a crushing stabilization, which hit white-collar workers and the middle classes particularly hard.[25] During the second half of the 1920s the Republic steadied itself as the German government gave in to the Allies, resumed reparations payments, and set up a new currency (the *Rentenmark*). Germany also made progress in foreign policy, due largely to the efforts of Gustav Stresemann, foreign minister from the fall of the Great Coalition in 1923 until his death in 1929.[26] For example, in 1924 the Dawes plan lowered the burden of reparations and secured French withdrawal from the Ruhr; in 1925 the Locarno treaties marked an important step towards Germany's reintegration into Europe; and in 1926 Germany became a member of the League of Nations. Despite some real accomplishments during the mid-1920s, the Great Inflation, its aftermath, and the continued weakness of the economy made all groups more jealous of their socioeconomic interests and more strident in their political demands. Middle-class and rural groups resented both workers and big business, which they viewed as having a disproportionate influence over the national government and political parties. The SPD presented itself primarily as a "worker's party," and its support for measures such as the eight-hour workday and better wages were viewed by middle-class and rural groups as serving workers' interests above all else.[27] Traditional liberal and conservative parties such as the DDP (the left liberal party), DVP (the National Liberals), and DNVP (the main conservative party), meanwhile, came to be seen by many middle-class and rural voters as the tools of big capitalists and financial interests, run by and for an unrepresentative elite.[28] Their vote accordingly dropped precipitously, especially during the latter part of the 1920s. By 1924 the DVP and DDP together attracted only about 15 percent of the vote, and splinter parties were capturing their alienated and fragmented constituency. By 1928—the high point of economic stabilization and supposedly the "golden age" of the Weimar Republic—splinter parties were outpolling the traditional parties of the middle.[29] The relative calm of the latter 1920s did, however, benefit the party most closely associated with the Republic—the SPD—and in the 1928 election, the last before the onset of the Depression, the Social Democrats scored a resounding victory, while the parties of the extreme right suffered significant losses. Critically, however, the parties of the bourgeois center did not recover[30] (see Figure 12.1) and the largely middle-class and rural voters who had previously voted for them remained without a political home.

During the latter part of the 1920s the NSDAP shifted course in response to these developments. Having failed to overthrow the Republic by force, and with its initial, heavily socialist appeal having failed to attract many urban workers, the NSDAP turned its attention to the middle-class, rural, and non-voters alienated from the Republic and traditional parties.[31] Particularly after 1928, the NSDAP toned down radical themes—for example, the expropriation plank in its official program was now interpreted as applying only to Jews and the party's support for private property was made explicit[32]—and instead emphasized national ones with greater cross-class appeal.[33] The NSDAP said it would serve the entire German *Volk* and create a united people, or a *Volksgemeinschaft*, that would never again suffer the divisions and defeat of the First World War. The party also promised to reverse the "decay and rottenness" caused by democracy,[34] eliminate the "enemies" of the people (for example, Jews, Communists), restore order, and reclaim Germany's "rightful" place in the world. The NSDAP gave Hitler firm control over major political decisions and its grassroots organization, and the party's ties to civil society groups expanded.[35] Indeed the Nazis masterfully infiltrated Weimar's rich associational life, using it to spread the party's message and cultivate cadres of activists with organizational skills and dense social networks.[36] By the early 1930s the NSDAP was a different party than it had been at the time of the Beer Hall putsch: it was deeply embedded in Weimar's bourgeois civil society, had "perhaps the most efficient and best equipped organizational structure in German politics,"[37] and an appeal designed to attract a broad range of disillusioned, disaffected voters.

An example of how these changes helped the NSDAP attract new supporters and reshape Weimar's political dynamics is reflected in the political evolution of the German peasantry. During the interwar years peasants joined and participated in a wide range of professional, special interest, and regional associations, a trend carried over from the prewar era. Early in the Republic the peasantry tended to vote liberal or conservative, but like many other groups it eventually abandoned traditional parties. During the second half of the 1920s most peasants either withdrew from the national political arena or gave their support to one of the new splinter parties.[38] As the economic situation worsened during the late 1920s and early '30s, the political situation in rural areas became increasingly volatile. Large landowners used their influence on the DNVP and other political organizations to secure a large amount of help, but the peasantry lacked a political champion that could secure aid for them.

Until late in the day the Nazis essentially ignored rural Germany, and certain aspects of the Nazi program such as land reform and expropriation drove farmers away. But by the end of the 1920s the NSDAP, clever and opportunistic in ways its competitors were not, noticed the political potential of the frustration and unrest spreading across the countryside. In 1928 it accordingly revamped its agricultural program, eliminating "offensive" planks and focusing instead on the needs and demands of rural inhabitants.[39]

R. Walther Darre was the key figure in Nazi agriculture policy, and by the end of 1930 he decided that the way to win the peasantry's support and box out potential opponents in rural areas was to capture agricultural associations. In November 1930 an instruction sheet ordered the NSDAP's agricultural apparatus (*agrarpolitische Apparat*, or aA) to:

> penetrate into all rural affairs like a finely intertwined root system. . . . [The aA] should embed itself deeply in [all rural organizations] and seek to embrace every element of agrarian life so thoroughly that eventually nothing will be able to occur in the realm of agriculture anywhere in the Reich . . . we do not observe. . . . Let there be no farm, no estate, no village, no cooperative, no agricultural industry, no local organization of the RLB [an agricultural organization], no rural equestrian association, etc., etc., where we have not—at the least—placed our [representatives].[40]

Darre became particularly interested in the *Reichslandbund* (RLB), a major player in German agrarian life which by the end of the 1920s had 5.6 million members. During the 1920s the RLB cooperated with a number of bourgeois parties including the DVP and DNVP. But eventually many RLB members grew disgusted with the organization's political vacillation and inept leadership, and began considering the NSDAP as a potential champion. During the latter part of 1930 Darre decided that the route to gaining control over the RLB was by "conquering one position after another from within."[41] The aA focused first on placing supporters in lower ranks of the RLB, then on capturing leadership positions; by 1932 one of the four presidents of the RLB was a Nazi and non-Nazis were increasingly scarce at the top of the organization. The RLB gradually moved into the Nazi fold, burnishing the NSDAP's image as the champion of Germany's "neglected" groups while opening up new avenues for recruiting supporters. "The RLB and other agricultural organizations became convenient conveyor belts for Nazi propaganda reaching deep into the rural population. In this way the intermediate groups facilitated the rise of Nazism."[42]

This Nazi infiltration of bourgeois civil society helped the NSDAP to achieve two goals that had long eluded German political parties—the creation of an effective political machine *and* a truly broad, cross-class coalition. In short, by the time the Great Depression hit, the NSDAP was well positioned to take advantage of the chaos that was about to consume Germany.

The Great Depression and the Collapse of the Weimar Republic

When the 1928 elections occurred during Weimar's "Indian summer," extremist parties did poorly while SPD did well enough to take power at the head of a Grand Coalition which included the SPD, DDP, DVP, the Center, and a regional party, the BVP. This government achieved some important successes, perhaps most notably the Young Plan, which revised reparations, set a time-limit on Germany's payment obligations, and pledged the Allies to evacuate the Rhineland five years ahead of schedule.[43] But as the Great Depression swept over Germany, tensions within the coalition over foreign, economic, and social policy grew. In particular, a rapid growth in unemployment led to a large deficit in the unemployment insurance system. The SPD argued that the best way to deal with these shortfalls was by increasing contributions, while the DVP argued for a substantial revision of the system. A compromise acceptable to all coalition parties could not be reached, and the SPD-led government resigned.

The September 1930 elections revealed a dramatically different political landscape than existed in 1928. The SPD remained the largest party, although its share of the vote dropped from about 30 percent to 24.5 percent, but the NSDAP had catapulted itself into second place (18.3 percent vs. 2.6 percent in 1928) and the KPD into third (13.1 percent vs. 10.6 percent in 1928). Together anti-democratic parties received almost 40 percent of the vote.[44] The party system's fragmentation also continued, with over thirty parties competing in the election and fifteen obtaining seats in the Reichstag. In response, the SPD declared that its most important task was defending the Republic and thus supported the chancellorship of Heinrich Brüning, a conservative from the Center party, as the lesser evil.[45] But while perhaps the lesser evil, Brüning was no friend to the SPD or democracy overall. Despite the devastating economic downturn, during his time in office Brüning chipped away at what remained of Germany's social support system and pursued what we would today consider austerity. The SPD responded by attacking the chancellor's "antisocial" agenda, but did not offer much in the way of an alternative. In fact, Brüning's memoirs make clear that he often turned to members of the SPD for support.[46] These policies were deeply unpopular and lacked the support of a majority in the Reichstag. As a result, Brüning governed with the help of emergency decrees issued by the president, which article forty-eight of the Weimar Constitution enabled him to issue without the support of the Reichstag. Brüning used the term "authoritative democracy" to describe this form of rule—based on the backing of the president rather than the active support of a majority in the Reichstag—but it was not very democratic at all.

The context within which this all occurred was the ever more devastating economic downturn. Indeed, the Great Depression hit Germany harder than probably any other major industrialized country; only the United States suffered nearly as much. From 1929 to 1932, industrial production dropped by almost half, national income decreased by about a third, stock prices collapsed, banks failed, savings evaporated, investment disappeared, and during the winters of both 1931/32 and 1932/33 unemployment shot above six million. This led to a rise in support for the KPD and emboldened its attacks on the Republic and capitalism, trends that frightened business, middle-class, and rural groups further. Meanwhile, the SPD—the Republic's largest and most important party—essentially sat on its hands. Having previously rejected explicit outreach to groups outside the working class, the party could not take advantage of the growing desperation of Germany's farmers and middle classes, and having rejected unorthodox policy options for dealing with the economic downturn, the party had little to offer an electorate desperate for an alternative to Brüning's austerity.[47] Into this void stepped the NSDAP.

During the early 1930s, the Nazis continued to reach out to almost all strata of German society, especially rural and middle-class groups. The party had already toned down its attacks on capitalism, though it did not eliminate criticism of free markets or calls for dramatic socioeconomic change. One way the Nazis attempted to square this circle was by stressing the difference between "rapacious" (*raffendes*) and "creative" (*schaffendes*) capital that National Socialists had developed generations before. The former was associated with finance, commerce, and Jews and was seen as serving no good purpose; the latter was linked to industry and production, reflected "German" values and virtues, and was necessary for a healthy society and economy. This distinction between *raffendes* and *schaffendes* capital was, as one observer notes, "indeed almost a stroke of genius; it permitted the Nazi party to assume an anticapitalist stance without frightening off the business world whose financial and political support it sought."[48]

As Germany's economic situation deteriorated, so too did its political situation. The Nazis attacked Brüning and the SPD for their passivity and promised that if they came to power they would jump-start the economy and alleviate the suffering of *all* Germans. Brüning, meanwhile, was trying to figure out some way to stay in power. His austerity policies and bypassing of the Reichstag alienated him from the SPD, but his willingness to even consider working with the SPD, unwillingness to fully eviscerate democracy, and attempts to ban paramilitary organizations, even those associated with the NSDAP, alienated the right. Ultimately unable to secure the support of a majority in the Reichstag or maintain the confidence of President Hindenburg, who, like much of the rest of the Junkers and military elite, increasingly viewed the chancellor as not conservative "enough," Brüning was forced to resign in May 1932, pushing the Republic even further away from democracy.[49]

With Brüning's departure, President Hindenburg appointed the even more conservative Franz von Papen as chancellor. In the run-up to the elections in the summer of 1932, von Papen allowed the Nazi paramilitary force (SA, or *Sturmabteilung*) almost free reign to violently clash with opponents, particularly its counterpart from the KPD, thus ensuring that the election would be Germany's bloodiest and most chaotic yet. Overall, the NSDAP's transformation over the previous years enabled it to fight an aggressive and versatile campaign. The party promised to fight the Depression and get rid of unemployment, contrasting these promises with the meekness of the government and the SPD. It distributed hundreds of thousands of copies of its economic program, which was organized around the basic principle that, "Our economy is not sick because there is a lack of production opportunities, but rather because the available production opportunities are not being put to use."[50] In addition to calling for an alternative to Brüning's austerity, the party also presented itself as the champion of all German citizens suffering from the Depression and the failures of the Republic. And thanks to its previous outreach efforts, the NSDAP could count on the support of many agricultural and middle-class associations during the campaign, including the RLB.[51] (Germany's peasants and small farmers were very critical of the deflationary policies of the early 1930s.[52]) The election results were remarkable: a clear majority of voters cast their votes for explicitly anti-democratic parties,[53] and for the first time since 1912 the SPD lost its status as the country's largest party, capturing only 21.6 percent of the vote and being replaced by the NSDAP with 37.3 percent of the vote; the KPD, meanwhile, got 14.5 percent of the vote. Electoral participation also shot up, as disillusioned voters stormed back to the polls (see Figure 12.2). As important as the *size* of the Nazi victory was its *nature*: the NSDAP had become a true "people's party": it received disproportionate support from the middle class, rural areas, and the young, but overall the party's voters were "more equally distributed among the different social and demographic categories than any other major party of the Weimar Republic."[54]

In the months following the election, von Papen eviscerated what remained of German democracy. He stayed in power after the election because he enjoyed the support of President Hindenburg, but had almost no support in the Reichstag or with the public at large. The only party willing to support him was the far-right DNVP, which received less than 6 percent

FIGURE 12.2 Voter turnout in Weimar Germany, 1919–1933.
Source: Dieter Nohlen and Philip Stover, *Elections in Europe: A Data Handbook* (Baden-Baden, Germany: Nomos, 2010).

of the vote in the July 1932 election. Although von Papen tried to appease the NSDAP by allowing the SA free reign, clamping down on freedom of the press and other civil liberties, and launching what was essentially a coup against the SPD-led government of Prussia, Hitler had little interest in playing second fiddle to him. And so in a bizarre and tragic move, the NSDAP joined its arch-rivals the KPD in September to support a vote of no-confidence against von Papen. The vote succeeded by an overwhelming majority and von Papen was forced to resign in September. Another set of elections were then called for November 1932.

Interestingly, for the first time in many years the NSDAP appeared to be faltering. Financial troubles and political differences, for example, over the conditions under which the party should take power, caused internal tensions, while the end of reparations payments in the summer of 1932 robbed the Nazi appeal of some of its force. As a result, for the first time in four years, the Nazi vote declined: In the November 1932 elections, the NSDAP lost two million votes, receiving about 33 percent of the vote vs. 37.3 percent in July and lost thirty-four Reichstag seats. This led many to breathe a sigh of relief, believing that the crest of the Nazi wave had been reached. Newspapers across Germany predicted that Hitler would never now gain power and that "the Republic has been rescued."[55] However, although the Nazi vote declined, support for the Republic did not increase. The SPD's vote fell again (to 20.6 percent) while the KPD's and anti-democratic DNVP's rose (to 17 percent and 8.3 percent, respectively). Thus, in November a majority of the electorate voted for anti-democratic parties with the NSDAP retaining its status as the largest of the bunch.

Nonetheless, while the NSDAP's status made it possible to appoint Hitler chancellor, it did not make it necessary. And in the weeks after the election Germany stumbled on, briefly under the chancellorship of General Kurt von Schleicher, a conservative confidant of Hindenburg's, who lacked any political base other than perhaps the military elite from whence he came,[56] but who hoped to remain in power by enticing the support of various groups, including the Strasserite (or "socialist") wing of the NSDAP. Hitler, however, had little interest in coming to power on anything but his own terms.[57] Meanwhile, behind the scenes, conservative elites[58] and in particular von Papen, Oskar von Hindenburg (the president's son), and Alfred Hugenberg were maneuvering to bring Hitler into a right-wing government that would be popular enough to finally put an end to democracy and "Marxism." Just as conservative elites in Italy (see chapter 11) believed they could control and manipulate Mussolini, so did their counterparts in Germany believe they could use Hitler and the NSDAP's support to mount a final attack against democracy and then shunt the Nazis to the sidelines. These machinations, combined with the fact that no other party was able to mount a convincing challenge to the Nazis or offer any real possibility of generating a working coalition in the Reichstag, led Hindenburg to finally name Hitler chancellor on January 30, 1933. As historian Henry Turner noted: "It was a triumphant conclusion to a remarkable political comeback. A mere month earlier, Hitler had appeared finished. His party had suffered a staggering setback in the last national election. . . . Dissension and rebellion had broken out among his disappointed followers. Signs of improvement in the economy threatened to deprive him of one of the issues he had so successfully exploited since the onset of the depression. . . . Upon attaining his goal, Hitler himself reportedly marveled at how, as so often before, he had been rescued just as all seemed lost."[59] As was the case in Italy, in short, although many factors contributed to democracy's decline in Germany, it is impossible to understand its final collapse without paying attention to the actions of a conservative elite that was unable or unwilling to reconcile itself with democracy, becoming desperate enough eventually to support a fanatic who would destroy them as well as much of Europe.

The Nazi Regime

Hitler became chancellor of a government including Nazis and conservatives on January 30, 1933. Hitler eviscerated his conservative "partners" and all other opposition much more quickly than did Mussolini. Two days after coming to power Hitler dissolved the Reichstag and insisted on holding another election. In the following weeks and particularly after the German parliament (Reichstag) building was set on fire in February 1933—which the Nazis claimed was part of a Communist plot to overthrow the government but was surely the work of an individual—the Nazis used their own shock troops as well as the powers of the state, control over the police, declaration of a permanent "state of emergency," banning of political meetings, limiting freedom of the press, and suspension of most remaining civil liberties to terrorize their political opponents, particular the SPD and KPD.[60] Despite this, the Nazis received only 43.9 percent of the vote in the March 5 elections, and so needed the support of the DNVP (which got 8 percent) for a majority in the Reichstag. This proved more than enough to get the job done. On March 23 all parties, with the exception of the SPD (and KPD, which had already been banned), voted to pass the Enabling Act giving Hitler essentially dictatorial powers. Hitler now spoke openly about the "revolution" to come: the transition from democracy to dictatorship was merely the first step on the road to transforming Germany's society, state, economy, and position in the world.[61]

Building on the NSDAP's already impressive infiltration of Weimar's civil society, after coming to power the Nazis extended their control over these organizations and formed a wide variety of new ones. Eventually Nazi organizations covered almost every imaginable area of social and cultural life: youth and women's groups, a "labor front" (replacing banned unions), and sports, leisure, and artistic associations. The Nazis reach into "civil" society gave the party an extensive and effective grassroots presence that enabled it to observe and shape society from the bottom up.[62] Meanwhile, Hitler's ability to re-shape Germany from the top down and eliminate any alternatives to Nazi rule was facilitated by the rapid consolidation of his hold over the state. Within a few months of coming to power, the government passed laws giving it control over the civil service, dissolving all other political parties, and creating a unitary rather than a federal state. In the summer of 1933 Hitler signed a Concordat with the Vatican, which promised that the Church and its affiliated organizations could work in Germany as long as they stayed out of politics and bishops swore an oath of allegiance to the new regime. Hitler also moved quickly against those within his own movement and coalition who were not viewed as completely loyal. The "Night of Long Knives," or Röhm Putsch, in June 1934 eliminated the "left-wing" or Strasserite faction of the NSDAP and the SA, whose independence threatened Hitler's monopoly of violence and relationship with the military. In addition, many conservative but non-Nazi elites, including von Papen and Schleicher, were killed or pushed aside. Soon after this bloodbath, President Hindenburg died and Hitler took over the presidency, leaving him the undisputed leader of a state already purged of most potential sources of opposition.

The only groups Hitler initially allowed to retain some independence were the military and business, mainly because their cooperation was necessary for the war effort to come and they were, in any case, eager to cooperate. The military shared Hitler's desire to rearm and get rid of democracy, "Bolshevism," and what remained of the hated Versailles treaty. In addition, soon after Hitler came to power, the head of the armed forces, Werner von Blomberg, dismissed officers who were not sufficiently pro-Nazi and the military took an oath of loyalty to him.[63] Despite its relative docility, Hitler had no intention of allowing the military any autonomy over the long term. He gradually chipped away at its independence[64] and in 1938 removed Blomberg as head of the armed forces and Colonel-General Werner von Fitsch as commander in chief of the army, and made himself chief of the *Wehrmacht*,

Goering field marshal, and the weak Walther von Brauschitsch head of the army.[65] Hitler also reshuffled the foreign ministry, placing a loyalist, Joachim von Ribbentrop, at its head. Germany's armed forces were finally fully under government control.

The business community's autonomy was also undermined. Like the military, the business community largely welcomed Hitler's rise, sharing with him the desire to eliminate democracy, the left, and the labor movement. It also benefited from the profits generated by the war preparations that began soon after he became chancellor. Nonetheless the business community paid a heavy price for these benefits: over time, decisions about what and how much to produce, levels and nature of investment, wages, prices, and the uses to which private property could be put were taken out of their hands and instead placed under the purview of the state.[66] Agriculture suffered a similar fate, but received less in exchange. Soon after the Nazis came to power, the entire agricultural sector was organized into cartels known as *Reichsnährstand*. Marketing boards (*Marktverbände*) fixed prices, regulated supplies, and oversaw almost all aspects of agricultural production. As time passed, regulation grew to the point where speaking of a market in agriculture became something of a misnomer since the state determined everything from what seeds and fertilizers were used to how land was inherited.[67] And even though farmers were granted a moratorium on debt payments and protection from food imports, the cumulative result of Nazi policies was a decline in agricultural production and rural standards of living and a record sell-off of farms.[68]

By the end of the 1930s the state touched every sphere of economic life, public spending as a share of the gross national product (GNP) had grown spectacularly,[69] and credit was politically distributed.[70] Even though the German economy remained nominally capitalist and private property was not fundamentally threatened, unless its owner was Jewish, "[t]he scope and depth of state intervention in Nazi Germany had no peacetime precedent or parallel in any capitalist economy, Fascist Italy included."[71] This transformed relationship between the state and the economy reflected the Nazis' long-standing insistence that all spheres of life had to be subordinated to the "national interest" ("*Gemeinnutz geht vor Eigennutz*").[72] The Nazi movement, according to Hitler, considered the economy "merely a necessary servant in the life of our people and nationhood. [The movement] feels an independent national economy to be necessary, but it does not consider it a primary factor that creates a strong state; on the contrary, only the strong nationalist state can protect such an economy and grant it freedom of existence and development." Hitler once remarked that "the fundamental idea in [the Nazi] economic program is the idea of authority. . . . I want everyone to keep the property that he has acquired for himself . . . [but] the Third Reich will always retain its right to control the owners of property."[73]

The Nazis' economic policies were quite popular, especially after their "successful" response to the Great Depression. Upon coming to power, the Nazis proclaimed full employment a central goal[74] and began a number of highly publicized work-creation programs, stepping up highway, canal, house, railway, and other types of infrastructure projects financed essentially by central bank credits,[75] exhorting "business to take on extra workers and restrict hours of work and overtime,"[76] and restarting the flow of credit.[77] Germany's economy rebounded and unemployment figures improved almost miraculously: when Hitler came to power in 1933, almost 6 million Germans were unemployed; by the end of 1934, this had dropped to 2.4 million; by 1938 the country enjoyed essentially full employment. Although most scholars now believe that much of this improvement was due to a simultaneous upswing in the international economy rather than the Nazis' policies,[78] *psychologically* the Nazi policies were critical. By showing that the government was committed to getting the economy moving again, these policies gave many Germans renewed confidence in the future, making the recovery something of a self-fulfilling prophecy.[79] And even more important were the political consequences of the regime's Depression-fighting policies. Many Germans gave the regime credit for the economic turnaround that occurred on its watch, and this boosted its popularity and legitimacy.[80]

The Nazis justified their economic policies in particular and the state's control over the economy more generally as part of their attempt to create a true *Volksgemeinschaft*—an order in which the good of the national community took precedence. This new *Volksgemeinschaft* would, the Nazis insisted, end the deep divisions and hierarchies long embedded in German society. As perverse as it seems, increasing social equality and mobility was central to the Nazi appeal. As Hitler, for example, once noted, with the Third Reich "we have opened the way for every qualified individual—whatever his origins— to reach the top if he is qualified, dynamic, industrious and resolute."[81] The Nazis would, Hitler declared, finally create "a socially just state" that would "eradicate [the social] barriers"[82] that had long divided Germans from each other. And indeed, during the Third Reich the old determinants of how far one rose in society—family, social status, wealth, education, etc.—were replaced by commitment to the cause and racial background. The Nazis also supported an extensive welfare state that included free higher education, help for families and child support, high pensions, health insurance, and a wide array of publicly supported entertainment and vacation options:

Seats in theater and concert halls were made available for a nominal entrance fee of 50 pfenning and for 7 marks one could take an eight-hour excursion on the Mosel River. In total, 9 million Germans availed themselves of the opportunity to join these cheap excursions and more people traveled abroad than ever before. This was an age of festivals. The Olympic games of 1936 and the annual party conventions in Nuremberg were the most widely publicized, but there were also harvest festivals and various parades celebrating some historical or current political event.[83]

This welfare state was of course only for "ethnically pure" Germans, designed to increase socioeconomic equality and solidarity among them, while differentiating them from Jews and other "undesireables"[84] who were subject to discrimination and violence. The welfare state was thus part of the Nazis' attempt to make race rather than class the key dividing line in modern society.[85] A clear classic statement of this view was made by Goebbels at the first Labor Day celebration held under Nazi auspices on May 1, 1933:

> On this day the whole nation at all levels, in all its professions, occupations, and estates, acknowledges the dignity and blessedness of labour. On a day when in former times we heard the rattle of machine-guns and the hate-inspired songs of the class struggle and the Internationale, in this first year of Hitler's government the German people is assembled in unanimous, unswerving loyalty to the state, the race (*Volk*), and the German nation to which we all belong. Every difference is wiped away. The barriers of class hatred and the arrogance of social status that for over fifty years divided the nation from itself have been torn down. Germans of all classes, tribes (*Stämme*), professions, and denominations have joined hands across the barriers that separated them and have vowed henceforth to live as a community, to work and fight for the fatherland that unites us all. . . . The class struggle is at an end. The idea of the national community rises above the ruins of the bankrupt liberal-capitalist state. . . . Thus the German people marches into the future.[86]

Especially up through 1939, most Germans' experience with the Nazi regime was probably positive. The Nazis had seemingly conquered the Depression and restored some semblance of economic and political stability. The Nazi welfare state "benefited probably around 95 percent of" all Germans, and real possibilities for social advancement for hitherto low-status individuals were opened up by the regime. In addition, as long as they could prove their ethnic "purity" and stayed away from overt shows of disloyalty, most individuals had little to fear from the regime's coercive apparatus. Most Germans, in short, "did not experience National Socialism as a system of tyranny and terror but rather as a regime of social warmth, a sort of 'warm and fuzzy' dictatorship (wohlfühl-Diktatur)."[87] In addition, support for the regime was bolstered by its foreign policy "successes," most notably getting rid of what remained of the Versailles treaty and (re)-integrating into Germany parts of Central and Eastern Europe with German-speaking populations. Indeed by 1938 and the *Anschluss* with Austria, Hitler had managed to achieve "the ultimate goal of German nationalism, the establishment of *Grossdeutschland*, something which had eluded even Bismarck, and he had done so without provoking a war."[88] Had Hitler stopped there, the Nazi regime might very well have gone down in history as Germany's most popular and successful yet.

Conclusions

Understanding the fate of the Weimar Republic requires understanding the problematic legacies bequeathed to it by the old regime: a conservative elite entrenched in the military, judiciary, and bureaucracy; a deeply divided population; an aggressive and virulently anti-Semitic nationalist movement that fed off the sense that Germany was threatened by enemies within and without; a plurality political party, the SPD, suspicious of "bourgeois" groups and institutions and lacking national governing experience; and a catastrophic failed war and a "stab in the back" legend to justify it. As if these legacies were not enough, upon coming to power Germany's first democracy immediately confronted extreme right- and left-wing radicalism, the fallout from a lost war and punitive peace, growing political disorder, and then a Great Inflation and a Great Depression. Even with more than "two strikes" against it, the Republic's ultimate fate still depended on the actions of conservative elites. Desperate to eviscerate democracy, but lacking the popular support to do so, landed, business, military, and other elites believed they could use Hitler and the NSDAP to achieve their goals and then push them aside to regain their "rightful" place at atop the German political order.

This did not happen, of course, and this is because they, like so many others, did not appreciate the revolutionary nature of the Nazis. The Nazis represented a powerful and truly modern alternative to liberal, capitalist democracy in a way traditional, elitist authoritarian movements did not. By the time of the Great Depression, the NSDAP had a sophisticated organizational infrastructure, deeps roots in civil society, a message designed to appeal to a wide range of dissatisfied voters, and a broad, cross-class support base. Rather than promising a return to an old order that largely excluded them, the Nazis instead promised Germans a new order that would provide stability, unity, solidarity, community, a sense of purpose, and international prominence. The price to be paid for this new order turned out to be the death of many of Germany's own citizens, particularly its Jews, and the destruction of much of the rest of Europe.

The Nazi project of course ultimately failed but not before transforming Germany's state, society, and economy and the rest of Europe to an unimaginable and appalling degree. Ironically some of these transformations would help clear the way for the rebirth of liberal democracy in Germany and Europe at the end of the Second World War. Before examining how and why that occurred (see chapter 14), another type of political path traversed during the interwar years must be examined: that which occurred in Spain.

CHAPTER 13

Political Development in Spain

The Second Republic was not a very democratic democracy.
—Javier Tussell[1]

THE COLLAPSE OF democracy in Spain was the last in a chain of democratic breakdowns during the interwar years that included Italy, Germany, and other countries (see chapter 9, table 9.1). The lateness of Spain's democratic breakdown contributed to some of its distinctive features, including the radicalization of the left and the right, and the foreign intervention in the civil war that followed democracy's collapse. The Spanish civil war, moreover, turned into a horrific prelude to the Second World War, left hundreds of thousands dead, and gave rise to a decades-long dictatorship that endured until the dictator, Franco, died in 1975. The demise of this dictatorship helped set off the "third wave" of democracy.

Why did democracy collapse in Spain, and why did this collapse lead to a conservative military dictatorship and not a revolutionary, mass-mobilizing fascist or National Socialist one as in Italy or Germany? Spain shared some important similarities with but also differed significantly from other countries where democracy failed during the interwar period. Like Italy and Germany, interwar Spain was plagued by disorder and violence, centrifugal tendencies within its party system, mass parties on the right and left lacking a firm commitment to democracy, and a growing sense by much of the population that the existing state was either unwilling or unable to protect their interests. Also like Italy and Germany, Spain lacked the strong sense of national identity that helps populations persevere through and reach compromises during difficult times. However, unlike Italy and Germany, Spain was an "old" country with the crown and state dating back to at least the fifteenth century, lacked simmering conflicts with its neighbors over borders or irredentist populations, and was neutral during the First World War. Thus despite a relatively weak state and sense of national identity, Spain lacked many of the characteristics and experiences that generated virulent, revisionist nationalism in Germany, Italy, and other "new" countries in Europe. Spain also differed socioeconomically from Germany and even Italy. It was extremely poor (see Figure 13.1), and lacked the large, disaffected middle class that provided the main support base for national socialism in Germany and to a somewhat lesser extent, fascism in Italy (see chapters 11 and 12).

Neither did it have a large working class, the group most likely to throw its support behind the other force opposed to liberal democracy, communism. The Spanish economy remained largely agricultural into the 1930s and its rural areas were dominated by traditional, conservative landowning elites who owned approximately two-thirds of the country's land and were semi-feudal in their attitudes and behavior.[2] Spain's low level of socioeconomic

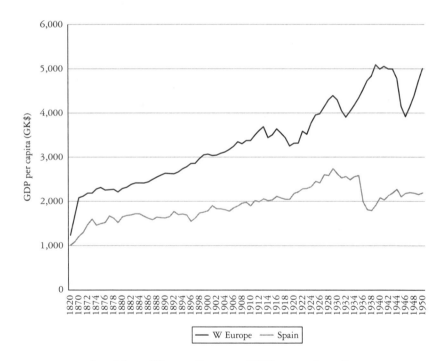

FIGURE 13.1 Spanish vs. Western European GDP per capita, 1820–1950.
Note: *GK$ hypothetical unit of currency that has the same purchasing power parity that the U.S. dollar had in the United States at a given point in time.
Source: The Maddison-Project, http://www.ggdc.net/maddison/maddison-project/home.htm, 2013 version.

development combined with its weak nation-state enabled other traditional conservative forces like the Church and military to retain significant power, and these groups preferred Catholic conservatism to fascism.

In addition to considering the interwar conditions that contributed to democracy's collapse, understanding Spain's political development during the 1930s also requires examining its prewar past. The challenges confronting the Second Republic were but the latest manifestation of political, social, and economic problems that had plagued Spain since long before the interwar era began.

Early Modern Spain

As noted in chapter 2, Spain entered the modern era with a relatively weak national state. This is perhaps surprising since Spain began the early modern period as one of Europe's great powers. Historians often date the birth of modern Spain to the uniting of the kingdoms of Aragon and Castile in 1469 with the marriage of Ferdinand II of Aragon and Isabella I of Castile.[3] Ferdinand and Isabella revived the power of the monarchy and built a powerful military that enabled them to lay the foundations for an overseas empire by financing the voyages of Christopher Columbus, reconquering Iberian territories previously captured by the Moors, and religiously "cleansing" the peninsula of Jews and Muslims. The latter two helped cement Catholicism as central to Spanish identity. Despite Ferdinand and Isabella's "achievements," they governed their territories in a fairly traditional manner, as a dynastic union or "composite kingdom"[4] through personal alliances with local and provincial elites and institutions.[5] Aragon, Castile, and the other regions under Ferdinand and Isabella's control retained their own customs, privileges, laws, currency, trade barriers, and political traditions rather than being merged into a unified political entity. The monarchy's need to fight the Moors partially explains this: in order to mobilize Spain's nobility and territories to participate in wars, ancient privileges or *fueros*[6] were strengthened or expanded.[7] This pattern continued even after Ferdinand and Isabella left the scene. When subsequent territories in Europe and the New World were added to Spain they were not forced to adopt Castilian or Spanish institutions or norms. Thus, the vaunted Spanish Empire remained "throughout the sixteenth century an agglomeration of unrelated States, with scarcely a trace of imperial unity or imperial mystique common to all."[8]

A dramatic attempt to centralize power in an absolutist monarchy along the lines of what was going on in other parts of Europe at the time was made in the middle of the seventeenth century under Philip (or Felipe) IV and his great minister, Olivares. Like his contemporary, Richelieu (see chapter 2),[9] Olivares sought to counteract the centrifugal tendencies that threatened to tear his country apart by consolidating authority in the monarchy.[10] Early in his reign Olivares secretly wrote to Philip IV that

> The most important thing in Your Majesty's monarchy is for you to become king of Spain: by this I mean, Sir, that Your Majesty should not be content with being king of Portugal, of Aragon, of Valencia and count of Barcelona, but should secretly plan and work to reduce these kingdoms of which Spain is composed to the style and laws of Castile, with no difference whatsoever. And if Your Majesty achieves this, you will be the most powerful prince in the world.[11]

Accomplishing this would require confronting the privileges, including freedom from much taxation, long enjoyed by Spain's regions and elites since they made it difficult for the crown to raise the fiscal resources necessary to compete in the conflict-prone seventeenth century.[12] The status quo also raised tensions among Spanish regions since it meant Castile, which the crown controlled most directly, bore a disproportionate share of the tax burden. Indeed by the early seventeenth century the growing cost of war combined with Castile's financial exhaustion created a financial crisis (see Figure 13.2).[13]

In order to deal with this crisis, Olivares came up with an ambitious reform program that would distribute military and fiscal burdens more equitably among Spain's regions, increase conformity among them, and pivot the monarchy away from its traditional Castilian base to a more truly Spanish one. Doing this would "require entirely new constitutional arrangements and the abandonment of treasured privileges" and consequently elicited fierce resistance.[14] Catalonia revolted, leading to over a dozen years of conflict that ended with the loss of part of its territory to France—and thereby the division of Catalan-speaking lands forever[15]—but also with its traditional privileges more or less re-confirmed by the Spanish crown. A rebellion in Portugal was even more successful, permanently ending its union with Spain. Faced with widespread resistance from its regions as well as its nobility, Philip IV backed down, dismissing Olivares in 1643 in what was a huge victory for "traditionalist" forces favoring the status quo. As one scholar put it, "the real significance of the fall of Olivares was not [merely] the fate of his policies but the manner of his going. The fall of Olivares was [caused by] aristocratic pressure. . . . It was symptomatic of a much broader process which some historians have described by the term 'refeudalisation.'" With Olivares's

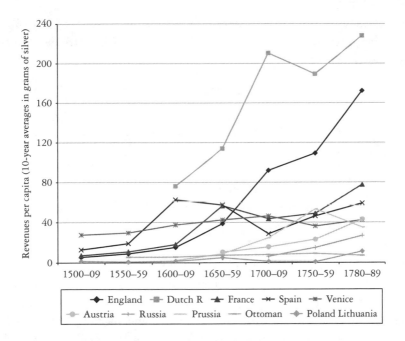

FIGURE 13.2 Annual revenues per capita of European states (10-year averages in tons of silver), 1500–1789.

Source: Kivanc, Karaman and Svket Pamuk, "Ottoman State Finances in European Perspective, 1500-1914," *Journal of Economic History*, 70, 2010, 593–629.

dismissal the decline of state power continued. Control over Spain's territory "re-fragmented," state functions and bureaucracies became "privatized," the power of privileged groups grew while that of the monarchy declined, and the loyalties of Spaniards became "increasingly diffused."[16]

Thus at the same time that central authority and institutions were being strengthened in France, Britain, and some other parts of Europe, Spain was going in the opposite direction.[17] Indeed by the late seventeenth century Spain seemed to many contemporaries to be "cast back into the fourteenth century"[18] with state building going in reverse, the power and efficacy of its army and navy shrinking,[19] its taxation capacity declining, and its regions, towns, and nobility[20] re-asserting their power and independence. Spain's internal market fragmentation and variegated monetary, tax, juridical, and other institutions also hindered economic development.[21] Spain's weak national state, in short, helps explain why it experienced a much-noted decline during the early modern period. The nature of Spanish state-building also helped create many of the political challenges—social divisions,[22] a weak sense of national identity, a recalcitrant and fractious nobility, a powerful and reactionary Church, a military that was one of country's few truly national institutions, and economic backwardness—the country faced during the modern era.[23]

Spain from the French Revolution to the First World War

As we know from previous chapters, the nineteenth century was turbulent. Even from a comparative perspective, however, Spain experienced a high degree of political instability.

The event with which the "long" nineteenth century[24] began—the French Revolution—undermined Spain's already weak political institutions and exacerbated existing socioeconomic and political cleavages. When Napoleon's troops came to Spain in 1808, disgust with the old order was widespread, and the reigning king, Charles IV, was weak and incompetent. Napoleon took advantage of this to march his troops into Spain, where they were initially greeted with enthusiasm.[25] However, rather than stabilizing Spain, the French invasion disrupted it further. Soon after the French invasion, a popular uprising forced Charles IV to abdicate in favor of his son, Ferdinand VII. But Napoleon wanted his own man on the throne and so forced Ferdinand VII to cede the crown to his own brother, Joseph Bonaparte.

With the old order gone and chaos reigning across much of the country Joseph attempted to put in place a new order that, although authoritarian, included many centralizing and liberalizing reforms that previous Spanish regimes had been unable to achieve, including equality of taxation, abolishing privilege and other feudal legacies, and eliminating barriers to a single market and a unified territory. Having long resisted attempts by the Spanish crown to centralize power, its regions, municipalities, and citizens fiercely resisted any attempt by foreigners to do the same. Uprisings spread, and Joseph found it almost impossible to control territory his troops did not physically occupy.[26] Not surprisingly given Spain's previous history and the collapse of the old order, resistance to French rule was decentralized, consisting primarily of what we would today consider guerilla warfare. (Indeed, the terms "guerilla" and "guerilla warfare" come from this period of Spanish resistance to French rule.[27]) Guerilla warfare is, of course, difficult to defeat using traditional armies, and Joseph was unable to do so: in fact, he was forced to flee the country several times when disorder got out of control. The way the Spanish fought was effective but chaotic and "reinforced rather than curbed Spain's long tradition of localism."[28] As one scholar notes, "between 1808 and 1814 Spain experienced the most devastating struggle in her entire history." Troops "marched and counter-marched across the face of the peninsula. City after city was [destroyed] by assaults and sieges. A savage guerrilla war and burgeoning social unrest reduced parts of the country to anarchy."[29]

Joseph was finally driven out in May 1813. As difficult and bloody as the struggle against the French was, it turned out to be easier than reaching agreement on the type of order that should replace the old and Napoleonic ones.

A first attempt came with the constitution of 1812, drafted by the Spanish national assembly while the country was still at war with France. This was Spain's first constitution and perhaps the most liberal in Europe at the time, calling for universal manhood suffrage, a constitutional monarchy checked by a national parliament (*Cortes*), the elimination of privilege, and institutionalizing important liberal rights, including equality before the law, freedom of the press, property rights, and so on.[30] This constitution did not, however, last very long. After Napoleon's defeat, the Allies restored Ferdinand VII to the throne in May 1814. He promptly rejected the 1812 constitution, replacing it with a conservative monarchical order closely tied to the Catholic Church.[31] This provoked uprisings, culminating in an 1820 revolt supported by troops under Colonel Rafael del Riego that transitioned Spain back towards a more liberal political order. In 1823 this liberal order was overthrown and Ferdinand was again restored to the throne, this time by French troops. He ruled until his death in 1833, but as he lay dying, his wife, Maria Christina, convinced him to set aside the Salic law barring female inheritance of the throne so that his infant daughter, Isabella II, could become queen. In response, Ferdinand's brother, Don Carlos, revolted, claiming this move to be illegitimate and that he was the rightful king. The division between Isabella's and Carlos's supporters led to a series of civil wars, often referred to as the Carlist wars (after Don Carlos) that contributed to giving Spain the dubious distinction of spending "more years at war than almost any other European country during the nineteenth century."[32] Carlists were drawn from the landed elite, regions like Catalonia and the Basque country eager to protect or restore "historic liberties," and small farmers and others threatened by capitalism and liberal economic reforms; these groups generally favored a political order closely allied with the Church that protected traditional privileges. Isabella's supporters were somewhat more liberal.

Between 1833 and 1868 Isabella II ruled Spain, but Carlists rejected her legitimacy, and patronage, corruption, and military intrigue were rife. In 1868 an uprising forced Isabella into exile but after she was gone divisions among her opponents quickly emerged. Some favored transitioning to a republic, others wanted a new monarch, but this latter group could not agree on whether this new monarch should be Isabella's son Alfonso or someone else.[33] Eventually, an Italian prince, Amadeo of Savoy, was invited to take the Spanish throne under a new constitution written by the Cortes in 1870. Almost as soon as he arrived, however, Amadeo learned that one of his key supporters, General Prim, a leader of the uprising against Isabella, had been assassinated and things went downhill from there. Amadeo was opposed by Republicans and faced uprisings by Carlists; unable to stabilize the situation he gave up after a couple of years and hightailed it back to Italy. With Amadeo's abdication another transition occurred, with the Cortes declaring Spain to be a federal Republic with universal manhood suffrage. This first Spanish Republic proved as unstable as its predecessors, quickly confronting another Carlist war and a major revolt in Cuba. After about a year and a half (May 1873–December 1874), the military intervened in support of a monarchical restoration under Isabella's son, Alfonso XII. During the nineteenth century military intervention became the dominant method of political change[34] in Spain. One scholar estimates that "between 1814 and 1874 there were 37 coup attempts, of which twelve were successful."[35]

With Alfonso's restoration in 1874 Spain seemed to have gone full circle in less than six years, from monarchy to Republic and back to monarchy again.[36] However, Alfonso's regime differed from its predecessors. It was a constitutional monarchy with a two-chamber parliament and equality before the law, freedom of assembly and association, and the protection of property rights embedded in the constitution. However, the new political order could not fix Spain's myriad problems, particularly the need to incorporate its people into political life. Stanley Payne fittingly characterized Spain during this period as being ruled by a "19th century oligarchy" confronting "20th century problems."[37] The political system was corrupt and exclusionary, and the country's two main parties, the liberals and conservatives, protected elites rather than responding to the people more generally. Spanish liberals and conservatives took turns governing, excluding other groups from power via "systemic and massive election rigging."[38] At the local level, politics was controlled by political bosses, or *caciques*, who acted as "agents of the political oligarchy" and doled out patronage in return for support.[39] So entrenched were these *caciques* that the introduction of universal male suffrage in 1890 did not change much.[40] Although corruption ensured some superficial stability, it also ensured that Spaniards learned to view voting as a "farce,"[41] which probably contributed to a tendency to resort to extra-parliamentary activity. Strikes, assassinations, church burnings, and uprisings became common, and "hardly a year [went] by without martial law being imposed somewhere in the country."[42] Spain's political order and parties thus resembled in many ways their Italian counterparts (see chapter 8), but differed from France and England where by the late nineteenth century liberals in both countries and conservatives in England had cultivated fairly broad bases of support, and political institutions provided regularized and predictable ways of channeling societal demands into political outcomes (see chapters 6, 9, and 10).

Alongside political disorder, Spain remained extremely poor,[43] with workers in urban and rural areas being particularly bad off.[44] Internationally, Spain fell further behind its erstwhile competitors, being crushed in the Spanish American war in 1898 and losing what remained of its once massive colonial empire at the same time as other European countries were expanding theirs. The year 1898 came to be known as "the Disaster," generating calls for national "regeneration" and increasing calls to turn back the clock to Spain's "glory days," when it was a traditional, Catholic monarchical dictatorship, free of the stain of democracy, liberalism, and other modern "corruptions."[45]

From the First World War to the Transition to Democracy

Spain did not participate in the First World War, but the shock waves produced by it destabilized the country nonetheless. As one observer put it, by 1914 the Spanish political order was like "an incapacitated person whose bodily resistance had become so reduced as to make him vulnerable to infection."[46] Economic dislocation[47] and the radicalization produced by the Bolshevik Revolution aggravated Spain's already high levels of social conflict. Between 1918 and 1920 the country was convulsed by labor unrest; these years came to be known as the "trienio bolchevique" or "Bolshevist Triennium."[48] The king and governments were unable to deal with this unrest or respond to the mass dissatisfaction causing it. Neither liberals nor conservatives were capable of mobilizing and organizing voters, and partially as a result, both declined during the early twentieth century.[49] Between 1917 and 1923 Spain had over a dozen governments with an average life-span of about five months. Meanwhile, the military, the traditional arbiter of Spanish political life, was aggrieved by low salaries and poor resources and suffered a humiliating defeat at Annual, Morocco, in 1921,[50] which many blamed on the lack of support provided by reigning elites and institutions.[51] By 1923 when Spain was hit with yet another wave of violence and unrest that reached "ominous proportions,"[52] many Spaniards had already concluded that their country had reached a political "dead-end."[53]

When General Miguel Primo de Rivera overthrew the existing government in September 1923 and declared himself dictator, his coup (or *pronunciamiento*) was generally welcomed, particularly by middle- and upper-class groups frightened by worker mobilization and the specter of Bolshevism.[54] Manuel Azaña, later prime minister in the Second Republic, "spoke of liberation from a state 'of impotence and imbecility'"[55] while the last prime minister, Manuel García-Prieto, is reported to have said that he was grateful to Primo de Rivera for "reliev[ing] him of the impossible task of governing Spain."[56] Primo de Rivera's coup can be interpreted as the latest in a long line of military interventions that followed impotent political regimes[57] or even perhaps as a half-hearted attempt to transition to a quasi-fascist regime. Primo de Rivera claimed to be a new kind of dictator, interested in serving the "national interest" and in promoting national "regeneration" and modernization.[58] He claimed to be

> neither of the Right nor Left; we do not come in response to a social or political ideology. . . . We come to purify the air, to re-establish discipline, to destroy the closed cliques of the professional politicians, so that the road cleared for them, civilians will be able to install a new politics.[59]

To the middle class and business, Primo de Rivera presented himself as a sort of "developmental dictator," offering a combination of economic nationalism, modernization, and protection against the "red menace."[60] To the landed elite, a group to which he belonged, Primo de Rivera offered a largely hands-off policy with regard to their inefficient, semi-feudal, and repressive estates. And to the military and other conservatives, Primo de Rivera offered a hard line vis-à-vis Spain's regions, rejecting political decentralization and suppressing local languages and other manifestations of cultural distinctiveness. Primo de Rivera aligned his regime with traditional Catholicism and supported the Church's role in educational, cultural, and other realms.

Primo de Rivera aspired, however, not merely to gain the support of Spain's traditional elites. He recognized that mass politics and a growing labor movement were here to stay[61] and hoped to attract the latter through a combination of economic interventionism and corporatism. Primo de Rivera believed that it was the state's role to "manage" the economy and ensure that neither the "ravings" nor "ambitions" of individuals stood in the way of the "national interest." He supported protectionism; updated Spain's woefully backward infrastructure, including its rail, road, and electricity networks as well as its education system; established corporatist institutions that included labor, business, and government representatives; and instituted a variety of social reforms, including public works, "cheap houses, a medical service, and above all a machinery of labour arbitration which the Socialist leaders accepted and dominated."[62] It is worth stressing, however, that these efforts were directed towards urban rather than rural workers. "No serious effort was made by the Dictator to tackle the social injustice inherent in *latifundismo*."[63]

Despite some successes, perhaps most notably resolving the conflict in Morocco, Primo de Rivera was unable to stabilize Spain. Although they initially welcomed an end to social disorder, the repression of the labor movement, and many of his other policies, landed and business elites as well as other conservatives became increasingly wary of Primo de Rivera's "modernizing" tendencies, economic interventionism, corporatist predilections, social reforms, and outreach to workers.[64] The labor movement, meanwhile, although willing to cooperate in return for concrete material gains, was frustrated by the suppression of political participation and Primo's unwillingness to challenge the power of landed, business, and other conservative elites.[65] In addition, although Primo de Rivera ultimately created a political movement, the *Unión Patriótica* (UP), he did so after he came to power, rather than before, and the UP was not a modern party with a distinct ideology backed by a powerful cross-class coalition along the lines of the fascists in Italy or the National Socialists in Germany (see chapters 11 and 12). As economic and financial problems mounted in the late 1920s causing a fresh wave of social unrest and economic suffering, Primo de Rivera's limited and conditional support melted away.[66] When the king and his own generals made clear they had lost confidence in him, Primo de Rivera resigned, leaving for Paris in January 1930 where he died less than two months later.

Primo de Rivera left behind a country "more troubled and difficult to govern than" when he took power. During the 1920s Spain experienced the most rapid economic growth in its modern history and Spanish society had accordingly become more urban, educated, and politically mobilized.[67] Meanwhile, Primo de Rivera's regime helped finish off the liberal and conservative parties around which Restoration politics had revolved, and because the king had supported Rivera, the monarchy was largely discredited as well.[68] When de Rivera's dictatorship collapsed in 1930 the king, Alfonso III, and his head of government, Dámaso Berenguer, no longer had the support of even the military elite, and when monarchists were soundly thrashed in municipal elections in April 1931, Alfonso simply left Spain. "Abandoned by the traditional pillars of the crown, the monarchy, which counted its origin in the ninth century, had ended with a whimper."[69]

With the old regime, Primo de Rivera's half-hearted quasi-fascist military dictatorship, and now the monarchy now gone, a transition to democracy occurred in April 1931. During the next five or so years the Second Republic had to deal with the problems left behind by previous regimes as well as the challenges posed by the interwar years. Between 1931 and 1936 the Second Republic passed through essentially three phases. The first, lasting from the transition to democracy through 1933, is often referred to as the "reformist biennium" (*bienio reformador*), and was dominated by governments of the center-left that aimed to transform Spain from a conservative Catholic into a secular socialist or at least social democratic society. During the second phase, lasting from the end of 1933 through the beginning of 1936, parties of the center and right took over in a period sometimes referred to as the "two black years" (*bienio negro*), during which Spain's traditional, conservative power holders re-grouped and attempted to turn the back the clock on many of the reforms passed during previous years. And the third phase, lasting from 1936 to 1939, began with the election of a Popular Front government and ended with civil war.

The Second Republic

The transition to democracy was relatively peaceful in Spain. Unlike many other new interwar democracies (see chapters 9–12), the Spanish transition did not occur at the end of a calamitous war, and in 1931 the "traditional" political alternatives in Spain—some type of monarchy or military dictatorship—had, for the time being, been discredited.[70] This was also, accordingly, the first time in "recent memory" that regime change in Spain was not accompanied by military intervention.[71] However, much else about the context within which the transition to democracy occurred was inauspicious. By 1931 Mussolini was already in power in nearby Italy, democracy was troubled in much of the rest of Europe, and the Great Depression was beginning to wreak havoc.[72] And of course, the Second Republic was burdened by problems left behind by its predecessors.

Economically, Spain remained extremely poor and pervaded by "brutal economic inequalities."[73] The single most important cause of economic underdevelopment was the country's inefficient and, in many areas, labor-repressive agriculture, which previous regimes did little to reform. There were relatively few medium-size or self-sufficient peasant farms of the type that dominated

France, Scandinavia, and parts of Germany; instead Spain's agricultural sector was dominated by micro-holdings too small for subsistence farming and, particularly in the south, large estates (*latifundios*) that were unproductive, inefficient, and required an army of landless laborers willing to accept wretched wages and living conditions in order for the estates to remain profitable.[74] It was precisely in the areas "where large owners monopolized the soil, [that] agrarian unrest was endemic, constantly upsetting the political life not only of the South, but also of the nation."[75]

Another unresolved problem inherited by the Second Republic was regionalism: Catalonia and the Basque country in particular harbored strong separatist sentiments, but previous regimes had rejected federalism and repressed local or regional languages, cultures, traditions, and so on.[76] That these regions were also Spain's most economically developed only exacerbated regional resentments. Much of the military opposed anything that threatened Spain's unity, which meant the Second Republic had to deal with conflicts between the military and other powerful political actors favoring centralism and regions favoring political decentralization and protective of their own identities and cultures.

The Second Republic also inherited an intensely polarized society. In addition to divisions between rich and poor, large landowners and landless laborers and peasants, centralizers and separatists, Spain was also riven by cleavages between committed Catholics and hardline secularists and between those who had historically opposed and favored Republicanism and democracy.

The anti-democratic camp included the landed elite since it depended on labor-repressive agriculture and therefore opposed any political regime that would empower labor or shift the balance of power in the countryside. The military, meanwhile, although initially not opposed to the Republic, had long played an independent role in Spain's political life and was wary of civilian oversight. And then there was the deeply conservative Spanish church—perhaps the most powerful in Europe.[77]

The Church's power was a product or reflection of the historical weakness of the Spanish state. Unlike in many other parts of Europe the Spanish state had not taken over the Church's traditional roles in education and the provision of social services, instead remaining allied with and dependent upon it. Spanish society was accordingly less secular than its counterparts even in other parts of Catholic Southern Europe.[78] And since the Spanish Church did not confront a powerful state, it was never forced to "modernize" or reform like most of its European counterparts; indeed, it retained "quasi-medieval"[79] scholastic positions and politically reactionary tendencies and was full of "incorrigible ultramontanes and *integristas* (essentially, fundamentalists) intent on returning Spain to a confessional society."[80] However, because the Church had allied with the Carlists in the first Carlist war, the liberal victors punished the Church by confiscating its lands. This made the Church dependent on the state for resources and thus even more interested in ensuring a pliant regime.[81] Also important is that Catholicism had historically been one of the few things unifying Spain's population—since the time of the "Catholic Monarchs" Ferdinand and Isabella, Catholicism had been integral to what it meant to be Spanish.[82]

In addition to leaving the Second Republic to cope with powerful anti-democratic and anti-liberal forces wedded to a vision of Spain as a traditional, hierarchical Catholic society,[83] previous regimes left behind limited proto-democratic legacies to counter them. By 1931 a parliament (*Cortes*) had long existed, but governments were not formed based on support in it or on election results (elections in any case being mostly rigged). Spain's two traditional political parties, the Liberals and Conservatives, remained elite organizations and did little to integrate the people into political life. With the transition to democracy, therefore, the task of leading Spain fell to parties largely unprepared for such a task. And, as we will see, the two largest and most important of them—the socialist PSOE (*Partido Socialista Obrero Español*) and the Catholic conservative CEDA (*Confederación Española de Derechas Autónomas*)—were not fully committed to liberal democracy. Instead, both had "instrumental," or what the Spanish literature refers to as "accidentalist," views of democracy: they accepted it only insofar as it enabled them to achieve other, more fundamental goals. Of the Republic's myriad parties only the PSOE had a history as a mass party but even it was relatively new compared to its European counterparts. It sent, for example, its first deputy to the Cortes in 1910 while in nearby Italy the socialists already had thirty-three seats in Parliament by the turn of the century. The Second Republic's political center, meanwhile, was divided among many parties that, although favoring democracy, differed in their views of the PSOE and (later) the CEDA and in the amount of social and economic reform they favored. These parties were also mostly new and lacked well-developed internal organizations or strong connections with voters.[84]

Between 1931 and 1933 Spain was governed by the PSOE and a collection of centrist, Republican parties. Within the initial provisional government (April–October 1931), a critical division emerged between the PSOE and left Republicans who believed the transition to democracy should begin socially and economically transforming Spain and more moderate Republicans who prioritized stabilizing democracy. The former were initially the dominant force and quickly began pursuing extensive social and economic reforms.[85]

The first article of Spain's new constitution declared the Republic to be one "of workers of all classes." Another article, forty-four, stated that all the country's wealth would be subordinated to the interests of the "national economy," that "the ownership of all kinds of goods is subject to forcible expropriation for the sake of social utility through adequate compensation," and that the "State may intervene by law [into the workings of industries and companies] when so required to streamline production and the interests of the national economy."[86] The constitution also committed the Republic to guaranteeing "every worker [the] conditions necessary for a dignified existence. Social legislation shall regulate: health insurance, accident, forced unemployment, old age, disability and death, the work of women and youth, and especially the protection of motherhood, working hours and minimum wage and family, paid annual holidays; conditions of the Spanish worker abroad; co-operatory institutions, the economic and judicial relationship of the factors that make up the production, the participation of workers in management, administration and the benefits of businesses, and everything that affects the defense of workers."[87]

Alongside major social and economic reforms, the constitution also promised Spain's regions significant autonomy. This had the greatest impact in Catalonia where substantial powers were devolved to a regional government and parliament.[88] The constitution also pledged to transform Church-state relations, not merely separating the two but subordinating the former to the latter and attempting to secularize society to a degree that had taken generations in France and other parts of Europe.[89] The constitution declared that Spain no longer had an official religion, introduced civil marriage and divorce, ended state payments to the clergy, took education out of Church hands, ordered all religious orders to register with the Ministry of Justice, limited their activities, and threatened those deemed dangerous with closure. The Jesuit order was, in fact, dissolved and its property nationalized.[90]

In addition to dramatic reforms enshrined in the constitution, the provisional government and the minister of labor, Francisco Largo Caballero, issued a series of decrees promising to shift power relationships in society and economy. For example, a "Municipal Boundaries Law" required all rural workers in a municipality to be employed before employers hired "immigrants," thereby hindering employers from shopping around for the most desperate workers; a "compulsory cultivation decree" declared that if owners refused to cultivate land according to "normal uses and customs," it could be confiscated and handed over to workers' organizations; arbitration panels were empowered to deal with labor-market disputes; an eight-hour workday was established; and more.[91] These policies were accompanied by a huge increase in unionization from about 13 percent in 1920 to about 45.5 percent in 1931,[92] an enormous rise in strikes and other forms of labor unrest, and the growing power of socialists in the rural labor market and political institutions.[93]

Moderate Republicans disagreed with many of changes pursued by the PSOE and left Republicans. The liberal philosopher and Republican leader José Ortega y Gasset,[94] for example, criticized these parties for treating themselves as "masters of the [current] situation" and "claiming the State for their own," rather than reaching out to and compromising with others. "The Republic is one thing," he insisted, "radicalism is another."[95] Indeed, discomfort with the provisional government's religious policies in particular led two Catholic Republican ministers to resign; that the authorities seemed unwilling or unable to control attacks against Churches, priests, and convents certainly did not help.[96] The Radicals (PRR, *Partido Republicano Radical*), the largest center party and the second-largest party in the Cortes, also left the government when the constitution passed.[97] With this, "the Republic's founding coalition [lost] . . . the last of the centrist parties and the chief representative of the liberal middle classes."[98]

With the Radicals gone, the government now consisted of left Republicans and the PSOE and was led by Manuel Azaña of the Republican Action (*Acción Republicana*) party. Azaña's government passed further military reforms, requiring army officers to swear an oath of allegiance to the Republic, downsizing the officer corps by voluntary retirement if possible but by forced removal if necessary, reducing the military budget, making promotions merit- rather than seniority-based, and closing the military academy, headed by Francisco Franco.[99] Probably the area most in need of reform, however, was agriculture. The "Law on Municipal Boundaries" and other legislation extending worker protection and social policies to agricultural laborers improved conditions in the countryside, but without land reform, particularly in the south, social peace and political stability would remain elusive. A basic problem, of course, was that satisfying the demands of Spain's large class of landless laborers and "micro" farmers for land and "justice"[100] was opposed by landed elites. A technical commission set up by the provisional government recommended a wide-ranging land reform to resettle 60,000–75,000 families annually on land from estates that exceeded a certain size, whether owned by nobles or non-nobles, absentee-owners or direct cultivators, but these proposals were vociferously opposed by the landed elite, the conservative and Catholic press, some center parties,[101] and also perhaps surprisingly, the left, which viewed them as not radical enough. As a result, the "potentially most revolutionary proposal produced by the Republic prior to 1936 was discarded mostly because the bourgeois Republicans would not accept the enormous political risks it entailed [and the Socialists were blind] to its revolutionary possibilities."[102] Azaña's government eventually put forward another Agrarian Law in September 1932 targeting fewer landowners and fewer types of land with expropriation,[103] but this law also generated opposition from the large absentee landowners it primarily targeted as well as smaller proprietors who worried expropriation would eventually affect them. Combined with the vacillation of the minister of agriculture, Marcelino Domingo, Azaña's own somewhat tentative commitment, and the inadequate budget the law provided for land purchase and redistribution, its impact turned out to be relatively limited.[104] Part of the reason for the government's lack of vigor is that by 1933 it was in trouble. The Church and its supporters were incensed by religious reforms,[105] with many viewing them as confirming that a "secret alliance of Jews, Freemasons and [Communists were] conspiring to destroy Christian Europe, with Spain as its principal target."[106] Many in the military were upset by the government's "attacks" on its traditional independence, and the landed elite declared "all-out war on the Republic" as a result of land and labor-market reforms.[107] But it was not merely the right that was increasingly opposed to the government; hostility from the left was growing as well.

After years of political exclusion and socioeconomic repression under previous regimes, the transition to democracy led to an explosion of political mobilization and rising expectations that even under the best of circumstances —for example, a regime with strong political institutions and parties, favorable international political and economic conditions—would have been extremely difficult to satisfy. As one contemporary observer noted, "The workers and peasants attributed a mythical significance to the republican form of government. To it they attached their yearning for social jus tice, and they believe it to be the cornerstone of a new society based on new economic and social precepts. They trust[ed] the Republic to rescue them from their misery."[108] Although the provisional and Azaña governments passed many reforms, these promised gradual rather than rapid and radical change. Thus alongside growing opposition from the right, including a serious coup attempt in 1932, the Azaña government confronted strikes, land occupations, assassinations, and attacks on factories, estates, and Churches, many of which were the work of anarchists.

Whereas in much of the rest of interwar Europe the left was divided between socialists and communists, in Spain the main split was between socialists and anarchists (or anarcho-syndicalists). This was partially because Spain had a relatively small industrial working class, obviously limiting the appeal of parties focused on the urban proletariat. In addition, the antipathy or indifference of both socialism and communism to regional and ethnic concerns diminished their appeal in Spain. Perhaps also relevant was that by flirting with revolutionary rhetoric and behavior particularly during the latter years of the Republic, the PSOE may have undercut the appeal of communism. In any case, anarchism—with its distrust of centralized authority and penchant for direct action—appealed to Spain's landless laborers, sharecroppers, and small tenant farmers as well as to those living in regions historically suspicious of the national government.[109] Catalonia, for example, was an anarchist hotbed, despite being among the most industrialized regions of Spain.

Anarchists despised the socialists, rejected democracy, and embraced violence. In January 1933 they engaged in another of their periodic insurrections. Like previous ones, it was poorly planned and lacked broad support, but during it a particularly tragic incident occurred at the village of Casas Viejas in Andalusia that dramatically affected the Azaña government and the Republic's political trajectory.

When anarchists rose up in Casas Viejas they were quickly beaten back, but after injuring a few of the Assault Guards sent in by the government to deal with the situation, some anarchists barricaded themselves in the home of one of their leaders. Reinforcement Guards ordered the leader's house set on fire, shot those trying to flee and then a dozen more villagers for good measure. This massacre elicited howls of protest from within the government and without[110] and, combined with a poor showing by the government in municipal elections and a weak vote of confidence in the Cortes, led the Republic's President, Niceto Alcalá-Zamora, to dismiss the Azaña government and call new elections for November 1933.

The election took place in a very different context from its predecessor. In 1931 the right was demoralized and divided but by 1933 it was revivified and united, led by a new Catholic Conservative party, CEDA (*Confederación Española de Derechas Autónomas*).[111]

The left Republicans and the PSOE, meanwhile, which had been united in 1931, were now demoralized and divided and unwilling to form electoral coalitions. Anarchists, meanwhile, advised their followers not to vote in the elections so as to accelerate democracy's demise. The election was extremely heated, with thousands of public meetings held, electioneering reaching all corners of the country, and new and varied forms of propaganda employed. The CEDA mounted a particularly impressive campaign, printing ten million leaflets and two hundred thousand color posters and using radio, cinema, and other forms of communication to mobilize Catholic voters and those wary of the left.[112] Since the Spanish electoral system greatly favored parties able to form electoral coalitions, the right gained a sweeping victory over the divided center and left and CEDA became the largest party. The PSOE, meanwhile, sunk to third place behind the Radicals.

The post-1933 parliament was extremely fragmented, with twenty-one parties; most deputies had no previous governing experience. Although the Cortes was now dominated by the moderate-center and right rather than the center and left, its largest party—now CEDA rather than the PSOE—was ambivalent about democracy.

Although the CEDA drew on previous Catholic political groupings, its motivating force was the attacks on the Church and religion undertaken by center-left governments, which, given the long-standing importance of the Church, the religiosity of many Spaniards, and the political power of forces committed to retaining Spain's Catholic identity, enabled it to gain the support of a fairly broad constituency.[113] Although many CEDA supporters opposed the Republic, the party initially took an accidentalist stance, insisting it would play by the democratic rules of the game—as long as these rules allowed it to achieve its goals. Its leader, Gil Robles, had, however, an unfortunate penchant for provocative, if not threatening rhetoric against "foreigners," Republicans, left-wingers, and others he viewed as bent on destroying Spain.[114] During the campaign he proclaimed that

> hardly an article of the Republic's legislation will be saved when the rightest reaction comes, a reaction that every day promises to be more terrible and intense, a total rectification will be carried out. . . . We are about to put democracy to the test, perhaps for the last time. It does not matter to us. We are going to parliament to defend our ideals, but if tomorrow parliament is against our ideals we shall go against parliament, because in politics, not the forms but the content is what interests us.[115]

Because of Robles's and the CEDA's accidentalism, the government that came to power after the 1933 elections was headed by Alejandro Lerroux of the Radicals rather than by Robles. The new government did not initially attempt to fully roll back the previous government's reforms, but it was clearly committed to reversing or watering down many of them. The CEDA was particularly intent on doing away with anti-clerical legislation, and during the *Bienio Negro* the substitution of secular for religious schools was halted; property was returned to the Jesuits and they were allowed resume teaching;

and state subsidies to the church were reinstated. In addition, the Agrarian Law as well as much labor market legislation was allowed to lapse or go unenforced, preparations for constitutional revisions were undertaken, local and regional officials out-of-step with the new government removed, and amnesty for those imprisoned as a result of the 1932 coup attempt declared.[116]

The left's response to the 1933 elections was rapid and radical: within days the PSOE's national committee began considering options including "armed insurrection," and the socialist press began speaking of the death of the "republican Republic" and the need for workers to "take all political power for themselves."[117] The PSOE's leader, Largo Cabellero, who had previously been a moderate, made clear he no longer believed it possible to achieve the party's goals via parliamentary means.[118] The increasingly dangerous international situation surely played a role in the PSOE's radicalization. By 1933 Hitler and Mussolini were in power, having destroyed the left in their respective countries with the help of traditional conservatives (see chapters 11 and 12). In addition, in February 1934 Austria collapsed into a civil war between socialists and Catholic conservatives, the latter bearing more than a passing resemblance to the CEDA. Reflecting the impact of the broader European context, the slogan "Better Vienna than Berlin"—better to go down fighting like the Austrian socialists then be meekly conquered like the Germans—became common on the Spanish left.[119] When three CEDA ministers joined the government in 1934 the left called a general strike. Catalonia, infuriated by the right's centralism as well as other policies, quickly joined. Luís Company, head of the autonomous Catalan government, declared "that monarchists and fascists had taken control of the government" and that as a result Catalonia was "breaking off all relations with [the Republic's] falsified institutions."[120] Uprisings broke out in other parts of Spain, but partially due to divisions on the left most of them quickly faltered. Internal PSOE discussions make clear, for example, that even within the party differences existed over what the actual goal of the uprising was.[121] In Asturias, however, miners turned the faltering strike movement into a full-scale insurrection, taking over the provincial capital and other small towns. In response, the government sent in General Francisco Franco and Moroccan troops known for their ferocity. These troops "gave themselves over to a repression which exceeded in horror and number any of the atrocities committed by the miners."[122] After putting down the revolt, Franco and his troops went on a rampage, killing over 1,000 people, wounding 2,000 to 4,000, taking perhaps another 30,000 to 40,000 prisoner, and engaging in looting, raping, and torture. Franco subsequently became known as the "butcher of Asturias." After Asturias, Company and other Catalan leaders were imprisoned, its separatist movement squashed and autonomy repealed, and martial law declared. Socialist and left Republican leaders, including Cabellero and Azaña, were arrested, most of the left's newspapers closed, and many town councils and arbitration boards suspended.[123]

The Asturias uprising and the ferocity of the government's response to it have led some to view the episode as the starting point of the Spanish civil war.[124] Certainly Asturias further deepened and hardened the left-right divide. For many on the left Asturias confirmed that only revolution and the elimination of "class enemies" could protect workers' interests, while for many on the right Asturias proved that the left was "foreign," sinister, hell-bent on "Bolshevism," and that the army was the only thing standing between Spain and communist revolution.[125] Asturias also further weakened and splintered the center, alienating the Radicals from left Republicans as a result of the former's alliance with CEDA and sanctioning of repressive measures.[126] After Asturias the government continued rolling back its predecessor's reforms, and when Robles took over the war ministry in 1935 conservative officers who would participate in the uprising against the Republic in July 1936[127] were given critical roles in the military. Robles's provocative rhetoric also intensified: in September 1935 he declared, for example, that he sought a "complete revision" of the constitution. "'And if the Cortes failed to pass this revision,' he added, 'the Cortes are dead and must disappear.'"[128]

In the fall of 1935 evidence of corruption by friends and relatives of the prime minister, Lerroux, as well as other leading Radicals helped discredit a party already weakened by its time in government and Asturias. With the Radicals in trouble, Robles, as the head of the largest party in Parliament, was the logical candidate to take over as prime minister. The Republic's president, Alcalá Zamora, did not however want to appoint Robles. Instead he dissolved the Cortes in January 1936 and gave a caretaker PM, Manuel Portela, the job of organizing new elections.

By the time of these elections Mussolini and Hitler were in power, left parties in these and other dictatorships had been destroyed, and the international situation was increasingly dangerous. As discussed in chapter 9, these conditions led to a course shift by the Soviets. Rather than encouraging communist parties to attack socialists and social democrats and actively attempt to overthrow democracy, the Soviets now advised communists to seek out Popular Front alliances to prevent fascist and National Socialist dictatorships. As noted above, up through the mid-1930s communism was a marginal political force in Spain: in the 1933 elections, for example, the Spanish communist party (PCE) received less than 2 percent of the vote. Advocating a Popular Front strategy, however, allowed the PCE to gain legitimacy on the left.

Meanwhile, Asturias, the growing power of the CEDA, and the frightening situation in Europe led other parties to consider a course change as well. The result was that by January 1936 the Republican left, the Republican Union, the Catalan left, and the socialist and communist parties agreed to fight the upcoming elections together behind a platform that essentially promised to restore the accomplishments of the "reformist biennium." Despite this, the Popular Front agreement did not signal a return to center-left unity. Indeed, the alliance was riven by different understandings of its rationale and purpose. For Azaña, protecting the Republic and restoring Spain to the path of peaceful reform was the goal, while for Largo Caballero defeating the right was paramount and the Republic of secondary, even questionable value.

Turnout for the 1936 election was unprecedented: 72 percent of eligible citizens voted, more than in 1931 or 1933. The election revealed a country almost evenly divided—or polarized—between left and right, with an eviscerated center. The Popular Front received about 47 percent of the vote; the CEDA and its "National Bloc" allies, which called for the restoration of a conservative, Catholic hierarchical political and social order, received about 46.5 percent; the Radical party, which had been the largest party of the center with 122 seats in the last Cortes, got only about 1 percent. Because of Spain's electoral law, the Popular Front, which had run a common slate throughout the country, ended up with over 100 more seats in the Cortes than the CEDA and the National Bloc. The left was also helped by anarchists urging their voters to go to the polls rather than abstain as in previous elections.[129] Also notable was the continued splintering of the Cortes: over thirty-three parties gained at least one seat; but only eleven got ten seats or more.

Despite being the largest party in the Cortes, the PSOE refused to join the government, as did the PCE. The PSOE's abstention was the result of deep internal divisions between its moderates, who believed the PSOE should focus on saving democracy, and its radicals, who were wary of "bourgeois" Republicans and the "bourgeois" Republic. The government that came to power after the 1936 elections thus included only the Republican left, Republican Union, and Catalan left parties and lacked a majority in the Cortes; it was dependent on support from the deeply divided PSOE and the deeply problematic PCE. As soon as Azaña, who initially again became prime minister, came to power he was confronted by a "trail of violence, murder and arson" that made governing extremely difficult.[130]

Despite the narrowness of the Popular Front's victory, many on the left acted as if "they had received a mandate for revolutionary change":[131] farm invasions and land seizures spread, gangs of workers forced farm managers to grant work, crop and animal theft increased, mobs freed political prisoners and forced the replacement of conservative municipal authorities, priests were harassed and churches and convents sacked and burned, and the socialist youth organization, which had merged with its communist counterpart, engaged in paramilitary training and clashes with its right-wing counterparts.[132] And beginning on May 1 Spain experienced what was perhaps the most severe strike wave in its history.[133] Dependent on support from the PSOE and PCE, the government needed to conciliate the left; the Cortes voted to restore all land taken from tenants during the *bienio negro,* passed a more extensive land reform bill than the 1932 Agrarian Law—more land was redistributed between March and July 1936 than in the preceding years of the Republic[134]—reinstated the anti-clerical legislation of the years 1931–1933, and restored provisions for regional autonomy. But despite these and other efforts, the PCE and anarchists remained intent on revolution as did the PSOE's radicals.[135] More generally the PSOE was weakened by splits between its radicals and moderates[136] and remained unwilling to join the government, despite the pleas of Azaña and others and the increasingly desperate situation in the country. Forces on the right, meanwhile, were also working to destabilize the Republic.

Just as the PSOE radicalized after losing the 1933 election, believing its opponents would use control of the government to eviscerate the labor movement and the previous government's reforms, so too did the right radicalize after the Popular Front's victory in 1936, viewing it as a sign of the bankruptcy of the CEDA's "accidentalism" and of the Republic's inability to protect their interests. Many within the monarchist movement, for example, who had tolerated Robles's and the CEDA's accidentalism when they believed it might enable them to achieve their goals, now began considering the Republic's forcible overthrow. More generally, the tendency on parts of the right to portray the Second Republic as "foreign and sinister" and the left and liberals as "existential threats" or even an "inferior race that had to be subjugated by . . . uncompromising violence," intensified.[137] The Popular Front's victory also helped bring together anti-Republican groups that had not previously cooperated.[138] As was the case with Spain's communist party, Spain's fascist party, the Falange, founded by José Antonio Primo de Rivera, a son of the previous dictator who updated his father's mixture of nationalism, corporatism, and opposition to liberal democracy for the 1930s, had been a marginal political force before 1936, receiving 0.07 percent of the vote in the 1936 elections. After the 1936 elections, however, sections of the CEDA and the monarchist movement, which had previously ignored or disdained the Falange, began to recognize shared interests with it.[139] The Popular Front's victory also brought a large increase in the Falange's membership: within six months it went from five thousand to five hundred thousand members.[140] When the Popular Front came to power the Falange stepped up its violence, assassinations, and street brawls with left-wing groups. In the countryside and elsewhere, meanwhile, landed and other elites increasingly used armed militias against workers and unions. And behind the scenes, some of CEDA's leaders, monarchists, and other reactionaries intensified negotiations with figures in the military about the possibility of a coup.[141]

Events in July provided the sparks that finally set this tinderbox aflame. By the summer parliamentary sessions had become chaotic with right- and left-wing deputies trading insults, blows, and even death threats. One of the latter was directed against a noted far-right leader, José Calvo Sotelo. Soon after this threat and the assassination of a high-profile anti-fascist figure named José Castillo by Falangist goons, a group of leftist militiamen, led by a member of the Assault Guards, arrived at Calvo Sotelo's home, telling him they were there to take him to an urgent meeting. Almost as soon as Calvo Sotelo got into the Assault Guard truck, he was killed by a young socialist.[142] Although evidence pointed to this being a spontaneous act by an unstable individual, the intense polarization reigning in the country combined with previous threats made against Calvo Sotelo led many on the right to view his assassination as further evidence that the left was hell-bent on revenge and revolution and that it was necessary, therefore, to get rid of the Republic.[143] On July 17, four days after Calvo Sotelo's murder, the army rose up under Francisco Franco and other generals.[144] Spain's civil war had begun.

Between 1936 and 1943 perhaps five hundred thousand Spaniards died. Both the left and right committed atrocities, dehumanized their opponents, and associated them with foreign elements hell-bent on destroying Spain; ultimately, however, the right was responsible for more deaths than the left during the war and the vicious reprisals that followed it. The right justified its actions as being part of a "crusade" or "religious war"[145] necessary to "disinfect"[146] the country of its enemies. Overall, the civil war brought to a violent culmination the growing tendency of left and right to deny the legitimacy or even basic humanity of the other: "political rather than ethnic cleansing"[147] was the consequence of democracy's collapse in Spain. Indeed, Franco's regime may have killed a higher proportion of its domestic political enemies than any other regime in Europe, including Hitler's.[148] In addition, although the civil war's origins were domestic, once it broke out it quickly became part of the larger European civil war. Foreign communists and fascists/National Socialists poured into the country, extending the war, the death and destruction associated with it, and setting the stage for the even more gruesome conflict of the Second World War.[149]

Conclusions

How can we understand the collapse of the Second Republic and why it led to civil war and the rise of a reactionary, military dictatorship in Spain? As in other countries where democracy failed, the Second Republic was unable to deal with the challenges it faced, including high levels of political disorder and violence, economic underdevelopment and inequality, and intense societal divisions between workers and business, large landowners and landless laborers and peasants, centralizers and separatists, committed Catholics and hardline secularists, and opponents and advocates of Republicanism and democracy. Such divisions existed, of course, in all European countries at some point or another; what was notable about Spain, and in different versions, many under-developed countries today, is that none had been tackled by the time the transition to democracy occurred. Even under the best of circumstances, tackling these challenges would have been difficult, but the Second Republic was not operating in the best of circumstances. When the transition to democracy occurred in 1931, democracy was already in retreat in much of Europe, and the Great Depression was beginning to wreak havoc across the continent. As inauspicious as the international situation was, the domestic one was even worse. Neither the main party on the right, the CEDA, nor the left, the PSOE, was committed to democracy. Instead, both viewed the Republic primarily in instrumentalist or "accidentalist" terms: as valuable only insofar as it enabled them to achieve other, more fundamental goals. The left, having long been barred from power, was determined to radically transform Spain's traditional, conservative, Catholic society. The right, meanwhile, was determined to defend "traditional" Spain and the forces most closely associated with it—landed elites, the Church, and the military. In addition, sectors of the right viewed Republicans and the left as sinister, foreign, existential threats, a tendency that increased as the Second Republic wore on.[150] Politics in the Second Republic thus quickly became a "zero-sum" game, with neither left nor right willing to accept electoral losses, the basic legitimacy of the opposition, or democracy as soon as it was no longer under their control. As a result, almost from its birth, the Second Republic was, as the historian Javier Tusell aptly put it, a "not very democratic democracy" ("un democracia poco democrática").[151]

Understanding why this was the case—why the Second Republic faced so many challenges and why its main political actors were not committed to the democratic rules of the game—required delving into the Spanish past. In particular Spain's intense regionalism, its persistent economic underdevelopment and inequality, tendency to slip into disorder and violence, the continued power of the Church, military, and landed elites—all had their roots in the relatively weak state and nation-building processes that began in the early modern period. These processes also help explain the political turbulence Spain experienced during the nineteenth century: lacking a strong state or sense of national identity made dealing with the political, economic, and social challenges of the period very difficult. None of the dizzying array of political regimes Spain experienced during the nineteenth century were able or perhaps even willing to deal with the country's problems. This created, in turn, a propensity for praetorianism: when the inefficacy of an existing regime caused it to lose support but its opponents were not yet powerful enough to take over on their own, the military stepped in and determined political outcomes.

By 1931 the inability of the monarchy, the old quasi-liberal constitutional political order, and Primo de Rivera's pseudo-fascist military regime to deal with Spain's problems led to a transition to democracy. But the Second Republic was burdened by problems inherited from previous regimes as well as a political left that distrusted "bourgeois" political institutions and actors and a political right dominated by landed elites, the Church, and a military committed to returning Spain to its conservative, Catholic, hierarchical past. Ultimately, these factors combined with an increasingly threatening international situation that further radicalized left and right and caused the Second Republic's collapse.

That this collapse eventually led to a transition to a conservative military dictatorship rather than a revolutionary fascist or National-Socialist one also required looking to Spain's past. Crucial was Spain's long-standing tradition of military intervention in politics, with the right in particular having a tendency to look to the army to protect its interests when it was unable to do so on its own. More fundamentally, however, because of Spain's previous economic and political development the constituencies favoring a traditional conservative regime—the Church, military and landed elites—remained strong in Spain, while those tending to favor revolutionary alternatives including fascism, national socialism, and communism—the middle and working classes—were relatively weak. Thus, while Franco's dictatorship is sometimes referred to as fascist, there were fundamental differences between it and the Italian and German dictatorships: it rested, as already noted, on a different social base, aimed to demobilize rather than mobilize the people, and aspired to (re)create a conservative, Catholic hierarchical political order rather than a modern, mass-based revolutionary one. In addition, while Franco incorporated the Falange as well as other rightist groups into a new political party, this party developed after rather than before the seizure of power and was not designed to mobilize a broad, cross-class following behind the dictator's revolutionary vision but instead to present a veneer of "public acquiescence" and provide supporters with a path to positions of power and influence.[152] Similarly, Franco functioned as a *caudillo* or "replacement" monarch, rather than as a revolutionary "fuhrer," "representative of the people," or the personification of the nation, as Mussolini and Hitler styled themselves. Moreover, unlike in Italy and Germany where the new regimes sidelined old elites, in Spain besides Franco, traditional conservative forces, including some monarchists, the military, and especially the Church—which regained control over education and many spheres of social life—retained power.[153]

Despite, or perhaps because of its conservative rather than revolutionary nature, Franco's regime far outlived its fascist and National Socialist counterparts, avoiding the Second World War and the democratic wave that swept across Western Europe at its end. Indeed, the dictatorship lasted as long as Franco did, collapsing only in the 1970s with his death.

CHAPTER 14

The Consolidation of Democracy
in Western Europe

"All of us have seen the great economic tragedy of our time. We saw
the worldwide depression of the 1930s. . . . We saw bewilderment and
bitterness become the breeders of fascism and finally of war." To prevent
a recurrence of this phenomenon, national governments would have to
be able to do more to protect people from capitalism's "malign effects."
—Henry Morgenthau, United States Treasury Secretary at the opening
of the Bretton Woods conference[1]

U P THROUGH NOW this book has examined the struggle to achieve
consolidated liberal democracy in Europe, a process that began in 1789
with the French Revolution. The revolution destroyed the political and legal
foundations of France's old order: absolutist monarchy was abolished, and the
institutional infrastructure of the system of privilege that lie at the heart of
its social and economic order was obliterated. However, despite successfully
destroying the political and legal foundations of the old order, the revolution was unable to construct a new one. An attempt was made to replace
the old order with a new democratic one, but this attempt quickly collapsed
into totalitarian terror and then populist military dictatorship. During the
nineteenth century the battle that began during the French Revolution between defenders of the old order and the advocates of a new democratic one
spread across Europe. Over time those defending the old order diminished
in number and power while those advocating democracy grew, but not by
enough to stabilize a new liberal democratic order. Instead, between 1789 and

1914 European political development proceeded in fits and starts, shifting back and forth between democracy and dictatorship as various groups battled to determine the shape of Europe's future.

The First World War was a critical juncture in this battle, eliminating the final political vestiges of the old order across Europe. Most obviously, after 1918, monarchies disappeared, continental empires crumbled, and a wave of democratization swept across Europe, but critical social and economic vestiges of the old order remained. In addition, as the interwar period progressed, the problems confronting new democracies grew and the ranks of its opponents swelled. But now rather than advocating monarchical dictatorships or a return of the old order more generally as their early nineteenth-century counterparts had, democracy's most dangerous opponents called for fascist or National Socialist dictatorships instead (see chapters 9–13). By the early 1930s many of Europe's new democracies were already in serious trouble, and the economic suffering and social chaos generated by the Great Depression pushed some over the edge. By the Depression's end the democratic wave that occurred at the end of the First World War was a dim memory, and soon Britain was standing alone against the Nazis, perhaps the most horrific political regime the world had ever known. If there was ever a time and place where democracy seemed to be a lost cause, Europe in 1940 was it.

The Second World War was inextricably intertwined with the collapse of interwar democracies and was an integral part of the struggle that had been going on since 1789 between democracy and its opponents. The period between 1914 and 1945 was thus an interregnum—a period when an old order died but a new one had not yet taken its place. The struggle among those with differing visions of what this new order should look like was so bloody and chaotic that many view this period as one of European civil war. If 1789 marked the beginning of the struggle between democracy and its opponents, 1945 can perhaps be seen as its end, at least in Western Europe (but see chapter 18). When fascism and national socialism went down in flames at the end of the Second World War, Western Europe finally made a transition to stable, liberal democracy. (Southern and Eastern Europe remained ruled by dictatorships, and their stories are told in chapters 15–17.) That it was only after the most destructive war in history that Western Europe was finally able to achieve consolidated liberal democracy may seem at first counterintuitive. But the war and its aftermath finally eliminated many remaining social and economic vestiges of the old order and hindrances to democracy that had long stymied democratic consolidation. It also, critically, helped create a consensus around the desirability of a new democratic one as well as a new understanding of what it would finally take to make it work.

Year Zero

The year 1945 in Europe is often referred to "Year Zero": a time when one era ended and another began.[2] Today, it can be hard to fathom how thoroughly devastated Europe was at the end of the Second World War. Surveying the postwar scene Winston Churchill, for example, asked, "What is Europe now? A rubble heap, a charnel house, a breeding ground of pestilence and hate." As was often the case, Churchill's description was colorful yet accurate. During the war the full force of the modern state was mobilized for the purpose of annihilating entire peoples, and the war's human and material costs were accordingly greater than anything the world had ever seen. Estimates range from fifty to eighty million dead, with at least two-thirds of these civilians.[3] Indeed, the Second World War was primarily a civilian experience: it was "a war of occupation, of repression, of exploitation and extermination in which soldiers, storm-troopers, and policemen disposed of the daily lives and very existence of tens of millions of" peoples. Much more than the First World War, the Second "was a near universal experience."[4] Bombing left entire cities and regions in ruins;[5] tens of millions homeless; and obliterated road, transportation, communication, and food supply networks. The war's end, moreover, did not bring an end to the suffering.[6] Here is George Kennan, for example, describing the situation in the areas "liberated" by the Soviets:

> The disaster that befell this area with the entry of the Soviet forces has no parallel in modern European experience. There were considerable sections of it where, to judge by all existing evidence, scarcely a man, woman or child of the indigenous population was left alive after the initial passage of Soviet forces. . . . The Russians . . . swept the native population clean in a manner that had no parallel since the days of the Asiatic hordes.[7]

In addition to slaughtering any men they came across, the Soviets engaged in an unprecedented campaign of violence against women: in Vienna and Berlin, for example, approximately ninety thousand women were raped within a week or so of the arrival of the Red Army; hundreds of thousands of women ultimately suffered this fate.[8] Postwar Europe was also plagued by famine and disease. In 1945 the residents of Budapest subsisted on about 550 calories a day, in Vienna 800,[9] and even in the Netherlands thousands of people starved. In some countries it became commonplace to see women and even children selling their bodies for scraps of food.[10] Conditions in Germany were particularly dire: the last months of the war were the bloodiest by far, and suffering continued after defeat.[11] During 1945 in Berlin, as many one-quarter of the children under the age of one died, thousands starved, malnutrition and disease were rampant, and about a quarter of the population was homeless.[12] Alongside unprecedented material destruction and suffering, the war also left much of Europe in a state of almost complete political, social, and economic collapse: governments, schools, civil society, libraries, post offices, newspapers, and markets simply ceased to exist. The consequences of Europe's almost total devastation and of the "zero hour" or "clean slate" produced by the war and its aftermath for postwar political development were profound.

One consequence was the discrediting of the revolutionary right. The destruction and suffering caused by fascist and National Socialist dictatorships and the Second World War undermined support for what had been democracy's most powerful prewar adversary. Since traditional conservatism had been in decline since the mid-nineteenth century, during the postwar period democracy found itself without a strong challenger on the right for the first time since 1789.[13] Alongside and probably to a large degree underlying this political shift were the social and economic consequences of the war and its aftermath. Between the mid-1930s and mid-1940s the socioeconomic vestiges of the old order—ruling classes and elites, status hierarchies, social norms, and relationships—had been more thoroughly destabilized than at any time since the French Revolution. This was particularly true and particularly consequential in Germany.

As discussed in chapter 12, even before the war the Nazis had undermined conservative elites' hold on political power and leadership positions in the civil service, judiciary, and army. In addition, Hitler established more complete "civilian" control over the military than had existed during the imperial or Weimar eras. The Nazi regime also dramatically limited the freedom of business elites, markedly increased state control over the economy, and broke down the class distinctions and social hierarchies that dominated Imperial and Weimar Germany, offering "racially pure" and politically committed Germans, regardless of birth, class, or educational background, a more "egalitarian" social order and more social mobility than they had previously enjoyed.[14] (Indeed the Nazis' success in "downgrading and ultimately destroying many of the hierarchies that had long defined German society" and in creating both a *Volksgemeinschaft*—a "people's community" where all "real" Germans enjoyed the same rights and responsibilities—and a *Leistungsgemeinschaft*—a society where achievement, defined as commitment to the führer and the party, rather than birth,[15] determined an individual's fate—was a key reason so many Germans found the regime attractive.[16])

Summing up some of the social consequences of the Nazi period Ralf Dahrendorf, for example, stressed,

> In order to maintain their power, the National Socialists had to turn against all traces of the social order that provided the basis for authoritarian rule. They destroyed inherited loyalties wherever they could; they co-ordinated all traditional institutions equipped with a life of their own; they generalized the social role of the *Volksgenosse* as far as they could. . . . National Socialism . . . finally abolished the German past as it was embodied in Imperial Germany. What came after it was free of the mortgage that burdened the Weimar Republic at its beginning. . . . There could be no return from the revolution of National Socialist times. . . . [Thus] however, brutal as it was, the break with tradition and thus a strong push toward modernity was the substantive characteristic of the social revolution of National Socialism. [The period of Nazi rule] gave German society an irreversible push, which exposed it to totalitarian dangers and opened it to liberal chances at the same time.[17]

The social "revolution" begun by the Nazis continued during and after the war. The mayhem accompanying the collapse of the Nazi regime helped delegitimize it in the eyes of many of its previous supporters and left Germany completely defeated and "atomized," further ensuring that any re-grouping of the forces of the old order, or revival of the stab-in-the-back legend, akin to what happened after 1918, was impossible.[18] More specifically, by the early postwar period two critical components of the old order that had long hindered democratic development in Germany, the Junkers and their traditional homeland, Prussia, were gone. The Nazis had already sidelined traditional conservative elites, and the war then killed a disproportionate number of them. And of those who survived, most were either killed by the incoming Red Army or fled westward to escape it; the property and estates they left behind were then burned and looted by the Soviets, destroying the final symbols of their economic and social power. As for Prussia, the Nazis had already undermined its independence and that of other *Länder* by centralizing authority in the national state and Nazi party. After the war Prussia disappeared from the map of Europe entirely, its territory carved up among various Eastern and Western *Länder* and Poland.[19]

Another critical social consequence of the war and its aftermath was massive ethnic cleansing. This was particularly true in Eastern and Central Europe, where the recent experience of empire had left behind states with ethnically, religiously, and linguistically mixed populations lacking national unity or social solidarity (see chapters 9 and 15). Between them Stalin and Hitler uprooted, transplanted, expelled, deported, and dispersed perhaps thirty to forty million people between 1939 and 1943,[20] and massive population transfers continued after the war's end.[21] As one observer put, Europe experienced nothing less than "a tidal wave of nomad peoples."[22] All told, tens of millions of people, the largest group of which were Germans (perhaps 16.5 million), fled their homes in the most brutal circumstances. Millions, including perhaps 2.25 million Germans, never made it where they were going.[23] These expulsions were partially motivated by vengeance and partially by a desire to further nation-building by homogenizing populations particularly in East and Central Europe (see chapter 15).

The consequences of ethnic cleansing for postwar political development were profound. As already noted, the Soviet army either killed or forced to flee any remaining Junkers in their path, putting the final touches on the elimination of a class that had played an outsized role in German political development. The Soviet advance also sent a huge number of ethnic Germans fleeing more generally: by 1950, expellees made up approximately one-fifth of Germany's population, and the economic and social integration of this group further shook up socioeconomic relationships and hierarchies. The ethnic cleansing of Germans also made Germany and Austria more like nation-states than they had ever been: by the postwar period they were finally the home of essentially all of Europe's Germans, finally fulfilling the goal proclaimed by German nationalists in 1848 (see chapters 5 and 8).

While the amount and consequences of ethnic cleansing were particularly dramatic in Germany and East and Central Europe, wartime and postwar population shifts impacted Western Europe as well. These shifts, along with the general destruction caused by the war, collapsed "the social distance upon which the rigid pre-war class systems of Europe had rested," destroyed identities, communities, social networks, and even families, and rendered much of Europe much more homogenous; Jews (and Gypsies), of course, were now essentially gone.[24]

In addition to discrediting the radical right, eliminating critical socioeconomic vestiges of the old order and hindrances to democracy, and creating more homogenous nation-states, another critical consequence of the war and its aftermath was the occupation and eventual "rehabilitation" of Europe's most problematic country: Germany. That the United States would commit to democratizing Germany was not a foregone conclusion. Up through the end of the war the Allies' main concern was preventing a revival of German power, and many assumed that Germany was incapable of becoming a peaceful, liberal democracy. Reflecting this, the original directive issued to

General Eisenhower in 1944 regarding the postwar occupation asserted that "Germany will not be occupied for the purpose of liberation but as a defeated enemy nation. . . . The aim is to prevent Germany from ever again becoming a threat to the peace of the world."[25] However, due partially to the onset of the Cold War, the Allies eventually shifted course and committed to a long-term, costly, and comprehensive occupation of Germany that recognized the need to put in place not merely the political and institutional infrastructure of democracy, but new social and economic foundations as well. It is only against the backdrop of Germany's utter destruction and prostration and the immense power enjoyed by the United States at the end of the war that such an ambitious project can be understood.

The Allied reform program is often referred to as "the four Ds": democratization, demilitarization, decartelization, and denazification.[26] The first D, democratization, aimed to correct the political and institutional mistakes that contributed to the failure of the Weimar Republic (see chapter 12).[27] For example, during the interwar years chancellors were frequently voted out of office even when a majority in the Reichstag was unable to agree on a new one, leading to political instability and often necessitating the use of emergency powers to get things done. The 1949 German "constitution" or Basic Law (*Grundgesetz*) addressed this by instituting a "constructive" vote of no confidence, which meant that a government could only be voted out of office if the Bundestag could agree on a new one. In addition, in order to avoid the conflicts between a Reichstag majority and a popularly elected president that had bedeviled the Weimar Republic, the postwar West German presidency became a symbolic post that was no longer popularly elected.[28] And, to prevent party fragmentation and extremism, Weimar's "pure" system of proportional representation (in which approximately 1 percent of the vote could entitle a party to a seat in the Reichstag) was replaced by an electoral system with higher representation thresholds and a ban on explicitly anti-democratic parties. There were other features of the Basic Law that were a direct or indirect reaction to the perceived failures of the past, including the incorporation of a long list of liberal rights.[29]

Notable about the Allied program is that it went beyond political and institutional reforms to include social and economic ones as well. For example, the second D, demilitarization, aimed to eliminate remaining vestiges of the politically powerful military that had been a critical part of German political life since Prussia's rise in the late seventeenth and early eighteenth century (see chapters 2 and 5). As noted above and in chapter 12, Hitler had already sidelined the military's traditional leadership and centralized his authority over it, but the Allies went further, reducing the size of the military, clearly subordinating it to civilian authority, and eventually integrating it into an American-led military alliance (NATO, see below). These reforms combined with the horrors produced by the collapse of the Nazi regime and the end of the war to "convert a nation once renowned for its reverence of the military into a nation which took a fundamental turn to pacifism."[30]

The "third D" of the Allied program, decartelization, was designed to eliminate economic blockages to democracy, most directly the large cartels that were viewed as having provided crucial support for Hitler and as being antithetical to a free-market economy.[31] And finally the "fourth D," denazification, aimed at "purging the Nazi evil from the German body politic."[32] (This part of the Allied program was eventually scaled down and only some high-level Nazis received punishment. The reasons for this were largely practical: probably 10 percent of the German population had been Nazi party members, and many millions more had been members of Nazi-affiliated youth, labor, professional, and other organizations, making investigating all Germans with a Nazi association a logistical nightmare. Relatedly, the Allies concluded that administering, much less rebuilding, Germany without the support or at least acquiescence of the millions of German teachers, civil servants, lawyers, members of the press, and so on, who had some Nazi association would be impossible.[33] And finally, the Cold War simply changed Allied calculations.)

In addition to committing itself to the democratization of Germany, another crucial consequence of the Second World War was a dramatic transformation of the United States' relationship with Europe. Unlike after the First World War when it shifted back to isolationism, after 1945 the United States accepted responsibility for protecting liberal democracy in Europe and ensuring the peace and prosperity that were critical prerequisites for it.

Triggered by a general fear that Western European states could not alone protect themselves from Soviet aggression and by Soviet threats to Turkey and Greece, President Truman declared to Congress in March 1947 that "it must be the policy of the United States to support free peoples who are resisting attempted subjugation by armed minorities or outside pressures."[34] This policy, which came to be known as the Truman Doctrine, cast aside the United States' traditional avoidance of foreign entanglements, committing it to protecting liberal democracy in Western Europe. (It was, as one scholar put it, "the greatest formal shift in U.S. policy . . . since the promulgation in 1823 of the Monroe doctrine."[35]) This led to the formation of NATO in 1949, which provided a formal institutional structure for the new American-led security order and, by eventually including West Germany, further anchored its democratic development and promoted European integration (see below). As NATO's first secretary general, Lord Ismay, pithily put it, NATO was founded "to keep the Russians out, the Americans in, and the Germans down."

In addition to accepting responsibility for ensuring its peace and security, the United States also committed itself to getting Western Europe back on track economically. Initially, these efforts focused on the construction of multilateral institutions and arrangements to integrate Western Europe into a new American-led liberal international economic order. The Bretton Woods system, for example, was devised to avoid the monetary chaos of the interwar years, ensure stable exchange rates, and provide support for economic reconstruction and development. (The International Monetary Fund [IMF] and the International Bank for Reconstruction and Development [IRBD] were set up to oversee these latter two goals.) The General Agreement on Tariffs and Trade (GATT) was the trade counterpart to Bretton Woods, devised to avoid the protectionism and beggar-thy-neighbor policies of the interwar years and provide the foundation for an open international trading order.[36] By 1947, however, it was clear that these multilateral institutions and arrangements, supplemented by a variety of relief programs, were not solving Western Europe's economic problems. Indeed 1947 was a particularly dismal year: the winter of 1946–1947 was the coldest since 1880, the spring's melting snows produced terrible flooding, and the summer was one of the hottest and driest on record;[37] the cumulative effect of these conditions was a worsening of Europe's already miserable agricultural and food situation. As William Clayton, the United States assistant secretary of state for economic affairs, wrote in May 1947:

> It is now obvious that we grossly underestimated the destruction of the European economy by the war. We understood the physical destruction, but we failed to take fully into account the effects of economic dislocation on production. . . . Europe is steadily deteriorating. The political position reflects the economic. One political crisis after another merely denotes the existence of grave economic distress.[38]

The recognition that without prosperity democratic stability would be impossible and that without American intervention prosperity might be impossible, provided the backdrop to the Marshall Plan. Marshall himself consistently stressed that without rapid and extensive American help, support for democracy would diminish and that for communism would grow.[39] It was necessary, therefore, that "the United States do whatever it is able to do to assist in the return of normal economic health in the world, without which there can be no political stability and no assured peace."[40] The Marshall Plan eventually provided an immense amount of aid—by 1952, $13 billion, equivalent to several hundred billion today and more than all other US aid packages combined[41]—designed to ensure that West European governments had funding to provide food, shelter, and basic services to their citizens and make the infrastructure investments necessary for long-term growth.[42]

Scholars have long-debated the impact of the Marshall Plan. It is certainly true that Europe began a remarkable economic recovery during the period the Plan was in force (1948–1951), but correlation does not equal causality and some argue aid came on line precisely as an upswing was on its way.[43] However, since the Marshall Plan's ends were primarily political—increasing support for democracy by showing it could generate prosperity—it is perhaps best judged by such criteria and here its success is clear. As one observer put it, at the onset of the Marshall Plan Europeans were

> [a] deeply beleaguered, dispirited people. By and large they felt vulnerable, insecure and lacked confidence in their future. Without the U.S. commitment tendered in the Marshall Plan, the imposition of even more draconian controls and sacrifices while they grappled with the internal Communist threat, political violence, and the external Soviet threat, would have fueled further desperation, insecurity and pessimism. It is possible that the Plan's most substantial contribution to Western Europe was intangible: the confidence that came with knowing that the region would not have to undergo further strident controls; that it would not be threatened with bankruptcy; that it would not descend once again into economic nationalism or even autarky; that it would not starve or freeze; that it would not be threatened with hyperinflation. The world's largest economy now stood with Western Europe and hitched its security and, in a large part, its destiny, to Europe's recovery and security.[44]

But the Marshall Plan did not just help overcome Europe's "crisis of confidence," it also helped spur European integration by mandating that participating states jointly decide how aid should be used.[45] The need to co-ordinate decision-making about aid led to the formation of the Organization for European Economic Co-operation (OEEC, later OECD),[46] which provided a foundation upon which future economic cooperation could be built. At the root of European integration, in short, was the recognition that Europe's problems were simply too large and too complicated to be solved by governments acting alone. Integration was the regional component of a larger, multifaceted effort to stabilize liberal democracy in postwar Europe.

Prosperity, for example, could only be achieved if, as the French statesman and EU architect Robert Schuman put it, France and Germany "worked together for common goals."[47] Similarly, peace required reconciling Germany with Europe and vice versa. As Winston Churchill put it, "to bring [Europe's horrible history] to an end, it would be necessary to re-create the European family . . . and provide it with a structure under which it can dwell in peace, safety and freedom." The goal had to be the creation of a "continent so integrated, so connected that war would be impossible."[48]

In short by discrediting the radical right, transforming class structures, status hierarchies, and social norms, creating more homogenous nation-states, producing a stable, peaceful Germany, transforming the relationship between the United States and Europe, and promoting European integration, the Second World War and its aftermath helped eliminate crucial social and economic vestiges of the old order and hindrances to democracy. However necessary these were, they were not alone sufficient for democratic consolidation. After eliminating the old order, a new one had to be constructed to take its place. American-led international economic and security institutions and European regional integration were critical parts of this new order. But without socioeconomic stability at the domestic level, the consolidation of liberal democracy would have been impossible. Thus, the final piece of the puzzle was provided by the restructuring of European political economies after 1945. During the postwar period a new social democratic order arose, providing a foundation upon which successful liberal democracy in Western Europe could finally be built.

The Social Democratic Order

After 1945, actors across the political spectrum recognized that if democracy was finally going to work in Europe, not merely a change in political forms and institutions but also a transformation of social and economic structures and relationships was necessary. This shifting view of what it would take to make democracy work was largely a consequence of the experience of the 1930s and '40s. There was widespread agreement, for example, that the political chaos and social dislocation of the 1930s had been caused by the Great Depression, which in turn had been the consequence of unregulated markets—so the idea of taking that path again was anathema. In addition, the war profoundly changed many people's views of the appropriate roles of states and markets. All European governments assumed responsibility for managing the economy during the war, and shared wartime suffering fostered national unity and a broad sense that states could and should provide for citizens' basic needs. And finally Europe's desperate postwar situation combined with the commanding position of the Soviet Union after the war and the heroic role played by many communist resistance movements during it, along with the sense that capitalism had failed during the 1930s, led many to fear that communism rather than democratic capitalism was the wave of the future. (Indeed, after 1945 many West European communist parties received much higher vote shares than they had before the war and were included in a number of postwar governments as a result.[49]) These experiences and conditions, combined with a broader sense that Europe could not allow itself to fall back into patterns that led to socioeconomic conflict and extremism in the past, reinforced the belief that a socioeconomic order capable of convincing citizens that liberal democracy could and would respond to their needs was necessary if postwar liberal democracy was not to meet the same fate as its predecessors.

Advocating a shift in the relationship between states, markets, and society had long been a staple of the left; what changed after 1945 is that others recognized that consolidated liberal democracy would require such a shift as well. The 1947 program of the German Christian Democrats, for example, declared that, "The new structure of the German economy must start from the realization that the period of uncurtailed rule by private capitalism is over." In France, meanwhile, the Catholic Mouvement Republican Populaire declared in its first manifesto in 1944 that it supported a "revolution" to create a state "liberated from the power of those who possess wealth."[50] Even the United States, least affected by the war and most committed to the restoration of a global free-trade order, recognized that democratic stability in Europe would require a break with the socioeconomic status quo ante. Reflecting this, in his opening speech to the Bretton Woods conference, United States treasury secretary Henry Morgenthau noted, "All of us have seen the great economic tragedy of our time. We saw the worldwide depression of the 1930s. . . . We saw bewilderment and bitterness become the breeders of fascism and finally of war." To prevent a recurrence of this phenomenon, Morgenthau argued, "national governments would have to be able to do more to protect people from capitalism's 'malign effects.' "[51]

After 1945, accordingly, West European nations constructed a new socioeconomic order, one that could generate economic growth while at the same time protecting citizens from capitalism's most destructive effects.[52] This order represented a decisive break with the past: states would not be limited to ensuring that markets could grow and flourish nor would economic interests be given the widest possible leeway. Instead, after 1945 the state was to become the guardian of society rather than the economy, and economic imperatives would sometimes have to take a backseat to social ones. This shift to a "social democratic" understanding of the relationship between states, markets, and societies[53] was based on a recognition that for liberal democracy to finally succeed, the socioeconomic conflict and economic inequalities and crises that had fed extremism and scuttled democratic experiments in the past would have to be confronted head-on. After 1945, therefore, democratic governments in Western Europe explicitly committed themselves to pursing policies designed to avoid these outcomes.

The two most oft-noted manifestations of this were Keynesianism and the welfare state. Keynesianism's significance lay in its rejection of the view that markets operated best when left alone and its recognition that state intervention in the economy was sometimes necessary to avoid the economic dislocation and crises that could threaten both democracy and capitalism. Having lived through the rise of the Soviet Union and the Great Depression, Keynes understood that unchecked markets could be socially and politically dangerous. As his biographer Robert Skidelsky noted, "Keynes was quite conscious in seeking an alternative to dictatorship . . . a programme on which to fight back against fascism and communism."[54] It is important to stress that Keynes favored a more active role for the state for political as much as economic reasons: he understood the appeal of communism's insistence that capitalism could not be rescued from its flaws and fascism's insistence that only a strong, non-liberal state could deal with challenges like the Great Depression. Keynes hoped that by designing a "system that held out the prospect that the state could reconcile the private ownership of the means of production with democratic management of the economy"[55] he could convince people that there was a democratic solution to capitalism's downsides.

Like Keynesianism, the welfare state helped transform the relationship among states, markets, and societies during the postwar era in ways that helped promote consolidated liberal democracy. As C.A.R. Crosland noted, after 1945, "it was increasingly regarded as a proper function and indeed obligation of Government to ward off distress and strain not only among the poor but almost all classes of society."[56] West European welfare states were significant not only because they protected individuals from economic distress, but also because they gave renewed importance to membership in a national community. Since they both required and fostered a sense of kinship and solidarity among citizens, welfare states could only be sustained if individuals believed that ensuring a basic level of well-being for all citizens was a worthy goal. The welfare state represented a new understanding of citizenship or a new "social contract" between governments and citizens with the former committing to ensuring the economic welfare and security of the latter, and the latter committing to supporting the welfare state and the larger liberal democratic system of which it was a part.[57] Welfare states thereby marked a significant break with a liberal *gesellschaft*—the anomie, dislocation, and atomization that had proved so politically destabilizing during the nineteenth and early twentieth centuries—and a move towards a more communitarian *gemeinschaft* where governments committed to taking care of their citizens. The postwar expansion of welfare states was thus not merely a reflection of a desire to rectify past mistakes, but also a deliberate attempt to undercut the support of extremist ideologies on the left and right that had played off anomie, dislocation, and atomization in the past in order to undermine support for liberal democracy.

Of course, Keynesianism and welfare states were not the only ways in which postwar European political economies changed. Each European country developed its own set of policies that used the power of the state to protect societies from capitalism's most destructive effects and promote social cohesion and stability. In France, for example, the Fourth Republic engaged in nationalization and planning, which were designed to ensure economic growth and that "the main sources of common wealth [were] worked and managed not for the profit of a few individuals, but for the benefit of all."[58] In Britain, where class distinctions remained immensely important up through the interwar years, the war had a significant leveling effect. Food and other essential items were rationed during the war on the basis of need rather than wealth or social standing and shared suffering boosted social solidarity. As one broadcaster put it, Britain had been "bombed and burned into democracy."[59] Similarly, observing the wartime social changes occurring in Britain the American war reporter Edward R. Murrow remarked, "You must understand that a world is dying, that old values, the old prejudices, and the old bases of power and prestige are going."[60] Against this backdrop the Beveridge report appeared in 1942, spurring a postwar commitment by British governments to ensuring "freedom from want." Beveridge had earlier been a critic of welfare capitalism, but like many others had been converted by the war to a belief that the governments could and should protect citizens from economic suffering and take responsibility for equitable economic development. After the war Britain expanded its welfare state, committed to full employment, and nationalized parts of the economy.[61] In Italy, meanwhile, a large state sector was carried over from the fascist period and viewed as part of a broader strategy for using the state to ensure economic growth and social well-being. The idea that democratic governments were responsible for steering the economy and protecting citizens was enshrined in Italy's postwar constitution, which declared the country a democratic republic "founded on labor," and promised that all "economic and social obstacles" to workers' advancement would be demolished. Recognizing the primacy of certain societal goals and needs, the constitution also refrained from according private property the status of "absolute right . . . instead emphasiz[ing] its social obligations and limitations."[62]

In Germany there was a clearer commitment to economic liberalism than in other parts of Europe because of the extreme statism of the Nazis and the more direct influence of the United States. (On the flipside, the West German state inherited from its Nazi predecessor a history of economic planning, crucial infrastructure investments in communications, transport, key industries, a business community used to state intervention or "coordination"—all of which influenced postwar developments.[63]) Nonetheless, West German governments also intervened in the economy in myriad ways and made a firm commitment to social protection and stability: the welfare state grew, and a number of innovative policies were implemented including codetermination, which gave workers the ability to oversee and in some cases even help direct, business decisions and activity and helped workers and management view each other as "social partners" rather than adversaries.

The most dramatic transformation in the relationship among state, market, and society occurred in Scandinavia and in Sweden in particular. The Swedish state was tasked with promoting growth, equity, and protecting society—goals that were seen as complementary rather than contradictory.[64] As Gunnar Adler-Karlsson, a well-known theorist of the postwar Swedish order, noted:

> All the parties of the economic process have realized that the most important economic task is to make the national cake grow bigger and bigger, because then everyone can satisfy his demanding stomach with a greater piece of that common cake. When instead, there is strong fighting between the classes in that society, we believe that the cake will often crumble or be destroyed in the fight, and because of this everyone loses.[65]

To achieve these goals, the Swedish state employed a wide range of tools including planning, the manipulation of investment funds and fiscal policy, and the encouragement of cooperation between labor market partners. (Interestingly, one tool that the Swedish state did not use much was nationalization, which was viewed as economically unnecessary and politically unwise.) But perhaps the two most distinctive features of Sweden's postwar political economy were the Rehn-Meidner model and a universal welfare state, both of which were distinguished by their focus on promoting economic growth, equity, and social solidarity.

The Rehn-Meidner model featured a centralized system of wage bargaining that set wages at what was seen as a "just" level (which in practice aimed to ensure "equal pay for equal work," consistently rising incomes, and improvements for the worse-off to reduce inequality). Wages were set "too high" for firms that were inefficient or uncompetitive and "too low" for firms that were highly productive and competitive. Firms in the former category faced the choice of either improving or going out of business, while those in the latter would increase their profitability (since the wages they paid would be less than they could otherwise afford). To compensate workers who lost their jobs, the state committed to retraining and relocating them for new ones. The system aimed to promote business efficiency and productivity while generating a more equal wage structure and social solidarity.[66]

The Swedish welfare state provided a range of programs and benefits that dwarfed most other welfare states and "socialized"—that is, brought into the public sector—services like health care, education, and child care in order to ensure the equitable distribution of resources, and the universal nature and high quality of social programs was designed to ensure the welfare state retained the support of a broad cross-sector of the population.[67]

For these and other reasons, Sweden was long recognized as a social democratic showplace. But while it may have been at one end of the spectrum, the postwar order across Europe marked a significant break with the past: capitalism remained, but it was capitalism of a very different type than had existed before the war—one tempered and limited by liberal democratic states and often made subservient to the goals of social stability and cohesion, rather than the other way around. This social democratic order worked remarkably well: despite fears after the war that it might take decades to recover economically,[68] by the early 1950s most of Europe had easily surpassed interwar economic figures and the thirty years after 1945 were Europe's fastest period of growth ever (see Figure 14.1).

Perhaps even more impressive than the postwar order's economic effects were its political ones. Social stability and a willingness to compromise—things that liberal democracy requires and that earlier in its history Europe had so often lacked—were now at hand. The restructured political economies of the postwar era seemed to offer something to everyone. More specifically, economic growth and growing economic equality facilitated compromises between workers and capitalists,[69] rich and poor, and attenuated the view, so prevalent during the nineteenth and early twentieth centuries (and back with a vengeance today), that capitalism was a zero-sum game. As Clas Offe put it,

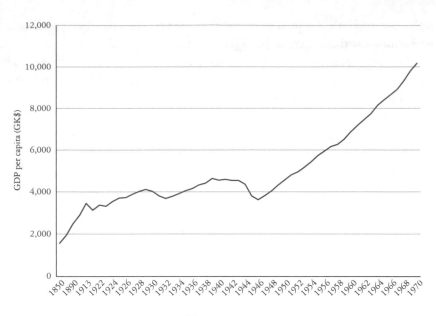

FIGURE 14.1 Western European GDP per capita, 1850–1970.
Note: *GK$ hypothetical unit of currency that has the same purchasing power parity that the U.S. dollar had in the United States at a given point in time.
Source: The Maddison-Project, http://www.ggdc.net/maddison/maddison-project/home.htm, 2013 version.

What was at issue in class conflicts [after 1945] was no longer the mode of production, but the volume of distribution, not control but growth, and this type of conflict was particularly suited for being processed on the political plan through party competition because it does not involve "either/or" questions, but questions of a "more or less" or "sooner or later" nature. Overarching this limited type of conflict, there was a consensus concerning basic priorities, desirabilities and values of the political economy, namely economic growth and social . . . security.[70]

Accordingly, the left- and right-wing extremism that plagued late-nineteenth- and early-twentieth-century Europe more or less disappeared: good times brought parties and voters back toward the political center and support for liberal democracy. As mentioned above, the war had largely discredited the fascist and National Socialist right, but communism was powerful after 1945 in parts of Western Europe. But over the postwar period West European communist parties moderated: even where they remained a significant electoral force, as in Italy and France, they made clear their commitment to democracy, gradually distanced themselves from the Soviet Union, and no longer engaged in insurrectionary behavior.[71] With right-wing extremism largely gone and left-wing extremism moderated, during the postwar decades West European party systems became dominated by parties of the center-left and center-right (generally social democratic and Christian Democratic, respectively), or what Otto Kirchheimer famously called "catch-all parties," that is, those that appealed to a broad, cross-class constituency and accepted the liberal democratic rules of the game.

In short, by reshaping the relationship between states, markets, and society the social democratic postwar order helped underpin democratic consolidation in Western Europe. It helped end social divisions and conflict, promote economic growth and equality, and thus dull the appeal of political extremism and promote satisfaction with liberal democracy. It undercut liberal fears that democracy "would lead by necessity to tyranny and expropriation by the poor and uneducated,"[72] Marxist assertions that giving the poor and workers the vote would lead inexorably to the end of bourgeois society, and fascism's claim that only dictatorships could produce national cohesion and social solidarity. The emergence of the social democratic postwar order, in short, played a crucial role in bringing an end to the struggle between democracy and its opponents that had begun in 1789—at least in Western Europe.

Conclusions

It was only after the most destructive war in history that Western Europe was finally able to put an end to the long-standing political and national struggles that it had suffered through since 1789. That Europe was able "to build a new world on the ashes of the old"[73] was partially because the Second World War and its aftermath eliminated many remaining legacies of the old order and hindrances to liberal democracy that had foiled consolidation in the past. By the postwar period the radical right was discredited, class structures, status hierarchies, and social norms transformed, more homogenous nation-states existed, a peaceful, stable Germany and a new relationship between the United States and Europe was emerging, and European integration had begun. In addition, the war and its aftermath produced a consensus on the desirability of liberal democracy as well as a new understanding of what it would take to make it work. An impressive learning process, in other words, was evident in the postwar reconstruction and consolidation of democracy. The Allied treatment of Germany reflected lessons learned from World War I as did the United States' commitment to Europe more generally. Similarly, European integration grew out of a recognition that the peace and prosperity necessary for liberal democracy could not be accomplished by European governments acting independently. And the postwar social democratic order emerged out of a recognition that consolidated liberal democracy required not merely reforming political institutions and relationships but social and economic ones as well.

Alongside the changes produced by the war and its aftermath, another factor contributing to democratic consolidation was that democracy did not have to be constructed from scratch after 1945. As previous chapters have made clear, the legacies of previous political regimes—both positive and negative—weigh heavily on the development of new ones. After 1945 many of the anti-democratic legacies of the old order were gone while some positive legacies from previous democratic experiments remained. Even in places like Germany and Italy, where dictatorships were home-grown and fairly long-lived, everything from political parties to civil society organizations, from national parliaments to local governments, could be reclaimed from the ashes of interwar democratic regimes. Neither the institutions nor the practices of democracy were new or unfamiliar to West Europeans; they just needed to be rebuilt, albeit in better ways. With all these pieces of the puzzle in place, Western Europe was finally able to achieve a goal that had eluded it since 1789: democratic consolidation. Southern and Eastern Europe, however, remained mired in dictatorships, and it is to their stories that we now turn.

| # The Transition to Communist Dictatorships in East-Central Europe[1]

This war is not as in the past; whoever occupies a territory also imposes upon it his own social system. Everyone imposes his own system as far as his army can reach. It cannot be otherwise.

—Joseph Stalin[2]

THE PREVIOUS CHAPTER examined why it was not until a century and a half after the French Revolution gave rise to modern Europe's first democratic experiment that liberal democracy finally consolidated across Western Europe. The old regime had been under attack since 1789, but the interwar years and the Second World War finally eliminated its remaining political, social, and economic legacies. The tragedies of the period also created a new consensus on the desirability of liberal democracy as well as a new understanding of what it would take to make it work. Domestically, not merely political institutions but also social and economic ones were restructured after the war in order to ensure that the socioeconomic and communal conflicts and political extremism that had undermined democracy in the past would not return. Regionally, European countries began a process of cooperation and eventually integration designed to ensure the peace and prosperity necessary to safeguard liberal democracy. And internationally, crucial changes also occurred, particularly regarding the relationship between the United States and Western Europe.

The United States occupied the Western half of the continent's most problematic country, Germany, constructed a wide range of international economic institutions, and encouraged European integration. In addition, recognizing that the Second World War had left West European countries unable to perform a critical function of modern states—self-defense—on their own, the United States assumed partial responsibility for the region's security with NATO, the Truman Doctrine, and other commitments. As with its economic support, American military assistance was not provided for purely altruistic reasons: the United States had a lot to lose if Western Europe slid into economic and political chaos and therefore became susceptible to communism. But because what was on offer after 1945 in Western Europe— a social democratic version of democratic capitalism—was attractive; the United States could stabilize the new order primarily via carrots rather than sticks. That there was, however, minimal overt coercion should not blind us to what happened. After 1945 the United States essentially assumed a sort of trusteeship over Western Europe. Or, as the scholar Geir Lunstad put it, what developed was a sort of "empire by invitation."[3]

If what existed in Western Europe was "empire by invitation," what developed in East-Central Europe[4] was more like empire of the traditional kind—but a uniquely ambitious one. The Soviet Union militarily dominated and economically exploited its colonies, as all imperialists do. But it did not stop there; the Soviet Union also transformed the political, social, and economic order in the European countries it dominated.[5] While both Western and East-Central Europe experienced profound transformations after 1945, the latter's was more far-reaching and externally directed than the former's. While Europe's thirty-year civil war robbed Western Europe of the ability to *alone* control its fate, much of East-Central Europe paid an even higher price, enduring not merely greater death and destruction during World War II but also losing its independence after it.

Political Development in East-Central Europe before World War II

During the nineteenth and early twentieth centuries the old order was still largely in place across East-Central Europe. Since the area was ruled over by Europe's continental empires—the Russian, Habsburg, German, and Ottoman—independent modern states, much less nation-states, did not exist. Neither did modern economies. Industrialization began relatively late

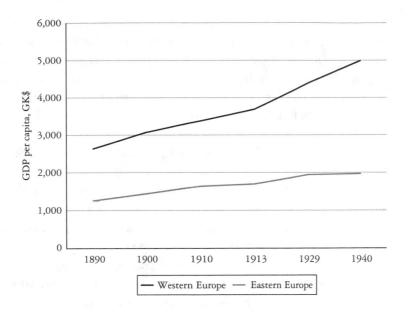

FIGURE 15.1 Western vs. Eastern European GDP per capita, 1890–1940.
Note: *GK$ hypothetical unit of currency that has the same purchasing power parity that the
U.S. dollar had in the United States at a given point in time.
Source: The Maddison-Project, http://www.ggdc.net/maddison/maddison-project/home.htm, 2013
version.

in East-Central Europe, and up through the early twentieth century the region was poorer, more agricultural, less urbanized, less literate, and less educated than Western Europe (see Figure 15.1).

The region's class structure reflected its relative "backwardness": its working and middle classes were small, its peasantries large, and in many places its landowning elite remained powerful; in Poland and Hungary in particular this group kept a significant part of the rural population in semifeudal conditions up through the twentieth century.[6] Reflecting these and other factors, nationalism also came relatively late to East-Central Europe. Empires, of course, repressed national aspirations, and within their borders very few of the groups we today consider as nationalities—Poles, Romanians, Czechs, Hungarians—lived in homogenous linguistic, ethnic, or religious areas; some, perhaps most notably the Poles, were not merely scattered across various territories, but across different empires. Since self-determination was incompatible with the continued existence of empires, when nationalism did come to East-Central Europe it was immensely destabilizing.[7] This became clear in 1848 (see chapter 5) when the demands of various groups for autonomy or even independence helped temporarily topple the old order in the Habsburg Empire—and then fatally divided the oppositional coalitions that had done the toppling. After 1848, peoples within the Habsburg Empire continued to demand greater control over their affairs and in some cases even their own states. As one observer put it: "A great power can endure without difficulty one Ireland, as England did, even three as imperial Germany did (Poland, Alsace, Schleswig). Different is the case when a Great Power is composed of nothing else but Irelands," as was the Habsburg Empire.[8] One particularly influential consequence of the destabilizing role of nationalism was the event that triggered the First World War: the assassination of the heir to the Habsburg throne and his wife by a Bosnian Serb nationalist.

As discussed in chapter 9, the First World War destroyed the political structures of the old order: monarchical dictatorships and empires. Out of the ashes of the latter, successor states including Czechoslovakia, Yugoslavia,[9] Austria, Hungary, Poland, Lithuania, Romania, and Estonia emerged.[10] These new countries began their existence as democracies, but in very difficult circumstances. To begin with, although the political infrastructure of the old order was gone, many social and economic legacies remained. As noted above, East-Central European countries inherited underdeveloped, largely agricultural economies with weak working and middle classes, large peasantries, and, in many places, powerful large landowners. The war weakened their economies further, destroying agricultural land, factories, roads, rails, and communication networks, generating food and raw material shortages, cutting off traditional trade and supply routes, and generating rampant inflation. Having just achieved independence, the new countries had to deal with these and other challenges while at the same time building states and nations. Herein lies a clear difference between Eastern Europe and Western and Southern Europe: although the sequencing and time-frame of state-, nation-, and democracy-building varied greatly in Western and Southern Europe, countries in these regions did not confront all three challenges at the same time, but those in Eastern Europe did. (The simultaneity of state-, nation-, and democracy-building is a common feature of newly decolonized regions.) Upon gaining independence East-Central European countries had to construct bureaucracies, taxation authorities, national armies, national communications and transport networks, educational institutions, and many other components of modern states, often from scratch.[11] They also had to build national unity in countries where state and national boundaries did not match. (This mismatch between state and national boundaries is also common in newly decolonized regions.) Further complicating matters, when the borders of Europe were redrawn after the war, many former minority groups (Poles, Czechs, Slovaks, Romanians, Serbs, Croats) became majorities, and some former majority groups (Hungarians, Germans) became minorities—a status change that increased resentments and conflict.[12] After the war Hungary, for example, lost two-thirds of its prewar territory and about 60 percent of its prewar population, which left about a third of all Magyars living as minorities in other countries (see Figures 15.2 and 15.3).[13] Yugoslavia, Romania, Czechoslovakia, and Poland, meanwhile, were left with extremely diverse populations.[14]

The mismatch between state and national boundaries not only created domestic problems in form of nation-building challenges, it also produced international conflicts as well. East-Central Europe was sandwiched between two of its former overlords, Germany and Russia, both of which were unhappy with postwar borders.[15] By 1919 Poland and the Soviet Union were already involved in a war over territories claimed by both.[16] Germans and Austrians, meanwhile, resented the Allies' refusal to allow Austria to join the new Weimar Republic, as it clearly wanted to do after 1918 as well as the "stranding" of German minorities in "foreign" countries, particularly Bohemia, Moravia, and Silesia in Czechoslovakia where they became minorities. These resentments would, of course, eventually provide the ostensible rationale for Hitler's invasion of East-Central Europe. But it was not just the region's great powers that rejected postwar borders: most of the new East-Central European countries did as well.[17] Hungary, for example, claimed

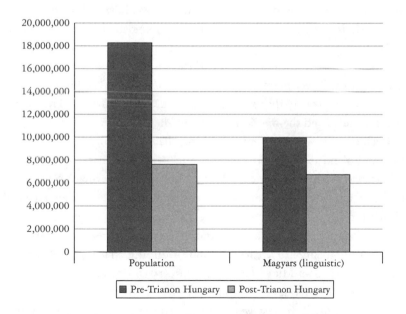

FIGURE 15.2 Population changes in Hungary post–Treaty of Trianon.
Source: Joseph Rothschild, *East Central Europe between the Two World Wars* (London: University of Washington Press, 1998), 155.

FIGURE 15.3 Territorial changes in Hungary post–Treaty of Trianon.
Source: Joseph Rothschild, *East Central Europe between the Two World Wars* (London: University of Washington Press, 1998), 155.

territory in Czechoslovakia, Romania, Yugoslavia, and Austria; Bulgaria coveted parts of Macedonia and Thrace, which were in Greece; and Poland and Czechoslovakia quarreled over Teschen, as well as over how to deal with Hungary and Russia. In short, East-Central Europe "abounded in potential conflicts" largely caused by its seemingly "arbitrarily drawn borders."[18] Each country "had one or more enemies within the area, and each of the 'victor' states among them also had a Great Power enemy—Poland even had two."[19] Watching the conflicts between the countries of the region unfold, Churchill remarked: "The war of the giants has ended and the war of the pygmies" has begun.[20]

Given this, it is perhaps not surprising that sustaining democracy proved difficult. Poland exemplified many of the dynamics characterizing the region. It had been reconstructed from parts of the German, Russian, and Habsburg Empires[21] and began its existence lacking well-defined borders and with territories characterized by different legal systems, currencies, armies, education systems, administrative infrastructure, and levels of economic development.[22] In addition to state-building challenges, Poland faced significant nation-building challenges. Post-1918 Poland was a multiethnic state:[23] of its twenty-seven million people, about 70 percent considered themselves Polish,[24] the rest were Ukrainians, Belorussians, Jews, Germans, Lithuanians, or something else. But even its ostensibly Polish citizens were

far from homogenous since they had lived in the extremely different social, economic, and political contexts of the German, Habsburg, or Russian
Empires for generations.[25] Moreover, in some regions of Poland, minorities
were the majority—and, with the exception of Jews, most had co-ethnics
in neighboring states, encouraging "separatism and even irredentism."[26]
Although the Polish constitution promised all citizens "legal equality and
protection by the State . . . irrespective of 'origin, nationality, language,
race or religion,'" the reality was that minorities were harassed, effectively
excluded from political power,[27] and subject to special taxes, repression,
and "Polonization" campaigns.[28] While real progress was made during the
interwar period unifying Poles from the German, Habsburg, and Russian
Empires, less progress was made reconciling the Polish majority with the
country's various minorities; instead relations remained tense, occasionally
erupting into violence.

For these and other reasons political stability proved elusive.[29] Dozens of
political parties, many representing either Poles *or* minorities, competed at
elections,[30] governments came and went, and political violence, corruption,
and electoral manipulation became commonplace.[31] By 1926 the country's
most respected political figure, Józef Piłsudski, decided enough was enough
and staged a coup. He originally claimed to have no intention of instituting
a dictatorship, merely wanting to "cleanse" or "heal" the political order.[32]
Initially the parliament (Sejm) and the opposition did remain in place, but
over time democratic procedures and institutions were undermined.[33] In
1935 Poland's slide towards dictatorship was "legalized" by a new constitution that enhanced the powers of the executive and minimized citizens'
ability to directly influence the government.[34] By the time Poland's independent existence was again ended by its two historic foes—Germany and
Russia—the democratic aspirations accompanying the country's rebirth had
long since disappeared.

Democracy disintegrated even more quickly in Hungary. Hungary began
the interwar years burdened by difficult legacies inherited from the old
order. While the Austrian half of the empire had experienced some political liberalization during the late nineteenth and early twentieth centuries,
the Hungarian half remained dominated by its nobility and gentry who
ruled over their lands and the people on them in a semi-feudal manner—in
Barrington Moore's terms, they engaged in labor-repressive agriculture—
blocked any meaningful political participation by the masses, controlled the
state apparatus, and repressed Hungary's minorities.[35] And as in much of the
rest of East-Central Europe, the Hungarian bourgeoisie or middle class was

largely Jewish, creating a potential divide between it and the rest of society that was easily exploited by demagogues.[36]

Hungary's postwar democratic government, led by Count Mihály Károlyi, received little elite or mass support and was quickly overwhelmed by dire economic problems—the currency plummeted to one-third its prewar value, agriculture and industry were in disarray, the country was cut off from its traditional markets, hunger and poverty were rampant, and disorder widespread[37]—and the backlash against the punitive peace settlement handed down by the Allies. After only a few months, Károlyi's government resigned and was replaced by a communist regime under Bela Kun.[38] With this, Hungary transitioned to Europe's first national-level communist dictatorship and only the world's second overall, after the Soviet Union. Kun immediately nationalized most industry, landholdings over forty hectares, and Church property; he also allowed a "red terror" to sweep parts of the country.[39] To deal with what most Hungarians viewed as the country's most pressing problem—the "unfair" treatment meted out by the Allies at the end of the war—he also quickly ordered the Red Army to invade Slovakia (previously "upper Hungary") and then continue on to Romania. Unlike in Poland, in other words, where the "national question" created domestic conflicts, in Hungary it created external conflicts with its neighbors.[40] The Allies forced Kun to retreat, and soon the Romanians were on their way to Budapest. Having alienated the peasantry by not distributing confiscated land to them, the nationalists and army by failing to recapture the territories and peoples lost after the war, and much of the rest of the country as a result of terror and repression, Kun fled on August 2 and the Soviet Republic collapsed.[41] After some months of chaos, a new regime led by Miklós Horthy resting on the support of the armed forces emerged.[42] Hungary now had the dubious distinction of transitioning from Europe's first communist dictatorship to its first postwar conservative-authoritarian one. Horthy's regime rapidly replaced its predecessor's "red terror" with an even more vicious "white" one: thousands were executed, seventy-five thousand jailed, and one hundred thousand citizens fled the country. It was, as the great historian of the region Joseph Rothschild put it, "a systematic, ferocious hunt, combining 'spontaneous' pogromist bestialities with a deliberate assault on those strata and institutions that . . . might challenge the traditional arrangements" that had long-reigned in Hungarian society and political life.[43] This dictatorship lasted longer than its communist and democratic predecessors but was also unable to solve the country's problems. By the 1930s its traditional, conservative nature was challenged by a rising radical right. Lured by the promise of regaining its lost territories, Hungary moved first economically and then politically into the Nazi sphere of influence.

Democracy suffered a similarly depressing fate in the rest of interwar East-Central Europe. The only exception was Czechoslovakia, which began the period with several advantages (see chapter 9, Figure 9.1). After Austria, it was the most economically developed, urbanized, and literate of the Habsburg Empire's successor states, it had a strong working and middle class,[44] its native landed nobility had been destroyed during the early modern period,[45] it was not overrun during the war,[46] and it had already developed a well "trained, honest and efficient" bureaucracy during the prewar period.[47] But even given these advantages, Czechoslovak democracy was not problem-free. Nation-building, for example, proved challenging. Czechoslovakia was the most ethnically diverse country in East-Central Europe: together Czechs and Slovaks made up about 64 percent of the population, but partially because the former was largely under Austrian rule (fairly liberal and tolerant of minorities) and the latter largely under Hungarian rule (less liberal and less tolerant of minorities), these two groups had very different economic, political, and social backgrounds.[48] The rest of Czechoslovakia's population was made up of Germans (23.4 percent), Magyars (5.6 percent), Ruthenians (3.4 percent), and Jews (1.3 percent). Despite constitutional pledges to protect minorities and ensure legal and political equality, top positions in the government and civil service were dominated by Czechs, electoral districts were gerrymandered to reduce minority voting power, Ruthenians denied the autonomy promised them after the war, and Germans treated as suspect or second-class citizens.[49] That the Germans and Magyar minorities had been members of dominant cultures during the prewar period and, along with the Ruthenians, had ties to "brother" populations in other successor states aggravated their resentment of their minority status in Czechoslovakia.[50]

Up through 1933 majority-minority conflicts and disagreements over Czechoslovakia's national identity compromised the liberal nature of its democracy; they did not, however, fundamentally threaten its existence. Hitler's rise to power changed this. Regardless of its internal politics, Czechoslovakia could not have resisted the Nazi juggernaut, especially once it was deserted by Europe's other big powers. A genuinely united society, however, one where all citizens' primary loyalty was to Czechoslovakia rather than to their own ethnic group or another state, would have been a less attractive target for the Nazis in 1938.[51] This was most obviously true of the country's Germans, most of whom supported nationalist German parties during the interwar period and then Hitler after he conquered the country. The same could be said of East-Central Europe more generally: even under the best of circumstances, resisting the Nazis probably would have been futile. However, these new countries' internal political, social, and communal divisions and the numerous conflicts among them weakened the individual and collective resistance they could mount against their enemies.

The Second World War and Its Aftermath

Having gained independence after the First World War, the countries of the region lost it during the Second to the Germans and then at its end to the Russians. The struggle between these great powers in the East-Central European *Bloodlands*[52] that lay between them generated the "worst acts of political violence in Europe in the twentieth century."[53] As Hitler put it, what occurred in the region was a "war of annihilation": the Nazis aimed to destroy the Soviet Union and enslave or exterminate its population as well as that of much of the rest of East-Central Europe; as the Soviet Union fought back, it responded in kind. The resulting death, destruction, and brutality was almost unimaginable: perhaps thirty million dead, about half of them civilians. Entire social groups disappeared: the Jews and Roma most notably, but also as a result of purposeful efforts by the Nazis and Soviets, a very high percentage of the region's intelligentsia and political and civil society leaders.[54] The region's landed elites were also decimated, "buried," as one observer put it, "under the ruins of war and fascism."[55] In short, even more than in Western Europe (see chapter 14) the war shattered East-Central European societies. Poland provides an extreme and frightening example of the region's fate. During the war, millions of Poles were forced from their homes, about 1.5 million were sent to Germany to work as slave laborers; by the war's end 17 percent of the Polish population was dead, including almost all its Jews and much of its educated and propertied classes;[56] its economy and transportation infrastructure were reduced to rubble.[57] As Norman Davies put it, in the nineteenth century the Poles had been faced with a life of deprivation. In the twentieth century they were faced with extinction.[58] By the end of the war, Poland like the rest of East Central Europe had been more radically transformed than "it had been in the century before or would be in the decades of communist rule that followed."[59]

The end of the war did not end the region's suffering. An unprecedented wave of ethnic cleansing that began during the war continued after it (see also chapter 14).[60] As Anne Applebaum has noted, "By 1945, the job of reordering [East-Central Europe] was already half completed. Hitler had already murdered most of the borderland Jews. Occupying Soviet officers had already sent over a million Polish officials, landowners and soldiers to Siberia and East Central Asia, along with over half a million West Ukrainians and half a million Balts. After the war, the deportations continued, grew, and developed into the largest mass movement of people in recorded history. . . . Call it ethnic cleansing . . . or call it cultural genocide. Either way, it was very successful."[61]

This was partially motivated by vengeance, particularly with regard to ethnic Germans since their presence had provided the pretext for Hitler's invasions and many supported the Nazis after they took power.[62] But along-side revenge existed a desire to homogenize populations so as to facilitate the nation-building that had proven so difficult during the interwar period. These motivations were often intertwined. In Czechoslovakia, for example, the large German-speaking population provided the pretense for Hitler's invasion and support for the Nazis once in power, but Germans had also long played a disproportionate role in the country's cultural, political, and economic life, leading many to view their presence as a hindrance to the development of a truly "Czechoslovak" nation-state. During the Second World War, President Edvard Beneš asserted that "national minorities are always . . . a thorn in the side of individual nations. This is especially true if they are German minorities." He made clear that at the war's end he intended "to eliminate the German problem in our Republic once and for all."[63] In this, he was largely successful: two million Germans were forced to flee Czechoslovakia after the war; several hundred thousand died along the way. These expulsions were supported by Stalin and the Allies, who, for the most part, believed that ho-mogenous states would have a better chance of survival than their ethnically mixed predecessors. Churchill, for example, told the House of Commons in 1944 that deportations would provide "the most satisfactory and lasting" solution to ethnic problems. There should not be a "mixture of populations to cause endless trouble. . . . A clean sweep will be made."[64] Referring to the Allied acceptance and supervision of ethnic cleansing, one observer, Anne McCormick of *The New York Times*, characterized it as "the most inhuman de-cision ever made by governments dedicated to the defense of human rights," noting that the "scale of this resettlement, and the conditions in which it takes place, are without precedent in history. No one seeing its horrors first hand can doubt that it is a crime against humanity for which history will exact a terrible retribution."[65]

Together wartime and postwar population shifts transformed East-Central Europe's ethnically mixed societies into homogenous ones; Yugoslavia was the exception.[66] By the late 1940s borders and peoples coincided in the re-gion more fully than ever before. The contrast with the post–World War I era was striking (see above and chapters 9 and 14). After 1918 "borders were invented and adjusted" but people left in place, while after World War II the opposite happened: for the most part, borders stayed in place and people moved.[67] As Mark Mazower put it, "War, violence and massive social dislocation had turned Versailles's dream of national homogeneity into realities."[68]

Although the costs were horrific, the prewar "mismatch" between people and borders had contributed to intense and often violent domestic conflicts in East-Central Europe and fed the rise of revisionist nationalism in Germany as well as Russia, Hungary, Austria, Bulgaria, and elsewhere.[69] In addition, while political stability, much less democracy, certainly does not *require* homogeneity, if citizens do not agree on the nature and boundaries of the national community—as was the case in much of East-Central Europe during the interwar period[70]—both are impossible. And thus far East-Central European societies had been unable to reach such agreements on their own. It is important to remember that such problems and dynamics were not limited to East-Central Europe: in Western Europe during the early modern period leaders forcibly homogenized populations by cleansing them of ethnic, religious, linguistic, and other minorities in order to create more easily controlled and cohesive societies. French kings, for example, expelled Protestants in order to create a more loyal and easily governed population (see chapter 2), and Spanish kings expelled Jews and Moors for a similar reason (see chapter 13). It was only when states had a high degree of legitimacy and infrastructural power that they could promote national identities and unity without the use of force but rather via education, the promotion of national culture and history, and the expansion of transport and communication networks, and by relying on flourishing civil societies that can create the sorts of cross-cutting ties and networks that can generate a sense of community and fellow-feeling among citizens. Alongside homogenizing East-Central European societies, ethnic cleansing also shattered existing class structures and social hierarchies. The elimination of Jews and Germans in particular, who played a disproportionately large role in the economic and cultural lives of the countries they inhabited, left gaping holes that majority populations could fill: Ethnic cleansing thus ironically "created opportunities for upward social mobility for skilled workers, artisans, entrepreneurs, and professionals that would not" otherwise have been available.[71] The few Jews who survived the war and tried to return home were often hounded out, their erstwhile neighbors putting the finishing touches on the process begun by Hitler.[72]

In short, World War II left East-Central Europe's old political, social, and economic order in ruins; it also left the Soviets on the ground. Russia had long viewed East-Central Europe as part of its natural sphere of influence and necessary for its defense—it was the route through which the country had been invaded from Napoleon through Hitler.[73] Such concerns, along with the presence of Soviet troops after a war that had cost more than twenty million Russian lives, meant Stalin was not going to let East-Central Europe go its own way[74] and the Allies were not in any case prepared to fight for control over the region. But that East-Central Europe ended up dominated, indeed colonized, by the Soviet Union was not merely a consequence of the latter's preferences; it depended on the history and characteristics of the former as well. East-Central European countries entered the Second World War with weak states, divided societies, and limited democratic experience; during the war they were brutalized, and almost all indigenous sources of resistance or even collective action—elites, political parties, civil society, armies—were wiped out; and at the war's end they were disrupted further by massive population shifts and horrific economic conditions—hunger, lack of shelter, and disease were prevalent.[75] East-Central Europe was not, in short, well positioned to resist external pressure. Also crucial was a receptivity to what communism claimed to offer. After 1945 East-Central Europeans were eager to eradicate the remnants of an old order that had left them mired in political instability, social conflict, and economic underdevelopment during the interwar years and replace it with a new order that would enable them not merely to catch up, but surpass the West. Communism promised just this: a quick path from backwardness to a socially just version of modernity. The plausibility of such promises was enhanced by the Soviet Union's accomplishments during the Second World War[76] and the seeming failures of democratic capitalism during the interwar period. The tendency of prewar dictators and elites to hurl the term "communist" at anyone who "stood up for the simple rights of the people . . . asked for reforms, protested against bureaucratic abuses, or resisted the gendarmerie in the execution of some wanton act of brutality,"[77] may also have solidified the connection between communism and progress for many East-Central Europeans. As one observer put it, "It is true that the Communist party dictatorship was brought to [East-Central Europe] by the victorious troops of Stalin, but we should admit that we were ready for it."[78]

After 1945, accordingly, control over East-Central Europe passed from the Nazis to the Soviets without ever really being in the hands of the region's peoples themselves. Unlike the Nazis and most colonizers, however, the Soviet Union did not merely want to control and extract resources from the region; it wanted to implant its own political, social, and economic order as well.[79] As Stalin put it in his conversations with Milovan Djilas, "This war is not as in the past; whoever occupies a territory also imposes upon it his own social system. Everyone imposes his own system as far as his army can reach. It cannot be otherwise."[80] (In fact, this was precisely as in the past, at least that part of the past when the principle of *cuius region, eius religio*— "Whose realm, his religion"—reigned. See chapter 2.[81]) And so after 1945 a revolution occurred in East-Central Europe. As with the French (1789), Russian (1917), and German (1933) revolutions, the one that occurred in East-Central Europe after 1945 followed on the heels of state collapse; involved immense violence; transformed politics, society, and the economy; and was accompanied by a utopian ideology promising a new and better world. But the revolution that occurred in East-Central Europe differed from previous revolutions in at least one critical way—it was imposed from the outside.[82] The revolution's external imposition, the nature of the communist system implanted by it, and the growing divergence between communism's reality and its utopian promises shaped East-Central Europe's political development during the postwar era.

The Transition to Stalinist Communism in East-Central Europe

As they did after the First World War, East-Central European countries began the post–World War II era as democracies. Stalin promised his Allies at Yalta that he would allow free elections; he hoped or believed these elections would produce communist majorities.[83] It quickly became clear, however, that communist parties could not gain majorities on their own. The Czechoslovaks came closest, receiving about 38 percent of the vote in the 1946 election—the party's high point. In other countries the results were worse: the Hungarian Communists got 17 percent in the 1945 elections (despite Soviet browbeating), and in Poland, Romania, and East Germany communist parties also did not come close to capturing majorities.[84] The realization that a legal route to power did not exist combined with the onset of the Cold War led communists to shift focus to gradually undermining democracy.[85] As Walter Ulbricht, who directed the communist takeover in East Germany, put it, "It's got to look democratic, but we must have everything in our control."[86] Although the nature and timing of this process varied from country to country, there were common elements and patterns.

Most notable was the use of "salami tactics" to slice up opponents piece by piece, like a salami, until nothing remained.[87] Across most of East-Central Europe this meant gradually dividing and weakening social democratic and peasant parties. Communists enjoyed many advantages over their opponents: they were more ruthless and united (many of their leaders had spent the war in the Soviet Union and came back after it knowing precisely what they wanted to achieve and how) and had access to financial, intelligence, and other resources provided by the Soviets that their opponents did not. (They also, of course, benefited from the presence of Soviet troops in the region.) Communists also infiltrated opposing parties, which gave them information about their internal deliberations and facilitated their ability to sow discord within them. This technique was particularly advanced in Hungary where, for example, József Révai (a party leader) informed the Cominform in September 1947 that "The National Peasant Party acts under our guidance. The secretary is a communist, and one of the two ministers representing it in the government is a communist. . . . The situation was similar with the Social Democratic left."[88]

Immediately after the war communists joined with social democratic, peasant, and other center and center-left parties in "National Front" coalitions, ostensibly to "eliminate the remnants of feudalism" and carry out much-needed reforms.[89] Once these coalitions were in power, communists insisted on controlling key ministries, most importantly the interior, which gave them power over the police and security forces and thus the tools for intimidating, blackmailing, and arresting opponents and rigging elections.[90] A contemporary Polish quip went: "What a magic ballot box!! You vote for Mikolajczyk [leader of the Peasant party] and Gomulka [the leader of the communist party] comes out!"[91] The ministries of justice and agriculture were also favorites, the former enabling communists to harass opponents with trumped-up charges and show trials and the latter providing access to patronage in the form of property confiscated from Nazis, fleeing minorities, and landed elites that could be used to bribe supporters.[92]

Harassment and intimidation weakened and divided non-communist parties, but finishing off social democratic parties—the communists' most serious opponents since they were clearly on the left and often the most popular parties, particularly among workers—could not be done via overt force. Instead, communists exploited divisions within social democratic parties about the desirability of left-wing alliances, and the guilt many social democrats felt about the left not working together before the war to prevent the rise of fascism, to pressure social democrats to join "left unity" parties. Often against much internal opposition and, with the exception of Czechoslovakia, under the watchful eye of Soviet troops, these mergers began in the Soviet zone of Germany with the joining of the SPD (social democratic party) and KPD (communists) into a "Socialist Unity Party" and then continued in Romania, Hungary, Czechoslovakia, and Poland. Once merged, communists shunted social democrats into positions of symbolic rather than real power, and then purged any members opposed to the merger from the "unity" parties. Once the mergers occurred, any real opposition to communism and any semblance of democracy came to an end.[93] By the late 1940s fairly uniform communist regimes subservient to the Soviet Union were in place across East-Central Europe.[94] These regimes then finished off what remained of the old order and began constructing a new political, social, and economic one.

The Stalinist Communist Order in East-Central Europe

One striking feature of all revolutions is the construction of new and powerful states after the collapse of old ones; this was certainly a consequence of the communist revolutions in East-Central Europe. For the first time states in the region obtained a monopoly over the use of violence and were able to eliminate traditional opponents to the centralization of power, like old elites and the Church.[95] Indeed, during the Stalinist period, all opposition—real and imagined—to communism was eliminated via hysterical and pervasive purges: "perhaps one in four party members suffered some form of persecution during the years 1948–1953. Without a doubt, more communists died at the hands of . . . communist governments . . . than under their interwar predecessors." But it was not just communists who suffered: purges affected almost all sectors of society. "No one was safe. Denunciations were rife, the definitions of crime all-embracing . . . and, most importantly, responsibilities for administering the purges were integrated into the everyday lives of all citizens."[96]

With alternative sources of power eliminated, communist states became immensely powerful. These states were dominated by the communist party and run by a "privileged" class that, like its ancien régime counterparts (see chapter 2), was granted access to political, economic, and social resources including high-status political and civil service positions, better schools, vacation facilities, and health care and special stores stocked with products available only to them,[97] in return for loyalty to the regime. Alongside monopolizing the means of violence, communist states used their immense "despotic" or coercive power to control the economy and society as well. This is a crucial way communist dictatorships differed from traditional authoritarian ones: whereas the latter controlled the political sphere but tended to intervene in the economy and society only to the degree necessary to maintain political power, the former aimed at "total" control—which is why, of course, they are often called "totalitarian."[98] By the end of the Stalinist period "no segment of the body social, economic, cultural, as well as no repressive institution escaped [the party-state's] continuous and systematic . . . intervention."[99]

Communism's control over the economy surpassed that of other totalitarian regimes like the German National Socialist or Italian fascist, which[100] aimed to contain or tame markets (see chapters 11 and 12), whereas communist dictatorships eliminated them and the broader capitalist order they were part of. In the place of a market-based, capitalist economic order, communists constructed a state-directed one focused on rapid industrialization. Industrialization and modernization more generally were certainly things East-Central Europe desperately needed: as noted above, the region had historically lagged far behind Western Europe, and the Second World War devastated its economies further.[101] Up through the war, agriculture remained the dominant sector, productivity within it was low, and inequality high.[102] In Hungary and Poland, moreover, large landholding elites dominated the agricultural sector and rural society more generally.[103] For both economic and social reasons, therefore, agricultural and particularly land reform were long overdue. Such reforms began during the interwar period in some parts of East-Central Europe,[104] but dramatically accelerated after the war with the confiscation of land owned by Nazis, expelled minorities, large landowners and other "fascist sympathizers,"[105] and its distribution to small peasants and rural laborers. In order to avoid alienating these groups, the next stage of communist land reform—nationalization of land and collectivization of agriculture—proceeded fairly slowly.[106] In 1953, when Stalin died, only Bulgaria had nationalized more than 50 percent of its land; it was not until the 1960s that state and collective farms encompassed more than 90 percent of agricultural land in the rest of East-Central Europe. (Poland was the exception, where the share remained at a very low 14 percent. See below.[107]) Nonetheless, the destruction of the old order in the countryside that began during the Second World War was largely completed by the 1950s: by this point, large landholding elites had been relegated to the dustbin of history and peasants were on their way there as well.[108] And as the traditional rural classes disappeared, so too did the "social institutions" and "cultural orientations" that had defined rural society.[109]

Industry fell under state control more quickly and completely: by 1949–1950, 96 percent of Czechoslovakia's, 81 percent of Hungary's, 92 percent of Poland's, and 76 percent of the GDR's industry was under state control; by

1952 it was essentially 100 percent across the region.[110] That communist states were able to so rapidly eliminate "private control of the means of production" is partially explained by the extensive control the Nazis had developed over East-Central European economies during the war. As Edvard Beneš, postwar president of Czechoslovakia, noted,

> The Germans simply took control of all main industries and banks. . . . If they did not nationalize them directly, they . . . put them in the hands of [Germans]. In this way they . . . prepared the economic and financial capital of our country for nationalization. . . . To return this property . . . to Czech individuals . . . was impossible. The state had to step in.[111]

Following the Soviet model, state control over the economy in East-Central Europe was directed at maximizing the output of heavy industry. Development was extremely one-sided: "all that grew was heavy industry to produce capital goods, to produce more capital goods, to produce more heavy industry. . . . The primary sector, agriculture . . . was blasted and blighted; and the tertiary, or service, sector was barely developed, as was that part of the secondary, or industrial sector devoted to consumer goods. So Soviet modernization meant essentially a hypertrophied secondary sector producing neither for an internal market nor for export but for itself and for the all-encompassing state, with just enough in the way of consumer goods and services to keep the population alive."[112] During the Stalinist period development was generated by extremely high investment rates of often up to a quarter of national income,[113] and the forced transfer of labor from agriculture, where productivity was much lower. This was an extreme example, in other words, of "extensive" growth—based upon a massive increase in the *quantity* of inputs, rather than "intensive" growth, based improving the *quality* of inputs like technology, industrial organization, managerial efficiency, and so on. The problem with extensive growth is that inputs cannot be increased indefinitely; it is inherently subject to diminishing marginal returns. At least in theory, this is not true of intensive growth since technology, productivity, and so on can be improved indefinitely.[114] In short, while economic development did occur during the Stalinist era, it was inefficient and unbalanced,[115] made possible by communist states' ability to coercively suck resources out of society, shift labor from one sector (agriculture) to another (industry), and keep wages, consumption, and overall improvements in living conditions artificially low.[116] In addition, during the Stalinist era, East-Central European economies were subjugated to the needs of the Soviet Union, which extracted more resources from the region than it put into it.[117]

There is thus an interesting comparison between what was going on in East-Central and Western Europe at this time. Whereas the United States was pumping resources into the latter with the Marshall Plan (see chapter 14), the Soviet Union was sucking resources out of former—up to 15–17 percent of national income in 1945 and still perhaps 7–10 percent in 1947—even though this intensified widespread shortages, distress, and, during the immediate postwar period, even famine in the region.[118]

East-Central Europe in the Post-Stalin Era

Stalin's death in 1953 ushered in a new period in East-Central Europe's political development. By the early 1950s the main features of Stalinist communism—the imperial relationship between the Soviet Union and East-Central Europe, relentless political repression and terror, and an economic model prioritizing heavy industry and military production over the needs of citizens—were generating growing discontent. Perhaps reflecting Tocqueville's adage that "the most dangerous moment for a bad government is when it begins to reform,"[119] when this discontent combined with the political opening accompanying Stalin's death and Khrushchev's subsequent rise to power, disorder spread. Sporadic strikes and demonstrations had occurred during the early 1950s, but the first major revolt broke out in East Germany in 1953.[120] That discontent had been building for some time is reflected in the 700,000 people who left East Germany between 1949 and 1952; in the first months of 1953 another 225,000 left. The spark that turned discontent into revolt was an announcement on June 16 that workplace conditions would be toughened and workers' quotas increased in response to economic slowdown.[121] Within a day, strikes broke out in East Berlin and spread across the country. The strikers' economic demands were quickly joined by political ones. As one observer recalled,

> I was just about to go . . . when a procession of . . . workers reached Unter den Linden. . . . It had grown mightily and, apart from building workers, many young people . . . were to be seen. . . . They had enthusiastically joined the protest. . . . They shouted in chorus: "We are workers and not slaves! Put an end to the extortionist norms. We want free elections!" And, always loudest of all, the sentence "We are not slaves!"[122]

The East German government was surprised by the revolt and unsure of how to respond; the Soviets therefore rapidly stepped in. By the end of June 17 their troops and tanks had rolled in and martial law had been declared. In the fighting that followed, four hundred workers were killed; dozens more were subsequently sentenced to death and thousands more to prison terms. This spurred Bertolt Brecht to write his famous poem:

> Following the June Seventeenth uprising
> the secretary of the Writers' League
> had leaflets distributed on Stalin Allee
> here one could read that the people
> had forfeited the confidence of the government
> and could regain it only through redoubled efforts.
> Wouldn't it be simpler under these circumstances
> for the government to dissolve the people
> and elect another one?[123]

Although the East Berlin revolt was crushed, the desire for change was not, and Khrushchev's denunciation of Stalinist "excesses" at the twentieth congress of the Communist party of the Soviet Union in February 1956 spurred further uprisings.[124] The first occurred in Poland. In June 1956 workers in Poznan marched out on strike, ostensibly over worsening work conditions and declining wages, but the movement quickly expanded beyond workers and beyond economic complaints. Perhaps one hundred thousand protestors gathered in Poznan's center chanting, "We want freedom," "Down with false Communism," and "Down with the Russians."[125] Troops were called in from Warsaw; by the time the fighting was over, between fifty and seventy-five people were dead and hundreds wounded.[126] Demonstrations continued into the fall when a new leader, Władysław Gomulka, came to power.

Soon after the uprising in Poland, an even more dramatic rebellion occurred in Hungary. As in other parts of East-Central Europe there had been rumblings of discontent amongst workers and peasants for many years, and the thaw following Stalin's death allowed differences within the communist party between reformists and hardliners, represented by Imre Nagy and Matyás Rákosi, respectively, over how to respond to such discontent and over Hungary's future more generally to emerge.[127] In 1953 Nagy was appointed chairman of the Council of Ministers and proposed a "new course" that included economic reform, lessening repression, and some political liberalization. Rákosi bided his time, waiting for the wheel to turn again in the Soviet Union, and when it did he pushed Nagy aside and returned to power in April 1955. But the balance of power shifted again after Khrushchev's 1956 speech and his reconciliation with the Yugoslavs (who despised Rákosi because of the prominent role he played in the anti-Titoist campaigns of the late 1940s), and Rákosi was pushed out again. Soon after Poland exploded; by October 1956 Hungary was in turmoil as well. Political mobilization spread like wildfire across the country: within days hundreds of thousands of Hungarians were on the streets demanding change and Nagy's return. This rapid mobilization surprised and overwhelmed the state and party.[128] Nagy was quickly called back as premier and along with Janos Kadar, who had been appointed secretary of the Communist party, tried to balance the demands of the Soviets and the people on the streets. When these proved incompatible, Nagy threw his hat in with the latter and Kadar with the former. On October 30 Nagy declared in a radio address that "the Cabinet abolishes the one-party system"; by the next day various parties were establishing or re-establishing themselves,[129] and the existing communist party disbanded. It is important to note that despite these moves, Nagy was a committed communist: as he declared over and over, he did not want to eliminate communism, but rather reform it. He believed that "the errors and mistakes of the communist era were simply the result of the usurpation and misuse of power by a group of evil and unprincipled leaders. The disease had only affected the elite: it was not a structural defect in the system itself. It could be cured by a 'changing of the guard,' enabling a return to the correct policies and noble ideas of socialism."[130] Despite protestations of communist loyalty, Nagy's reforms and the situation in Hungary generally proved more than the Soviets could countenance; at the beginning of November Soviet troops and tanks rolled into the country.[131] Nagy tried to gain support from the West and the U.N. and declared that Hungary would withdraw from the Warsaw Pact and become neutral,[132] but he was essentially ignored. After fighting that cost between 2,500 and 4,000 Hungarian lives and about 20,000 wounded and close to 700 Russian lives and about 1,450 wounded, Hungary's brief attempt at reformist, national communism came to an end.[133] At this point Nagy fled to the Yugoslav Embassy, where he had been promised safe passage. He was nonetheless arrested, spirited out of Hungary, and eventually executed—a crime and betrayal that would play an important role in later Hungarian history (see chapter 17). A wave of terror washed over Hungary after the Soviet invasion: between 1956 and 1959 thirty-five thousand people were arrested, twenty-two thousand sentenced to jail, and hundreds executed. Hundreds of thousands of Hungarians also fled the country. Violence, repression, and emigration successfully eliminated any remnants of resistance.[134]

The emergence and crushing of uprisings during the 1950s made several things clear. First: as long as the Soviets were willing to intervene, little would change in East-Central Europe. The balance of power between the metropole and its satellites was simply too skewed for the latter to be able to implement reforms that the former were willing to violently oppose. Second: since the political, economic, and social spheres were inexorably intertwined in communist regimes, it was difficult to keep demands for change in one sphere from spilling into the others. Third: the leaders of the 1950s uprisings claimed to want to reform the reigning order, purging it of its "Stalinist excesses," colonial nature, and economic inefficiencies and inequities, not destroy it. Their inability to do so, however, began to raise questions about the feasibility of reform. Fourth: below the surface significant discontent existed, and if the Soviets and local communist leaders wanted to avoid future uprisings and the need to use force to crush them, buying the support or at least quiescence of East-Central European populations would be necessary. And so after the uprisings of the 1950s were brutally put down and the hegemony of communist party-states re-established, gradual, grudging, and primarily economic reforms began in East-Central Europe. This mixture of primarily economic concessions and continued coercion did pacify populations during the late 1950s and 1960s, but as will be discussed in chapter 17, over time the cost of both became increasingly high.

Conclusions

After two devastating world wars, Europe lost its autonomy: its postwar political development was determined not *merely* in the case of Western Europe, and not *primarily* in the case of East-Central Europe, by the wishes of its people themselves, but rather by the interests of the two superpowers created by the wars—the United States and the Soviet Union. In Western Europe American influence occurred primarily via carrots and cooperation rather than sticks and coercion. In order to help consolidate liberal democracy, the United States offered Western Europe a variety of material benefits through the Marshall Plan, the creation of a new international economic order, and the construction of myriad international economic institutions; it also took over partial responsibility for Western Europe's defense and security. Cumulatively these arrangements helped support "social democratic" domestic orders and the most prosperous, peaceful, and politically successful period in modern West European history. In East-Central Europe Soviet influence occurred in a more overtly coercive and colonial manner, and the states of the region lost more of their sovereignty than their West European counterparts. Nonetheless, at least initially communism enjoyed some legitimacy or at least acceptance as a result of its promise to eradicate the remnants of the regions' backward, corrupt, and unequal old orders and create modern, just, and humane new ones. Although the price paid in terms of political freedom and national sovereignty was very high, communist regimes did destroy what remained of the old order and initiate a period of rapid, if warped, economic development and social modernization after the Second World War. By the 1950s, however, the limits of the Stalinist-communist model were becoming clear, and the dissatisfaction generated by this, particularly once Stalin died, led to uprisings throughout the region—most notably in East Germany in 1953 and in Poland and Hungary in 1956. These uprisings were spontaneous, lacked organization, and were easily crushed, but revealed that below the surface the legitimacy communist regimes had initially enjoyed was eroding.[135]

Social scientists differentiate among different kinds of legitimacy. One is "systemic" or "diffuse." This type of legitimacy comes from citizens believing in a particular system itself—separate from the "ups and downs" of government performance, short-term fluctuations in economic conditions, or the particular policies or leaders characterizing it at any given time. Seymour Martin Lipset describes this type of legitimacy as involving "the capacity of the system to engender and maintain the belief that the existing political institutions are the most appropriate ones for society."[136] Because it is anchored in political values, attachments, and identities rather than in short-term evaluations of particular outcomes, "systemic" or "diffuse" legitimacy is fairly durable. This is the type of legitimacy embedded in the definition of democratic consolidation laid out in chapter 1 and used throughout this book: democracy is considered consolidated when citizens believe in its inherent superiority or suitability for their society, separate from the particular outcomes it produces or the leaders and governments in power at particular times. Communist regimes seem initially to have enjoyed at least some of this type of legitimacy from citizens who believed or hoped communism would create a new and better world out of the ashes of the old one.

Another type of legitimacy is "performance" or "output" legitimacy. Here citizens support a regime and a regime justifies its existence not on ideological but practical grounds: the promotion of economic growth, the maintenance of order, protecting the interests of a "threatened" group, defeating an external enemy, and so on. Since this type of legitimacy is subject to continual re-evaluation, it is less durable or dependable than its "systemic" or "diffuse" counterpart: if output or performance does not match promises, citizens will relatively quickly withdraw their support, leaving force as the only way for a regime to stay in power.[137] Despite, in other words, differing from traditional dictatorships in critical ways, during the post-Stalinist era East-Central European communist regimes became more like them in their increasing reliance on "performance" or "output," rather than "systemic" or diffuse" legitimacy. This shift may have begun as early as the 1950s, but as we will see in chapter 17, it accelerated dramatically after 1968 with the crushing of the Prague Spring. By the 1970s and 1980s there were few "true believers" or ideologically committed communists left in East-Central Europe, even within communist parties. Once communist regimes were no longer able to rely on a reservoir of citizen belief in the inherent legitimacy or desirability of communism, and had to instead buy citizen support with promises of better output or performance, they came to share with other dictatorships a *potentially* dangerous vulnerability. Should they be unable to produce better output or performance—particularly ever-improving living conditions—lacking reserves of "systemic" or "diffuse" legitimacy, the only way communist regimes could remain in power was via force. To paraphrase Ernst Gellner, during the post-Stalinist era East-Central Europeans gradually lost faith in communism's transcendental claims—its promise to deliver a better world—and its continued existence therefore increasingly came to depend on "promises testable in this world rather than the next"—a precarious and perilous situation indeed.[138]

CHAPTER 16 | The Transition to Democracy
in Spain

Spain is characterized by its anarchic spirit, negative critique, lack of
solidarity among men, extremism, and mutual hostility.
—Francisco Franco[1]

AFTER 1945 WESTERN Europe finally achieved consolidated liberal democracy. As discussed in chapter 14, this was partially because during
the 1930s and '40s, and particularly as a result of the Second World War and
its aftermath, remaining social and economic legacies of the old order and
hindrances to democracy were eliminated. In addition, the horrors produced
by fascist and National Socialist dictatorships and war produced a renewed
appreciation for the virtues of democracy as well as a better understanding
of what it would take to make it work. A learning process, in other words,
contributed to the postwar consolidation of democracy in Western Europe.
Also crucial was the fact that after 1945 democracy did not have to be
constructed from scratch: with most of the anti-democratic legacies of the old
order now gone, other legacies from previous democratic experiments—political parties, civil society organizations, a free press, elites with experience
working within democratic institutions—could be rebuilt and contribute to
the consolidation of liberal democracy.

At the same time that the foundations of consolidated liberal democracy
were being laid in Western Europe, Eastern Europe was making a transition
to communism (see chapter 15). This transition was the result primarily of
external factors, namely the influence of the Soviet Union, but internal factors

also played a role—the countries of the region were extremely weak and extremely eager for radical change at the end of the war. Eastern European communist regimes differed greatly from traditional dictatorships: they monopolized not merely political power, but controlled and transformed societies and economies as well.

Southern Europe's political trajectory differed from both Western and Eastern Europe's: neither democratic nor communist, Spain, Portugal, and Greece (between 1967 and 1974) were ruled by conservative dictatorships during the postwar period. This chapter focuses on Spain. As discussed in chapter 13, when Spain's democratic experiment collapsed in 1936, the Soviet Union, Fascist Italy, and National Socialist Germany were ready to intervene, making the ensuing civil war longer and more brutal than it otherwise might have been. The civil war eventually killed hundreds of thousands of Spaniards and gave rise to a dictatorship that endured until the dictator, Franco, died in 1975.

Spain's transition to democracy turned out to be remarkably successful. To a large degree this was because many of the problems or hindrances to democracy that foiled the Second Republic during the interwar years had disappeared by the 1970s. Domestically Spain's economy and society had changed dramatically, and the international environment had shifted from being hostile to democracy to being favorable to it. Along with these structural changes, the nature and success of the Spanish transition was also shaped by the behavior of key political actors. As in Western Europe's transition to democracy after World War II, a significant learning process influenced the Spanish transition in the 1970s. The memory of the Second Republic and the civil war made key political actors aware of the fragility of democracy and led to a new understanding of what it would take to make it work this time around.

Franco's Regime

Although supported by fascist Italy and National Socialist Germany and coming to power with the support of the army, Franco's regime was neither a fascist/National Socialist dictatorship nor a traditional military one. Instead, particularly during its early years, Franco's regime was essentially a personal dictatorship.[2] During the civil war Franco "ran the entire government . . . via personal decrees" and when the war ended in 1939 all powers were handed over to him. Over the following years he consolidated his control over the state,[3] systematically killing or imprisoning what remained of the Republican opposition,[4] insisting that he had saved Spain from its internal and external enemies and was the only one who could do so going forward,[5] and dominating the various groups supporting the Nationalist cause—landed, industrial, and banking elites, monarchists, the military, and the Church.

The military, of course, was Franco's original power base and was responsible for victory in the civil war; it was celebrated as the defender of the nation, and was charged with the maintenance of public order when the war was over. However, Franco kept the military subservient to him, instilling in it "the attitude that the function of the military was to serve rather than to dominate." Franco thereby ironically succeeded in achieving a goal that had long eluded his predecessors: "demilitarizing" the political process and keeping the military out of day-to-day political life.[6] Even the many officers who served in government were forced to do so as individuals rather than as representatives of the military (see Figure 16.1).[7]

Alongside the military, the other main pillar of Franco's regime was the Church. During the civil war the Church openly condemned the republic and supported the Nationalists, and Franco returned the favor by identifying his cause with the Church and the defense of Catholicism. When the war ended, Franco promoted the spread of Catholic rites and rituals throughout society, brought laws into closer alignment with Church doctrine, and integrated ecclesiastical figures into government.[8] Franco also signed a concordat

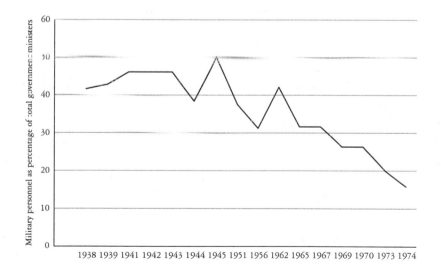

FIGURE 16.1 Military personnel in government, 1938–1974.
Source: Stanley G. Payne, *The Franco Regime, 1936–1975* (Madison: University of Wisconsin Press, 1987), 567.

with the Catholic Church that granted it control over primary education alongside its dominant role in secondary education (at one point Catholic schools educated almost half of all secondary school students); guaranteed the Church independence in its activities and freedom from state censorship for its publications; and provided it with financial subsidies, tax exemptions, and special legal privileges for the clergy.[9] In essence, the concordat returned the Spanish Church to its pre–Second Republic stature and gave it a degree of social influence probably unmatched by any other national church since the nineteenth century. As significant as these benefits were, Franco also profited immensely from the concordat: he gained the right to review bishops and thus gained significant control over the Church, and his regime received an immense legitimacy boost. As one observer put it, after the concordat, the symbiosis of Catholicism and Francoism in "national Catholicism" seemed complete.[10]

Having eliminated his Republican opponents during the civil war and its aftermath and having dominated/co-opted Spain's traditionally two most powerful institutions—the military and the Church—Franco had, by the mid-1940s, probably more "power than any previous ruler of Spain," and his state was more "centralized" and had more control over society than any other "in Spanish history."[11] During the decade or so after the civil war the regime was at its most oppressive[12] and also pursued a state-directed program of economic autarky. For Franco "autarky was the reflection in economic policy of paranoia in politics; for Spain, surrounded by a conspiring hostile world, autarky was presented as a patriotic necessity."[13] Autarky further devastated a Spanish economy that had not recovered from the civil war: industrial output, agricultural production, and national income remained below prewar levels; the country's infrastructure was in a state of near collapse; and the black economy was close to outpacing the real one.[14] Continued economic suffering threatened to erode the regime's popularity; by the mid-1950s Franco had accepted the need for a course shift. In 1957 he brought into his government a team of Opus Dei technocrats and began "a completely new phase of the dictatorship."[15]

Although conservative and monarchical, the Opus Dei team lacked ties to the traditional Nationalist coalition and were mostly professionals with university and technical backgrounds. They modernized "'the entire state administration', imbuing the Ministries of the Economy and Finance" in particular with "'modern economic thought' at the highest levels,"[16] and restructured the relationship between the state and economy. State intervention was not eliminated, but economic liberalization and internationalization began. Spain joined the OEEC, the Export-Import Bank, and the

IMF. The Spanish currency, the peseta, was devalued; government controls, regulations, and oversight of investment pared down; the tax system reformed and simplified; and antimonopoly rules imposed to encourage competition.[17] Spain's communication and transportation infrastructures were expanded and modernized. Partially as a result of these reforms and Spain's concomitant ability to take advantage of the growth going on in Western Europe, between 1960 and 1973 Spain's overall GDP increased about 7.5 percent per year, industrial production shot up about 10 percent per year, and service sector growth about 6.7 percent per year; agriculture's share of national production and employment declined significantly. Tourism became a major industry, drawing millions of visitors to Spain, bringing in large amounts of foreign currency and investment, transforming entire regions of the country and probably forcing Franco to exercise some political restraint in order to keep the tourists coming.[18] This period is often referred to as Spain's economic "miracle"[19] since it represented "the greatest sustained economic development and general improvement in living standards in all of [Spain's] history. . . . Only Japan made greater proportionate progress than Spain during this" time.[20] As a result, by the 1970s Spain's closed, backward, agrarian economy had been transformed into an open, middle-income, industrial, and service-sector-based one (see Figures 16.2–16.6).

The social consequences of economic development were profound: "Spanish society changed more rapidly between 1950 and 1970 than in the previous century":[21] it was transformed from a traditional society dominated by a

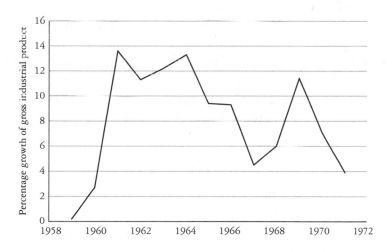

FIGURE 16.2 Growth of Spanish gross industrial product, 1958–1972.
Source: Stanley G. Payne, *The Franco Regime, 1936–1975* (Madison: University of Wisconsin Press, 1987), 477.

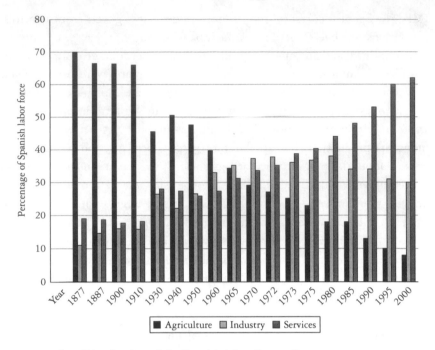

FIGURE 16.3 Distribution of the Spanish labor force, 1877–2000.
Source: Joseph Harrison, *The Spanish Economy in the Twentieth Century* (London: Palgrave, 1985); and R. Gunther, J. R. Montero, and J. Botella, *Democracy in Modern Spain* (New Haven, CT: Yale University Press, 2004).

powerful and reactionary landowning elite, a large class of (radical) farm laborers, and a relatively small middle and working class into one dominated by its middle and working classes, with rural/agricultural groups in terminal decline (see table 16.1).

This shift in class structure was accompanied by massive urbanization. During the postwar period, and particularly from about 1960, entire rural areas depopulated as marginal farmers and agricultural laborers moved to cities or other parts of Europe in search of better jobs and lives. During the 1960s approximately one hundred thousand to two hundred thousand Spaniards left Spain per year; by 1973 millions had left overall.[22] In 1960 about 58 percent of Spaniards lived in towns with fewer than ten thousand residents, but by 1981 this had fallen to 36 percent; during the same period residents in cities with more than one hundred thousand residents grew from 15 percent to 42 percent. By the 1980s Spain's urbanization rate was about the European average.[23] This rural exodus was the most successful agrarian reform of all time: demands for land redistribution essentially vanished. In addition, as agricultural laborers gradually disappeared, so too did the

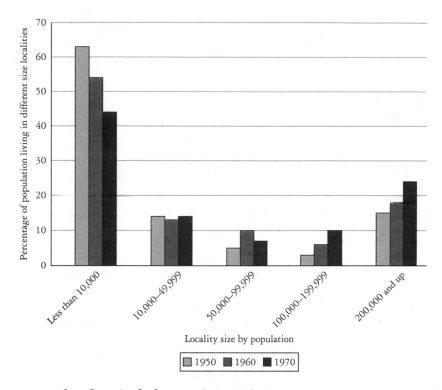

FIGURE 16.4 Growth of urban population in Spain, 1950–1970.
Source: John Coverdale, *The Political Transformation of Spain after Franco* (New York: Praeger, 1979), 3.

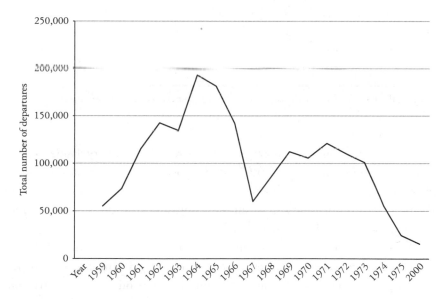

FIGURE 16.5 Emigration out of Spain, 1959–2000.
Source: Joseph Harrison, *The Spanish Economy in the Twentieth Century* (London: Palgrave, 1985), 151.

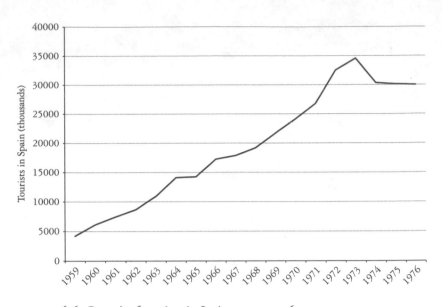

FIGURE 16.6 Growth of tourism in Spain, 1959–1976.
Source: José Amodia, *Franco's Political Legacy: From Dictatorship to Façade Democracy* (London: Allen Lane, 1977), 133; and Harrison, *The Spanish Economy in the Twentieth Century*, 156.

TABLE 16.1 Class and employment section, 1860, 1950, and 1970

	1860	1950	1970
Urban upper and middle classes	24%	26%	41%
Self-employed farmers	29%	17%	14%
Industrial workers	13%	24%	35%
Farm laborers	34%	33%	11%
Employed in industry/services	27%	50%	75%

Source: Payne, *The Franco Regime*, 488, and Aceña and Ruiz, "The Golden Age," 33.

radicalism and anarchism they long supported. Reactionary landed elites lost social and economic power,[24] and the patron-client relationships long characterizing rural Spain collapsed.[25] By the early 1970s "traditional" Spain, the heartland of Francoism, and long a bastion of anti-democratic norms and activity, had essentially disappeared.[26]

Alongside economic development, urbanization, and changes in class structure, education also transformed Spanish society during the postwar period. By 1970 the government was spending more on education than on the armed forces.[27] In the 1930s a quarter of Spaniards were illiterate; by the 1960s 12 percent, and by the early 1970s perhaps 5 percent.[28] Higher education also expanded: in 1960 there were 71,000 university students, in 1970 the total grew to 175,000, and in 1980 to 277,000.[29] Rising education levels spread new ideas and values throughout Spanish society and increased secularization.[30] Economic development broke down the isolation of many parts of Spain, particularly its rural areas, and welded the country's various "geographic regions into one interconnected economic unit." Moreover, just as migration was filling the cities with "workers from all parts of the country, government agencies, banks, and corporations were [becoming populated by] a single interlocking elite of state officials, bankers and corporation executives. . . . In a very real sense, the regionalism which had marked Spain since medieval times was under mortal attack."[31]

These economic and social changes generated increasing unrest. Illegal workers' organizations (Workers' commissions), strikes, protests by students and professors,[32] and regional dissatisfaction with the Franco regime's extreme centralization grew. The most worrying manifestation of the latter was the terrorism of the Basque ETA.[33] The Catholic Church was also transformed. Beginning in the 1960s a generational shift produced a new cadre of priests "susceptible to the new currents of liberalization coming from abroad and from the international Roman Catholic Church."[34] Particularly after the liberalizing Second Vatican Council, the Spanish Church began accepting "the necessity of political change"[35] and used its relative freedom, particularly from censorship, to provide a forum for the airing of new ideas and dissident voices. In 1971 an assembly of priests and bishops pronounced itself in favor of civil rights and against continued participation in the Francoist regime.[36]

By the early 1970s, in short, Spain resembled the situation Eric Hobsbawm described facing Europe in 1848 (see chapter 5): it was "out of balance." Two of the main supports of the old regime—the Church and landed elites—either ceased to support it or had faded away, and dissatisfaction with the dictatorship was growing within Spain's middle and working classes and various regions. Also contributing to this "Hobsbawmian imbalance" was the international environment Spain faced by the early 1970s: Western Europe was now home to prosperous consolidated liberal democracies that viewed Franco's dictatorship as a backward anachronism and kept Spain out of the EEC; this isolation carried a heavy economic price and, for Spain's increasingly educated and well-informed citizens, a psychological one as well. "'Europismo' became an almost mythical aspiration for" many Spanish citizens.[37] In short, although few things in politics are "irresistible" or "inevitable" (pace Hobsbawm), by the early 1970s a "malaise was afflicting the Francoist state" as pressure for political change mounted as did an acceptance within at least some sectors of the regime that the status quo was untenable. As the ultra right-winger Blas Piñar said in October 1972, "In Spain, we are suffering from a crisis of identity of our own state."[38]

The Transition

During the 1960s a tentative political opening (*Apertura*) began: restrictions on workers' and non-political associations, press censorship, and repression were loosened.[39] Franco also gradually ceased making all major decisions, turning day-to-day policy making over to technocrats and bureaucrats—initially, as mentioned above, in the economic sphere, but increasingly in other areas as well.[40] Franco remained, however, the pivot of the regime and nothing significant happened without his approval. However, his withdrawal from everyday politics and his age (he was born in 1892) placed the issue of succession, and the regime's future, front and center.

In June 1973 Franco appointed the loyal Luis Carrero Blanco prime minister to ensure "the continuation of Francoism after Franco."[41] This was the first time someone other than Franco was prime minister. (Franco remained head of state and the military.) Within about six months, however, Carrero Blanco was dead, assassinated by ETA terrorists. But because Carrero Blanco had been chosen as "the most promising candidate for ensuring the continuation of Francoism,"[42] his assassination again thrust the question of the regime's future to the forefront. Meanwhile, the regime confronted a serious economic downturn during this time partially as a result of the oil price shock, growing strikes and other forms of social unrest, and a middle class that increasingly seemed to believe that "political change was of the greatest urgency."[43] These and other problems aggravated tensions within the ruling elite between hardliners and liberalizers. Opposition forces began thinking about a post-Franco future. In 1974 the Communist party joined with several other groups to form the *Junta Democrática*; somewhat later the Socialist party united with other leftist, liberal, and regional groups in the *Plataforma de Convergencia Democrática*. The reemergence of the Socialist party (PSOE) was particularly important: in 1972 the party held a conference in France and elected Felipe González as its secretary general. González's election represented a crucial shift: he was very young (only thirty years old), represented a break with the civil war generation, and came from the more reformist wing of the party.

However, growing discontent manifested in strikes, terrorist attacks, and other forms of social unrest as well as the church's distancing itself from the regime, and the increasing confidence and organization of the opposition could not alone produce political change. Indeed during 1974 and 1975 the regime responded to discontent with repression. When Franco upheld death sentences for five terrorists in 1975, protests broke out across Europe, several countries recalled their ambassadors, and the EEC voted to freeze trade with Spain. The political situation seemed stalemated—and then in November 1975, Franco died.

Once the dictator was gone, pent-up pressures exploded. Strikes increased from 14.5 million working days lost in 1975 to 150 million in 1976; demonstrations broke out across the country; ETA assassinations continued; and armed groups associated with the right-wing Fuerza Nueva beat up liberal students and bombed "Marxist" bookstores.[44] Spanish and foreign observers feared disorder would lead the army to intervene as it had in the past. Raymond Carr, for example, a well-known expert on Spain, confessed that he "had feared 'the worst' given . . . the number of confrontations between demonstrators and the police and the acts of terrorism committed by both left and right."[45] This did not, however, happen. Instead, over the coming years Spain experienced such a successful transition to democracy that it came to be viewed as "paradigmatic."[46] Rather than retrenching or holding out until it collapsed, the old regime instead initiated a gradual process of political liberalization, holding extended negotiations with the democratic opposition. The shadow of the Second Republic hung heavy over this process: both regime insiders and the opposition were strongly committed to maintaining order and avoiding the polarization and extremism that had doomed Spain's last democratic experiment. As one perspicacious observer put it, "revisiting the past with an eye toward applying its lessons to the present was critical to the making of every major decision concerning . . . the new democratic regime."[47]

One particularly important actor in this transition was Franco's handpicked successor, Juan Carlos I, grandson of Spain's last ruling monarch, Alfonso XIII (see chapter 13). Juan Carlos was brought to Spain at an early age to ensure his loyalty to the Francoist regime: he was educated in the armed forces' academies and watched over by Franco and his supporters. Yet already at his swearing in as Franco's successor on November 27, 1975, the pressure for change was visible: the archbishop performing the ceremony, Cardinal Enrique y Tarancón, urged Juan Carlos to be "king of all Spaniards" and for his reign be characterized by "justice for all, with everyone subjected to the rule of law and with the law always in the service of the community."[48] Juan Carlos luckily turned out to be anything but the loyalist Franco and his supporters expected him to be. Perhaps his most important move after coming to power was replacing the head of government he inherited from Franco, Carlos Arias Navarro, who was unwilling to go beyond extremely cautious reforms, with Adolfo Suarez in the summer of 1976.[49] Like Juan Carlos, Suarez did not initially appear a likely reformer: he was a Franco-era technocrat who had held many positions within the old regime. But unlike many of his colleagues, Suarez recognized the need for democratization and that its success would depend on bringing *both* the old regime and the democratic opposition on board.

Suarez's first step was getting the Cortes to agree to a "Law for Political Reform" (*Ley para la Reforma Política*), which established the ground rules for democratic elections and other components of a new democratic political order. Suarez urged his erstwhile Francoist colleagues in the Cortes to recognize that this law, and the controlled transition it would initiate, was the lesser of two evils. If the Cortes did not see the writing on the wall and accept political change, radicalization and social conflict would be the result. The violence and terrorism Spain experienced during the transition heightened such concerns. Post-Franco Spain was more violent than neighboring Portugal, where the transition was ushered in by a "revolutionary" coup rather than pacted negotiations between the old regime and the opposition. More than 460 politically motivated, violent deaths occurred in Spain "between 1975 and 1980 and about 400 people died in right- and left-wing terrorist acts."[50] Suarez declared, "We cannot allow ourselves the luxury of ignoring" the changes in Spanish society. "We would entrench ourselves into an absurd blindness if we refuse to" recognize the growing "pluralism of our society" and the growth of opposition parties that aim "to assume power." If a legal road to power is not opened to these parties, we will only have secured "an apparent peace, below which will germinate the seeds of subversion."[51]

Alongside urging his colleagues to recognize the advantages of reform over revolution, other factors helped Suarez convince the Cortes to move forward. One was the law's "backward legitimacy": it was presented to the Cortes to be considered and passed in accordance with the existing procedures of the Francoist regime. In addition, Suarez helped found a new party—the UCD (Union of the Democratic Center or *Unión de Centro Democrático*)—leading many on the right to believe that they would be able to retain some power under new democratic rules of the game.[52] Also critical was the behavior of the democratic opposition. As was the case with Suarez and the regime insiders supporting him, memories of the Second Republic and the civil war and fear of radicalization led the democratic opposition to recognize the importance of compromise, negotiation, and tolerance.[53] In return for a full transition to democracy, the opposition agreed to play by the rules of the game: maintain the monarchy, amnesty for Francoist functionaries, and an electoral system skewed towards rural areas. As one observer noted, "Suarez and Juan Carlos were able to take the risks of democratization despite" the existence of some extremism and violence because the moderation of the main opposition forces led them to "forecast that continued democratization would not lead to the triumph of radical[ism]."[54] The PSOE, the largest opposition force, played a crucial role. Although it had a radical past and a radical wing, the party recognized that neither it nor the opposition more generally could achieve a transition on their own. Full democratization therefore required moderation in order to maintain the support or at least acquiescence of the old regime's supporters. The PSOE's restraint and willingness to compromise was also influenced by the tutelage of other West European social democratic parties, which in the years before Franco's death had trained and supported Spanish socialists and prepared them for democratic politics. And so, with these pieces of the puzzle in place, the Cortes voted itself out of existence in December 1976, passing the "Political Reform Law" with 425 votes in favor, 59 against, and 13 abstentions and then sending it to the public for a referendum, where it was approved by 94 percent of voters. Turnout was 78 percent. Spain's first free elections in forty years were set for the summer of 1977.

Before those could occur, however, a critical sticking point remained: the status of the communist PCE. The hatred Franco and his supporters felt for communism made including the PCE in elections anathema to the right, and Suarez initially promised to exclude the party from the transition. Over time, however, it became clear that this would imperil the election's legitimacy[55] since the PCE had made an explicit commitment to "multiparty democratic government" and stressed the learning process it had undergone since the civil war.[56] Santiago Álvarez, for example, a communist leader who had been tortured and sentenced to death by Franco, noted that

> The memory of the past obliges us . . . to follow a policy of moderation. We feel responsibility for this process of democratization and the need to make a superhuman effort so that this process is not truncated. This is a unique moment in Spanish history. After more than a century of civil wars and a vicious cycle of massacres among Spaniards, which began after the War of Independence . . . this is the moment when it is possible for us to end this cycle and to open a period of civilized life, politically speaking. In this sense we cannot allow ourselves the luxury of expressing opinions which might be misunderstood, which could be, or appear to be, extremist.[57]

Ultimately recognizing that he had run out of options (he tried to fob the decision off to the Supreme Court, for example, but it threw it back at him), and that excluding the PCE might generate a public backlash (opinion polls showed many more Spaniards in favor of legalizing the PCE than against),[58] Suarez legalized the PCE in April 1977. This turned out to be a wise decision: the PCE stuck to its pro-democratic stance, proclaiming during the electoral campaign, for example, that "A Vote for Communism is a Vote for Democracy," and avoided mass demonstrations or other actions that might provoke the army or the extreme right.[59] The elections were a remarkable success. The parties of the center-right (UCD, led by Suarez, age forty-three) and center-left (PSOE, led by Felipe Gonzalez, age thirty-six) gained the largest share of the votes, 34.5 percent and 29.3 percent, respectively, while more extreme parties like the Francoist AP, *Alianza Popular*, on the right, and the PCE, on the left, gained only 8.3 percent and 9.3 percent, respectively. The election also revealed that many of the hindrances to democracy that had existed in the past had either disappeared or been greatly attenuated. Most obviously, radical and not fully democratic (or "accidentalist," see chapter 13) parties of the type that stymied the Second Republic attracted only minimal support.[60] Also notable was the absence of critical cleavages that had plagued Spain in the past: Neither the clerical-anticlerical nor the institutional monarchist-republican cleavage played a significant role in the election. Instead the election revealed the most important issues to be socioeconomic and center-periphery or regional ones.[61] With regard to the former, in order to deal with serious economic problems, Suarez reached out to the political opposition and trade unions to form Moncloa pacts in 1977. Moncloa basically traded austerity—wage increases were kept below the rate of inflation, public spending was reduced, credit restricted— for promises of progressive tax and welfare reforms. The pacts helped cement a "collaborative approach to policy making"[62] that aimed to prevent the socioeconomic divisions and polarization that might undermine democratization or provoke old-regime hardliners.[63] Moncloa's import was therefore as much political as economic. As one of the key participants in the pacts put it, the aim was to "neutralize" political threats and keep Spain on track towards "the acceptance of a democratic constitution by all political forces."[64] These pacts grew out of a desire to not repeat the mistakes of the past: both the government and the opposition recognized that a failure to "responsibly deal with the economic problems that plagued the Second Republic . . . was one of the principle causes behind [the failure of] democratic consolidation" during the 1930s.[65] Along with Suarez's victory in the 1977 election and the passing of an amnesty law that released existing political prisoners and protected Francoist officials,[66] the moderation of the opposition placated old regime supporters, despite ongoing unrest and terrorism. Against this backdrop, a new constitution was overwhelmingly approved by the Cortes in 1978 and then approved in a referendum by approximately 88 percent of the voters. Unlike its Second Republic predecessor (see chapter 13), this one was "a negotiated settlement involving all the major political parties" and included numerous compromises.[67] Among the constitution's most important provisions were the establishment of a constitutional monarchy, a parliamentary system with a two-chambered Cortes, and a constitutional court and a more decentralized state.[68] Soon after the constitution's approval in March 1979 Suarez called for another general election. Spanish voters again gave their overwhelming support to moderate, centrist parties, with the UCD gaining 35.5 percent of the vote and the PSOE 31 percent (the PCE received 11 percent and the CD [former AP] 6 percent of the vote). Regionalist parties also gained seats, most notably Herri Batasuna and Euzkadiko Ezkerra in the Basque country, reflecting continuing conflicts over the nature and structure of the Spanish state and identity.

Because the civil war was in part a victory of Spanish nationalists over regionalists, all manifestations of regionalism were suppressed by Franco's regime. This did not make regional resentments disappear; it just pushed them underground, eventually exploding as noted above into terrorist activity in the years preceding and following the transition. The new constitution provided for significant regional autonomy, but this did not satisfy Basque nationalists who rejected the constitution and continued their campaign of violence. Basque terrorism, which was largely directed at the military,[69] continued strikes, demonstrations, and other signs of unrest, leading a minority in the military to conclude that Spain was once again sliding into disorder. On February 23, 1981, Lieutenant Colonel Antonio Tejero led a force into the Cortes and took the deputies hostage with the intent of overthrowing the constitution.[70] While this seemed an almost predictable reversion to an all-too-prevalent Spanish pattern, what followed reflected how much other political actors and the political context more generally had changed in Spain.

All major political parties and the king stood together to condemn the coup and declare their support for democracy. At an hour past midnight Juan Carlos appeared on television in full military regalia, declaring that he would not tolerate interruptions to the democratic process and demanding that the rebels "uphold the constitutional order." Without the king or other traditional right-wing forces willing to support them, Tejero and his co-conspirators quickly surrendered. As discussed in chapter 13, often in Spain's past the military stepped in when political authorities lost control of the situation; military intervention was as much a consequence of political weakness or collapse, in other words, as it was its cause. In 1981, in contrast, political leaders and parties stood together behind democracy and, unable to exploit the disunity or weakness of other political actors, the coup quickly collapsed.[71] Also notable was the role of the public. A few days after the coup, a million citizens marched in the capital and hundreds of thousands in other parts of Spain to show their support for the king and their new democracy.[72] Up until then, the Spanish civil society had played relatively little of a direct role in the transition. Perhaps ironically, therefore, the attempted coup accomplished what Spain's ostensibly democratic-minded leadership thus far had not—indeed had in many ways sought to avoid—namely mobilizing Spaniards in support of democracy. By doing this and by reminding political actors how crucial continued cultivation of democratic norms and procedures was, the military rebels "unwittingly helped . . . consolidate the democratic regime they had tried to overthrow by force of arms."[73]

Democratic consolidation was furthered by another successful election in October 1982, the outcome of which must have had Franco rolling in his grave. The PSOE gained 48 percent of the vote and a majority of seats in parliament—the first time democratic elections had produced a single-party majority and the first time socialists had received a majority since the Cortes's founding in 1879.[74] The UCD, on the other hand, collapsed, gaining only 6.8 percent of the vote, and was replaced as Spain's "second" party by the "People's Coalition" (*Coalición Popular*), an alliance of center-right and right groups that would eventually morph into a new mainstream conservative-right party, the *Partido Popular*. Also crucial was that this election resulted in the first alternation in power since the transition.

The PSOE remained in power until 1996 and passed myriad reforms that furthered the liberal nature of Spanish democracy.[75] For example, the PSOE government increased civilian control over the military[76] and punished the coup plotters for their actions. During the PSOE's tenure Spain also joined NATO—something the party had previously opposed. The 1981 coup attempt seems to have convinced many socialists as well as many Spanish citizens that the democratization of the armed forces that NATO promised outweighed some of its purported disadvantages.[77] The PSOE also oversaw Spain's admittance into the European Economic Community in 1986. Membership provided much-needed access to regional development funds, of which Spain became the largest recipient.[78] Partially as a result of this, and other economic reforms put in place by Gonzalez, including a currency devaluation, wage restraint, and a reduction in public sector jobs and state expenditures,[79] Spain experienced a mini-boom during the late 1980s, growing about 4 percent per year. EEC membership was not, however, merely of economic significance. Spain was long viewed by outsiders and its own citizens as "different" from Western Europe, backwards and unstable, and Franco's dictatorship differentiated and isolated the country further.[80] Prime Minister González noted in 1987 that since the nineteenth century Spaniards had lived in political and cultural isolation.

> That was a breeding ground for authoritarianism . . . and explains the fragility of our democratic experiments. Political isolation was accompanied by economic isolation. . . . The result was comparatively less development than our European neighbors. That process of political isolationism and economic protectionism was negative for Spain. Opening the political frontiers and becoming part of broader areas is the consistent response for those of us who seek a better, democratically stable and economically developed Spain. Here is the real foundation for our wish to join the Communities.[81]

Joining the EEC in short, "provided external validation" of Spain's status as a "normal" country and crucial support for the consolidation of its liberal democracy.[82]

After winning three consecutive elections, the PSOE lost to the People's Party in 1996. By this point, Spanish citizens and elites professed consistently democratic attitudes as evinced by myriad public surveys;[83] several successful elections and alternations in power between political parties had occurred; and while regionalism remained a serious problem, with the exception of Basque terrorists, political actors remained within the democratic "rules of the game."[84]

When the PSOE came back into power in 2004 it further deepened the liberal nature of Spanish democracy, partially by confronting some of the remaining illiberal legacies from its past. PSOE prime minister Zapatero revisited the "pact of forgetting" that accompanied Spain's transition, supporting efforts to "recover" Spain's historical memory and confront the crimes of the past.[85] Zapatero also abolished many vestiges of traditional Catholic Spain, banning the display of religious symbols in public places, eliminating compulsory religious education in schools, ending state subsidies for private schools, the vast majority of which were Catholic, relaxing abortion and divorce laws, signing a law allowing same-sex marriages (which made "Spain the first Catholic country and only the third country in Europe after the Netherlands and Belgium to allow such marriages"[86]), "advance[ing] an ambitious agenda of women's rights in a country famous for having invented macho culture,"[87] appointing women to half of all cabinet posts, "crusading" against domestic violence, passing laws to promote gender equality in government and the workplace, and instituting paternity and maternity leave.[88] In addition, Zapatero supported greater regional autonomy and cultural diversity, and oversaw a further devolution of power to Catalonia. Not long ago such policies might well have destabilized Spain,[89] but by the early 2000s this was no longer in the cards. Given that Spain's first attempt at liberal democracy occurred with the 1812 Constitution of Cadiz[90] and was followed by over a century and a half of seemingly intractable political instability, the relative ease of Spain's late-twentieth-century transition and consolidation of liberal democracy must be considered remarkable.

Conclusions

Why was Spain able to achieve consolidated, liberal democracy during the late twentieth century when it had previously been unable to do so? Spain had been so politically unstable and violent during the late nineteenth and much of the twentieth century that many within the country and without considered it intrinsically "different": unsuited for the liberal, democratic institutions and practices that (eventually) became the norm in Western Europe. (A tendency, of course, we see still see in analyses of many other parts today.) As an old adage attributed to Talleyrand put it, "Europe ends at the Pyrenees."[91] So deep-seated was this view that it often took on a racial or at least cultural tinge. Observers characterized Spaniards as "cruel and intolerant," "inherently violent and fanatical," and simply unsuited for "modern civilization." Franco himself described the Spanish character as distinguished by "an anarchic spirit, negativ[ism], lack of solidarity among men, extremism and mutual hostility"—which made a strongman like himself necessary to control and guide the country.[92] Yet despite such views, Spain did make a break with the past during the last decades of the twentieth century and became a liberal democracy. As we have seen, this is largely because by this point many problems that had foiled democratic consolidation in the past, and created the negative characteristics long associated with Spaniards, had been eliminated.

During the postwar era Spain's society and economy were transformed. During its previous try at democracy in the 1930s, Spain was a largely agrarian country and its rural areas were dominated by large landowners and landless laborers, neither of whom supported democracy and both of whom were prone to engage in violent conflicts. The diminution of the agricultural sector removed from the political agenda an issue that had helped destroy the Second Republic—land reform.[93] By the 1970s Spain's economy and society were dominated by working and middle classes that were educated, urbanized, and secularized, and increasingly favored democracy. The Spanish Church also changed dramatically, finally making its peace with democracy and modernity. And the military, which had helped bring many regimes, including the Second Republic, to an end during the late nineteenth and early twentieth centuries, had been largely "depoliticized" by the 1970s.[94] Also critical was that the international context had shifted dramatically since Spain's last try at democracy: during the 1930s Europe was dominated by weak or crumbling democracies and seemingly vibrant dictatorships, but by the 1970s Spain was surrounded by successful, prosperous democracies that made clear their preference for a democratic Spain.

The elimination of many hindrances to democracy did not ensure that a transition would occur—but it did make it possible. Also necessary was commitment to creating a new democratic order and agreement on how to do so. The Spanish case highlights the importance of a key variable in this process: political actors. Franco, or rather his death, was key in getting the democratic ball rolling and the transition of political actors on both the right and left from "accidentalist" (that is, prioritizing maximization of their own goals rather than the maintenance of democracy) to committed democrats was crucial not only in pushing democratization forwards but also in creating conditions within which consolidation could occur. This commitment to making democracy work was also true of key civil society groups and other organized interests, perhaps most notably unions, which also shifted from "accidentalism" to a full commitment to democracy by the 1970s.[95] The attitudes and behavior of key political actors in Spain was profoundly influenced by memories of the Second Republic and the civil war. An impressive learning process, in other words, influenced Spanish political development during the late twentieth century: a desire to break with the past shaped political actors' behavior during the transition and their understanding of what it would take to achieve consolidated liberal democracy in Spain.[96]

Structural changes in Spain's society and economy, a favorable international context, and a full commitment to democracy by key political actors created favorable conditions for democratic consolidation. This does not mean that Spain's new democracy lacked challenges: regionalism, particularly in the form of Catalonian and Basque nationalism, did raise fundamental questions about the legitimacy and future of the Spanish state and Spain's national identity. These problems have their roots deep in Spain's past—in the state-building process that occurred during the early modern era (see chapter 13). That a problem is long-standing does not mean that it cannot be solved: indeed, the consolidation of democracy in Spain during the late twentieth century after a century and a half of political instability and violence shows that breaking with the past is indeed possible. Unlike other problems facing Spain, regionalism did not dissipate during the postwar period; indeed it was exacerbated by the extreme centralization and complete denial of regional and cultural diversity characterizing Franco's regime. By the 1970s regional resentments had already generated a violent terrorist movement in the Basque country. However, democracy consolidated rapidly in Spain, and so the challenges presented by Basque and more recently Catalonian nationalism have not fundamentally threatened Spanish democracy. The Spanish case thus highlights the importance of sequencing and avoiding political "overload": by the time the transition occurred most of the traditional hindrances to democracy—a weak state, economic backwardness, deep social cleavages, a politicized military, reactionary Church, and landed elites—had disappeared in Spain, leaving regionalism as the only major challenge confronting Spanish democracy. As the next chapter makes clear, other European countries that democratized in the third wave did not have it so easy.

CHAPTER 17

The Transition to Democracy
in East-Central Europe

People, your government has returned to you.
—Václav Havel, president of Czechoslovakia, 1990[1]

A FTER THE SECOND World War East-Central Europe experienced both
revolution and colonization, transitioning to communism and becoming part of the Soviet Empire. As discussed in chapter 15, this was
primarily determined by the interests and power of the Soviet Union, but
the region's previous political development was also crucial. During the
interwar period East-Central Europe had weak states, divided societies,
under-developed economies, and limited experience with either democracy
or liberalism. During the Second World War the region was brutalized, and
almost all indigenous sources of resistance or even collective action—elites,
political parties and civil society, armies—were destroyed. At the war's
end the region was disorganized and disrupted further by ethnic cleansing
and desperate material conditions; hunger, lack of shelter, and disease were
prevalent.[2] East-Central Europe was not, in short, well positioned to resist
Soviet pressure. Also important was a widespread desire among East-Central
Europeans to eliminate the remnants of the old orders that had left them
in turmoil during the interwar years and replace them with new ones that
could finally create modern, developed, but also equal, just, and cohesive
societies. Communism promised to do just this: destroy the ancien régime,
"generate" a high level of development more quickly and efficiently than

could capitalism,[3] and create a new and better world—leading some East-Central Europeans initially to support it.

Unfortunately, in history as in economics there is no free lunch. Communist regimes did eradicate what remained of the old order and jumpstart socioeconomic modernization in East-Central Europe, but the price paid for these accomplishments was extremely high: economic inefficiency, political repression, and societal violence. By the 1950s populations were already dissatisfied with "actually existing" communism. But as we have seen throughout European history, dissatisfaction alone does not regime change make. One reason is that during the early postwar decades many believed that dissatisfaction could be dealt with by reforming communism rather than destroying it. Particularly after Stalin's death in 1953, Khrushchev and various East-Central European leaders attempted to improve communism and purge it of Stalinism's "excesses." Another reason dissatisfaction did not lead to regime change was that opposition to it was unorganized. The aspirations and actions of workers, students, and other groups discontented with the reigning order were disparate and uncoordinated, and uprisings accordingly tended to be spontaneous, usually triggered by a particular event, like a change in working conditions or Khrushchev's 1956 speech denouncing Stalinism, rather than planned. This made them relatively easy to crush and participants in them more easily bought off afterwards by vague and minor concessions.[4] (See chapter 5 for a discussion of 1848 for an analysis of a similar dynamic.) The third and most obvious reason dissatisfaction did not lead to regime change during the 1950s was the continued willingness of the Soviet Union to use overwhelming military force to block it.

As the postwar period wore on and particularly after the Prague Spring, the factors promoting regime stability began to change. First, after 1968, faith that communism could be reformed declined dramatically. By the 1970s and especially 1980s communism's opponents were questioning not merely features of the reigning order, but its overall viability and desirability. But it was not just the opposition: after 1968, faith in communism's superiority and ability to create a better world declined dramatically even within party-states. As one observer put it, "In the late 1940s, the Communist establishments across Eastern Europe formed small minorities, yet their members seemed deeply assured. They had resisted and defeated fascism; they were part of the movement of history; therefore, their theories and actions were right, even if majorities of their compatriots did not appreciate it, and in the name of the cause they could (and did) lie at will." By the 1970s, on the other hand, these establishments were enormous and controlled their countries, yet they were rapidly losing faith that history was on their side, or that they had the ability to create a better future.[5] Communist regimes could no longer, in other words, count on ideological conviction or "systemic" legitimacy to stabilize their hold on power. Instead they had to rely on a mix of repression and "performance" legitimacy—promises of increasing prosperity and improving living conditions—to maintain the support or at least the quiescence of their populations.

By the 1980s, however, the performance of communist economies was dismal, something citizens were increasingly aware of *and* increasingly unwilling to tolerate.[6] As Figures 17.1–17.5 make clear, the significant, if warped and inefficient, development that occurred during the initial postwar decades made East-Central European populations wealthier, more industrialized, urbanized, and well-educated. Blue- and white-collar workers rather than landed elites and peasantries became the dominant social groups.[7]

With a basic level of economic security assured, East-Central Europeans were increasingly unwilling to tolerate shoddy consumer goods; collapsing housing, health care, educational, and transportation infrastructures; the privileges and corruption of elites; political repression; endless lies;

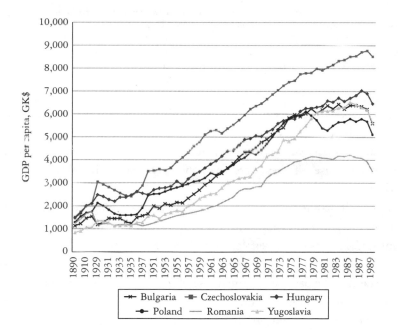

FIGURE 17.1 Eastern European GDP per capita, 1890–1990.
Note: *GK$ is a hypothetical unit of currency that has the same purchasing power parity that the U.S. dollar had in the United States at a given point in time.
Source: The Maddison-Project, http://www.ggdc.net/maddison/maddison-project/home.htm, 2013 version.

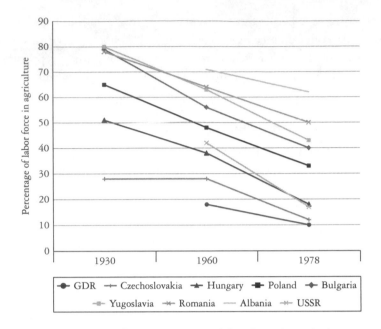

FIGURE 17.2 Percentage of Eastern European labor forces in agriculture, 1930–1978.

Source: David S. Mason, *Revolution and Transition in East-Central Europe* (Boulder, CO: Westview, 1992); The Maddison-Project, http://www.ggdc.net/maddison/maddison-project/home.htm, 2013 version; Charles Gati, *The Politics of Modernization in Eastern Europe* (New York: Praeger, 1975); and Jeffrey Kopstein and Michael Bernhard, "Post-Communism, the Civilizing Process, and the Mixed Impact of Leninist Violence," *East European Politics and Societies*, 29, 2, 2014.

environmental degradation; and the other obvious downsides of communism. Moreover, by the 1970s and especially 1980s increasing access to television, radio, and tourists was making it painfully clear to East-Central Europeans how much worse off they were than their Western neighbors (see Figures 17.6 and 17.7).

But while communism's dismal record and growing awareness and re-sentment of it were crucial, these too were not alone enough to cause regime change. Constants cannot explain variables: dissatisfaction grew throughout the postwar period, yet transitions did not occur until 1989. Also crucial to understand is the pattern of transitions: Why did the East-Central European "wave" began in Poland, move next to Hungary, and then sweep rapidly across the region? Why were some transitions negotiated and others pushed forward by mass mobilization and protest? And why, particularly given their violent pasts, did communist regimes collapse so peacefully?

These questions cannot be answered by "snapshot" analyses of the transitions themselves. Instead, answering these questions requires examining

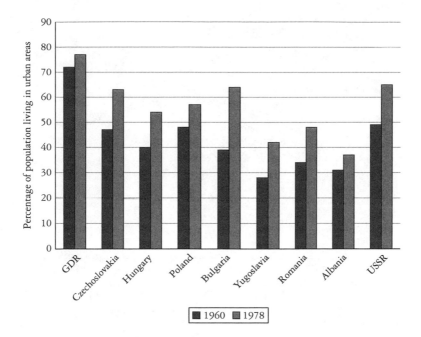

FIGURE 17.3 Percentage of Eastern European population living in urban areas, 1960–1978.

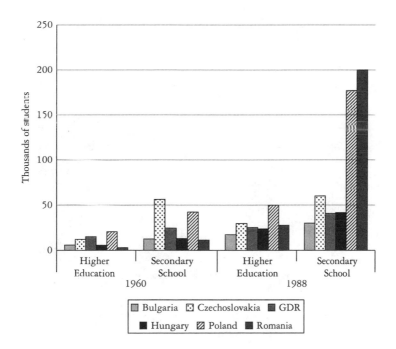

FIGURE 17.4 Higher education in East-Central Europe by thousands of students, 1960–1988.

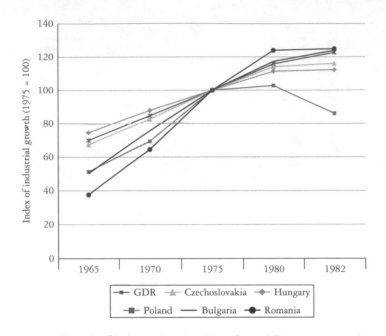

FIGURE 17.5 Growth of industry in select East-Central European countries, 1965–1982; 1975 = 100.

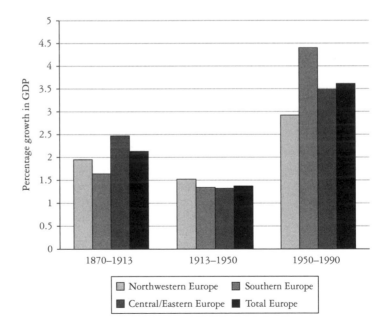

FIGURE 17.6 Comparative GDP growth by region, 1870–1990.

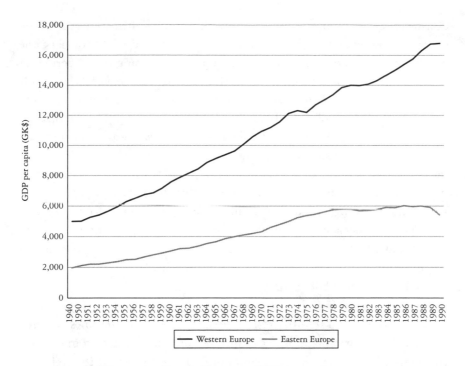

FIGURE 17.7 Western vs. Eastern European GDP per capita, 1940–1990.
Source: The Maddison-Project, http://www.ggdc.net/maddison/maddison-project/home.htm, 2013 version.

political development in the decades—if not longer—preceding 1989. By the late 1980s East-Central European communist regimes had lost systemic as well as performance legitimacy, leaving repression as their primary means of staying in power. But in Poland and Hungary communist regimes had been significantly weakened, and organized, independent socioeconomic actors existed by the late 1980s, complicating and raising the cost of repression. In the past, of course, the Soviet Union stepped in to (re)stabilize East-Central European communist regimes that had gotten themselves into "trouble." But by the late 1980s this option was no longer available. The stage was thus set for another revolution.

The Prague Spring: The End of Reformism

As noted above and in chapter 15, during the 1950s dissatisfaction with communism had already generated uprisings in East-Central Europe. These early uprisings shared several features: they aimed to reform rather than destroy existing regimes, were unorganized, and were ultimately crushed by overwhelming external force. All these factors came together to shape the development and outcome of the most important uprising of the period, in Hungary in 1956. Imre Nagy, for example, who led and personified the revolt was a committed communist whose goal was improving communism, and in particular purging it of its Stalinist "excesses," not getting rid of it entirely. The uprising from below that propelled Nagy to power was unplanned and unorganized. And finally, despite this uprising and the Communist party's quick collapse, Soviet forces quickly marched in and re-installed the communist regime. As one observer put it, what Hungary in 1956 and other uprisings across East-Central Europe during this time revealed was that communist regimes were "both stable and precarious, monolithic and brittle": despite widespread dissatisfaction, as long as the opposition remained unorganized and overwhelming Soviet military power was available, communist regimes could maintain their hold on power.[8]

After the uprisings in Hungary and elsewhere in the 1950s were crushed and political stability re-established, communist regimes engaged in some "reform from above,"[9] the specifics of which varied from country to country. In general, however, communist leaders believed that reforms, particularly those that improved living standards, would quell dissatisfaction: although some modifications might be necessary, communism remained the "most successful system in the world, able to provide citizens with everything they needed."[10] For a while, this new "social contract" or trade-off between communist regimes and their populations seemed to work: in the decade after 1956 political stability was re-established in the GDR, Poland, and Hungary, repression diminished, and living standards improved.[11]

Czechoslovakia was not part of these developments. After transitioning to communism in the late 1940s, the Czechoslovak regime became perhaps the most Stalinist in the region. After a series of spectacular show trials in the early 1950s, government ministers were hanged, 60,000 party members imprisoned, and 120,000 citizens sent to labor camps.[12] This repression, along with Czechoslovakia's relatively advanced and successful economy (as noted previously, it was the wealthiest and most industrialized of the Habsburg Empire's East-Central European successor states), enabled it to avoid the uprisings that occurred in other parts of the region during the 1950s— and thus the de-Stalinization and other reforms that followed them. By the 1960s, however, the initial advantages enjoyed by the Czechoslovak economy had dissipated, and the inherent flaws of the communist economic model taken their toll: growth stagnated, and in 1963 Czechoslovakia became the first communist country to experience negative growth.[13] The severity of the downturn shook the party leadership and emboldened a reformist group within it. What developed in Czechoslovakia in the 1960s was thus in many ways a delayed version of what had developed in the rest of East-Central Europe a decade previously. But largely because the Czechoslovak regime was so repressive, rather than demands from change emerging from below, pressure for reform had to emerge from within the party itself.[14]

In 1968, reformist forces, now led by Alexander Dubček, issued an "Action Program," setting off the chain of events known as the Prague Spring. The program argued that the time had come for Czechoslovakia to embark on a new phase: "socialism with a human face." Dubček and his colleagues favored a course similar to Nagy's in 1956: de-Stalinization, diminished political repression and censorship, reform of the security forces (particularly to end their role in persecuting "political" crimes), greater political freedom, normalization of Church-state relations, lessening the state's role in the economy and central planning, empowering trade unions, and focusing on consumer interests. The Action Program also called for greater national autonomy for Slovaks and federalization.[15] Dubček and other reformists insisted, however, that they remained communists and that reforms would not threaten the leading role of the party or Czechoslovakia's alliance with Soviet Union. Despite these reassurances, and the fact that unlike in the GDR, Poland, and especially Hungary in the 1950s, the Czechoslovak Communist party remained in control and the police and security forces in place,[16] the Soviets invaded anyway. On August 20–21 "help" arrived in the form of Soviet troops, accompanied by contingents from the GDR, Hungary, Poland, and Bulgaria in what turned into the largest military operation in Europe since the end of the Second World War. In response, the Czechoslovak leadership unanimously opposed resistance, and so rather than an armed uprising the population engaged primarily in passive resistance: road signs were removed, troops denied supplies, and so on.[17] (Partially as a result, "only" 100–200 lives were lost.[18]) Despite this, the invasion's aftermath followed a predictable pattern: a hard-line, practically neo-Stalinist regime was re-established and all reformists and suspected reformists (approximately 22 percent of the membership) were purged from the party. In December 1970 the party adopted a document fully accepting the Soviet interpretation of the Prague Spring as a "counterrevolution" and praising the external intervention crushing it as "international assistance to the Czechoslovak people in defense of socialism."[19] The only real reform that survived the Prague Spring was federalism.[20] The end of the Prague Spring also led to the proclamation of what came to be known as "the Brezhnev doctrine" justifying the right of the Soviet Union and the communist bloc to intervene in the internal affairs of other countries. In Brezhnev's words:

> When forces hostile to socialism try to turn the development of a . . . socialist country in the direction of restoration of the capitalist system, when a threat arises to the cause of socialism in that country— a threat to the security of the socialist commonwealth as a whole—this is no longer merely a problem for that country's people, but a common problem, the concern of all socialist countries. . . . [In such a situation] military assistance to . . . end a threat to the socialist system [may be necessary].[21]

The crushing of the Prague Spring had enormous consequences. First and most obviously, it made clear that the Soviets were not willing to give up control over their empire. As with the imposition of communism in East-Central Europe after the Second World War, its maintenance continued to depend on external force. The neo-colonial character of Soviet–East-Central European relations thus re-emerged clearly in 1968: the GDR, Poland, Hungary, and Czechoslovakia enjoyed at best limited sovereignty. (Reflecting this, the Brezhnev doctrine was sometimes referred to as the "doctrine of limited sovereignty."[22]) A second consequence was to destroy hopes that communism could be reformed. After 1968, dissidents and opposition movements no longer focused primarily on obtaining concessions from existing regimes or achieving some version of "socialism with a human face." Instead of improving, modernizing, or liberalizing communism, the goal increasingly became eliminating it entirely.[23] "For many the Prague Spring had meant a rebirth of faith" in communism, an attempt to overcome past disillusionment. The crushing of the reform movement thus made "disenchantment permanent. . . . revisionism was finished and had given way to rejectionism." Few any longer believed a new and better future could be created by communism. Socialism with a human face turned out to be "the last attempt to rejuvenate communism in central Europe."[24]

In short, the crushing of the Prague Spring eliminated most of the "systemic" legitimacy communist regimes still had. It was now clear to almost everyone, both within existing regimes and without, that communism no longer had a positive vision to offer: party-states were primarily interested in maintaining the status quo and could only do so through a mixture of repression and bribes.

East-Central Europe in the 1970s and 1980s: Consumerism and Crisis

Although repression had again crushed an attempt at reformism and a hard-line communist regime had been re-established in Czechoslovakia, as in East Germany, Poland, and Hungary a decade earlier there was no going back to the status quo ante. Repression can be effective, but it is blunt and expensive. However, with faith in communism's utopian goals as well as its reformability largely gone, the only way other than force to stay in power was via bribes or performance legitimacy. As one observer put it, by the 1970s and especially the 1980s communist regimes were increasingly forced to make "decisions in response to a single question: What have you done for me lately?"[25] The problem of course was that it was becoming increasingly clear that communist economies could not generate the requisite prosperity or improvement in living conditions. First, extensive growth had reached its limit—there were only so many workers who could be transferred from agriculture to industry, only so many resources that could be extracted and exploited, and only so much working hours could be increased and working conditions intensified.[26] Second, the Soviet Union had become less willing and able to subsidize East-Central Europe's economies: it ended below-market prices for its oil, began insisting on payment in Western currency, and stopped acting as the default buyer for shoddy East-Central European goods.[27] And third, a technological "revolution" swept the advanced industrial world during the 1970s and 1980s, and the more sophisticated consumer and military products produced by the capitalist West simply could not be matched by communist economies designed for the heavy industrialization of the "second" industrial revolution. As one Czech economist put it, communist development policies had turned East-Central Europe into "one large 'museum' of the industrial revolution."[28] Making matters worse, East-Central Europeans were increasingly aware of how poorly communist economies were faring compared to their Western capitalist counterparts. "Films, television, printed material," and other forms of media "brought home to East-Central Europeans how far behind they were not merely Western but also Southern Europe, which had begun the post-war period at a similar economic level. Foreign travel and tourism made East-Central Europe's continued 'backwardness' clear as well. Psychologically this was quite devastating . . . it meant the majority of the population began to understand that there was nothing to be done with the communist system, except to get rid of it."[29]

Economic stagnation set off a vicious cycle: governments had less money to spend on wages, housing, transport, health care, education, and other public goods that would improve citizens' quality of life, but cutbacks and austerity further undercut the "performance" legitimacy communist regimes needed. During the 1970s communist regimes tried to "square this circle" with Western loans. Borrowing did enable communist regimes to keep up a flow of economic goodies to their populations for a while, but without fundamental reforms that could improve economic performance over the long term, this credit-fueled boom was bound to crash. And indeed by the late 1970s it was clear that borrowing had simply provided communism's "inner contradictions . . . time . . . to mature and . . . wreck the system."[30] This dynamic played out most clearly and consequentially in Poland.

Poland: A New Type of Opposition Emerges

Throughout the postwar period Poland was the most contentious country in East-Central Europe: strikes, protests, and other forms of popular mobilization occurred fairly regularly. This had its roots deep in the Polish past: after Poland was partitioned in the late eighteenth century Poles developed a habit of rising up against their overlords and developed a particular antipathy against Russia, which was one of these overlords. Alongside these long-standing legacies, dynamics set in motion after the 1950s uprisings also shaped Poland's political development in the 1970s and 1980s.[31] After the 1956 uprising (see chapter 15), Władysław Gomułka initiated what came to be known as "Gomułka's thaw," halting the collectivization of agriculture, promising to include workers in economic decision-making, granting the Catholic Church more independence than allowed any other Church in the region, and extracting financial and other concessions from the Soviet Union that left Poland with some national autonomy.[32] But Gomułka eventually backtracked, cracked down on domestic dissent, and sent Polish troops to help crush the Prague Spring, thereby squashing expectations after raising them.[33] What ultimately did Gomułka in, however, was his inability to increase prosperity or improve living conditions enough to compensate for his broken promises. By December 1970 Poland's economic problems were so severe that Gomułka had no choice but to announce an increase in food prices and other austerity measures. Food prices were particularly explosive in Poland because the agricultural sector's inefficiency made them extremely high; workers spent perhaps half their wages on food.[34] The reaction to the price increases—especially since they were announced so close to Christmas—was immediate and explosive. By December 15 a general strike was underway in the Gdánsk shipyards; a close associate of Gomułka's ordered the police to fire on strikers, dozens were killed, workers stormed the Gdánsk party headquarters, and battles exploded throughout the city. By December 16 Gdánsk was at a standoff, with troops on one side and workers' committees on the other. Gomułka asked the Soviets for aid but was instead forced to resign and was replaced by Edward Gierek who immediately announced economic concessions. Protests nonetheless continued, and in January 1971 another strike wave broke out in Gdánsk; workers demanded the dismissal of those who had given the orders to shoot, the release of arrested strikers, an end to reprisals against strike leaders and participants, and democratic elections to trade unions and workers' councils.[35]

Gierek personally held talks with workers and asked for their help solving Poland's problems. This, along with vague promises of a new course combining "consultation" in the form of a pledge to keep the party-state in closer contact with society and "consumerism" in the form of an end to austerity and a commitment to rising prosperity and improved living standards, appeased the protestors.[36] But any attempt to improve economic performance over the long term would require structural reforms that would undermine the communist nature of the economy and the communist party's political control over it[37]—and this Gierek, like Gomułka before him, was unwilling to pursue. (As discussed below, such reforms did occur in Hungary with precisely the predicted result.) Gierek instead turned to Western loans to fund his promises to Polish society. One observer colorfully characterized Gierek's strategy as using "crack cocaine–style borrowing from the West to mollify the restive population"; another more soberly characterized it as substituting more consumer goods "for economic reform, and wage increases for political change."[38] During the early 1970s these loans enabled the Polish regime to raise wages, put more consumer goods on the shelves, and improve housing and transport. But by the mid-1970s growth rates were plummeting and foreign debt was exploding.[39] By 1976 the situation was so bad that Gierek felt he had no choice but to resort to some of the same policies that had doomed his predecessor, including increasing food prices. Almost a third of the money Poland borrowed in the 1970s had paid for food imports.[40] As in the past, the response was immediate and explosive: strikes broke out and within twenty-four hours the government rescinded austerity measures. It also, however, brutally cracked down, firing perhaps 10,000 to 20,000 workers from their jobs, detaining another 2,500, and putting hundreds on trial. Despite important similarities to past protests, this one had different consequences: the crackdown following it clearly ended the "fragile reconciliation" that had existed between Gierek and Polish society[41] and a new type of opposition emerged.[42]

In the fall of 1976 a group of intellectuals formed the Workers' Defense Committee (Komitet Obrony Robotników, or KOR) to support strike victims and bring public officials responsible for violence to account.[43] The KOR was not merely organized, it was cross-class, explicitly allying intellectuals to the workers' cause, characteristics previous opposition movements lacked. The KOR's goals also differed from most previous oppositions': rather than demanding reforms or concessions from the regime, it focused on changing society instead. Adam Michnik characterized this as the "new evolutionism":

> A programme of evolution should be addressed to independent public opinion and not the totalitarian authorities. Instead of acting as a prompter to the government, telling it how to improve itself, this programme should tell society how to act. As far as the government is concerned, it can have no clearer counsel than that provided by social pressure from below.[44] [No longer did we speak] about "socialism with a human face." [All that remained was] communism with its teeth knocked out.[45]

The KOR was also transparent, non-hierarchical, and eventually expanded to include an underground press and other activities. It represented, in short, the seeds of a real civil society. And its impact was far-reaching: other associations followed, focused on everything from human rights, to "documenting abuses of power, incompetence and corruption" by the communist party, to publishing underground newspapers,[46] to organizing workers (the "Committee of Free Trade Unions for the Baltic Coast," formed in 1978, included among its leaders an electrician named Lech Walesa).[47]

Alongside the growth of a new opposition and civil society, another important factor influencing Polish political development during this period was the election of the archbishop of Kraków, Karol Józef Wojtyła, as pope in 1978. When Pope John Paul II came to visit his home country in 1979 he was greeted by outpourings of mass fervor that, while not explicitly political, were in their size, expression of collective solidarity, and enthusiasm a clear rebuke to the communist regime. As one observer recalled: for the first time "a whole generation experienced . . . a feeling of collective power and exaltation of which they had never dreamt. It gave them a sense of confidence, unity and strength to take up their causes even more decisively."[48] So significant was the pope's visit and the upsurge of religious nationalism and collective solidarity accompanying it that Timothy Garten Ash and others date the beginning of the end of the communist regime to it: "Here for the first time, we saw that massive, sustained, yet supremely peaceful and self-disciplined manifestation of social unity, the gentle crowd against the Party-state, which was both the hallmark and the essential domestic catalyst of change in 1989. . . . The Pope's visit was followed, just over a year later by the birth of Solidarity."[49]

By the early 1980s, in short, there was a widespread sense within the Polish regime and society that something had to change:[50] the opposition was growing; organized; included workers, intellectuals, and the Church; and was energized by the pope's visit. In addition, the economy was in a nosedive. These factors did not, of course, make regime change inevitable, but they did significantly narrow the range of options available to the communist leadership.

Poland in the Early 1980s: The Balance of Power between Regime and Opposition Shifts

By 1980 Poland's foreign debt had jumped to state which currency 23.5 billion from 1.2 billion in 1971, and debt servicing was eating up almost all the country's hard currency earnings.[51] In response to this and other economic problems the regime again resorted to cutbacks and raised food prices; as in the past, the reaction was immediate and explosive. Protests spread and were particularly large at the shipyards on the coast: by mid-August about sixteen thousand workers led by Lech Walesa were out on strike at the Lenin shipyards. These protests differed from their predecessors. workers, students, intellectuals, housewives, and peasants came together, were organized, and were supported by the Catholic Church.[52] This broad, united, and organized opposition also presented the regime with more concrete and far-reaching demands than had its predecessors. Rather than merely democratic elections to unions, it demanded "free" unions, independent of the party-state. Instead of merely ending reprisals against strikers, it demanded the right to strike. Instead of an end to the security service's harassment of strikers, it demanded the release of political prisoners. The opposition also called for "freedom of speech, print and publication" and more—its demands covered "practically the whole range of Polish discontents."[53] The unity and organization of the opposition also "fundamentally changed the rules of the political game."[54] To end the protests the regime had to negotiate directly with the opposition and agree to the Gdánsk accords, which committed it to economic and political reforms including wage increases and price rollbacks, an end to many elite privileges, an expansion of press freedom, increasing government transparency so that citizens would know, for example, what was actually going on in the economy, and the right for workers to form their own independent organizations and strike.[55] It was from these accords that Solidarity emerged.

After the Gdánsk accords Poland found itself in uncharted territory. The accords signaled a new type of relationship between the regime and the opposition, and the formation of Solidarity marked the end of the regime's hegemony over the public sphere and the emergence of a true civil society in Poland.[56] More groups, including university students, professional organizations, and even members of the police and military, began forming independent associations. It was as if society began encroaching on the party-state using the same "salami-tactics" communists had used to take over society after World War II (see chapter 15). For sixteen months Solidarity "slowly sliced one professional organization or public institution after another from [the party-state's] control."[57] Solidarity did not, however, challenge the regime head-on, focusing instead on transforming Poland from below—a wise tactic when an opposition confronts a state too strong to attack directly.[58] Even though Solidarity did not engage in direct political confrontation, its activity and that of civil society more generally fundamentally threatened the balance of power. Reflecting this, the Soviets made clear that they expected the Poles to re-gain control of the situation, and in December 1981 the Polish military staged a coup.

In January 1982 the Sejm (parliament) confirmed the legality of martial law and dissolved Solidarity. Although this was a setback for the opposition, the price paid by the regime for it was very high. The coup made the regime's political bankruptcy clear:[59] only the use of force was keeping it in power. It also made clear that the regime had become more or less like any other traditional dictatorship: it lacked ideological justification or a positive vision and its main goal was merely retaining control. Like most traditional dictatorships, in other words, the Polish regime was thus both strong and weak: it had a monopoly of force (despotic power) but lacked legitimacy or widespread popular support.[60] As one Polish worker put it, "We've got all the symbols, and they've got all the guns and tanks."[61] Force can "solve" some problems but not others—and Poland in the 1980s had a lot of problems. Also reflecting the Polish regime's increasing resemblance to a traditional dictatorship was the decline of one of communism's most distinctive features during this period—the domination of the state by the communist party. The party lost over a third of its members, and the state became increasingly independent. "In this way the most fundamental principle" and institutional component "of state socialist regimes was forsaken."[62]

The country's new military ruler, Wojciech Jaruzelski, recognized that ruling by force alone would be difficult if not impossible—as he put it, "How long can [we] hang on by just threatening workers with tanks and police truncheons?"[63]—but the country's continued economic decline limited his options. During the 1980s debt rose, wages and national product per head declined, the welfare, educational, and health systems deteriorated, poverty grew, and environmental problems worsened.[64] Narrowing the regime's options further, the organization and determination of the opposition enabled it to continue its activities—samizdat publications, radio broadcasts, videotape recordings, discussion groups, underground universities—covertly during martial law.[65] By the mid-1980s Poland was thus in a sort of political stalemate, re-igniting debates within the regime and opposition about what it would take to move forward. These debates were critically influenced by changes occurring outside its borders.

In the mid-1980s the Soviet Union—the external power necessary for the establishment and maintenance of communism in Poland and the rest of East-Central Europe—began its own transformation. Like other parts of its empire, by this time the Soviet Union was in crisis: its economy was in a tailspin, production of oil, its most important export, had leveled off and world oil prices were falling; it was bogged down in a war in Afghanistan; and under Ronald Reagan the United States challenged it more directly with increased spending, advanced technology, and by moving away from détente and openly calling for regime change in the "evil empire." These problems helped bring Mikhail Gorbachev to power in 1985. Gorbachev wanted to revitalize communism, and abandoning the Brezhnev doctrine was one of the reforms he hoped would accomplish this. Some jokingly referred to Gorbachev's new approach as the "Sinatra doctrine" since he promised to allow the Soviet Union's satellites to do things "their own way." As he put it, his policy was "based on unconditional independence, fully equal rights, strict non-interference in others' internal affairs, and the righting of earlier wrongs."[66] Gorbachev hoped that East-Central European countries would use their national autonomy to experiment with various ways of rejuvenating communism. But East-Central Europe had already tried the reform route and found it a dead-end. And so when Gorbachev made clear that the Soviet Union would not backstop communist regimes if they became unable to stay in power on their own, the door was open for major change. And the Poles were best positioned to walk through it.

The Collapse Begins

By 1989 Poland was in a full-fledged crisis. The dictatorship was unable to get rid of Solidarity or solve the country's economic problems. It hoped to introduce major economic reforms but doing so would require austerity, price increases, and other hardships in the short term, and without popular support or legitimacy, gaining acceptance for such sacrifices was impossible. Worsening economic conditions contributed to the outbreak of another strike wave in the summer 1988.[67] Unable to demobilize these strikes and with the Soviets no longer pushing for a military solution, the dictatorship reached out to Solidarity, leading to the Roundtable Talks in February–April 1989. (Western pressure also helped: the Polish government needed foreign aid and credits which the United States made clear would not be forthcoming if force was used against the strikers. The United States also supported Solidarity with printing presses, radios, computers, and other resources.[68]) Important also was that both the government and Solidarity had learned from previous confrontations and the stalemates following them and were eager to take advantage of the opportunity provided by Gorbachev's abandonment of the Brezhnev doctrine.[69] Indeed, most of the people at the 1989 Roundtable talks were involved in the negotiations in the 1980–1981 period as well. In particular, Solidarity understood the need to avoid a military crackdown, and the government understood that force alone would neither get rid of the opposition nor solve the country's problems. The Roundtable Talks were therefore not merely a consequence of the 1988 strikes, but rather the culmination of decades-long developments.

The agreement that came out of these talks, signed on April 7, 1989, re-legalized Solidarity, its publications, and other activities, and called for new parliamentary elections in June. In these elections the Solidarity-led opposition would be able to compete for 35 percent of seats in Sejm and all the seats in a reconstituted upper house, the Senate. After these elections, the two houses of parliament would elect a president, with an understanding this would be Jaruzelski. At the signing of the Roundtable Agreement Lech Walesa said, "This is the beginning of democracy and a free Poland."[70] His prediction was fulfilled more rapidly than he imagined.

When the agreement was signed, neither the government nor the opposition had a clear sense of the balance of power. In addition, given the time-frame (there were only a couple of months between the signing of the Agreement and the elections), the opposition had little opportunity to prepare for elections; its expectations accordingly were modest. Nonetheless the elections were a disaster for the communists and an overwhelming victory for the opposition: the latter won all the contested seats in the Sejm and ninety-nine out of one hundred seats in the Senate. It is hard to overplay the shock that followed. As Timothy Garten Ash put it, three things happened at once: "the communists lost an election; Solidarity won; the communists acknowledged that Solidarity won; almost until the day before, anyone who had predicted these events would have been universally considered a lunatic."[71] From here political developments barreled forward. Jaruzelski was chosen as president on July 19 by a single vote (the election's outcome caused many of the communist party's allies to defect), and in August he appointed a prime minister from the opposition, Tadeusz Mazowiecki. For the first time in forty years Poland had a non-communist government.

The collapse of communism in Poland shook the rest of East-Central Europe. Hungary's communist regime was the next to go—its "runner-up" status a consequence of developments dating back at least to the 1950s.[72] After the 1956 uprising (see chapter 15), Janos Kádár engaged in a brutal crackdown, but Hungary did not fully return to the status quo ante. The regime eventually instituted some reforms, primarily economic.[73] Indeed, by the 1960s Hungary had become East-Central Europe's leading economic reformer.[74] In 1968 the regime put in place the region's most ambitious attempt yet to deal with the myriad problems facing communist economies with the New Economic Mechanism (NEM), which abandoned mandatory planning, gave enterprises autonomy in day-to-day decision-making, freed internal trade, and moved to quasi-market prices. Public ownership remained dominant, but cooperative, private, and other forms of ownership were allowed as well. Going forward the state's role would be limited to setting the economy's macro parameters and making major, long-term economic decisions. Just as in Poland, in other words, after the 1950s a new social compact developed between the regime and its citizens in Hungary, based on the former's commitment to provide the latter with a new "consumerism."[75]

Also as in Poland, this new "social contract" developed a momentum of its own, with reforms gradually accumulating and altering the regime, society, and the relationship between them. After 1968 the next major innovation came in 1982 with a property rights reform that changed private entrepreneurship and business ownership from a privilege determined by political decisions to a right enshrined in law.[76] In 1984 enterprise governance was reformed, in 1985 an individual income tax introduced, and in 1988 business owners were allowed to form new economic associations.[77] The cumulative impact of these reforms was enormous: by the mid-1980s Hungary had a hybrid economy with a legal private sector and businesses and private entrepreneurs who engaged in activism to support their economic interests.[78]

As in Poland, "salami tactics" thus significantly hollowed out the regime, eroding its control over the economy and allowing groups with some degree of organization, independence, and even legal recognition to emerge.[79]

Nonetheless, like the rest of East-Central Europe, Hungary experienced significant economic and other problems in the mid-1980s: rising inflation; massive foreign debt; increasing poverty; decaying housing and health care; high rates of alcoholism, drug use, and suicide; widespread corruption; and pervasive pollution.[80] These problems, along with Gorbachev's encouragement of national autonomy and experimentation, led reformers within the Hungarian communist party to press for change. In contrast to Poland where society led and the party followed, in Hungary the reform drive in the late 1980s began within the party since Hungarian civil society had not developed to the same degree as its Polish counterpart. In March 1988 Kádár was pushed aside as general secretary of the communist party and reformists began a process of political liberalization that included a commission to study the 1956 uprising—the "third rail" of Hungarian politics. Hitherto the party had insisted 1956 was a counter-revolution, the crushing of which should be celebrated. But in March 1989 the party admitted it was wrong about 1956 and the repression that followed. Roundtable talks then began to discuss further political and constitutional reform, but because the regime and opposition were fragmented and the former was quickly revealed to be little more than an empty shell, extended negotiations were not as important in the Hungarian transition as they had been in the Polish. In Poland the elections called after the Roundtable Agreement had made clear that the "emperor had no clothes" and marked the point of no return for the communist regime; in Hungary a similar dynamic unfolded because of a funeral.

In June a now rehabilitated Imre Nagy, leader of the 1956 uprising (see chapter 15), and four others were taken from the anonymous graves they had been dumped in thirty-one years earlier and reburied as national heroes in Budapest; hundreds of thousands of Hungarians came out on the streets to participate. "Exactly a year earlier, when opposition activists held a demonstration to mark the anniversary of Nagy's execution they had been violently dispersed by the police. Now these same police assisted opposition activists in preparing an extraordinary ceremonial reburial of the hero of 1956."[81] The floodgates had opened.[82] By August the communist party accepted the transition to a market economy; by September it completed the dismantling of the Iron Curtain (see below); and in the beginning of October it essentially dissolved itself. In mid-October legislation establishing elections for parliament and the presidency was passed, and on October 23—the thirty-third anniversary of the beginning of the 1956 uprising—the Hungarian

People's Republic was officially renamed Republic of Hungary. As in Poland, the elections were a crushing defeat for what remained of the communist party, and a coalition of center-right parties came to power. Communism had collapsed and Hungary transitioned to democracy.

Events in Poland and Hungary ignited a revolutionary wave across Eastern Europe: Poland's transition unfolded over years, Hungary's months, and the GDR's and Czechoslovakia's weeks. Alongside their rapidity, these latter revolutions were also characterized by mass mobilization and protests rather than negotiations and gradualism. One way of understanding this has been offered by Timur Kuran. Kuran argues that as growing numbers of people participate in a potentially dangerous activity like calling for regime change, the costs of repression go up and its likelihood therefore goes down, thereby lowering the cost of participation. Once a critical mass of participants is reached, a "tipping point" occurs, emboldening those who had previously kept their dissatisfaction hidden to participate in protests.[83] From this perspective, previous transitions are critical in showing that "it can be done" and encouraging the bravest and/or most discontented citizens to mobilize and begin the chain reaction that will eventually encourage regime change in other countries.

However helpful this perspective may be in explaining the rapidity of communism's collapse, particularly in the post-Polish cases, it does not fully explain why mass mobilization and protests played a much greater role in later transitions than the earlier Polish (and Hungarian) ones. To understand this, an examination of previous political development is necessary. Whereas by the late 1980s communist regimes in Poland and Hungary had already been hollowed out and groups with some degree of organization and even legal recognition existed, in East Germany and Czechoslovakia regimes remained repressive and thus organized independent groups did not exist. In East Germany in particular the scale of the repressive apparatus was impressive: up through the 1980s the *Stasi* had close to one hundred thousand employees, or about one for every 180 East Germans, much larger than Hitler's Gestapo,[84] as well as a massive network of informants. The formation of a significant opposition in East Germany was also blunted by the "safety valve" of West Germany: dissidents either left or were forced to leave. West Germany also granted the GDR trade and tariff advantages, financial subsidies and easy credit, access to advanced technology and high-quality consumer goods, thereby enabling the regime to provide its citizens with relatively high living standards up through the 1980s.

Nonetheless by the mid-1980s the GDR was facing massive problems[85] including a stagnant economy, high debt, out-of-date technology, and colossal pollution. Dissatisfaction stemming from these problems was aggravated by increasing awareness of how far the GDR had fallen behind West Germany. By the 1980s access to West German television was pervasive and West German visitors and tourists common. Despite this the East German regime initially maintained a hard line, but the cost of doing so mounted. One reason was events in nearby Hungary.

In the spring of 1989 Hungary repudiated its long-standing agreement with the GDR to treat East Germans fleeing the country as refugees (who would therefore be repatriated), and by the fall it had opened its border to Austria, thereby allowing East Germans safe passage to Austria and then West Germany. This spurred masses of East Germans to cram themselves into trains, buses, Trabbies—anything that could get them to Hungary or diplomatic missions in Prague or Warsaw, where they assumed they would be granted passage west. Accompanying the flood of East Germans were growing mass protests across the country. Mass mobilization was then jolted forward by another external shock in the form of visit from Gorbachev on the occasion of festivities organized by the regime to mark its fortieth anniversary in early October.

These festivities were a disaster for the regime. Massive crowds celebrated not the GDR but Gorbachev, screaming, "Gorbi, Gorbi," as he passed by. And Gorbachev pointedly warned his hosts that "life punishes those who come too late,"[86] a not-so subtle reminder about the price to be paid by those who ignore the way the political winds are blowing. The GDR's hard-line leader, Erich Honecker, nonetheless refused to budge, pointedly meeting a Chinese dignitary a few days later, discussing the similarities between the Chinese and East German situations, and making clear his preference for a Tiananmen Square–style crackdown. However, when seventy thousand East Germans came out on the streets on October 9 in Leipzig, other party officials overruled Honecker's orders to use troops against them. During the following week, criticism against Honecker mounted, and on October 17–18 he was forced to resign. His replacement, Egon Krenz, desperately tried to reform his way out of the growing chaos, but by this point it was too late. By early November hundreds of thousands of citizens were out on streets in East Berlin and other parts of the GDR and were no longer chanting, "We are the people"—indicating their desire for an end to dictatorship—but "We are one people"—indicating their desire to do away with the GDR entirely and join their West German brethren. When on November 9 rumors began flying that free travel would be allowed, citizens massed at the Berlin Wall. Unsure of what to do, border guards simply let them pass. With this, the Berlin Wall crumbled and soon after it the regime that built it.

As in East Germany, the collapse of communism in Czechoslovakia was accompanied by mass mobilization and occurred rapidly. Up through the 1980s Czechoslovakia also had a hard-line, repressive regime that allowed little economic or political liberalization or organized opposition. There were, of course, dissidents in Czechoslovakia, as there were in East Germany, but they were isolated, largely intellectuals, and focused primarily on human rights and counter-cultural activities rather than political or economic reform. Charter 77 was the best-known dissident group; it was small and focused on highlighting the disjuncture between the government's human rights behavior and its own laws and international commitments.

The year 1989 began in Czechoslovakia with several thousand people defying a government ban to commemorate a student who had set himself on fire in protest against the crushing of the Prague Spring. The police arrested almost one hundred people and beat more in the melees that followed; among those jailed was Václav Havel. Despite the regime's hard-line stance, the Polish elections in June, the fleeing of East Germans during the summer, and the huge demonstrations in the GDR in the fall encouraged Czechoslovaks to continue protesting. These protests came to a head on November 17 when student groups brought perhaps fifteen thousand out on the streets and rumors spread that a student had been killed by the police. Within forty-eight hours a general strike was underway that included students, intellectuals, artists, and others and led to the formation of a new organization, Civic Forum, to represent the opposition going forward. "If an independent society had been slow in forming in Czechoslovakia in comparison to Poland and Hungary, it almost caught up in the ten days following the November 17 events."[87] Demonstrations accelerated with huge crowds now gathering every night in Prague and other cities and Civic Forum holding frantic meetings at the Magic Lantern Theater. By the end of November the regime decided it had no choice but to concede: on November 29 the federal assembly revoked the constitutional provisions guaranteeing the communist party's political hegemony, and on December 10 a coalition government dominated by non-communists took power. After further negotiations, Alexander Dubcek (the leader of the Prague Spring) was appointed chairman of the National Assembly, which then unanimously elected Václav Havel Czechoslovakia's new president. On January 1, 1990, Havel ended his New Year's address to the nation with the words: "People, your government has returned to you!"[88]

Conclusions

After 1945 a revolution occurred in East-Central Europe. This revolution resembled previous ones in many ways, most notably in transforming politics, economics, and society, but differed in one crucial way: it was imposed from the outside (see chapter 15). The revolution's external imposition, the nature of the communist system implanted by it, and the growing divergence between what communism meant in practice and its utopian promises shaped the political development of the region during the postwar period as well as the revolution that brought communism to an end. Specific features of the 1989 revolution, on the other hand—why it began in Poland before moving on to Hungary and then sweeping across the rest of East-Central Europe, and why the demise of the old regime was negotiated in Poland and to a lesser degree Hungary but dominated by mass mobilization and protests in East Germany and Czechoslovakia—were shaped by variations in the political development of East-Central European countries during the postwar communist era.

By 1950s the divergence between communism's promises and reality had led to strikes, protests, and even uprisings in much of East-Central Europe. But as we have seen throughout European history, dissatisfaction alone is not sufficient to cause regime change, much less revolution. In East-Central Europe pressure for regime change was blunted during the 1950s and 1960s by a belief that communism could be reformed—that it was possible to create "socialism with a human face." Second, the opposition was simply weaker than the regime. Political power is relative: even a regime facing significant dissatisfaction can stay in power if its opposition is divided and disorganized, as the opposition in East-Central Europe during this time was. And third, when all else failed—as it almost did in Hungary in 1956—the Soviet Union stepped in to ensure communist regimes remained in power.

Particularly after the crushing of the Prague Spring in 1968 these conditions changed. First, faith in the possibility of reforming communism dissipated; by the 1980s few "true believers" in communism's utopian promises remained. Over time East-Central European communist regimes lost their "systemic legitimacy" and increasingly depended on "performance legitimacy," that is, promises to raise prosperity and improve living conditions, to maintain the support or at least quiescence of their populations. But by the 1980s even performance legitimacy was slipping out of their grasp as communist economies fell into crisis. And once performance legitimacy was gone, the only way to hold on to power was repression. Force can be very effective: the Chinese communist regime successfully used it to crush an uprising in 1989 at the same time communist regimes were collapsing in the Soviet Empire. In East-Central Europe, however, the impetus for the use of force as well as the troops necessary for it had been provided by the Soviet Union. But by the late 1980s Gorbachev had revoked the Brezhnev doctrine and left communist leaderships to "go their own way." The withdrawal of the coercive power backstopping communist regimes created an unprecedented opportunity—and the opposition best prepared to take advantage of this opportunity existed in Poland.

By the late 1980s a broad, organized opposition existed in Poland. Indeed this opposition had become such a threat that, pushed by the Soviet Union, the regime felt it had no choice but to engage in a military crackdown against it, which made crystal clear that force was now the only thing keeping the regime in power. But Poland's military ruler, Wojciech Jaruzelski, quickly recognized that he could not get rid of Solidarity through force alone and this, combined with a continued economic crisis and the subsequent withdrawal of Soviet insistence on, and potential assistance with, military repression, created an opportunity for change. When the economic crisis led to another round of strikes in the summer of 1988 Jaruzelski agreed to negotiate with Solidarity at the Roundtable talks. Within months of these talks, the regime was gone.

The next regime to go was Hungary's. Like Poland, Hungary experienced significant, particularly economic, liberalization after the crushing of the 1956 uprising, and by the 1980s economic reforms had weakened the regime's control over the economy and society. Thus, when Gorbachev and developments in Poland created an opportunity, reformists within the Hungarian communist party and some organized groups (albeit primarily focused on economic issues and interests) were already in place. Such conditions did not exist in East Germany or Czechoslovakia. Here regimes remained repressive up through the 1980s, and organized, independent groups did not exist. When discontent emerged in 1989, regimes initially reacted towards it as they had in the past: with repression. But encouraged by Gorbachev's reforms and transitions in Poland and Hungary, opposition in East Germany and Czechoslovakia grew, but without pre-existing opposition groups or leaders to guide it, it took the form of mass mobilization and protest. As mobilization and protest grew, and without pressure from the Soviet Union to crush it, moderates within the East German and Czechoslovak communist parties were able to push aside hardliners and unwilling and indeed perhaps unable to use force to maintain power, their regimes quickly and peacefully collapsed.

The remarkable and unusually non-violent nature of the 1989 revolutions was thus primarily a consequence of the most unusual feature of the revolution that ushered in communism—its external imposition. Not merely revolution but also colonization occurred in East-Central Europe after 1945: the imposition and survival of communist regimes depended on the overwhelming military power of the Soviet Union. Once that disappeared with Gorbachev's reforms in the mid-1980s, political dynamics and calculations shifted. With the Soviets no longer insisting on or supporting military intervention, staying in power meant East-Central European communist regimes would have to use force against their own citizens on their own initiative. The withdrawal of colonial pressure also meant that "moderates" who opposed the use of force could now do so without fearing repercussions as Nagy, Dubček, and many others had in the past.

If examination of the past is critical to understanding how and when the transition to democracy occurred in East-Central Europe, it is equally critical to understanding the challenges the region faced after the transition. A key theme of this book is how legacies of the old regime shape the political challenges facing and thus the fate of new ones. And it would be hard to exaggerate the depth and extent of the legacies communism and colonialism left behind in East-Central Europe.[89]

Most obviously, after 1989 East-Central Europe faced the challenge of having to make a transition not merely to democracy but also to capitalism. And for either democracy or capitalism to flourish, societies would have to be transformed as well. On the "positive" side of the ledger, decades of communism left East-Central European societies wealthier, more industrialized, more educated, and more literate than ever before and they were dominated by working and white-collar classes, rather than peasantries and landed elites as most had been before the war. But communism had also erased the distinction between the public and private spheres and between state and society—divisions required not only for democracy and capitalism but also for liberalism.[90] Decades of communism also left problematic habits and norms embedded in East-European societies. Perhaps most obviously, understandings or expectations of democracy differed greatly from those characteristic of consolidated liberal democracies, but that are fairly common in "new" democracies. Surveys conducted after the transitions "showed that 40–70 percent of the population emphasized social and economic rather than liberal rights in their definitions of democracy." Governments were viewed as being responsible not merely for prosperity "but also for guaranteeing employment and the basic material needs of individual citizens."[91] In addition, decades of communism left East-Central Europeans distrustful of each other, political elites, and institutions, and lacking traditions of political independence, compromise, or toleration.[92] And with the partial exception of Czechoslovakia, these were not habits or norms East-Central European countries could recover from their pre-communist pasts, having been subsumed in illiberal, undemocratic empires before independence.

Also necessary for consolidated liberal democracy (and well-functioning capitalism) is a strong state. On the "positive" side, unlike most revolutions 1989 was not ushered in by state collapse. Moreover, one crucial "achievement" of communist regimes was building strong states in a region hitherto lacking them. Although the strength of communist states was overwhelmingly anchored in despotic or repressive power, they did maintain order, develop (overly large and intrusive) administrative institutions, extract resources, and establish civilian control over the military.[93] On the other side of the ledger, post-communist states needed "slimming down" in both size and reach in order to enable a distinction between the public and private spheres and for an independent civil society to develop. In addition, states needed to be purged of recalcitrant communists and the corrupt and venal practices embedded in them. In most of the region, the meritocratic, impartial governance associated with consolidated liberal democracies again needed to be built from scratch.

Another crucial pre-condition for consolidated liberal democracy is agreement on the nature and boundaries of the national community. As discussed in chapter 15, East-Central European countries were much more homogenous during the postwar period than they had been during the interwar one as a result of the violence and genocide carried out by the Nazis during the war and the massive ethnic cleansing that occurred under Soviet (and Allied) auspices after it. This, along with communist-era repression, largely (but not entirely) eliminated the communal conflicts that had destabilized political life during the interwar era. But national identities and communities built on violence, repression, and ethnic cleansing are brittle and inflexible: minorities, influxes of new people, and even shifts in the norms and values "traditionally" associated with national cultures (for example, acceptance of homosexuality or equal status for women) are perceived as threats. And of course, given the region's history, it has little experience dealing peacefully with minorities or immigrants/refugees and is extremely wary of outside intervention. Given these legacies and putting East-Central Europe's experience in historical and comparative perspective, how can we best understand and assess the region's post-transition political development? East-Central Europe first gained its independence in 1918, at which point it faced the challenge of eliminating the remnants of the old regime and building states, nations, and democracies almost from scratch. These challenges, particularly in the context of the difficult interwar years, proved overwhelming and most of the region collapsed into dictatorship even before it once again lost its independence—first to the Nazis and then to the Soviets. After 1989 East-Central Europe regained its independence. Given the region's long experience of external domination (longer in fact that most colonized regions, in other parts of the world having been ruled over by the Habsburg, Nazi, and Soviet Empires), permanently regaining its sovereignty—which looks more likely than at any time in the past—would be an accomplishment of historic significance.[94] National sovereignty, of course, is also the most basic precondition for consolidated liberal democracy.

As noted throughout this book, democratic consolidation is best understood as a two-stage process: eliminating the old (dictatorial) order and building up a new (democratic) one. In East-Central Europe the political infrastructure of the old Habsburg order disappeared after World War I, and its social and economic remnants were eliminated during the Second World War and the communist era. Communists then built a new order. After it collapsed in 1989, East-Central Europe thus once again found itself facing the challenge of eliminating the remnants of an old, communist order and having to construct new ones.

The conditions for so doing are surely better than during the region's last period of independence after the First World War: it is more economically advanced and socially modern, does not have to build states or nations from scratch, Germany is no longer a danger, and while Russia is a menace, it represents nowhere near the threat it has in past. The European Union, on the other hand, which played such an important role in facilitating East-Central Europe's transitions to democracy, has been horrifically inept these past years, allowing significant backsliding to occur under its watch. Whether it can regain its role as a promoter or at least protector of liberal democracy remains unclear. (For more on this, see chapter 18.)

But key challenges remain: first, as noted above, dealing with the legacies of the old, communist regimes, and second, building up a consensus around a new one. As we saw, East-Central European citizens were fairly united in wanting to rule themselves—to get rid of dictatorships and foreign rule—but, as has so often been the case in the past, they are less united on the form "self-rule" should take. As discussed in chapter 1, liberal democracy is a form of self-rule or rule by the people—it requires not merely that citizens get to choose their leaders and governments, but also that they accept liberal values and norms, including limitations on political power, minority and individual rights, the rule of law, the political equality of all citizens, rights to free speech, press, religion, and so forth.[95] And so while there was a broad consensus on the desirability of democracy—Poles, Hungarians, Czechs, and others wanted to rule themselves and not be ruled over by others as they had throughout their modern history—there was little consensus on liberalism. As a result democracy and liberalism began to diverge in Eastern Europe, as they have so often in Europe's past. Indeed, as we have seen in previous chapters, reaching a consensus on liberal norms and values was harder and took longer to achieve than gaining support for the overthrow of dictatorships and transitions to democracy. The latter began in Europe in 1789, but throughout the nineteenth and early twentieth centuries most transitions never made it past the electoral or illiberal level; many simply collapsed. It took until the second half of the twentieth century to eliminate the legacies of old, dictatorial regimes in Western and Southern Europe and build up a consensus around not just democracy but liberal democracy as well as an understanding of what it would take to make this type of regime finally work. With liberal democracy in Western Europe and the United States once again being questioned and the European Union in crisis, Eastern Europe has been largely left to figure out its political path forward on its own.

| Lessons from Europe

The present enables us to understand the past, not the other way round.
—A.J.P. Taylor[1]

The tradition of all dead generations weighs like a nightmare on the brains of the living.
—Karl Marx[2]

T HIS BOOK HAS analyzed the development of democracies and dictatorships in Europe from the ancien régime through the collapse of communism. By examining history through the prism of current debates about democracy we can, as A.J.P. Taylor noted, better understand the past. Having now done so, it is indeed clear that certain patterns, even lessons, emerge from European history. These patterns and lessons can, in turn, help us better understand what is going on with democracy today.

At the end of the twentieth century with the collapse of communism many believed the story of European political development had come to an end with the entire continent united in the democratic camp for the first time in history. By the early twenty-first century this story had already begun to unravel as some of the continent's newer democracies slid towards illiberalism and even dictatorship, and citizens in many of its older democracies began questioning democracy's functioning and even legitimacy.[3] And of course it is not merely in Europe where democracy is under siege. Across the globe the immense optimism accompanying the third wave has been replaced by pessimism as new democracies in Latin America, Africa, and Asia have run into difficulties, the Arab Spring quickly turned into the Arab winter, and many wonder if Donald Trump threatens liberal democracy in the United States.[4] Indeed, it has become increasingly common for leaders, intellectuals, commentators, and others to claim that, rather than democracy, some form of dictatorship, perhaps of the "authoritarian capitalist" variety that exists in places like China and Russia, or illiberal democracy, as in Hungary or Turkey, is the wave of the future.[5]

As described throughout this book, such cycles of optimism and pessimism are not new: they have accompanied previous democratic waves and the backsliding that followed them. What can we learn from these previous cycles? Why did liberal democracy flourish in some parts of Europe and at some times but not others? What patterns of political development emerge, and what lessons can be derived from Europe's past that can help us better understand the state of democracy today?

What Can We Learn from Europe?

The first and perhaps the most obvious lesson of European political development is that consolidated liberal democracy most often comes at the end of a long and difficult process that involves missteps and even failures along the way. What we commonly expect of new democracies today, in other words—a quick, simple, irreversible jump from dictatorship to consolidated liberal democracy—is not only unusual but essentially the opposite of what has most often occurred. Historically, most initial transitions have been the *beginning* of a country's path to liberal democracy, not its *end*.

Take France. The modern struggle for democracy is usually dated as beginning with the French Revolution in 1789 (see chapter 4). Just as the third wave and the Arab Spring were greeted with jubilation by observers around the globe, so too was the collapse of France's monarchical dictatorship in 1789. In the "Prelude," William Wordsworth remembered the time as one when "all Europe was thrilled with joy, / France standing at the top of golden hours, / And human nature seeming born again." Yet despite the initial optimism, the transition quickly went awry. In 1791, with the proclamation of a constitutional monarchy, France made its first attempt to create a new political order, but this moderate political regime was rejected by reactionaries and radicals. The latter gained the upper hand and in 1793 executed the king and declared a republic with universal suffrage and a commitment to a broad range of liberal rights. Europe's first modern democracy did not last long, however, descending quickly into illiberalism and a Reign of Terror in which twenty thousand to forty thousand people were executed for "counter-revolutionary" activities. This is not what most people had hoped for when the old regime collapsed, and by 1799 an exhausted France submitted to a coup by General Napoleon Bonaparte.

In the space of a decade, France moved from monarchical dictatorship to democracy, to war and domestic chaos, and then back to dictatorship, albeit in a new form: a populist military dictatorship. This regime also eventually collapsed and France then returned to a monarchy, but of a different type than existed before 1789. When a new Bourbon king, Louis XVIII, took over from Napoleon in 1814, he ruled under a constitution that provided for a two-chamber parliament; granted suffrage to men of means; and established equality before the law, freedom of the press, and other civil liberties. Over time, however, Louis XVIII and his successor Charles X began "backsliding" or chipping away at representative institutions, resorting to increasing repression and seeking an alliance with religious conservatives. The government's disconnect from popular needs sparked a civil war. In 1830 Charles X was shipped off to exile and France transitioned to a more moderate political order under a new king, Louis-Philippe. The new regime expanded the suffrage to include the middle, but not the lower, classes. But such a political order—which might now be characterized as "competitive authoritarianism" or a hybrid regime—was rejected by reactionaries, democrats, and the lower classes, and was ultimately unable to satisfy much of the middle class. The result was renewed instability and violence. By 1848 pressure for political change reached a critical juncture in France and much of the rest of Europe (see chapter 5). Initially, demands for change took relatively peaceful forms, with middle-class groups organizing "reform banquets" featuring anti-regime rhetoric and discussions of alternative policies. The king tried to ignore discontent, but as that became more difficult he switched to trying to shut it down. This pushed discontent in a more chaotic and violent direction. Facing growing turmoil, the king fled. Although the protestors of 1848 were united in their opposition to the existing political order, they disagreed on much else. The newly elected National Assembly was determined to prevent disorder and radicalism and so called out the National Guard to deal with workers who demanded sweeping political and economic reforms. By the time the dust settled, about 4,500 people were dead and 12,000 arrested. This allowed the government to maintain control, but only at the price of alienating much of the lower classes. When presidential elections under universal suffrage were held in December 1848, the populist Louis-Napoleon Bonaparte (the previous Napoleon's nephew) emerged as the winner.

Following what would come to be a pretty standard authoritarian-populist playbook, Louis-Napoleon recognized the need for some popular or democratic legitimacy, but he rejected the "constraints" that would be imposed by liberal democracy and so circumvented the Republic's institutions and appealed directly to the people. After the assembly refused to revise the constitution to allow him a second four-year presidential term, he attacked it head-on. In December 1851, forces loyal to him occupied Paris and arrested his opponents. After suppressing uprisings, he offered the public a plebiscite to ratify his rule. A majority voted to keep him in office, and in the coming months he promulgated a new constitution. This gave France an authoritarian-populist regime in which the president's term of office and powers were greatly extended and the powers of the legislative branch diminished.

Louis-Napoleon's regime lasted until France's military defeat by Germany in 1870. The collapse of this political regime set off battles within French society and led to the Paris Commune's takeover of the capital from March to May 1871. Like the original Communards of Revolutionary-era Paris eight decades before, the latter-day Communards demanded radical change. This allowed their opponents to recoup support and organize a military assault on the capital. By the time the dust settled, twenty thousand were dead, the Commune had been extinguished, and the country set about once again trying to reconstruct a functioning political order. A new democracy, the Third Republic, was established in 1875 (see chapter 6), and in the ensuing decades carried out important educational, cultural, and economic reforms. Perhaps most notably, it was under this regime that national unification was essentially completed and "peasants finally became Frenchmen."[6] But the Third Republic had to contend with hostility from conservative, monarchical, and religious forces, as well as deep political and social divisions that exploded in the Dreyfus Affair, which lasted from 1894 to 1906. In short, although the Third Republic was France's longest-lived regime since the French Revolution, it cannot be considered a fully consolidated liberal democracy since significant sectors of the population did not accept basic liberal values or play by the democratic rules of the game.

The Third Republic lasted throughout the interwar years but became weaker and French society more divided as the period rolled on, making the country easier prey for the Nazi war machine and the Vichy regime that followed in 1940 (see chapter 9). When the war ended, France again transitioned to democracy with the Fourth Republic, but despite important successes, political instability returned; between 1946 and 1958 there were twenty-one governments. This instability hindered the Republic's ability to deal with the country's problems, and when war broke out in Algeria in 1958 and a section of the army rebelled, Charles de Gaulle stepped in, the

Fourth Republic collapsed, and a Fifth Republic, under a new constitution featuring a strong presidency, emerged. With this Fifth Republic France finally achieved the political stability and consolidated liberal democracy that had eluded it for so long.

Although France's struggle to achieve consolidated liberal democracy was particularly long and difficult, similar patterns characterized other European countries. During the 1848 wave, for example, some of the states on the Italian peninsula made brief transitions to democracy. When these various states came together to form a unified Italy in the early 1860s, the new country was ruled by a hybrid regime that featured a constitutional monarchy, parliamentary government, and a lower house elected by limited suffrage (see chapter 7). As with most new states, however, the Italian one was weak and unloved by many of its ostensible "people," whose identities remained more closely tied to their regions or religion than to their new country. State weakness made it difficult to create a cohesive national identity or deal with Italy's myriad other problems: economic backwardness, deep regional divides, immense socioeconomic inequality, and widespread crime and violence. Governments became mired in a form of corruption and inefficiency termed *trasformismo*. During the late nineteenth and early twentieth centuries dissatisfaction with these conditions led to political instability and extremism. Despite a transition to essentially universal manhood suffrage in 1912, little progress was made toward consolidating liberal democracy. To begin with, the state remained unable to maintain political order or enforce the rule of law, and political stability thus remained elusive, becoming even more so after the First World War (see chapter 11). In urban areas, battles reached epic proportions by the *biennio rosso* ("two red years") of 1919 and 1920 when approximately 1.3 million workers marched off their jobs and declared that they, rather than owners and managers, were in charge. The situation in rural areas was perhaps even more chaotic, as peasants and agricultural workers rebelled against large landowners and took over unoccupied or underutilized land; large landowners engaged private militias to keep the lower classes in check. In addition, Italy's main political actors never fully accepted the democratic rules of the game, the legitimacy of their opponents, or the desirability of liberal democracy overall. Indeed the two largest parties, the Socialists and Catholics, were unwilling to work together, even to save democracy from its opponents; they remained, instead, primarily interested in protecting their own constituencies and interests. (The Catholic Popular party's focus was protecting religion and the Church while Socialists remained convinced that workers had little to gain from the "bourgeois" state or cooperation with "bourgeois" political forces.)

Radicals on both the left and right blamed Italy's problems on democracy, but it was the right that gained the upper hand. In October 1922 democracy's opponents finally got what they wanted when the Italian king, urged on by conservatives, asked Mussolini to form a government. With this, Italy's democratic experiment came to an end. The shift to fascism was applauded by many within Italy and without who believed that dictatorship was more likely to provide the stability and development the country desperately needed. It was only after the Second World War that something resembling consolidated liberal democracy emerged in Italy.

The same was true of Germany. Like many other European countries, Germany's first attempt at democracy and political unification occurred in 1848 (see chapter 5), when delegates from across the German-speaking lands met in Frankfurt to convene the first democratically elected parliament in German history, which issued a "Declaration of Fundamental Rights" calling for freedom of speech and religion, equality before the law, and representative government. But radicals and moderates disagreed over whether to call for a republic, while other factions debated who the "people" of the new Germany should be. (Concretely this meant battles over the borders of the new Germany and the populations to be included in it.) The Prussian king, Frederick William IV, bided his time, recognizing that the longer reformers argued, the stronger his position would be. When the Frankfurt parliament finally offered him the crown of a new, united Germany in April 1849, he turned it down, dismissed the parliament, crushed the uprisings that broke out in response, and re-instated a dictatorship.

Although it failed in 1848, German unification remained on the political agenda and was finally achieved in 1871—although not as the result of the deliberations of a liberal parliament but rather as a consequence of war and the efforts of the profoundly anti-liberal Otto von Bismarck (see chapter 8). The new Germany had what we would now characterize as a hybrid or semi-authoritarian regime, mixing democratic and non-democratic elements. However, the dominance of Prussia, within the new Germany, and the Junkers' (large landowners') dominance of Prussia enabled a conservative elite to hold on to political power even as Germany's economy and society changed dramatically. Germany's political order began running into trouble even before Bismarck was pushed into retirement in 1890. Growing sectors of the population became increasingly frustrated by the unrepresentative and unresponsive nature of government. The regime attempted to silence advocates of political change, particularly social democrats and Catholics, but ultimately this solidified and increased these groups' political support while deepening social divisions and increasing political discontent. As is often the case, frustration with the existing political order led increasing numbers of Germans to turn away from it and channel their political energy instead into increasingly polarized and extremist civil society organizations, most worryingly radical nationalist movements, during the late nineteenth and early twentieth centuries. By the eve of the First World War, Germany faced governmental deadlock, rising social tension, growing political alienation and extremism, and a willingness on the part of some conservatives to embrace radical ideologies and risky military adventures to head off growing pressures for democratization.

Germany finally democratized in the democratic wave that swept across Europe at the end of the First World War, but the new Weimar Republic was burdened by myriad problems as well as anti-democratic and illiberal legacies inherited from its predecessor (see chapter 12). Within months of its founding, communists declared a Soviet republic in Bavaria, which was soon overthrown by the *Freikorps*, a right-wing militia largely beyond the central government's control. The *Freikorps* continued their rampages, engaging in assassinations and violent demonstrations and eventually supporting an attempted coup in 1920; other right-wing uprisings followed, including Hitler's infamous Beer Hall putsch in 1923. Worker rebellions and communist uprisings were also widespread. And to top it off, the government's default on reparations debts in 1923 caused the French and Belgians to invade the country, setting off the Great Inflation—which disoriented and angered the German middle classes and further delegitimized the government and other mainstream political institutions.

Some stabilization occurred in the late 1920s, but the Republic barely had time to breathe before being buffeted by the Great Depression. When mainstream political parties dithered in the face of looming economic and political catastrophe, extremists gained ground, and in the fall of 1932 the Nazis, running on a platform marrying attacks on democracy with promises to tackle the country's economic problems and heal its social divisions, became Germany's largest party. In January 1933 Hitler was offered the chancellorship and Germany's democratic experiment came to an end. It was only after enduring perhaps the most evil regime and most brutal war in history that Germany finally made a transition to consolidated liberal democracy (see chapter 14), and even then, of course, only its western half, since its eastern half remained mired under a communist dictatorship for decades to come (see chapter 15).

Spain also followed a long and difficult path to consolidated liberal democracy, experiencing a dizzying array of political transitions, military interventions, and civil wars during the nineteenth and early twentieth centuries (see chapter 13). None of the various regimes that emerged in Spain during this period made real progress dealing with the country's economic backwardness, extreme socioeconomic inequality and divisions, violent clerical/anti-clerical split, and need for state- and nation-building. The result, predictably, was growing extremism and even violence. In 1931 Spain made a transition to democracy for the second time (the first being the short-lived First Republic of the years 1873–1874), but the Second Republic was weak and divided from birth, burdened by a huge number of problems and anti-democratic and illiberal legacies inherited from its predecessors; political instability, extremism, and violence quickly grew. In 1939 the military, urged on by conservatives, overthrew the Republic and set off a civil war that eventually killed approximately five hundred thousand Spaniards. After a dictatorship that lasted for decades, Spain made another transition to democracy in the mid-1970s, which, due to social and economic changes that occurred during the previous decades and lessons learned by political actors about what it would take to make democracy work, consolidated remarkably quickly (see chapter 16).

Although the countries of the region are relatively young, thus far the political development of East-Central Europe has been as difficult and non-linear as that of Western and Southern Europe. East-Central European countries only emerged after the First World War when the Habsburg, German, Russian, and Ottoman Empires collapsed (see chapter 15). Like many newly decolonized countries, but unlike their counterparts in Western and Southern Europe, Poland, Czechoslovakia, Hungary, and the empires' other successor states had to deal with the challenges of state-, nation-, and democracy-building simultaneously. Perhaps not surprisingly, therefore, during the interwar period these new countries were wracked by socioeconomic and communal divisions, political instability, extremism, and international conflicts. With the exception of Czechoslovakia, democracy collapsed in all of them even before they were invaded by the Nazis and then the Soviets. With these invasions East-Central European countries lost the independence they gained in 1918 and did not regain it until the Soviet Empire collapsed in 1989 (see chapter 17). The region was in better shape in 1989 than in 1918: it was more economically developed and socially modern; had more homogenous populations and stronger states; and its European neighbors were democratic, peaceful, and willing to integrate it into a larger regional entity, the European Union. But the countries of the region had little experience with democracy and even less with liberalism and also, of course, inherited myriad problems and anti-democratic and anti-liberal legacies from previous communist dictatorships, including non-capitalist economies, weak or non-existent civil societies, fragile national identities, and populations riven by distrust and alienation. Given how long and difficult the path towards liberal democracy was in other parts of Europe—only being achieved after 1945 in Western and during the late twentieth century in Southern Europe—and the "disadvantages" Eastern European countries were burdened with after 1989, it is perhaps not surprising that consolidating liberal democracy has been difficult. Making matters worse has been the weakening of the postwar European order (see below). The European Union in particular played a powerful role in supporting democracy in Eastern Europe after 1989, and its weakening since the financial crisis has hindered its ability to promote consolidation; indeed, it has proven powerless to prevent democratic backsliding in the region—a sad irony since it was formed as part of an effort to prevent the re-emergence of dictatorships after the Second World War (see below).

In short, a pattern that emerges clearly from the European past and a crucial lesson for the contemporary period is that achieving consolidated liberal democracy easily or quickly is extremely unusual. Even the cases most often heralded as having done so had far more trouble and took much longer than most observers recognize. As discussed in chapter 3, for example, even in Britain the development of democracy had a turbulent backstory—once you take into account the English Civil War, Cromwell's republican but dictatorial Commonwealth, and other political developments leading up to the Glorious Revolution in 1688. It is hard to imagine how the peaceful political development that Britain (but of course not Ireland or other British colonies) experienced during the nineteenth and twentieth centuries would have been possible without the political turmoil of the seventeenth. And it is important to remember how much time it actually took to achieve full democracy in Britain: whether the process is dated from 1688—with the Glorious Revolution's establishment of parliamentary dominance and constitutionalism—or 1832—with the first reform act—it took literally hundreds of years until a fully liberal democracy was achieved (see chapter 10).

In addition to making clear how long and difficult the path to consolidated liberal democracy has been, a second lesson of European political development is that it is much easier to topple dictatorial regimes than build new, democratic ones, particularly of the liberal democratic variety. Beginning in 1789 and occurring with increasing frequency during the nineteenth and early twentieth centuries, regime change in general and transitions to democracy in particular became increasingly common in Europe. As chapter 6, for example, pointed out, in France—the birthplace of modern democracy— political transitions occurred so often after the French Revolution that a long-standing joke had it that the National Library kept its copies of the constitution in the periodicals section.[7] None of the countries examined in this book, with the exception of Britain, which, as noted above, went through its own period of political turmoil and rapid regime change in the seventeenth century, achieved consolidated liberal democracy on its first try. Indeed, there were two continent-wide waves of democracy during the nineteenth and early twentieth centuries that left few stable democracies, much less liberal democracies, in their wake. The 1848 democratic wave quickly toppled many of Europe's seemingly sturdiest monarchical dictatorships, yet it proved impossible to build stable democratic regimes to replace them (see chapter 5). Europe's next democratic wave, which occurred between 1917 and 1920, brought an end to the Russian, German, and Austro-Hungarian Empires and swept away the last hindrances to democratization in other parts of Europe as well. But while this ended the era of monarchical dictatorship in Europe, it did not usher in an era of consolidated liberal democracy. Indeed, few of the democratic regimes produced by the 1917–1920 wave survived; some collapsed into fascist or National Socialist dictatorships (see chapter 9, Figure 9.1).

A third lesson of European political development is that most transitions to democracy, particularly initial ones, either fail or give rise to electoral or illiberal rather than consolidated liberal democracy. On one level, this makes perfect sense considering the more stringent requirements of liberal as opposed to electoral or illiberal democracy. As discussed in chapter 1, electoral or illiberal democracies are distinguished from dictatorships by the *procedures* or *institutions* used to choose rulers: elections rather than heredity, nepotism, or the preferences of an elite or privileged group. Considerations beyond this—for example, what policies governments actually pursue, whether governments discriminate between citizens from majority and minority groups, whether citizens view each other as political equals—are not part of this definition of democracy.

More than procedures or institutions, on the other hand, distinguishes liberal democracy from dictatorship. Unlike dictatorships, but also unlike electoral or illiberal democracies, liberal democracy requires governments and citizens to behave in accordance with the tenets of liberalism: the rule of law must be guaranteed, minorities protected, individual civil liberties respected, and the political equality of all citizens accepted. There have been *very few* liberal democracies in European history; indeed, it was not until the second half of the twentieth century that this regime type became common. Before this, the democracies that existed were primarily of the electoral or illiberal variety. This was true from the very beginning: Europe's first democratic experiment during the French Revolution never made it past the electoral or illiberal stage, persecuting many of its own citizens as "enemies of the nation" during a horrific "Reign of Terror" (see chapter 4). Although France made two other transitions to democracy before the Second World War, neither became a fully consolidated liberal democracy. Even the Third Republic, France's most durable regime since the revolution and the one that came closest to achieving consolidated liberal democratic status, was plagued by significant groups that rejected liberal values, and its government was unable to consistently ensure the impartial application of the rule of law or protect minorities (see chapter 6). The same was true of most other democracies examined in this book: none of the democratic regimes that existed in Germany, Italy, or Spain before the second half of the twentieth century were consolidated liberal democracies. It was only after 1945 that liberal democracy consolidated across Western Europe (see chapter 14) and only in the late twentieth century in Spain (see chapter 16). (And of course in Eastern Europe, liberal democracy remains elusive.)

Beyond the more stringent requirements of liberal as opposed to electoral or illiberal democracy, a fourth lesson of European political development is that liberal democracy is so rare and difficult to achieve because it requires transforming not merely the political procedures and institutions of dictatorship, but societies and economies as well.

Dictatorships are not just a type of political regime: they are generally embedded in and rest upon particular social and economic foundations. This was clearly true of the monarchical dictatorships that emerged in Europe in the early modern period (see, for example, chapter 2). Central to these dictatorships was the system of privilege. Privilege was sanctified by law; one contemporary definition described it as "distinctions, whether useful or honorific, which are enjoyed by certain members of society and denied to others."[8] These distinctions extended into almost all spheres of life, governing everything from access to economic resources in general and property in particular, to the payment or non-payment of taxes, to the type of justice system and punishment one was subjected to. Rather, in other words, than in liberal democracies where rights are generally viewed either as national (that is, deriving from membership in a particular state) or universal (that is, inhering in all human beings), in the old regimes of Europe rights were inherited or sometimes bought and depended on one's membership in a particular group (or estate). This was, in other words, an inherently illiberal and unequal world where economic, social, and political power were inextricably intertwined. Interestingly twentieth-century totalitarian regimes resembled their early modern absolutist predecessors in this regard: in fascist, National Socialist, and communist regimes, economic, social, and political power were inextricably intertwined, and the regime's support was based in a privileged class that enjoyed special access to economic resources, high-status jobs, preferential legal treatment, and so on (see chapters 11, 12, and 15).

This system reached its apogee in ancien régime France (see chapter 2). It was precisely because economic, social, and political power were so deeply entwined and the society created by the system of privilege so deeply divided that the ancien régime proved impossible to reform (see chapter 4). Instead, once things started to unravel, pressure for change built in all spheres of life and among most social groups, leading to the revolution that engulfed France and spilled over into the rest of Europe.

After the French Revolution and the upheavals unleashed by Napoleon, the old order in Europe began to crumble, but getting rid of the political institutions of monarchical dictatorship turned out to be only the first, and in many ways the easiest, of the many steps it would take to eradicate the old regime. Indeed, even in France, where the revolution eliminated absolutism as well as the legal infrastructure of the system of privilege, critical social and economic legacies of the old regime, including a resentful elite, reactionary Church, and a deeply divided society, remained, hindering the development of liberal democracy in France up through the twentieth century. In most other parts of Europe, the breakdown of the old order began later than in France and proceeded in fits and starts throughout the nineteenth and early twentieth centuries since, unlike in post-revolutionary France, unreconstructed monarchs, privileged nobilities, and churches remained to fight for it.

The old order also often created societies riven by national and communal cleavages. This was especially true in Europe's continental empires (the Austro-Hungarian, Russian, and Ottoman), where "divide and rule" tactics were used to forestall the formation of coalitions opposed to the old order (see, for example, chapter 5). When these empires collapsed after the First World War, their successor states were accordingly burdened by diverse populations deeply suspicious of each other. Communal conflict thus became endemic in newly independent East-Central European countries, contributing to illiberalism and the rapid collapse of democracy. That national unity only emerged in many of these countries *after* the murderous ethnic cleansing of the Second World War and its aftermath left them ethnically homogenous meant that "challenges" to homogeneity were perceived as threats to national unity and identity, helping to explain why resistance to immigration and liberal understandings of citizenship and minority rights can be easily whipped up today.

"Divide-and-rule" tactics were also employed in the German Empire where Bismarck waged a *Kulturkampf* against Catholics and ignored or even encouraged the demonization of Jews and Poles as well as the left (see chapter 8) in order to weaken and fragment his opposition. In Italy, meanwhile, political elites made deals with southern landowners, facilitating the persistence and perhaps even deepening of regional divisions and socioeconomic inequalities (see chapter 7). And in Spain, rulers and governments up through the twentieth century were unable and/or unwilling to overcome the country's deep regional and social divisions or to create a strong national identity (see chapter 13). Even in France and Britain, where national unity preceded the furthest, communal divisions hindered democratic development up through the twentieth century, as chapter 6's discussion of the Dreyfus Affair (and the anti-Semitism it revealed and whipped up) and chapter 10's discussion of conflicts over Ireland made clear. The persistence of communal divisions, especially when combined with socioeconomic ones, made it difficult for societies to agree on who was a member of the national community—or who "the people" were—and thus entitled to the benefits of citizenship, which in turn made consolidation of democracy, particularly of the liberal kind, almost impossible.

A fifth lesson of European political development is that it often takes major structural shocks or changes like war or economic development to overcome the anti-democratic and illiberal legacies of the old order, a crucial prerequisite for the emergence of liberal democracy. There were, however, cases where political actors played a key role in this process.

Many scholars and political commentators agree that economic development changes societies in ways that lead to democratization and/or consolidation. In political science such arguments are generally grouped under the rubric of "modernization theory." Where such arguments are weak or differ is in understandings of precisely *how* broad structural trends like economic development matter. One crucial way reflected in European history was by diminishing the power of the supporters of the old regime, particularly landed elites and the Church. These groups were weakened by the decline of agriculture, rise in urbanization and literacy, increases in political mobilization and awareness, and the spread of ideas about individual freedom, personal mobility, and self-interest accompanying economic development. The political impact of these socioeconomic changes was not, however, simple or direct. In some European countries, landed elites and the Church were able to successfully fend off challenges for a very long time, which is one reason why political development was less linear and more conflictual than modernization theories based on economic development predict. Indeed, in some cases, like ancien régime France and Imperial Germany (see chapters 4, 12, and 13), so persistent and effective was the resistance of the old regime's supporters that it took revolutions to get rid of them. The determined opposition of landed elites in particular to liberal democracy can be thought of as an example of the "resource curse" dynamic familiar to observers of political development today—when a group's wealth is "immobile" and depends on controlling the state and keeping the masses from access to it, liberal democracy is extremely difficult to achieve.

In addition to challenging the old regime's strongest supporters, economic development strengthens its opponents—the middle and working classes. However, here again European political development reveals a more complicated picture than portrayed in most modernization accounts. Although both the middle and working classes opposed unrepresentative and unresponsive old regime dictatorships, they rarely agreed that liberal democracy was the best alternative to it. This was particularly true of the middle classes, which generally favored a liberal order that gave them political power, but not one coupled with full democratization since that would give the working class access to political power as well. (Barrington Moore's famous line "No bourgeois, no democracy" is thus perhaps more accurately stated as "No bourgeoisie, no liberalism.") It is therefore worth stressing something European history makes clear—liberalism and democracy are not the same thing, nor did they develop at the same time. Indeed, they were only fully united in Western Europe after 1945, in Southern Europe in the late twentieth century, and they remain in conflict in much of Eastern Europe today. In addition, the tension between liberalism and democracy shaped the outcome of many critical junctures in European history, perhaps most notably and fatefully 1848—the "turning point at which modern history failed to turn."[9]

By 1848 discontent with the old order was widespread among the middle and working classes, but these groups differed over the type and degree of change they wanted: the middle classes wanted limited political opening and the institutionalization of particular liberal rights, while the working classes demanded democratization and significant socioeconomic reforms (see chapter 5). These differences broke apart the alliance between the middle and working classes: faced with a choice between democratization (and empowering the working class) and throwing their lot back in with conservative defenders of the old regime, European middle classes for the most part chose the latter. This tendency continued throughout the late nineteenth and early twentieth centuries as the middle classes grew increasingly frustrated with regimes that denied them political power, but remained wary of democratization and the socioeconomic changes working-class political empowerment would bring. In some countries, like Spain and Italy, the middle classes attempted to square this circle by accepting or acquiescing in institutionalized political corruption in order to insulate governments from popular pressure (see chapters 7 and 13). The antipathy not only of traditional old regime supporters—the landed elites and the church—to democratization, but the middle classes as well, radicalized workers in many European countries, furthering societal distrust and divisions, extremism, and political instability up through the first half of the twentieth century.

Alongside economic development another crucial factor contributing to the elimination of anti-democratic and illiberal vestiges of the old order was violence, often via war.[10] This was clear, for example, in the modern era's first great political revolution—the French—which did away with the political and legal infrastructure of the ancien régime and marked the beginning of the end of the old order in the rest of Europe as well (see chapter 4). During the nineteenth century dissatisfaction with the old regime grew, but it took the First World War to permanently eliminate the old regime's political infrastructure—monarchical dictatorships and continental empires (see chapter 9). Fascism, national socialism, and the Second World War then eradicated remaining social and economic legacies of the old regime (see chapter 14). The fascist and especially the National Socialist regime sidelined conservative elites and the military and broke down the status hierarchies that had long defined and divided their societies (see chapters 11 and 12). But it was not just Italy and Germany that were transformed during this period: the Second World War "collapsed the social distance upon which the rigid pre-war class systems of Europe had rested" and homogenized many European societies. By the end of the 1940s Jews (and Gypsies) had been mostly killed off, and many other minorities—Hungarians, Slovaks, Ukrainians, Serbs, Croats, Poles, Finns, Italians—had been eliminated or expelled from their traditional homelands, making borders and populations coincide, particularly in Eastern and Central Europe, to a greater degree than ever before. This process was particularly clear and particularly consequential in Germany. The Junkers and traditional conservative elites were weakened by the Nazi regime, the war then killed a disproportionate number of them, and of those who survived, most were either eliminated by the incoming Red Army or fled westward to escape it; the property and estates they left behind were then burned and looted by the Soviets, destroying the final remnants of their economic and social power. Prussia, meanwhile, which had long dominated Germany and which had long been dominated by conservative Junkers, had its independence undermined by Hitler, who centralized authority in the national government and Nazi party, and after the war Prussia was eliminated from the map of Europe entirely, its territory carved up among various Eastern and Western *Länder* and Poland.[11] The war's aftermath also forced ethnic Germans from their traditional homelands in Eastern and Central Europe, making, as noted above, the states of the region more homogenous as well as making Germany and Austria more like nation-states than ever before: by the postwar period they were the home of essentially all of Europe's Germans, finally fulfilling the goal proclaimed by German nationalists in 1848 (see chapters 5 and 8). And in East-Central Europe, the Soviets eliminated the remnants of the old order—landed elites, peasantries, multiethnic states, and more—via violence at the end of the war and via an unprecedented process of social and economic engineering during the postwar period (see chapter 15).

In short, because the economic and social legacies of the old order are often so deeply rooted, it often takes powerful structural forces like economic development or violent events like war or revolution to uproot them. There were, however, cases where political actors played a key role in this process. The clearest and perhaps most unusual example of this is Britain. Unlike in most of Europe, during the nineteenth and early twentieth centuries Britain's old order peacefully and progressively transitioned to a liberal democratic one. This was partially due to the violence and upheavals of the seventeenth century—civil wars, religious conflict, military dictatorship, regicide, and the Glorious Revolution—which transformed the power of and relationship among the monarchy, Parliament, and Anglican Church. But it was also due to the comparatively puzzling behavior of the British landowning elites (see chapter 10). Unlike their counterparts in much of the rest of Europe who responded to decline with intransigent and reactionary behavior, British elites gradually, if grudgingly, went into a sort of "voluntary retirement," agreeing to reforms that slowly eliminated their political and more slowly their economic and social dominance and other vestiges of the old order and hindrances to liberal democracy. This helped forestall the radicalism and instability that plagued most of the continent during the nineteenth and early twentieth centuries and helped Britain weather the storms of the interwar years much more successfully than many other European countries.

If an important lesson of European political history is that liberal democracy requires eliminating not merely the political institutions and procedures of the old regime but also its social and economic legacies, another lesson is that the *nature* of these legacies and the *difficulty* of eradicating them depended largely on the stages in which political development occurred. In particular, the sequencing of state-, nation-, and democracy-building mattered.

As noted, liberal democracy requires governments able to enforce the democratic rules of the game, guarantee the rule of law, protect minorities and individual liberties, and, of course, implement policies. Liberal democracy requires, in other words, a relatively strong state. Liberal democracy also requires that citizens view their governments as legitimate, respect the democratic rules of the game, obey the law, and accept other members of society as political equals. Liberal democracy also requires, in other words, a consensus on who belongs to the national community—who "the people" are—and is therefore entitled to participate in the political process and enjoy the other rights and responsibilities of citizenship.[12] Reflecting this, throughout European history liberal democracy—but not illiberal or electoral democracy—has consolidated only in countries possessing relatively strong states and national unity. Britain's unusually gradual and peaceful development towards liberal democracy during the nineteenth and early twentieth centuries, for example, was possible only because it began state- and nation-building earlier than almost anywhere else in Europe. By the time pressure for democracy began to build in the nineteenth century, Britain already had a strong and legitimate state as well as a fairly strong sense of national identity that facilitated compromises and the incorporation of new groups into the political order.

In comparison to England, France faced greater hurdles to state- and nation-building during the early modern era (see chapters 2 and 4). Up through the sixteenth century many French provinces were largely independent of the central government, retaining their own customs, privileges, languages, and laws; attempts to alter the status quo provoked civil and religious conflict. This began to change in the seventeenth century, but because opposition to centralization was relatively high, French kings had to make more unpalatable, even counterproductive, concessions to the opponents of centralization than their British counterparts. For example, French kings left in place and even enhanced the privileges enjoyed by provinces, the nobility, and the Church, thereby embedding critical (perhaps fatal) flaws in the state they constructed and the society they ruled over. It took a revolution to destroy these privileges and clear the way for further state- and nation-building (see chapter 4). But the violence and destruction of the revolution also left behind legacies that hindered state- and nation-building, including a tendency towards radicalism and violence, a deeply divided society, and a large peasantry that could potentially be mobilized for conservative causes. Indeed, despite the immense progress made as a result of the revolution, it was only under the democratic Third Republic that the French state became strong *and* legitimate enough to unify France's still diverse citizenry into more of a truly national community—without the direct coercion that dictatorships like the Bourbon monarchy relied on to push this process forward.

Unlike France and Britain, many other European countries confronted the challenge of democratization with only a weak state and/or national identity in place. Italy, for example, only unified in the second half of the nineteenth century (see chapter 7). Previously, the peninsula was divided into a large number of separate states, with very different political, economic, social, and cultural histories. Complicating matters further, Italy was created largely from above, by the leaders of the peninsula's most powerful state, Piedmont, which imposed what was essentially a foreign system (its own) on the rest of the peninsula via a top-down, heavy-handed, non-democratic process. As a result, the new Italy met with almost immediate resistance—by areas of the peninsula that felt colonized and exploited by Piedmont, and by the Catholic Church, which rejected the idea of a superior secular authority governing Italians. Italy began its existence, in short, with a weak state and sense of national identity, which both contributed to and made it difficult to deal with the violence, disorder, divisions, and corruption pervading the country. When Italy made a transition to democracy on the eve of the First World War, its weak state and national identity made dealing with the problems it confronted extremely difficult; within a few years, it collapsed into dictatorship (see chapter 11).

Like Italy, Germany also unified in the second half of the nineteenth century, and was also formed from above under the auspices of its most powerful state, the conservative and militaristic Prussia (see chapter 8). While the new German state was stronger than its Italian counterpart, its domination by Prussia and Prussia's domination by its landowning elite embedded critical flaws in it. The semi-authoritarian German state also created strong incentives to engage in "divide-and-rule" tactics. Bismarck was a master of this, holding together a conservative, anti-democratic coalition of the large land-owning *Junker* elite and heavy industrialists while demonizing his socialist and Catholic opponents, thereby deepening divisions between Protestants and Catholics, between religious and secular Germans, and between workers and others. Bismarck's "enemies of the state" policy exerted a pernicious influence over German nationalism, helping cement the idea that the country faced enemies within and without. These flaws hindered the state's ability to create a cohesive national community; instead radical, anti-Semitic national movements stepped in to fulfill this task. The type of state- and nation-building that occurred in the late nineteenth and early twentieth centuries thus burdened Germany's first democratic experiment, the Weimar Republic, with crippling legacies—a divided society, an aggressive and racialist nationalism obsessed with internal and external enemies, and left- and right-wing extremism—that made building liberal democracy in face of the admittedly vast challenges the country faced during the interwar period almost impossible (see chapter 12).

Spain represents another variation on this theme. Spain also confronted the turmoil of the nineteenth and early twentieth centuries without a strong state or national identity, but unlike Italy and Germany, it was an "old" country rather than a "new" one. Its "founders," Ferdinand II of Aragon and Isabella I of Castile, and their early modern successors engaged in little state- or nation-building, ruling instead in a fairly traditional manner through personal alliances with local and provincial elites and institutions that left Spain a "composite kingdom"[13] rather than a proto nation-state (see chapter 13). This did not prevent Spain from accumulating an immense empire during the early modern period—indeed there was probably an inverse correlation between the growth of the empire and the progress of or at least perceived need for state- and nation-building—but it severely hindered political and economic development later on. Spanish monarchs, for example, lacked a state with the power to create a unified national market or taxation system or to encourage agricultural modernization. And weak state- and nation-building left traditional privileged groups—the nobility, church, regional authorities—strong and central governments weak: except for the military, Spain lacked robust national institutions, and Spanish rulers were unable to fully control their territory or peoples, making political stability, much less liberal democracy, extremely difficult to achieve. And of course, the lack of a strong state or national identity was reflected in the persistence of deep regional divisions and societal cleavages, leaving a deeply troubling legacy for the interwar Second Republic.

If creating liberal democracy was more difficult where states and national identities were weak, East-Central European countries had it even worse since they had to deal with state-, nation-, and democracy-building simultaneously upon gaining independence at the end of the First World War (see chapter 15)—a typical situation in decolonizing countries. The lack of a strong state or sense of national identity generated myriad problems during the interwar years, including economic crises, class and communal conflict, and political disorder and violence, making consolidating democracy, particularly of the liberal variety, impossible. (Czechoslovakia was a partial exception.[14])

European political development makes clear, in short, that sequencing matters: without strong states and national identities, liberal democracy is difficult if not impossible to achieve.[15] It is important to remember, however, that regardless of how sequencing occurred, there was no easy or peaceful path to liberal democracy. The difference between Western and Southern, and East-Central Europe was not *whether* violence and instability were part of the backstory of liberal democracy, but rather *when* and over *how long* a period they occurred. In Western Europe state- and nation-building were extremely violent and coercive, involving what today would be characterized as colonization and ethnic cleansing, that is, the destruction or absorption of weaker political entities into stronger ones (for example, Brittany, Burgundy, and Aquitaine into France, Scotland, and Wales, and especially Ireland into Britain), and the suppression or elimination of traditional communities, loyalties, languages, traditions, and identities in the process of creating new, national ones (see chapters 2–4).[16] But in much of Western Europe these processes occurred or at least began during the early modern period (but not, notably, in Italy and Germany), and so unlike Southern and Central Europe, Western Europe did not experience the violence and coercion associated with state- and nation-building during the modern era at the same time the challenge of democratization appeared on the political agenda. By the nineteenth century in France and England, and by the second half of the twentieth century in the rest of Western Europe, states were strong and legitimate enough to advance nation-building without overt coercion but instead via education, promoting national culture, language, and history, improved transport and communication networks, and by supporting a flourishing civil society within which potentially cross-cutting cleavages and networks could develop, strengthening the bonds among citizens. East-Central Europe, on the other hand, got started on these processes much later, and only achieved a semblance of national unity as a result of the violent ethnic cleansing that occurred during and after World War II. They were then re-colonized by the Soviets and their national identities suppressed until 1989, helping to explain why many in these countries feel threatened by ethnic diversity and liberal notions of citizenship and minority rights today.

This reflects a seventh lesson of European history—democratic and dictatorial regimes often pursue state- and nation-building differently. As discussed in chapter 2, state-building in Europe began under monarchical, particularly absolutist, dictatorships. Successful state-builders used both carrots and sticks to centralize power and undermine their opponents: the use or threat of force was necessary but not sufficient: bribes, often in the form of enhanced privileges, were also needed to get the job done. Early-modern state building thus produced states that in crucial ways resemble those existing in many parts of the world today: dictatorial and pervaded by corruption, venality, and entrenched status-hierarchies. These kinds of states can be brittle because while they have "despotic"[17] or coercive power, their infrastructural power and legitimacy are limited by the social, economic, and political foundations they are built upon. For example, in otherwise different dictatorships like those that existed in ancien régime France (see chapters 2 and 4) and the German Empire (see chapter 8), the wealthiest members of society were exempt from direct taxation, limiting the tools available to states to raise revenue. The differential treatment of citizens that often characterizes dictatorships creates deep divisions among them, leaving these regimes vulnerable to attack when conditions shift to enable the mobilization of discontent—as for example occurred with the debt and economic crises that preceded the French Revolution (see chapter 4), or the economic downturn that preceded the 1848 wave (see chapter 5), or the pressures of war that proceeded the Russian Revolution and the democratic wave of 1917 and 1918—or in the contemporary period when democratization finally occurs and divisions long suppressed under dictatorships are able to emerge.

As for nation-building, dictatorial states had a limited repertoire of tools to pursue this goal and also often ruled in ways antithetical to it. Dictatorships rely heavily on coercive means to create national unity: compulsory conversions, ethnic cleansing, discrimination against minorities, and suppression of their cultures, languages, and so on were employed by European dictatorships from the early modern period up through the twentieth century. Alongside dictatorships' limited, largely coercive repertoire, their nation-building efforts were often hindered by the means they used to stay in power: supporting the power and privileges of traditional elites (which hindered their ability to directly control their territories and peoples); using "divide-and-rule" tactics (which weakened national cohesion and state legitimacy); and relying on threats and force rather than voluntary cooperation with society to govern.

For these and other reasons, some of the most striking advances in state- and nation-building in European history occurred only *after* dictatorships were overthrown—post–Glorious Revolution Britain and post-revolutionary France being the most obvious examples (see chapters 3 and 4). As opposed to dictatorships, democratic and particularly liberal-democratic regimes have at least the *potential* to promote national unity and cohesion without coercion as well as *potentially* a greater ability to integrate diverse groups into a national whole. A long-term examination of European political development enables us to see such differences between regime types playing out even within the same country: early modern French kings, for example, promoted nation- and state-building via ethnic cleansing, expelling or converting Protestants, while the Third Republic (see chapter 6) incentivized the use of a national language, broke down the isolation of rural areas via new transportation networks, brought citizens from different regions and classes together in the army, and provided a common education to all.[18] Similarly, during the interwar period East-Central European states lacked the strength or legitimacy to integrate minorities into the national community, instead repressing or discriminating against them. These countries were then homogenized as a result of the ruthless ethnic cleansing pursued by the Nazi and Soviet dictatorships. This did eventually produce a sense of national unity during the postwar period, but alongside its obvious brutality it is simply a less effective and robust way of nation-building than non-coercive measures. Eradicating or expelling minorities, for example, "creates" a national community by eliminating from the nation those who appear different. But what differences are seen to be relevant changes over time: during the early modern period religion was the most salient cleavage, but during the modern era ethnicity and language became critical national markers as well. Repression or ethnic cleansing thus creates a "thin" or fragile type of national identity based on ascriptive characteristics and creates a national community that lacks the tools or traditions to respond to new social cleavages or integrate new groups. Democratic and particularly liberal democratic regimes, in contrast, at least have the *potential* to knit peoples together on the basis of particular ideals, or various policies that promote solidarity without coercion, or through a free, vibrant civil society that can involve citizens from various backgrounds in collective endeavors. Alongside the Third Republic mentioned above, another critical example was postwar Western Europe, where welfare states were designed to overcome societal divisions and deepen national unity and solidarity (see chapter 14, and see more on this below).

A final lesson of European political development that flows directly from previous ones is that destroying an old dictatorial order and building a new liberal democratic one are neither equivalent nor necessarily coterminous. In Europe, for example, by 1918, monarchical dictatorships and empires were gone, but across most of Europe it proved impossible to reach a consensus on what should replace them. Instead democrats, communists, fascists, National Socialists, anarchists, and others battled it out to determine the path Europe should take into the future (see chapters 9–13). These battles finally ended after 1945 (see chapter 14) in Western Europe as the war and its aftermath eliminated not only the social and economic remnants of the old order, but also finally generated a consensus on the desirability of a new liberal democratic one as well as a new consensus on what it would take to make it work.

In Southern and East-Central Europe the process of destroying the old order continued under postwar dictatorships, and the process of constructing new democratic ones began at the end of the twentieth century. In Spain, the monarchy disappeared in the 1930s and a transition to democracy occurred, but this democracy collapsed largely because critical social and economic legacies of the old remained (see chapter 13). Despite coming to power as the old order's defender, Franco's dictatorship ended up undermining many of its legacies (see chapter 16). During the postwar period Spain's society and economy were transformed; by the time Franco died in 1975 not much of "traditional" Spain remained. The process of building a new liberal democratic order then commenced, facilitated by the immense social and economic changes that had occurred during the previous decades and by the memories of the collapse of the Second Republic and the civil war that followed. As in Western Europe after 1945, these horrible experiences helped generate a consensus among actors across the political spectrum on the desirability of liberal democracy as well as on what it would take to make it work. And so after 1975, representatives from the old regime and the opposition worked together to reach compromises on a wide range of political, economic, and social reforms that gradually transitioned Spain from dictatorship to liberal democracy while the encouragement, funds, and institutions of the European Community helped speed the process along. In East-Central Europe, finally, the Second World War largely destroyed the old order, with the Soviets mopping up its remnants at the war's end. The communist regimes the Soviets helped install then constructed new ones to take their place (see chapter 15). These communist regimes collapsed during the third wave, leaving behind anti-liberal and anti-democratic legacies (see chapter 17). During the late twentieth and early twenty-first centuries East-Central Europe began confronting these legacies and the challenge of generating a consensus around a new, order, a process the region remains mired in today.

Democracy Today

This brings us to the present. Recently new democracies in Eastern Europe have slid towards illiberalism and even populist dictatorship while many long-standing democracies in Western Europe have become mired in social conflict and political extremism. What is going on? Just as we can gain a new perspective on political development in the past by re-examining it through the prism of debates we are having about democracy today, so too can we better understand the present if we know the past. And indeed, if we reflect on what it took to make liberal democracy work after 1945, its weakening over the past decades becomes easier to understand.

As discussed in chapter 14, by the end of the Second World War most of the anti-democratic and anti-liberal vestiges of the old order were gone. This was a necessary but not sufficient condition for consolidating liberal democracy. The tragedy of the interwar years and the Second World War also contributed to the consolidation of liberal democracy by producing a new commitment to making liberal democracy work *and* a new understanding of what it would take to do so. Just as getting rid of the old regime meant not just eliminating its political infrastructure but also its social and economic legacies, so too consolidating liberal democracy was now understood to require more than changing political institutions and procedures—it would require new social and economic arrangements and relationships as well. In particular, the economic crises, inequality, and social divisions that had generated the socioeconomic and communal conflicts and political extremism that had undermined democracy in the past needed to be avoided— and to achieve this, new domestic, regional, and international orders would be necessary.

The United States played a key role in constructing new international security and economic arrangements. Triggered by fears that Western Europe could not alone protect itself from Soviet aggression, President Truman committed the United States to defending Western Europe and liberal democracy with the "Truman Doctrine" and in 1949 NATO was formed, linking West European countries to each other and the United States, and eventually integrating Germany into the Western security bloc. The United States also helped construct international economic institutions, including the Bretton Woods system, GATT, and the IMF, to jumpstart postwar economic reconstruction, promote growth, and link Western Europe and the United States together.

These new American-led international security and economic arrangements were designed to undergird peace and prosperity and also, along with the Marshall Plan, which required recipient nations to decide together how aid was to be used, contributed to the formation of the regional pillar of the postwar order—European integration. Fundamentally, European integration stemmed from the recognition that successful liberal democracy required overcoming challenges too great to be achieved by the uncoordinated efforts of individual governments acting alone. In particular, reconciling Germany to Europe and vice versa and ensuring postwar economic reconstruction and growth would necessitate cooperation and coordination among European nations. This led to the formation of a series of agreements and institutions, beginning with Council of Europe (1949) and the European coal and steel community (1951), that gradually propelled the process of European integration forward (see below).

The final pillar of the tripartite foundation upon which consolidated liberal democracy was built was a new "social democratic" domestic political order.[19] After 1945 West European political economies were reconstructed in a novel way. They were capitalist, but in a different way than before the war—democratic states now tempered or limited capitalism in order to avoid the economic crises, inequality, and social divisions that had led to domestic conflict and political extremism and undermined democracy in the past. This new social democratic order not only generated unprecedented prosperity—the thirty years after 1945 were Europe's fastest period of growth ever—but by spreading the benefits of capitalism more widely it helped eliminate the belief, which as we have seen was prevalent among liberals, Marxists, fascists, and others throughout the nineteenth and first half of the twentieth centuries, that liberal democracy could not or would not respond to all citizens' interests, rather than merely a subset of them. By showing how broadly responsive liberal democracy could be, the postwar order helped undercut the appeal of anti-democratic extremists on the left and right who claimed only non-liberal democratic regimes could truly represent "the people."[20] As a result, during the decades after 1945 the centrifugal political dynamics of the interwar years were transformed into centripetal ones, as good times brought parties and voters back toward the political middle.

During the 1970s, however, all three pillars of the tripartite foundation upon which liberal democracy had been rebuilt after 1945 began to decay, and during the last decade or so they have threatened to disintegrate entirely. As this has occurred many of the pernicious dynamics the postwar order was designed to counteract have reappeared.

The decay of the US-led international order probably began in the 1970s when President Richard Nixon "closed the gold window," bringing an end to the postwar–Bretton Woods monetary system.[21] While this did not signal a wholesale abandonment by the United States of its commitment to Western Europe, it did reflect a decline in the United States' willingness or ability to shoulder the burdens of hegemonic leadership. It also coincided with the rise of neoliberalism, which, as discussed below, weakened the postwar liberal international economic order. And during the last years, the Trump administration has thrown the United States' commitment to this order and its postwar security counterpart into question entirely. (As Germany's former foreign minister Joschka Fischer recently lamented, "The American president is deliberately destroying the American world order."[22]) The decline of American leadership, and of the postwar security and economic arrangements it helped construct, has contributed to a number of destructive trends, including the re-emergence of Russia as a destabilizing force on Europe's periphery and a decline in the West's ability to solve "collective action" problems on issues as varied as globalization, immigration, the environment, and nuclear proliferation.

The regional component of the postwar order—European integration—has also decayed over the past years. This is because the integration process developed a complex set of economic institutions that promoted economic interdependence but neglected to develop a set of political institutions that could promote corresponding political authority or legitimacy.[23] A political deficit appeared during the earliest stages of the integration process. The very foundation of the European project—the 1951 European Coal and Steel Community (ECSC)—set a pattern whereby economic integration far outpaced the development of corresponding political institutions. The goals of the ECSC were explicitly political—ensuring peace and stability in Europe by binding France and Germany so closely together so as to make conflict between them unthinkable. But the means chosen to achieve these ends were economic—the creation of a common market for coal and steel. As Europe's common market expanded to include more countries and more sectors of the economy, the pattern continued. In the 1957 Treaty of Rome, for example, France, Germany, Italy, Belgium, Luxembourg, and the Netherlands agreed to remove all restrictions on trade, institute common external tariffs, reduce barriers to the free movement of people, services, and capital, and develop common agricultural policies, but did little to integrate political decision-making. The result was that by the 1960s, European economic integration had gone further than even early architects of the process could have hoped while political integration and the development of regional political institutions lagged further and further behind.

The bills started to come due in the 1970s. After thirty years of growth and progress, European political economies sank into a noxious bog of unemployment and inflation. As noted above, partially in response, the United States abandoned the gold standard, throwing the postwar monetary order into chaos. European governments responded to these developments with various policies, none of which worked well and some of which, like floating currencies, threatened to lead to conflict among them. In response, European leaders decided to move forward with monetary cooperation and eventually integration.[24]

At the time, this was seen by many as merely the next logical step in the process of economic integration. But with hindsight we can see now that it sowed the seeds of many contemporary problems. It furthered and deepened the political deficit already embedded in the European project, even more so than might have been expected thanks to the spread of neoliberal thinking from the 1970s on.[25] The development of a European monetary union also deprived national governments of a critical economic policy tool: the ability to manipulate the value of their currencies. When the financial crisis hit, along with the overall technocratic and non-democratic nature of the EU, this created terrible economic and political consequences.

Economically, the failure to tie monetary integration to the development of a corresponding regional political authority and the fiscal powers that would go along with it deprived the EU of the ability to respond effectively to the financial crisis. Indeed, the EU's undemocratic, technocratic nature probably made policy-making during the crisis even less effective by insulating "experts" from popular pressure, and hence, the need to reconsider unpopular and ineffective policies.[26]

Politically, however, the consequences of the nature of European integration for the health of liberal democracy were even worse. The EU's technocratic rather than democratic nature generated a backlash against the EU as it became associated with economic problems rather than prosperity. As discussed in previous chapters, non-democratic political orders have two ways to remain in power—via the outcomes they produce, that is, their performance legitimacy, and repression. Lacking coercive abilities, the EU's support came primarily from the former—for much of the postwar period it was associated with the promotion of peace and prosperity. But as memories of the Second World War faded, appreciation of fragility of peace did as well, and the financial crisis largely severed the EU's relationship with prosperity. As the EU's performance legitimacy declined, so did support for it, generating growing demands for a return of national sovereignty and thereby feeding the nationalism and populism that threaten liberal democracy in Europe today. And of course, declining support for the EU has also hindered its ability to take forceful action against democratic backsliding in the East.

The domestic component of the postwar order—social democratic political economies—has also decayed over the past decades. The economic difficulties of the 1970s provided an opening for a neoliberal right that had been organizing and thinking about what it saw as the drawbacks of the postwar order and was ready with explanations for the West's problems as well as solutions to them. This helped it capture the ideological high ground on economic issues during the last decades of the twentieth century and begin freeing markets from many of the restrictions placed on them after 1945. In an ironic echo of postwar convergence, both mainstream left and right broadly accepted this shift. Unfortunately, the shift from a social democratic to a more neoliberal order contributed not only to the financial crisis but helped generate the economic opposite of what existed during the postwar period: slow *and* inequitable growth. In addition, by dialing back social protections at the same time that economic insecurity as well as immigration were increasing, neoliberalism aggravated the potential for social scapegoating and socioeconomic conflict, and weakened social cohesion and national unity. And of course, neoliberal politicians like Ronald Reagan and Margaret Thatcher proclaimed that government was the problem rather than solution, further undermining a central premise of the postwar order, namely that it was the job of democracy to secure the "public good." But as those who lived through the interwar period learned the hard way, when citizens feel "left behind," unsure about their and their country's future, and convinced that their politicians, parties, and governments cannot or will not respond to their needs, polarization and extremism increase, and the foundations of liberal democracy erode.

In short, underlying many of liberal democracy's current problems is a decline of the institutions, structures, and insights of the postwar order. The very success of this order and the "naturalness" with which many of its accomplishments came to be taken, combined with the lack of success of its key competitor—communism—led many to forget how distinctive it was and how important to defend. The result was that by the late twentieth century much of the political establishment forgot what it took to make liberal democracy work after 1945: a democratic state willing and able to assert its authority over markets to ensure that capitalism produced growth and equity, economic and social needs were balanced, and social peace and unity were preserved.

We have also forgotten that before this postwar order emerged, few believed liberal democracy, particularly when paired with capitalism, could satisfy the needs of all citizens. This was of course true of communists, fascists, and National Socialists, all of whom agreed that only some type of dictatorship could protect the interests of "the people" (where they differed was in how they defined the "people" in whose name they would rule—the workers versus an ethnically or culturally defined nation). It was also, however, as we saw in previous chapters, true of many liberals and others on the left: the former because they believed democracy would lead to tyranny of the majority and expropriation by the poor, and the latter because they believed the middle and upper classes would never allow workers to gain power and take away their economic power and privileges. It was only under the postwar order that the idea that liberal democracy could satisfy the needs of all citizens became broadly accepted throughout society and across the political spectrum (see chapter 14).

As this order has declined and many of the problems it had been designed to deal with have reappeared—social and economic divisions and conflict, scapegoating, and extremism—so too have voices on the left and right once again begun questioning the viability and even desirability of liberal democracy.

Populist parties, of course, are the most obvious and dangerous manifestation of this trend. Populist leaders and parties are in power in many parts of Eastern Europe. In Western Europe populism has been growing for decades, but since 2008 such parties have moved from the margins of politics to its center. Populist parties have been included in governments in Austria, Denmark, Norway, and Italy, and the far-right populist AfD became the main opposition party in the German parliament after the 2017 elections. In the Netherlands, France, Sweden, and other European countries populist parties' vote shares continue to rise. Moving from the electoral to the intellectual sphere, criticism of liberal democracy has also exploded. On the right, neo-Hayekian libertarians and public choice scholars criticize the "irresponsibility" of politicians who cater to an uneducated electorate by interfering in otherwise efficient markets. While few would go as far as Hayek, who at times seemed to favor abolishing democracy to "save" markets, concerns about "irresponsible" masses have become commonplace. Books like David Van Reybrouck's *Against Elections*, Jason Brennan's *Against Democracy*, and David Harsanyi's *The People Have Spoken (And They Are Wrong)* no longer raise eyebrows, and voices across the political spectrum increasingly express disdain for rule by "the people." Even mainstream intellectuals like Fareed Zakaria, Alan Blinder, and Andrew Sullivan have argued that the solution to the West's problems lies in making democracy less democratic: more like the European Union or the Federal Reserve—institutions run by elites and insulated from "uninformed" voters and popular pressures. On the left, meanwhile, scholars have argued that the West's current problems are simply a "manifestation of a basic underlying tension" between capitalism and democracy and that "disequilibrium and instability" are the rule rather than the exception. As Wolfgang Streeck, perhaps the most forceful advocate of this view, has put it, it is a "utopian" fantasy to assume democracy and capitalism can be reconciled.[27]

If liberal democracy is once again to flourish—and prove its superiority over its internal (populist) and external (autocratic) critics—a renewed appreciation for what it took to make it work in the past is absolutely necessary. The postwar order was based on a recognition that successful liberal democracy required states that could exert authority over markets in order to ensure that capitalism produced growth and equity, economic and social needs were balanced, and social peace and unity were preserved. Social democratic political economies were embedded in larger regional and international orders that were also crucial for ensuring the peace and prosperity necessary to make liberal democracy work. The decline of the domestic, regional, and international pillars of the postwar order had the predictable, if not predicted[28] result of bringing back many of the problems that undermined liberal democracy before the Second World War. While we are nowhere near the kind of political crisis that characterized the interwar years—since postwar domestic, regional, and international arrangements have decayed but are not yet dead—the consequences for liberal democracy have already been dire.

Conclusion: The Importance of Knowing the Past

This book has argued for the value of a historical perspective—what used to be known as a "political development" approach—for the study of democracy. Such a perspective provides at least three things lacking from many analyses today.

First and most obvious is an appreciation for how much the past influences the present. It is simply impossible to understand the challenges new democracies face as well as the difficulty of overcoming them without knowledge of their pasts. As Marx put it, "The tradition of all dead generations weighs like a nightmare on the brains of the living." Getting rid of these traditions—the legacies of the old regime—is, as we have seen, an extremely long and difficult process. And new democracies' ability to deal with these legacies also depends on their pasts, in particular on the degree and nature of state- and nation-building they have experienced at the time of transition and on whether they have previous democratic experience to build on. "Snapshot" analyses of new democracies that focus on the present, in short, provide incomplete or even misleading accounts of the challenges facing and fate of new democracies.

A second and related contribution of a historical perspective is to provide more realistic criteria by which to judge new democracies. Without knowledge of the past we cannot know what aspects of contemporary cases are distinctive to these cases or the particular time we are living in, rather than fairly common characteristics of political development. For example, there is a strong tendency on the part of contemporary commentators to set high expectations for new democracies—to view post-transition violence, corruption, confusion, and incompetence as signs that countries are not "ready" for democracy; the implicit historical assumption here, of course, is that "normal" democratic transitions lead smoothly to stable liberal democracy and countries that stumble along the way must have something wrong with them—and would therefore be better off under dictatorships. But as we have seen, viewing post-transition problems as a sign that a country is not "ready" for democracy is unwise—such problems often reflect the difficulty of eliminating the social and economic as well as political legacies of dictatorship. In addition, countries that stumble along the way to democracy are the norm rather than the exception: liberal democracy usually emerges only at the end of long, often violent, struggle, with many twists, turns, false starts, and detours from the high road.

Americans have particular difficulty grappling with the chaotic and circuitous nature of democratic development, and here too a better understanding of the past can help. We commonly think of our country as having always been a liberal democracy and thus assume democracy is "natural" or at least fairly easy to achieve. But using common political science standards, the United States was not, in fact, a fully liberal democracy until the second half of the twentieth century. Before the Civil War an entire section of the United States—the South—was a tyrannical oligarchy and it took the bloodiest conflict in our history—the Civil War—to *begin* changing this, and another century before the political and legal infrastructure of liberal democracy was fully in place. It was only in the 1960s that the national government was able, or willing, to ensure that democratic and liberal rights were enjoyed by *all* citizens, including African Americans. Moreover, even though the political and legal infrastructure of liberal democracy was finally in place by the 1960s, the economic and social legacies of our old regime—in the form of racial inequalities and animosities and a national identity that while inclusive in theory had long been exclusionary in practice—remained, and continue to mar the functioning of American liberal democracy up through the present day.

A third contribution of a historical perspective is to provide a better understanding of what it actually took to make democracy work in Europe— and thus insight into the problems facing its established democracies today.

Consolidated liberal democracy only came to Europe in the second half of the twentieth century. As we have seen, this occurred in two "stages." The first, getting rid of the political, social, and economic legacies of the old regime, began in 1789 and was essentially completed by the end of the Second World War. This was a necessary but not sufficient condition for consolidating liberal democracy. The second stage was building the political, social, and economic infrastructure of a new liberal democratic order to replace the old one. It took the tragedies of the interwar period and the Second World War to achieve this: by 1945 a consensus emerged on the desirability of liberal democracy as well as a new understanding of what it would take to make it work. New domestic, regional, and international orders were accordingly constructed during the postwar period and were designed to avoid the economic crises and social divisions that had led to extremism and dissatisfaction with democracy in the past. Over the past decades these orders have declined, and with this decline has come a return of some of the problems that undermined liberal democracy in the past.

The consolidation of liberal democracy after 1945 depended not only on its performance—although the period of peace and prosperity characterizing the postwar decades was crucial—but rather on the more general sense that liberal democracy was capable of responding to the needs of all citizens. As noted in chapter 1, democracy literally means "rule by the people." While this term is more ambiguous or complicated than it may initially seem, at the very least it means that people get to choose their own leaders and governments, and that these leaders and governments are able and willing to respond to their needs and concerns. But what if people no longer feel like they rule? If they come to view leaders and governments as impotent and/or unresponsive? If rather than the needs of average citizens, political outcomes are seen as being determined by markets, technocrats, international organizations, businesses, or the wealthy? As we have seen over and over again in European history, when there is a mismatch between citizens' demands and expectations and the willingness or ability of political institutions to respond to them, the outcome is disorder and instability.[29]

This is, of course, the situation much of Europe and the United States are in today. A belief in the efficacy and responsiveness of liberal democracy has declined, and with this has come a willingness to support politicians and parties with serious, even radical critiques, of the reigning order. This is not the first time since 1945 that the liberal democratic order has come under attack: in the 1960s, significant critiques of the status quo were raised by myriad groups in Western Europe and the United States, accompanied by protests, disorder, and even violence. But liberal democracy was able to respond to demands for fuller incorporation of hitherto excluded groups like women and minorities and fuller recognition of new concerns like environmentalism, and so dissatisfaction and extremism diminished over time. Whether or not we are living in the midst of another such cycle or are experiencing a true interregnum—a time when an old order is dying but a new one has not yet taken its place—is unclear. Here

European political history might have one final lesson to teach: societies cannot overcome their problems unless and until they are squarely faced. Throughout European history it has often taken tragedies like democratic collapse, violent dictatorships, and war to force elites and publics to recognize the value of liberal democracy and what it takes to actually make it work. Let's hope this is one lesson of history that does not need to be re-learned.

NOTES

Chapter 1

1. C.E. Sagan, author and presenter, Episode 2: "One Voice in the Cosmic Fugue," in *Cosmos: A Personal Voyage*, produced by Adrian Malone (Arlington, VA: Public Broadcasting Service, 1980).

2. State of the Union Address 1992. https://www.nytimes.com/1992/01/29/us/state-union-transcript-president-bush-s-address-state-union.html?pagewanted=all.

3. See, e.g., Edward Luce, *The Retreat of Western Liberalism* (New York: Atlantic Monthly Press, 2017), who invokes Wordsworth's words to capture the mood as he rushed with his friends to watch the wall collapse.

4. See, e.g., William Drozdiak, *Fractured Continent: Europe's Crises and the Fate of the West* (New York: W.W. Norton, 2017).

5. Lucan Way, "The Authoritarian Threat," *Journal of Democracy* 37, no. 1 (January 2016); Christian von Soest, "Democracy Prevention: The International Collaboration of Authoritarian Regimes," *European Journal of Political Research* 54, no. 4 (November 2015); Rachel Vanderhill, *Promoting Authoritarianism Abroad* (New York: Lynne Reiner, 2013); Larry Diamond, Marc Plattner, and Christopher Walken, eds., *Authoritarianism Goes Global* (Baltimore: Johns Hopkins University Press, 2016); Roberto Stephan Foa and Yascha Mounk, "The Danger of Deconsolidation," *The Journal of Democracy* 27, no. 3 (July 2016); and Foa and Mounk, "The Signs of Deconsolidation," *Journal of Democracy* 33, no. 1 (January 2017).

6. "Secure in Hungary, Orban Readies for Battle with Brussels," *New York Times*, May 11, 2018. https://www.nytimes.com/2018/05/11/world/europe/hungary-victor-orban-immigration-europe.html.

7. The work of such historians and political scientists is therefore embedded deeply in all chapters of this book.

8. See, e.g., Yascha Mounk, *The People versus Democracy* (Cambridge, MA: Harvard University Press, 2018) and Steven Levitsky and Daniel Ziblatt, *How Democracies Die* (New York: Penguin, 2018).

9. Hector Schamis and Ariel Armory, "Babel in Democratization Studies," *Journal of Democracy* 16, no. 4 (2005): 113–28; David Collier and Robert Adcock, "Democracy and Dichotomies: A Pragmatic Approach to Choices about Concepts," *Annual Review of Political Science* 2 (1999): 537–65; David Collier and Steven Levitsky, "Democracy with Adjectives: Conceptual Innovation in Comparative Research," *World Politics* 49 (1997): 430–51.

10. Actually, the etymology seems to be a little more complicated, with the English word derived from the Middle French *democratie* (*démocratie*), which comes in turn from the Medieval Latin *democratia*, which came from the Ancient Greek δημοκρατία (*dēmokratia*).

11. Because Schumpeter's views have been so influential, this definition of democracy is sometimes referred to as the "Schumpeterian definition of democracy." Schumpeter's views are concentrated in chapters 21 and 22 of *Capitalism, Socialism and Democracy* (New York: Harper and Brothers, 1942), 250–52.

12. Edward Djerejian, "The U.S. and the Middle East in a Changing World: Address at Meridian House International," U.S. Department of State Dispatch, June 2, 1992.

13. Quoted in Fareed Zakaria, *The Future of Freedom* (New York: Norton, 2007), 18.

14. As always, in other words, there is a price to pay. In particular, some scholars believe that the benefits of the liberal definition's greater accuracy are outweighed by costs in terms of parsimony. Once the Pandora's box of democratic "requirements" is opened, it is hard to know how to close it. While most observers would probably agree that things like the protection of minority rights, the rule of law, and limitations on government power belong in any definition of liberal democracy, other qualities are less easily agreed upon. So for example, should limits on the military be included in a definition of democracy? How about a minimum level of welfare provision? Or, what about explicit limits on executive power (vis-à-vis the legislature)? All of these have been proposed by some scholars as necessary to ensure that citizens are "truly" able to enjoy/exercise basic liberal rights. What "background conditions," in other words, are truly necessary to ensure the full flourishing of individual liberal rights? And then, of course, we must be sure not to confuse the development of democracy and the development of liberalism. Find more on this below.

15. All the main rating agencies, including Freedom House, Polity, and the Varieties of Democracy Institute, accordingly differentiate between liberal and electoral democracies, or their equivalent, e.g., free, partly free, and unfree countries.

16. Sheri Berman, "The Pipe Dream of Undemocratic Liberalism," *Journal of Democracy* 28, no. 3 (July 2017).

17. Fareed Zakaria for example has argued that democratic experiments embarked on in countries without a prior history of liberalism (operationalized as the rule of law and a state willing and able to protect individual freedom) are likely to run into trouble. Similarly Ed Mansfield and Jack Snyder have argued that "ill-prepared attempts to democratize" countries "where the institutional requisites for successful consolidation are not yet in place . . . may lead to costly warfare in the short run, and may delay or prevent real progress toward democracy over the long term." Zakaria, *The Future of Freedom*; Mansfield and Snyder, *Electing to Fight*, pages 265, 3.

18. Andreas Schedler, "What Is Democratic Consolidation?" *Journal of Democracy* 9, no. 2 (April 1998).

19. See, e.g., Juan Linz and Alfred Stepan, "Toward Consolidated Democracies," *Journal of Democracy* (1996); Larry Diamond, *Developing Democracy: Toward Consolidation* (Baltimore: Johns Hopkins University Press, 1999).

20. Assuming the English commonwealth doesn't count, a question that will be taken up in chapter 3.

Chapter 2

1. Turgot in a confidential report to the king, quoted in Tocqueville, *The Old Regime and the French Revolution*, p. 107, with some help from Hilton Root, *The Fountain of Privilege: Political Foundations of Markets in Old Regime France and England* (Berkeley: University of California Press, 1994), 236.

2. Alexis de Tocqueville, *The Old Regime and the French Revolution* (New York: Anchor Books, 1985), Part 3, chapter 8, p. 210.

3. William Doyle, *The Ancien régime* (New York: Palgrave Macmillan, 2001), 1.

4. As one influential advocate of royal absolutism described it: "Consider the Prince in his cabinet. From there issue the orders which set in motion together the magistrates and the captains, the citizens and the soldiers, the provinces and the armies by sea and land. This is the image of God, who directs all nature from his throne in the highest heaven." Jacques Bossuet, *Politics Drawn from the Holy Scripture* (New York: Cambridge University Press, 1990), 160.

   As discussed further below, the term "absolutism" can be misleading, since the king's power was not truly absolute. Most obviously in France, as in most other "absolutist" monarchies, the king still had to contend with the nobility and the Church. See, e.g., Richard Bonney, "Absolutism: What's in a Name?" *French History* 1, no. 1 (1987).

5. Theodore Rabb, *The Struggle for Stability in Early Modern Europe* (New York: Oxford University Press, 1975); Geoffrey Parker, "Crisis and Catastrophe: The Global Crisis of the Seventeenth Century," *American Historical Review* 113, no. 4 (October 2008).

6. Of course, they did not view themselves as laying the foundation of modern states; this is a retrospective observation. What kings were interested in was increasingly their power and authority and extracting the resources necessary to do so.

7. Norman Davies, *Vanished Kingdoms: The Rise and Fall of States and Nations* (New York: Viking, 2011).

8. M.S. Anderson, *War and Society in Europe of the Old Regime 1618–1789* (Montreal: McGill-Queen's University Press, 1998), 15; Mark Greengrass, *Conquest and Coalescence* (New York: Edward Arnold, 1991), 2; Saskia Sassen, *Territory, Authority, and Rights: From Medieval to Global Assemblages* (Princeton, NJ: Princeton University Press, 2006).

9. I use the term "king" for convenience sake, but rulers could also be princes, dukes, or bishops.

10. Reflecting this, the political units of the time are often referred to as "composite monarchies." See Dan Nexon, *The Struggle for Power in Early Modern Europe* (Princeton, NJ: Princeton University Press, 2009), 7; J.S. Elliot, "A Europe of Composite Monarchies," *Past and Present* 137 (November 1992).

11. J.H. Elliot, *Europe Divided 1559–1598* (New York: Harper and Row, 1968), 73.

12. Janice Thomson, *Mercenaries, Pirates, and Sovereigns* (Princeton, NJ: Princeton University Press, 1994), 3.

13. S.R. Epstein, *Freedom and Growth: The Rise of States and Markets in Europe, 1300–1750* (New York: Routledge, 2000).

14. Janice Thomson, *Mercenaries, Pirates, and Sovereigns* (Princeton, NJ: Princeton University Press, 1994).

15. Peter H. Wilson, *The Thirty Years War: Europe's Tragedy* (Cambridge, MA: Harvard University Press, 2009).

16. In fact, because of the confused and changing nature of authority during this time, it can be difficult to distinguish between international and civil wars. The most important conflict of this time, the Thirty Years' War, is a good example of this. Anderson, *War and Society*, pp. 14–15. Also Charles, Louise, and Richard Tilly, *The Rebellious Century, 1830–1930* (Cambridge, MA: Harvard University Press, 1975); Michael Mann, *The Sources of Social Power*, vol. II (New York: Cambridge University Press, 1993), chapter 12; and Geoffrey Best, *War and Society in Revolutionary Europe* (New York: St Martin's Press, 1982).

17. Geoffrey Parker and Lesley Smith, *The General Crisis of the Seventeenth Century* (New York: Routledge, 1997), 47; Perez Zagorian, *Rebels and Rulers, 1500–1660* (New York: Cambridge University Press, 1982); see also Theodore K. Rabb, *The Struggle for Stability in Early Modern Europe* (New York: Oxford University Press, 1975); Trevor Aston, ed., *Crisis in Europe 1560–1660* (New York: Basic Books, 1965); Jack Goldstone, *Revolution and Rebellion in the Early Modern World* (Berkeley: University of California Press, 1991); Geoffrey Treasure, *The Making of Modern Europe* (New York: Methuen, 1985).

18. A Parisian judge in 1652, quoted in Geoffrey Parker, "Crisis and Catastrophe: The Global Crisis of the Seventeenth Century," *American Historical Review* 113, no. 4 (October 2008): 1057.

19. Nannerl Keohane, *Philosophy and the State in France: The Renaissance to the Enlightenment* (Princeton, NJ: Princeton University Press, 1980), 70; Thomas Hobbes, *Leviathan* (New York: Penguin Classics, 1982), part 1, chapter 13.

20. A classic "Tilley-esque" situation. Charles Tilly, "Reflections on the History of European State-Making," in Tilly, ed., *The Formation of National States in Western Europe* (Princeton, NJ: Princeton University Press, 1975), 42; also Tilly, *Coercion, Capital, and European States, AD 990–1990* (Cambridge, MA: Blackwell Publishers, 1990).

21. Encyclopédie methodique: jurisprudence, quoted in Peter M. Jones, *Reform and Revolution in France: The Politics of Transition, 1774–1791* (Cambridge: Cambridge University Press, 1995), 58.

22. David Parker, *The Making of French Absolutism* (New York: St. Martin's Press, 1983); Samuel Clark, *State and Status* (Montreal: McGill-Queen's University Press, 1995), 33ff.

23. Ann Katherine Isaac and Maarten Prak, "Cities, Bourgeoisies and States," in Wolfgang Reinhard, ed. *Power Elites and State Building* (New York: Oxford Unversity Press, 1996), ed. Reinhard, 214; Clark, *State and Status*, 38ff.

24. R.J. Knecht, *French Renaissance Monarchy* (London: Longman Group, 1996), 1; Robin Briggs, *Early Modern France 1560–1715* (New York: Oxford University Press, 1998).

25. Philip Hoffman, "Early Modern France, 1450–1700," in *Fiscal Crises, Liberty, and Representative Government, 1450–1789*, ed. Philip Hoffman and Kathryn Norberg (Palo Alto, CA: Stanford University Press, 1994), 227. Huguenot areas went perhaps the furthest in this regard, being allowed to keep their own troops, fortresses, and authority structures. Zagorin, *Rebels and Rulers*; A.D. Lublinskaya, *French Absolutism* (New York: Cambridge University Press, 1968); Pierre Goubert, *Louis XIV and Twenty Million Frenchmen* (New York: Pantheon Books, 1996).

26. And lest we romanticize these nobles, especially in comparison to their contemporary counterparts, here is one scholar's description of them: "Many noblemen . . . were nothing short of petty tyrants or gangsters who embraced violence as a way of life. Not only did they take up arms against royal magistrates and tax officials . . . they also waged war against the peasantry, and frequently fought to the death among themselves as a matter of course . . . Moliere, of course, has given us an enduring image of this petty tyrant in the character of Don Juan, a blasphemer, womanizer, duelist, thief and murderer who recognizes no law, either earthly or divine, except that of his own sadistic will." Robert Schneider, "Swordplay and Statemaking," in *Statemaking and Social Movements*, ed. Charles Bright and Susan Harding (Ann Arbor: University of Michigan Press, 1984), 273–74.

27. Bendix, *Kings or People*, 339; Zagorin, *Rebels and Rulers*, esp. 6; Greengrass, *Conquest and Coalescence*; and James Collins, *The State in Early Modern France* (New York: Cambridge University Press, 1995).

28. Donna Bohanan, *Crown and Nobility in Early Modern France* (New York: Palgrave, 2001), 32.

29. Edward Fox Whiting, *The Emergence of the Modern European World* (Cambridge: Blackwell, 1991), 6; Douglas Johnson, "The Making of the French Nation," in *The National Question in Europe in Historical Context*, ed. Mikulas Teich and Roy Porter (New York: Cambridge University Press, 1993), 43. See also William Church, "Introduction," in *The Impact of Absolutism in France*, ed. Church (New York: John Wiley & Sons, 1969).

30. This is not to say that centralization was a unilinear process, nor that some centralization had not occurred during earlier periods, but during the early modern period a new era began. Clark, *State and Status*.

31. Woloch, *Eighteenth Century Europe*, 8–10.

32. Richelieu in his *Testament Politique*, quoted in J.H. Elliott, *Richelieu and Olivares* (New York: Cambridge University Press, 1984), 64–65.

33. Charles Tilly, *Contention and Democracy in Europe, 1650–2000* (New York: Cambridge University Press, 2004), 99.

34. Again to quote Bacon on this period: "The Kingdom of France . . . is now fallen into those calamities, that, as the prophet saith, 'From the crown of the head to the sole of the foot, there is no whole place.'" Quoted in Zagorin, *Rebels and Rulers*, vol. II, p. 58.

35. William Doyle, *Old Regime France, 1648–1788* (New York: Oxford University Press, 2001), 3. Peter Bickle, *Resistance, Repression and Community* (Oxford: Clarendon Press, 1997), 68ff.

36. In addition, the destructiveness of the *Fronde*, against the backdrop of so much previous conflict, created a strong desire for peace, order, and stability, which the king seemed most likely to be able to provide. Blickle, *Resistance, Repression and Community*; Richard Dunn, *The Age of Religious Wars, 1559–1689* (New York: W.W. Norton, 1970), 31.

37. Bohanan, *Crown and Nobility*, 61; Root, *The Fountain of Privilege*, 14, 15, and 18; Edgar Kiser and April Linton, "The Hinges of History: State-Making and Revolt in Early Modern France," *American Sociological Review* 67 (2002).

38. Root, *The Fountain of Privilege*, 14, 15, and 18.

39. Zagorin, *Rebels and Rulers, 1500–1660*, vol. 1 (New York: Cambridge University Press, 1982); Kiser and April, "The Hinges of History."

40. Louis XIII and XIV were not the first French monarchs to make use of venality, but they expanded the practice in politically consequential ways. William Doyle, *Venality: The Sale of Offices in Eighteenth Century France* (New York: Oxford University Press, 1996); William Doyle, *Officers, Nobles, and Revolutionaries* (London: Hambledon Press, 1995); Colin Jones, *The Great*

Nation (New York: Columbia University Press, 2002), 57; and K.W. Swart, *Sale of Offices in the Seventeenth Century* (The Hague: M. Nijhoff, 1949).

41. John Gagliardo, *Enlightened Despotism* (New York: Thomas Cromwell, 1970), 62.

42. Doyle, *Venality*, 9–10.

43. Barrington Moore, *Social Origins of Dictatorship and Democracy* (Boston: Beacon Press, 1966), 59.

44. Hence, the title of Root's *Fountain of Privilege*; see Doyle, *Old Regime France*, 52.

45. Doyle, *Venality*, 12.

46. Alfred Cobban, *A History of Modern France, Volume I: 1715–1799* (Baltimore: Penguin Books, 1961), 13; Root, *Fountain*, esp. 18.

47. William Beik, *Absolutism and Society in Seventeenth Century France* (New York: Cambridge University Press, 1985); William Doyle, "The Sale of Offices in French History," *History Today*, September 1996, p. 42.

48. Charles Loyseau, quoted in Robert Harding, *Anatomy of a Power Elite* (New Haven, CT: Yale University Press, 1978), 7.

49. Bohanan, *Crown and Nobility*, 57.

50. Kettering, *Patrons, Clients and Brokers*, esp. 99ff.

51. Kettering, *Patrons, Clients and Brokers*, 75.

52. These *intendants'* positions were salaried rather than venal and appointed rather than purchased. Since they were "removable at the King's pleasure, they were in every respect the King's men and could at least rival if not altogether displace the local elites." Isser Woloch, *Eighteenth Century Europe* (New York: W.W. Norton, 1982), 8–10; Vivian Gruder, *The Royal Provincial Intendants* (Ithaca, NY: Cornell University Press, 1968). Although they had existed in the past, by the 1630s *intendants* had become more numerous and more powerful and began developing "many of the features of a permanent organization." Briggs, *Early Modern France*, 119–20; Richard Bonney, *Political Change in France under Richelieu and Mazarin 1624–1661* (New York: Oxford University Press, 1978), 30; Harding, *Anatomy*, 216–17; and Charles Godard, "The Historical Role of the Intendants," in *The Impact of Absolutism*, ed. Church.

53. Dunn, *The Age of Religious Wars*, 138ff; Antoni Maczak, "The Nobility-State Relationship," in *Power Elites and State Building*, ed. Reinhard, 245; Beik, *Absolutism and Society*, 318; Goubert, *Louis XIV*, 89.

54. William Doyle, *The Oxford History of the French Revolution* (New York: Oxford University Press, 2002), 41–42.

55. Collins, *The State in Early Modern France*, 136ff.

56. Kettering, *Patronage in Sixteenth and Seventeenth Century France*, 159ff.

57. Doyle, *Old Regime France*, 59. As one observer put it, "A nobleman, if he lives at home in his province, lives free but without substance; if he lives at court, he is taken care of, but enslaved," quote in Franklin Ford, *Robe and Sword: The*

Regrouping of the French Aristocracy after Louis XIV (Cambridge, MA: Harvard University Press, 1953), vii.

58. Alexis de Tocqueville, *The Old Regime and the French Revolution* (New York: Anchor Books, 1955), 30, 204.

59. Jones, *The Great Nation*, 53.

60. Parker, *The Making of French Absolutism*, 122.

61. The edict had granted toleration to Protestants. With this move, Louis XIV forced Protestants to choose between conversion and exile: after 1685 French Protestants no longer had civil rights; their clergy were exiled or jailed, their possessions could be confiscated, and their children were encouraged to convert to Catholicism. Of course, the departure of many Huguenots had many negative consequences as well, especially in the economic realm.

62. As noted earlier, religious conflict had torn France apart during the previous century and the Huguenots had resisted encroachments upon their privileges. As Richelieu put it, "As long as the Huguenots have a foothold in France, the king will never be master in his own house." Quoted in Victor-L. Tapié, *France in the Age of Louis XIII and Richelieu* (New York: Praeger, 1975), 148.

63. See, e.g., H.G. Koeningsberger and George Mosse, *Europe in the Sixteenth Century* (New York: Holt, Rinehart and Winston, 1968), 252.

64. At the time of Louis XIV's accession the French Army had about 20,000 men; by 1688 it had between 150,000 and 400,000 men (depending on whether it was peace or wartime). See, e.g., Woloch, *Eighteenth Century Europe*, 51; H.G. Koenigsberger, *Early Modern Europe* (London: Longman Group, 1987), 185; Briggs, *Early Modern France*, 141–42; Parker, *The Making of French Absolutism*, 149; Guy Rowlands, *The Dynastic State and the Army under Louis XIV* (New York: Cambridge University Press, 2002).

65. This transformation is the reason why so many praised Louis XIV as the savior of France. As Voltaire put it, "the spirit of faction, strife and rebellion which had possessed the people since the time of Francis II, was transformed into a rivalry to serve their king." Voltaire, "Louis XIV: Builder of France," in *The Impact of Absolutism*, ed. Church, 137–38. See also William Church, ed., *The Greatness of Louis XIV* (Boston: Heath and Co., 1959); and Pierre Goubert, *Louis XIV and Twenty Million Frenchmen* (New York: Pantheon Books, 1966).

66. Unusual since after disappearing during the early modern period, Poland was resurrected during the twentieth century, which helps explain why it is easier studied than those that disappeared forever.

67. Norman Davis, *God's Playground: A History of Poland* (New York: Columbia University Press, 1982), 160, 386. Or, as Gale Stokes put it, "The Polish nobility considered themselves the freest men in Europe, and they were, but they also ruled what increasingly became the weakest state in Europe." Stokes, *Three Eras of Political Change in Eastern Europe* (New York: Oxford University Press, 1997), 12.

68. Jan Glete, *War and the State in Early Modern Europe* (New York: Routledge, 2002).

69. George Rude, *Europe in the Eighteenth Century: Aristocracy and the Bourgeois Challenge* (London: Phoenix Press, 2002); I.A.A. Thompson, "Absolutism in Castille," in *Crown and Cortes*; and E.N. Williams, *The Ancien Régime in Europe* (New York: Harper and Row, 1970).

70. I.A.A. Thompson, "The Government of Spain in the Reign of Philip IV," reprinted in *Crown and Cortes* (Brookfield, VA: Ashgate, 1993), 84.

71. E.N. Williams, *The Ancien Régime in Europe* (New York: Harper and Row, 1970), 67, 121–22. Also, Geoffrey Treasure, *The Making of Modern Europe, 1648–1780* (New York: Methuen, 1985), 340; I.A.A. Thompson, "Castile: Polity, Fiscality and Fiscal Crisis," in *Fiscal Crises, Liberty, and Representative Government, 1450–1789*, ed. Hoffman and Norberg; and H.M. Scott, *Enlightened Absolutism: Reform and Reformers in Later Eighteenth Century Europe* (Ann Arbor: University of Michigan Press, 1990).

72. Thompson, "Absolutism in Castille," 89–90.

73. Hans Rosenberg, *Bureaucracy, Aristocracy and Autocracy* (Boston: Beacon, 1958), 27–28.

74. Christopher Clark, *Iron Kingdom: The Rise and Downfall of Prussia, 1600–1947* (Cambridge, MA: Harvard University Press, 2006), xvi; Williams, *The Ancien*, 292.

75. Clark, *Iron Kingdom*, 111.

76. Clark, *Iron Kingdom*, 63.

77. Friedrich von Schrötter (1743–1815), Prussian Junker and government minister. Very few officers came from outside the nobility.

78. Rude, *Europe in the Eighteenth Century*, 75.

79. Clark, *Iron Kingdom*, 99. Also see Isser Woloch, *Eighteenth Century Europe* (New York: Norton, 1982), esp. 89ff; Mary Fulbrook, *Piety and Politics: Religion and the Rise of Absolutism in England, Wurttemberg and Prussia* (New York: Cambridge University Press, 1983).

80. Rosenberg, *Bureaucracy, Aristocracy and Autocracy*; Robert Berdhal, *The Politics of the Prussia Nobility* (Princeton, NJ: Princeton University Press, 1988).

81. Clark, *Iron Kingdom*, 155. Interestingly, the only nobility with a similar share of land was the English. This will be discussed below and in subsequent chapters.

82. Williams, *The Ancien Régime*, 326.

83. Liah Greenfeld, *Nationalism: Five Roads to Modernity* (Cambridge, MA: Harvard University Press, 1992), 289, 292.

84. Although this refers only to England. If we include Scotland and Ireland in the equation things look much more complicated. And indeed, unifying all the territories of the British Isles was a long and difficult process that dragged on until the eighteenth century and beyond. This will be discussed below and in subsequent chapters.

85. H.G. Koeningsberger, *Medieval Europe, 400–1500* (London: Longman, 1987); Clark, *State and Status*; Deborah Boucoyannis, *Laws, Courts and*

Parliaments: The Hidden Sinews of Power in the Emergence of Constitutionalism (New York: Cambridge University Press, forthcoming).

86. Pitrim Sorokin, quoted in Christopher Hill, *Reformation to Industrial Revolution* (Baltimore: Penguin Books, 1969), 119. See also J.H. Plumb, *The Growth of Political Stability in England 1675–1725* (London: MacMillan, 1967), 1. Also see James Mervyn, *Society, Politics, and Culture: Studies in Early Modern England* (New York: Cambridge University Press, 1986).

87. G.R. Elton, *England under the Tudors* (London: Methuen, 1955), 10, but again see Boucoyannis and Clark, *State and Status*, for longer-term perspectives.

88. Elton, *England under the Tudors?*; Boucoyannis and Clark, *State and Status?* But also Christopher Coleman and David Starkey, *Revolution Reassessed* (Oxford: Clarendon Press, 1986); Breden Bradshaw, "The Tudor Commonwealth: Reform and Revision," *The Historical Journal* 22, no. 2 (June 1979). As Lawrence Stone notes, the move to London "distracted them from the dangerous rural pastimes of riot and rebellion and . . . occupied them in time-consuming ceremony and intrigue, both of which centered round the Prince and tended to enhance his prestige and his authority. As the Earl of Northumberland was told in 1566, an absentee landlord could not command the same personal loyalty as a man living on the spot, and in any case potential traitors were more easily watched and their plots more swiftly intercepted if they were at Court than if they were lurking undisturbed in their rural strongholds . . . [By] attracting the nobility to court by the lure of office and rewards [the King helped] turn them from haughty and independent magnates into a set of shameless mendicants." Stone, *Crisis of the Aristocracy, 1558–1641* (New York: Oxford University Press, 1965), 191, 218.

89. W.T. MacCaffery, "Place and Patronage in Elizabethan Politics," in *Elizabethan Government and Society*, ed. J. Hurstfield, C.H. Williams, and S.T. Bindoff (London: University of London Press, 1961); Diarmaid MacColluh, *Suffolk and the Tudors* (Oxford: Clarendon Press, 1986). It is important to stress, however, that the scale of venality in England was not in the same category as in France. See Swart, *The Sale of Offices and Ertman, Birth of the Leviathan.*

90. John Gay, *Tudor England* (New York: Oxford University Press, 1988), 157, 352.

Chapter 3

1. J.H. Plumb, *The Growth of Political Stability in England, 1675–1725* (London: The Macmillan Press, 1967), xviii.

2. J.G.A. Pocock, *The British Revolutions 1641, 1688, 1776* (Princeton, NJ: Princeton University Press, 1980), 24; Jonathan Scott, *England's Troubles: Seventeenth Century English Political Instability in European Context* (New York: Cambridge University Press, 2000), esp. 29.

3. Or as Edward Thompson put it, the English entered the modern age "at the genteel pace of a cricket match, with breaks for lunch and tea, instead of in one massive upheaval." Quoted in Philip Hoffman and Kathryn Norberg, *Fiscal Crises, Liberty and Representative Government, 1450–1789* (Palo Alto, CA: Stanford University Press, 1994), 15.

4. Mark Kishlansky, *A Monarchy Transformed: Britain 1603–1714* (New York: Penguin Books, 1996), 55–56. But see also Deborah Boucoyannis on the long history and "backstory" of Parliament, and how that affected the relationship between the king and nobility in England.

5. The Star Chamber was originally set up to deal with cases that could not be dealt with by the regular justice system. Its sessions were held in secret and controlled by the monarch and his counselors.

6. David Smith, *A History of the Modern British Isles* (Malden, MA: Blackwell, 1998), 80.

7. Conrad Russell, *The Causes of the English Civil War* (Oxford: Clarendon Press, 1990), 183. Also see Michael Howard, *War in European History* (New York: Oxford University Press, 2009); Brian Downing, *The Military Revolution and Political Change* (Princeton, NJ: Princeton University Press, 1992).

8. Simon Schama, *A History of Britain, Vol. II: The Wars of the British 1603–1776* (New York: Hyperion, 2001), 80.

9. See, e.g., H.G. Koeningsberger and George Mosse, *Europe in the Sixteenth Century* (New York: Holt, Rinehart and Winston, 1968), 252.

10. Russell, *The Causes of the English Civil War*, 63.

11. Edwin Jones, *The English Nation: The Great Myth* (London: Sutton, 1998); Christopher Hill, *The Century of Rebellion, 1603–1714* (New York: W.W. Norton, 1982), 2; and Derek Hirst, *Authority and Conflict: England 1603–1658* (Cambridge, MA: Harvard University Press, 1986), esp. 60ff. Although covering a later period, see also Linda Colley, *Britons: Forging the Nation 1707–1837* (New Haven, CT: Yale University Press, 1992). (Fears of Catholicism were, of course, furthered by the fact that many of the most powerful states of the day [e.g., France and Spain] were resolutely Catholic.)

12. Lawrence Stone, *Causes of the English Revolution, 1529–1642* (New York: Routledge, 2002), 116. See also Michael Walzer, *The Revolution of the Saints: A Study in the Origin of Radical Politics* (Cambridge, MA: Harvard University Press, 1965); G.E. Aylmer, *Rebellion or Revolution: England from Civil War to Restoration* (New York: Oxford University Press, 1987), esp. 45–46.

13. Schama, *A History of Britain*, vol. II, p. 102.

14. Mary Fulbrook, *Piety and Politics: Religion and the Rise of Absolutism in England, Wurttemberg and Prussia* (New York: Cambridge University Press, 1983); Daniel Nexon, *The Struggle for Power in Early Modern Europe* (Princeton, NJ: Princeton University Press, 2009).

15. Stone, *Causes of the English Revolution*, 129.

16. Stone, *Causes of the English Revolution*, 131; Jack Goldstone, *Revolution and Rebellion in the Early Modern World* (Berkeley: University of California Press, 1993).

17. H.G. Koeningsberger, *Medieval Europe, 400–1500* (London: Longman, 1987); Deborah Boucoyannis, "From Roving to Stationary Judges: Power, Land, and the Origins of Representative Institutions," book manuscript, forthcoming.

18. Kishlansky, *A Monarchy Transformed*, 78.

19. Gordon Donaldson, "Foundations of the Anglo-Scottish Union," in *Elizabethan Government and Society: Essays Presented to John Neale*, ed. J. Hurstfield, C.H. Williams, and S.T. Bindoff (London: University of London Athlone Press, 1961), 283–84.

20. Fulbrook, *Piety and Politics*, 92.

21. Russell, *The Causes of the English Civil War*, 34.

22. John Adamson, *The Noble Revolt: The Overthrow of Charles I* (London: Weidenfeld & Nicolson, 2007).

23. And, if the king refused to call a Parliament, Parliament now had the right to come into session without the Crown's explicit consent.

24. What is odd about the British Isles during this time is that several different kinds of political relationships co-existed. Wales had been more or less fully integrated into the English state: the Welsh and English shared one Parliament, one Church, and one legal system. Ireland was in a pseudo-colonial relationship with England, clearly subordinate to it but having still its own Parliament, legal system, and of course, religion (although the first two were not fully independent and the last was repressed). Scotland, finally, occupied yet a third position vis-à-vis England. Although clearly weaker than England, it was an equally sovereign state, despite being under the rule of the same monarch. Its Parliament, legal system, and Church remained separate from England's, and unlike Ireland's, fairly independent of it. Of course, it was precisely Charles's desire to "move" Scotland in an "Irish" or perhaps even "Welsh" direction that started the conflict in the first place.

25. The king's supporters came to be known as "Cavaliers," reflecting their purportedly aristocratic pretensions and dress, while Parliament's supporters were called "Roundheads," which derived from the closely cropped hair favored by Puritans (which made their heads look round and contrasted with the fancy hairstyles favored by aristocrats).

26. Hirst, *Authority and Conflict*, 257; Smith, *A History of the Modern British Isles*, 147.

27. Extracts from the debates at the General Council of the Army, Putney, October 29, 1647, accessed at http://www.constitution.org/lev/eng_lev_08.htm.

28. Schama, *A History of Britain*, vol. II, p. 156.

29. Quoted in Aylmer, *Rebellion or Revolution?*, 99.

30. Schama, *A History of Britain*, vol. II, p. 155.

31. Christopher Hill, *The World Turned Upside Down: Radical Ideas during the English Revolution* (New York: Penguin, 1991).

32. During the war Charles sent an emissary to Ireland. The emissary promised the Irish religious toleration in return for their support of the royalist cause. Although Charles later said the emissary had gone too far, the Irish clearly felt they would get a better deal from Charles than from the New Model Army.

33. As was the case with most wars of the time, the bulk of the deaths were caused by the side-effects of war (e.g., disease, famine).

34. Michael Mann, *The Dark Side of Democracy* (New York: Cambridge University Press, 2005), 50–52. See also Eric Strauss, *Irish Nationalism and British Democracy* (New York: Columbia University Press, 1951).

35. Toby Barnard, *The English Republic 1649–1660* (New York: Addison Wesley, 1997), esp. 72.

36. Scott, *England's Troubles*, 47; Smith, *A History of the Modern British Isles*, 147; and Blair Worden, *Roundhead Reputations: The English Civil Wars and the Passions of Posterity* (London: Penguin, 2001), 3. These figures reflect the entire period, and most of the deaths come from the consequences of war, rather than the fighting itself.

37. For an analysis of how dictatorial this regime was, see Austin Woolrych, "The Cromwellian Protectorate: A Military Dictatorship?" *History* 75, no. 244 (January 1990): 207–31.

38. Again, it is worth stressing that would have been less true in Ireland or Scotland, where the consequences of the New Model Army's conquests had significantly changed the political facts on the ground.

39. Jack Green and Robert Forster, *Preconditions of Revolution in Early Modern Europe* (Baltimore: Johns Hopkins University Press, 1979), 107–108. Christopher Hill, *The Century of Revolution 1603–1714* (New York: W.W. Norton, 1982), 163.

40. Kishlansky, *A Monarchy Transformed*, 225–26: Stone, *Causes of the English Revolution*, 49, 146–47.

41. Steve Pincus, *1688: The First Modern Revolution* (New Haven, CT: Yale University Press, 2009), 104. Also see Tim Harris, *Revolution: The Great Crisis of the British Monarchy, 1685–1720* (London: Allen Lane, 2006), 61ff.

42. W.A. Speck, *Reluctant Revolutionaries: Englishmen and the Revolution of 1688* (Oxford: Oxford University Press, 1988), 9.

43. Pincus, *1688*, 160. But again see Boucoyannis for an argument about the pre-seventeenth-century period.

44. Jonathan Israel, *The Anglo-Dutch Moment: Essays on the Glorious Revolution and Its World Impact* (Cambridge: Cambridge University Press, 1991), 70; Tim Harris, *Revolution: The Great Crisis of the British Monarchy, 1685–1720* (London: Allen Lane, 2006), 96.

45. Pincus, *1688*, 145 and 149–50.

46. Pincus, *1688*, 158. Also Speck, *Reluctant Revolutionaries*, 8.

47. Pincus, *1688*, pp. 150–51.

48. Quoted in Pincus, *1688*, 153. See also pp. 150–52.

49. G.M. Trevelyan, *The English Revolution 1688–1689* (New York: Oxford University Press, 1965), 48.

50. It is worth stressing that James's absolutism extended to Scotland and Ireland as well as England, evoking particularly hostile reactions in the former.

51. Pincus, *1688*, 162, 178. See also Harris, *Revolution*; Speck, *Reluctant Revolutionaries*.

52. Indeed, so hysterical was the reaction to the birth of James's son that conspiracy theories arose claiming that the birth was "supposititious" and that a baby had, in fact, been smuggled into the birthing room in a warming pan.

53. Harris, *Revolution*, 485.

54. Robert Beddard, ed., *The Revolutions of 1688* (Oxford: Clarendon Press, 1991).

55. *House of Commons Journal* 10 (January 1689). Accessed at http://www.british-history.ac.uk/report.aspx?compid=28740#s10.

56. In May they accepted the Crown in Scotland. Ireland, not surprisingly, was a different story. Catholic support for James was greatest here, and fighting here continued until 1691.

57. Holmes, *The Making of a Great Power*, 215.

58. Bill of Rights, accessed at http://www.constitution.org/eng/eng_bor.htm.

59. Speck, *Reluctant Revolutionaries*, esp. 20, 246. See also Trevelyan, *The English Revolution*, 71.

60. Michael Barone, *Our First Revolution: The Remarkable British Upheaval That Inspired America's Founding Fathers* (New York: Crown, 2007), 229.

61. J.G.A. Pocock, *Three British Revolutions: 1641, 1688, 1776* (Princeton, NJ: Princeton University Press, 1980), 237.

62. Pincus, *1688*, is the most influential recent study of this process.

63. John Brewer, *The Sinews of Power: War, Money and the English State, 1688–1783* (New York: Knopf, 1989), 137. See also John Brewer and Eckhart Hellmuth, *Rethinking Leviathan: The Eighteenth-Century State in Britain and Germany* (New York: Oxford University Press, 1999); Lawrence Stone, *An Imperial State at War: Britain from 1689 to 1815* (New York: Routledge, 1994).

64. Michael Mann, "The Autonomous Power of the State: Its Origins, Mechanisms and Results," *European Journal of Sociology* (Archives européennes de sociologie) 25 (1984); Michael Mann, *The Sources of Social Power, vol. 1: A History of Power from the Beginnings to AD 1760* (New York: Cambridge University Press, 1986).

65. The Scottish government and Parliament were merged with the English. The Scots did get to keep their Church, however. It is important to note that this did not end all uprisings against the throne. Jacobite rebellions did emerge in the years to come, but they did not threaten the Crown or overall political stability as they had earlier during the seventeenth century.

66. See, e.g., Douglass North, *Structure and Change in Economic History* (New York: W.W. Norton, 1982); Douglas North and Barry Weingast, "Constitution and Commitment: The Evolution of Institutions Governing Public Choice in Seventeenth Century England," *The Journal of Economic History* 49, no. 4 (December 1989). For not dissimilar reasons, Marxists therefore also viewed the Glorious Revolution as a bourgeois or capitalist revolution, since it eventuated in the triumph of the bourgeoise and capitalism. Christopher Hill is probably the most influential representative of this school. See, e.g., Christopher Hill, *The Century of Revolution, 1607–1714* (New York: W.W. Norton, 1982).

67. Smith, *A History of the Modern British Isles*, 313; Patrick O' Brien and Philip Hunt, "The Rise of a Fiscal State in England, 1485–1815," *Historical Research* 66, no. 160 (June 1993); Richard Bonney, "England 1485–1815," in *The Rise of the Fiscal State in Europe*, ed. Richard Bonney (New York: Oxford University Press, 1999). For comparative numbers see Mark Dinecco, "Fiscal Centralization, Limited Government and Public Revenues in Europe, 1650–1913," *The Journal of Economic History* 69, no. 1 (March 2009).

68. Brewer, *The Sinews of Power*; Michael Braddick, *The Nerves of State* (Manchester: Manchester University Press, 1996); Smith, *A History of the Modern British Isles*, 306; and Scott, *England's Troubles*, 470ff.

69. It also further stipulated that the monarch be "in communion with the Church of England."

70. Barone, *Our First Revolution*, 234.

71. Trevelyan's *The English Revolution*, for example, emphasizes this long-term effect of the revolution.

72. On this debate see Lois Schowerer, *The Revolution of 1688–1689: Changing Perspectives* (New York: Cambridge University Press, 1992): Beddard, ed., *The Revolutions of 1688*.

73. It is important to note, however, that the British aristocracy was not entitled to the social or economic privileges many of their European counterparts enjoyed. In Britain, political power came from landownership or wealth, rather than from being a member of a particular caste. Hannah Schissler, "The Junkers," in *Peasants and Lords in Modern Germany*, ed. Robert Moeller (Boston: Allen and Unwin, 1986); F.M.L. Thompson, *English Landed Society in the Nineteenth Century* (London: Routledge, 1971); Rudolf Vierhaus, *Adel vor der Revolution* (Göttingen: Vandenhoeck and Ruprecht, 1971); Albert Goodwin, *European Nobility in the Eighteenth Century* (New York: Black, 1967); David Spring, *European Landed Elites in the Nineteenth Century* (Baltimore: Johns Hopkins University Press, 1977).

74. Plumb, *The Growth of Political Stability in England, 1675–1725* (London: The Macmillan Press, 1967), xviii, 1, 19. See also Scott, *England's Troubles*.

Chapter 4

1. This is a paraphrase. The original quote is: "European (or indeed world) politics between 1789 and 1917 were largely the struggle for and against the principles of 1789, or the even more incendiary ones of 1793." E.J. Hobsbawm, *The Age of Revolution 1789–1848* (New York: Mentor, 1962), 74.

2. E.J. Hobsbawm, *The Age of Revolution 1789–1848*, 74.

3. Quoted in Pierre Rosanvallon, *The Society of Equals* (Cambridge, MA: Harvard University Press, 2013), 12.

4. Reinhard Bendix, *Kings or People? Power and the Mandate to Rule* (Los Angeles: University of California Press, 1978).

5. David J. Sturdy, *Fractured Europe 1600–1721* (Malden, MA: Blackwell, 2002), 395–96.

6. Beloff, *The Age of Absolutism*, 168.

7. John Gillis, *The Development of European Society 1770–1870* (New York: University Press of America, 1983), 61.

8. G.J. Cavanaugh, "Nobles, Privileges and Taxes in France: A Revision Reviewed," *French Historical Studies* 8, no. 4 (1974): 689.

9. William Doyle, *The Oxford History of the French Revolution* (New York: Oxford University Press, 2002), 22–23. The population grew about 25% during this time.

10. Colin Lucas, "Nobles, Bourgeois and the Origins of the French Revolution," in *The French Revolution: Recent Debates and New Controversies*, ed. Gary Kates (London: Routledge, 1998).

11. Leon Trotsky, *The History of the Russian Revolution*, vol. II (New York: Monad Press), vii.

12. Theda Skocpol, *States and Social Revolutions* (New York: Cambridge University Press, 1979).

13. "David Harris Sacks, "The Paradox of Taxation: Fiscal Crises, Parliament and Liberty in England," in Kathryn Norberg, "The French Financial Crisis of 1788 and the Financial Origins of the Revolution of 1789," in Phillip Hoffman and Kathryn Norberg, *Fiscal Crisis, Liberty, and Representative Government, 1450–1789* (Stanford: Stanford University Press, 1994), 7.

14. Alfred Cobban, *A History of Modern France*, vol. 1 (Baltimore: Penguin Books, 1961), 55.

15. M. Prestwich, "The Making of Absolute Monarchy (1559–1683)," in *France Government and Society*, ed. J.M. Wallace-Hadrill and J. McManners (London: Methuen, 1957), 121; Gordon Wright, *France in Modern Times* (New York: W.W. Norton, 1981), 8.

16. This was double debt servicing's share of the budget before the war. Norberg, "The French Financial Crisis of 1788 and the Financial Origins of the Revolution of 1789," in *Fiscal Crisis, Liberty, and Representative Government*, ed.

Hoffman and Norberg, 284. Rafe Blaufarb, "Noble Privilege and Absolutist State Building: French Military Administration after the Seven Years' War," *French Historical Studies* 24, no. 2 (Spring 2001).

17. William Doyle, *The Old European Order 1660–1800* (London: Oxford University Press, 1978), 317.

18. Georges Lefrebvre, *The Coming of the French Revolution* (Princeton, NJ: Princeton University Press, 1947), 9–10.

19. The war added more than 1 billion livres to state debt, which translated into an additional 100–130 million livres annually in debt payments.

20. Philip Hoffman and Kathryn Norberg, "Conclusion," in *Fiscal Crisis, Liberty and Representative Government*, ed. Hoffman and Norberg, 300–301. Jean-Laurent Rosenthal, "The Political Economy of Absolutism Revisited," in *Analytic Narratives*, ed. Robert Bates, Avner Grief, Margaret Levi, Jean-Laurent Rosenthal, and Barry Weingast (Princeton, NJ: Princeton University Press, 1998); Peter Claus Hartmann, "Die Steursysteme in Frankreich und England am Vorabend der Französischen Revolution," in *Vom Ancien Régime zur Französischen Revolution*, ed. Ernst Hinrichs, Eberhard Schmitt, and Rudolf Verhaus (Göttingen: Vandenhoeck & Ruprecht, 1978).

21. Peter Mathias and Patrick O'Brien, "Taxation in Britain and France 1715–1810: A Comparison of the Social and Economic Incidence of Taxes Collected for the Central Governments," *Journal of European Economic History* 5, no. 3 (Winter 1976): 610, 634, 635; Norberg, "French Fiscal Crisis," 272–74; and for a general analysis of differential taxation capabilities and political implications see Deborah Boucoyannis, "From Roving to Stationary Judges: Power, Land, and the Origins of Representative Institutions," book manuscript, forthcoming.

22. François Velde and David Weir, "The Financial Market and Government Debt Policy in France, 1746–1793," *The Journal of Economic History* 52, no. 1 (March 1992): 19.

23. Cavanaugh, "Nobles, Privileges, and Taxes in France," 692; Norberg, "French Fiscal Crisis," 265; Boucoyannis, "From Roving to Stationary Judges." Also important were the different types of taxation employed by Britain and France, with the latter relying more on direct than indirect taxes (which were less politically problematic). Mathias and O'Brien, "Taxation in Britain and France," esp. 636.

24. The *parlements* were not parliaments in the English or contemporary sense of the word. They were primarily judicial bodies that registered and recorded royal edicts and laws. The most important was the Paris *parlement*, but *parlements* also existed in regional capitals as well.

25. Quoted in Doyle, *The Oxford History of the French Revolution*, 66.

26. Fraçois Furet, *Revolutionary France 1770–1880* (Malden, MA: Blackwell, 1988), 26.

27. There were others who succeeded Turgot as controller-general since Necker could not officially take that position since he was a Protestant. But Necker was the key adviser.

28. He did this, presumably, to make his own financial stewardship appear more successful than it was. Eugene Nelson White, "Was There a Solution to the Ancien Régime's Financial Dilemma?" *The Journal of Economic History* 44, no. 3 (September 1989): 559.

29. William Doyle, *The Origins of the French Revolution* (New York: Oxford University Press, 1989), 52.

30. Betty Behrens, "Nobles, Privileges and Taxes in France at the end of the Ancien Régime," *The Economic History Review* 15, no. 3 (1963): 468.

31. Michael Fitzsimmons, *The Remaking of France: The National Assembly and the Constitution of 1791* (New York: Cambridge University Press, 1994); Vivian Gruder, "Paths to Political Consciousness: The Assembly of Notables of 1787 and the 'Pre-Revolution' in France," *French Historical Studies* 13, no. 3 (Spring 1984).

32. Vivian Gruder, "No Taxation Without Representation: The Assembly of Notables of 1787 and Political Ideology in France," *Legislative Studies Quarterly* 7, no. 2 (May 1982): 265.

33. Velde and Weir, "The Financial Market and Government Debt Policy," 7; Pierre Goubert, *The Course of French History* (New York: Franklin Watts, 1988).

34. Quoted in Norberg, "French Fiscal Crisis of 1788," 264.

35. Another option was default, which the crown had resorted to in the past. But it was deemed too great a risk to France's international position at this time. See, e.g., White, "Was There a Solution?" 566.

36. Gaetano Salvemini, *The French Revolution 1788–1792* (New York: W.W. Norton, 1962), 325; Cobban, *A History of Modern France*, vol. 1, p. 134.

37. Alexis de Tocqueville, *The Old Regime and the French Revolution* (New York: Anchor Books, 1955), 205.

38. Hilton Root, *Fountain of Privilege*, 236.

39. Turgot in a confidential report to the king, quoted in Tocqueville, *The Old Regime*, 107.

40. Norberg, "French Fiscal Crisis," 295.

41. As Samuel Huntington pointed out in his classic study *Political Order in Changing Societies* (New Haven, CT: Yale University Press, 1968) over a generation ago, when rates of social mobilization and political participation are high, but rates of political organization and institutionalization are low, the result is political disorder.

42. Israel, *Revolutionary Ideas*, 26.

43. Dominique Joseph Garat, paraphrased in Israel, *Revolutionary Ideas*, 15–16.

44. On "conservative" advocates of reform, see Jacques Godechot, *The Counter-Revolution: Doctrine and Action, 1789–1804* (New York: Howard Fertig, 1971).

45. Although it did invite members of the other two estates to join them, which some did, especially from the ranks of the lower clergy.

46. The storming of the Bastille also sent a first wave of conservative nobles fleeing France to begin plotting their revenge against the new regime from abroad.

47. François Furet, "Night of August 4," in *A Critical Dictionary of the French Revolution*, ed. François Furet (Cambridge, MA: Harvard University Press, 1988), 107.

48. Of course, this was 1789 so this did not include women or many minorities.

49. Furet, *Revolutionary France*, 89. This does mean that the peasants were the only ones to purchase this land; far from it. But they did purchase some and this helped solidify small-scale land ownership, which in turn affected France's subsequent economic, social, and political development.

50. D.M.G. Sutherland, *France 1789–1815* (New York: Oxford, 1986), 95.

51. Fitzsimmons, *The Making of France*, xi; John Merriman, *A History of Modern Europe*, vol. 2 (New York: W.W. Norton, 2004), 484.

52. Arno Mayer, *The Furies: Violence and Terror in the French and Russian Revolutions* (Princeton, NJ: Princeton University Press, 2000), 423, 426.

53. George Rudé, *Revolutionary Europe* (New York: Harper and Row, 1964), 108.

54. P.M. Jones, *Reform and Revolution in France: The Politics of Transition, 1774–1791* (New York: Cambridge University Press, 1995). Also R.R. Palmer, *The Age of the Democratic Revolution: A Political History of Europe and America, 1760–1800* (Princeton, NJ: Princeton University Press, 1959), esp. 501.

55. Doyle, *The Oxford History of the French Revolution*, 180.

56. Doyle, *The Oxford History of the French Revolution*, 194–95.

57. R.R. Palmer, *Twelve Who Ruled: The Year of Terror in the French Revolution* (Princeton, NJ: Princeton University Press, 1969), esp. 23.

58. After Louis XVI had been captured, the Legislative Assembly called for a national convention to draw up a new constitution.

59. The Montagnards, or the Mountain, was a group within the National Convention known for its opposition to the more moderate Girondists and eventual support for the policy of terror. (This term is also sometimes used interchangeably with "Jacobin.") Key leaders were Marat, Danton, and Robespierre.

60. Doyle, *The Oxford History*, 257; Mayer, *The Furies*, 324ff.

61. Maximilien Robespierre, "On the Principles of Political Morality," February 1794.

62. This is, of course, a crude characterization of a number of more sophisticated arguments. But it does, I think, cover authors from Edmund Burke (*Reflections on the Revolution in France* [1790]) to J.L. Talmon (*The Origins of Totalitarian Democracy* [New York: Norton, 1970]).

63. Mona Ozouf, "War and Terror in French Revolutionary Discourse, 1792–1794," *Journal of Modern History* 56 (December 1984); François Furet, "Terror," in *A Critical Dictionary of the French Revolution*, ed. François Furet.

64. Barrington Moore, *Social Origins of Dictatorship and Democracy: Lord and Peasant in the Making of the Modern World* (Boston: Beacon Press, 1966), 103. Also see John Markoff, "Violence, Emancipation and Democracy," in *The French Revolution*, ed. Gary Kates.

65. Palmer, *Twelve Who Ruled*, 5.

66. The name comes from the month in the revolutionary calendar when the transition occurred.

67. Colin Jones, *The Great Nation: France from Louis XV to Napoleon* (New York: Columbia University Press, 2002), 517.

68. Recognizing this, Benjamin Constant wrote to Sieyès warning of this "man . . . who is . . . a threat to the Republic. His proclamations, in which he speaks only of himself and says that his return has raised hopes that in everything he does he sees nothing but his own elevation . . . [H]e has on his side the generals, the soldiers, aristocratic riffraff and everyone who surrenders enthusiastically . . . [to] the appearance of strength." Quoted in Jones, *The Great Nation*, 577.

69. Malcolm Crook, *Napoleon Comes to Power: Democracy and Dictatorship in Revolutionary France* (Cardiff: University of Wales Press, 1998).

70. Owen Connelly, *The French Revolution and the Napoleonic Era* (Fort Worth: Holt, Reinhart, and Winston, 1991), 209.

71. Another reflection of the seeming contradiction between Napoleon's status as emperor and his commitment to the Republic was the inscription on many of the empire's gold coins (known as "Napoleons") which read, "Napoleon, Emperor of the French Republic."

72. Michael Broers, *Europe under Napoleon 1799–1815* (London: Arnold, 1996).

73. In his notes for the never completed second volume of his study of the revolution, Tocqueville also apparently commented that "for the sake of rest and order, the nation throws itself into the arms of a man who is believed sufficiently strong to arrest the Revolution and sufficiently generous to consolidate its aims." Jack Hayward, *After the French Revolution* (Hertfordshire: Harvester Wheatsheaf, 1991), 36–37.

74. Louis Bergeron, *France under Napoleon* (Princeton, NJ: Princeton University Press, 1981); Connelly, *The French Revolution and the Napoleonic Era*, esp. 210.

75. Apparently, he used the verb *"achever,"* which has a somewhat ambiguous meaning. Edward Fox, *The Emergence of the Modern European World* (Cambridge: Blackwell, 1991), 84.

76. Skocpol, *States and Social Revolutions*, 179ff.; Robert Gildea, *Barricades and Borders* (Oxford: Oxford University Press, 1987); Fox, *The Emergence of the Modern European World*, 86; S.J. Woolf, *Napoleon's Integration of Europe* (London: Routledge, 1991).

77. Merriman, *A History of Modern Europe*, 536.

78. Napoleon was smart enough to realize that a tamed Church and clergy could prove useful.

79. Gildea, *Barricades and Borders*, 54.

80. George Rudé, *Revolutionary Europe 1783–1815* (New York: Harper, 1964), 179–80; E.J. Hobsbawm, *The Age of Revolution 1789–1848* (New York: Mentor, 1962), 116. Also see Woolf, *Napoleon's Integration of Europe*; Broers, *Europe Under Napoleon*; Connelly, *The French Revolution*.

81. Woolf, *Napoleon's Integration of Europe*, 243ff.

82. Hobsbawm, *The Age of Revolution*, 117.

83. Tocqueville, *The Old Regime*, 210, x.

84. R.R. Palmer, for example, lamented the "inability of the Revolutionists to work together. Had the Jacobins been a revolutionary party of the modern kind, drilled to a mechanical obedience, the whole French Revolution might have been different." *Twelve Who Ruled*, 306.

85. Turgot in a confidential report to the king, quoted in Tocqueville, *The Old Regime*, 107.

86. Here again Tocqueville: "[I]n no other country had the private citizen become so completely out of touch with public affairs and so unused to studying the course of events, so much so that not only had the average Frenchman no experience of 'popular movements' but he hardly understood what 'the people' meant. Bearing this in mind, we may find it easier to understand why the nation as a whole could launch out into a sanguinary revolution, with those very men who stood to lose the most by it taking the lead and clearing the ground for it." Tocqueville, *The Old Regime*, 205. Or, for those who prefer their analyses in somewhat more "social scientific" terms, Huntington: "A society with weak political institutions lacks the ability to curb the excesses of personal and parochial desires . . . Without strong political institutions, society lacks the means to define and realize its common interests . . . [Countries] with low levels of institutionalization and high levels of mobilization and participation are systems where social forces using their own methods act directly in the political sphere." Huntington, *Political Order*, 24, 79–80.

Putting aside Burke and other conservative historians mentioned above, there is a long tradition of viewing the ancien régime's collapse and the violence and chaos that followed it as avoidable and unnecessary. The analysis presented here disagrees with this view. A recent, influential example of this viewpoint is Simon Schama's *Citizens: A Chronicle of the French Revolution* (New York: Knopf, 1989).

87. Its most recent iteration came with the revolution's bicentennial in 1989. In the English-speaking world Schama's *Citizens* helped reignite the debate. The quotes come from a review by Norman Hampson in *The New York Review of Books* on April 13, 1989, of two books on opposite side of the debate, George Rudé's *The French Revolution* (London: Weidenfeld and Nicolson, 1989) and Schama's *Citizens*. See also Kates, ed., *The French Revolution*; Peter Davies, *The Debate on the French Revolution* (Manchester: Manchester University Press, 2006).

88. Salvemini, *The French Revolution*, 330.

89. Skocpol, *States and Social Revolutions*, 178–79; Connor Cruise O'Brien, *The Decline and Fall of the French Revolution* (Cambridge, MA: Harvard University Press, 1990), 14.

90. Max Beloff, *The Age of Absolutism 1660–1815* (New York: Harper, 1962), 179. Also, E.J. Hobsbawm, "The Making of a 'Bourgeois Revolution,' " *Social Research* 56, no. 1 (Spring 1989).

91. Robert Darnton, "What Was Revolutionary about the French Revolution?" *The New York Review of Books*, January 19, 1989. On the development of the French nation after the revolution see Patrick Weil, *How to Be French: Nationality in the Making since 1789* (Durham, NC: Duke University Press, 2008).

92. If we return again to taxation, it also seems that taxation was higher in non-absolutist states (e.g., England and the Netherlands) than in more absolutist ones (e.g., France and even Spain). See Hoffman and Norberg, "Conclusion," 299, 310; Boucoyannis, "From Roving to Stationary Judges."

93. John Markoff, *The Abolition of Feudalism* (University Park: Pennsylvania State University Press, 1991). This chapter therefore agrees with those who view the revolution as essentially being "a political revolution with social consequences and not a social revolution with political consequences." Doyle, *Origins*, 17.

94. This assessment is shared by many if not most analysts of the revolution, but one of the best comparative analyses of this social shift and its political implications remains Moore's *Social Origins*.

95. Roger McGraw, *France 1815–1914: The Bourgeois Century* (New York: Oxford University Press, 1986); Hobsbawm, "The Making of a 'Bourgeois Revolution.' "

96. Jones, *The Great Nation*, 538.

97. Moore, *Social Origins*; Hobsbawm, *The Age of Revolution*, 93; and William Doyle, *The Old European Order 1660–1800* (London: Oxford University Press, 1978), 365.

Chapter 5

1. G.M. Trevelyan, *British History in the Nineteenth Century* (New York: Longmans, 1927), 292. A.J.P. Taylor later paraphrased this as in "1848 Germany History reached its turning point and failed to turn." *The Course of German History* (London: Routledge, 1961), 69.

2. Karl Marx and Frederick Engels's *The Communist Manifesto* was first published in 1848.

3. Theodore Hamerow, *The Birth of a New Europe: State and Society in the Nineteenth Century* (Chapel Hill: University of North Carolina Press, 1983).

4. Paul Bairoch and Gary Goertz, "Factors of Urbanisation in the Nineteenth Century Developed Countries," *Urban Studies* 23 (1986).

5. It is important to note that the working class during this time was still small (estimates range, for example, from about 400,000 to 500,000 in France and Germany).

6. Peter Jones, *The 1848 Revolutions* (London: Longman Group, 1991), 7–10.

7. Jonathan Sperber estimates that between the mid-1820s and the mid-1840s workers' wages and the incomes of master craftsmen probably declined about 20 percent. Sperber, *The European Revolutions 1848–1851* (New York: Cambridge University Press, 1994).

8. Peter Stearns, *1848: The Revolutionary Tide in Europe* (New York: W.W. Norton, 1974), part 1, esp. pp. 24, 27. William Sewell, *Work and Revolution in France: The Language of Labor from the Old Regime to 1848* (Cambridge: Cambridge University Press, 1980), 160.

9. Sperber, *The European Revolutions*, chapter 1.

10. Some political scientists identify these conditions as being correlated with democratization. See Carles Boix, *Democracy and Redistribution* (New York: Cambridge University Press, 2003); Daron Acemoglu and James Robinson, *Economic Origins of Dictatorship and Democracy* (New York: Cambridge University Press, 2006).

11. On how mass mobilization, distributive conflicts, and inequality interact to produce political outcomes see Stephen Haggard and Robert Kaufman, "Inequality and Regime Change: Democratic Transitions and the Stability of Democratic Rule," *American Political Science Review* 106 (August 2012); Stephen Haggard, Robert Kaufmann, and Terence Teo, "Inequality and Regime Change: The Role of Distributive Conflict," *Comparative Democratization Newsletter* 11, no. 3 (October 2013).

12. The other major country to escape the 1848 wave was Russia, which had not yet experienced the degree of economic growth or social change that had begun transforming much of the rest of Europe.

13. E.J. Hobsbawm, *The Age of Revolution* (New York: Mentor, 1962), 356.

14. Carl von Clausewitz, *On War*, ed. and trans. Michael Howard and Peter Paret (Princeton, NJ: Princeton University Press, 1984), 591–92.

15. Fejtö, "Europe on the Eve of Revolution," in *The Opening of an Era 1848*, ed. François Fejtö (New York: Howard Fertig, 1966), 2.

16. Ernst Gellner, *Nationalism* (New York: New York University Press, 1997).

17. Elie Kedourie, *Nationalism* (New York: Wiley-Blackwell, 1993).

18. Benedict Anderson, *Imagined Communities* (New York: Verso, 2006).

19. Eric Hobsbawm, *The Age of Capital, 1848–1875* (New York: Meridian Books, 1984), esp. 6–7.

20. John Gillis, *The Development of European Society, 1770–1870* (Lanham, MD: University Press of America, 1983), 138; John Merriman, *A History of Modern Europe, Volume II: From the French Revolution to the Present* (New York: W.W. Norton, 2004), 671; William Langer, *Political and Social Upheaval, 1832–1852* (New York: Harper and Row, 1969), esp. chapter 6.

21. William Langer, *The Revolutions of 1848* (New York: Harper and Row, 1969), 4–5. The Irish suffered the most during this time with the "great hunger" claiming perhaps a million and a half victims.

22. Quoted in G.P. Gooch, "The Centenary of 1848 in Germany and Austria," in *1848: A Turning Point?* ed. Melvin Kranzberg (Boston: D.C. Heath, 1959), 82.

23. Louis XVII, Louis XVI's son, died in prison in 1795.

24. J.P.T. Bury, *France 1814–1940* (London: Cox and Wyman, 1969), 3; Roger Magraw, *France 1815–1914* (New York: Oxford University Press, 1986), 23.

25. William Fortescue, *Revolution and Counter-Revolution in France, 1815–1852* (New York: Basil Blackwell, 1988), esp. 25ff. See also Mark Traugott, *The Insurgent Barricade* (Berkeley: University of California Press, 2010), for a discussion of the role played by barricades and other collective action in the July Revolution.

26. The size of the electorate more or less doubled to about 170,000 (rising to about 240,000 by 1846), but it was still small. But because the electorate did expand to include part of the middle class, this regime has been called the "bourgeois monarchy." As we will see, this is at least partially a misnomer since much of the middle class remained excluded from political life.

27. Quoted in Pierre Léveque, "The Revolutionary Crisis of 1848/51 in France," in *Europe in 1848: Revolution and Reform*, ed. Dieter Dowe et al. (New York: Berghahn Books, 2001).

28. De Tocqueville, speech to the Chamber of Deputies, January 29, 1848. (Accessed at http://www.speeches-usa.com/Transcripts/091_deTocqueville .html.)

29. For a comparative analysis of the extent and nature of barricades and other forms of collective protest in France and other parts of Europe, see Traugott, *The Insurgent Barricade.*

30. This was a familiar pattern. See, e.g., Guillermo O'Donnell and Philippe Schmitter, *Transitions from Authoritarian Rule: Tentative Conclusions about Uncertain Democracies* (Berkeley: University of California Press, 1986).

31. Geoffrey Ellis, "The Revolution of 1848–1849 in France," in *The Revolutions in Europe 1848– 1849*, ed. R.J.W. Evans and Hartmut Pogge von Strandmann (New York: Oxford University Press, 2000).

32. Charles Breunig, *The Age of Revolution and Reaction, 1789–1850* (New York: W.W. Norton, 1970), 174; William Fortescue, *Revolution and Counter-Revolution in France, 1815–1852* (New York: Basil Blackwell, 1988).

33. Merriman, *A History of Modern Europe*, 676.

34. Hobsbawm, *The Age of Capital*, 4 and 8.

35. I use the term "Austrian Empire" for convenience, even though the term empire is inexact. The other options, however (Habsburg Monarchy or Austria), are probably more confusing. See Grete Klingenstein, "The Meanings of 'Austria' and 'Austrian' in the Eighteenth Century," in *Royal and Republican*

Sovereignty in Early Modern Europe, ed. R. Oresko (New York: Cambridge University Press, 2006).

36. On growing pressure during the Vormärz period see Arthur May, The Habsburg Monarchy (New York: Cambridge University Press, 1951); R.J.W. Evans, The Making of the Habsburg Monarchy 1550–1700 (New York: Oxford University Press, 1991); R.J.W. Evans, Austria, Hungary and the Habsburgs (New York: Oxford University Press, 2006); Jean Bérenger, A History of the Habsburg Empire (New York: Longman, 1990).

37. Istvan Deak, The Lawful Revolution: Louis Kossuth and the Hungarians, 1848–1849 (New York: Columbia University Press, 1979).

38. March because they were presented in March, April because they were accepted by the Habsburg emperor in April (see below). See the document in Peter Jones, The 1848 Revolutions (New York: Longman, 1991), 112.

39. Quoted in Francois Fejtö, "Hungary," in The Opening of an Era 1848, ed. Francois Fejtö (New York: Howard Fertig, 1966), 315.

40. Budapest did not become a unified city until 1873 when the cities of Buda, Pest, and Obuda were unified, but it is customary to write their names together or join them with a hyphen.

41. The text of Petöfi's poem in English can be found at http://www.fordham.edu/halsall/mod/1848hungary-natsong.asp.

42. Evans, Austria, Hungary and the Habsburgs, 147, 151.

43. A view, by the way, that Marx, Engels, and many other intellectuals of the day shared. Even Kossuth, for example, a firm liberal and generally tolerant, rejected Slovak claims for autonomy, arguing that they had no history of their own. See Deak, Lawful Revolution, 45.

44. For example, after 1848 Magyar was to be enforced as the language of Parliament, thereby eliminating all those who did not speak the very difficult language from serving.

45. Deak, Lawful Revolution, 121.

46. Letter sent by Palacký to the Committee of Fifty in Frankfurt (1848), reprinted in Slavonic and Eastern European Review 26 (1947/48): 308. http://spinnet.eu/images/2010-12/letter_by_palacky.pdf.

47. Indeed, since the Magyar nobility were the direct oppressors of the Slav peasantry they were viewed as worse than the Habsburgs.

48. George Fasel, Europe in Upheaval: The Revolutions of 1848 (Chicago: Rand McNally, 1970), 125.

49. Fasel, Europe in Upheaval, 304.

50. R.J.W. Evans, "1848–1849 in the Habsburg Monarchy," in The Revolutions in Europe, ed. Evans and Von Strandmann.

51. Evans, "1848–1849 in the Habsburg Monarchy," 306.

52. For the declaration issued at the end of the congress (and other documents from the period 1848–1849) see Frank Eyck, The Revolutions of 1848–49 (Edinburgh: Oliver & Boyd, 1972), 96–97.

53. David Blackbourn, *The Long Nineteenth Century: A History of Germany, 1780–1918* (New York: Oxford University Press, 1997), 71.

54. Brian Vick, *Defining Germany: The 1848 Frankfurt Parliamentarians and National Identity* (Cambridge, MA: Harvard University Press, 2002).

55. Christopher Clark, *Iron Kingdom* (Cambridge, MA: Harvard University Press, 2006), 111.

56. Robert Berdahl, *The Politics of the Prussian Nobility* (Princeton, NJ: Princeton University Press, 1988).

57. Friedrich von Schrötter (1743–1815) was a Prussian Junker and government minister.

58. Reprinted in Eyck, *The Revolutions*, 68–69.

59. The assembly was elected by all "independent" males, a provision that was interpreted differently by the different confederation states, but it is estimated that as many as three-fourths of all adult males were eligible.

60. Lewis Namier, *1848: The Revolution of the Intellectuals* (London: Oxford University Press, 1944). On the social makeup of the Parliament see also Theodor Hamerow, "The Elections to the Frankfurt Parliament," *Journal of Modern History* 33, no. 1 (1961). The German version of Wikipedia has a complete list of all the members of the Frankfurt Parliament as well as the fraction they belonged to: http://de.wikipedia.org/wiki/Mitglieder_der_Frankfurter_Nationalversammlung.

61. Theodore Hamerow, *Restoration Revolution Reaction* (Princeton, NJ: Princeton University Press, 1958), 62.

62. On the background of the democratic movement see, e.g., Jonathan Sperber, *Rhineland Radicals: The Democratic Movement and the Revolution of 1848–1849* (Princeton, NJ: Princeton University Press, 1991).

63. Hagen Schulze, "The Revolution of the European Order and the Rise of German Nationalism," in *Nation-Building in Central Europe*, ed. Schulze (New York: Berg, 1987), 13.

64. The literature on the Frankfurt Parliament and the national question is huge. In addition to Vick, *Defining Germany,* and Namier, *1848,* see Günter Wollstein, *Das 'Grossdeutschland' der Paulskirche: Nationale Ziele in der bürgerlichen Revolution von 1848/49* (Düsseldorf: Droste, 1977).

65. Bejamin Goriely, "Poland," in *The Opening of an Era 1848*, ed. Fejtö, 353.

66. John Merriman, *The Agony of the Republic: The Repression of the Left in Revolutionary France, 1849–1851* (New Haven, CT: Yale University Press, 1978).

67. He was the nephew of the original Bonaparte. The extent and scale of Louis-Napoleon's victory was truly stunning; he won about 75 percent of all votes cast and got support from almost all social groups.

68. Maurice Agulhon, *The Republic Experiment, 1848–1852* (New York: Cambridge University Press, 1989). To be fair, Louis-Napoleon also moved against

conservatives, who tried to chip away at universal suffrage and thwart his bid for a prolongation of his term of office (see below).

69. About 7.5 million voted "yes" and about 640,000 "no," with about 1.5 million abstentions.

70. Napoleon III because Napoleon's son, Napoleon II, had died, and his elder brother Joseph died without sons.

71. Karl Marx, *The Eighteenth Brumaire of Louis Bonaparte*. A more extended version of the quote: "Hegel remarks somewhere that all great world-historic facts and personages appear, so to speak, twice. He forgot to add: the first time as tragedy, the second time as farce. . . . Men make their own history, but they do not make it as they please; they do not make it under self-selected circumstances, but under circumstances existing already, given and transmitted from the past. The tradition of all dead generations weighs like a nightmare on the brains of the living. And just as they seem to be occupied with revolutionizing themselves and things, creating something that did not exist before, precisely in such epochs of revolutionary crisis they anxiously conjure up the spirits of the past to their service, borrowing from them names, battle slogans, and costumes in order to present this new scene in world history in time-honored disguise and borrowed language. Thus . . . the Revolution of 1848 knew nothing better to do than to parody, now 1789, now the revolutionary tradition of 1793–95. . . . The French, so long as they were engaged in revolution, could not get rid of the memory of Napoleon. . . . Now they have not only a caricature of the old Napoleon, but the old Napoleon himself, caricatured as he would have to be in the middle of the nineteenth century."

72. Charles Breunig, *The Age of Revolution and Reaction* (New York: W.W. Norton, 1970), 231.

73. Arnost Klima, "Bohemia," in *The Opening of an Era 1848*, ed. Fejtö, 294–95.

74. Langer, *The Revolutions of 1848*, 52.

75. Gunther Rothenberg, quoted in Deak, *Lawful Revolution*, 131. As another observer put it, "[t]he Croats were to the Hungarians what the Hungarians were to Austria, with the difference that the Croats were . . . ardent nationalists full of bitterness against those who refused to recognize that they constituted a nation." Fejtö, "Hungary," in *The Opening of an Era 1848*, ed. Fejtö, 326.

76. Fejtö, "Hungary," 341–42.

77. Romanian nationalist leaders had been arrested by the Hungarian government in August, and the animosity of the Romanians towards the Hungarians had been encouraged by the Habsburgs.

78. "Declaration of the Russian Government on Hungary," reprinted in Eyck, *Revolutions of 1848–49*, 167–68.

79. Attributed to Karl Marx, but really Engels, *Revolution and Counterrevolution in Germany* (Chicago: Charles Kerr, 1907), 79.

80. Hagen Schulze, *The Course of German Nationalism* (New York: Cambridge University Press, 1993), 74–75.

81. In a letter to his sister, quoted in Clark, *Iron Kingdom*, 494.

82. Karl Marx, *The Class Struggles in France* (part 1). However, it is important to note that the revolt was essentially unplanned and lacking in leadership by socialists or anyone else. Later studies also seem to indicate that the majority of the insurgents were skilled workers and artisans rather than unskilled or migrant workers. See, e.g., Roger Price, *The French Second Republic: A Social History* (Ithaca, NY: Cornell University Press, 1972).

83. Sperber, *The European Revolutions*, 138.

84. Roger Price, "The Holy Struggle Against Anarchy," in *Europe in 1848*, ed. Dowe et al.

85. Heinz-Gerhard Haupt and Dieter Langewiesche, "The European Revolution of 1848," in *Europe in 1848*, ed. Dowe et al.

86. Charles Tilly, "Did the Cake of Custom Break?" in *Consciousness and Class Experience in Nineteenth Century Europe*, ed. John Merriman (New York: Holmes & Maier, 1979); Heinz-Gerhard Haput and Dieter Langewiesche, "The European Revolution of 1848," Heinrich Best, "Structures of the Parliamentary Representation in the Revolutions of 1848," Michael Wettengel, "Party Formation in Germany," and Edward Berenson, "Organization and 'Modernization' in the Revolutions of 1848," in *Europe in 1848: Revolution and Reform*, ed. Dieter Dowe (New York: Berghahn Books, 2001).

87. Fejto, "Conclusion," and Endres, "Austria," in *The Opening of an Era*, ed. Fejtö, 426; Jean Bérenger, *A History of the Habsburg Empire* (New York: Longmans, 1997), 173; and Evans, *Austria, Hungary and the Habsburgs*, chapter 15.

88. The suffrage system used to elect Parliament was extremely skewed, but overall these changes altered political dynamics in the kingdom and were quite popular with both liberals and conservatives. Clark, *Iron Kingdom*, 502; Blackbourn, *The Long Nineteenth Century*, 173.

89. Sperber, *The European Revolutions*, 191; Stearns, *1848*, 247.

90. As L.B. Namier put it, 1848 was a "seed-plot of history. It crystallized ideas and projected the pattern of things to come; it determined the course of the century which followed." Namier, "1848: Seed-plot of History," in *1848*, ed. Kranzberg, 70.

91. L. Ranke, quoted in Robert C. Binkley, *Realism and Nationalism 1852–1871* (New York: Harper & Row, 1935), 124.

92. Hobsbawm, *Age of Capital*, 15–16.

93. In 1850, for example, in their "Address to the Central Committee of the Communist League" in London, Marx and Engels noted that they had predicted "that the German liberal bourgeoisie would soon come to power and would immediately turn its newly won power against the workers. You have seen how this forecast came true." And so "to be able forcefully and threateningly

to oppose [the bourgeoisie], whose betrayal of the workers will begin with the very first hour of victory, the workers must be armed and organized," https://www.marxists.org/archive/marx/works/1847/communist-league/1850-ad1.htm.

Chapter 6

1. See, e.g., Maurice Agulhon, *The French Republic 1879–1992* (Cambridge: Blackwell, 1993); James McMillan, *Dreyfus to DeGaulle* (London: Edward Arnold, 1985).
2. Daniel Bell, "Pogroms of Words," *The New Republic*, June 24, 2010, p. 32.
3. Switzerland is the possible exception.
4. Karl Marx, *The Eighteenth Brumaire of Louis Bonaparte.*
5. Stuart Campbell, *The Second Empire Revisited: A Study in French Historiography* (New Brunswick: Rutgers University Press, 1978).
6. Alain Plessis, *The Rise and Fall of the Second Empire, 1852–1871* (New York: Cambridge University Press, 1985), 21.
7. Sudhir Hazareesingh, *From Subject to Citizen: The Second Empire and the Emergence of Modern French Democracy* (Princeton, NJ: Princeton University Press, 1998), 27.
8. Repression during the empire was fairly mild. See Howard Payne, *The Police State of Napoleon Bonaparte 1851–1860* (Seattle: University of Washington Press, 1966).
9. Stephen Hanson, "The Founding of the French Third Republic," *Comparative Political Studies* 43 (2010): 1029; Philip Nord, *The Republican Moment: Struggles for Democracy in Nineteenth-Century France* (Cambridge, MA: Harvard University Press, 1995), 251.
10. Pierre Goubert, *The Course of French History* (New York: Franklin Watts, 1988), 392ff.; Alain Plessis and Jonathan Mandelbaum, *The Rise and Fall of the Second Empire* (New York: Cambridge University Press, 1985).
11. Of course, much of this redesign was a response to the revolutionary tradition that had grown up in Paris. Street fighting and barricades made sense in a city with narrow and winding streets; wide straight boulevards were designed to prevent this and facilitate the movement of troops. D.P. Jordan, *Transforming Paris* (New York: Free Press, 1995); Stephane Kirland, *Paris Reborn: Napoleon III, Baron Haussmann, and the Quest to Build a Modern City* (New York: St. Martin's Press, 2013).
12. Roger Price, *The French Second Empire: An Anatomy of Political Power* (New York: Cambridge University Press, 2001).
13. Roger Price, *The French Second Empire.*
14. John Merriman, *Massacre: The Life and Death of the Paris Commune* (New York: Basic Books, 2014).
15. Ruth Harris, *Dreyfus* (New York: Metropolitan Books, 2010), 60.

16. The monarchists were divided between Legitimists (who supported the heirs of Charles X) and Orleanists (who supported the heirs to Louis Phillipe I) and were ultimately unable to put forward either a viable leader or program. They did come to a compromise whereby the childless heir of Charles X, Henri, Comte de Cambord, would first become king and then, when he died, be followed by the heir of Louis Philippe, but Henri had no interest in ruling as a constitutional monarch and so insisted on conditions that made him unacceptable to the populace. By the time he died and a more pliable Orléanist might have come to the throne, the constituency for any form of monarchy had diminished too greatly to make it a possibility.

17. See, e.g., Maurice Agulhon, *The French Republic 1879–1992* (Cambridge: Blackwell, 1993); James McMillan, *Dreyfus to DeGaulle* (London: Edward Arnold, 1985).

18. Michael Mann, "The Autonomous Power of the State: Its Origins, Mechanisms and Results," *European Journal of Sociology (Archives européennes de sociologie)* 25 (1984); Agustin Goenaga Orrego, "Trajectories of State Capacity in France and Mexico, 1830–1950" (Paper presented at 2013 Annual Meeting of the American Political Science Association).

19. Before this time "many rural communities remained imprisoned in semi-isolation, limited participants in the economy and politics" of France. Eugen Weber, *Peasants into Frenchmen: The Modernization of Rural France, 1870–1914* (Palo Alto, CA: Stanford University Press, 1976), 195.

20. Before this time some scholars estimate that as many as one half of France's citizens did not speak standard French. See Weber, *Peasants into Frenchmen*.

21. David Bell, *The Cult of the Nation in France* (Cambridge, MA: Harvard University Press, 2003), 207. This is why these teachers were vilified by the Church and right more generally as "professors of atheism," "seasoned revolutionaries," and "masters of demagogy." Frederik Brown, *For the Soul of France: Culture Wars in the Age of Dreyfus* (New York: Anchor Books, 2011), 56.

22. Douglas Johnson, "The Making of the French Nation," in *The National Question in Europe in Historical Context*, ed. Roy Porter and Mikulas Teich (New York: Cambridge University Press, 1993), 53.

23. B.R. Mitchell, *European Historical Statistics 1750–1970* (New York: Columbia University Press, 1978).

24. Interestingly, despite their being among France's best-known advocates of Marxism, neither Guesde nor Lafargue had extensive firsthand knowledge of Marx's oeuvre nor much in the way of sophisticated economic or philosophical training, despite the fact that Lafargue was Marx's son-in-law. Joy Hudson Hall, "Gabriel Deville and the Development of French Socialism" (PhD diss., Auburn University, 1983).

25. Guesde (1886), quoted in Louis Levine, *Syndicalism in France* (New York: Columbia University Press, 1912), 56.

26. Guesde (1886), quoted in Louis Levine, *Syndicalism in France* (New York: Columbia University Press, 1912), 56.

27. Zeev Sternhell, *Neither Right nor Left: Fascist Ideology in France* (Princeton, NJ: Princeton University Press, 1995); Zeev Sternhell, *The Birth of Fascist Ideology* (Princeton, NJ: Princeton University Press, 1995); and Sheri Berman, *The Primacy of Politics: Social Democracy and the Making of Europe's Twentieth Century* (New York: Cambridge University Press, 1994).

28. C. Stewart Doty, *From Cultural Rebellion to Counterrevolution: The Politics of Maurice Barrès* (Athens: Ohio University Press, 1976), 94.

29. Michael Curtis, *Three Against the Third Republic: Sorel, Barrés and Maurras* (Princeton, NJ: Princeton University Press, 1959), esp. chapter 2; Patrick H. Hutton, "Popular Boulangism and the Advent of Mass Politics in France, 1866–90," *Journal of Contemporary History* 11 (1976); René Rémond, *The Right Wing in France: From 1815 to de Gaulle* (Philadelphia: University of Pennsylvania Press, 1969), esp. chapter 6.

30. Charles Sowerwine, *France since 1870* (London: Palgrave, 2001), esp. p. 62. Also see Ze'ev Sternhell, "Paul Deroulede and the Origins of Modern French Nationalism," *Journal of Contemporary History* 6, no. 4 (1971): 68.

31. Howard Jack, *After the French Revolution: Six Critics of Democracy and Nationalism* (Hertfordshire: Harvester Wheatsheaf, 1991), 284.

32. René Rémond, *The Right Wing in France: From 1815 to de Gaulle* (Philadelphia: University of Pennsylvania Press, 1969), 60.

33. See Brown, *For the Soul of France*; Brown, *The Embrace of Unreason* (New York: Alfred Knopf, 2014).

34. Although most of Alsace had been part of France since the Treaty of Westphalia, it had earlier been part of the Holy Roman Empire and retained crucial ties to German-speaking lands. After the war, some inhabitants chose to adopt French citizenship, but others did not. In addition, most of its Jews spoke Yiddish and many German, including Dreyfus's family (which also included members who chose not to take French citizenship), leading them to be labeled "foreign" or un-French).

35. Harris, *Dreyfus*, 61.

36. Louis Begley, *Why the Dreyfus Affair Matters* (New Haven, CT: Yale University Press, 2009), 7, 9.

37. Over a hundred years later, the paper officially apologized for its anti-Semitic writings in the Dreyfus Affair. http://www.nytimes.com/1998/01/13/world/world-news-briefs-french-paper-apologizes-for-slurs-on-dreyfus.html.

38. http://exhibits.library.duke.edu/exhibits/show/dreyfus/intro/anti-semiticpress.

39. Ruth Harris, *Dreyfus: Politics, Emotion, and the Scandal of the Century* (New York: Henry Holt, 2010).

40. Gildea, 4. Douglas Johnson, *France and the Dreyfus Affair* (New York: Walker and Co., 1966).

41. *J'accuse* and other writings of Zola's concerning the Dreyfus Affair are collected in Emile Zola, *The Dreyfus Affair*, ed. Alain Pagès (New Haven, CT: Yale University Press, 1996).

42. Michael Marrus, *The Politics of Assimilation: A Study of the French-Jewish Community at the Time of the Dreyfus Affair* (New York: Oxford University Press, 1981), 208–09, quoted in Begley, *Why the Dreyfus Affair Matters*, 75; Brown, *For the Soul of France*, 207.

43. Robert Lynn Fuller, *The Origins of the French Nationalist Movement, 1886–1914* (Jefferson, NC: MacFarland, 2012).

44. Fuller, *The Origins of the French Nationalist Movement, 1886–1914*, 57.

45. Eugen Weber, *Action Français: Royalism and Reaction in Twentieth Century France* (Palo Alto, CA: Stanford University Press, 1962), 52. Also Stephen Wilson, "History and Traditionalism: Maurras and the Action Français," *Journal of the History of Ideas* 29, no. 3 (July–September 1968).

46. Begley, *Why the Dreyfus Affair Matters*, 154–55.

47. Fuller, *The Origins*, 102.

48. Interestingly, he maintained his belief in Dreyfus's guilt despite what he had found.

49. Esterhazy, meanwhile, was never prosecuted and died in England.

50. Quoted in J.P. Mayer, *Political Thought in France: From the Revolution to the Fourth Republic* (London: Routledge and Kegan Paul, 1943), 99.

51. Quoted in David Thomson, *Democracy in France: The Third Republic* (New York: Oxford University Press, 1946), 49–50.

52. Sheri Berman, *The Primacy of Politics: Social Democracy and the Making of Europe's Twentieth Century* (New York: Cambridge University Press, 1994).

53. Sowerwine, *France since 1870*, 83.

54. Although governments during the Third Republic rarely lasted more than a few months (there were over ninety governments over the lifetime of the Third Republic), government ministers changed less often than governments, making levels of instability deceptive. John Scott, *Republican Ideas and the Liberal Tradition in France, 1870–1914* (New York: Columbia University Press, 1951); Suhir Hazareesingh, *Political Traditions in Modern France* (New York: Oxford University Press, 1994); Sanford Elwitt, *The Third Republic Defended* (Baton Rouge: Louisiana State University Press, 1986).

55. Maurice Agulhon, *The French Republic 1879–1992* (Cambridge: Blackwell Publishers, 1993), 62; Sanford Elwitt, *The Making of the Third Republic* (Baton Rouge: Louisiana State University Press, 1975).

56. David Thomson, *Democracy in France* (New York: Oxford University Press, 1946), 171–72.

57. Jews gained full legal equality in France during the revolutionary era, a status they did not achieve in Austria until 1867, 1871 in the new Germany, and 1858 in England.

58. See, e.g., Shlomo Avineri, *Herzl: Theodor Herzl and the Foundation of the Jewish State* (London: Weidenfeld and Nicolson, 2013); Amos Elon, *Herzl* (New York: Holt, Rinehart and Winston, 1975).

59. Robert Gildea, "How to Understand the Dreyfus Affair," *New York Review of Books*, June 10, 2010.

Chapter 7

1. This is a colloquial translation from his memoirs first published in 1866. Republished by Forgotten Books (London, 2012).

2. Victor von Unruh, Prussian civil servant and politician, quoted in Blackbourn, *The Long Nineteenth Century*, 138.

3. John Davis, *Conflict and Control: Law and Order in Nineteenth Century Italy* (Atlantic Highlands, NJ: Humanities Press, 1988).

4. Alexander Grab, "The Napoleonic Legacy in Italy," in *Tosca's Prism*, ed. Deborah Burton, Susan Vandiver Nicassio, and Agustino Zino (Boston: Northeastern Press, 2003); Alexander Grab, *Napoleon and the Transformation of Europe* (New York: Palgrave Macmillan, 2003); Alexander Grab, "From the French Revolution to Napoleon," in *Italy in the Nineteenth Century*, ed. John Davis (New York: Oxford University Press, 2000).

5. David Gilmour, *The Pursuit of Italy* (New York: Farrar, Straus and Giroux, 2012), 137; Martin Clark, *The Italian Risorgimento* (New York: Pearson, 2009).

6. Metternich apparently first used this term in 1814 in his "Memorandum to the Great Powers," but it was repeated later in his memoirs and letters.

7. David Laven, "The Age of Restoration," in *Italy in the Nineteenth Century*, ed. Davis, 54.

8. G.F.-H. Berkeley, *Italy in the Making* (Cambridge: Cambridge University Press, 1940).

9. Mazzini in Mack Smith, *The Making of Italy*, 41.

10. Derek Beales, "Garibaldi and the Politics of Italian Enthusiasm," in *Society and Politics in the Age of the Risorgimento*, ed. John Davis and Paul Ginsborg (New York: Cambridge University Press, 1991).

11. Before 1848 the Neo-Guelph movement had championed the pope as leader of a unified Italy but his actions during the period 1848–49 eliminated this possibility.

12. Beales and Biagini, *The Risorgimento*, 110.

13. For example, the three leaders of the National Society, Manin, Giorgio Pallavcino, and Giuseppe La Farina, were exiles.

14. Daniele Manin in a letter to Lorenzo Valerio, reprinted in Mack Smith, *Risorgimento*, 215.

15. Raymond Grew, *A Sterner Plan for Italian Unity: The Italian National Society in the Risorgimento* (Princeton, NJ: Princeton University Press, 1963), 105.

16. This also seemed to support jettisoning the radical social and political goals and mass-based strategies of 1848 so as to avoid antagonizing the non-democratic, anti-revolutionary regimes in these countries.

17. At this point unification did not mean unifying the whole peninsula but rather consolidating it, pushing out the Austrians, and putting its northern regions under Piedmontese control.

18. This sympathy seems to have had a variety of sources: regret at restoring theocratic papal rule in the Papal States after 1848, reconsideration of his position after an assassination attempt by an Italian nationalist in 1848, and his own roots in Italy, which included time spent with the Carbonari in the 1830s.

19. Part of the problem was that wealthy, non-noble families rather than peasants ended up with land. The peasants did not have the money to buy the land offered by the government and so ended up worse off than before since now they were under the thumb of landowners who had no obligations towards them while the Crown was too weak to provide protection.

20. Luigi Blanch quoted by John Davis, "The South, The Risorgimento and the Origins of the 'Southern Problem,'" in *Gramsci and Italy's Passive Revolution*, ed. John Davis (New York: Routledge, 2014), 92.

21. *A Letter to the Earl of Aberdeen on the State Prosecutions of the Neapolitan Government* (1851), Oxford Essential Quotations 2014 (online version: http://www.oxfordreference.com/view/10.1093/acref/9780191735240.001.0001/q-oro-00004876).

22. Lucy Riall, *Sicily and the Unification of Italy* (Oxford: Clarendon Press, 1998), 60.

23. Diego Gambetta, *The Sicilian Mafia: The Business of Private Protection* (Cambridge, MA: Harvard University Press, 1996).

24. Mack Smith, *Risorgimento*, 361.

25. Riall, *Sicily and the Unification of Italy*, 75.

26. Edgar Holt, *Risorgimento: The Making of Italy 1815–1870* (London: Macmillan, 1970), 249.

27. Frederick Schneid, *The Second War of Italian Unification 1859–1861* (Oxford: Osprey, 2012).

28. Denis Mack Smith, *Cavour and Garibaldi 1860: A Study in Political Conflict* (New York: Cambridge University Press, 1985); Denis Mack Smith, *Italy and Its Monarchy* (New Haven, CT: Yale University Press, 1992); Denis Mack Smith, *Mazzini* (New Haven, CT: Yale University Press, 1996).

29. Graziano, *The Failure of Italian Nationhood*, 14, 81.

30. Mazzini, quoted in Robert Pearce and Andrina Stiles, *The Unification of Italy* (London: Hodder Education, 2008).

31. Quoted in Moe, "The Emergence of the Southern Question," 53.

32. In any case, geography made Italy no more "preordained to unite" than Scandinavia, the Balkan Peninsula, North America, or any other geographically contiguous region. Gilmour, *The Pursuit of Italy*, 147. Also see Derek

Beales and Eugenio Biagini, *The Risorgimento and the Unification of Italy* (London: Pearson, 2002), chapter 1.

33. Beales and Biagini, *The Risorgimento*, 33. Most people spoke a variety of dialects, some related to Italian, others less so. Beale and Biagini, *The Risorgimento*, chapter 4.

34. Benedict Anderson, *Imagined Communities* (New York: Verso, 1991).

35. Manilio Graziano, *The Failure of Italian Nationhood* (New York: Palgrave, 2010), 137. Also see Lucy Riall, *Risorgimento: The History of Italy from Napoleon to Nation-State* (London: Palgrave, 2009), esp. chapter 6.

36. See the first note in this chapter.

37. Harry Hearder, *Italy in the Age of the Risorgimento* (London: Longman, 1983); Denis Mack Smith, *Italy* (Ann Arbor: University of Michigan Press, 1959); Christopher Seton-Watson, *Italy from Liberalism to Fascism* (London: Butler and Tanner, 1967); Salvatore Saladino, *Italy from Unification to 1919* (New York: Thomas Crowell, 1970); Denis Mack Smith, *Victor Emanuel, Cavour and the Risorgimento* (New York: Oxford University Press, 1971).

38. Graziano, *The Failure of Italian Nationhood*, 79; Holt, *Risorgimento*, 255.

39. Daniel Ziblatt, *Structuring the State: The Formation of Italy and Germany and the Puzzle of Federalism* (Princeton, NJ: Princeton University Press, 2006). Also see Lucy Riall, "Elite Resistance to State Formation," in *National Histories & European History*, ed. Mary Fullbrook (Boulder, CO: Westview, 1993).

40. Gilmour, *The Pursuit of Italy*, 17.

41. Mack Smith, *Cavour and Garibaldi*.

42. Mack Smith, *Italy*, 58.

43. Riall, *Sicily and the Unification of Italy*, 83.

44. Denis Mack Smith, *The Making of Italy, 1796–1870* (New York: Harper and Row, 1968), 3.

45. In his *Prison Notebooks* Gramsci, for example, referred to the Risorgimento as a "passive revolution" made by elites rather than the masses that led to a deep division between state and civil society. Also see Stuart Woolf, *A History of Italy 1700–1860* (London: Methuen & Co., 1979), esp. 479.

46. Luigi Barzini, "Romance and the Risorgimento," *The New York Review of Books*, October 5, 1972.

47. Gabriella Gribaudi, "Images of the South," in *The New History of the Italian South*, ed. Robert Lumley and Jonathan Morris (Exeter, England: University of Exeter Press, 1997), 88–89.

48. Holt, *Risorgimento*, 271; J. Dickie, "A World at War: The Italian Army and Brigandage," *History Workshop Journal* 33 (1992).

49. John Dickie, "Stereotypes of the Italian South 1860–1900," in *The New History of the Italian South*, ed. Lumley and Morris.

50. Quoted in Mack Smith, *Risorgimento*, 328, 330.

51. Quoted in Dickie, "Stereotypes," 122.

52. D'Azeglio to C. Matteucci, August 1861, in Mack Smith, *Risorgimento*, 367.

53. *Trasformismo* was also a partial inheritance from Piedmont. Cavour had coopted potential opponents in order to rule from the "conservative middle"; he disliked opposition and party politics more generally.

54. Judith Chubb, *Patronage, Power and Poverty in Southern Italy* (New York: Cambridge University Press, 1982), 16.

55. Christopher Duggan, *A Concise History of Italy* (New York: Cambridge University Press, 2014), 160.

56. Newer research on the south has complicated the issue of "backwardness," but the region's poverty, illiteracy, isolation, etc. are not in doubt. See, e.g., Lumley and Jonathan, eds., *The New History of the Italian South*; and Jane Schneider, ed., *Italy's "Southern Question": Orientalism in One Country* (New York: Berg, 1998).

57. The "alliance" that developed between Northern and Southern elites has been identified as one of the key features and flaws of post-unification Italy by many analysts, of which Gramsci is perhaps the most well known.

58. The later imposition of protectionism also worked to the North's rather than the South's benefit. As Stefano Jacini put it, these policies represented a "plunder of the rural south by Italy's politicians." Quoted in Marta Petrusewicz, "The Demise of *Latifondismo*," in *The New History of the Italian South*, ed. Lumley and Morris, 33. Also see Davis, "The South, The Risorgimento and the Origins of the 'Southern Problem.'"

59. Leopold Franchetti and Sidney Sonnino, "Peasant Life and Local Government in the Abruzzi," in Mack Smith, *Risorgimento*, 374–78. The full report is available at http://www.intratext.com/ixt/ita2434/_INDEX.HTM. Also see Paolo Pezzino, "Local Power in Southern Italy," in *The New History of the Italian South*, ed. Lumley and Morris; and Nelson Moe, "The Emergence of the Southern Question in Villari, Franchetti and Sonnino," in *Italy's Southern Question*, ed. Schneider.

60. David Roberts, *The Syndicalist Tradition and Italian Fascism* (Chapel Hill: The University of North Carolina Press, 1979), 37. Also see Martin Clark, *Modern Italy 1871–1982* (New York: Longman, 1984), 159.

61. By 1900, illiteracy rates were down to about 70 percent in the south and 40 percent in the north. Italian speakers were now about 15–20 percent of the population. Oddly by this point Italy had the highest percentage of university graduates and illiterates in Western Europe.

62. Davis quoting from a report by Francesco Saverio Merlino, *Conflict and Control*, 4. Also see Roger Absalom, *Italy since 1800* (New York: Longman, 1995), esp. 67.

63. Sheri Berman, *The Primacy of Politics: Social Democracy and the Making of Europe's Twentieth Century* (New York: Cambridge University Press, 2006), chapter 3.

64. Ronald Cunsolo, *Italian Nationalism* (Malabar, FL: Krieger, 1990); Alexander De Grand, *The Nationalist Association and the Rise of Fascism in Italy* (Lincoln: University of Nebraska Press, 1978); Armand Patrucco, *The Critics of the Italian Parliamentary System, 1860–1915* (Dusseldorf: Bertelsmann

Universitätsverlag, 1973); John A. Thayer, *Italy and the Great War: Politics and Culture, 1870–1915* (Madison: University of Wisconsin Press, 1964).

65. David Roberts, *The Syndicalist Tradition and Italian Fascism* (Chapel Hill: University of North Carolina Press, 1979), 118.

66. Cunsolo, *Italian Nationalism*, 104.

67. Roth, *The Cult of Violence*, 92.

68. Quoted in Salvatore Saladino, *Italy from Unification to 1919: The Growth and Decay of a Liberal Regime* (New York: Thomas Cromwell, 1970), 98. For an introduction to Giolitti and the controversies surrounding him, see G. Giolitti, *Memoirs of My Life* (London: Sydney, Chapman and Dodd, 1923); Ronald Consolo, "The Great Debate on Prime Minister Giovanni Giolitt and Giolittian Italy," *Canadian Review of Studies in Nationalism* 18, nos. 1–2 (1991).

69. Frank Coppa, *Planning, Protectionism and Politics: Economics and Politics in the Giolittian Age* (Washington, DC: Catholic University Press, 1971).

70. Coppa, *Planning, Protectionism, and Politics in Liberal Italy*, 164. Maria Sophia Quine, *Italy's Social Revolution: Charity and Welfare from Liberalism to Fascism* (New York: Palgrave, 2002).

71. A. William Salomone, *Italian Democracy in the Making* (Philadelphia: University of Pennsylvania Press, 1945), chapter 5.

72. Alexander de Grand, *The Hunchback's Tailor: Giovanni Giolitti and Liberal Italy from the Challenge of Mass Politics to the Rise of Fascism* (New York: Praeger, 2001).

73. Paul Corner, "Liberalism, Fascism, Pre-Fascism," in *Rethinking Italian Fascism*, ed. David Forgacs (London: Lawrence and Wishart, 1986), 16.

74. This was particularly true after 1907–1908 when an economic crisis made many businessmen fed up with Giolitti's social policies and toleration of the workers' movement.

75. Quoted in Emilio Gentile, "From the Cultural Revolt of the Giolittian Era to the Ideology of Fascsim," in *Studies*, ed. Koppa, 103.

76. Enrico Corridini, "The Principles of Nationalism" (Report to the First National Congress in Florence on December 3, 1910), reprinted in Adrian Lyttelton, ed., *Italian Fascisms* (New York: Harper and Row, 1973), 146–48.

77. Duggan, *A Concise History of Modern Italy*, 186–87.

78. Alexander De Grand, *The Italian Left in the Twentieth Century* (Indianapolis: Indiana University Press, 1989), 24; Maurice Neufeld, *Italy: School for Awakening Countries—The Italian Labor Movement in Its Political, Social, and Economic Setting from 1800 to 1960* (Ithaca, NY: Cayuga Press, 1961), 240; Ronald Cunsolo, "Libya and the Undoing of the Giolittian System," in *Studies in Modern Italian History*, ed. Frank Coppa (New York: Peter Lang, 1986).

79. All men over twenty-one who were literate or had completed military service would have the vote as well as all men over thirty, whether literate or not.

80. A. William Salomone, *Italy from the Risorgimento to Fascism* (New York: Anchor, 1970); John Davis, "Remapping Italy's Path to the Twentieth Century,"

Journal of Modern History 66 (June 1994); Davis, ed., *Gramsci and Italy's Passive Revolution*.

81. The only close competitor here might be Spain, where as we will see Catholicism was intricately tied up with Spanish identity and the Church played an extremely powerful role. There may also be some overlap with what Muslim societies are experiencing today.

82. Gaetano Salvemini, "Introductory Essay," in Salomone, *Italian Democracy in the Making*, vii.

83. Patrucco, *The Critics of the Italian Parliamentary System*, 126.

84. Samuel Huntington, *Political Order in Changing Societies* (New Haven, CT: Yale University Press, 1968). Another issue was the tendency of the state to respond to discontent with force rather than reform, i.e., with despotic rather than infrastructural power, a clear sign of state weakness rather than strength. Michael Mann, "The Autonomous Power of the State: Its Origins, Mechanisms and Results," *European Journal of Sociology* 25 (1984). Also see Riall, *Sicily and the Unification of Italy*, 226; Riall, "Elite Resistance to State Formation," esp. 64; Riall, "Garibaldi and the South," in *Italy in the Nineteenth Century*, ed. Davis, 151; Davis, *Conflict and Control*, 5, 264; Geoffrey Haywood, *Failure of a Dream: Sidney Sonnino and the Rise and Fall of Liberal Italy* (Florence: Leo Olschki, 1999), 34.

Chapter 8

1. Speech in the Prussian parliament (1862). Excerpts at http://germanhistorydocs .ghi-dc.org/sub_document.cfm?document_id=250.

2. Text of the 1850 Prussian constitution: http://en.wikisource.org/wiki/ Constitution_of_the_Kingdom_of_Prussia.

3. Heinrich August Winkler, *Germany: The Long Road West 1789–1933* (New York: Oxford, 2006), 115.

4. Henry Kissinger, "The White Revolutionary: Reflections on Bismarck," *Daedalus* 97, no. 3 (1968): 888.

5. Dennis Showalter, *The Wars of German Unification* (London: Bloomsbury Academic, 2015).

6. This war also influenced Italian unification—see chapter 7.

7. Nicholas Sambanis, Stergios Skaperdas, and William Wohlforth, "Nation-Building through War," *APSR* 109, no. 2 (May 2015).

8. Daniel Ziblatt, *Structuring the State: The Formation of Germany and Italy and the Puzzle of Federalism* (Princeton, NJ: Princeton University Press, 2008).

9. http://ourworldindata.org/data/education-knowledge/literacy/.

10. Hans-Ulrich Wehler, *The German Empire, 1871–1918* (New York: Berg Publishers, 1985), 55. Similarly but more colorfully Marx and Engels referred to it as a "police-guarded, military despotism, embellished with parliamentary forms, alloyed with a feudal admixture, already influenced by the

bourgeoisie, and bureaucratically carpentered . . . where the government is almost omnipotent and the Reichstag and other representative bodies have no real power." Quoted in Christopher Henning, *Philosophy after Marx* (Bielefeld, Germany: Transcript Verlag, 2005), 92.

11. A.J.P. Taylor, *Bismarck: The Man and the Statesman* (New York: Vintage Books, 1955), 98.

12. Schmitt, *Staatsgefüge und Zusammenbruch des Zweiten Reiches* (1934), quoted in Dieter Grosser, *Vom monarchischen Konstitutionalismus zur parlamentarischen Demokratie* (The Hague: Martinus Nijhoff, 1970), 3. Also Marcus Kreuzer, "Parliamentarization and the Question of German Exceptionalism," *Central European History* 36, no. 3 (2003).

13. Larry Diamond, "Thinking about Hybrid Regimes," *Journal of Democracy* 13, no. 2 (April 2002); Steven Levitsky and Lucan Way, "Assessing the Quality of Democracy," *Journal of Democracy* 13, no. 2 (April 2002).

14. Daniel Ziblatt, *Structuring the State: The Formation of Germany and Italy and the Puzzle of Federalism* (Princeton, NJ: Princeton University Press, 2008); John Breuilly, "Sovereignty and Boundaries: Modern State Formation and National Identity in Germany," in *National Histories and European Histories*, ed. Mary Fulbrook (Boulder, CO: Westview, 1993); Geoff Eley, "Bismarckian Germany," in *Modern Germany Reconsidered*, ed. Gordon Martel (New York: Routledge, 1992).

15. They did lose control over their militaries.

16. As Gordon Craig put it, the military was "a law unto itself, acquiescing in directions issued by the political heads of the state for the most part only when it suited its purpose to do so." *The Politics of the Prussian Army, 1640–1945* (New York: Oxford University Press, 1955), 468.

17. Highly undemocratic voting systems existed in a couple of other states as well. Thomas Kühne, *Dreiklassenwahlrech and Wahlkultur in Preussen, 1867–1914* (Düsseldorf: Droste, 1994).

18. Joseph Biesinger, *Germany: A Reference Guide* (New York: Infobase, 2006), 637.

19. Manfred Rauh, *Föderalismus und Parlamentarismus im Wilhelminischen Reich* (Düsseldorf: Droste, 1973); Elmar M. Hucko, ed., *The Democratic Tradition: Four German Constitutions* (New York: Berg, 1987), 29–30; and Nipperdey, *Nachdenken über die deutsche Geschichte* (Munich: C.H. Beck, 1986).

20. Christopher Clark, *Iron Kingdom* (Cambridge, MA: Harvard University Press, 2006), 561.

21. Wolfgang Mommsen, *Imperial Germany, 1867–1918* (London: Arnold, 1995), 199; John Snell, *The Democratic Movement in Germany, 1789–1914* (Chapel Hill: University of North Carolina Press, 1976).

22. Hucko, ed., *The Democratic Tradition*; Klaus Erich Pollman, *Parlamentarismus in Norddeutschen Bund, 1867–1870* (Düsseldorf: Droste, 1985).

23. Arthur Rosenberg, *Imperial Germany* (Boston: Beacon, 1964), 19.

24. Alexander Gerschenkron, *Bread and Democracy in Germany* (Ithaca, NY: Cornell University Press, 1989); H.-J. Puhle, *Agrarische Interessenpolitik und preussischer Konservatismus im wilhelminischen Reich* (Bonn: 1966).

25. Wehler, *The German Empire*, 94.

26. Michael Gross, *The War Against Catholicism* (Ann Arbor: University of Michigan Press, 2004), 1. Also see Rebecca Bennette, *Fighting for the Soul of Germany* (Cambridge, MA: Harvard University Press, 2012); Ronal Ross, *The Failure of Bismarck's Kulturkampf* (Washington, DC: Catholic University of America, 2000); Margaret Lavina Anderson, "The Kulturkampf and the Course of German History," *Central European History* 19, no. 1 (March 1986); and Clark, *Iron Kingdom*, 568.

27. Vernon Lidtke, *The Alternative Culture: Socialist Labor in Imperial Germany* (New York: Oxford University Press, 1985), 81.

28. Sheri Berman, *The Social Democratic Moment: Ideas and Politics in the Making of Interwar Europe* (Cambridge, MA: Harvard University Press, 1998); Sheri Berman, *The Primacy of Politics: Social Democracy and the Making of Europe's Twentieth Century* (New York: Cambridge University Press, 1994).

29. Anderson, *Practicing Democracy*, 86. See also Anderson, "Piety and Politics: Recent Work on German Catholics," *Journal of Modern History* (December 1991); Anderson, *Windthorst: A Political Biography* (New York: Oxford University Press, 1981); Ronald Ross, "Enforcing the Kulturkampf in the Bismarckian State and the Limits of Coercion in Imperial Germany," *Journal of Modern History* 56 (September 1984); Jonathan Sperber, *Popular Catholicism in Nineteenth Century Germany* (Princeton, NJ: Princeton University Press, 1984).

30. Anderson, *Practicing Democracy*, 246; Michael Stürmer, ed., *Bismarck und die preussisch-deutsche Politik, 1871–1890* (Munich: Deutscher Taschenbuch, 1970); Michael Stürmer, "Staatsstreichgedanken im Bismarckreich," *Historische Zeitschrift* 209 (1969).

31. As Wehler put it, the German "constitution was tailored to [Bismarck's] abilities . . . and without him it no longer had a point of coordination. A power vacuum was created and subsequently a climate arose in which various personalities and social forces appeared in an attempt to fill it. Since, in the long run, neither they nor Parliament succeeded, there existed in Germany a permanent crisis of the state behind its façade of high-handed leadership." *The German Empire*, 62.

32. In England property restrictions disenfranchised at least one-third of all male voters, while in the United States voluntary registration lowered turnout and African Americans were effectively barred from meaningful political participation. Stanley Suval, *Electoral Politics in Wilhelmine Germany* (Chapel Hill: University of North Carolina Press, 1985); Jonathan Sperber, *The Kaiser's Voters* (New York: Cambridge University Press, 1997).

33. Suval, *Electoral Politics*, 21, 17.

34. David Blackbourn, *Class, Religion and Local Politics in Wilhelmine Germany* (New Haven, CT: Yale University Press, 1980), p. 12.

35. Anderson, "The Kulturkampf" and Anderson, *Practicing Democracy*, chapter 5.

36. Sperber, *The Kaiser's Voters*, 123; James Sheehan, *German Liberalism in the Nineteenth Century* (Chicago: University of Chicago Press, 1978).

37. Estimates of the German unemployment rate at the turn of the century are as low as 2.7 percent and wages were creeping up during this era. Such figures show just how tight the labor market was, giving German workers some flexibility.

38. Geoff Eley, *Reshaping the German Right: Radical Nationalism and Political Change after Bismarck* (Ann Arbor: University of Michigan Press, 1991), chapter 2; Sheehan, *German Liberalism*, part 6; Daniel Ziblatt, *Conservative Parties and the Birth of Modern Democracy* (New York: Cambridge University Press, 2017).

39. Daniel Ziblatt, "Shaping Democratic Practice and Causes of Electoral Fraud: The Case of Nineteenth Century Germany," *American Political Science Review* 103, no. 1 (2009): 15, 18.

40. Sheehan, *German Liberalism*, 236.

41. See, e.g., Friz Stern, *The Politics of Cultural Despair: A Study in the Rise of the Germanic Ideology* (Berkeley: University of California Press, 1961). On the proliferation of civil society organizations and their implications for German political development, see Sheri Berman, "Civil Society and the Collapse of the Weimar Republic," *World Politics* 49, no. 3 (April 1997).

42. Peter Stachura, *The German Youth Movement 1900–1945: An Interpretive and Documentary History* (New York: St. Martin's Press, 1981), 17.

43. Such ideas combined with the power and independence of the army to produce horrific massacres and even genocide in parts of German-occupied Africa. Isabell Hull, *Absolute Destruction: Military Culture and the Practices of War in Imperial Germany* (Ithaca, NY: Cornell University Press, 2004).

44. Puhle, *Agrarische Interessenpolitik*.

45. Stern, *The Politics of Cultural Despair*, xi, xxiii, 169; Eley, *Reshaping the German Right*.

46. Eley, *Reshaping the German Right*, xix.

47. This was rejected by government ministers, key figures in state governments, and others. Anderson, *Practicing Democracy*, 247–48.

48. Quoted in Winkler, *Germany*, 269–70.

49. Rosenberg, *Imperial Germany*, 52–54.

50. James Retallack, "The Road to Philippi," in *Between Reform, Reaction and Resistance: Studies in the History of German Conservatism from 1789 to 1945*, ed. Larry Eugene Jones and James Retallack (Providence, RI: Berg, 1993). Also see P.-C. Witt, *Die Finanzpolitik des deutschen Reiches von 1903 bis 1913* (Hamburg: Matthiesen, 1970); Katharine Lerman, *The Chancellor As Courtier: Bernhard von Bülow and the Governance of Germany, 1900–1909* (New York: Cambridge University Press, 1990); Beverly Heckert, *From*

Basserman to Bebel: The Grand Bloc's Quest for Reform in the Kaiserreich, 1900–1914 (New Haven, CT: Yale University Press, 1974), 79ff.

51. Quoted in Rauh, *Föderalismus*, 245. Bülow later wrote of this period that he feared that it was "'the starting point of a trend that creates embittered party conflicts, brings forth unnatural party groupings, and is detrimental to the welfare of the nation.' To the Conservatives he declared: 'We will see each other at Philippi.'" Quoted in Retallack, "The Road," 268.

52. Heckert, *From Basserman to Bebel*. Such coalitions appeared in a number of the more liberal states, further increasing the apprehension of conservatives (and radicals within the SPD).

53. Retallack, "The Road," 271.

54. On the SPD and the 1912 election, see Berman, *The Social Democratic Moment*, 128–30. Also see Jürgen Bertram, *Die Wahlen zum Deutschen Reichstag von Jahre 1912* (Düsseldorf: Droste, 1964); James Retallack, "'What Is to Be Done?' The Red Specter, Franchise Questions, and the Crisis of Conservative Hegemony in Saxony, 1896–1909," *Central European History* 23 (December 1990).

55. For an explanation of why the party failed to make this shift, see Berman, *The Social Democratic Moment*, chapters 4, 6.

56. Daniel Ziblatt, "Does Landholding Inequality Block Democratization? A Test of the 'Bread and Democracy' Thesis and the Case of Prussia," *World Politics* 60 (July 2008).

57. Berghahn, *Imperial Germany*, 274.

58. Kreuzer, "Parliamentarization," 339ff. and Mark Hewitson, "The Kaiserreich in Question: Constitutional Crisis in Germany before the First World War," *The Journal of Modern History* 73, no. 4 (December 2001): 765ff.

59. Lenin, quoted in Schoenbaum, *Zabern*, 172.

60. Niall Ferguson, "Public Finance and National Security: The Domestic Origins of the First World War Revisited," *Past and Present* 142 (February 1994): 153, 155–56.

61. Ferguson, "Public Finance and National Security," 158.

62. Theobald von Bethmann-Hollweg, *Betrachtungen zum Weltkrieg*, vol. 1 (Berlin: R. Hubbing, 1919–1921).

63. In the spring/summer of 1913 the Crown Prince apparently passed a memo to the emperor and Bethmann calling for this but it was rejected by both. V.R. Berghahn, *Germany and the Approach of War in 1914* (New York: St. Martin's Press, 1973), esp. 22ff. and 162ff.; Schoenbaum, *Zabern*, 11–12.

64. Robert Bergdahl, *The Politics of the Prussian Nobility* (Princeton, NJ: Princeton University Press, 1988), 3.

65. Reflecting this, characterizations of politics during the imperial era range from a "fragile equilibrium," to a "single long armistice in an undeclared war," to Friedrich Stampfer's famous quip that Germany was the "best administered but worst governed country in Europe." Schoenbaum, *Zabern*, 34, 36; John

C.G. Rohl, *The Kaiser and His Court* (New York: Cambridge University Press, 1987), 2.

66. There is debate on whether anti-Semitism was more central to German nationalism than other European nationalisms. Jacob Katz, *From Prejudice to Destruction* (Cambridge, MA: Harvard University Press, 1982); Peter Pulzer, *The Rise of Political Anti-Semitism in Germany and Austria* (London: Peter Halban, 1988); Meyer Weinberg, *Because They Were Jews* (New York: Greenwood Press, 1986); Robert Wistrich, *Anti-Semitism: The Longest Hatred* (New York: New York University Press, 1990).

67. Niall Ferguson has argued that this caused the German military to fall dangerously and provocatively behind its rivals, indirectly contributing to the outbreak of WWI. See "Public Finance and National Security"; Ferguson, *The Pity of War: Explaining World War I* (New York: Basic Books, 1999).

68. In 1913, for example, the moderate leader of the National Liberals, Ernst Bessermann, wrote to Chancellor Bülow that "the internal difficulties of Germany" had become "so enormously large that they can no longer be overcome within the present-day system." Quoted in Hewitson, "The Kaisserreich in Question," 765.

69. The most influential advocate of such views is Fritz Fischer, *War of Illusions* (New York: W.W. Norton, 1975). Also see Fischer, *Germany's Aims in the First World War* (New York: W.W. Norton, 1967); Eckert Kehr, *Battleship Building and Party Politics in Germany, 1894–1901* (Chicago: University of Chicago Press, 1983); Gordon Craig, ed., *Economic Interest, Militarism and Foreign Policy* (Berkeley: University of California Press, 1977); Wehler, *The German Empire*. On the controversy over this thesis see John A. Moses, *The Politics of Illusion* (London: George Prior Publishers, 1975).

70. This argument probably began with Karl Marx. See, e.g., "The Bourgeoisie and the Counter-Revolution," *Neue Rheinische Zeitung*, December 14, 1848, in Karl Marx, *The Revolutions of 1848* (London: Harmondsworth, 1973); and Marx, "A Radical German Revolution," in "Toward the Critique of Hegel's Philosophy of Law: Introduction," *Deutsch-Französische Jahrbucher*, 1844, reprinted in Saul K. Padover, *Karl Marx on Revolution* (New York: McGraw-Hill, 1971), 422–26. More recent advocates include Wehler, *The German Empire*; H.A. Winkler, "Bürgerliche Emanzipation und nationale Einigung," in *Probleme der Reichsgründungszeit 1848–1879*, ed. H. Böhme (Berlin: Kiepenheuer und Witsch, 1968); Ralf Dahrendorf, *Society and Democracy in Germany* (Garden City, NY: Doubleday, 1969); Fritz Fischer, *From Kaiserreich to Third Reich* (Boston: Allen and Unwin, 1986); and Talcott Parsons, "Democracy and Social Structure in Pre-Nazi Germany," in Talcott Parsons, *Essays in Sociological Theory* (Glencoe, IL: The Free Press, 1954). For discussions of the *Sonderweg* thesis see Thomas Nipperdey, *Nachdenken*; Richard Evans, "The Myth of Germany's Missing Revolution," in Evans, *Rethinking German History*; Martel, ed., *Modern*

Germany Reconsidered, chapters 1–3; and Geoff Eley, *From Unification to Nazism* (Boston: Allen and Unwin, 1986).

71. The most influential critique, particularly in English, came from David Blackbourn and Geoff Eley, *The Peculiarities of German History* (New York: Oxford University Press, 1984), which of course also explicitly takes a comparative perspective. Also, Robert G. Moeller, "The Kaiserreich Recast?" *Journal of Social History* 17 (1984); Roger Fletcher, "Recent Developments in German Historiography," *German Studies Review* 7 (1984).

72. Arno Mayer, *The Persistence of the Old Regime* (New York: Pantheon, 1981).

73. For a recent discussion of "continuities" see Helmut Walser Smith, *The Continuities of German History* (New York: Cambridge University Press, 2008).

Chapter 9

1. Apparently first published in his memoirs, but it is unclear if Grey remembered uttering them. http://www.telegraph.co.uk/history/world-war-one/11006042/How-darkness-descended-over-Europe-in-August-1914.html.

2. There are a few minor exceptions to this, i.e., places where some form of monarchy persisted past 1918—e.g., Spain, Romania—but these did not last very long.

3. Arno Mayer, *The Persistence of the Old Regime* (New York: Pantheon Books, 1981).

4. Eric Hobsbawm, *The Age of Extremes: A History of the World, 1914–1991* (New York: Pantheon Books, 1994), part 1.

5. Quoted in John Merriman, *A History of Modern Europe* (New York: W.W. Norton, 2004), 1056.

6. *The Economic Consequences of the Peace* (New York: Harcourt, Brace and Howe, 1920), 296–97.

7. Sheri Berman, "European Powers Forced Artificial borders on More Than the Middle East," *Washington Post*, Monkey Cage, May 18, 2016. https://www.washingtonpost.com/news/monkey-cage/wp/2016/05/18/european-powers-forced-artificial-borders-on-the-middle-east-they-did-the-same-thing-to-europe-itself/?utm_term=.b8e388009454.

8. Probably about 3.5 million Greeks, Armenians, and Assyrians were killed and then in 1923 the process was "finished off" when the "convention concerning the exchange of Greek and Turkish populations" was signed in Lausanne, Switzerland, leading to the transfer of approximately 1.5 Christians (Greeks) and Muslim Turks from Turkey to Greece and approximately 500,000 Muslim (Turks) from Greece to Turkey. See also Heather Rae, *State Identities and the Homogenisation of Peoples* (New York: Cambridge University Press, 2002).

9. Arno Mayer, *The Persistence of the Old Regime* (New York: Pantheon Books, 1981).

10. Eugen Weber, *Peasants into Frenchman* (Palo Alto, CA: Stanford University Press, 1976); Augustin Alonso Goenega Orrego, "The Social Origins of State Capacity: Civil Society, Political Order and Public Goods in France

(1789–1970) and Mexico (1810–1970)" (PhD diss., University of British Columbia, 2015).

11. Maurice Agulhon, *The French Republic 1879–1992* (Cambridge: Blackwell, 1993), 178–79.

12. Gordon Wright, *France in Modern Times* (New York: W.W. Norton, 1995), 306.

13. James McMillan, *Dreyfus to DeGaulle* (London: Edward Arnold, 1985), 78.

14. Wright, *France,* 306.

15. During the 1920s the Treasury seems to have borrowed more money from French citizens than it did during the war. Wright, *France,* 344.

16. Weber, *The Hollow Years,* 13.

17. Weber, *The Hollow Years,* 13. Pierre Goubert, *The Course of French History* (New York: Franklin Watts, 1988), 448.

18. Charles Sowerwine, *France since 1870* (London: Palgrave, 2001), 139.

19. Sheri Berman, *The Primacy of Politics: Social Democracy and the Making of Europe's Twentieth Century* (New York: Cambridge University Press, 1994).

20. See, e.g., Robert Soucy, *French Fascism: The First Wave, 1924–1933* (New Haven, CT: Yale University Press, 1986), 28, 161ff.

21. Soucy, *French Fascism,* 30.

22. Soucy, *French Fascism,* 69.

23. Soucy, *French Fascism,* 69

24. Soucy, *French Fascism,* 92.

25. Robert Soucy, *French Fascism: The Second Wave* (New Haven, CT: Yale University Press, 1997), 184. Also see Kevin Passmore, *From Liberalism to Fascism* (New York: Cambridge University Press, 1997), chapter 8; Kalus-Juergen Mueller, "French Fascism and Modernization," *Journal of Contemporary History* 11 (1976); and Frederick Brown, *The Embrace of Unreason* (New York: Knopf, 2014).

26. Ibid., 167.

27. Sheri Berman, *The Primacy of Politics: Social Democracy and the Making of Europe's Twentieth Century* (New York: Cambridge University Press, 2006), chapter 6.

28. Joel Colton, *Léon Blum: Humanist in Politics* (New York: Alfred Knopf, 1966), 66.

29. Michael Dobry, "France: An Ambiguous Survival," in *Conditions of Democracy in Europe,* ed. Dirk Berg-Schlosser and Jeremy Mitchell (New York: St. Martin's Press, 2000), 168.

30. Julian Jackson, *The Politics of Depression in France 1932–1936* (New York: Cambridge University Press, 1985).

31. http://socialdemocracy21stcentury.blogspot.com/2013/07/the-great-depression-in-europe-real-gdp.html.
   http://www.britannica.com/event/Great-Depression.
   https://en.wikipedia.org/wiki/Great_Depression_in_France#/media/File:PIB_1929-1939.gif.

http://krugman.blogs.nytimes.com/2009/10/09/modified-goldbugism-at-the-wsj/?_r=0.

http://thinkprogress.org/yglesias/2010/01/01/195635/leveling-up-or-leveling-down-with-china/.

https://en.wikipedia.org/wiki/Great_Depression#/media/File:Graph_charting_income_per_capita_throughout_the_Great_Depression.svg.

https://fportier.files.wordpress.com/2012/02/french-depression.pdf.

http://www.zum.de/whkmla/region/france/france19291939ec.html.

http://www.nber.org/chapters/c11482.pdf.

32. This was how it was viewed by many on the left, but some scholars characterize it this way as well, e.g. Alfred Cobban, *A History of Modern France*, vol. 3 (New York: Penguin, 1986), 142.

33. Soucy, *French Fascism: The Second Wave*.

34. Berman, *The Primacy of Politics*, chapter 6.

35. Julian Jackson, *The Popular Front in France* (New York: Cambridge University Press, 1988), 29.

36. Jackson, *The Popular Front in France*, 112; William Shirer, *The Collapse of the Third Republic* (New York: DaCapo Press, 1994).

37. Stanley Hoffman, *In Search of France* (New York: Harper Torchbooks, 1963), 25.

38. Jackson, *The Popular Front*, 169.

39. Its leader, Jacques Doriot, was a former communist. Jackson, *The Popular Front in France*, 236, 247.

40. There is debate about whether the CF and PSF should be considered fascist. See my *Primacy of Politics* but also Soucy, *French Fascism: The Second Wave,* and William Irvine, "Fascism in France and the Strange Case of the Croix de Feu," *Journal of Modern History* 63 (June 1991).

41. Stanley Payne, *A History of Fascism, 1914–1945* (Madison: University of Wisconsin Press, 1995), 295. Also see Irvine, "Fascism in France."

42. Soucy, *French Fascism: The Second Wave*, 178.

43. Soucy, *French Fascism: The Second Wave*, 36. See also Soucy, *French Fascism: The First Wave*, xii.

44. Joel Colton, *Léon Blum: Humanist in Politics* (Durham, NC: Duke University Press, 1987), 273, citing John Morton Blum, ed., *From the Morgenthau Diaries* (New York: Houghton Mifflin, 1959), 474.

45. Wright, *France in Modern Times*, 321–22.

46. Berman, *The Primacy of Politics*; Mazower, *Dark Continent*; Wolfgang Schivelbusch, *Three New Deals: Reflections on Roosevelt's America, Mussolini's Italy and Hitler's Germany* (New York: Henry Holt, 2006).

Chapter 10

1. Quoted in Pearce, *Reform!* 88.

2. Universal manhood suffrage came in 1918, but women under thirty were excluded until 1928. Plural voting and other anachronisms were fully eliminated in 1948. It is important to note that each part of the United Kingdom had somewhat different voting requirements until 1884 and so the reforms discussed below had somewhat differential effects on England, Scotland, Wales, and Ireland. This will be discussed further below.

3. See, e.g., John Garrard, *Democratisation in Britain* (New York: Palgrave, 2002). Or in the terminology of Robert Dahl, it was a competitive oligarchy. Dahl, *Polyarchy* (New Haven, CT: Yale University Press, 1973).

   I use the term "landed elites" but the terminology can be confusing. Britain's nobility differed from that of most other European countries in that it lacked legal privileges as a class; power came from the ownership of land (the loss of a landed estate therefore meant the loss of power and privilege). There were no "poor" aristocrats in England as there were in so many other European countries. Landowning elites were also divided into (at least) two main categories: peers (who had a right to sit in the House of Lords) and gentry. M.L. Bush, *The English Aristocracy* (Manchester: Manchester University Press, 1984).

4. David Spring, "Landed Elites Compared," in *European Landed Elites in the Nineteenth Century*, ed. David Spring (Baltimore: Johns Hopkins University Press, 1977); Hannah Schissler, "The Junkers," in *Peasants and Lords in Modern Germany*, ed. Robert Moeller (Boston: Allen and Unwin, 1986); G.E. Mingay, *English Landed Society in the Eighteenth Century* (London: Routledge, 1963); F.M.L. Thompson, *English Landed Society in the Nineteenth Century* (London: Routledge, 1971); Albert Goodwin, *European Nobility in the Eighteenth Century* (New York: Black, 1967).

5. David Cannadine, ed., *Patricians, Power and Politics in Nineteenth-Century Towns* (New York: St. Martin's Press, 1982).

6. O.F. Christie, *The Transition from Aristocracy* (London: Seeley, Service & co., 1927), 19. P.K. O'Brien and D. Heath, "English and French Landowners," in *Landowners, Capitalists and Entrepreneurs*, ed. F.M.L. Thompson (Oxford: Clarendon Press, 1994).

7. David Cannadine, *The Decline and Fall of the British Aristocracy* (New York: Vintage Books, 1999), 16, 21.

8. Russell, "The Rotten Boroughs of England," in *Famous Orators of the World and Their Orations*, ed. Charles Morris (Philadelphia: John Winston, 1933), 529–30. One indication of how much districting mattered is that in 1831 (the last election before the Great Reform Act) of the 658 seats up for grabs, only one-third were actually contested. House of Commons, "The History of the Parliamentary Franchise," Research Paper 13/14, March 2013, p. 3 (http://researchbriefings.parliament.uk/ResearchBriefing/Summary/RP13-14).

9. Derek Beales, *From Castlereagh to Gladstone* (New York: W.W. Norton, 1969), 49; John Hostettler and Brian Block, *Voting in Britain* (Chichester, England: Barry Rose, 2001), esp. chapter 6.

10. Evans, *The Great Reform Act*, 8–9; Michael Brock, *The Great Reform Act* (London: Hutchinson, 1973), 17ff.; Hostettler and Block, *Voting in Britain*.

11. Thompson, *English Landed Society*, 47. See also W.L. Guttsman, *The British Political Elite* (New York: Basic Books, 1963).

12. Britain's political order may actually have become less representative over time since due to population shifts and other developments the proportion of the citizenry actually entitled to vote in the early nineteenth century was probably less than in 1688. See, e.g., Evans, *The Great Reform Act*, 10–11.

13. In fact, by the early nineteenth century many of these restrictions were being ignored in practice.

14. Lord Holland to Henry Fox, quoted in J.C.D. Clark, *English Society, 1688–1832: Ideology, Social Structure and Political Practice during the Ancien Régime* (Cambridge: Cambridge University Press, 1985), 396–97.

15. G.I.T. Machin, "Resistance to the Repeal of the Test and Corporation Acts, 1828," *The Historical Journal* 22, no. 1 (1979): 128. Also see Machin, *The Catholic Question in English Politics 1820 to 1830* (Oxford: Clarendon Press, 1964).

16. Linda Colley, *Britons: Forging the Nation* (New Haven, CT: Yale University Press, 1992), chapter 8. Lord John Russell, for example, declared in 1828 that "what was at stake in the debate over Catholic emancipation was the principle that every man . . . should be at liberty to worship God according to the dictates of his conscience, without being subject to any penalty of disqualification whatsoever; that any restraint or restriction imposed on any man on account of his religious creed is in the nature of persecution, and is at once an offence to God and an injury to man. . . . If Parliament should say, "Nothing can be alleged against the Dissenters" . . . and if you afterwards decide against the Roman Catholics . . . whose only crime is that they adhere to a particular religious belief—if you decide against the admission of Roman Catholics to full civil privileges—I cannot very well conceive on what fair ground such a decision could rest." Parliamentary Debates February 26 and 28, 1828, in Russell, *Political Opinions on the Roman Catholic Question* (London: Richardson and Son, 1850), 2–3 (accessed as Google book https://books.google.com/books?id=8TGgAAAAMAAJ&dq=Lord%20Russell%20%22the%20great%20principle%2C%20involved%20in%20the%22&pg=PA3#v=onepage&q=Lord%20Russell%20%22the%20great%20principle,%20involved%20in%20the%22&f=false).

17. There were, for example, few English Catholics, and the Catholic Relief Act was coupled with increased property qualifications for voting in Ireland in an attempt to blunt further political organizing and agitation there. And as stressed below, the landowning elite's political domination extended at least until the end of the nineteenth century.

18. Evans, *The Great Reform Act*, 43; Brock, *The Great Reform Act*, 55.

19. They were more pro-reform partially because the existing political system favored the Tories. See, e.g., Stephen Lee, *Aspects of British Political History* (New York: Routledge, 1995), 57.

20. Edward Pearce, *Reform! The Fight for the 1832 Reform Act* (London: Jonathan Cape, 2003); R.W. Davies, "The Tories, the Whigs, and Catholic Emancipation," *English Historical Review* (1982).

21. Thomas Ertman, "The Great Reform Act of 1832 and British Democratization," *Comparative Political Studies* 43 (2010).

22. See, e.g., Robert Goldstein, *Political Repression in 19th Century Europe* (London: Routledge, 1983), 158.

23. Quoted in Pearce, *Reform!* 88.

24. Quoted in Brock, *The Great Reform Act*, 336.

25. Henry Cockburn, *Letters Chiefly Connected with the Affairs of Scotland* (London: William Ridgway, 1864), 259 (accessed as Google book https://books.google.com/books?id=bWcVAAAAQAAJ&lpg=PA258&ots=SvAB023NX-&dq=%22the%20object%20of%20an%20extension%20of%20the%20Elective%20franchise%22&pg=PA259#v=onepage&q=%22the%20object%20of%20an%20extension%20of%20the%20Elective%20franchise%22&f=false).

26. Hostettler and Block, *Voting in Britain*, chapter 9.

27. Walter Arnstein, *Britain Yesterday and Today: 1830 to the Present* (New York: Houghton Mifflin, 2001), 13.

28. Guttsman, *The British Political Elite*, 35–36.

29. Eric Evans, *The Great Reform Act of 1832* (London: Routledge, 1983), 2.

30. Estimates range from about one in five to about one in seven adult men now had the right to vote. The Reform initially covered England and Wales, equivalent acts were passed for Scotland and Ireland. For a fuller description of the effects of the 1832 reform see "The History of the Parliamentary Franchise"; Blackburn, *The Electoral System*; and Hostettler and Block, *Voting in Britain*. Text of the Bill and a list of changes in the distribution of seats can be found, for example, in Evans, appendices.

31. John Merriman, *A History of Modern Europe* (New York: W.W. Norton, 2004), 664. Similarly, Gaetano Mosca wrote that "In the course of the nineteenth century England adopted peacefully and without the violent shocks almost all the basic civil and political reforms that France paid so heavily to achieve through the great revolution. Undeniably, the great advantage of England lay in the greater energy, the greater practical wisdom, the better political training that her ruling class possessed." Quoted in Guttsman, *British Political Elite*, 75.

32. William Langer, *Political and Social Upheaval 1832–1852* (New York: Harper, 1969), 57, quoting George Young, *Victorian Essays* (London: Oxford University Press, 1936).

33. Simon Schama, *A History of Britain,* vol. 3 (New York: Miramax, 2002), 139; Eric Evans, *The Forging of the Modern State* (New York: Longman, 1996), 223;

Garrad, *Democratisation*, 37, and also Garrad, "Democratization in Britain," in *European Democratization Since 1800*, ed. Garrard, Vera Tolz, and Ralph White (New York: St. Martin's Press, 2000), 29; Beales, *From Castlereagh to Gladstone*, 84; Hugh Cunningham, *The Challenge of Democracy* (London: Longman, 2001), 32.

34. Many activists viewed repealing the Corn Laws an economic and a political necessity, since they both hindered free trade and prevented economic modernization as well as protected (and symbolized) the power of the landowning elite. Asa Briggs, *The Making of Modern England 1783–1867* (New York: Harper and Row, 1959), 314.

35. Robert Blake, *The Conservative Party from Peel to Thatcher* (London: Methuen, 1985), 57–58.

36. Langer, *Political and Social Upheaval*, 65; Cunningham, *The Challenge*, 54; N. McCord, *The Anti–Corn Law League* (London: Unwin, 1958).

37. These distinctions between the relative stability of Britain and the upheavals on the continent were remarked upon by many; such views became a standard part of the popular "Whig" school of history in Britain. Thomas Babington Macauley, for example, in his *The History of England* published in 1848, remarked: "All around us the world is convulsed by the agonies of great nations. Governments which lately seemed likely to stand during ages have been on a sudden shaken and overthrown. The proudest capitals of Europe stream with blood. . . . Meanwhile, in our island the regular course of government has never been for a day interrupted. . . . We have order in the midst of anarchy." *Selections from the Writings of Lord Macauley*, vol. 1, ed. G.O. Trevelyan (London: Longmans, Green and Co., 1876), 279.

38. The passing of the Poor Laws after the Great Reform Act was also a major spur to working-class organization.

39. Asa Briggs, *Chartist Studies* (London: Macmillan, 1958); J. Epstein and D. Thompson, eds., *The Chartist Experience* (London: MacMillan, 1982).

40. A parliamentary grouping in the mid-nineteenth century that supported Catholic Emancipation, political reform, free trade, and other forms of liberalization.

41. The former was primarily a working-class organization, while the latter included middle- and working-class members.

42. By this point France, Switzerland, and parts of Scandinavia had broader franchises.

43. Hostettler and Block, *Voting in Britain*, chapter 12; Cunningham, *The Challenge*, esp. 72; and Maurice Cowling, *1867: Disraeli, Gladstone and Revolution* (New York: Cambridge University Press, 1967).

44. Robert Saunders, *Democracy and the Vote in British Politics, 1848–1867* (Burlington, VT: Ashgate, 2011), 1, 4; Robin Blackburn, *The Electoral System in Britain* (New York: Palgrave Macmillan, 1995), 66; and Jonathan Parry, *The Rise and Fall of Liberal Government in Victorian Britain* (New

Haven, CT: Yale University Press, 1993). Even the Reform League, which called for "manhood suffrage," called for residence qualification and excluded criminals, paupers, and others incapable of acting "rationally" and independently. F.B. Smith, *The Making of the Second Reform Bill* (London: Cambridge University Press, 1966), 26.

45. Maurice Cowling, *1867: Disraeli, Gladstone and Revolution* (New York: Cambridge University Press, 1967); Cunningham, *The Challenge of Democracy*.

46. This meant, essentially, the most highly skilled and educated members of the working class. Catherine Hall, Keith McClelland, and Jane Rendall, "Introduction," in *Defining the Victorian Nation: Class, Race, Gender and the British Reform Act of 1867*, ed. Hall, Mclelland, and Rendall (New York: Cambridge University Press, 2000).

47. Gladstone's speech reprinted in Thomas Barnes and Gerald Feldman, eds., *Nationalism, Industrialization and Democracy* (Latham, MD: University Press of America, 1980), 204–05.

48. In the words of another Liberal MP quoted by Henry Miller in a review of Saunders, *Democracy and the Vote in British Politics*, http://www.history.ac.uk/reviews/review/1131 (date accessed: October 29, 2015).

49. Quoted in Smith, *Second Reform Act*, 48–49 and 81.

50. There had, of course, previously been mass demonstrations in favor of reform, but the size, timing, and nature of the 1866 protests highlighted the potentially high cost of further delaying reform. Even the Queen, for example, apparently wanted the issue settled. See Smith, *The Second Reform Bill*, 135.

51. Overall, however, protests remained moderate. As Gertrude Himmelfarb snarkily put it, "other demonstrations must have been pacific indeed for contemporaries and historians alike to have been so outraged by little more than broken railings and trampled flower beds." Reflecting a similar sentiment, albeit from the opposite perspective, Karl Marx observed at the time that if only the railings had been used "offensively and defensively" against the police and a score of policemen had been killed, "there would have been some fun." Himmelfarb, "The Politics of Democracy: The English Reform Act of 1867," *Journal of British Studies* 6, no. 1 (November 1966): 104–105.

52. Maurice Cowling, *1867: Disraeli, Gladstone and Revolution* (London: Cambridge University Press, 1967); Smith, *The Making of the Second Reform Bill*; Saunders, *Democracy the Vote*; John Walton, *The Second Reform Act* (London: Methuen, 1987); and Hall, McClelland, and Rendall, *Defining the Victorian Nation*.

53. Arnstein, *Britain*, 126; Eric Evans, *Forging the Modern State: Early Industrial Britain* (New York: Longman, 1996), 365ff.; Saunders, *Democracy and the Vote*, esp. chapter 8; and Cowling, *1867*. "In a progressive country," Disraeli once noted, "change is constant, and the question is not whether you should resist change which is inevitable, but whether that change should be carried out in deference to the manners, the customs, the laws and the traditions of the

people, or whether it should be carried out in deference to abstract principles and arbitrary and general doctrines." Quoted in Robert Rhodes James, *The British Revolution* (London: Hamish Hamilton, 1976), 17.

54. Saunders, *Democracy and the Vote*, 107, and especially chapter 8.

55. As was the case with the 1832 reform, the 1867 reform act originally applied only to England and Wales; separate legislation was passed for Scotland and Ireland.

56. For a fuller discussion of the bill's provisions see "The History of the Parliamentary Franchise."

57. See, e.g., Saunders, *Democracy and the Vote*, 13. "We do not," Disraeli declared to his colleagues in Parliament, "live—and I trust it will never be the fate of this country to live—under a democracy." Disraeli, *Selected Speeches*, vol. 1 (London: Longmans Green and Co., 1882), 546. Also see Cowling, *1867*, e.g. 48ff.

58. "What is the Tory party," Disraeli once said, "unless it represents national feeling? If it does not represent national feeling, Toryism is nothing." Quoted in Saunders, *Democracy and the Vote*, 278. Disraeli's paternalism, and in particular his belief that as long as the elite played its natural role in looking out for the national interest it would have nothing to fear from the working class, probably played a role in his relatively benign view of suffrage expansion. See, e.g., Himmelfarb, "The Politics of Democracy."

59. Theodore Happen, "The Franchise and Electoral Politics in England and Ireland," *History* 70 (1985): 201, 215.

60. Smith, *The Making of the Second Reform Bill*, 2, 3.

61. Martin Pugh, *The Making of Modern British Politics 1867–1939* (Oxford: Basil Blackwell, 1982); Parry, *The Rise and Fall,* esp. 221ff.; Saunders, *Democracy and the Vote in British Politics*. The fate of governments also became dependent on elections rather than votes in Parliament.

62. Cannadine, *The Decline and Fall*.

63. L.T. Hobhouse, *Liberalism* (New York: Oxford University Press, 1964), 110.

64. Sheri Berman, "The Primacy of Politics vs. the Primacy of Economics: Understanding the Ideological Dynamics of the Twentieth Century," *Perspectives on Politics* 7, no. 3 (2009); Guido De Ruggiero, *The History of European Liberalism* (Boston: Beacon Press, 1959); Richard Bellamy, *Liberalism and Modern Society* (University Park, PA: Penn State Press, 1992); James Kloppenberg, *Uncertain Victory: Social Democracy and Progressivism in European and American Thought, 1870–1920* (New York: Oxford University Press, 1986); Daniel Rogers, *Atlantic Crossings* (Cambridge: Belknap, 2000); Anthony Arblaster, *The Rise and Decline of Western Liberalism* (Oxford: Basil Blackwell, 1984); Steven Seidman, *Liberalism and the Origin of European Social Theory* (Berkeley: University of California Press, 1983).

65. The Ballot Act was officially known as the Parliamentary and Municipal Elections Act.

66. Cannadine, *The Decline and Fall*, 27, and John Habakkuk, *Marriage, Debt and the Estates System: English Landownership 1650–1950* (Oxford: Clarendon Press, 1994), 632.

67. To put it more correctly, between county (rural) and borough (urban) constituencies.

68. Speech accessed here: http://archive.org/stream/lifeofdavidlloyd04dupauoft/lifeofdavidlloyd04dupauoft_djvu.txt (#640).

69. In 1908 the government had already passed the Old-Age Pension Act, which granted all persons over the age of seventy a weekly benefit. Although the sums provided were low, the bill was significant since pensions "were granted as a right, rather than as something for which the elderly poor had to make a special request" as had been the case with poor relief. T.O. Lloyd, *Empire, Welfare State, Europe* (New York: Oxford University Press, 1993), 15.

70. http://www.parliament.uk/about/living-heritage/evolutionofparliament/houseoflords/house-of-lords-reform/from-the-collections/peoples-budget/budget/.

71. Speech accessed at http://archive.spectator.co.uk/article/14th-august-1909/14/the-limehouse-speech.

72. Speech accessed at https://books.google.com/books?id=pDzmAAAAMAAJ&pg=PA1049#v=onepage&q&f=false. Also, Bentley Brinkeroff Gilbert, "David Lloyd George: Land, the Budget, and Social Reform," *The American Historical Review* 81, no. 5 (December 1976).

73. David Spring, "Land and Politics in Edwardian England," *Agricultural History* 58, no. 1 (January 1984): 33–34.

74. Cannadine, *The Decline and Fall*, 54. Also see Cunningham, *The Challenge*, 207–208, and Robert Rhodes James, *The British Revolution* (London: Hamish Hamilton, 1976), 245–50.

75. Daniel Ziblatt, *Conservative Political Parties and the Birth of Modern Democracy in Europe, 1848–1950* (New York: Cambridge University Press, 2017).

76. Quoted in Cunningham, *The Challenge*, 113. See also Anthony Sneldon and Peter Snowden, *The Conservative Party* (Gloucestershire: Sutton, 2004).

77. Accessed at http://www.europeana.eu/portal/record/9200175/BibliographicResource_3000004631925.html.

78. P. Smith, *Disraelian Conservatism and Social Reform* (London: Routledge, 1967).

79. This government went on to pass "a range of social legislation which . . . equaled or even surpassed those of other governments of the period" in areas including housing, labor relations, public health, and sanitation; it also liberalized trade union rights. Lee, *Aspects*, 153–54, and Smith, *Disraelian Conservatism*.

80. Quoted in Janet Hendersen Robb, "The Primrose League, 1883–1906" (PhD diss., Columbia University, 1942), 148.

81. Blake, *The Conservative Party*, 118, 360, 130; Martin Pugh, *The Tories and the People, 1880–1935* (Oxford: Basil Blackwell, 1985), 42.

82. This was because at the time, the working-class movement was too weak to elect MPs on its own. Even after an independent Labour party was formed, co-operation between Liberals and Labour continued. The prominent role played by members of the middle class, most notably the Fabians, in many working-class organizations and social reform movements probably also helped diminish class conflict in Britain. See, e.g., Trygve Tholfsen, "The Transition to Democracy in Victorian England," in *The Victorian Revolution*, ed. Peter Stansky (New York: New Viewpoints, 1973).

83. Ziblatt, *Conservative Political Parties*.

84. J.L. Hammond and M.R.D. Foot, *Gladstone and Liberalism* (London: English Universities Press, 1966).

85. Gladstone urged his colleagues to recognize that Home Rule was a "conservative" move "in the highest sense of the term, as tending to the union of the three Countries . . . and to stability of the Imperial throne and institutions." Quoted in Eric Strauss, *Irish Nationalism and British Democracy* (New York: Columbia University Press, 1951), 242.

86. Hammond and Foot, *Gladstone and Liberalism*, 142.

87. Together the two parties held 394 seats (317 Conservative, 77 Liberal Unionist) to the Liberals 191.

88. In 1892 when Gladstone formed a minority government dependent on Irish Nationalist support that once again tried and failed to pass Home Rule (as discussed above). Alvin Jackson, *Home Rule: An Irish History* (London: Weidenfeld & Nicolson, 2003); James Loughlin, *Gladstone, Home Rule and the Ulster Question* (Dublin: Gill and Macmillan, 1986).

89. Ulster was basically the Protestant-majority areas of Northern Ireland.

90. Quoted in Joseph Finnan, *John Redmond and Irish Unity* (Syracuse, NY: Syracuse University Press, 2003), 37. See also P.J. Buckland, "The Southern Irish Unionists, the Irish Question and British Politics, 1906–14," *Irish Historical Studies* 15, no. 59 (March 1967).

91. Quoted in "Starting Out on the Road to Partition," *Irish Times*, April 25, 2012. Accessed on December 11, 2015. http://www.irishtimes.com/news/starting-out-on-the-road-to-partition-1.508371. Also see Rhodes, *The British Revolution*, 273; Strauss, *Irish Nationalism*.

92. By the summer, apparently about two million signatures had been obtained. Text and pictures can be found at http://brianjohnspencer.tumblr.com/post/126495482058/citizen69-mass-rally-for-ulster-at-hyde-park. See also Spring, "Land and Politics in Edwardian England," 39; Cannadine, *Decline and Fall*, 528.

93. See, e.g., "If the First World War had not broken out in 1914, something like a unilateral declaration of independence would have been made in Ulster— and made, moreover . . . with the full backing of the leader of the Conservative party, and the vast majority of his followers." Blake, *The Conservative Party*, 195; Mathew and Morgan, *The Oxford History of Britain*, 65; Cunningham, *Challenge*

of Democracy, 209; Arnstein, *Britain*, 241; Pugh, *State and Society*, 143; H.C.G. Mathew and Kenneth Morgan, *The Modern Age* (New York: Oxford University Press, 1992), 65; and George Dangerfield, *The Strange Death of Liberal England* (New York: Perigree, 1980), esp. chapter 2.

94. David Close, "The Collapse of Resistance to Democracy: Conservatives, Adult Suffrage and the Second Chamber Reform, 1911–1928," *The Historical Journal* 20, no. 4 (December 1977).

95. As the (Conservative) Home Secretary, George Cave, put it:

> War by all classes of our countrymen has brought us nearer together, has opened men's eyes, and removed misunderstandings on all sides. It has made it, I think, impossible that ever again, at all events in the lifetime of the present generation, there should be a revival of the old class feeling which was responsible for so much, and, among other things, for the exclusion for a period, of so many of our population from the class of electors. I think I need say no more to justify this extension of the franchise. Hansard HC Debs (May 21, 1917) vol. 94, col 2135, quoted in https://en.wikipedia.org/wiki/Representation_of_the_People_Act_1918.

96. The vote in the Commons was 385 to 55. It also easily passed the House of Lords.

97. It had never really disappeared of course. In 1916, for example, the famous Easter Rising or Rebellion occurred against British rule.

98. Essentially *Freikorps* (as the Germans called them), this force was officially known as the Royal Irish Constabulary Special Reserve and unofficially as the "Black and Tans."

99. Estimates range from about 1,400 to about 2,500 overall deaths, depending on the source and time frame. Michael Hopkinson, *The Irish War of Independence* (Montreal: McGill, 2004), and Charles Townshend, *The Republic: The Irish Fight for Independence* (London: Allen Lane, 2013).

100. The new United Kingdom became the United Kingdom of Great Britain and Northern Ireland rather than the United Kingdom of Great Britain and Ireland.

101. Britain had about 723,000 deaths or about 1.8% of its population (France 4.3%, Italy 3%, Russia 1.8%, Germany 3.5%, and Austria-Hungary 3.5%).

102. See, e.g., Barry Eichengreen, "The Interwar Economy in a European Mirror," in *The Economic History of Britain since 1700*, vol. 2, ed. Rodrick Floud and Paul Johnson (New York: Cambridge University Press, 1994); Richard Overy, *The Twilight Years: The Paradox of Britain Between the Wars* (New York: Penguin, 2010).

103. About one in five of the sons of British and Irish peers who served during the war were killed as opposed to one in eight for all members of the services. A. Lambert, *Unquiet Souls: The Indian Summer of the British Aristocracy* (London: Macmillan, 1984), 186, 188, 205; Cannadine, *The Decline and Fall*, 35, 37, 83, and 704.

104. Cannadine, *The Decline and Fall*, 229–30 and 711. Also see Bush, *The English Aristocracy*, 150–52.

105. One-third came from the professions, one-fifth from the services, another fifth from commerce, and the rest from industry. Cannadine, *The Decline and Fall*, 184.

    To some degree, the elite was able to compensate by turning to the empire, where they continued to play a disproportionate role in high-status governmental and administrative positions.

106. Cannadine, *The Decline and Fall*, 272.

107. Cannadine, *Decline and Fall*, 111 and 89; Bush, *The English Aristocracy*, 155–57; Thompson, *English Landed Society*, 332–33; and Habakkuk, *Marriage, Debt*, chapter 8.

108. One reflection of this is that up through the late nineteenth century the vast majority of British millionaires were landowners but by the interwar period this was no longer the case. Cannadine, *Decline and Fall*, 91.

109. This two-party dominance was surely also a result of the fact that Britain did not adopt a proportional representation system, as did so many other European countries. The classic analysis of the role of various electoral systems in structuring interwar political outcomes is F.A. Hermens, *Democracy or Anarchy? A Study of Proportional Representation* (Notre Dame, IN: The Review of Politics, 1941).

110. Reflecting this, interwar Conservative governments moved further towards an acceptance of the welfare state, even instituting some new social reforms of their own.

111. Arthur Marwick, *The Deluge: British Society and the First World War* (New York: W.W. Norton, 1965).

112. Cunningham, *Challenge of Democracy*, 252.

113. Robert Skidelsky, *Politicians and the Slump: Labour Government 1929–1931* (New York: Papermac, 1994).

114. Winston Churchill, of course, coined the phrase "the darkest hour" to describe the period after the fall of France when Britain stood alone against Nazi Germany.

115. Douglas Allen, *The Institutional Revolution* (Chicago: University of Chicago Press, 2012), 75. See also Cannadine, *The Decline and Fall*, 21; Spring, "Landed Elites Compared," 2; Thompson, *English Landed Society*, 27.

116. Tocqueville, *Democracy in America*, book 2, chapter 3.

117. The political science literature relating inequality in general and concentrated resource wealth in particular to a lack of democracy is very large. A good place to begin is with the somewhat contrasting analyses provided by Carles Boix, *Democracy and Redistribution* (New York: Cambridge University Press, 2002); Daron Acemoglu and James Robinson, *Economic Origins of Dictatorship and Democracy* (New York: Cambridge University Press, 2009).

118. Thus while I agree with scholars like Spring, Dangerfield, and others that the conservative reaction to Home Rule must be taken seriously, I think a comparative perspective highlights how weak this reaction actually was. Spring, "Land and Politics," and Dangerfield, *The Strange Death*.

119. Bush, *The English Aristocracy*, 12–13. At least some members of this elite retreated to the empire, where they were able to exert immense political, economic, and social power for another generation or so.

120. The comparatively puzzling political behavior of the British landowning elite raises the question of why it acted so differently than many of its European counterparts. One common and influential approach to understanding modern British political development and the landowning elite's role in it focuses on the country's early commercialization of agriculture, which is seen as having two crucial consequences. First, it eliminated the peasantry and thus the landed elite's need to use political power to control or repress a large, and potentially antagonistic class in rural areas. Second, it created a landed elite that was more "bourgeois" and therefore less divided from and more sympathetic to the interests of the middle classes than many of its European counterparts. While such factors were probably critically important, they are also probably alone not enough to explain the British landowning elite's behavior during the modern era. There may not have been a peasantry to fear and repress, but up through the nineteenth century the British elite certainly used its immense political power to control rural areas and the people living on them. In addition, while the commercialization of agriculture certainly occurred earlier in England than in many other parts of Europe, by the nineteenth century most landed elites (particularly in Western and Central Europe) had turned to commercial agriculture and lost their seigneurial privileges. Moreover, unlike in most of the rest of Europe, the British aristocracy's status came from land ownership rather legal privilege, and so anything that threatened its estates or the viability of agriculture more generally was a potentially existential threat.

Thus alongside a focus on the early commercialization of agriculture, understanding British political development during the nineteenth and twentieth centuries requires an appreciation of the country's early modern political history as well. Since 1688, Britain had a political order in which the landowning elite enjoyed a remarkable amount of power. Up through the nineteenth century this order in general and Parliament in particular enabled this elite to further its interests vis-à-vis the Crown as well as other social groups. It seems, accordingly, to have developed a remarkable stake in this order and thus a strong aversion to doing anything that might risk its overthrow, even if this meant accepting reforms of it. The elite was also remarkably confident of this order's ability to socialize and moderate the behavior of hitherto excluded groups. (And because this order was constitutional and liberal it allowed these groups to press their demands in an organized and legal fashion, thereby diminishing the fear that change would push Britain down a slippery slope to disorder and revolution.) And for yet another account of why British elites acted so differently than their counterparts elsewhere, see Ziblatt, Conservative Parties.

Chapter 11

1. Antonio Gramsci, Prison Notebooks.
2. Francesco L. Galassi and Mark Harrison, "Italy at War, 1915–1918," in *The Economics of World War I*, ed. Stephen Broadberry and Mark Harrison (New York: Cambridge University Press, 2005); Martin Clark, *Modern Italy* (New York: Longman, 1984), 156ff. Inflation ranged from about 20 to about 35 percent between 1917 and 1919.
3. Michele Fratianni and Franco Spinelli, *A Monetary History of Italy* (New York: Cambridge University Press, 1997); R.J.B. Bosworth, *Mussolini's Italy* (New York: Penguin, 2006), 124.
4. Anthony Cardoza, *Agrarian Elites and Italian Fascism: The Province of Bologna, 1901–1926* (Princeton, NJ: Princeton University Press, 1982), chapter 6; Martin Clark, *Modern Italy 1871–1982* (New York: Longman, 1984), 206ff.; Alexander De Grand, *Italian Fascism* (Lincoln: University of Nebraska Press, 1982), 24.
5. Alexander De Grand, *In Stalin's Shadow* (DeKalb: Northern Illinois University Press, 1986), and Albert Lindemann, *The "Red Years": European Socialism Versus Bolshevism* (Berkeley: University of California Press, 1974), 59–60.
6. Sheri Berman, *The Primacy of Politics: Social Democracy and the Making of Europe's Twentieth Century* (New York: Cambridge University Press, 2006), 102ff.
7. Berman, *The Primacy of Politics*; Christopher Seton-Watson, *Italy from Liberalism to Fascism* (London: Butler and Tanner, 1967), 548; Denis Mack Smith, *Italy: A Modern History* (Ann Arbor: University of Michigan Press, 1959), 328.
8. Stathis Kalyvas, *The Rise of Christian Democracy in Europe* (Ithaca, NY: Cornell University Press, 1996).
9. Mario Tarchi, "Italy: Early Crisis and Fascist Takeover," in *Conditions of Democracy in Europe, 1919–1939*, ed. Dirk Berg-Schlosser and Jeremy Mitchell (New York: St. Martin's Press, 2000), 309, 312.
10. A. Rossi, *The Rise of Italian Fascism 1918–1922* (London: Methuen, 1938), 53.
11. Richard Bellamy and Darrow Schecter, *Gramsci and the Italian State* (Manchester, UK: Manchester University Press, 1993); John M. Cammett, *Antonio Gramsci and the Origins of Italian Communism* (Stanford, CA: Stanford University Press, 1967); Gwyn A. Williams, *Proletarian Order: Antonio Gramsci, Factory Councils and the Origins of Italian Communism, 1911–1921* (London: Pluto Press, 1975).
12. Maurice Neufeld, *Italy: School for Awakening Countries* (Ithaca, NY: Cayuga Press, 1961), 379.
13. Horowitz, *The Italian Labor Movement*, 149.
14. Horowitz, *The Italian Labor Movement*, 151.

15. Horowitz, *The Italian Labor Movement*, 151–52; Rossi, *The Rise of Italian Fascism*, 70.

16. Giovanni Giolitti, *Memoirs of My Life* (London: Chapman and Dodd, 1923), 437–38.

17. Cammett, *Antonio Gramsci and the Origins of Italian Communism*, 133ff.; Alastair Davidson, *The Theory and Practice of Italian Communism*, vol. 1 (London: Merlin Press, 1982), 97ff.; Spencer Di Scala, *Italy from Revolution to Republic* (Boulder, CO: Westview Press, 1998), 218; Horowitz, *The Italian Labor Movement*, 157–59.

18. Berman, *The Primacy of Politics*, chapter 3.

19. Berman, *The Primacy of Politics*, 207–08.

20. A. James Gregor, *Contemporary Radical Ideologies* (Berkeley: University of California Press, 1968), 131.

21. A. James Gregor, *Young Mussolini and the Intellectual Origins of Fascism* (Berkeley: University of California Press, 1979), 191–92.

22. A. James Gregor, *The Fascist Persuasion in Radical Politics* (Princeton, NJ: Princeton University Press, 1974), 176–78.

23. Clarence Yarrow, "The Forging of Fascist Doctrine," *Journal of the History of Ideas* 3, no. 2 (April 1942): 170.

24. "Platform of the Fasci di Combattimento," in *Italian Fascism*, ed. Jeffrey Schnapp (Lincoln: University of Nebraska Press), 3–5. Also see Ivanoe Bonomi, *From Socialism to Fascism* (London: Martin Hopkinson, 1924), 102; F.L. Carsten, *The Rise of Fascism* (Berkeley: University of California Press, 1982), 50; Edward Tannenbaum, "The Goals of Italian Fascism," *American Historical Review* 74, no. 4 (April 1969): 1185.

25. Michael A. Leeden, *The First Duce: D'Annunzio at Fiume* (Baltimore: Johns Hopkins University Press, 1977).

26. Lucy Hughes-Hallet, *Gabrielle D'Annunzio: Poet, Seducer, and Preacher of War* (New York: Alfred A. Knopf, 2013); Sheri Berman, "Fascist Designs: Gabrielle D'Annunzio by Lucy Hughes-Hallet," *New York Times*, August 30, 2013.

27. Frank Snowden, "On the Social Origins of Agrarian Fascism in Italy," *European Journal of Sociology* 13 (1972): 270.

28. Edward Tannenbaum, *The Fascist Experience: Italian Society and Culture, 1922–45* (New York: Basic Books, 1972), 35. Also see Anthony L. Cardoza, *Agrarian Elites and Italian Fascism: The Province of Bologna, 1901–1926* (Princeton, NJ: Princeton University Press, 1982); Frank Snowden, *The Fascist Revolution in Tuscany 1919–1922* (New York: Cambridge University Press, 1989).

29. The liberal movement included Liberals-Democrats-Radicals, Radicals, the Italian Liberal Party, the Democratic Liberal party, the Republican party, and others.

30. Tarchi, "Italy," 304–305.

31. Cardoza, *Agrarian Elites and Italian Fascism*; Paul Corner, *Fascism in Ferrara* (New York: Oxford University Press, 1975).

32. Snowden, "On the Social Origins of Agrarian Fascism in Italy," 279. Also see Corner, *Fascism in Ferrara*, 146ff; Adrian Lyttelton, *The Seizure of Power: Fascism in Italy 1919–1929* (London: Weidenfeld and Nicolson, 1973); Snowden, *The Fascist Revolution*, 81ff.; C.F. Delzell, ed., *Mediterranean Fascism* (New York: Harper and Row, 1971).

33. Snowden, *The Fascist Revolution*, 82.

34. Denis Mack Smith, *Italy: A Modern History* (Ann Arbor: University of Michigan Press, 1959), 342, 345. Also see Charles Maier, *Recasting Bourgeois Europe* (Princeton, NJ: Princeton University Press, 1975), 317ff; Paolo Farneti, "Social Conflict, Parliamentary Fragmentation, Institutional Shift, and the Rise of Fascism: Italy," in *The Breakdown of Democratic Regimes: Europe*, ed. Juan Linz and Alfred Stepan (Baltimore: Johns Hopkins University Press, 1978), 23.

35. Frederico Chabod, *A History of Italian Fascism* (London: Weidenfield and Nicolson, 1963), 57.

36. Tarchi, "Italy," 311.

37. Mack Smith, *Italy*, 345.

38. "Program of the National Fascist Party, 1921," in *A Primer of Italian Fascism*, ed. Jeffrey Schnapp (Lincoln: University of Nebraska Press, 2000), 10–18.

39. "Program of the National Fascist Party, 1921," 15.

40. Carl T. Schmidt, *The Corporate State in Action* (New York: Oxford University Press, 1939), 40.

41. Stanley Payne, *A History of Fascism, 1914–1945* (Madison: University of Wisconsin Press, 1995), 104; Bosworth, *Mussolini's Italy*, 151; E. Spencer Wellhofer, "Democracy and Fascism: Class, Civil Society and Rational Choice in Italy," *American Political Science Review* 97, no. 1 (2003).

42. Anthony James Joes, *Fascism in the Contemporary World* (Boulder, CO: Westview Press, 1978), 40. See also Margot Hentze, *Pre-Fascist Italy* (New York: W.W. Norton, 1939), and Rossi, *The Rise of Italian Fascism*.

43. Quoted in Carsten, *The Rise of Fascism*, 60.

44. Bosworth, *Mussolini's Italy*, 180–81.

45. See, e.g., Gaetano Salvemini, *The Fascist Dictatorship in Italy* (New York: Howard Fertig, 1967).

46. Quoted in Rossi, *The Rise of Italian Fascism*, 122. Pace Banchelli's assertion, authorities did not intervene simply due to weakness and confusion, rather than active support for fascism. Regardless of the motivation, the result was a gradual fascist takeover of many towns and provinces. See, e.g., Snowden, *The Fascist Revolution*.

47. Lyttelton, *The Seizure of Power*, 149. Contrary to popular belief and fascist legend, the March on Rome thus happened after all the important political decisions had been made. It was more of a victory parade than a seizure of power.

48. This section is drawn from Berman, *The Primacy of Politics*, 131–36.

49. The Acerbo Law gave the party that won the largest share of the vote two-thirds of the seats in parliament.

50. Carsten, *The Rise of Fascism*; F. Allen Cassells, *Fascist Italy* (London: Routledge and Kegan Paul, 1986); Federico Chabod, *A History of Italian Fascism* (London: Weidenfield and Nicolson, 1963); Lyttleton, *The Seizure of Power*.

51. Adrian Lyttleton, "Fascism in Italy: The Second Wave," *Journal of Contemporary History* 1, no. 1 (May 1966): 76.

52. Paul Corner, *The Fascist Party and Popular Opinion in Mussolini's Italy* (New York: Oxford University Press, 2012).

53. Corner, *The Fascist Party*, 61, 65, 66–67; Renzo De Felice, *Mussolini il fascista* (Turin: Giulio Einaudi, 1968), 55–68, reprinted in Sarti, *The Ax Within*, 87–99; Tannenbaum, *The Fascist Experience*, 73; Martin Clark, *Modern Italy* (New York: Longman, 1984), 238; Delzell, *Mediterranean Fascism*, 742.

54. Corner, *The Fascist Party*, 74 and also Alberto Aquarone, *L'organizzasione dello Stato totalitario* (Turin: Giulio Einaudi, 1965), selections reprinted in Sarti, *The Ax Within*.

55. Alberto Aquarone, "The Rise of the Fascist State," and Renzo de Felice, "From the Liberal Regime to the Fascist Regime," in *The Ax Within*, ed. Roland Sarti (New York: New Viewpoints, 1974); Lyttelton, "Fascism in Italy." Mussolini himself later wrote that it was during this time that the "foundations of the totalitarian state were laid." Carsten, *The Rise of Fascism*, 73.

56. This was a term constantly invoked by fascist theoreticians and activists. See, for example, Roger Griffin, ed., *Fascism* (New York: Oxford University Press, 1995).

57. Mussolini, "The Achievements of the Fascist Revolution," in *Fascism*, ed. Griffin, 64. Document collections can be found in Adrian Lyttleton, *Italian Fascisms* (New York: Harper, 1973); Marla Stone, *The Fascist Revolution in Italy* (Boston: St. Martin's 2013), and John Pollard, *The Fascist Experience in Italy* (New York: Routledge, 1998).

58. Marla Stone, *The Fascist Revolution in Italy* (New York: St. Martin's Press, 2013), 16 and section 3.

59. Corner, *The Fascist Party,* and Aqaurone, *L'organizzazione.*

60. Stone, *The Fascist Revolution*, 19. Text of the pacts on p. 69. Also see Francesco Margiotta Broglio, *Italia e Santa Sede dalla Grande Guerra all Conciliazione* (Bari: Laterza, 1966), excerpts reprinted in Sarti, *The Ax Within*, 33–40.

61. Achille Starace, "Going Toward the People" (1933) reprinted in Stone, *The Fascist Revolution*, 87; Victoria De Grazia, *The Culture of Consent: Mass Organization of Leisure in Fascist Italy* (New York: Cambridge University Press, 1981), 3.

62. Corner, *The Fascist Party*, 128–29, 132.

63. Katherine Hite and Leonardo Morlino, "Problematizing the Links Between Authoritarian Legacies and 'Good' Democracy," in *Authoritarian Legacies and*

Democracy in Latin America and Southern Europe, ed. Hite and Paola Cesarini (Notre Dame, IN: University of Notre Dame Press, 2004), 35ff.

64. See, e.g., Mario Palmieri, *The Philosophy of Fascism*, excerpts reprinted in Cohen, ed., *Communism, Fascism, Democracy*, 381. Also see Dick Pels, "Fascism and the Primacy of the Political," *Telos* 10 (Winter 1998), and Ze'ev Sternhell, *The Birth of Fascist Ideology* (Princeton, NJ: Princeton University Press, 1994).

65. Lyttelton, "Fascism in Italy: The Second Wave"; Payne, *A History of Fascism*, 121; Roland Sarti, *Fascism and the Industrial Leadership in Italy, 1919–1940* (Berkeley: University of California Press, 1971), 58.

66. Sarti, *Fascism and the Industrial Leadership in Italy*, 72.

67. Gaetano Salvemini, *Under the Axe of Fascism* (New York: Viking Press, 1936), 90.

68. "The Labour Charter," in Benito Mussolini, *The Corporate State* (Florence: Vallecchi, 1938), 122–26.

69. Alexander De Grand, *Italian Fascism* (Lincoln: University of Nebraska Press, 1982), 107. Also see A. James Gregor, *Italian Fascism and Developmental Dictatorship* (Princeton, NJ: Princeton University Press, 1979).

70. Cesare Vannutelli, "The Living Standard of Italian Workers 1929–1939," in *The Axe Within*, ed. Sarti; Schmidt, *The Corporate State in Action*, 86.

71. Roger Eatwell, *Fascism* (New York: Penguin, 1995), 79; Schmidt, *The Corporate State in Action*, 128.

72. Martin Clark, *Modern Italy* (New York: Longman, 1984), 271; Sarti, *Fascism and the Industrial Leadership in Italy,* 124; John Whittan, *Fascist Italy* (Manchester, UK: Manchester University Press, 1995), 65.

73. Corner, *The Fascist Party*; Christopher Duggan, *Fascist Voices* (New York: Oxford, 2013).

74. Eatwell, *Fascism*, 79. See also Max Gallo, *Mussolini's Italy* (New York: Macmillan, 1973), 168.

75. Quoted in Stone, *The Fascist Revolution*, 1.

Chapter 12

1. Quoted in Deist et al., eds., *Germany and the Second World War*, 148–49.

2. Martin Kitchen, *The Silent Dictatorship: The Politics of the German High Command Under Hindenburg and Ludendorff, 1916–1918* (London: Croom Helm, 1976); Frank Tipton, *A History of Modern Germany* (Berkeley: University of California Press, 2003).

3. Sheri Berman, *The Social Democratic Moment: Ideas and Politics in the Making of Interwar Europe* (Cambridge, MA: Harvard University Press, 1998), esp. 134–42.

4. Quoted in Heinrich August Winkler, *Die Sozialdemokratie und die Revolution von 1918/1919* (Berlin: J.H.W. Dietz, 1979), 57.

5. Friedrich Stampfer, *Die Vierzehn Jahre der Ersten Deutschen* (Karlsbad: Verlagsanstalt Graphia, 1936), 304. As a result of the lack of thought given to what achieving stable, consolidated democracy would require, Ebert (and much of the SPD leadership) viewed the party's role during the immediate postwar period primarily in a "negative" sense—focused on dealing with the myriad problems the collapse of the old regime and the war left behind—rather than in a "positive" sense—dedicated to constructing a new and fully democratic Germany. Reflecting this, Ebert tellingly characterized the SPD as acting during this time as the "bankruptcy trustees of the old regime." Quoted in Heinrich August Winkler, *Germany: The Long Road West* (New York: Oxford University Press, 2000), 345.

6. The research on the council movement is extensive. See Eberhard Kolb, *Die Arbeiterräte in der deutschen Innenpolitik 1918 bis 1919* (Düsseldorf: Droste, 1962); Susanne Miller, *Die Bürde der Macht*; Peter von Oertzen, *Betriebsräte in der Novemberrevolution* (Berlin: J.H.W. Dietz, 1976); Detlev Lehnert, *Sozialdemokratie und Novemberrevolution: Die Neuordnungsdebatte 1918/1919 in der politischen Publizistik von SPD und USPD* (Frankfurt: Campus, 1983); Reinhard Rürup, "Problems of the German Revolution 1918–1919," *Journal of Contemporary History* 3 (1968). On the demands of the congress in general see also Holger Herwig, "The First German Congress of Workers and Soldiers' Councils and the Problem of Military Reforms," *Central European History* 1 (June 1968); Wolfgang Mommsen, "The German Revolution 1918–1920: Political Revolution and Social Protest Movement," in *Social Change and Political Development in Weimar Germany*, ed. Richard Bessel and E.J. Feuchtwanger (London: Croom Helm, 1981); Richard Löwenthal, "The 'Missing Revolution' in Industrial Societies: Comparative Reflections on a German Problem," in *Germany in the Age of Total War*, ed. Volker Berghahn and Martin Kitchen (London: Croom Helm, 1981), esp. 251.

7. D.K. Buse, "Ebert and the German Crisis," *Central European History* 5 (1972); Richard Hunt, "Friedrich Ebert and the German Revolution of 1918," in *The Responsibility of Power: Historical Essays in Honor of Hajo Holborn*, ed. Leonard Krieger and Fritz Stern (New York: Doubleday, 1967).

8. For Groener's recollection of the agreement, see his *Lebenserinnerungen*; relevant sections are reprinted in Miller and Ritter, eds., *Die deutsche Republik*, 98–99.

9. The First National Congress of Workers' and Soldiers' Councils (*Reichsrätekongress*).

10. Reprinted in Ritter and Miller, *Die deutsche Revolution*, 155–56.

11. Cabinet meeting in joint session with the Zentralrat, December 20, 1918, reprinted in Burdick and Lutz, eds., *The Political Institutions*, 110.

12. Obuch's statement was made at a meeting of the Executive Committee in the Presence of the Cabinet, December 7, 1918, and Haase's at a joint meeting of the Cabinet and Zentralrat, December 28, 1918. Burdick and Lutz, eds., *The*

Political Institutions, 87–88 and 161–62. See also the joint cabinet meeting of the Cabinet and Zentralrat on December 28, pp. 149–63.

13. Halperin, *Germany Tried Democracy*, 121; Richard Hunt, *German Social Democracy, 1918–1933* (Chicago: Quadrangle Books, 1964), 29–30.

14. Arthur Rosenberg argues that Noske's decision to use the Freikorps "sealed the fate of the Republic." *A History of the German Revolution*, 81. In addition, he asserts that Noske decided to rely primarily on the Freikorp troops despite the fact that he could have used troops made up largely of majority Socialists. See also Theodore Wolff's account of this episode reprinted in Meyer, ed., *The Long Generation*, 88–91. For the cabinet discussion of the events (December 28, 1918) see Burdick and Lutz, eds., *The Political Institutions*, 137–48.

15. These parties came to be known as the Weimar coalition. They had, in fact, begun working together in the Reichstag towards the end of the war.

16. Like the Nazis, the KPD developed its own "paramilitary" units that it eagerly employed, particularly toward the end of the Republic. See Ben Fowkes, *Communism in Germany* (London: Palgrave Macmillan, 1984), and Eric Weitz, *Creating German Communism* (Princeton, NJ: Princeton University Press, 1996).

17. Kolb, *The Weimar Republic*, 20–21; Rosenberg, *A History of the German Republic*, 35–53; and Berlau, *The German Social Democratic Party*, 245–54.

18. As Ludendorff noted, "Let them [the Reichstag parties] now conclude the peace that has to be negotiated. Let them eat the broth they have prepared for us." Recounted in the diary of Obersten von Thaer, sections reprinted in Gerhard A. Ritter and Susanne Miller, eds., *Die deutsche Revolution: Dokumente* (Hamburg: Hoffman und Campe, 1975), 27.

19. There was one area of Germany where some action was taken, however, and that was Prussia. When the "new rulers [of Prussia] did undertake energetic reforms [of the civil service] after the Kapp putsch had exposed their earlier mistakes, the Prussian civil service helped the state to become the democratic bulwark that it was to be during the crisis-ridden years of the 1920s." Dietrich Orlow, *Weimar Prussia 1918–1925: The Unlikely Rock of Democracy* (Pittsburgh: University of Pittsburgh Press, 1986), 115.

20. Werner Angress, "Weimar Coalition and Ruhr Insurrection, March–April 1920: A Study of Government Policy," *The Journal of Modern History* 29 (1957).

21. By this point many voters in particular saw the MSPD in particular not as the leader of a new Germany, but rather as a group of unimaginative, "so-called revolutionaries" unable to control a situation that was rapidly slipping out of their hands. Observing the unfolding events Rainer Maria Rilke wrote: "Under the pretense of a great upheaval, the old want of character persists." Quoted in Peter Gay, *Weimar Culture: The Outsider as Insider* (New York: Harper and Row, 1970), 9–10. For a semi-fictional account which captures the disappointment and anger on the Left regarding the revolution see Alfred Döblin,

November 1918: A German Revolution, trans. John Woods (New York: Fromm International, 1983).

22. Program reprinted in J. Noakes and G. Pridham, eds., *Nazism 1919–1945. Vol. 1: The Rise to Power* (Exeter, UK: University of Exeter Press, 1994), 14–16.

23. Sheri Berman, *The Primacy of Politics* (New York: Cambridge University Press, 2006), esp. chapters 4 and 6; Zeev Sternhell, *Neither Right nor Left* (Princeton, NJ: Princeton University Press, 1996); Sternhell, *The Birth of Fascist Ideology* (Princeton, NJ: Princeton University Press, 1995).

24. It should be emphasized, however, that the collapse of the German currency had its origins in the government's financing of the First World War. Gerald Feldman, *Vom Weltkrieg zur Weltwirtschaftskrise* (Göttingen: Vandenhoeck and Ruprecht, 1984); Feldman, *Iron and Steel in the German Inflation, 1916–1923* (Princeton, NJ: Princeton University Press, 1977); Feldman, ed., *Die Nachwirkungen der Inflation auf die deutsche Geschichte, 1924–1933* (Munich: R. Oldenburg, 1985); Feldman, ed., *Die Erfahrung der Inflation im internationalen Zusammenhang und Vergleich* (Berlin: Walter de Gruyter, 1984); Feldman, *The Great Disorder: Politics, Economics, and Society in the German Inflation, 1914–1924* (New York: Oxford University Press, 1995).

25. Gerald Feldman, *The Great Disorder: Politics, Economics and Society in the German Inflation, 1919–1924* (New York: Oxford University Press, 1993); Jürgen von Krüdener, "Die Entstehung des Inflationstraumas: Zur Sozialpsychologie der deutschen Hyperinflation 1922–23," in *Consequences of Inflation*, ed. Feldman et al. (Berlin: Colloquium Verlag, 1989); Jones, "The Dying Middle," 25; also see Kocka, "The First World War and the Mittelstand."

26. Stresemann was also the head of the DVP, a right-liberal party with close ties to big business and, at least originally, an ambiguous commitment to democracy. On the DVP and other liberal parties during the interwar period see Larry Eugen Jones, *German Liberalism and the Dissolution of the Weimar Republic* (Chapel Hill: University of North Carolina Press, 1988). On Stresemann see Henry Turner, *Stresemann and the Politics of the Weimar Republic* (Princeton, NJ: Princeton University Press, 1963).

27. The SPD itself did much to preserve its image as a workers' rather than a people's party. See Sheri Berman, *Ideas and Politics: Social Democratic Parties in Interwar Europe* (Cambridge, MA: Harvard University Press, 1998); Donna Harsch, *German Social Democracy and the Rise of Fascism* (Chapel Hill: University of North Carolina Press, 1993); Richard Hunt, *German Social Democracy, 1918–1933* (Chicago: Quadrangle, 1964); Hans Kremdahl, "Könnte die SPD in der Weimarer Republik eine Volkspartei Werden?" in *Reformsozialismus und Sozialdemokratie*, ed. Horst Heimann and Thomas Meyer (Berlin: Verlag J.H.W. Dietz, 1982); Heinrich August Winkler, "Klassenbewegung oder Volkspartei?" *Geschichte und Gesellschaft* 8 (1972).

28. The twenties even saw something of a resuscitation of the old Bismarckian coalition of iron and rye, which like its predecessor was able to secure a

wide range of subsidies and tariffs, the most infamous of which being the *Osthilfe*. See Dietmar Petzina, "Elemente der Wirtschaftspolitik in der Spätphase der Weimarer Republik," *Vierteljahrshefte für Zeitgeschichte*, vol. 21 (1973); and Gerald Feldman, *Vom Weltkrieg zur Weltwirtschaftskrise* (Göttingen: Vandenhoeck & Ruprecht, 1984).

29. Jones, *German Liberalism*; Jones, "'The Dying Middle': Weimar Germany and the Fragmentation of Bourgeois Politics," *Central European History* 5 (1972); Jones, "In the Shadow of Stabilization: German Liberalism and the Legitimacy of the Weimar Party System," and Thomas Childers, "Interest and Ideology: Anti-System Parties in the Era of Stabilization," both in *Die Nachwirkungen der Inflation auf die deutsche Geschichte*, ed. Gerald Feldman (Munich: R. Oldenburg Verlag, 1985). See also Hans Mommsen, "The Decline of the Bürgertum in Late Nineteenth and Early Twentieth Century Germany," in *From Weimar to Auschwitz*, ed. Mommsen (Princeton, NJ: Princeton University Press, 1991).

30. On the collapse of the bourgeois middle see Jones, *German Liberalism and the Dissolution of the Weimar Party System*; Jones, "'The Dying Middle': Weimar Germany and the Fragmentation of Bourgeois Politics," *Central European History* 5 (1972); Jones, "In the Shadow of Stabilization: German Liberalism and the Legitimacy of the Weimar Party System"; and Thomas Childers, "Interest and Ideology: Anti-System Parties in the Era of Stabilization," both in *Die Nachwirkungen der Inflation*, ed. Feldman.

31. On the party's changing social profile see Michael Kater, *The Nazi Party. A Social Profile of Its Members and Leaders, 1919–1945* (Cambridge, MA: Harvard University Press, 1983).

32. Werner Angress, "The Political Role of the Peasantry," *Review of Politics* 21 (July 1959); J.E. Farquharson, *The Plough and the Swastika* (London: Sage, 1976); Horst Gies, "The NSDAP and Agrarian Organization in the Final Phase of the Weimar Republic," in *Nazism and the Third Reich*, ed. Henry Turner (New York: New Viewpoints, 1972); Charles Loomis and J. Allan Beegle, "The Spread of Nazism in Rural Areas," *American Sociological Review* 11 (December 1946).

33. Peter Stachura, *The Shaping of the Nazi State* (New York: Barnes and Noble, 1978); Jeremy Noakes, *The Nazi Party in Lower Saxony* (New York: Oxford University Press, 1971); Dietrich Orlow, *The History of the Nazi Party*, vol. 1 (Pittsburgh: University of Pittsburgh Press, 1971).

34. Hans Mommsen, "The Breakthrough of the National Socialists as Mass Movement," in *German History, 1933–1945*, ed. Hermann Mau and Helmut Krausnick (London: O. Wolff, 1964), 104.

35. Sheri Berman, "Civil Society and the Collapse of the Weimar Republic," *World Politics* 49, no. 3 (1997).

36. Sheri Berman, "Civil Society and the Collapse of the Weimar Republic," *World Politics* 49, no. 3 (1997); Fritzsche, *Rehearsals for Fascism*, 13.

37. Stachura, *Gregor Strasser and the Rise of Nazism*, 71. See also Orlow, *The History of the Nazi Party*.

38. In the 1928 elections, for example, the NSDAP share of the vote in the pre-dominantly rural districts of East Prussia, Pomerania, East Hannover, and Hesse-Darmstadt was below its national average. Horst Gies, "The NSDAP and Agrarian Organizations in the Final Phase of the Weimar Republic," in *Nazism and the Third Reich*, ed. Henry A. Turner (New York: New Viewpoints, 1972), 75 n. 2. See also Richard J. Evans and W.R. Lee, eds., *The German Peasantry* (New York: St. Martin's Press, 1986); Robert G. Moeller, *German Peasants and Agrarian Politics, 1914–1924* (Chapel Hill: University of North Carolina Press, 1986); Shelley Baranowski, *The Sanctity of Rural Life: Nobility, Protestantism, and Nazism in West Prussia* (New York: Oxford University Press 1995); and Werner Angress, "The Political Role of the Peasantry," *Review of Politics* 21, no. 3 (1959).

39. On Nazi agricultural policy during this period see J.E. Farquharson, *The Plough and the Swastika: The NSDAP and Agriculture in Germany, 1928–1945* (London: Sage, 1976). For a discussion of why other parties such as the SPD passed up this opportunity see Berman, *Ideas and Politics*.

40. Quoted in Gies, "The NSDAP and Agrarian Organizations in the Final Phase of the Weimar Republic," 51.

41. Gies, 62. See also Zdenek Zofka, "Between Bauernbund and National Socialism: The Political Orientation of the Peasantry in the Final Phase of the Weimar Republic," in *The Formation of the Nazi Constituency*, ed. Childers.

42. Hagtvet, "The Theory of Mass Society," 91.

43. Despite the obvious advantages to Germany, the nationalist right mounted a vicious campaign against the Young Plan and forced a referendum on the issue. However, in the December 1929 referendum only 13.8 percent of the electorate voted with the Nationalist, right-wing parties. One side effect of the campaign, however, was that it brought the Nazis into national prominence.

44. If we only include the NSDAP and KPD the share is 31.4 percent; including the DNVP brings the total to 38.4 percent. Some small splinter parties probably also deserve the characterization of "extremist."

45. Eberhard Kolb, "Die Sozialdemokratische Strategie in der Ära des Präsidialkabinetts Brüning: Strategie ohne Alternative?" in *Das Unrechtsregime: Internationale Forschung über den Nationalsozialismus*, vol. 1, ed. Ursula Büttner (Hamburg: Christians, 1986), and Heinrich August Winkler, *Der Weg in die Katastrophe: Arbeiter und Arbeiterbewegung in der Weimarer Republik, 1930–1933* (Berlin: J.H.W. Dietz, 1987), chapter 2, section 3.

46. Heinrich Brüning, *Memoiren 1918–1934* (Stuttgart: Deutsche, 1970), for example 105, 115–16, 118, 133, 315, 501–502, and also Gottfried Reinhold Treviranus, *Das Ende von Weimar* (Düsseldorf: Droste, 1968), 156–61.

47. Berman, *The Social Democratic Moment*, chapter 8, and Berman, *The Primacy of Politics*, chapter 6.

48. Avraham Barkai, *Nazi Economics* (New Haven, CT: Yale University Press, 1990), 23.

49. Winkler, *The Long Road*, 454.

50. Winkler, 40, and Heinrich August Winkler, *Der Weg in die Katastrophe: Arbeiter und Arbeiterbewegung in der Weimarer Republik, 1930–1933* (Berlin: J.H.W. Dietz, 1987), 638.

51. Angress, "The Political Role of the Peasantry"; Martin Broszat, *Hitler and the Collapse of Weimar Germany* (Berg: Lexington Spa, 1989), 72–73; Jens Flemming, "Großagarische Interessen und Landarbeiterbewegung: Überlegungen zur Arbeiterpolitik des Bundes der Landwirte und des Reichslandbundes in der Anfangsphase der Weimarer Republik," in *Industrielles System*, ed. Mommsen et al.; Dietrich Orlow, *History of the Nazi Party: 1919–1933* (Pittsburgh: University of Pittsburgh Press, 1969), 151ff.; Charles P. Loomis and J. Allan Beegle, "The Spread of Nazism in Rural Areas," *American Sociological Review* 11 (December 1946); and J.E. Farquharson, *The Plough and the Swastika: The NSDAP and Agriculture in Germany, 1929–1945* (London: Sage, 1976).

52. Hans Beyer, "Die Agrarkrise und das Ende der Weimarer Republik," *Zeitschrift für Agrargeschichte und Agrarsoziologie* 13 (1965).

53. If we include only the NSDAP, KPD, and DNVP it is about 57 percent.

54. Jürgen Falter, "The First German Volkspartei," in *Elections, Parties and Political Traditions: Social Foundations of German Parties and Party Systems*, ed. Karl Rohe (Providence, RI: Berg, 1990), 79, 81; Thomas Childers, "National Socialism and the New Middle Class," in *Die Nationalsozialisten: Analysen faschistischer Bewegungen*, ed. Reinhard Mann (Stuttgart: Klett-Cotta, 1980); Kater, *The Nazi Party*; Richard Hamilton, *Who Voted for Hitler?* (Princeton, NJ: Princeton University Press, 1982); Thomas Childers, "Who, Indeed, Did Vote for Hitler?" *Central European History* 17, no. 1 (1984); Paul Madden, "Some Social Characteristics of Early Nazi Party Members," *Central European History* 15, no. 1 (March 1982); Detlef Muhlberger, "The Sociology of the NSDAP," *Journal of Contemporary History* 15, no. 3 (July 1980).

55. Quoted in Henry Ashby Turner, *Hitler's Thirty Days to Power: January 1933* (New York: Addison Wesley, 1996), 1. Within the party itself, many were concerned that time was limited. Goebbels, for example, believed that if the party did not achieve power soon, its ability to hold itself together was in doubt. Mommsen, "The Breakthrough," 248.

56. Gordon Craig, *The Politics of the Prussian Army* (New York: Oxford University Press, 1955), chapter 11.

57. On Schleicher's machinations and the SPD see Richard Breitman, "On German Social Democracy and General Schleicher 1932–1933," *Central European History* 9 (December 1976); Gerard Braunthal, "The German Free Trade Unions during the Rise of Nazism," *Journal of Central European Affairs* 15 (1956).

58. Winkler, *The Long Road West*, 489; Alexander Gerschenkron, *Bread and Democracy in Germany* (Ithaca, NY: Cornell University Press, 1989); Farquharson, *The Plough*; and Adam Tooze, *The Wages of Destruction* (New York: Penguin, 2008), 29–30.

59. Turner, *Hitler's Thirty Days*, 160. On the problems facing the Nazi party during 1932 and 1933 see also Orlow, *The History of the Nazi Party*, 233ff.; Thomas Childers, "The Limits of National Socialist Mobilization," in *The Formation of the Nazi Constituency*, ed. Childers (London: Croom and Helm, 1986).

60. Klaus Hildebrand, *The Third Reich* (London: Allen & Unwin, 1984), 4ff.

61. The debate about how revolutionary the Nazis really were remains a live one. Although this chapter does not wade directly into it, the subsequent sections discuss the remarkable and far-reaching changes wrought by Hitler's regime. For assessments, see below and Thomas Saunders, "Nazism and Social Revolution," in *Modern Germany Reconsidered 1870–1945*, ed. Gordon Martel (New York: Routledge, 1992); Jeremy Noakes, "Nazism and Revolution," in *Revolutionary Theory and Political Reality*, ed. Noël O'Sullivan (New York: St. Martin's Press, 1983); Mau and Krausnick, *German History*, 31ff.; David Schoenbaum, *Hitler's Social Revolution* (New York: W.W. Norton, 1966); Karl Dietrich Bracher, "The Role of Hitler," in *Fascism*, ed. Walter Laqueur (Berkeley: University of California Press, 1976).

62. Peter Fritzsche, *Life and Death in the Third Reich* (Cambridge, MA: Harvard University Press, 2008), esp. 49ff.; Wolfgang Benz, *A Concise History of the Third Reich* (Berkeley: University of California Press, 2006), chapter 4.

63. Noakes, "Nazism and Revolution," 82.

64. Schoenbaum, *Hitler's Social Revolution*, 247ff.

65. Wilhelm Dienst, Manfred Messerschmidt, Hans-Erich Volkmann, and Wolfram Wetter, *Germany and the Second World War* (Oxford: Clarendon Press, 1990), 521–22. On the men involved see Correlli Barnett, *Hitler's Generals* (London: Weidenfeld and Nicolson, 1989).

66. As several observers have noted:

    there is no question that, compared to other strata, the industrial community enjoyed a preeminent and protected position under Nazi rule and was less exposed to . . . terror. It is also true that the Nazis allowed that community a considerable measure of self-management as long as it kept to the straight and narrow and painstakingly strove to achieve the prescribed objectives. However, to describe this state of affairs as a "coalition of equal partners" is a gross exaggeration.

    Avraham Barkai, *Nazi Economics* (New York: Berg, 1990), 16–17.

67. Stolper, *The German Economy*, 137.

68. David Schoenbaum, *Hitler's Social Revolution* (New York: W. W. Norton, 1966), 174.

69. For comparison, the comparable figures for Great Britain and the United States were 23 percent and 10 percent, respectively. See Walter Laqueur,

Fascism: Past, Present, Future (New York: Oxford University Press, 1996), 67; Overy, *The Nazi Economic Recovery*, 35.

70. Overy, *The Nazi Economic Recovery*, 42.

71. Barkai, *Nazi Economics*, 3. Also see Berman, *The Primacy of Politics*, chapter 6; Tooze, *The Wages of Destruction*; Götz Aly, *Hitler's Beneficiaries* (New York: Henry Holt, 2007); Barkai, *Nazi Economics*; R.J. Overy, *War and Economy in the Third Reich* (Oxford: Clarendon Press, 1994); Alan Milward, *The German Economy at War* (London: Athlone Press, 1965); Timothy Mason, "The Primacy of Politics," in *The Nature of Fascism*, ed. S.J. Woolf (New York: Random House, 1958); Mason Timothy, *Social Policy in the Third Reich* (Oxford: Berg, 1993); Ian Kershaw, *The Nazi Dictatorship* (New York: Routledge, 1993), chapter 3.

72. Or, to put it another way, Hitler once said that "there was no need to nationalize German businesses, if the population itself could be nationalized," and this is precisely what the Nazis set out to do. Tooze, *Wages of Destruction*, 134.

73. Barkai, *Nazi Economics*, 26–27.

74. Timothy Mason, "The Primacy of Politics," in *The Nature of Fascism*, ed. S.J. Woolf (New York: Random House, 1958), and Mason, *Social Policy in the Third Reich* (Oxford: Berg, 1993). See also Barkai, *Nazi Economics*, 168–69, and R.J. Overy, *War and Economy in the Third Reich* (Oxford: Clarendon Press, 1994), 38.

75. C.W. Guillebaud, *The Social Policy of Nazi Germany* (New York: Howard Fertig, 1971), 15–16 and chapter 3; Overy, *War and Economy in the Third Reich*; Dan Silverman, *Hitler's Economy: Nazi Work Creation Programs, 1933–1936* (Cambridge, MA: Harvard University Press, 1998).

76. Overy, *War and Economy in the Third Reich*, 55. When work-creation programs were originally proposed during the end phase of the Weimar Republic, many businesses objected, viewing the government spending and intervention in the market that they implied as dangerous. However, once the Nazis came to power, such criticism essentially stopped. As one observer notes:

> by August 1933 businessmen who had resisted work creation two years earlier were now doing their part to support the Hitler government's battle for jobs. The new attitude reflected not only an improved economic outlook, but also the fact that under the developing Nazi dictatorship "the price of insurance against unpleasant forms of government intervention had risen considerably." By destroying the German trade unions, Hitler had finished the job begun by Brüning. In return, the government expected industry to cooperate in providing jobs for the unemployed. If that cooperation had not been forthcoming . . . German industrialists might have faced unpleasant consequences.
>
> Silverman, *Hitler's Economy*, 8.

77. Silverman, *Hitler's Economy*, chapter 2. Barkai, *Nazi Economics*, 166; Gustav Stolper, *The German Economy* (London: Weidenfeld and Nicolson, 1967), 143. For a more circumspect judgment, see Overy, *War and Economy in the Third Reich*, e.g., 56.

78. It is also worth noting that many of these policies, as well as the funding for them, were in place even before Hitler came to power. R.J. Overy, *The Nazi Economic Recovery* (London: Macmillan, 1982); Overy, *War and Economy in the Third Reich*, 38; Silverman, *Hitler's Economy*, 245; Tooze, *Wages of Destruction*.

79. Overy, *War and Economy in the Third Reich*, 80.

80. Kater, *The Nazi Party*, 83–84; Aly, *Hitler's Beneficiaries*.

81. Kater, *The Nazi Party*, 238.

82. Aly, *Hitler's Beneficiaries*, 13.

83. Laqueur, *Fascism*, 68–69. Also see Mason, *Social Policy in the Third Reich*; Schoenbaum, *Hitler's Social Revolution*, chapter 3; and Fritzsche, *Life and Death*, chapter 1.

84. These excluded groups as well as those Germans conquered were forced to help pay for the welfare state. Aly, *Hitler's Beneficiaries*.

85. Aly, for example, calls it a "racist-totalitarian" welfare state. See, e.g., *Hitler's Beneficiaries,* and Michael Burleigh and Wolfgang Wippermann, *The Racial State: Germany 1933–1945* (Cambridge: Cambridge University Press, 1991).

86. Quoted in Deist et al., eds., *Germany and the Second World War*, 148–49.

87. Götz Aly, "Die Wohlfühl-Diktator," *Der Spiegel*, October 2005, 56. Also, Fritzsche, *Life and Death*, chapters 1 and 2.

88. Tooze, *Wages of Destruction*, 285.

Chapter 13

1. Quoted in Stanley Payne, *Civil War in Europe, 1905–1949* (New York: Cambridge University Press, 2011), 120.

2. Walther Bernecker, "Spain: The Double Breakdown," in *Conditions of Democracy in Europe*, ed. Dirk Berg-Schlosser and Jeremy Mitchell (New York: St. Martin's Press, 2000).

3. William and Carla Rahn Phillips, *A Concise History of Spain* (New York: Cambridge University Press, 2010), 116; J.H. Elliot, *Imperial Spain, 1469–1716* (New York: St Martin's, 1963).

4. J.S. Elliot, "A Europe of Composite Monarchies," *Past and Present* 137 (November 1992).

5. Indeed, this is related to their accomplishments. In order to unite the forces against the Moors, the monarchy had to promise them privileges or *fueros* that continued to shape political development up through the modern era. John Elliot, "The Spanish Monarchy," in *Conquest and Coalescence*, ed. Mark Greengrass (New York: Edward Arnold, 1991); Elliot, *Imperial Spain*; David Sturdy, *Fractured Europe* (Oxford: Blackwell Publishers, 2002); Henry Kamen, *Spain 1469–1714: A Society in Conflict* (Harlow, England: Pearson, 2005); Kamen, *Spain's Road to Empire* (London: Penguin, 2002); John Lynch, *Spain 1516–1598* (Cambridge: Blackwell, 1992); J.N. Hillgarth, *The Spanish Kingdoms*, vol. 2 (Oxford: Clarendon Press, 1978).

6. Historic laws or freedoms might be a more accurate name.

7. E. Ramón Arango, *The Spanish Political System* (Boulder, CO: Westview Press, 1978), chapter 1.

8. J.H. Elliot, *The Revolt of the Catalans* (New York: Cambridge University Press, 1963), 7–8. On the logic of this rule, see also J.B. Owens, *By My Absolute Royal Authority* (Rochester, NY: University of Rochester Press, 2005). Contributing to the maintenance of this state of affairs may have been what contemporary social scientists refer to as the "resource curse": when rulers have access to resource revenues they have less need to build taxation and administrative institutions or extract resources from society in order to finance their endeavors. The Spanish monarch's access to silver from the New World meant that it had hitherto faced less pressure than other European monarchs to confront the opponents of centralization and build institutions capable of extracting resources from them up through the early modern period. Mauricio Drelichman and Hans-Joachim Voth, *Lending to the Borrower from Hell* (Princeton, NJ: Princeton University Press, 2014). Similarly, the "resource curse" probably also helps explain why frequent warfare did not lead to state-building in Spain, as Tilly and other scholars would predict since with significant resource revenue at its disposal, Spanish rulers faced less pressure to build proto-state institutions to finance warfare. Charles Tilly, *Coercion, Capital and European States* (New York: Blackwell, 1990).

9. Elliot, *Revolt of the Catalans*, 193; Elliot, *Richelieu and Olivares* (New York: Cambridge University Press, 1984); and Elliot, *The Count-Duke of Olivares* (New Haven, CT: Yale University Press, 1986).

10. I.A.A. Thompson, *Crown and Cortes* (Hampshire, England: Variorum, 1993).

11. Quoted in Elliot, *Revolt of the Catalans*, 200.

12. During the first decades of the seventeenth century Spain was involved in approximately ten conflicts: the Anglo-Spanish war, Irish Nine Years' War, Acoma war, Dutch-Portuguese War, War of Julich Succession, Thirty Years' War, Genoese-Savoyard, War of Mantuan Succession, and Franco-Spanish.

13. Elliot, *Imperial Spain*, 323. But see also Helen Nader, *Liberty in Absolutist Spain* (Baltimore: Johns Hopkins University Press, 1990).

14. Elliot, *Revolt of the Catalans*, 193; Elliot, *Imperial Spain*, 324.

15. Peter Sahlins, *Boundaries: The Making of France and Spain in the Pyrenees* (Berkeley: University of California Press, 1989).

16. Thompson, *Crown and Cortes*, chapter 4, pp. 51, 79, 80, 82, 84. Also, Ruth Mackay, *The Limits of Royal Authority: Resistance and Obedience in Seventeenth-Century Castile* (New York: Cambridge University Press, 1999); Elliot, *Imperial Spain*, 357.

17. For a discussion of the overall implications of this trend, see S.R. Epstein, *Freedom and Growth: The Rise of States and Markets in Europe, 1300–1750* (New York: Routledge, 2000).

18. Thompson, *Crown and Cortes*, chapter 4, p. 85, and chapter 5, p. 89. J.H. Elliot, "The Decline of Spain," reprinted in Elliot, *Spain and Its World* (New Haven, CT: Yale University Press, 1989).

19. Mark Dinecco, "Fiscal Centralization, Limited Government, and Public Revenues in Europe, 1650–1913," *The Journal of Economic History* 69, no. 1 (March 2009); Dinecco, "Fragmented Authority from Ancien Régime to Modernity: A Quantitative Analysis," *Journal of Institutional Economics* 6, no. 3 (September 2010).

20. Reflecting their views of their own position vis-à-vis the crown, Aragonese nobles swore this oath of allegiance to a new king:

We, who are as good as you,
Swear to you, who are no better than us,
To accept you as our king and sovereign,
Provided you observe all our liberties and laws,
But if not, not.

Quoted in Drelichman and Voth, *Lending to the Borrower from Hell*, 258, and Richard Herr, *An Historical Essay on Modern Spain* (Berkeley: University of California Press, 1974).

21. Grafe, *Distant Tyranny*. The Spanish nobility was, as noted above, an extremely fractious and divided class, including great nobles who owned vast estates as well as relatively poor *Hildagos* who often owned little or no property at all. Raymond Carr, *Spain 1808–1975* (New York: Oxford University Press, 1966), 46; Geoffrey Treasure, *The Making of Modern Europe, 1648–1780* (New York: Methuen, 1985), 349; E.N. Williams, *The Ancien Régime* (New York: Harper and Row, 1970), chapter 3; Drelichman and Voth, *Lending to the Borrower from Hell*, 80; H.M. Scott, *Enlightened Absolutism* (Ann Arbor: University of Michigan Press, 1990), 120–21.

22. R.A. Stradling, *Europe and the Decline of Spain* (London: George Allen and Unwin, 1981); Kamen, *Spain*; Ortiz Antonio Dominguez, *The Golden Age of Spain, 1516–1659* (New York: Basic, 1971); and Regina Grafe, *Distant Tyranny: Markets, Power and Backwardness in Spain, 1650–1800* (Princeton, NJ: Princeton University Press, 2012). Also see the work of Mark Dinecco on how centralization and fragmentation influenced the "strength" and capacity of various European states, e.g., Mark Dinecco, "Fiscal Centralization, Limited Government and Public Revenues in Europe, 1650–1913," *The Journal of Economic History* 69, no. 1 (March 2009); Dinecco, "Fragmented Authority from Ancien Régime to Modernity," *Journal of Institutional Economics* 6, no. 3 (September 2010); Dinecco, "Warfare, Fiscal Capacity, and Performance," *Journal of Economic Growth* 17 (2012); and Dinecco, "The Rise of Effective States in Europe," *The Journal of Economic History* 75, no. 3 (September 2015).

23. Drelichman and Voth, *Lending to the Borrower from Hell*, chapter 8.

24. This is what Eric Hobsbawm called the period 1789–1914. See, e.g., his trilogy *The Age of Revolution, 1789–1848; The Age of Capital, 1848–1875*; and *The Age of Empire, 1875–1914*.

25. Those supporting the French and the principles of the French Revolution were called *afrancescados* in Spain, those who had "turned French."

26. Michael Broers, *Europe Under Napoleon, 1799–1815* (London: Arnold, 1996).

27. Guerilla referring in Spanish to a "body of skirmishers, skirmishing warfare": diminutive of Guerra (war) as in "little war" (http://www.etymonline.com/index.php?term=guerrilla).

28. Geoffrey Jensen, *Irrational Triumph* (Las Vegas: University of Nevada Press, 2002), 18.

29. Charles Esdaile, *Spain in the Liberal Age: From Constitution to Civil War, 1808–1939* (London: Blackwell, 2000), 21.

30. Charles Esdaile, *Spain in the Liberal Age* (London: Blackwell, 2000), 32.

31. Peter Pierson, *The History of Spain* (Westport, CT: Greenwood, 1999), 93ff.; William Callahan, *Church, Politics and Society in Spain, 1750–1874* (Cambridge, MA: Harvard University Press, 1984).

32. Stanley Payne, *Spain's First Democracy* (Madison: University of Wisconsin Press, 1993), 6; Mary Vincent, *Spain 1833–2002* (New York: Oxford University Press, 2007), 1.

33. Esdaile, *Spain in the Liberal Age*, 121ff.; E. Christiansen, *The Origins of Military Power in Spain* (New York: Oxford University Press, 1967).

34. Vincent, *Spain*, 35.

35. Anthony Beevor, *The Battle for Spain* (New York: Penguin, 2006), 8.

36. Esdaile, *Spain in the Liberal Age*, 123.

37. Stanley Payne, "Spanish Conservatism, 1834–1923," *Journal of Contemporary History* 13 (1978): 787.

38. Robert Goldstein, *Political Repression in 19th Century Europe* (New York: Rowman and Littlefield, 1983), 287. Julián Casanova and Carlos Gil Andés, *Twentieth Century Spain* (New York: Cambridge University Press, 2014); Phillips and Phillips, *A Concise History of Spain*, 201; Esdaile, *Spain in the Liberal Age*, 147ff.; Herr and Herr, *An Historical Essay*, 115ff.; Carr, *Spain 1808–1975*, 352ff.; and Carr, *Modern Spain* (New York: Oxford University Press, 1980), 8–13.

    One crucial difference between liberals and conservatives concerned views of the Church, with the former opposed to its immensely powerful role in Spanish life and the latter supportive of it.

39. Georgina Blakeley, "Clientelism in the Building of State and Civil Society in Spain," in *Clientelism, Interests and Democratic Representation: The European Experience in Comparative and Historical Perspective*, ed. Simonia Piattoni (New York: Cambridge University Press, 2001), 83; Xavier Tusell Gómez, "The Functioning of the Cacique System in Andalusia," in *Politics and Society in Twentieth-Century Spain*, ed. Stanley Payne (New York: Franklin Watts, 1976).

40. Hugh Thomas, *The Spanish Civil War* (New York: Harper and Row, 1963), 14.

41. Sociologist Adolfo Posada, quoted in D.J. Walker, *Spanish Women and the Colonial Wars of the 1890s* (Baton Rouge: Louisiana State University Press, 2008), chapter 4, p. 2.

42. Goldstein, *Political Repression*, 295. Also see Arango, *The Spanish Political System*, 33.

43. James Simpson, "Economic Development in Spain, 1850–1936," *The Economic History Review* 50, no. 2 (May 1997); Carr, *Modern Spain*, chapter 2; and Javier Moreno-Luzón, *Modernizing the Nation* (Brighton, England: Sussex Press, 2012).

44. Martin, *The Agony*, 51.

45. Martin Blinkhorn, *Democracy and Civil War in Spain* (London: Routledge, 1988), 3; Nigel Townson, "Introduction," in *Is Spain Different?* ed. Townson (Chicago: Sussex Press, 2015), 1; and Jensen, *Irrational Triumph*.

46. Martin, *The Agony*, 175.

47. For instance, between 1914 and 1920 the cost of living almost doubled and wages did not keep up with rising prices. An inflationary crisis also followed. Malefakis, *Agrarian Crisis*, 145.

48. Benjamin Martin, *The Agony of Modernization: Labor and Industrialization in Spain* (Ithaca, NY: ILR Press, 1990), xv.

49. Payne, "Spanish Conservatism," esp. 784.

50. Carolyn Boyd, *Praetorian Politics in Liberal Spain* (Chapel Hill: University of North Carolina Press, 1979).

51. Boyd, *Praetorian Politics*; Sebastian Balfour, *The End of the Spanish Empire, 1898–1923* (Oxford: Clarendon Press, 1997); and Balfour, *Deadly Embrace: Morocco and the Road to the Spanish Civil War* (New York: Oxford University Press, 2002).

52. James Rial, *Revolution from Above: The Primo de Rivera Dictatorship in Spain* (Fairfax, VA: George Mason University Press, 1986), 33–34, and Malefakis, *Agrarian Crisis*, 152.

53. Martin, *The Agony*, 227, and Vincent, *Spain*, 106.

54. Gerald Brennan, *The Spanish Labyrinth: The Social and Political Background to the Spanish Civil War* (New York: Cambridge University Press, 1943), 78. On Primo de Rivera and his regime more generally see Sholomo Ben-Ami, *Fascism from Above* (New York: Oxford University Press, 1983) and J. Rial, *Revolution from Above* (London: Associated University Presses, 1986).

55. Martin, *The Agony*, 264.

56. Bernecker, "The Double Breakdown," 411.

57. Carr, *Spain 1808–1975*, 501.

58. Rial, *Revolution from Above* and Herr and Herr, *An Historical Essay*, 141.

59. Rial, *Revolution from Above*, 51.

60. Shlomo Ben-Ami, *Fascism from Above: The Dictatorship of Primo de Rivera in Spain, 1923–1930* (New York: Oxford University Press, 1983).

61. Ben-Ami, *Fascism from Above*.

62. Ben-Ami, *Fascism from Above*, esp. chapters 7 and 8, and Carr, *Spain*, 570.

63. Ben-Ami, *Fascism from Above*, 299.

64. Ben-Ami, *Fascism from Above*; Carr, *Modern Spain*, 101.

65. Gerald Brenan, *The Spanish Labyrinth* (New York: Cambridge University Press, 1943), 81ff.

66. Ben-Ami, *Fascism from Above*, chapter 9.

67. Esdaile, *Spain in the Liberal Age*, 272, 280; Shlomo Ben-Ami, "The Republican 'Take-Over': Prelude to Inevitable Catastrophe?" in *Revolution and War in Spain*, ed. Paul Preston (New York: Methuen, 1984).

68. Moreno-Luzón, *Modernizing the Nation*, esp. 173.

69. Herr and Herr, *An Historical Essay*, 156; Rial, *Revolution from Above*, 232; Casanova and Andrés, *Twentieth Century Spain*, 102.

70. Juan Linz, "From Great Hope to Civil War: The Breakdown of Democracy in Spain," in *The Breakdown of Democratic Regimes: Europe*, ed. Linz and Stepan (Baltimore: Johns Hopkins University Press, 1978), 143; Carr, *Spain 1808–1939*, 592.

71. Martin, *The Agony*, 297.

72. Stanley Payne, *Spain's First Democracy: The Second Republic, 1931–1936* (Madison: University of Wisconsin Press, 1993), 372.

73. Paul Preston, *The Coming of the Spanish Civil War* (New York: Routledge, 1994), 1; Bernecker, "The Double Breakdown," 398ff.

74. On the nature and dynamics of Spain's agricultural sector, see Edward E. Malefakis, *Agrarian Reform and Peasant Revolution in Spain* (New Haven, CT: Yale University Press, 1970).

75. Malefakis, *Agrarian Reform*, 33.

76. Michael Mann, *Fascists* (New York: Cambridge University Press, 2004), 302–03.

77. As one scholar put it, "few institutions have played so central a role in the history of a people as has the Spanish Church." Callahan, *Church, Politics and Society*, 1.

78. Nigel Townson, "Anticlericalism and Secularization," in *Is Spain Different?* ed. Townson, 82.

79. Callahan, *Church, Politics and Society*, 183.

80. Martin, *The Agony*, 147.

81. Arango, *The Spanish Political System*, 23.

82. José Alvarez Junco, "The Debate over the Nation," in *Is Spain Different?* ed. Townson. Also see Alvarez Junco, *Spanish Identity in the Age of Nations* (Manchester, UK: Manchester University Press, 2011); Carolyn Boyd, *Historia Patria* (Princeton, NJ: Princeton University Press, 1997).

83. Some scholars, like Paul Preston, argue that by the early twentieth century these groups were increasingly embracing apocalyptic, racialist views of groups opposed to this traditional vision of Spain, portraying them as "neither really Spanish nor even really human," as existential threats to the "nation's

existence," and as worthy of "extermination." See his *The Spanish Holocaust* (New York: Harper Press, 2012).

84. Luis Arranz Notario, "Could the Second Republic Have Become a Democracy?" and Gabriel Ranzato, "The Republican Left and the Defense of Democracy," in *The Spanish Second Republic Revisited*, ed. Manuel Álvarez Tardío and Fernando Del Rey Regullo (Portland, OR: Sussex Press, 2012); Nigel Townson, *The Crisis of Democracy in Spain* (Portland, OR: Sussex Press, 2000).

85. "Never before had Spain experienced such an intense period of change and conflict, democratic advances of social conquests." Julián Casanova, *The Spanish Republic and Civil War* (New York: Cambridge University Press, 2010), 37. Also see José Manuel Macarro, "The Socialists and Revolution," and Nigel Townson, "A Third Way? Centrist Politics Under the Republic," in *The Spanish Second Republic Revisited*, ed. Tardio and Del Rey Regullo.

86. https://www.scribd.com/doc/123469543/Constitution-of-the-Republic-of-Spain-1931.

87. Text of constitution, accessed at https://www.scribd.com/doc/123469543/Constitution-of-the-Republic-of-Spain-1931.

88. In 1932 the Catalan Statute was passed by the Cortes granting Catalonia autonomy. A similar process dragged on in the Basque country due largely to divisions among Basque parties themselves.

89. Townson, "Anticlericalism and Secularization," 89. Or, as Juan Linz put it: "the Azaña government attempted to quickly secularize [Spain] by decree." Linz, "From Great Hopes," 152.

90. Thomas, *The Spanish Civil War*, 46; Blinkhorn, *Democracy and Civil War*, 17; Frances Lannon, "The Church's Crusade Against the Republic," in *Revolution and War*, ed. Preston.

91. Adrian Shubert, *A Social History of Modern Spain* (New York: Routledge, 1990), 99; Joseph Harrison, *An Economic History of Modern Spain* (Manchester, UK: Manchester University Press, 1978), 134.

92. Martin, *The Agony*, 306.

93. Townson, "A Third Way?" 101.

94. He led a group called Group at the Service of the Republic (*Agrupación al Servicio de la República*). Carolyn P. Boyd, "The Republicans and the Left," in *Spain in Conflict, 1931–1939*, ed. Martin Blinkhorn (London: Sage, 1986).

95. Townson, "A Third Way?" 99.

96. Maria Thomas, *The Faith and the Fury: Popular Anticlerical Violence and Iconoclasm in Spain* (Brighton: Sussex Press, 2013).

97. Nigel Townson, *The Crisis of Democracy in Spain* (Portland, OR: Sussex Press, 2000).

98. Townson, "A Third Way?" 100.

99. In 1931, 21,000 out of a total of 118,000 troops were officers. Preston, *The Coming of the Spanish Civil War*, 49; Esdaile, *Spain in the Liberal Age*, 291–92; Payne, *Spain's First Democracy*, 92.

100. Malefakis, *Agrarian Reform*.

101. Malefakis, *Agrarian Reform*, 175–76.

102. Malefakis, *Agrarian Reform*, 179.

103. Malefakis, *Agrarian Reform*, chapters 7–10; Beevor, *The Battle*, 21–22: Martin, *The Agony*, 330; Esdaile, *Spain in the Liberal Age*, 291–314.

104. As perhaps the foremost scholar of agrarian reform in the Second Republic put it: "Though milder than some of the bills which preceded it, the Agrarian Law was nevertheless revolutionary in its implications. It seriously threatened the strongest economic class in Spain . . . and awakened the hopes of the impoverished peasantry. To have been consistent with so revolutionary a measure, revolutionary means should have been used to put it into effect. But the Azaña government lacked the emotional commitment necessary to accept the risks involved. . . . [The fear] was that if the reform were implemented too rapidly it might lead to massive owner resistance or degenerate into a chaotic series of peasant assaults on large estates. Either of these eventualities would produce enormous dislocations . . . and condemn Spain to . . . one or two years of Russian hunger." Malkefakis, *Agrarian Reform*, 255.

105. The reactionary primate of Spain, Cardinal Pedro Segura, for example, declared that Spain would be "either a Catholic country or nothing at all" and urged Spaniards to vote against parties determined to destroy the Church. Beevor, *The Battle for Spain*, 22–24.

106. Preston, *The Spanish Holocaust*, 4 and 10.

107. Preston, *The Coming of the Spanish Civil War*, 101; Payne, *Spain's First Democracy*, 114ff.; Martin, *The Agony*, 300–301.

108. Manuel Villar, an anarchist during the Second Republic, quoted in Shubert, *The Role to Revolution*, 141. See also Julián Casanova, *Anarchism, the Republic and Civil War in Spain: 1931–1939* (New York: Routledge, 2005).

109. Martin, *The Agony*, 80. See Casanova, *Anarchism, the Republic, and Civil War*; Robert Kern, *Red Yeas/Black Years: A Political History of Spanish Anarchism* (Philadelphia: ISHI, 1978); and Murray Bookchin, *The Spanish Anarchists* (New York: Free Life, 1977).

110. Casanova, *The Spanish Republic*, 62.

111. Manuel Álvarez Tardío, "The CEDA: Threat or Opportunity," in *The Spanish Second Republic*, ed. Tardío and Del Rey Raguillo.

112. Casanova, *The Spanish Republic*, 90 and Roberto Villa García, "The Limits of Democratization: Elections and Political Culture," in *The Spanish Second Republic*, ed. Tardío and Del Rey Raguillo.

113. Gabriel Jackson, *The Spanish Republic and Civil War* (Princeton, NJ: Princeton University Press, 1967), e.g., 30; Richard Robinson, *The Origins of Franco's Spain* (Plymouth, UK: Latimer and Trend, 1970).

114. He said, e.g., "We must found a new state, purge the fatherland of Judaizing Freemasons. . . . We must proceed to a new state and this imposes duties and

sacrifices. What does it mean if we have to shed blood!" Preston, *The Spanish Holocaust*, 48.

115. Ben-Ami, "The Republican 'Take Over,' " 28; Lannon, "The Church's Crusade," 39, in *Revolution and War*, ed. Preston.

116. Brenan, *The Spanish Labyrinth*, 266ff.; Herr and Herr, *An Historical Essay*, 174ff.; Phillips and Phillips, *A Concise History*, 420ff.; Jackson, *The Spanish Republic*, 123ff.; and Robinson, *The Origins*, chapter 5.

117. Adrian Shubert, *The Road to Revolution in Spain: The Coal Miners of Asturias* (Urbana: University of Illinois Press, 1987). Also see Casanova and Andrés, *Twentieth-Century Spain*, 131–32, 149ff.; Macarro, "The Socialists and Revolution."

118. Martin, *The Agony*, 346–47; Preston, *The Coming of the Spanish Civil War*, 117; and Carr, *Modern Spain*, 129.

119. Jackson, *The Spanish Republic*, 147.

120. Norman Jones, "Regionalism and Revolution in Catalonia," in *Revolution and War*, ed. Preston, 107.

121. See, e.g., Shubert, *The Road to Revolution*, 13ff.

122. Thomas, *The Spanish Civil War*, 83; Linz and Stepan, *The Breakdown*, 191.

123. Vincent, *Spain*, 133.

124. Adrian Shubert, "The Epic Failure: The Asturian Revolution of October 1934," in *Revolution and War*, ed. Preston.

125. Beevor, *The Battle for Spain*, 32.

126. Beevor, *The Battle for Spain*, 32; Esdaile, *Spain in the Liberal Age*, 325–26.

127. Casanova, *The Spanish Republic*, 117–19.

128. Quoted in Casanova, *The Spanish Republic*, 120.

129. Xavier Tusell Gómez, "The Popular Front Elections in Spain," in *Politics and Society*, ed. Payne.

130. Thomas, *The Spanish Civil War*, 98.

131. Beevor, *The Battle for Spain*, 38.

132. Jackson, *The Spanish Republic*, e.g., 32–35.

133. Malefakis, *Agrarian Reform*, 371, 374; Martin, *The Agony*, 365.

134. Malefakis, *Agrarian Reform*, 375–79; Payne, *Spain's First Democracy*, 302–306.

135. Macarro, "The Socialists and Revolution," in *The Spanish Second Republic*, ed. Tardío and Del Rey Raguillo, 55–56.

136. Payne, *Spain's First Democracy*, 334; Carr, *Spain*, 642–43; and Richard Gillespie, *The Spanish Socialist Party* (Oxford: Clarendon Press, 1989).

137. Preston, *The Spanish Holocaust*, xii, 10ff.

138. Robinson, *The Origins*.

139. José Parejo Fernández, "The Mutation of Falangism," in *The Spanish Second Republic*, ed. Tardío and Del Rey Reguillo; Stephen Lyman, "Moderate Conservatism and the Second Republic," Paul Preston, "Alfonsist Monarchism and the Coming of the Spanish Civil War," and Martin Blinkhorn, "Right-Wing

Utopianism and Harsh Reality: Carlism, the Republic and the 'Crusade,'" in *Spain in Conflict*, ed. Blinkhorn.

140. Sheelagh Ellwood, "Falange Española," in *Spain in Conflict*, ed. Blinkhorn.

141. To use terms common in the Spanish literature, the right moved from the "accidentalist" into the "catastrophist" camp, no longer viewing the Republic instrumentally but rather as fundamentally or irredeemably flawed.

142. "It was indeed, in many ways, an unprecedented event—a key opposition leader being killed by the state's own police. As one observer put it, 'it is perhaps hard to convey the enormity of the deed. . . . Sir Alec Douglas-Home kidnapped and murdered by Special Branch detectives? Senator Robert Kennedy kidnapped and murdered by the F.B.I.? Unthinkable, one might say. And that is the point: in Spain in the summer of 1936, the unthinkable had become normal.' " Brian Crozier, *Franco* (London: Eyre and Spottiswoode, 1967), 165, quoted in Arango, *The Spanish Political System*, 77.

143. Robles, for example, portentously accused the left in Parliament of "carrying out a policy of persecution, violence and extermination against anything that is rightist. But you are profoundly mistaken: however great may be the violence, the reaction will be greater still. For everyone killed another combatant will rise up. . . . You who are today fostering violence will become the first victims of it. The phrase that revolutions . . . devour their children is commonplace, but not less true for being so." Payne, *Spain's First Democracy*, 358–59.

144. A coup, of course, had been planned for a while; the question was when it would begin.

145. Mann, *Fascists*, 344.

146. Javier Tusell, *Spain from Dictatorship to Democracy* (Malden, MA: Blackwell, 2007), 21; Michael Seidman, "The Spanish Civil War: A Unique Conflict?" in *Is Spain Different?* ed. Townson; Preston, *The Spanish Holocaust*.

147. Mann, *Fascists*, 297. Preston refers to it as a "holocaust" (see his *The Spanish Holocaust*).

148. See, e.g., Michael Mann, *Fascists* (New York: Cambridge University Press, 2004), 343–44. This may be wrong, however, depending on the time frame used. Proportionally more Finns, for example, may have been killed during and after the Finnish civil war than Spaniards during and after the Spanish. Aapo Roselius and Tuomas Tepora, *The Finnish Civil War* (Leiden: Brill, 2014); Gerwarth Robert and John Horne, eds., *War and Peace: Paramilitary Violence in Europe after the Great War* (New York: Oxford University Press, 2013); Anthony Upton, *The Finnish Revolution* (Minneapolis: University of Minnesota Press, 1980).

149. Julian Casanova, *The Spanish Civil War* (London: I.B. Taurus, 1913); Michael Alpert, *A New International History of the Spanish Civil War* (New York: St. Martins, 1994); Preston, *The Spanish Holocaust*.

150. Preston, *The Spanish Holocaust*.

151. Quoted in Stanley Payne, *Civil War in Europe, 1905–1949* (New York: Cambridge University Press, 2011), 120.

152. Ben-Ami, *Fascism from Above*, 396.

153. Raymond Carr, *The Spanish Tragedy* (London: Weidenfeld and Nicolson, 1977), esp. chapter 7; Stanley Payne, *Fascism in Spain* (Madison: University of Wisconsin Press, 1999).

Chapter 14

1. G. John Ikenberry, "A World Economy Restored," *International Organization* 46, no. 1 (Winter 1992); Ikenberry, "Workers and the World Economy," *Foreign Affairs* (May/June 1996).

2. See, e.g., Ian Buruma, *Year Zero* (New York: Penguin Press, 2013).

3. Tony Judt, *Postwar* (New York: Penguin Press, 2005), 13–14; Donald Bloxham and Robert Gerwarth, *Political Violence in Twentieth Century Europe* (New York: Cambridge University Press, 2011); Keith Lowe, *Savage Continent* (New York: St. Martin's Press, 2011), 13–17.

4. Judt, *Postwar*, 13–14.

5. William Hitchcock, *The Bitter Road to Freedom* (New York: Free Press, 2008), 190.

6. Hitchcock, *The Bitter Road to Freedom*, 3.

7. Quoted in Judt, *Postwar*, 19.

8. Judt, *Postwar*, 20; Lowe, *Savage Continent*, 51ff.

9. Giles Macdonogh, *After the Reich* (New York: Basic, 2007).

10. Judt, *Postwar*, 21–22; Hitchcock, *The Bitter Road*, 99, 111; and Lowe, *Savage Continent*, 41ff.

11. Richard Bessel, *Germany 1945* (New York: Harper, 2010), 11.

12. Macdonogh, *After the Reich*; Bessel, *Germany 1945*; Manfred Malzahn, ed., *Germany 1945–1949* (New York: Routledge, 1990).

13. There was, however, a strong postwar shift to the left, including increased support for communism. This will be discussed below.

14. David Schoenbaum, *Hitler's Social Revolution* (New York: W.W. Norton, 1966), 286.

15. Schoenbaum, *Hitler's Social Revolution*, 234.

16. N. Kogan, "Fascism as a Political System," in S.J. Woolf, ed., *The Nature of Fascism* (London: George Weidenfeld & Nicolson, Ltd., 1968), 123. Also Götz Aly, *Hitler's Beneficiaries* (New York: Metropolitan Books, 2005).

17. Ralf Dahrendorf, *Society and Democracy in Germany* (New York: Anchor Books, 1969), 395–96.

18. Bessel, *Germany*, 66.

19. Christopher Clark, *Iron Kingdom* (Cambridge, MA: Harvard University Press, 2006), 675–79; Alexander Gerschenkron, *Bread and Democracy in Germany*, preface to the 1966 edition (New York: Fertig, 1989), xxxii.

20. Philipp Ther, *The Dark Side of Nation-States* (New York: Berghahn, 2014); Michael Maurras, *The Unwanted: European Refugees in the Twentieth Century* (New York: Oxford University Press, 1985).

21. Judt, *Postwar*, 24–25.

22. Hitchcock, *The Bitter Road*, 249.

23. Macdonogh, *After the Reich*, 1, 162; R.M. Douglas, *Orderly and Humane: The Expulsion of Germans after the Second World War* (New Haven, CT: Yale University Press, 2012); and Donald Bloxham and Robert Gerwarth, *Political Violence in Twentieth-Century Europe* (New York: Cambridge University Press, 2011); Ben Shepard, *The Long Road Home* (New York: Alfred Knopf, 2011); Alfred Rieber, ed., *Forced Migration in Central and Eastern Europe* (New York: Frank Cass, 2000); and Robert Gerwarth, *Political Violence in Twentieth-Century Europe* (New York: Cambridge University Press, 2011). The numbers are hard to calculate because chaos did not facilitate record keeping and what scholars include in their estimates, e.g., prisoner of war deaths, varies.

24. Mark Mazower, *Dark Continent: Europe's Twentieth Century* (New York: Knopf, 1998), 185.

25. Hitchcock, *The Bitter Road to Freedom*, 170ff.

26. Sometimes a fifth is added—decentralization, referring to the federal nature of postwar Germany—and sometimes the exact nature of the four varies. See, e.g., Bessel, *Germany*.

27. Michael Bernhard, *Institutions and the Fate of Democracy: Germany and Poland in the Twentieth Century* (Pittsburgh: University of Pittsburgh Press, 2005).

28. Instead, the president is chosen by the Bundestag and parliaments of the Länder.

29. Karlheinz Niclauss, "Political Reconstruction at Bonn," in *From Dictatorship to Democracy*, ed. John Herz (Westport, CT: Greenwood Press, 1982).

30. Bessel, *Germany*, 399.

31. The intertwining of political and economic goals was reflected, for example, in the law (56) authorizing decartelizing promulgated by the occupation authorities, which state that "concentrations of economic power as exemplified, in particular, by cartels, syndicates, trusts, combines, and other types of monopolistic or restrictive arrangements" are to be dissolved so as to avoid them being used by Germany in the future "as instruments of [either] political or economic aggression." John Stedman, "The German Decartelization Program," *University of Chicago Law Review* 17, no. 3 (1950): 441.

32. MacDonogh, *After the Reich*, 344.

33. One observer writes, e.g., that "Within a very short time after the liberation it became clear that Germany (and Austria) could not be returned to civil administration and local self-government, even under Allied supervision, if the purging of [all] Nazis was undertaken in a sustained and consistent manner. Moreover . . . the Social Democratic and Christian Democratic parties . . . could not be expected to ignore [all] the votes of former Nazis" if they wanted to

rebuild their voter base and eventually democracy in Germany and Austria." Judt, "The Past in Another Country," in *The Politics of Retribution*, ed. Deak et al., 297.

34. Speech accessed at http://www.americanrhetoric.com/speeches/harrystrumantrumandoctrine.html.

35. Greg Behrman, *The Most Noble Adventure*: The Marshall Plan and How America Helped Rebuild Europe (New York: Free Press, 2008), 243–44.

36. John Ikenberry, "A World Economy Restored," *International Organization* 46, no. 1 (1992); Richard Gardner, *Sterling Dollar Diplomacy* (New York: Columbia University Press, 1980); Michael Bordo and Barry Eichengreen, *A Retrospective on the Bretton Woods System* (Chicago: University of Chicago Press, 2007); Benn Steil, *The Battle of Bretton Woods* (Princeton, NJ: Princeton University Press, 2013).

37. Mills, *Winning the Peace*, 69–73.

38. Alan Milward, *The Reconstruction of Western Europe* (Berkeley: University of California Press, 1984), 2. Memorandum accessed at http://digicoll.library.wisc.edu/cgi-bin/FRUS/FRUS-idx?type=goto&id=FRUS.FRUS1947v03&isize=M&submit=Go+to+page&page=230.

39. See, e.g., Nicolaus Mills, *Winning the Peace: The Marshall Plan and America's Coming of Age as a Superpower* (New York: Wiley, 2008).

40. Quoted in Mills, *Winning the Peace*, 21.

41. Mills, *Winning the Peace*, 3–4.

42. Milward, *The Reconstruction*; Mills, *Winning the Peace*.

43. This position is argued perhaps most notably by Milward.

44. Behrman, *The Most Noble Adventure*, 335.

45. As Marshall put it, "It would be neither fitting nor efficacious for this Government to undertake to draw up unilaterally a program designed to place Europe on its feet economically. This is the business of the Europeans. The initiative, I think, must come from Europe." Text of the Marshall Plan speech, delivered at Harvard University, June 5, 1947, http://www.oecd.org/general/themarshallplanspeechatharvarduniversity5june1947.htm.

In this regard too, the Marshall Plan represented a significant change in American policy: "from being an indifferent or hostile observer of plans for European integration, the United States became a vigorous advocate." Peter Stirk, *History of European Integration since 1914* (New York: Pinter, 1996), 83.

46. OEEC was an organization that itself represented, at least in the words of Arthur Schlesinger, "perhaps the most remarkable example of international cooperation in the history of the world." Quoted in Behrman, *The Most Noble Adventure*, 216.

47. Schuman declaration https://europa.eu/european-union/about-eu/symbols/europe-day/schuman-declaration_en.

48. Winston Churchill, "I Wish to Speak to You Today About the Tragedy of Europe," address delivered at Zurich, Switzerland, September 19, 1946.

49. In the first postwar elections, communists won 12 percent of the vote in Norway and Denmark, 13 percent in Belgium, 19 percent in Italy, 23.5 percent in Finland, and 28.8 percent in France (in the November 1946 election). Lowe, *Savage Continent*, 278.

50. Donald Sassoon, *One Hundred Years of Socialism* (New York: New Press, 1998), 140.

51. G. John Ikenberry, "A World Economy Restored," *International Organization* 46, no. 1 (Winter 1992); Ikenberry, "Workers and the World Economy," *Foreign Affairs* (May/June 1996).

52. Philip Armstrong, Andrew Glyn, and John Harrison, *Capitalism since 1945* (New York: Basil Blackwell, 1991); Stephen Marglin and Juliet Schor, eds., *The Golden Age of Capitalism* (New York: Clarendon Press, 1991).

53. Sheri Berman, *The Primacy of Politics: Social Democracy and the Making of Europe's Twentieth Century* (New York: Cambridge University Press, 2006). This section draws on chapter 8.

54. Robert Skidelsky, "The Political Meaning of Keynesianism," in *The Political Power of Economic Ideas*, ed. Peter Hall (Princeton, NJ: Princeton University Press, 1989), 35–36.

55. Adam Przeworski, *Capitalism and Social Democracy* (New York: Cambridge University Press, 1985), 207.

56. C.A.R. Crosland, *The Future of Socialism* (London: Fletcher and Son, 1967), 98.

57. The best statement of this probably remains T.H. Marshall, *Citizenship and Social Class* (New York: Cambridge University Press, 1950).

58. De Gaulle, quoted in Andrew Shennan, *Rethinking France: Plans for Renewal 1940–1946* (Oxford: Clarendon Press, 1989), 251.

59. Simon Schama, *A History of Britain: The Fate of Empire, 1776–2000* (New York: Hyperion, 2002), 529.

60. Lowe, *Savage Continent*, 66–67.

61. Martin Pugh, *State and Society: British Political and Social History* (London: Bloomsbury, 2012), 228ff.; T.O. Lloyd, *Empire, Welfare State, Europe* (New York: Oxford University Press, 1993).

62. Spencer M. Di Scala, *Italy: From Revolution to Republic* (Boulder, CO: Westview Press, 1998), 283, and Harold James, *Europe Reborn* (New York: Longman, 2003), 257.

63. Simon Reich, *The Fruits of Fascism* (Ithaca, NY: Cornell University Press, 1990).

64. Lars Trädgårdh, "Statist Individualism: On the Culturality of the Nordic Welfare State," in *The Cultural Construction of Norden*, ed. Bo Stråth (Gothenburg, Sweden: Gothenburg University, 1990), 261, and also Korpi, *The Working Class in Welfare Capitalism*, esp. 48–9.

65. Gunnar Adler-Karlsson, *Functional Socialism* (Stockholm: Prisma, 1967), 18.

66. Magnus Ryner, *Capital Restructuring, Globalisation and the Third Way* (London: Routledge, 2002), 85.

67. Huber and Stephens, *Development and Crisis of the Welfare State*, 103. Esping-Andersen, *Politics Against Markets*, and Esping-Andersen, *The Three Worlds of Welfare Capitalism*.

68. German residents polled in the American zone after World War II expected that it would take at least twenty years for the country to recover. De Gaulle had similarly informed French citizens that it would take twenty-five years of "furious work" before France would be back on its feet again. Judt, *Postwar*, 1005, 89.

69. Charles Maier, "The Two Postwar Eras," *American Historical Review* 86, no. 2 (April 1981).

70. Maier, "The Two Postwar Eras," 237.

71. Sheri Berman, "Taming Extremist Parties: The Lessons from European Communism," *Journal of Democracy* 18, no. 5 (January 2008).

72. Clas Offe, "Competitive Party Democracy and the Keynesian Welfare State: Factors of Stability and Disorganization," *Policy Sciences* 15 (1983): 225–26.

73. Bessel, *Germany*, 147.

Chapter 15

1. The is some debate about what this region of the world should be called: Eastern Europe, East-Central Europe, or Central Europe. I use the term "East-Central Europe" mostly because this chapter will not directly examine all the countries that emerged out of the former Habsburg Empire or were subsumed in the Soviet Empire. Instead it focuses primarily on Hungary, Czechoslovakia, East Germany, and Poland. East-Central Europe, therefore, seemed to the most logical appellation but admittedly the choice is somewhat arbitrary.

2. Milovan Djilas, *Conversations with Stalin* (New York: Harcourt Brace, 1963).

3. Geir Lundstad, "Empire by Invitation? The United States and Western Europe, 1945–1952," *Journal of Peace Research* 33, no. 3 (1986). See also Charles Maier, "Empires or Nations? 1918, 1945, 1989," in *Three Postwar Eras in Comparison*, ed. Carl Levy and Mark Roseman (London: Palgrave, 2002).

4. The concept of "Eastern Europe" appeared after WWI with the appearance of successor states. For the purposes of this book, Eastern Europe will refer to those countries that fell under Soviet influence after 1945.

5. Another way to think about it, further elaborated below, would be that unlike with traditional empires, the Soviets made use of "infrastructural" rather than merely "despotic" power to maintain their rule. Michael Mann, "The Autonomous Power of the State," *European Journal of Sociology* 25, no. 2 (1984).

6. In return for promising to support him militarily after 1867, the emperor essentially allowed the Magyar nobility to control both the country's minorities and its rural population. For example, up through 1914 Hungary's landowning elite controlled 40 percent of the country's land, ruled over the peasants and

laborers on their estates in a semi-feudal manner, manipulated elections, and dominated the government and civil service. Joseph Rothschild, *East Central Europe Between the Two World Wars* (Seattle: University of Washington Press, 1974); Gale Stokes, "The Social Origins of East European Politics," *East European Politics and Societies* 1, no. 1 (1986); Hugh Seton-Watson, *The East European Revolution* (New York: Praeger, 1951); Zygmunt Bauman, "Intellectuals in East-Central Europe," *Eastern European Politics and Societies* 1, no. 2 (1987); Robert Bideleux and Ian Jeffries, *A History of Eastern Europe* (New York: Routledge, 2007), 242ff.; Hugh Seton-Watson, *Eastern Europe Between the Wars* (Hamden, CT: Archon Books, 1962), 40ff.; Arnold Dámoe, "The Agrarian Problem in Hungary," *The Slavonic Review* 1 (June 1922).

7. Ernst Gellner, "Ethnicity and Faith in Eastern Europe," *Daedalus* 119, no. 1 (1990).

8. "In this vast empire, which concentrated more than fifty-one million inhabitants in an area of two hundred and sixty thousand square miles, were almost ten nations and twenty more or less divergent nationalities in political or moral bonds. These constituted two distinct states (Austria and Hungary), seventeen provinces or crownlands in Austria, an 'associated country' with Hungary (Croatia-Slavonia), a 'separate body' (city and harbor of Fiume) annexed to Hungary, and a province of colonial nature (Bosnia-Herzegovina)—all of them with distinct historical consciousness and more or less extended territorial autonomy." Oscar Jaszi, *The Dissolution of the Habsburg Monarchy* (Chicago: University of Chicago Press, 1929), 3. Quote in text from p. 379. Also see Beatrice Manz, "Empires and the Formulation of Identity," *Ethnic and Racial Studies* 26, no. 1 (2003).

9. Initially it was called the "State of Slovenes, Croats and Serbs."

10. Anne Applebaum, *Between East and West* (New York: Pantheon, 1994), xii. Whereas in Western Europe nationalism tended to consolidate many smaller political units into larger ones—e.g., France, Germany, and Italy—in Eastern Europe "it . . . tended to have the opposite effect," fragmenting larger units into many smaller ones. This has left Eastern Europe with many more states than Western Europe, for example, despite being much smaller, area-wise.

11. Empires tended, to use Michael Mann's characterization, to rely more on despotic and less on infrastructural power to rule. This was less true of the Habsburg than of the Ottoman or Russian Empires. Valerie Bunce, "The National Idea: Imperial Legacies and Post-Communist Pathways in Eastern Europe," *East European Politics & Societies* 19, no. 3 (2005); Ben Fowkes, *Eastern Europe, 1945–1969* (London: Person Education, 2000), 5; and Jochen Böhler, "Generals and Warlords, Revolutionaries and Nation-State Builders," in *Legacies of Violence*, ed. Böhler et al., 63.

There is a debate in the literature about how much state- and nation-building had actually gone on in the Habsburg Empire during the prewar period. See, e.g., Pieter Judson, *The Habsburg Empire* (Cambridge,

MA: Harvard University Press, 2016); Gary Cohen, "Our Laws, Our Taxes, and Our Administration," in *Shatterzones of Empires*, ed. Bartov and Weitz; Jeremy King, *Budweisers into Czechs and Germans* (Princeton, NJ: Princeton University Press, 2005).

12. Julius Rezler, "Economic and Social Differentiation and Ethnicity," in *Ethnic Diversity and Conflict*, ed. Sugar, 305; Bideleux and Jeffries, *A History of Eastern Europe*, 254–56; and Joseph Rothschild, *Return to Diversity* (New York: Oxford University Press, 1993), 10.

13. Gabriella Illonski, "Hungary: Crisis and Pseudo-Democratic Compromise," in *Conditions of Democracy in Europe, 1919–39*, ed. Dirk Berg-Schlosser and Jeremy Mitchell (London: Palgrave, 2000).

14. Andrew Janos, *East Central Europe in the Modern World* (Stanford, CA: Stanford University Press, 2000), 9.

15. Rothschild, *East Central Europe*, 10.

16. Applebaum, *Between East and West*, xii.

17. Applebaum, *Between East and West*, xii.

18. Sheri Berman, "European Powers Forced Artificial Borders on More Places than the Middle East," Monkey Cage, *Washington Post*, May 2016, https://www.washingtonpost.com/news/monkey-cage/wp/2016/05/18/european-powers-forced-artificial-borders-on-the-middle-east-they-did-the-same-thing-to-europe-itself/?utm_term=.f008972017d8; Walker Conner, "The Ethnopolitical Challenge and Government Response," in *Ethnic Diversity and Conflict in Eastern Europe*, ed. Peter Sugar (Santa Barbara, CA: ABC-Clio, 1980); and John Bradley, "Czechoslovakia: External Crisis and Internal Compromise," in *Conditions of Democracy*, ed. Berg-Schlosser and Mitchell, 92.

    Particularly conflict-prone were those regions that had been the borderlands of the old empires—which some historians have referred to as "shatterzones"—since these tended to have particularly diverse populations and be difficult for new states to control. Omer Bartov and Eric Weitz, eds., *Shatterzones of Empires* (Bloomington: Indiana University Press, 2013); Jochen Bohler et al., eds., *Legacies of Violence: Eastern Europe's First World War* (Munich: Oldenbourg, 2014).

19. Rothschild, *Return to Diversity*, 9.

20. Applebaum, *Between East and West*, xi–xii; Tismaneanu, 54.

21. Molotov called it "'the monstrous bastard of the Peace of Versailles.' Stalin called it 'pardon the expression,' a state. J.M. Keynes . . . called it 'an economic impossibility whose only industry is Jew-baiting.' Lewis Namier called it 'pathological' [and] E.H. Carr called it 'a farce.' . . . In 1919, Lloyd George was reported as saying that he would no more give Upper Silesia to Poland [it had been part of Prussia and then the German Empire] 'than he would give a clock to a monkey.' As Norman Davies remarked, "rarely, if ever, has a newly independent country been subjected to such eloquent and gratuitous abuse." See Davies, *God's Playground: A History of Poland, Volume 2: 1795 to the Present* (New York: Columbia University Press, 2005).

22. Davies, *God's Playground*, 298; Z.A.B. Zeman, *The Making and Breaking of Communist Europe* (Cambridge, MA: Basil Blackwell, 1991), 92; and Andrzej Korbonski, "Poland," in *The Columbia History*, ed. Held, 231.

23. This was true of pre-partition Poland as well.

24. About two-thirds of these were literate, which means about 44 percent of the overall population consisted of literate Poles. Davies, *God's Playground*, 309.

25. On any of these measures of status, all were generally higher in the territories that came from the German than Austro-Hungarian or Russian empires. Janos, *East Central Europe in the Modern World*, 340; Davies, *God's Playground*, 307; and R.J. Crampton, *Eastern Europe in the Twentieth Century* (New York: Routledge, 1994), 40–41.

26. Jerzy Tomaszewski, "The National Question in Poland in the Twentieth Century," in *The National Question in Europe in Historical Context*, ed. Roy Porter and Mikulás Teich (New York: Cambridge University Press, 1993), 306.

27. In 1923, for example, 111,300 of Poland's 121,000 state employees were Poles (the vast majority of the remainder being teachers in minority schools) and during the interwar period not a single government included a minister from a national minority. Davies, *God's Playground*, 298–300.

28. Zeman, *The Making and Breaking*, 105; Winkler, *The Age of Catastrophe*, 259.

29. This despite Poland beginning with some advantages: citizens coming from the German and Habsburg Empires had experience with elections and political participation and representative institutions and elected bodies had a long history in Poland, even if they had been limited to the nobility and gentry. See chapter 2 and Korbonski, "Poland," 237–38.

30. Rothschild, *East Central Europe*, 31.

31. Seton-Watson, *Eastern Europe*, 161; Crampton, *Eastern Europe*, 45.

32. Hence it became known as the sanacja—cleansing or healing—regime.

33. Jerzy Holzer, "Poland: From Post-War Crisis to Authoritarianism," in *Conditions of Democracy in Europe, 1919–39*, ed. Berg-Schlosser and Mitchell. It is worth noting that Piłsudski did not share the ethnic view of Polishness common on the right, instead believing that minorities could be incorporated into Poland. Nonetheless, during this regime, the political participation of minorites decreased.

34. The 1935 constitution gave the president the right to name the prime minister, appoint one-third of all members of the Senate, and control over the armed forces, courts, and more. Voting was circumscribed and its impact on the selection of leaders minimized. Ironically, Piłsudski, the man upon whom these powers were meant to devolve died a few weeks after the constitution was put in place.

35. See, e.g., Charles Gati, "Hungary: The Dynamics of Revolutionary Transformation," in *The Politics of Modernization in Eastern Europe*, ed. Gati (New York: Praeger, 1973).

36. Stokes, *Three Eras of Political Change*, chapter 3.

37. Peter Hanak, "Hungary," in *The Columbia History*, ed. Held, 168.

38. Officially the government was led by Sándor Garbai, but Kun was really in charge.

39. Rather than giving the land to peasants, however, and thereby perhaps buying some support for the regime, Kun's dogmatic interpretation of Marxism led him to disdain small farms, Crampton, *Eastern Europe*, 81.

40. Emil Niederhauser, "The National Question in Hungary," in *The National Question in Europe*, ed. Porter and Teich.

41. Kun ultimately ended up in the Soviet Union, where he was murdered in 1937 during the Great Purge.

42. Officially, Horthy was acting as regent for the deposed king of Hungary and so the new regime was known as the Kingdom of Hungary. Practical realities ensured, however, that the latter would never return, and so Horthy assumed the dictatorial powers that would otherwise have been exercised by the king.

43. Rothschild, *East Central Europe*, 153.

44. Sharon Wolchik, "Czechoslovakia," in *The Columbia History of Eastern Europe in the Twentieth Century*, ed. Joseph Held (New York: Columbia University Press, 1992); Tomak Jankowski, *Eastern Europe!* (Williamstown, MA: New Europe, 2013), 289; and George Schöpflin, "The Political Traditions of Eastern Europe," *Daedalus* 119, no. 1 (1990): 66–67.

45. The Czech nobility was deposed after the battle of White Mountain in 1620 and its estates parceled out over the next century to nobles from other parts of the Habsburg Empire. Gale Stokes, *The Origins of East European Politics* (New York: Oxford University Press, 1997), 39.

46. Rothschild, *East Central Europe*, 86.

47. Rothschild, *East Central Europe*, 87; Janos, *East Central Europe*, 112.

48. Wolchik, "Czechoslovakia," 123–24; Stokes, *The Social Origins of European Politics*, 33–41; Rotschild, *East Central Europe*, 75; and Jaszi, *The Dissolution of the Habsburg Monarchy*, 385.

49. Bradley, *Czechoslovakia*; Rezler, "Economic and Social Differrentiation," 312.

50. Rothschild, *East Central Europe*, 87; John Bradley, "Czechoslovakia: External Crisis and Internal Compromise," in *Conditions of Democracy*, ed. Berg-Schlosser and Mitchell.

51. Schöpflin, *The Political Traditions*, 23, 73–74.

52. Timothy Snyder, *Bloodlands: Europe Between Hitler and Stalin* (New York: Basic Books, 2012).

53. Timothy Snyder, "The Historical Reality of Eastern Europe," *East European Politics & Societies* 23, no. 1 (February 2009): 9; Snyder, *Bloodlands: Europe Between Hitler and Stalin* (New York: Basic Books, 2012).

54. Jan Gross, "Social Consequences of War: Preliminaries to the Study of Imposition of Communist Regimes in East Central Europe," *East European Politics & Societies* 3, no. 2 (1989); Ben Fowkes, *Eastern Europe 1945–1969* (New York: Pearson, 2000), 17–18.

55. Berend, *East Central and Eastern Europe*, 4.

56. At least 57% of Poland's lawyers, 39% of its doctors, 27% of its clergy, and 29% of its university teachers were gone. Winkler, *The Age of Catastrophe*, 852. Anton Kaminski and Bartlomiej Kaminski, "Road to 'People's Poland': Stalin's Conquest Revisited," in *Stalinism Revisited*, ed. Vladimir Tismaneanu (New York: CEU Press, 2009). In comparison Romania lost 3% of its population, Hungary over 6%, and Yugoslavia about 10%.

57. Zeman, *The Making and Breaking*, 158–61; Applebaum, *Iron Curtain*, 11; E.A. Radice, "Economic Developments in Eastern Europe under German Hegemony," in *Communist Power in Europe, 1944–1949*, ed. Martin McCauley (London: Macmillan, 1979).

58. Davies, *God's Playground*, vol. 2, 49.

59. Davies, *God's Playground*, vol. 2, 365.

60. See numerous citations on this process in chapter 14. On Eastern Europe in particular see Tara Zahra, *The Great Departure: Mass Migration from Eastern Europe and the Making of the Free World* (New York: W.W. Norton, 2016).

61. Applebaum, *Iron Curtain*, xiv, xv.

62. Lowe, *Savage Continent*; Istvan Deak, Jan Gross, and Tony Judt, *The Politics of Retribution in Europe* (Princeton, NJ: Princeton University Press, 2000).

63. Judt, *Postwar*, 25–26; Douglas, *Orderly and Humane*, 21; see also Normal Naimark, *Fires of Hatred* (Cambridge, MA: Harvard University Press, 2001), chapter 4.

64. Quoted in Michael Mann, *The Dark Side of Democracy* (New York: Cambridge University Press, 2005), 353. Also see Naimark, *Fires of Hatred*, 109–10.

65. Lowe, *Savage Continent*, 234; Judt, *Postwar*, 26.

66. Minorities made up less than 10 percent of the populations of Czechoslovakia, Hungary, Bulgaria, and Poland; in Romania they were now about 12 percent. Lowe, *Savage Continent*, 22, 211, 248; Mazower, *Dark Continent*, 218–19; Judt, "The Past Is Another Country," in *The Politics of Retribution in Europe*, ed. Deak et al.; Rieber, ed., *Forced Migration*, esp. 20ff.

67. Judt, *Postwar*, 27; Lowe, *Savage Continent*, 247; and J.F. Brown, *Eastern Europe and Communist Rule* (Durham, NC: Duke University Press, 1988), 3.

68. Mazower, *Dark Continent*, 218.

69. Indirect support for this might be Yugoslavia, which remained ethnically mixed after the war and exploded as soon as the communist dictatorship disappeared.

70. Dankwart Rustow, "Transitions Towards Democracy: Towards a Dynamic Model," *Comparative Politics* 2, no. 3 (April 1970): 350–51. See also Michael Bernhard and Jeffrey Kopstein, "Revolutionary Change and the Prospects for Democracy," unpublished ms, p. 7; Michael Bernhard and Jeffrey Kopstein, "Post-Communism, the Civilizing Process, and the Mixed Impact of Leninist Violence," *East European Politics and Cultures* 29, no. 2 (2015); Judt, *Postwar*, p. 39.

71. Jan Gross, "War as Revolution," in *The Establishment of Communist Regimes in Eastern Europe, 1944–1949*, ed. Norman Naimark and Leonid Gibianskii (Boulder, CO: Westview, 1997), 22–23.

72. Between 1948 and 1951 another 332,000 Jews left Europe.

73. Mark Kramer, "Stalin, Soviet Policy, and the Consolidation of a Communist Bloc in Eastern Europe," in *Stalinism Revisited*, ed. Tismaneanu, 59.

74. Bronislas Geremek, "Between Hope and Despair," *Daedalus* 119, no. 1 (1990): 93–94.

75. Schöpflin, *Politics in Eastern Europe*, 58ff. Instructive here is a comparison with Finland and Austria which also fell under Soviet influence at the end of the war but managed to retain (at least some) independence. Both had stronger states and societies and would have been able to marshal greater resistance to Soviet colonization. Other interesting counterfactuals are Albania and Yugoslavia, two countries where indigenous resistance movements fought the Nazis and the Soviets did not control at the end of the war. Although both turned communist, they ended up outside the Soviet sphere of influence.

76. Rothschild, *Return to Diversity*, 75.

77. Seton-Watson, *Eastern Europe*, 262–63. It is also possible that the extreme brutality of the war and the Nazi occupation might have made the "methods of the Communist *Machtergriefung* in the subsequent period more acceptable than" they otherwise might have been. Gross, "War as Revolution," 24.

78. G.M. Tama, quoted in Stokes, *Eastern Europe*, 164.

79. Vladimir Tismaneanu, "Introduction," in *Stalinism Revisited*, ed. Tismaneanu, 3–4.

80. Milovan Djilas, *Conversations with Stalin* (New York: Harcourt Brace, 1963).

81. Ferenc Fehér, "Eastern Europe's Long Revolution Against Yalta," *Eastern European Politics & Societies* 2, no. 1 (1988): 19. As noted above and discussed in chapter 14, a new political, social, and economic order also appeared in Western Europe under American auspices, but this new order reformed rather than revolutionized what had existed in the region in the past and was not imposed, but rather developed in cooperation between West European and American leaders within a democratic framework.

82. In this sense, it shared some similarities to the fascist consolidation of power in Italy after 1922. See chapter 11.

83. "Report of the Crimea conference (Yalta)," in *From Stalinism to Pluralism*, ed. Gale Stokes (New York: Oxford University Press, 1991), 15.

84. Kramer, "Stalin, Soviet Policy and the Consolidation of a Communist Bloc," 70.

85. There is a debate in the literature about whether Stalin had decided in advance to do away with any semblance of democracy in the region or whether this decision was only taken as a result of the onset of the Cold War. For the purposes of this book, however, what is relevant is that he did do away with democracy.

86. Quoted in Wolfgang Leonhard, *Child of the Revolution* (London: Collins, 1957), 381.

87. Fowkes, *Eastern Europe*, 24ff.; Thomas Hammond, "The History of Communist Takeovers," in *The Anatomy of Communist Takeovers*, ed. Fowkes (New Haven, CT: Yale University Press, 1971); and Hugh Seton-Watson, *The Pattern of Communist Revolution* (London: Methuen, 1953), chapter 13.

88. Ben Fowkes, *The Rise and Fall of Communism in Eastern Europe* (New York: St. Martin's Press, 1993), 32.

89. Kramer, "Stalin, Soviet Policy, and the Consolidation of a Communist Bloc," 78ff.; Alfred Rieber, "Popular Democracy: An Illusion?"; Kaminski and Kaminski, "Road to 'People's Poland,'" in *Stalinism Revisited*, ed. Tismaneanu.

90. Appleabaum, *Iron Curtain*, 67; Karel Kaplan, *The Short March: The Communist Takeover in Czechoslovakia* (New York: St. Martin's Press, 1987).

91. Kaminski and Kaminski, "Road to 'People's Poland,'" 195.

92. Ivan Berend and Gyorgy Ranki, *Economic Development in East-East Central Europe in the 19th and 20th Centuries* (New York: Columbia University Press, 1974), chapter 14; Norman Davies, "Poland," in *Communist Power in Europe*, ed. McCauley.

93. Seton-Watson, *The East European Revolution*, chapter 8.

94. As Jowitt, for example, characterized the situation: "For more than a decade, most communist countries were . . . colonies of the Soviet Union. The presence of Soviet troops, advisers and secret police officials; economic plans establishing the priority of Soviet interests; and the imposition of Soviet political and economic models meant direct Soviet domination." *New World Disorder*, 44.

95. Kopstein, Bernhard, and Rothschild, *East-Central Europe*, 96–97, 103.

96. Crampton, *Eastern Europe*, 263, 267.

97. Schöpflin, *Politics in Eastern Europe*, 8.

98. Hannah Arendt, *The Origins of Totalitarianism* (New York: Harcourt, Brace, Jovanovich, 1973); Franz Borkenau, *The Totalitarian Enemy* (New York: Ams Pr Inc., 1940); Karl Dietrich Bracher, "The Disputed Concept of Totalitarianism," in Ernest Menze, ed., *Totalitarianism Reconsidered* (New York: Associated Faculty Press, 1981); and Carl Friedrich and Z.K. Brzezinski, *Totalitarian Dictatorship and Autocracy* (New York: Praeger, 1966).

99. Vladimir Tismaneanu, "Diabolical Pedagogy and the (Il)logic of Stalinism in Eastern Europe," in *Stalinism Revisited*, ed. Tismaneanu, 26. Also see Francöis Fejtö, *A History of the People's Democracies* (New York: Praeger Publishers, 1971).

100. János Kornai, *The Socialist System* (Princeton, NJ: Princeton University Press, 1992).

101. Before the war the per capita national income in 1948 U.S. dollars was $70 in Romania, $104 in Poland, $112 in Hungary, and $176 in Czechoslovakia. In comparison the UK was $378 and France $236.

102. 70 percent of the holdings in East-Central Europe, accounting for 20 percent of acreage, were subsistence farms under five hectares, and less than 1 percent of holdings accounted for 40 percent of the acreage. Inequality was most extreme in Hungary, where 85 percent of holdings were under five hectares and larger estates were upwards of 3,000 hectares. Alan Smith, *The Planned Economies of Eastern Europe* (New York: Holmes and Meier, 1983), 18–19.

103. Gyorgy Ranki, "Has Modernity Made a Difference?" in *The Politics of Modernization*, ed. Gati.

104. Rezler, "Economic and Social Differentiation,"; Crampton, *Eastern Europe*, 34; C.A. Macartney and A.W. Palmer, *Independent Eastern Europe* (New York: St. Martin's, 1962), chapter 5.

105. Smith, *The Planned Economies*, 28–29; Ross, *Constructing Socialism*, chapter 2; Berend and Ranki, *Economic Development*, chapter 14.

106. There were different types of socialized farms: collective farms where farmers pooled land and resources and state farms owned and operated by the government. The latter were generally favored by the state. David Mason, *Revolution and Transition in East-Central Europe* (New York: Westview, 1996), 15.

107. Mason, *Revolution and Transition in East-Central Europe*, 29–30; Hammond, *The Anatomy*, 27ff.

108. Ken Jowitt, "Stalinist Revolutionary Breakthroughs in Eastern Europe," in *Stalinism Revisited*, ed. Tismaneanu, 20; Berend, *East Central and Eastern Europe*, 207ff.

109. Jowitt, *New World Disorder*, 29ff.

110. Fowkes, *The Rise and Fall*, 56.

111. Chris Harman, *Bureaucracy and Revolution in Eastern Europe* (London: Pluto, 1974), 28–29, 27.

112. Z, "To the Stalinist Mausoleum," *Daedalus* 119, no. 1 (1990): 311–12. Particular sectors were governed by multi-year plans which set targets for growth, levels of investment, etc. These plans created perverse incentives, most notably to do anything to fulfill or over-fulfill quantity targets no matter the impact on quality or the potential for innovation. Applebaum, *Iron Curtain*, chapter 10; Smith, *The Planned Economies*, 47; and Berend, *East Central and Eastern Europe*, 72ff. and chapter 5. On the impact on society see Kathryn Verdery, *What Was Socialism, and What Comes Next?* (Princeton, NJ: Princeton University Press, 1996).

113. See, e.g., Fowkes, *The Rise and Fall*, 63.

114. Fowkes, *The Rise and Fall*, chapter 3.

115. Janos, *East Central Europe*.

116. Mark Pittaway, *Eastern Europe 1939–2000* (New York: Oxford University Press, 2004), 59–60; Ferenc Fehér, "Eastern Europe's Long Revolution Against Yalta," *East European Politics & Societies* 2, no. 1 (1988): esp. 23; and Fowkes, *The Rise and Fall*, 64.

117. Janos, *East Central Europe*, 265.

118. Berend, *East Central and Eastern Europe*, 24; Harman, *Bureaucracy and Revolution*, 50–51; Bideleux and Jeffries, *A History of Eastern Europe*, 461.

119. Tocqueville, *The Old Regime*, 214.

120. In 1950 real wages may have been about half of what they were in 1936 and declined even further in 1951 and 1952. Harman, *Bureaucracy and Revolution*, 80.

121. Jeffrey Kopstein, "Chipping Away at the State: Workers' Resistance and the Demise of East Germany," *World Politics* 48, no. 3 (1996); Ross, *Constructing Socialism*, chapter 4.

122. Quoted in Harman, *Bureaucracy and Revolution*, 71.

123. Karl Reyman, "The Special Case of East Germany," in *Communism and Eastern Europe*, ed. Frantisek Silnitsky, Larisa Silnitsky, and Karl Reyman (New York: Karz, 1979), 160–61.

124. Also crucial here was Khrushchev's reconciliation with Tito. Many communist parties had torn themselves apart "extirpating the evils of Titoism," and the reconciliation between Moscow and Belgrade therefore further shook up old certainties that had already begun crumbling after Stalin's death. Crampton, *Eastern Europe*, 282.

125. Harman, *Bureaucracy and Revolution*, 102–03; and Paul Zinner, ed., *National Communism and Popular Revolt* (New York: Columbia University Press, 1956), chapter 2.

126. Fowkes, *The Rise and Fall*, 95.

127. Grzgorz Ekiert, *The State Against Society: Political Crises and Their Aftermath in East Central Europe* (Princeton, NJ: Princeton University Press, 1996), chapter 2; and Bill Lomax, *Hungary 1956* (New York: St. Martin's Press, 1976), 19.

128. Ekiert, *State Against Society*, chapter 4.

129. Steven Kotkin, *Uncivil Society: 1989 and the Implosion of the Communist Establishment* (New York: The Modern Library 2009), 17; and Imre Nagy, "Radio Address," reprinted in Zimmer, *National Communism*, 428–32, 453–54.

130. Lomax, *Hungary*, 67. Nagy, "Reform Communism," in *From Stalinism to Pluralism*, ed. Stokes.

131. Rothschild, *Return to Diversity*, 159.

132. Lomax, *Hungary 1956*. Telegram from Nagy to Secretary General of UN and Radio Address declaring neutrality, reprinted in Zimmer, ed., *National Communism*, 462–64.

133. Frenec Fehér and Agnes Heller, *Hungary 1956 Revisited* (London: George Allen and Unwin, 1983); J. Schöpflin, "Hungary," in *Communism*, ed. Silnitsky et al.

134. Ekiert, *State Against Society*, chapter 4.

135. Bideleux and Jeffries, *A History of Eastern Europe*, 478.

136. Seymour Martin Lipset, *Political Man* (New York: Anchor Books, 1984), 77; David Easton, "A Re-Assessment of the Concept of Political Support," *British Journal of Political Science* 5, no. 4 (1975); Min-hua Huang et al., "Identifying

Sources of Democratic Legitimacy," *Electoral Studies* 27, no. 1 (2008); and Robert Mattes and Michael Bratton, "Learning About Democracy in Africa," *American Journal of Political Science* 51, no. 1 (2007).

137. Vivien Schmidt, "Democracy and Legitimacy in the European Union," *Political Studies* 61, no. 1 (March 2013).

138. Ernst Gellner, "Islam and Marxism: Some Comparisions," *International Affairs* 67, no. 1 (1991): 1–6.

Chapter 16

1. Richard Gunther, José Ramón Montero, and Joan Botella, *Democracy in Modern Spain* (New Haven, CT: Yale University Press 2004), 3.

2. Payne, *The Franco Regime*; Guy Hermet, "Spain Under Franco," *European Journal of Political Research* 4 (1976); and Juan Linz, "An Authoritarian Regime: Spain," in *Cleavages, Ideologies and Party Systems*, ed. E. Allart and Y. Littuen (Helsinki: Academic, 1964).

3. Stanley Payne, *The Franco Regime* (London: Phoenix, 2000), 342.

4. The 1939 "Law of Political Responsibilities," for example, criminalized anyone who had belonged to a Republican political party or trade union or supported the Republican cause in anyway. The regime's own figures suggest that perhaps four hundred thousand people passed through its prisons between 1939 and 1945, and anywhere from twenty-five thousand to two hundred thousand were killed. Julián Casanova and Carlos Gil Andrés, *Twentieth-Century Spain* (New York: Cambridge University Press, 2014), Part IV; Raymond Carr, *The Spanish Tragedy* (London: Weidenfeld & Nicolson, 1977), Epilogue, part 1; Jean Grugel and Tim Rees, *Franco's Spain* (New York: St Martin's, 1977), 26; Julius Ruiz, *Franco's Justice* (Oxford: Clarendon, 2005).

5. Aguilar, *Memory and Amnesia*, chapter 2.

6. John Coverdale, *The Political Transformation of Spain after Franco* (New York: Praeger, 1979), 4–5.

7. Raymond Carr, *Modern Spain, 1875–1980* (New York: Oxford University Press, 1980), 166; Grugel and Rees, *Franco's Spain*, 53, 35; Javier Tusell, *Spain: From Dictatorship to Democracy* (Malden, MA: Blackwell, 2007).

8. Payne, *The Franco Regime*, 362–68.

9. Richard Herr, *An Historical Essay on Modern Spain*, chapter 15. The Library of Iberian Resources Online (http://libro.uca.edu/herr/essay.htm); Casanova and Andrés, *Twentieth-Century Spain*, chapter 11.

10. Alongside the army and the Church, the Falange is sometimes mentioned as a third pillar of Franco's regime, but its influence never approached that of the other two. In 1937 the Falange was incorporated into a new Nationalist party (*Falange Española Tradicionalista y de las Juntas de Ofensiva Nacional Sindicalista*), but this party was not integrated into the regime like its Italian fascist, German

National Socialist, or especially its communist counterparts were. In addition, although some Falangist policies, like national syndicalism, were initially incorporated into the Francoist state, these were watered down or withered away over time, especially after the Axis powers' defeat in 1945 and the subsequent (re)-emphasis on National-Catholicism as the regime's legitimating doctrine. Carr, *The Spanish Tragedy*, 261.

11. Payne, *The Franco Regime*, esp. 342–43, 231; Javier Tusell, *Spain from Dictatorship to Democracy* (Malden, MA: Blackwell, 1977); and Raymond Carr, *The Spanish Tragedy* (London: Weidenfeld & Nicolson, 1977), Epilogue, part 1. On the institutional infrastructure of the regime see José Amodia, *Franco's Political Legacy* (London: Allen Lane, 1977).

12. Nigel Townson, "Introduction," in *Spain Transformed: The Late Franco Dictatorship*, ed. Nigel Townson (New York: Palgrave, 2007), 2.

13. Raymond Carr, *Spain 1808–1975* (New York: Oxford University Press, 1966), 740.

14. Payne, *The Franco Regime*, 390; Carr, *Modern Spain*, 155; Herr, *An Historical Essay*, 237.

15. Grugel and Rees, *Franco's Spain*, 64.

16. Richard Gunther, *Policy-Making in a No-Party State* (Berkeley: University of California Press, 1980), 183, 86–87; Omar Encarnación, "Social Concertation in Democratic and Market Transitions," *Comparative Political Studies* 30, no. 4 (August 1997): 397.

17. Fred López III, "Bourgeois State and the Rise of Social Democracy in Spain," in *Transitions from Dictatorship to Democracy*, ed. Ronald Chilcote et al. (New York: Taylor and Francis, 1990), 29ff.

18. Sasha Pack, "Tourism and Political Change in Franco's Spain," in *Spain Transformed*, ed. Townson.

19. Payne, *The Franco Regime*, chapters 19 and 20; Herr and Herr, *An Historical Essay*, 20ff., 237ff.; William Phillips and Carla Rahn Phillips, *A Concise History of Spain* (New York: Cambridge University Press, 2010), 268ff.; Mary Vincent, *Spain* (New York: Oxford University Press, 2007), 180ff.; Grugel and Rees, *Franco's Spain*, 118ff.

20. Payne, *The Franco Regime*, 463; Joseph Harrison, *An Economic History of Modern Spain* (New York: Homes & Meier, 1978); Pablo Martín Aceña and Elena Martínez Ruiz, "The Golden Age of Spanish Capitalism: Economic Growth without Political Freedom," in *Spain Transformed*, ed. Townson.

21. Carr, *The Spanish Tragedy*, 282; José Maravall and Julián Santamaría, "Political Change in Spain and the Prospects for Democracy," in *Transitions from Authoritarian Rule*, ed. Guillermo O'Donnell, Philppe Schmitter, and Laurence Whitehead (Baltimore: Johns Hopkins University Press, 1986), 74–75; and Adrian Shubert, *A Social History of Modern Spain* (Boston: Unwin, Hyman, 1990).

22. Tusell, *Spain*, 190; Vincent, *Spain*, 183.

23. Gunther et al., *Democracy in Modern Spain*, 71.

24. Casanova and Andrés, *Twentieth-Century Spain*, 260; Phillips and Phillips, *A Concise History*, 270; Paul Preston, *The Triumph of Democracy in Spain* (London: Metheun 1986), 5.

25. Gunther et al., *Democracy in Modern Spain*, 8.

26. Vincent, *Spain*, 183.

27. Payne, *The Franco Regime*, 487.

28. Peter Pierson, *The History of Spain* (Westport, CT: Greenwood, 1999), 166–67 and Amodia, *Franco's Political Legacy*, 31.

29. Amodia, *Franco's Political Legacy*, 31.

30. Walter Bernecker, "The Change in Mentalities," in *Spain Transformed*, ed. Townson.

31. Herr, *An Historical Essay*, 247.

32. Jose Maravall, *Dictatorship and Political Dissent* (New York: St. Martin's Press, 1978); Jose Maravall, *The Transition to Democracy in Spain* (New York: St. Martin's Press, 1982), chapter 1; and Foweraker, *Making Democracy.*

33. In 1966 1.5 million hours were lost to strikes, and by 1970 this had risen to 8.7 million. Maravall and Santamaria, "Political Change in Spain," 77–78.

34. Payne, *The Franco Regime*, 499–500.

35. William Callahan, "The Spanish Church," in *Spain Transformed*, ed. Townson, 181.

36. Donald Share, *The Making of Spanish Democracy* (New York: Praeger, 1986).

37. Share, *The Making*, 51.

38. Raymond Carr and Juan Pablo Fusi Aizpurua, *Spain: Dictatorship to Democracy* (London: George Allen & Unwin, 1979), 194.

39. Pamela Radcliff, "Associations and the Social Origins of Transition," in *Spain Transformed*, ed. Townson; Radcliff, *Making Democratic Citizens in Spain* (New York: Palgrave Macmillan, 2011); Joe Foweraker, *Making Democracy in Spain* (New York: Cambridge University Press, 1989); and Juan Linz, "An Authoritarian Regime: Spain," in *Mass Politics: Studies in Political Sociology*, ed. Erik Allardt and Stein Rokkan (New York: Free Press, 1970).

40. Christina Palomares, "New Political Mentalities in the Tardofranquismo," in *Spain Transformed*, ed. Townson.

41. Payne, *The Franco Regime*, 587.

42. Palomares, "New Political Mentalities," in *Spain Transformed*, ed. Townson, 128.

43. Preston, *The Triumph*, 26; Sidney Tarrow, "Mass Mobilization and Regime Change," in *The Poltiics*, ed. Gunther et al., 218ff.

44. Maravall and Santamaría, "Political Change," 82; Herr, "Epilogue," in *An Historical Essay on Modern Spain.*

45. Quoted in Paloma Aguilar, "Justice, Politics, and Memory in the Spanish Transition," in *The Politics of Memory and Democratization* (New York: Oxford University Press, 2001). *Oxford Scholarship Online*, 2003. Date accessed January

9, 2017, http://www.oxfordscholarship.com.ezproxy.cul.columbia.edu/view/
10.1093/0199240906.001.0001/acprof-9780199240906-chapter-4>, 93.

46. Jaun Linz and Alfred Stepan, *Problems of Democratic Transition and Consolidation* (Baltimore: Johns Hopkins University Press, 1996), chapter 6.

47. Omar Encarnación, *Spanish Politics* (Malden, MA: Polity Press, 2008), 32; Paloma Aguilar, *Memory and Amnesia: The Role of the Spanish Civil War in the Transition to Democracy* (New York: Berghahn Books, 2002).

48. Paul Preston, *Juan Carlos: A People's King* (London: Harper Collins, 2004), 325.

49. John Coverdale, *The Political Transformation of Spain after Franco* (New York: Praeger, 1979); Gunther et al., *Democracy*, chapter 3.

50. Aguilar, "Justice, Politics, and Memory," 97; Nancy Bermeo, "Myths of Moderation: Confrontation and Conflict during Democratic Transitions," *Comparative Politics* 29, no. 3 (April 1997); and Share, *The Making*, 121.

51. Quoted in Linz and Stepan, *Problems*, 93–94.

52. Gunther et al., *Democracy*, esp. 86–87; Encarnación, *Spanish Politics*, 35; Daniel Ziblatt, *Conservative Parties and the Birth of Democracy* (New York: Cambridge University Press, 2017).

53. Aguilar, *Memory and Amnesia*, 151.

54. Bermeo, "Myths," 317.

55. Linz and Stepan, *Problems*, 96–97; Herr, *An Historical Essay*, 294.

56. Coverdale, *The Political Transformation*, 19, 58.

57. Quoted in Encarnacion, *Spanish Politics*, 29–30.

58. Javier Tussell, "The Legalization of the PCE," http://www.artehistoria.com/ v2/contextos/7462.htm.

59. Coverdale, *The Political Transformation*, 65.

60. Richard Gunther, Giacomo Sani, and Goldie Shabad, *Spain after Franco: The Making of a Competitive Party System* (Berkeley: University of California Press, 1988).

61. Maravall and Santamaría, "Political Change," 85. More generally, Gunther, Sani, and Shabad, *Spain after Franco*.

62. Encarnación, *Spanish Politics*, 37.

63. Grugel and Rees, *Franco's Spain*, 185.

64. Enrique Fuentes-Quintana, deputy PM, quoted in Encarnación, "Social Concertation," 407.

65. Encarnación, "Social Concertation," 407.

66. Omar Encarnación, "Reconciliation after Democratization: Coping with the Past in Spain," *Political Science Quarterly* 123, no. 3 (2008): 438–39, 440.

67. Encarnación, *Spanish Politics*, 39–40.

68. O'Donnell et al., *Transitions*, 88–89; Grugel and Rees, *Franco's Spain*, 184.

69. Aguilar, "Justice, Politics, and Memory," 107.

70. Herr, *An Historical Essay*, Epilogue, 296.

71. Felipe Agüero, "Democratic Consolidation and the Military in Southern Europe and South America," in *The Poltics*, ed. Gunther et al.

72. Ibid Agüero, "Democratic Consolidation"; Gunther et al., *Democracy*, 110ff.

73. Casanova and Andrés, *Twentieth-Century Spain*, 322.

74. López, "Bourgeois State," 62; Share, "The Making," 187.

75. Sebastian Balfour, *The Politics of Contemporary Spain* (New York: Routledge, 2005).

76. Linz, Stepan and Gunther, "Democratic Transition," 97; Felipe Agüero, "Authoritarian Legacies: The Military's Role," in *Authoritarian Legacies and Democracy in Latin America and Southern Europe*, ed. Katherin Hite and Paola Cesarini (Notre Dame, IN: University of Notre Dame Press, 2004). Also see Narcis Serra, *The Military Transition: Democratic Reform of the Armed Forces* (New York: Cambridge University Press, 2010); and Agüero, "Consolidation and the Military," 161–62.

77. Herr, *An Historical Essay*, Epilogue, 297; Share, "The Making," 190–91.

78. Annual transfers rose from 13.7 billion pesetas in 1986 to 160 billion by 1988 and increased infrastructural investment in the country by approximately 8 percent during these years. Geoffrey Pridham, "The International Context of Democratic Consolidation," in *The Politics*, ed. Gunter et al., 183.

79. Share, "The Making," 192–93; Encarnación, *Spanish Politics*, 114ff.

80. Pridham, "The International Context," 177–78.

81. Pridham, "The International Context."

82. Pridham, "The International Context."

83. Encarnación, *Spanish Politics*; Linz, Stepan, and Gunther, "Democratic Transition," 97; Leonardo Molino and José R. Montero, "Legitimacy and Democracy in Southern Europe," in *The Politics*, ed. Gunther et al.; Peter McDonough, Samuel Barnes, Antonio López Pina, et al., eds., *The Cultural Dynamics of Democratization in Spain* (Ithaca, NY: Cornell University Press, 1998).

84. Gunther et al., eds., *The Politics*, 78ff.

85. Gunther et al., eds., *The Politics*, 152.

86. Gunther et al., eds., *The Politics*, 154.

87. Gunther et al., eds., *The Politics*, 153.

88. Gunther et al., eds., *The Politics*, 153–54.

89. Encarnación, *Spanish Politics*, 150 and chapter 9; Bonnie Field, ed., *Spain's Second Transition* (New York: Routledge, 2010).

90. The Constitution of Cadiz called for universal male suffrage, a constitutional monarchy, and the institutionalization of myriad civil and political rights and liberties (see chapter 13).

91. Kenneth Maxwell and Steven Spiegel, *The New Spain* (New York: Council on Foreign Relations, 1994), 4.

92. Gunther et al., *Democracy*, 2–3; E. Ramón Arango, *The Spanish Political System* (Boulder, CO: Westview Press, 1978), 2.

93. Aguilar, *Memory and Amnesia*, 154.

94. Agüero, "Consolidation and the Military," 142.

95. Philippe Schmitter, "Organized Interests and Democratic Consolidation in Southern Europe," in *The Politics*, ed. Gunther et al.; Víctor Pérez-Diaz, *The Return of Civil Society* (Cambridge, MA: Harvard University Press, 1993); Radcliff, *Making Democratic Citizens*; Foweraker, *Making Democracy*; Edward Malefakis, "Spain and Its Francoist Heritage," in *From Dictatorship to Democracy*, ed. John Herz (Westport, CT: Greenwood Press, 1994); Foweraker, *Making Democracy*.

96. David Goldblatt, "Democracy in the Long Nineteenth Century," in *Democratization*, ed. David Potter et al.

Chapter 17

1. In his 1990 New Year's address. Adapting words from the seventeenth-century Czech scholar Comenius originally quoted by Tomás Masaryk in his inaugural address as first president of Czechoslovakia in 1918. https://chnm.gmu.edu/1989/archive/files/havel-speech-1-1-90_0c7cd97e58.pdf. See also Timothy Garten Ash, *The Magic Lantern* (New York: Random House, 1990).

2. George Schöpflin, *Politics in Eastern Europe 1945–1992* (Cambridge, MA: Blackwell, 1993), 58ff. Instructive here is a comparison with Finland and Austria, which also fell under Soviet influence at the end of the war but managed to retain (at least some) independence. Both had stronger states and societies and would have been able to marshal greater resistance to Soviet colonization. Other interesting counterfactuals are Albania and Yugoslavia, two countries where indigenous resistance movements fought the Nazis and the Soviets did not control at the end of the war. Although both turned communist, they ended up outside the Soviet sphere of influence.

3. Daniel Chirot, "Introduction," in *The Crisis of Leninism and the Decline of the Left*, ed. Chirot (Seattle: University of Washington Press, 1991), 5.

4. Grzegorz Ekiert, *The State against Society: Political Crises and Their Aftermath* (Princeton, NJ: Princeton University Press, 1996), 9.

5. Ekiert, *The State against Society*, 25. Reflecting this loss of faith, communist regimes were increasingly dominated by aged, sclerotic, bureaucratic, and even corrupt career rather than convinced communists. J.F. Brown, *Surge to Freedom* (Durham, NC: Duke University Press, 1991), 25: Schöpflin, *Politics in Eastern Europe*, 187, 192, 199; Nancy Bermeo, "Introduction," in *Liberalization and Democratization*, ed. Bermeo (Baltimore: Johns Hopkins University Press, 1992), 2; Guiseppe Di Palma, "Legitimation from the Top to Civil Society," in Bermeo, ed. *Liberalization and Democratization*, 56.

6. Barrington Moore, *Injustice: The Social Bases of Obedience and Revolt* (New York: M.E. Sharpe, 1978); Michael H. Bernhard, *The Origin of Democratization in Poland* (New York: Columbia University Press, 1993), esp. 151–52, 158.

7. Gender relations also became more equal during the period. Women's employment rates approached men's, and women were integrated into "traditionally male" professions like engineering and manufacturing. Women also made up more than 50 percent of the students in higher education in many East-Central European countries. Robin Okey, *The Demise of Communist East Europe* (New York: Oxford University Press, 2004), 26–28.

8. Steven Kotkin, *Uncivil Society—1989 and the Implosion of the Communist Establishment* (New York: Modern Library, 2009), 17 and 18.

9. Jeremy Azrael, "Varieties of De-Stalinization," in *Change in Communist Systems*, ed. Chalmers Johnson (Stanford, CA: Stanford University Press, 1970).

10. Schöpflin, *Politics in Eastern Europe*, 142.

11. Okey, *The Demise of Communist East Europe*, 15.

12. Chris Harman, *Bureaucracy and Revolution in Eastern Europe* (London: Pluto Press, 1974), 188–89; Ekiert, *State against Society*, 129.

13. Harman, *Bureaucracy and Revolution*, 194; Ben Fowkes, *Eastern Europe, 1945–1969* (New York: Routledge, 2000), 76; Schöpflin, *Politics in Eastern Europe*, 227.

14. Schöpflin, *Politics in Eastern Europe*, 152: Ekiert, *State against Society*, 121–22.

15. Francöis Fejtö, *A History of the People's Democracies* (New York: Praeger, 1971), 146ff.; Milan Hubl, "The Legacy of 1968," in *Communism and Eastern Europe*, ed. F. Silnitsky, L. Silnitsky, and K. Reyman (New York: Karz, 1979); Zdeněk Mlynář, *Night Frost in Prague* (New York: Karz, 1980); Kurt Weisskopf, *The Agony of Czechoslovakia* (London: Elek, 1968), chapter 23.

16. Ekiert, *State against Society*, part II.

17. Fowkes, *Eastern Europe*, 80.

18. Jiri Valenta, *Soviet Intervention in Czechoslovakia* (Baltimore: Johns Hopkins University Press, 1991); Crampton, *Eastern Europe*, 336ff.

19. Ben Fowkes, *The Rise and Fall of Communism in Eastern Europe* (New York: St. Martin's Press, 1993), 139–40; Ekiert, *State against Society*, 181 and chapter 6.

20. And federalism's legacy was ambiguous, since many Czechs saw it rewarding Slovaks' less than full-hearted enthusiasm for the reform movement and many Slovaks viewed it as overdue payback for Czech domination and centralization. Joseph Rothschild, *Return to Diversity* (New York: Oxford University Press, 1993), 173.

21. Leonid Brezhnev, "Speech to the Fifth Congress of the Polish United Workers' Party" (The "Brezhnev Doctrine"), reprinted in Gale Stokes, ed., *From Stalinism to Pluralism* (New York: Oxford University Press, 1991), 132–34.

22. Fejtö, *A History of the People's Democracies*, part II.

23. Fowkes, *Eastern Europe*, 81ff.; Bronislaw Geremek, "Between Hope and Despair," *Daedalus* 119, no. 1 (1990): esp. 102ff.; and Tony Judt, "The Dilemmas of Dissidence," in *Crisis and Reform in Eastern Europe*, ed. Ferenc Fehér and Andrew Arato (New Brunswick, NJ: Transaction, 1991).

24. Crampton, *Eastern Europe*, 341; Schöplfin, *Politics in Eastern Europe*, 159, 180; Gale Stokes, *Three Eras of Political Change in Eastern Europe* (New York: Oxford University Press, 1997), 168, 186; and Okey, *The Demise of Communist East Europe*, 19.

25. Bunce, *Subversive Institutions*, 56–57.

26. Alec Nove, Hans-Hermann Höhmann, and Gertraud Seidenstecher, eds., *The East European Economies in the 1970s* (London: Butterworths, 1982).

27. David Mason, *Revolution and Transition in East-Central Europe* (Boulder, CO: Westview, 1996), 31–32.

28. Quoted in Bunce, *Subversive Institutions*, 21.

29. Schöpflin, *Politics in Eastern Europe*, 189; Charles Gati, ed., *The Politics of Modernization in Eastern Europe* (New York: Praeger, 1973), chapter 11.

30. Crampton, *Eastern Europe*, 346.

31. Bernard, *The Origins of Democratization*, 25; Ekiert, *State against Society*; Anna Seleny, *The Political Economy of State-Society Relations in Hungary and Poland* (New York: Cambridge University Press, 2006).

32. R.J. Crampton, *Eastern Europe in the Twentieth Century* (New York: Routledge, 1994), 318; Bernhard, *The Origins of Democratization*, 36ff.; Inessa Iazhborovskaia, "The Gomułka Alternative," in *The Establishment of Communist Regimes in Eastern Europe*, ed. Norman Naimark and Leonid Gibianskii (New York: Westview, 1997).

33. Alain Touraine, *Solidarity: Poland 1980–1981* (New York: Cambridge University Press, 1983), esp. 26–27.

34. Seleny, *The Political Economy*, 79, 90.

35. Fowkes, *The Rise and Fall*, 149.

36. Bernhard, *The Origins of Democratization*, 41ff.; Ekiert, *State against Society*, 222ff.

37. Hans-Hermann Höhmann, "Economic Reform in the 1970s—Policy with No Alternative," in *The East European Economies*, ed. Nove et al., 10.

38. Fowkes, *The Rise and Fall of Communism*, 150.

39. Wlodzimierz Brus, "Aims, Methods and Political Determinants of the Economic Policy of Poland, 1970–1980," in *The East European Economies*, ed. Nove et al. A Poland "supposedly led by national communists had become dependent on western finance capitalists." Kotkin, *Uncivil Society*, 102; Crampton, *Eastern Europe*, 363.

40. Seleny, *The Political Economy*, 79.

41. Rothschild, *Return to Diversity*, 197.

42. Aleksander Smolar, "The Polish Opposition," *Crisis and Reform*, ed. in Fehér and Arato.

43. Jan Józef Lipski, *KOR: A History of the Workers' Defense Committee in Poland* (Berkeley: University of California Press, 1985), which contains its "appeal to society": a list of complaints about and demands on the government, 474–79. Bernhard, *The Origins*, chapter 4.

44. Quoted in Bernhard, *The Origins*, 93.

45. Quoted in Mason, *Revolution and Transition*, 29.

46. Ekiert, *State against Society*, 232.

47. Timothy Garton Ash, *The Polish Revolution: Solidarity* (New York: Charles Scribner's Son, 1983); David Ost, *Solidarity and the Politics of Anti-Politics* (Philadelphia: Temple University Press, 1990).

48. Bogdan Szajkowski, quoted in Bernhard, *The Origins*, 139.

49. Garton Ash, *The Magic Lantern*, 133.

50. Fowkes, *The Rise and Fall*, 156; Okey, *The Demise*, 38; Ekiert, *State against Society*, 236.

51. Crampton, *Eastern Europe*, 363; Schöpflin, *Politics in Eastern Europe*, 184.

52. Rothschild, *Return to Diversity*, 198; Mason, *Revolution and Transition*, 27; Bernhard, *The Origins*, chapter 8.

53. Fowkes, *The Rise and Fall of Communism*, 158–59.

54. Ekiert, *State against Society*, 236. "The sporadic outbursts of the past were transcended, because the strikes of 1980 came under the control of a worker counter-elite that channelled discontent into the institutionalization of new structures like Solidarity, which later were able to advance democratization even further." Barbara Geddes, "A Comparative Perspective on the Leninst Legacy in Eastern Europe," *Comparative Political Studies* 28, no. 2 (July 1995): 248–49.

55. Gdańsk Agreement, reprinted in Stokes, ed. *From Stalinism to Pluralism*. See also Abraham Brumberg, ed., *Poland: Genesis of a Revolution* (New York: Random House, 1983).

56. Ekiert, *State against Society*, 238; David Ost, *Solidarity and the Politics of Ant-Politics* (Philadelphia: Temple University Press, 1991), esp. 73.

57. Richard Spielman, "The Eighteenth Brumaire of General Wojcich Jaruzelski," *World Politics* 37, no. 4 (1985): 570, quoted in Ekiert, *State against Society*, 242.

58. Sheri Berman, "Islamism, Revolution and Civil Society," *Perspectives on Politics* 1, no. 2 (June 2003).

59. Brown, *Surge to Freedom*, 33.

60. Timothy Garton Ash, *The Uses of Adversity* (New York: Random House, 1989), 55.

61. Kotkin, *Uncivil Society*, 123; Jan Kubik, *The Power of Symbols Against the Symbols of Power: The Rise of Solidarity and the Fall of State Socialism in Poland* (University Park: Pennsylvania State University Press, 1994).

62. Ekiert, *State against Society*, 277.

63. Kotkin, *Uncivil Society*, 124; Teresa Rakowska-Harmstone, *Communism in Eastern Europe* (Bloomington: Indiana University Press, 1979), 57ff., 334ff.

64. Ivan Berend, *Central and Eastern Europe* (New York: Cambridge University Press, 1996), chapters 6 and 7; Ekiert, *State against Society*, 295.

65. Stokes, *Three Eras*, 172.

66. Quoted in Fowkes, *The Rise and Fall*, 171.

67. Wiktor Osiatynski, "The Roundtable Talks in Poland," in *The Roundtable Talks and the Breakdown of Communism*, ed. Jon Elster (Chicago: University of Chicago Press, 1996), 23.

68. Gregory Domber, "Poland: International Pressure for a Negotiated Transition," in *Transitions to Democracy*, ed. Kathryn Stoner and Michael McFaul (Baltimore: Johns Hopkins University Press, 2013).

69. In symbolic reflection of this, a Polish eagle was situated on the wall between where the regime and opposition were positioned at the roundtable. Valerie Bunce, "The National Idea: Imperial Legacies and Post-Communist Pathways in Eastern Europe," *East European Politics and Societies* 19, no. 3 (2005): 484.

70. Mason, *Revolution and Transition*, 53.

71. Garton Ash, *The Magic Lantern*, 29.

72. Gregorz Ekiert, "Patterns of Post-Communist Transitions," in *Conflict, Cleavage and Change in Central Asia and the Caucaus*, ed. Karen Dawisha and Bruce Parrot (New York: Cambridge University Press, 1997); Sorin Antohi and Vladimir Tismaneanu, eds., *Between Past and Future: The Revolutions of 1989 and Their Aftermath* (Budapest: CEU Press, 2000).

73. The Hungarian regime was able to draw on legacies from Nagy's efforts and a group of reform economists that had emerged during that time. Seleny, *The Political Economy*, chapter 5.

74. Seleny, *The Political Economy*; János Kornai, *The Socialist System* (Princeton, NJ: Princeton University Press, 1992).

75. Seleny, *The Political Economy*, 75.

76. Seleny, *The Political Economy*, 12, 37, and 197.

77. Seleny, *The Political Economy*, 38.

78. Seleny, *The Political Economy*, 204, 231–32.

79. Ekiert, *State against Society*, 326–27; Stokes, *Three Eras*, 157ff.

80. Rothschild, *Return to Diversity*, 240.

81. Garton Ash, *Magic Lantern*, 47.

82. András Sajó, "The Roundtable Talks in Hungary," in *The Roundtable Talks and the Breakdown of Communism*, ed. Jon Elster (Chicago: University of Chicago Press, 1996). Rothschild, *Return to Diversity*, 242.

83. See, e.g., Timur Kuran, "Now out of Never: The Element of Surprise in the East European Revolution of 1989," *World Politics* 44, no. 1 (October 1991).

84. Kotkin, *Uncivil Society*, 53.

85. Jeffrey Kopstein, *The Politics of Economic Decline in East Germany, 1945–1989* (Chapel Hill: University of North Carolina Press, 1997).

86. Speech in East Berlin (October 7, 1989) (*"Wer zu spät kommt, den bestraft das Leben"* (Frankfurter Allgemeine, 3 October 2004).

87. Stokes, *The Walls Came Tumbling Down*, 156.

88. See note 1, this chapter.

89. See references above, but see also Zoltan Barany and Ivan Volges, *The Legacies of Communism in Eastern Europe* (Baltimore: Johns Hopkins University Press, 1996); James Millar and Sharon Wolchik, *The Social Legacies of Communism* (New York: Cambridge University Press, 1994); Barbara Geddes, "A Comparative Persepctive on the Leninist Legacy in Eastern Europe," *Comparative Political Studies* 28, no. 2 (July 1995); Grzegorz Ekiert and Daniel Ziblatt, "Democracy in Central and Eastern Europe, One Hundred Years On," *East European Politics and Societies and Cultures* 27, no. 1 (February 2013); *East European Politics and Societies and Cultures* 13, no. 2 (March 1999); Beverly Crawford and Arend Lijphart, "Explaining Political and Economic Change in Post-Communist Eastern Europe: Old Legacies, New Institutions, Hegomonic Norms, and International Pressures," *Comparative Political Studies* 28, no. 2 (1995).

90. Jean Cohen and Andrew Arato, *Civil Society and Political Theory* (Cambridge, MA: MIT Press, 1992); Marc Morjé Howard, *The Weakness of Civil Society in Post-Communist Europe* (New York: Cambridge University Press, 2003).

91. Millar and Wolchik, "Introduction," in *Social Legacies*, ed. Millar and Wolchik, 16–17.

92. Ken Jowitt, *New World Disorder* (Berkeley: University of California Press, 1992), 287–94; Millar and Wolchik, *Social Legacies*.

93. Zoltan Barany, *Soldiers and Politics in Eastern Europe, 1945–1990* (New York: St. Martin's Press, 1993).

94. During its previous period of independence during the interwar years, many, particularly within Germany and Russia, refused to accept these countries' sovereignty. Molotov, for example, contemptuously dismissed interwar Poland as "this ugly offspring of the Versailles treaty," while many Germans, particularly on the right, refused to accept the borders of Poland or Czechoslovakia. Rothschild, *Return to Diversity*, 23.

95. Jacques Rupnik, "Surging Illiberalism in the East," *Journal of Democracy* 27, no. 4 (October 2016); Ivan Krastev, "The Strange Death of the Liberal Consensus," *Journal of Democracy* (2007); Ivan Krastev, "Liberalism's Failure to Deliver," *Journal of Democracy* 27, no. 1 (January 2016); James Dawson and Sean Hanley, "The Fading Mirage of the 'Liberal Consensus,'" *Journal of Democracy* 27, no. 1 (January 2016); Ivan Krastev, "The Unraveling of the Post-1989 Order," *Journal of Democracy* 27, no. 4 (2016).

Chapter 18

1. A.J.P. Taylor, http://quotes.yourdictionary.com/author/a-j-p-taylor/110864#uqHvT11O3awefZG6.99.

2. Karl Marx, *The Eighteenth Brumaire of Louis Napoleon.*

3. Roberto Stephan Foa and Yascha Mounk, "The Danger of Deconsolidation," *Journal of Democracy* 27, no. 3 (July 2016); Foa and Mounk, "The Signs of Deconsolidation," *Journal of Democracy* 28, no. 1 (2017).

4. Fareed Zakaria, *The Future of Freedom: Illiberal Democracy at Home and Abroad* (New York: W.W. Norton, 2003); Edward Mansfield and Jack Snyder, *Electing to Fight: Why Emerging Democracies Go to War* (Cambridge, MA: MIT Press, 2005); Francis Fukuyama, Thomas Carothers, Edward D. Mansfield, Jack Snyder, and Sheri Berman, "The Debate on Sequencing," *Journal of Democracy* 18, no. 3 (July 2007).

5. Michael McFaul and Kathryn Stoner-Weiss, "The Myth of the Authoritarian Model," *Foreign Affairs* 87, no. 1 (January/February 2008); Azar Gat, "The Return of Authoritarian Great Powers," *Foreign Affairs* (July/August 2007). http://www.huffingtonpost.com/daniel-wagner/whether-democracy-or-auth_b_1181149.html; http://thediplomat.com/2009/06/western-vs-authoritarian-capitalism/; http://www.chinausfocus.com/foreign-policy/the-challenge-from-authoritarian-capitalism-to-liberal-democracy; http://faculty.insead.edu/michael-witt/documents/Witt_Redding_China_2012.pdf; http://www.hoover.org/research/authoritarian-capitalism-versus-democracy. On democratic pessimism more generally see Larry Diamond, Mark Plattner, and Christopher Walken, eds., *Authoritarianism Goes Global: The Challenge to Democracy* (Baltimore: Johns Hopkins University Press, 2016); Larry Diamond and Marc Plattner, eds., *Democracy in Decline* (Baltimore: Johns Hopkins University Press, 2015).

6. Eugen Weber, *Peasants into Frenchmen* (Stanford, CA: Stanford University Press, 1976).

7. Daniel Bell, "Pogroms of Words," *The New Republic*, June 24, 2010, 32.

8. Encyclopédie methodique: jurisprudence, quoted in Peter M. Jones, *Reform and Revolution in France: The Politics of Transition, 1774–1791* (Cambridge: Cambridge University Press, 1995), 58.

9. Originally attributed to G.M. Trevelyan but later used by many scholars, perhaps most influentially A.J.P. Taylor with regard to Germany. See, e.g., Melvan Kranzberg, ed., *1848: A Turning Point* (New York: Heath, 1959).

10. Walter Scheidel, *The Great Leveler: Violence and the History of Inequality from the Stone Age to the 21st Century* (Princeton, NJ: Princeton University Press, 2017).

11. Christopher Clark, *Iron Kingdom* (Cambridge, MA: Harvard University Press, 2006), 675–79; Alexander Gerschenkron, *Bread and Democracy in Germany*, preface to the 1966 edition (New York: Fertig, 1989), xxxii.

12. David Andersen, Jørgen Møller, and Svend-Erik Skaaning, "The State Democracy Nexus: Conceptual Distinctions, Theoretical Perspectives and Comparative Approaches," *Democratization* 21, no. 7 (2014).

13. J.S. Elliot, "A Europe of Composite Monarchies," *Past and Present* 137 (November 1992).

14. Czechoslovakia began the interwar period in the most advantageous position among the Habsburg Empire's successor states, with a fairly developed economy, weak landed nobility, fairly strong working and middle classes, a relatively well-developed sense of national identity, and a somewhat well-functioning bureaucracy inherited from the prewar period.

15. Francis Fukuyama, *Political Order and Political Decay. From the Industrial Revolution to the Globalization of Democracy* (New York: Farrar, Straus, and Giroux, 2015); "The Debate on Sequencing," *Journal of Democracy* 18, no. 3 (July 2007).

16. This has, of course, been stressed by other scholars. Classics include Moore, *Social Origins*; Eugene Weber, *Peasants into Frenchmen* (Palo Alto, CA: Stanford University Press, 1976); and Mark Mazower, *The Dark Side of Democracy* (New York: Cambridge University Press, 2005).

17. Michael Mann, "The Autonomous Power of the State: Its Origins, Mechanisms and Results," *European Journal of Sociology* (Archives européennes de sociologie) 25 (1984).

18. Weber, *Peasants into Frenchmen*.

19. This draws on Sheri Berman, *The Primacy of Politics* (New York: Cambridge University Press, 2006), especially chapter 8.

20. Sheri Berman, "Taming Extremist Parties: Lessons from Europe," *Journal of Democracy* 19, no. 1 (January 2008).

21. Joanna Gowa, *Closing the Gold Window* (Ithaca, NY: Cornell University Press, 1983).

22. http://www.spiegel.de/international/germany/former-german-foreign-minister-american-president-is-destroying-american-order-a-1208549. html#ref=nl-international.

23. Kathleen McNamara, *The Politics of Everyday Europe* (New York: Oxford University Press, 2015).

24. Kathleen McNamara, *The Currency of Ideas* (Ithaca, NY: Cornell University Press, 1999).

25. Mark Blyth, *The Great Transformation* (New York: Cambridge University Press, 2002) and Mark Blyth, *Austerity, The History of a Dangerous Idea* (New York: Oxford University Press, 2015).

26. Matthias Mattjis and Mark Blyth, "Theresa May's Horrible, No Good, Very Bad Day Explains Why Democracy Is Better Than Technocracy," The Monkey Cage, *Washington Post*, October 5, 2017; Matthias Mattjis and Mark Blyth, "When Is It Rational to Learn the Wrong Lessons? Technocratic Authority, Social Learning, and Euro Fragility," *Perspectives on Politics* (2017): 1–17.

27. See, e.g., Wolfgang Streeck, "The Crises of Democratic Capitalism," *New Left Review* 71 (September–October 2011), and many other writings. For overviews, see Sheri Berman, "Populism Is a Problem: Elite Technocrats Are Not the Solution," *Foreign Policy*, December 2017; Jonathan Chait, "Why

Trump's Assault on Democracy Doesn't Bother the Radical Left," *New York Magazine*, May 2018; and Eric Levitz, "America's Version of Capitalism Is Incompatible with Democracy," *New York Magazine*, May 2018.

28. Peter Hall, "Varieties of Capitalism and the Euro Crisis," *West European Politics* 37, no. 6 (2014): 1228.

29. Samuel Huntington, *Political Order in Changing Societies* (New Haven, CT: Yale University Press, 1968).

INDEX

Christian Democratic Party
(Germany), 295
Churchill, Winston, 286, 294,
308, 313
Civic Forum organization, 369
Civil Constitution of the Clergy
(France, 1790), 62
Clausewitz, Carl von, 83
Clayton, William, 292
Cockburn, Henry, 194
Cohen-Reuss, Max, 237
Colbert, Jean-Baptiste, 23
Cold War
liberal democracy and, 10, 13,
285, 290, 294–97, 299–302,
324, 327, 386, 389, 395, 397,
399–400, 403–5
Marshall Plan and, 292–93, 321,
324, 399, 491n45
reconstruction of Western Europe
after Second World War
and, 289–91
Committee of Free Trade Unions for the
Baltic Coast (Poland), 360
Committee on Public Safety (French
Revolution), 64–65
communism
Brezhnev Doctrine and, 356,
363–64, 371
collapse (1989–91) of, 1, 10–11,
365–72, 376
democratization challenged by
legacies of, 372–75, 398
legitimacy of regimes in, 325–26,
349, 353, 358, 370
privileged elites' special access to
resources and, 386–87
protests against regimes of,
350, 353–54
reform efforts within, 348–49,
354–56, 370
repression of political opponents and,
318, 357

state control of the economy
in, 319–21
Third Republic France and,
177–78, 180–82
Western Europe in Cold War era and,
295, 300–301
Company, Luís, 276
Confederación Española de Derechas
Autónomas (CEDA, Spain)
Catholics as primary constituents of,
274–75, 278
coalition government (1933–36)
of, 274–78
election (1936) and, 278–79
lack of commitment to democracy in,
270, 275, 279–81
Radical Party and, 277
Confederation of Fascist Unions
(Italy), 229
Confederation of the Rhine, 92. See also
German Confederation
Confindustria (CGII, Italy), 229
Congress of Vienna (1815), 77, 84, 93,
95, 127
Conservative Party (Germany)
direct taxation opposed by, 162
electoral performance (1890s–1900s)
of, 159, 161, 163–64, 167
finance bill (1913) and, 165
National Liberal Party and, 163–64
Zentrum Party and, 162
Conservative Party (Great Britain). See
also Tories
Corn Laws and, 196–97, 199
early twentieth-century strength
of, 209–11
First World War and, 207
Ireland policy and, 206
landed elites and, 197, 208–9
modernization of the organizational
infastructure of, 200, 203–4,
209–10, 265
nationalism and, 209–10

twenty-first century declines in, 2,
398, 400–405, 407
Denmark, 81, 95, 99, 148, 174, 404
dictatorship
ancien régime absolutism and, 11,
15–16, 20, 26, 28, 34, 41, 43,
50–51, 57, 61, 386, 396
coercion and, 395–96
national identity and, 396
state building and, 395–96
twenty-first century increases in, 3
Di Lampedusa, Giuseppe, 212
The Directory (French Revolution
government), 67–68
Disraeli, Benjamin, 199, 203–4,
459n53, 460nn57–58
Dittmann, Wilhelm, 238
Djerejian, Edward, 5
Domingo, Marcelino, 273
Don Carlos (Carlist war claimant to
Spanish throne), 263
Doriot, Jacques, 182
Dreyfus Affair (France, 1890s)
anti-Semitism as the motivating
force of, 107, 114–15, 117–20,
123–24, 388
Boulangism as predecessor of, 113
Catholic Church and, 115, 118
Dreyfus's biographical background
and, 114
espionage charges at core
of, 114–15
nationalist and populist forces'
actions in, 113, 118–20,
122–23, 175
pardon of Dreyfus and, 120
Patriot's League and, 118–19
socialist parties in France
and, 121
trials of Dreyfus and, 115, 120
Zola and, 117–19
Drumont, Edmund, 115, 118–19
Dubček, Alexander, 355, 369, 372

Eastern Europe in Cold War era. *See also*
specific countries
agricultural sector in, 319, 350
Brezhnev Doctrine and, 356,
363–64, 371
collapse of communism (1989–90)
in, 1, 10–11, 365–72, 376, 398
communisms' appeal in, 315, 324–
25, 328, 347–48
communist regimes in, 10–11,
13, 315–25, 327–28, 348–49,
353–58, 398
consumer goods and, 357–58
democratization following, 14, 347,
372–75, 383–84, 398
economic development and, 349,
352–53, 357–58
education levels and, 351
ethnic cleansing in, 314
industrialization and, 320–21,
349, 352
legacy of economic
underdevelopment in, 304–6
postwar Popular Front governments
and, 317
social democratic parties eliminated
in, 317–18
Soviet hegemony in, 286, 304–5,
314–18, 320–25, 327–28, 347,
353–56, 362–63, 370–72,
499–500n85
state-building in, 10, 373
state control of economies in, 319–21
urbanization and, 351
East Germany
agricultural sector in, 350
collapse of communist regime
(1989–90) in, 368, 370
communist regime in, 316–18
economic development and economic
conditions in, 367–68
education levels in, 351
industrialization in, 352

Hitler, Adolf (*Cont.*)
    ascension to presidency (1934)
        of, 251
    Beer Hall putsch (1923) and,
        241–42, 382
    Concordat with the Vatican and, 251
    conservative elites manipulated by,
        249–50, 252, 287
    consolidation of control in Nazi Party
        by, 242–43, 390–91
    consolidation of power (1930s)
        by, 180
    dictatorship consolidated by, 250–51
    Eastern European territories
        conquered by, 311–15
    ethnic cleansing and, 288–89
    ethnic German population in Eastern
        Europe and, 307
    First World War and, 172
    military leaders and, 251–52,
        287, 290–91
    Mussolini and, 231
    on Nazi economic policies, 252–53
    as personification of German
        nation, 283
    von Papen and, 249
Hobbes, Thomas, 18, 38
Hobhouse, L.T., 201
Hobsbawm, Eric, 49, 83, 170, 335
Hohenzollern Dynasty, 26–27,
    146–47
Holbrooke, Richard, 5
Holstein, 95, 99, 149
Honecker, Erich, 368
Horthy, Miklós, 310
Hugenberg, Alfred, 249
Hugh Capet (king of France), 20
Huguenots, 20, 24
Hungary
    1848 uprisngs and, 89–91, 98–100
    agricultural sector in, 350, 501n102
    border disputes in interwar era and,
        307–8, 310

collapse of communist regime
    (1989–90) in, 366–67, 370–71
communist regime during Cold
    War era in, 316–17, 322–23,
    353–54, 383
economic development and
    conditions in, 80, 349, 366
economic reform efforts during
    communist era in, 359,
    365–66, 371
education levels in, 351
ethnic and religious diversity in, 91
illiberal democracy's rise in, 2,
    5–6, 377
independence (1919) of, 306
industrialization in, 352
interwar demise of democracy
    in, 309–11
Kun's communist regime (1919)
    in, 310
landed elite in, 305, 309, 319,
    493–94n6
Magyarization policy in, 91
March Laws (1848) and, 89
nationalism and, 89–90, 305, 314
Nazi regime in Germany and, 311
rebellion (1956) quelled by Soviet
    Union in, 322–23, 325, 354,
    365–66, 370
state control of economy during
    communist era in, 319
urbanization in, 81, 351
Versailles Treaty and, 171
Hyde Park Railings Affair
    (1866), 199

illiberal democracy, 2, 5–7,
    377, 385–86
Il Regno journal, 140
Institute for Industrial Reconstruction
    (Italy), 230
International Bank for Reconstruction
    and Development (IBRD), 292

International Monetary Fund (IMF),
    292, 399
Ireland
    Act for the Settlement of Ireland
        (1652) and, 38–39
    Act of Union (1707) and, 45
    Catholic majority population
        marginalized before modern era in,
        39, 47, 205
    Home Rule and, 205–9, 212,
        384, 388
    interwar democracy in, 174
    Irish Free State established (1922)
        in, 208
    Irish Republican Army and, 208
    Irish revolts (1640s) and, 35–36, 38
    nationalism in, 206–8
    potato blight and famine (1840s)
        in, 196–97
Isabella I (queen of Spain), 259, 394
Isabella II (queen of Spain), 263
Islamic Salvation Front (FIS), 5
Ismay, Lord, 292
Italian Communist Party (PCI), 219, 223
Italian Credit Institute, 230
Italian Financial Society, 230
Italian Nationalist Association, 142
Italian National Society, 130
Italian Socialist Party (PSI)
    Bolshevik Revolution and, 216–17
    cooperation with liberal forces and,
        140–42, 216–17
    decline (1920s) of, 225, 232
    election (1919) and, 217–18
    factory council movement
        and, 218–19
    founding of, 139
    international socialist movement
        and, 219
    Libya War (1911) and, 142
    Maximalist faction of, 217, 219
    nationalization of agriculture
        advocated by, 222–23

Italy
    1848 uprisings in, 88, 90, 97–98,
        127–28, 143, 380
    Austro-Prussian War and, 132
    Biennio Rosso period (1919–20) in,
        217–18, 221–22, 380
    Catholic Church and, 135–36,
        143–44, 217, 225, 228, 393
    Charter of Labor (1927) in, 229–30
    communist parties during Cold War
        era in, 300
    debt and inflation during interwar
        era in, 216, 232
    economic development in, 80, 82,
        141, 149, 380
    factory council movement in, 218–19
    fascism in, 13, 143, 174, 214,
        219–33, 381
    Habsburg control of states in,
        126, 128–31
    Libyan War (1911) and, 142
    Napoleon's conquests and reordering
        of, 72, 84, 126–28, 143
    nationalism and, 84, 104, 124, 126,
        128–30, 132–34, 393, 395
    nationalist and populist forces in,
        140–42, 144–45, 215–16, 404
    party system in, 138–39
    "Piedmontization" during nation-
        building in, 134–36
    regional variation in, 133–34,
        143, 388
    Risorgimento period in, 129–30,
        141, 143, 227–28
    Rome Treaty (1957) and, 401
    socialist parties and mobilization in,
        139–42, 144–45, 216–20, 222–
        23, 225, 232
    "southern question" in, 136–38
    state-building in, 10, 12, 126–27,
        134–35, 138–39, 143–44, 215,
        227–32, 302, 395
    suffrage expansions in, 138, 380

state-building and, 227–28
US ambassador's praise (1928)
    for, 231
Versailles Treaty and, 221

Nagy, Imre, 322–23, 354–55, 366, 372
Naples, 126, 132, 136–37
Napoleon Bonaparte
    Catholic Church and, 69–71
    Consulate government and, 68
    coup of 18 Brumaire (1799) by,
        68, 378
    David's painting of, 69
    European conquests of, 49
    European political systems
        reordered by, 71–72, 84, 92–93,
        127, 387
    fall (1815) of, 74, 77, 378
    Germany and, 72, 84, 92–93
    Italy and, 72, 84, 126–28, 143
    military accomplishments of, 69
    Napoleonic code and, 70–71, 85
    plebiscites and, 68–69
    popular support for, 68–70
    royalist uprising (1795)
        quelled by, 67
    Spain and, 262–63
    state building and, 70–72
    tax systems and, 70–71
Napoleon III (Louis-Napoleon
        Bonaparte, emperor of France)
    ascension (1852) of, 96–97, 378
    Franco-Prussian War and, 109,
        132, 379
    Italy and, 130–32
    liberal democracy and, 103,
        108–9, 378–79
National Assembly (France),
    59–63, 109–10
National Convention (France),
    64–65, 67
National Fascist Party (PNF, Italy),
    224, 227–28

nationalism
    1848 uprisings and, 77–78, 83–84,
        89–90, 99, 102, 104–6, 146
    anti-Semitism and, 114, 123–24,
        160–61, 176, 180
    ethnic cleansing and, 397
    First World War and, 171–72
    France and, 75, 83, 105, 110–13,
        123, 175, 388, 392, 395–97, 404
    Germany and, 84, 94–95, 99, 104,
        124, 149, 168, 172, 395
    Hungary and, 89–90, 305, 314
    interwar period and, 172–73
    in Ireland, 206–8
    liberal democracy and, 124, 373,
        392, 397
    public education and, 84
National Liberal Party (Germany, DVP)
    Bismarck and, 153–54
    civil liberties restrictions passed
        by, 154
    Conservative Party and, 163–64
    declining electoral performance
        (1870s–1910s) of, 159, 161, 167
    electoral performance in Weimar
        Germany of, 239, 241, 243, 245
    establishment of, 153
    Great Depression and, 245
    middle-class disenchantment
        with, 242–43
    Reichslandbund and, 244
    Social Democratic Party and, 162
National Peasant Party (Hungary), 317
National Reform Union (Great
        Britain), 197
Navarro, Carlos Arias, 338
Nazi Party (NSDAP)
    agricultural sector and rural
        supporters of, 244–45, 248, 252
    Anschluss (union of Germany and
        Austria) and, 255
    anti-Semitism and, 236, 241, 243,
        247, 254, 256, 393

Nazi Party (NSDAP) (*Cont.*)
  Beer Hall Putsch (1923) and,
    241–42, 382
  broad base of support for, 214,
    245–48, 255–56
  conservative elites marginalized
    by, 287–88
  dictatorship consolidated by, 250–51
  Eastern European territories
    conquered by, 311–15
  electoral performance in Weimar
    Republic of, 239, 245–46, 248–
    50, 382, 475n38
  ethnic German population in Eastern
    Europe and, 307
  First World War and, 167
  German economy controlled
    by, 252–53
  Great Depression and,
    246–47, 253–55
  Hitler's consolidation of control in,
    242–43, 390–91
  membership levels in, 182–83
  parastatal organizations and, 251
  privileged elites' special access to
    resources and, 386–87
  race and racism in, 234, 243,
    253–54, 287
  Reichslandbund and, 244–45, 248
  social welfare policies and, 253–54
  state control of the economy and,
    287, 478n76
  Sturmabteilung (SA, paramilitary
    force), 247, 249, 251
  terrorism against political opponents
    by, 251
  Versailles Treaty provisions attacked
    by, 251, 255
Necker, Jacques, 56, 60
neoliberalism, 402–3
The Netherlands
  Calvinism and, 47
  First World War and, 170, 174
  French Revolution and, 66
  interwar democracy in, 174
  populist parties in, 404
  same-sex marriage and, 343
  Treaty of Rome and, 401
New Model Army (England), 37–39
Nicholas I (tsar of Russia), 99
Night of Long Knives (Germany,
    1934), 251
Nineteen Propositions
    (England,1641), 37
Nitti, Francesco Saverio, 217, 221–22
Nixon, Richard, 400
North Atlantic Treaty Organization
    (NATO), 291–92, 304,
    342, 399
North German Confederation, 149–50
Norway, 81, 174, 404
Noske, Gustav, 238–40

O'Connell, Daniel, 192–93
Olivares, Count-Duke of, 260–61
Opera Nazionale Dopolavoro
    (OND), 228
Orbán, Viktor, 2, 5
Organization for European Economic
    Co-operation (OEEC), 293
Orlando, Vittorio Emanuele, 139, 222
Ortega y Gasset, José, 272
Ottoman Empire, 142, 170–72, 304,
    383, 387

Pact of Plombières (1858), 130
Palacký, František, 91–92
Palazzo Vidoni Pact (1925), 229
Palmer, R.R., 66–67
Palmerston, Viscount, 199
Pan-German League, 160
Pan-Slavic Congress (1848), 92, 97
Papal States, 126, 129, 131
Pareto, Vilfredo, 138–39
Paris Commune (1870–71), 109–10,
    112, 379

Parliament Act of 1911 (Great Britain),
201, 203, 205
Parliamentary Reform Act (Great
Britain, 1884), 201
Partido Popular (Spain), 342
Partido Republicano Radical (PRR,
Spain), 272, 275, 277–78
Partido Socialista Obrero Español
(PSOE, Spain)
coalition government (1931–33) led
by, 270–72
electoral performance during 1930s
of, 275, 278
indifference to regional and ethnic
concerns among, 274
lack of commitment to democracy
during interwar era among, 270,
276, 281
military reforms (1980s)
implemented by, 342
re-emergence during Spain's
democratization (1970s) of,
336, 339
social reforms promoted during
twenty-first century by, 343
as Spain's majority party
(1977–96), 340–43
splits between radical and moderates
in, 279
threats of armed insurrection by,
276, 279
Parti Ouvrier Français (POF), 112
Parti Populaire Français (PPF), 182
Parti Social Français (PSF),
180, 182–83
Partito Popolare Italiano (PPI), 217,
222, 225, 232
Patriot's League (France), 118–19
Peel, Robert, 193, 196–97
The People Have Spoken (Harsanyi), 404
People's Budget (Great Britain, 1909),
202–3, 205
People's Party (PP, Spain), 343

Petőfi, Alexander (Petőfi
Sándor), 89–90
Philip IV (king of Spain), 260
Picquart, Georges, 116–17
Piedmont
1848 uprisings and, 90, 98
Italian unification and, 129–37, 143,
150, 393
liberal democratic reforms in,
128–29, 134
Piłsudski, Józef, 309
Piñar, Blas, 336
Pincus, Steven, 43
Pius IX (pope), 135
Pius VII (pope), 71
Platforma de Convergencia Democrática
(Spain), 336
Plumb, J.H., 29
Poincarè, Raymond, 178
Poland
agricultural sector in, 350, 358
border disputes in interwar era
and, 307–8
Catholic Church and, 358, 360–61
collapse of communism (1989) in,
365, 370
communist regime during Cold
War era in, 317, 322, 353–54,
360–63, 383
coup (1981–82) in, 362
economic development and
conditions in, 349, 358–59, 361,
363–64, 371
education levels in, 351
ethnic diversity in, 308–9
Gdánsk accords and, 361–62
illiberal democracy's rise in, 5–6
independence (1919) of, 306, 308
industrialization in, 352
interwar demise of democracy in,
174, 308–9
landed elite in, 25, 45, 305, 319
nationalism in, 305